Exclusionary Rules in Comparative Law

IUS GENTIUM

COMPARATIVE PERSPECTIVES ON LAW AND JUSTICE

VOLUME 20

For further volumes:
http://www.springer.com/series/7888

Stephen C. Thaman
Editor

Exclusionary Rules in Comparative Law

Springer

Editor
Stephen C. Thaman
School of Law
Saint Louis University
St. Louis, MO, USA

ISBN 978-94-007-5347-1 ISBN 978-94-007-5348-8 (eBook)
DOI 10.1007/978-94-007-5348-8
Springer Dordrecht Heidelberg New York London

Library of Congress Control Number: 2012954419

Printed on acid-free paper

Springer is part of Springer Science+Business Media (www.springer.com)

To the memory of my dear friend and colleague Prof. Dr. Günter Heine (Ravensburg, 4 June 1952 : Freiburg im Breisgau, 25 June 2011), a great criminal law scholar, who paved the way for my academic career and whom I sorely miss.

Acknowledgements

I would like to thank my two research assistants who helped me in the 2 years it took me to edit this book: Joshua Walker, who also worked on the translations of the chapters on Belgium and France from French to English, and Emily Williams, who worked on the final citechecking and formatting.

Introduction

Stephen C. Thaman

This book, *Exclusionary Rules in Comparative Law*, grew out of excellent country studies on the criminal exclusionary rule prepared for the XVIII Congress of the International Academy of Comparative Law (IACL), which was held in Washington, D.C., from July 25 through August 1, 2010. I had the honor of being the general rapporteur for criminal procedure for the congress and also chose the topic for the congress.

What is controversial about what are called "exclusionary rules" in American law, prohibitions on the use of evidence (*Beweisverwertungsverbote*) in German, or simply "non-usability" (*inutilizzabilità*) in Italy, is that they end up depriving the factfinders in criminal trials, whether professional judges, jurors, or lay judges sitting with professional judges in mixed courts, of relevant, material evidence of guilt, because of errors committed by law enforcement personnel in the collection of this evidence. We thus have a real confrontation of two principles of criminal procedure, that of truth-finding, often called the principle of material truth in civil law countries, and that of "due process" to use the Anglo-American term, or the principle of a state under the rule of law or *Rechtsstaatlichkeit*, to use the German term.

The sacrifice of truth in favor of other important values not only occurs through the use of exclusionary rules. In the area of plea bargaining and other abbreviated and consensual methods of avoiding a full trial on the truth of the charges, truth is sacrificed at the altar of efficiency and procedural economy, that is, in order to save time and money.[1] Many criticize the common law jury system with its non-reasoned

[1] I chose this topic when I was general rapporteur for criminal procedure at the XVII Congress of the International Academy of Comparative Law which was held in Utrecht, The Netherlands. See Thaman, S.C. (ed.)(2010), *World Plea Bargaining*, Durham, North Carolina: Carolina Academic Press.

S.C. Thaman (✉)
School of Law, Saint Louis University,
3700 Lindell Blvd., St. Louis, MO 63108, USA
e-mail: thamansc@slu.edu

verdicts and non-appealable acquittal judgments as a system that places ideas of popular democracy above truth-finding.[2] These three topics were traditionally the most disputatious in the academy and served to distinguish adversarial common law systems, which were considered to be the cradle of each of these procedural arrangements, and the inquisitorial civil law systems, which held all three to be anathema. Today, especially in the area of plea bargaining and exclusionary rules, this is no longer the case. As this book shows, exclusionary rules are part and parcel of nearly all criminal procedure systems in Europe and are also becoming more prevalent in other parts of the world.

After I was chosen as general rapporteur on the subject of exclusionary rules, I prepared a questionnaire and sent it to the various country reporters who were either nominated by their country's section of the IACL, or were recruited by me from friends and colleagues. Although I asked the country reporters to address the issues in the questionnaire, I gave them freedom to arrange their reports as they wished so as to make them more readable when published in book form. In the questionnaire I wanted to know, in general, whether the principle of material truth had a constitutional foundation in their countries, whether it was explicitly spelled out in the Code of Criminal Procedure (CCP), or whether if had been developed from the academic literature or in the case law of the high courts. I also wanted to know whether the exclusion of illegally gathered evidence was included as a constitutional mandate, or was introduced by high court jurisprudence, or by legislative enactment. I was interested, as well, in whether the country had a generally worded rule excluding evidence gathered in violation of the law, and whether such exclusionary rule was limited to fundamental or constitutional violations, or was applicable, in addition, to violations of statutory rules.

With respect to more particular exclusionary rules applying to specific violations of laws relating to the gathering or admissibility of evidence, I decided to narrow the scope of the country reports to what I thought were the two most critical areas in which exclusionary rules are used to enforce important human rights protected by both national constitutions and international human rights conventions, that is: (1) where police acquire evidence by violating the universally protected right to privacy in one's home or in one's private conversations and (2) where police violate human dignity, the privilege against self-incrimination and/or the right to silence in obtaining confessions.

This book will not touch on another important exclusionary rule, despite its grounding in constitutional and international human rights law: the exclusion of inculpatory hearsay evidence in the form of witness statements, where the defendant was deprived of the opportunity to confront or examine the witness. Although there is substantial statutory and case law dealing with this exclusionary rule, rooted, *inter alia*, in the Sixth Amendment of the U.S. Constitution, Art. 14(3)(e) of the International Covenant on Civil and Political Rights, and Art. 6 (3)(d) of the

---

[2] See, for instance, Thaman, S.C. (2011), "Should Criminal Juries Give Reasons for their Verdicts": The Spanish Experience and the Implications of the European Court of Human Rights Decision in *Taxquet v. Belgium*, *Chicago-Kent Law Review*, Vol. 86, 613–668.

European Convention of Human Rights I felt that this important material does not as glaringly pose the question of truth against due process. This is because the right to confrontation is a purely procedural right that has no impact beyond criminal procedure, unlike the right to human dignity or the right to privacy, and also because the violation of the right to confrontation can never lead to the exclusion of physical evidence of guilt, but only to words, which, whether in the form of prior witness testimony, confessions, or intercepted telephone conversations, are not always reliable and credible indicia of guilt.

In the end, 24 country reports and a report on the jurisprudence of the European Court of Human Rights (hereafter ECtHR) were submitted and temporarily published on the website of the XVIII Congress of the IACL. I wrote the general report for the Washington congress and referred to the wealth of information that I learned in these reports.[3] Although much of the groundwork for Chap. 17 of this book, my general theoretical treatment of the exclusionary rule, is based on my general report for the conference, they are in no way identical. I have expanded and re-organized the material in the general report in a more concise and theoretically consistent manner, giving Chap. 17 a closer likeness to an article I later wrote, which was published in the University of Toronto Law Journal.[4]

I received the following reports as general rapporteur for the Washington conference: Belgium, written by Marie-Aude Beernaert, of the Catholic University of Louvain and Philip Traest, of the University of Ghent; Brazil, written by Ana Paula Zomer Sica, State Procurator in São Paulo and Leonardo Sica, a lawyer in São Paulo; the Czech Republic, written by Jaroslav Fenyk of Masaryk University in Brno; England and Wales, written by Andrew Choo, University of Warwick; Finland, written by Hannu Kiuru, Helsinki, Vice-President of the Finnish Section of the Comparative Law Association; France, written by Jean Pradel, Professor Emeritus of the University of Poitiers; Germany, written by Sabine Gless, University of Basel, Switzerland; Greece, written by George Triantafyllou, University of Athens; Ireland, written by Yvonne Daly, Dublin City University and Arnaud Cras, University College Dublin; Israel, written by Rinat Kitai Sangero, Academic Center of Law and Business, Jerusalem and Yuval Merin, College of Management School of Law, Rishon LeZion; Italy, written by Giulio Illuminati, University of Bologna; Macao, written by Paulo Martins Chan, Public Prosecutor, University of Macao; the Netherlands, written by Lonneke Stevens and Matthias J. Borgers, Free University of Amsterdam; Norway, written by Runar Torgersen, Public Prosecutor, Oslo; Poland, written by Maria Rogacka-Rzewnicka, University of Warsaw; Portugal, written by Maria João da Silva Baila Madeira Antunes, University of Coimbra; Russia, written by Vladimir I. Rudnev, Institute of Legislation and Comparative

[3] See Thaman, S.C. (2012), "The Exclusionary Rule", in: K.B. Brown & D.V. Snyder (eds.), *General Reports of the XVIII Congress of the International Academy of Comparative Law*, Dordrecht, Heidelberg, London, New York: Springer, 657–704.

[4] Thaman, S.C. (2011), "Constitutional Rights in the Balance: Modern Exclusionary Rules and the Toleration of Police Lawlessness in the Search for Truth", 61 *Univ. of Toronto L. J.*, Vol. 61, 691–735.

Law, Moscow; Scotland, written by Fiona Leverick, University of Glasgow and Findlay Stark, Ph.D. Candidate, University of Edinburgh; Serbia, written by Snežana Brkić, University of Novi Sad; Slovenia, written by Ana Pauletič, University of Ljubljana; Spain, written by Lorena Bachmaier Winter, Complutense University, Madrid; Taiwan, written by Jaw-perng Wang, National Taiwan University, Taipei; Turkey, written by Adem Sözüer and Öznur Sevdiren, Istanbul University; United States, written by Mark Cammack, Southwestern School of Law, Los Angeles; and the European Court of Human Rights, written by Pinar Ölçer, University of Leiden, the Netherlands.

I would also like to acknowledge, that the country reporter for Croatia, Prof. Ivo Josipović, University of Zagreb, graciously excused himself for being unable to submit his report. His excuse was rather compelling: he was elected President of Croatia in the meantime! We wish him the best of luck!

Due to space constraints, I could not publish all of the reports in this book, so my choice was based on two factors: (1) what I thought was the importance of the country's approach to the issue of exclusionary rules, and (2) the quality of the report both in the sense of its coverage of the material and its stylistic merits. I regret that we had to leave out many countries, but what I learned from the reports that have not entered this volume will appear in my synthetic, theoretical chapter, which concludes it. For the 16 reports that make up the other chapters of this book, I will cite directly to these chapters when I refer to the law reflected therein. If I cite to the work of the writers who are not published herein, I will cite to the legal sources they cited, or to my general report for the IACL Congress.

Part I of the book will deal with court-made exclusionary rules, and begins with Chap. 1 on the United States, whose famous court-crafted exclusionary rules have had considerable influence in other common law countries, as well as in the civil law world. I will then deal with other common law countries which also have judicially created exclusionary rules: Chap. 2 deals with Ireland, Chap. 3 with Scotland and Chap. 4 with Israel (which has been greatly influenced by common law procedural models). Part I concludes with Chap. 5 on Germany, where the courts have developed a sophisticated balancing test which determines which evidence will be excluded and which will not.

Part II of the book, the longest part, deals with the development in the civil law world which took place from the traditional theory of "nullities" to modern exclusionary rules. It begins, as it should, with Chap. 6 on France, where the concept of "nullities" originated, and where they remain the only vehicles to exclude evidence. It continues with Chap. 7 on Belgium, which inherited the concept of "nullities" from France, but whose courts have gradually developed a balancing test when deciding on the admissibility of illegally gathered evidence. Chapter 8 on the Netherlands, deals with a country coming from a similar tradition, but which has introduced a statutory exclusionary rule which gives judges wide discretion in balancing various factors. Chapter 9 on Spain, Chap. 10 on Italy, and Chap. 11 on Greece present countries coming from the "nullity" tradition, which have enacted modern statutory exclusionary rules which have been the subject of some fascinating judicial interpretations by the high courts of those countries. Finally, Chap. 12 on

Turkey and Chap. 13 on Serbia depict countries emerging from military or authoritarian political systems, which have codified categorical exclusionary rules and whose courts are wrestling with these new developments.

Part III deals with tests for exclusion which, by and large, look at the larger picture in order to determine whether a failure to exclude illegally gathered evidence would violate the defendant's right to a fair trial. Chapter 14 deals with the application of this test in England and Wales, where it was introduced in the Police and Criminal Evidence Act of 1984. The new general exclusionary rule adopted by Taiwan's legislature, described in Chap. 15, can also be seen as a balancing test where the ultimate fairness of the proceedings is the crucial factor. Finally, Chap. 16 deals with the fair trial test applied by the European Court of Human Rights, which was perhaps influenced by the approach in England and Wales. The book then concludes with my synthetic, theoretical approach to exclusionary rules, where I treat all exclusionary rules as results of balancing carried out at the different levels of international and national institutions, whether we are dealing with exclusion of the fruits of torture, or those of mere statutory violations which do not rise to constitutional stature.

And, as we shall see, the most difficult step for any state or even international court to take is to exclude physical evidence—contraband, instruments of crime, or fruits of crime—which is gathered in violation of the law, even of constitutional and human rights guarantees. For physical evidence—if not tampered with—does not lie, it speaks for itself (*res ipsa loquitur*): the murder weapon, the body of a murder victim, the fingerprints, DNA residue, the stolen loot, the illegal stash of drugs. Thus, the treatment of especially these "fruits of the poisonous tree" is the most controversial aspect in most countries, and is the area where truth most clearly begs to be heard, and is reluctant to cede to respect for human rights.

It may surprise readers, that exclusionary rules were traditionally more common in inquisitorial non-jury systems in civil law jurisdictions, in the form of what are called "nullities". If a procedural actor, such as a police officer, investigating magistrate or prosecutor violated a rule of criminal procedure, this could lead to the nullity of the procedural act, and, in some cases, the inadmissibility of evidence related to this violation. Some of these "nullities" are specifically related to certain violations, and others are expressed in general form.

Chapter 1
The United States: The Rise and Fall of the Constitutional Exclusionary Rule

Mark E. Cammack

1.1 The General Theory of Admissibility of Illegally Gathered Evidence

In 1961 the US Supreme Court (USSC) held in *Mapp v. Ohio*[1] that the exclusion of evidence obtained as a result of an unconstitutional search or seizure is required in state criminal trials as a matter of federal constitutional law. The *Mapp* holding applied only to evidence acquired in violation of the search and seizure protections of the Fourth Amendment. Before the decade was over, however, the Court decided cases creating constitutional exclusionary rules for evidence obtained as a result of violations of two other rights. The 1964 case of *Massiah v. United States*[2] interpreted the right to counsel guaranteed by the Sixth Amendment to require exclusion of statements elicited from the accused in the absence of an attorney after the filing of formal criminal charges. Two years later in *Miranda v. Arizona*[3] the Court relied on the Fifth Amendment right against compelled self-incrimination to mandate exclusion of statements made in response to custodial interrogation unless the suspect had been advised of her rights and voluntarily waived them.

The constitutional exclusionary rules created in *Mapp, Massiah*, and *Miranda* were not the first to require exclusion of illegally obtained evidence in the United States (US). Confessions obtained by means that operated to "deprive [the accused] of that freedom of will or self-control essential to make his confession voluntary"

[1] 367 U.S. 643 (1961).

[2] 377 U.S. 201 (1964).

[3] 348 U.S. 436 (1966).

M.E. Cammack (✉)
Southwestern Law School, 3050 Wilshire Boulevard, Los Angeles, CA 90010-1106, USA
e-mail: mcammack@swlaw.edu

S.C. Thaman (ed.), *Exclusionary Rules in Comparative Law*, Ius Gentium: Comparative Perspectives on Law and Justice 20, DOI 10.1007/978-94-007-5348-8_1,

were inadmissible under the common law of evidence.[4] At the end of the nineteenth century the USSC held that the Fifth Amendment self-incrimination right required the exclusion of involuntary confessions from federal prosecutions as a matter of constitutional law,[5] and in the 1930s the Court established a constitutional exclusionary rule for involuntary confessions in state courts based on the due process clause of the Fourteenth Amendment.[6] Exclusion of evidence obtained as a result of an unlawful search or seizure was required in federal court for nearly 50 years before *Mapp* extended the rule to the states,[7] and a minority of states had required the exclusion of such evidence as a matter of state law prior to the establishment of the Fourth Amendment exclusionary rule in *Mapp*.[8]

The imposition of the constitutional mandates stated in Mapp, Massiah, and Miranda does not foreclose the existence of additional exclusionary rules for illegally obtained evidence based on state law. Because the federal constitution is superior to both constitutional and non-constitutional state laws, the rights protections contained in the US constitution establish a minimum standard that the states must honor. States are free, however, to provide greater protection than federal law requires. But while some states require exclusion of illegally seized evidence beyond what is mandated by the US constitution, in the years since the Supreme Court decided *Mapp, Massiah*, and *Miranda*, the federal constitution has served as the primary standard for admissibility of illegally obtained evidence.

The requirement that the evidentiary fruits of official illegality be excluded from trial has functioned as the principal mechanism for enforcing limitations on the actions of police for nearly 50 years. However, the exclusion of illegally obtained evidence has always been controversial in US law, and while the exclusionary remedy retains its central importance in regulating the conduct of the police, the USSC's approach toward the exclusion of illegally obtained evidence has undergone a major transformation in recent decades. The decisions in *Mapp*, *Massiah*, and *Miranda* generally reflect the view that the exclusion from trial of evidence derived through illegal means is required as a constitutional mandate. In the years since those cases were decided a different interpretation has emerged as a result of a shift in the ideological balance on the USSC beginning in the 1970s. The approach of the current USSC majority to the exclusion of illegally obtained evidence is characterized by a parsimonious conception of the rights guaranteed by the constitution based on (or justified by) a textualist theory of constitutional interpretation. The upshot of this approach has been to demote the exclusionary rule from the status of a right to that of a remedy. In evaluating whether to apply the exclusionary

[4] See, e.g., Hopt v. Utah, 110 U.S. 574, 585 (1884).

[5] Bram v. United States, 168 U.S. 532 (1897).

[6] Brown v. Mississippi, 297 U.S. 278 (1936).

[7] Weeks v. United States, 232 U.S. 383 (1914).

[8] See, e.g., Tucker v. State, 128 Miss. 211 (1922).

rule the Court has applied a balancing test that weighs the deterrent benefits of exclusion against its costs measured in terms of lost evidence. The practical consequence has been to significantly restrict the use of exclusion of illegally obtained evidence as a response to violations of the constitution.

1.2 Rules of Exclusion/Admissibility in Relation to Violations of the Right to Privacy

1.2.1 General Provisions Protecting the Right to Privacy

Because of its federal structure, the US has 51 separate legal systems: the federal system and the 50 state legal systems. Each of the 51 jurisdictions has its own constitution, many of which include protections against governmental intrusions on privacy and personal security. There are also a variety of statutes that protect privacy. While some state laws have significance within the particular state, by far the most important source of legal protection for privacy as it relates to the prosecution of crime is the Fourth Amendment to the federal Constitution.

The text of the Fourth Amendment is brief, speaks in broad generalities, and is notoriously ambiguous. The full Fourth Amendment states: "The right of the people to be secure in their persons, houses, papers, and effects against unreasonable searches and seizures, shall not be violated, and no Warrants shall issue but upon probable cause, supported by Oath or affirmation, and particularly describing the place to be searched, and persons or things to be seized." There is, however, a vast body of USSC jurisprudence applying the commands of the Amendment in particular cases, and it is these decisions that contain the positive doctrine relating to search and seizure.

The ambiguity of the Fourth Amendment arises from the fact that it includes two seemingly distinct rights or commands. The first part of the Amendment—the "unreasonableness" clause—guarantees the right of the people to be secure against searches and seizures that are "unreasonable"; the second part of the Amendment—the warrant clause—specifies requirements for a valid warrant. The most important requirement is that the warrant be supported by probable cause.

The language of the Fourth Amendment does not, on its face, clarify the relationship between the prohibition against unreasonable searches and seizures and the requirement of probable cause for warrants. While the correct interpretation of the Fourth Amendment continues to be debated, the USSC's application of the Amendment has generally assumed that the two clauses should be construed together as expressing a unified rule for the legality of government searches and seizures. Although the syntax of the Fourth Amendment would seem to indicate two separate norms, the second, warrant clause, has generally been taken as establishing the standard for when a search or a seizure is reasonable under the first clause. The assumption underlying much of the Court's Fourth Amendment jurisprudence is that in order to be constitutionally reasonable, a search or seizure must be carried out pursuant to a warrant that is supported by probable cause.

The first ten amendments to the constitution known collectively as the Bill of Rights were added in 1791, 2 years after the constitution itself was ratified. At the time of their enactment the Bill of Rights were clearly intended as limitations on the powers of the federal government, and for the better part of a century had no relevance to the states. The relationship between the states and the federal government changed dramatically in the latter part of the nineteenth century as a result of amendments to the US constitution following the civil war. The most important change as it relates to criminal procedure is language in the Fourteenth Amendment that guarantees a right against state deprivations of life, liberty or property without "due process of law". The full implications of this provision were not realized for many decades, but it eventually resulted in the extension of most of the criminal procedure protections in the Bill of Rights to the states. Today the terms of the Fourth Amendment limit the actions of state officials in precisely the same way they limit the federal government.

The substantive protections of the Fourth Amendment apply to "*searches* and *seizures*" of "persons, houses, papers, and effects" (emphasis added). This language encompasses several distinct interests; a search entails interference with privacy, while a seizure relates to possessory interests or the interest in personal liberty. Fourth Amendment doctrine has developed to reflect the different interests involved in a search and a seizure as well as the different interests implicated by particular types of searches and seizures.

Although the Fourth Amendment has been in existence for more than two centuries, most of the contemporary law of search and seizure is contained in USSC decisions rendered in the past 50 years. Much of the current Fourth Amendment doctrine relating to searches traces its source to the USSC's 1967 decision in *Katz v. United States*.[9] Under the framework established in *Katz*, the threshold question is whether the means by which the challenged evidence was acquired infringed the defendant's reasonable expectation of privacy. If the evidence was obtained as a result of a search subject to Fourth Amendment regulation, and if the search was not conducted pursuant to a valid warrant, then the discovery of the evidence is unlawful unless the facts satisfy an exception to the general requirement of a warrant and probable cause.

The reasonable expectation of privacy test announced in *Katz* represents an advance over the Court's earlier approach, but it has nevertheless been justly criticized as both circular and difficult to apply. The crux of the inquiry requires a determination whether an individual's expectation that certain facts shall remain private is one that society is prepared to recognize as reasonable or legitimate. The Court has devised a number of ostensibly objective criteria for answering that question, but the application of those criteria has been inconsistent and based on dubious assumptions, and the nearly inescapable impression is that the stated grounds for the decisions conceal an implicit balancing of the burden of a particular investigative technique on privacy against its utility in obtaining evidence of crime.

---

[9] 389 U.S. 347 (1967).

As one leading commentator has written, the determination whether particular police conduct constitutes a search inevitably involves a "value judgment" as to "whether, if the particular form of surveillance practiced by the police is permitted to go unregulated by constitutional constraints, the amount of privacy and freedom remaining to citizens would be diminished to a compass inconsistent with the aims of a free and open society".[10]

In the 40-odd years since the *Katz* test was first announced the USSC has applied it to a variety of forms of police investigation. The Court has found, for example, that the Fourth Amendment is not implicated in the gathering of evidence through the use of informers or undercover police posing as partners in crime.[11] The reason given for this rule is that the defendant assumes the risk that his misplaced confidences will be communicated to the police and used as evidence. The Court relied on the same assumption of the risk rationale to find that it is not a search for police surreptitiously to record the numbers dialed from the defendant's home telephone through the use of a pen register.[12] The Court has held that the use of an airplane[13] or a helicopter[14] to view the defendant's yard is not a search on the grounds that one could not reasonably expect privacy from such observations since the facts seen by the police could have been observed by any member of the public who happened to fly over the defendant's yard. By the same logic, the use of an electronic tracking device to track the progress of a car on public streets is not a search since the car's movements are plainly visible.[15] The Court reached a different conclusion in a case in which a tracking device placed inside a container revealed that the container was moved inside a home.[16] The fact that the investigation focused on the home was also apparently the critical factor in a decision that the use of a thermal imaging device to measure relative amounts of heat emanating from various parts of the defendant's house was a Fourth Amendment search.[17]

Although the USSC continues to reiterate that a search is considered unreasonable unless it is carried out pursuant to a warrant based on a judicial finding of probable cause the requirement of a search warrant is subject to significant exceptions.[18] The USSC has long recognized that it is constitutionally reasonable for police to search without a warrant based on their own evaluation of probable cause when an immediate search is necessary because of exigent circumstances.[19]

---

[10] Amsterdam (1974, 403).

[11] United States v. White, 401 U.S. 745 (1971).

[12] Smith v. Maryland, 442 U.S. 735 (1979).

[13] California v. Ciraolo, 476 U.S. 207 (1986).

[14] Florida v. Riley, 488 U.S. 445 (1989).

[15] United States v. Knotts, 460 U.S. 276 (1983).

[16] United States v. Karo, 468 U.S. 705 (1984).

[17] Kyllo v. United States, 533 U.S. 27 (2001).

[18] As Justice Clarence Thomas commented in one recent case, "our cases stand for the illuminating proposition that warrantless searches are *per se* unreasonable, except, of course, when they are not." Groh v. Ramirez, 540 U.S. 551, 573 (2004) (Thomas, J., dissenting).

[19] See, e.g., Warden v. Hayden, 387 U.S. 294 (1967).

be so ephemeral and so neatly severed from its conceptual nexus with the freedom from all brutish means of coercing evidence as not to merit this Court's high regard as a freedom 'implicit in the concept of ordered liberty'".[34]

These statements suggest that the admission of illegally seized evidence in state criminal trials is itself a violation of the federal constitution. There is other language in *Mapp*, however, that supports the understanding of the exclusionary rule articulated in *Wolf* as a judicially created prophylactic mechanism for effectuation of constitutional privacy protections. The Court quoted language from a case decided the year before describing the exclusionary rule as designed "to deter—to compel respect for the constitutional guarantee in the only effectively available way—by removing the incentive to disregard it".[35] A substantial portion of the opinion is devoted to an argument that the experience of states with alternatives to the exclusionary rule has proven other remedies to be ineffective. The premise of this argument is that the exclusionary rule is constitutionally required or justified not because admission of illegally seized evidence violates the constitution but because all other enforcement mechanisms have failed. While the Court labeled these "factual considerations" as "not basically relevant" to the decision, the inclusion of the argument would seem to indicate a degree of ambivalence over the grounds for the decision.

Although the constitutional exclusionary rule has served as the principal enforcement mechanism for violations of the law of search and seizure for nearly half a century, the jurisprudential foundations and legitimacy of the rule continue to be disputed. While the membership of the USSC has always included both supporters and critics of the exclusionary rule, the balance of views has shifted in recent decades. In the years after *Mapp* a majority of the USSC seemed to regard the admission of illegally seized evidence as a violation of the constitution. Although the timing of the shift cannot be pinpointed with precision, the current USSC majority clearly takes a different view. The Court has unequivocally rejected the proposition that exclusion of illegally seized evidence is required by the Fourth Amendment, and regards the exclusionary rule as a judicially created deterrent remedy designed to protect the right against unreasonable search and seizures.

The contrasting understandings of the exclusionary rule received particularly clear expression in the opinions filed in the 1984 decision in *United States v. Leon*,[36] the case in which the Court first recognized the so-called "good faith" exception to the exclusionary rule. The majority opinion in the case was written by Justice Byron White, a long-time advocate for the view that the benefits of the exclusionary rule, in deterring violations of the Fourth Amendment, should be weighed against the costs of lost evidence, and that application of the rule should be limited to situations where its deterrent potential is significant. Justice White rejects the view that

---

[34] Ibid.

[35] Ibid, 656 (quoting Elkins v. United States, 364 U.S. 206, 217 (1960)).

[36] 468 U.S. 897 (1984).

"the exclusionary rule is a necessary corollary of the Fourth Amendment".[37] The exclusion of illegally seized evidence is not itself a part of the Fourth Amendment guarantee since "the wrong condemned by the Amendment is 'fully accomplished' by the unlawful search or seizure itself".[38] That conclusion is based on the text of Fourth Amendment, which "contains no provision expressly precluding the use of evidence obtained in violation of its commands", and on an examination of the Amendment's origins and purposes, which "makes clear that the use of fruits of a past unlawful search or seizure 'work[s] no new Fourth Amendment wrong'".[39] Because a violation of the Fourth Amendment is complete upon the occurrence of an unlawful search or seizure, the exclusionary rule cannot and was not intended to serve as a "cure" for the constitutional violation. Much like a civil suit for damages, the rule "operates as 'a judicially created remedy designed to safeguard Fourth Amendment rights generally through its deterrent effect, rather than a personal constitutional right of the party aggrieved'".[40]

The dissenting opinion of Justice Brennan in *Leon* sets forth the alternative understanding of the Fourth Amendment exclusionary rule that regards the right against governmental interference with privacy or liberty and the right to exclude the fruits of that interference as "coordinate components of the central embracing right to be free from unreasonable searches and seizures".[41] Justice Brennan's conclusion that the exclusionary remedy is inseparable from the underlying substantive guarantee is premised on a belief that the prohibition against unreasonable search and seizure is directed at the government as a whole, including the courts, and that exclusion of illegally obtained evidence is necessary to give effect to the Amendment's essential purpose.

> The judiciary is responsible, no less than the executive, for ensuring that constitutional rights are respected.... Because seizures are executed principally to secure evidence, and because such evidence generally has utility in our legal system only in the context of a trial supervised by a judge, it is apparent that the admission of illegally seized evidence implicates the same constitutional concerns as the initial seizure of that evidence. Indeed, by admitting unlawfully seized evidence, the judiciary becomes a part of what is in fact a single governmental action prohibited by the terms of the Amendment.[42]

Thus, when courts admit illegally obtained evidence they become complicit in a violation of the constitution. As Judge (later Justice) Benjamin Cardozo stated in a case rejecting the exclusionary rule as a matter of state law, "[t]he thought is that in appropriating the results, [the court] ratifies the means".[43]

---

[37] Ibid, 905.

[38] Ibid, 906 (quoting United States v. Calandra, 414 U.S. 338, 454 (1974)).

[39] Ibid, (quoting United States v. Calandra, 414 U.S. 338, 454 (1974)).

[40] Ibid, (quoting United States v. Calandra, 414 U.S. 338, 348 (1974)).

[41] Leon, 468 U.S. at 935 (Brennan, J., dissenting).

[42] Ibid, 932–933.

[43] People v. Defore, 242 N.Y. 13, 22 (1926).

themselves suffered a Fourth Amendment violation are entitled to assert the violation and secure a remedy. In order to obtain the benefit of the exclusionary rule the party seeking exclusion "must have been a victim of a search or seizure … as distinguished from one who claims prejudice only through the use of evidence gathered as a consequence of a search or seizure directed at someone else".[49]

The rule that only those who have suffered an unlawful search or seizure are entitled to invoke the exclusionary rule is arguably in tension with the current rationale for the rule as designed to deter Fourth Amendment violations. The logic of deterrence would seem to dictate that applying the exclusionary rule more widely would have the effect of further reducing the frequency of Fourth Amendment violations. Indeed, limiting the exclusionary rule to the victims of unlawful searches or seizures opens the possibility that police will conduct searches they know are unlawful in anticipation that those against whom the unlawfully obtained evidence is to be used will lack standing to seek exclusion.[50]

The Supreme Court has acknowledged that expanding the scope of the exclusionary rule by making it available to parties against whom unlawfully seized evidence is being used would increase the rule's deterrent impact. In explaining its refusal to extend exclusion beyond those who have suffered a Fourth Amendment violation the Court has emphasized that the gains in deterrence achieved through applying the exclusionary rule more broadly must be balanced against its cost in terms of lost evidence and possibly lost convictions. The Court has held that the balance of costs and benefits does not warrant expanding exclusion beyond the victims of unlawful searches or seizures. It has adhered to that view even when it had the effect of permitting the government to use the evidentiary fruits of a deliberate violation of the Fourth Amendment. In *United States v. Payner*[51] investigators for the Internal Revenue Service conducted a search of a banker's briefcase that they knew was unlawful after being advised that the standing doctrine would prevent bank customers against whom the illegally obtained documents were to be used from objecting to their admission at trial. Although acknowledging the interest in deterring "deliberate intrusions into the privacy of persons who are unlikely to become defendants in a criminal prosecution,"[52] the USSC concluded that that interest "does not justify the exclusion of tainted evidence at the instance of a party who was not the victim of the challenged practices".[53]

Just as states may provide greater protection against searches and seizures under their own constitutions than is guaranteed by the Fourth Amendment, states may also apply their own exclusionary rules more broadly than the federal rule. Nearly

---

[49] Jones v. United States, 362 U.S. 257, 261 (1960).

[50] See, e.g., Rakas v. Illinois, 439 U.S. 128, 157 (1978) (White, J. dissenting) (stating that decision that passengers qua passengers do not have standing to contest search of car amounts to declaring "open season" on search of cars as far as passengers are concerned).

[51] 447 U.S. 727 (1980).

[52] Ibid, 733.

[53] Ibid, 735.

40 years before the USSC extended the federal exclusionary rule to the states in *Mapp v. Ohio*, the Supreme Court of California held that evidence obtained in violation of the state constitution could not be used in a criminal prosecution.[54] When presented with the question of who is entitled to claim the benefit of the exclusionary rule, the California Court expressly rejected the federal rule that standing is limited to victims of unlawful search or seizure.[55] California's "vicarious exclusionary rule" remained in effect until 1985 when it was abolished as a result of a ballot measure that added language to the California constitution providing that, subject to a few stated exceptions, "relevant evidence shall not be excluded in any criminal proceeding".[56]

1.2.5 The Independent Source Doctrine

The fruit of the poisonous tree doctrine extends the reach of the Fourth Amendment exclusionary rule to include indirect or derivative fruits of unconstitutional searches and seizures. The doctrine also functions as a limitation on the exclusionary rule by limiting the rule's operation to evidence that was discovered as a causal result of a constitutional violation. The fact that an individual has suffered a violation of her constitutional rights does not immunize her from being prosecuted provided the evidence is acquired through lawful means.

The application of the exclusionary rule has always required proof of a causal connection between the challenged evidence and a violation of the Fourth Amendment. There is room for disagreement about what that requirement means, however, and in recent years the Supreme Court has narrowed the scope of the exclusionary rule by expanding the circumstances in which evidence will be deemed to have been acquired by means that are independent of the constitutional violation.[57] In its most recent decision on the independent source doctrine the Supreme Court extended the rule to circumstances in which the police discovered evidence unlawfully and then re-discovered the same evidence through lawful means. In *United States v. Murray*[58] police had probable cause to believe that there was

---

[54] People v. Mayen, 188 Cal. 237 (1922).

[55] People v. Martin, 45 Cal.2d 755 (1955).

[56] California Constitution Article 1 Section 28(f)(2). The California Supreme Court held in In re Lance W., 37 Cal.3d 873, (1985) that this language was intended to permit exclusion of relevant, but unlawfully obtained evidence, only if exclusion is required by the United States Constitution.

[57] The independent source doctrine was first recognized by the USSC in dicta in Silverthorne Lumber Co. v. United States, 251 U.S. 385 (1920). After holding that the prosecution could not use information gleaned from documents that were obtained through an illegal search to subpoena those same documents, the Court stated, "Of course this does not mean that the facts thus obtained become sacred and inaccessible. If knowledge of them is gained from an independent source they may be proved like any others". Ibid, 392.

[58] 487 U.S. 533 (1988).

attenuated to warrant admission. The majority did not, however, attempt to relate its dissipation analysis to the purposes of the exclusionary rule. In a concurring opinion written by Justice Powell the significance of attenuation is explained in terms of its effect on the deterrent value of exclusion. "The notion of the 'dissipation of the taint' attempts to mark the point at which the detrimental consequences of illegal police action become so attenuated that the deterrent effect of the exclusionary rule no longer justifies its cost".[65] Thus, when the question of attenuation is viewed from the perspective of deterrence the nature of the constitutional violation becomes the primary focus of the analysis. The deterrent value of the exclusionary rule can be expected to be greatest in cases in which official conduct was flagrantly abusive of Fourth Amendment rights. Evidence obtained as a consequence of a flagrant violation should be admitted only with the "clearest indication of attenuation". In the absence of police conduct that is willful or at least negligent, however, "the deterrence rationale of the exclusionary rule does not obtain" and there is "no legitimate justification for depriving the prosecution of reliable evidence".[66]

The USSC added a new wrinkle to the attenuation doctrine in the recent case of *Hudson v. Michigan*.[67] The issue in *Hudson* concerned the applicability of the exclusionary rule to violations of the so-called knock-and-announce rule, the requirement that police executing a search warrant provide the occupants an opportunity to admit them into the house before entering by force. The Court gave as one reason for holding that the exclusionary rule is never applicable to violations of the knock-and-announce rule that by its nature the constitutional violation is attenuated from the evidence. The attenuation identified in *Hudson* is different from attenuation recognized in prior cases, however. This second form of attenuation is not based on the character of the causal links between the constitutional violation and the discovery of the evidence but on the relationship between the purposes served by the rule that was violated and the exclusion of evidence. Specifically, there is attenuation in this second sense when "the interests protected by the constitutional guarantee that has been violated would not be served by suppression of the evidence obtained".[68] The interests served by the knock-and-announce rule include protection against violence that could occur if the occupant mistakenly believed that the officers were intruders, the protection against the destruction of property caused by an unnecessary forced entry, and protection of privacy and dignity interests that can be compromised by a sudden entrance. Since the exclusion of evidence obtained following a violation of the knock-and-announce rule furthered none of those interests the Court found the discovery of the evidence to be attenuated.

[65] Ibid, 609 (1975) (Powell, J. concurring in part).

[66] Ibid, 612.

[67] 547 U.S. 586 (2006).

[68] Ibid, 594.

1.2.8 *The Good Faith Exception*

In the past several decades the conservative majority on the USSC has increasingly emphasized deterrence as the sole justification for excluding evidence obtained in violation of the Fourth Amendment. The Court took the logic of deterrence furthest when in *United States v. Leon*[69] it created an exception to the Fourth Amendment exclusionary rule for evidence seized by police while acting in good faith reliance on a search warrant that was later declared to be invalid. Under the good faith exception recognized in *Leon*, the exclusion of evidence based on an invalid warrant is not required if a reasonably well-trained police officer would have believed that the warrant was valid.

The majority opinion in *Leon* takes as its starting point the premise that the exclusionary rule is not "a personal constitutional right of the aggrieved party" but rather "a judicially created remedy designed to safeguard Fourth Amendment rights generally through its deterrent effect".[70] Because an "unbending application of the exclusionary sanction to enforce ideals of governmental rectitude would impede unacceptably the truth-finding functions of judge and jury",[71] the applicability of the exclusionary rule is to be determined through a weighing of the deterrent benefits of exclusion against the costs in terms of lost evidence. In applying this balancing test to the situation in which police seize evidence under a warrant that is later found to be invalid the Court first rejects the view that exclusion is justified in order to deter misconduct or errors by judges. The exclusionary rule, according to the Court, "is designed to deter police misconduct rather than to punish the errors of judges and magistrates".[72] Furthermore, there is no evidence that judges and magistrates are inclined to ignore or subvert the Fourth Amendment and no basis for believing that excluding evidence seized pursuant to a warrant would have a significant deterrent effect on the issuing judge or magistrate. Thus, "[i]f exclusion of evidence pursuant to a subsequently invalidated warrant is to have any deterrent effect … it must alter the behavior of individual law enforcement officers or the policies of their departments".[73]

The Court's evaluation of the likely impact on police misconduct of excluding evidence obtained in reliance on a facially valid warrant concludes that the deterrent benefit of exclusion is minimal at best. "The deterrent purpose of the exclusionary rule necessarily assumes that the police have engaged in willful, or at the very least negligent, conduct".[74] For that reason, "where the officer's conduct is objectively reasonable, 'excluding the evidence will not further the ends of the exclusionary rule

---

[69] 468 U.S. 897 (1984).

[70] Ibid, 906 (quoting United States v. Calandra, 414 U.S. 338, 348 (1974)).

[71] Ibid, 907 (quoting United States v. Payner, 447 U.S. 727, 734 (1980)).

[72] Ibid, 916.

[73] Ibid, 918.

[74] Ibid, 919 (quoting United States v. Peltier, 422 U.S. 531, 539 (1975)).

in any appreciable way'", and "[e]xcluding the evidence can in no way affect his future conduct unless it is to make him less willing to do his duty".[75] But application of the exclusionary rule to evidence obtained pursuant to a warrant that was later found to be invalid would not be appropriate even if exclusion did deter some police misconduct or create incentives for adherence to the commands of the Fourth Amendment. This is so because "when an officer acting with objective good faith has obtained a search warrant from a judge or magistrate and acted within its scope" there is in most cases "no police illegality and thus nothing to deter".[76]

The *Leon* case involved a search pursuant to a warrant that was later found to be invalid because the evidence on which the warrant was based was found to be insufficient to establish probable cause. In *Massachusetts v. Shepherd*,[77] a case decided on the same day as *Leon*, the Court applied the good faith exception to uphold the admission of evidence discovered under a warrant that was defective because it did not particularly describe the items subject to seizure.[78] In the years since *Leon* the USSC has extended the good faith principle to a number of other contexts. In *Illinois v. Krull*[79] the Court held the good faith exception applicable to warrantless administrative searches carried out in good faith reliance on a statute that was later declared to be unconstitutional, and in *Arizona v. Evans*[80] the Court held that the good faith rule applied to police who reasonably relied on mistaken information in a court database that an arrest warrant was outstanding. Finally, in the 2009 decision of *Herring v. United States*[81] the Court extended the good faith exception to the situation in which police rely on mistaken information regarding the existence of a warrant in a database maintained by police.

1.2.9 Knock-and-Announce

In *Hudson v. Michigan*,[82] decided in 2006, the USSC took the unusual step of abolishing the exclusionary rule for an entire category of Fourth Amendment violations. The defendant in Hudson sought suppression of evidence seized during a search of his house under a search warrant. The suppression claim was based on a failure on the part of the officers executing the warrant to comply with what's known as the knock-and-announce rule. Although not expressly stated in the Fourth Amendment, the USSC has found that

[75] Ibid, 920 (quoting Stone v. Powell, 428 U.S. 465, 539–540 (1976)) (White, J., dissenting).

[76] Ibid, 920–21.

[77] 468 U.S. 981 (1984).

[78] The error resulted from the magistrate's failure to strike out inapplicable language contained in form warrant application. The police officer who executed the warrant failed to discover the error because he relied on the magistrate's assurance that the necessary modifications had been made.

[79] 480 U.S. 340 (1987).

[80] 514 U.S. 1 (1995).

[81] 555 U.S. 135 (2009).

[82] 547 U.S. 586 (2006).

knock-and-announce was considered a necessary part of a reasonable search at the time the constitution was adopted, and on that basis the Court has held knock-and-announce to be a requirement for a lawful search under current law. The rule requires that police executing a warrant provide the occupants of the search premises an opportunity to admit the officers and comply with their demands before using force to gain entry. The Michigan courts found that the rule had been violated because the police waited for just 3–5 s after announcing their arrival before entering the house.

The USSC accepted the state courts' conclusion that the police violated the Fourth Amendment but held that the violation did not require suppression of the evidence seized during the search. Justice Scalia's opinion for the Court provided three separate reasons for holding that the exclusionary rule does not apply to violations of the knock-and-announce rule. The first two reasons were based on an application of existing exclusionary rule doctrine. The Court gave as its first reason for not requiring exclusion its conclusion that "the constitutional violation of the illegal manner of entry was not a but-for cause of obtaining the evidence".[83] That is, the police would have discovered the gun and the drugs inside the house whether the "preliminary misstep [of failing to allow the occupants an opportunity to respond] had occurred or not".[84] The Court next found that even if but-for causation between the constitutional violation and the discovery of the evidence were established suppression should be denied under the attenuation doctrine. Here the Court distinguished two meanings of attenuation. Attenuation can occur "when the causal connection is remote",[85] but even if the connection between the illegality and the evidence is direct, attenuation occurs when "the interest protected by the constitutional guarantee that has been violated would not be served by suppression of the evidence obtained".[86] Since the knock-and-announce rule serves interests wholly distinct from "the interest in preventing the government from seeing or taking evidence described in a warrant", the exclusionary rule is inapplicable.[87]

The third reason given by the Court for eliminating the exclusionary rule for violations of the knock-and-announce rule carries the greatest implications for the future of the exclusionary rule. The Court applied the balancing test used in *United States v. Leon* and other cases and concluded that costs of excluding evidence following a violation of knock-and-announce outweigh the benefits. The costs of exclusion include not only "the grave adverse consequences that exclusion of relevant incriminating evidence always entails (viz., the risk of releasing dangerous criminals into society)" but also "a constant flood [of claims] of alleged failures to observe the rule" raising questions that are "difficult for the trial court to determine and even more difficult for an appellate court to review".[88] Application of the

[83] Ibid, 592.

[84] Ibid.

[85] Ibid.

[86] Ibid.

[87] Ibid, 594.

[88] Ibid, 595.

exclusionary rule to violations of knock-and-announce could also result in preventable violence against *Mapp* police and destruction of evidence, since "officers would be inclined to wait longer than the law requires" to avoid the "massive" consequences of running afoul of the rule.[89] In weighing the benefits of the exclusion the Court stated that "[m]assive deterrence is hardly required" since police could be expected to have little incentive to violate the knock-and-announce rule.[90] Finally, the Court argued that because of changed circumstances since the decision extended the Fourth Amendment exclusionary rule to the states exclusion may no longer be necessary to deter at least some police illegality. In particular the Court pointed to the increased availability of civil suits and the greater professionalism and internal discipline of police.[91]

1.3 Rules of Admissibility/Exclusion in Relation to Illegal Interrogations

1.3.1 Involuntary Confessions

Under the common law of evidence, as applied in the United States, confessions of the accused that were found to be involuntary were excluded as presumptively unreliable.[92] In 1897 in *Bram v. United States*[93] the USSC constitutionalized the common law rule of evidence holding that exclusion of involuntary confessions was required by the privilege against compelled self-incrimination contained in the Fifth Amendment.

At the time *Bram* was decided the Fifth Amendment prohibition against compelled self-incrimination was not understood to be applicable to the actions of state officials. However, in *Brown v. Mississippi*[94] decided in 1936 the USSC held that the use of an involuntary confession at a state criminal trial violates the due process clause of the Fourteenth Amendment. In 1964 the right against compelled self-incrimination became available as a second basis for exclusion of involuntary confessions in state court when the USSC held that the Fifth Amendment privilege was applicable to the states through the Fourteenth Amendment.[95] Initially, at least,

---

[89] Ibid.

[90] Ibid, 596.

[91] Ibid, 597–599.

[92] See Hopt v. Utah, 110 U.S. 574 (1884)

[93] 168 U.S. 532 (1897).

[94] 297 U.S. 278 (1936).

[95] Malloy v. Hogan, 378 U.S. 1 (1964).

the due process clause and the self incrimination privilege established different standards: the self-incrimination standard was based on the broad definition of involuntariness adopted from the common law as the measure of a Fifth Amendment violation; the due process test has always been narrower than the common law rule. The two constitutional texts are now understood as defining a single test for the voluntariness of a confession based on the test developed in cases decided under the due process clause.

The test for whether a confession is involuntary in violation of due process is whether the suspect's will was overborne as a result of official coercion.[96] Resolution of that issue is based on a case-by-case analysis of the totality of the circumstances, including the actions of the police in obtaining the confession and the characteristics or susceptibilities of the individual suspect. The use of deception to induce a confession, although relevant to whether the suspect's will has been overborne, does not necessarily render a confession involuntary. Similarly, promises of leniency or threats of harsh treatment are evaluated in terms of their effect in overbearing the suspect's will and do not invariably result in exclusion of a confession. The USSC has drawn a clear line when it comes to confessions obtained through threats or use of violence. A confession given in response to actual or threatened use of physical violence against the accused is involuntary.[97]

The USSC has addressed the scope of the exclusionary rule for violations of the due process right against the use of involuntary confessions only rarely. The only cases to address the issue directly involved the admissibility of an involuntary confession to impeach the defendant's trial testimony. In *Mincey v. Arizona*[98] the Court held that an involuntary confession is inadmissible for all purposes, including impeachment. Although the USSC has never decided the issue, it is generally assumed that the fruit of the poisonous tree doctrine applies to involuntary confessions and requires suppression of evidence obtained as an indirect result of an involuntary confession as well as the confession itself. It is also generally assumed that the limitations on the fruit of the poisonous tree doctrine developed in the Fourth Amendment context apply to secondary fruits of due process violations. Thus, evidence discovered as a result of an involuntary confession is admissible if the causal connection between the illegality and the discovery of the evidence is attenuated, and the evidence discovered as a consequence of a due process violation may be admitted if the same evidence would inevitably have been discovered through lawful means.

[96] Spano v. New York, 360 U.S. 315 (1959).

[97] Arizona v. Fulminante, 499 U.S. 279 (1991).

[98] 437 U.S. 385 (1978). *See also* New Jersey v. Portash, 440 U.S. 450 (1979).

1.3.2 The Protection Against Unknowing Self-Incrimination: The Miranda Paradigm

In its 1966 decision in *Miranda v. Arizona*[99] the USSC established the rule that a statement made in response to custodial interrogation may not be used at trial unless the suspect has first been advised of certain rights and knowingly and voluntarily waived those rights. Specifically, the suspect must be informed that she has a right not to speak and that if she does speak what she says may be used against her. As a further protection against official compulsion to speak the suspect must be told that she has a right to have an attorney present during interrogation, and that if she cannot afford to hire an attorney one will be provided. These rights can be waived, and statements obtained following a knowing and voluntary waiver may be used at trial. If the suspect invokes either the right to silence or the right to have an attorney present during interrogation further protections come into play. A decision by the suspect to waive her rights and answer questions can be reversed at any point during the interrogation, and statements obtained after the suspect has indicated that she will no longer answer questions or wishes to have an attorney present are inadmissible.

The *Miranda* doctrine was born of the USSC's frustration with the due process standard as the exclusive mechanism for regulating the conduct of the police and adjudicating the admissibility of pre-trial confessions. With *Miranda* the Court sought to establish a clear, easily administered rule to replace the fact-specific case-by-case approach required under the due process approach.[100]

The requirements set forth in *Miranda* are based on the Fifth Amendment right against compelled self-incrimination made applicable to the states through the due process clause of the Fourteenth Amendment. While the imposition of the *Miranda* rule on the states necessarily means that it is based on the constitution, there is some uncertainty in the decision as to the precise relationship between the procedures it prescribes and the right to be free from compelled self-incrimination. The Court explained the need for the procedures mandated in the case in terms of the compulsion that is inherent in custodial interrogation. The general tenor of the opinion suggests that any statement obtained in the absence of warnings and waiver is compelled in violation of the Fifth Amendment. At one point in the opinion, for example, the Court writes that "[u]nless adequate protective devices are employed

[99] 384 U.S. 436 (1966).

[100] The *Miranda* doctrine was controversial from the start. Even the rule's supporters acknowledge that the Court's decision has a legislative quality to it that is atypical of the incrementalism and case-by-case approach to law making that generally characterizes common law decision-making. *Miranda*'s critics contend that the USSC has the power to enforce the commands of the constitution but it does not have the authority to establish procedures to prevent the constitution from being violated. The *Miranda* scheme has also been criticized on the ground that it goes too far in discouraging suspects from making lawful, voluntary confessions. While the impact of *Miranda* in reducing the frequency of confessions is disputed, the case clearly has not eliminated police interrogation as a mechanism for gathering evidence for trial, as some opponents had predicted.

to dispel the compulsion inherent in custodial surroundings, no statement obtained from the defendant can truly be the product of his free choice".[101] There is also language in the opinion, however, supportive of the view that the rule requires the exclusion of statements when there is a risk of compulsion in order to prevent the use of statements that are in fact compelled. The Court refers to the "potentiality for compulsion" and acknowledges that the statements made by Miranda and the other defendants that were ruled inadmissible in the case might not have been "involuntary in traditional terms".[102]

The USSC's current approach to defining the scope of exclusion for violations of *Miranda* parallels the approach followed in the Fourth Amendment context. Just as the reach of the Fourth Amendment exclusionary rule has come to turn on the constitutional status of the rule, the Court has linked the question of the evidentiary consequences of a *Miranda* violation to the question of the relationship between *Miranda*'s requirements and the constitution. Over the four decades since the case was decided, the Court's *Miranda* jurisprudence has increasingly come to reflect a conservative understanding of the rule as a mechanism for preventing constitutional violations rather than as a statement of what the constitution requires. Because a violation of *Miranda*'s prophylactic procedures is not a violation of the constitution, *Miranda*'s exclusionary rule is limited to statements obtained as a direct result of a *Miranda* violation.

The premises of the *Miranda* rule have been contested from the beginning, and the evolution of the balance of views held by members of the USSC is reflected in the Court's decisions over the past 50 years. The Court first imposed limits on the *Miranda* exclusionary in a case decided in 1971. In *Harris v. New York*[103] the Court held that a statement obtained in violation of *Miranda* may be used to impeach a defendant who testifies inconsistently with the out of court statement. The Court majority based its decision on a balancing of the costs of exclusion in denying the prosecution the means to test the credibility of the defendant's testimony against the benefits of deterring "proscribed police conduct". Although the *Harris* Court did not address the constitutional status of *Miranda*, the decision to allow the use of statements obtained in violation of *Miranda* for impeachment rests on an implicit assumption that a violation of *Miranda* is not a violation of the Fifth Amendment, since a statement that has been compelled contrary to the Fifth Amendment cannot be used for any purpose, including impeachment.[104]

The scope of the *Miranda* exclusionary rule came before the Court again 3 years after *Harris* in *Michigan v. Tucker*.[105] The issue in *Tucker* was whether the *Miranda* rule prevented the prosecution from presenting the testimony of a witness who was discovered as a result of a statement made by the defendant without adequate warnings.

---

[101] *Miranda*, 384 U.S. at 458.

[102] Ibid, 457.

[103] 401 U.S. 222 (1971).

[104] Mincy v. Arizona, 437 U.S. 385 (1978).

[105] 417 U.S. 433 (1974).

Although the significance of the decision is somewhat muddied by the procedural posture of the case when it reached the Court,[106] the opinion by Justice (later, Chief Justice) William Rehnquist proved to be a harbinger of the Court's approach to the *Miranda* exclusionary rule. The Court's analysis of the admissibility of the witness's testimony focused on the jurisprudential underpinnings of the *Miranda* rule. The Court based its holding that the testimony was admissible in large part on a conclusion that the warnings mandated by *Miranda* are "not themselves rights protected by the Constitution but instead measures to insure that the right against compulsory self-incrimination [is] protected".[107] Because the violation related to "prophylactic" standards, the fruit of the poisonous tree analysis that might have required exclusion of the evidence did not apply since a violation of a prophylactic rule is not a poisonous tree.

The USSC addressed the scope of the *Miranda* exclusionary rule once again in *Oregon v. Elstad*.[108] The issue in *Elstad* concerned the effect of a statement obtained without *Miranda* warnings on the admissibility of a later statement made after the suspect had been informed of his rights and made a valid waiver. The Court held that the first unwarned statement did not require suppression of the second warned statement, but the majority opinion does not provide a clear explanation of the reason for the result or the principles that govern the admissibility of derivative fruits of *Miranda* violations. The opinion could be read as establishing that the consequences of a *Miranda* violation do not extend beyond exclusion of the statement that is a direct result of the violation. The Court questioned the relevance of the derivative fruits doctrine to violations of *Miranda* on the grounds that the fruit of the poisonous tree analysis "assumes the existence of a constitutional violation",[109] and distinguished the treatment of secondary fruits of *Miranda* violations from the approach applicable to violations of the Fourth Amendment on the ground that the *Miranda* exclusionary rule is a prophylactic measure that "serves the Fifth Amendment and sweeps more broadly than the Fifth Amendment itself".[110] While these statements and other parts of the opinion could be taken as indicating that the *Miranda* exclusionary rule is limited to those statements obtained in violation of its requirements, other parts of the Court's opinion suggest that the admissibility of the defendant's second statement was based on the same attenuation analysis applied to the secondary fruits of Fourth Amendment violations. As support for its conclusion the Court emphasized the significance of police compliance with *Miranda* prior to the second statement in establishing

---

[106] The questioning of the defendant that produced the statement occurred before the *Miranda* decision was announced, but its requirements were nonetheless applicable retroactively because the trial occurred afterwards. The Court cited as one reason for finding that the *Miranda* rule did not require exclusion of the testimony of the witness discovered as a result of the *Miranda* violation the fact that the deterrent benefit of exclusion was diluted by the fact that officer who obtained the confession was acting in good faith.

[107] Michigan v. Tucker, 417 U.S. 433, 444.

[108] 470 U.S. 298 (1985).

[109] Ibid, 305.

[110] Ibid, 306.

that it was voluntary and "cures the condition that rendered the unwarned statement inadmissible".[111] And after having seemingly dismissed the approach to the admissibility of secondary fruits developed in the Fourth Amendment context, the Court relied on a leading Fourth Amendment attenuation case in support of its conclusion that the defendant's second statement was a product of his own volition.

The USSC's characterization of *Miranda* in *Tucker*, *Elstad* and other cases[112] undermined its jurisprudential basis and, by extension, the rule itself. In 2000 the Court was required to confront the implications of its decisions disparaging *Miranda*'s foundations when it agreed to review a lower court decision that had held that *Miranda* could be and had been overruled by an act of Congress. The case arose as a result of a statute enacted in 1968 that sought to displace *Miranda* by declaring any confession to be admissible provided it is voluntary. It is, of course, fundamental that an act of Congress cannot permit that which the constitution forbids. Because the USSC is the final authority on the meaning of the constitution, and because the Court's decision in *Miranda* was commonly understood as a statement of what the constitution requires, the 1968 statute was for many years dismissed as an empty gesture. That began to change, however, as the Court's repeated characterization of the *Miranda* warnings as a prophylactic safeguard and the Court's statements that a violation of those safeguards is not a violation of the constitution raised doubts about the constitutional foundations of the decision. The issue was finally joined in 1999 when the US Court of Appeals for the Fourth Circuit held in *United States v. Dickerson*[113] that the *Miranda* decision had been overruled by the 1968 statute, and therefore the defendant's voluntary statement obtained in violation of *Miranda* was admissible. Upon the defendant's appeal to the USSC the Court's conservative majority was presented with the opportunity to carry the implications of its deconstitutionalization of *Miranda* to their logical conclusion and overrule it.

The USSC released its much-anticipated decision in *Dickerson v. United States*[114] in 2000. The majority opinion by Chief Justice Rehnquist—the author of the opinion that had first described Miranda warnings as prophylactic safeguards rather than constitutional rights—rejected the argument that the case had been overruled. In an effort to navigate a course that would permit it to uphold the *Miranda* decision without disavowing the decisions that impugned its foundations the Court sought to finesse the issue of *Miranda*'s constitutional underpinnings by describing it as a

---

111 Ibid, 310–311.

112 Another case that seemed to deny the core premises of *Miranda* is New York v. Quarles, 467 U.S. 649 (1984). In *Quarles* the Court held that a statement obtained without *Miranda* warnings is admissible if the questioning that elicited the statement was "reasonably prompted by a concern for the public safety." As the dissent pointed out, it is one thing to approve questioning without warnings in the interest of public safety, but it does not follow that the suspect's response be admissible at a later criminal trial.

113 166 F.3d 667 (4th Cir. 1999).

114 530 U.S. 428 (2000).

"constitutional rule",[115] "constitutionally based",[116] and "a constitutional decision".[117] This seeming equivocation drew a contemptuous response from Justice Scalia, who filed a dissent contending that fidelity to post-*Miranda* precedents required that *Miranda* be overruled, and condemning the view that the Court can establish prophylactic rules to protect against the violation of constitutional rights as "an immense and frightening antidemocratic power [that] does not exist".[118]

The opinion in *Dickerson* seemed intended to preserve both the *Miranda* rule itself and the limitations the Court had imposed on the *Miranda* exclusionary rule. Some courts concluded nonetheless that the USSC's affirmation of *Miranda*'s constitutional grounding carried with it as a necessary consequence a reinvigoration of the *Miranda* exclusionary rule. That view was undercut in 2003 when a plurality of the Court declared in *Chavez v. Martinez*[119] that obtaining a statement in violation of *Miranda* does not implicate the self incrimination right unless and until the statement is introduced at trial, and then was laid to rest entirely with the decision the following year in *United States v. Patane*.[120] The issue in *Patane* was whether the defendant's statement obtained in violation of *Miranda* that revealed the location of a gun required suppression of the gun. Justice Thomas' opinion in *Patane* is as clean and decisive as the *Elstad* opinion is obscure. The Court declared unequivocally that the fruit of the poisonous tree doctrine developed in the Fourth Amendment context is inapplicable to violations of the *Miranda* rule. Exclusion of the derivative fruits of illegal searches and seizures is justified by the need to deter violations of the Fourth Amendment. But *Miranda* is a prophylactic designed to protect against the admission of compelled statements. To that end, statements obtained in violation of *Miranda* are presumed to be compelled and inadmissible. A mere failure to give *Miranda* warnings, however, even if deliberate, "does not, by itself, violate a suspect's constitutional rights or even the *Miranda* rule."[121] "Thus, unlike unreasonable searches and seizures under the Fourth Amendment or actual violations of the Due Process Clause or the Self-Incrimination Clause, there is, with respect to mere failures to warn, nothing to deter."[122]

---

[115] Ibid, 438.

[116] Ibid, 440.

[117] Ibid, 432.

[118] Ibid, 446 (Scalia, J., dissenting).

[119] 538 U.S. 760 (2003).

[120] 542 U.S. 630 (2004).

[121] Ibid, 641 (plurality opinion).

[122] Ibid, 642 (plurality opinion). On the same day the Court announced the *Patane* decision it issued its decision in Missouri v. Seibert, 542 U.S. 600 (2004). *Seibert* involved the admissibility of a statement which, though preceded by *Miranda* warnings and a waiver by the defendant, was obtained through the use of a deliberate two-stage interrogation technique in which police first obtain a statement without giving *Miranda* warnings and then elicit substantially the same statement after an administration of warnings. The Court held the second statement inadmissible on the grounds that the deliberate elicitation of the first statement in violation of *Miranda* rendered the *Miranda* warnings given prior to the second statement ineffective. Although the case was not

1.3.3 The Right to the Assistance of Counsel During Pre-trial Interrogation

In *Massiah v. United States*[123] the USSC held that the Sixth Amendment right to the assistance of counsel applies to efforts by police to obtain incriminating admissions from the defendant prior to trial. The case arose as a result of the enlistment of Massiah's co-defendant, who had agreed to cooperate with the prosecution, to elicit statements that were later admitted at Massiah's trial. The Court held that this deliberate elicitation of incriminating statements in the absence of counsel after the state had initiated formal criminal charges violated the defendant's right to counsel under the Sixth Amendment. Although *Massiah* was a federal prosecution, the *Massiah* rule applies in state cases as a result of the incorporation of the Sixth Amendment right to counsel through the Fourteenth Amendment due process clause.[124]

The circumstances that trigger the protections of *Miranda* often overlap with the circumstances that trigger the *Massiah* right to counsel, but the two rules serve different interests and have distinct requirements. *Miranda*'s focus on custody as the condition for the necessity of warnings and the combination of custody and interrogation as constituting a violation reflect the rule's underlying concern with official compulsion to speak. *Massiah* seeks to give effect to the principle that a person accused of a crime should not be required to stand alone before the power of the state, and for that reason its protections attach only after there has been a formal accusation. Unlike interrogation, deliberate elicitation under *Massiah* need not entail the application of pressure to speak.[125]

The USSC opinion in *Massiah* did not explain the nature or justification for the exclusion of evidence obtained in violation of the Sixth Amendment. In a later case the Court characterized the opinion in *Massiah* as "equivocal on what precisely constituted the violation",[126] and pointed to language in the opinion supportive of the view that the violation occurs at the point at which the statement is obtained and to other statements in the opinion indicating that the violation occurs when the defendant's uncounseled statement is admitted in evidence. As one commentator has trenchantly shown, however, the most (if not only) plausible interpretation

---

decided on exclusionary rule grounds, a clear majority of the Justices in *Seibert* endorsed the view that the poisonous tree doctrine is not relevant "for analyzing the admissibility of a subsequent warned confession following 'an initial failure . . . to administer the warnings required by Miranda'". Ibid, 612, n.4, (plurality opinion) (quoting Oregon v. Elstad, 470 U.S 298, 300 (1985)).

[123] 377 U.S. 201 (1964).

[124] *Massiah* was decided in 1964, 2 years before the Court decided *Miranda*, and it was generally assumed that *Miranda*'s Fifth Amendment based approach to the regulation of pre-trial interrogation had entirely supplanted the right to counsel doctrine announced in *Massiah*. However, the Supreme Court breathed new life into the *Massiah* doctrine in the 1977 case of Brewer v. Williams, 430 U.S. 387 (1977).

[125] See Fellers v. United States, 540 U.S. 519 (2004).

[126] Kansas v. Ventris, 129 S.Ct. 1841, 1846 (2009).

is that the Court regarded the Sixth Amendment to be violated upon the admission of the defendant's statement at trial and not when it is elicited by police.[127] That conclusion is based on the Court's response to the government's argument that "law enforcement agents had the right, if not indeed the duty, to continue the investigation" following the defendant's indictment. The Court agreed that it was "entirely proper" to continue to investigate the defendant and his confederates after defendant was indicted. "All that we hold", the Court stated, "is that the defendant's own incriminating statements … could not constitutionally be used by the prosecution as evidence against him at his trial".[128]

The USSC has addressed the scope of the exclusionary rule for a Massiah violation in two cases.[129] The first case, *Nix v. Williams*,[130] involved the admissibility of derivative fruits of a violation of the *Massiah* right to counsel. The Court assumed that the fruit of the poisonous tree doctrine applies to violations of *Massiah*, but then held that the evidence at issue in the case was admissible under the inevitable discovery doctrine.

The Court's opinion in *Nix v. Williams* does not address the underpinnings of the *Massiah* exclusionary rule directly, and the Court's language and reasoning do not reflect a completely coherent vision of the basis for exclusion. In the recent case of *Kansas v. Ventris*,[131] however, the Court addressed the character of the *Massiah* exclusionary rule head-on and delivered an unequivocal answer to the question. The issue in *Ventris* was whether a statement obtained in violation of *Massiah* is admissible to impeach the defendant's credibility. The resolution of that question, according to the Court, "depends on the nature of the constitutional guarantee that is violated".[132] Sometimes, as in the case of the Fifth Amendment right against compelled self-incrimination, the constitutional rule "explicitly mandates exclusion from trial".[133] When exclusion is constitutionally mandated the use of illegally obtained evidence is prohibited for all purposes, including impeachment. Impeachment use is not prohibited, however, when "exclusion comes by way of deterrent sanction", as in the case of the Fourth Amendment protection against unreasonable search and seizure and the *Miranda* rule. Admissibility for these violations is determined through the application of "an exclusionary rule balancing test",[134] and the Court's "precedents make clear that the game of excluding tainted evidence for impeachment purposes is not worth the candle".[135]

---

[127] Tomkovicz (2007, 746–747).

[128] Massiah v. United States, 377 U.S. 201, 207.

[129] A third case, Michigan v. Harvey, 494 U.S. 344 (1990) dealt with the exclusionary rule for violations of the rule announced in Michigan v. Jackson, 475 U.S. 625 (1986) that limited the defendant's ability to waive the right to counsel after it had been invoked. The *Jackson* gloss on the *Massiah* rule was abolished in 2009. Montejo v. Louisiana, 556 U.S. 778, 129 S.Ct. 2079 (2009).

[130] 467 U.S. 431 (1984).

[131] 556 U.S. 586, 129 S.Ct. 1841 (2009).

[132] Ibid, 1845.

[133] Ibid.

[134] Ibid.

[135] Ibid, 1846.

The issue in *Ventris* thus reduces to a single question: Is the exclusion of evidence obtained as a result of a violation of *Massiah* guaranteed as a constitutional right, or is exclusion a mechanism for deterring the police from eliciting statements from uncounseled defendants after the initiation of formal charges? The Court holds that "the *Massiah* right is a right to be free of uncounseled interrogation, and is infringed at the time of interrogation."[136]

The question decided in *Ventris* is not inconsequential, and the implications of the decision extend beyond the use of evidence for impeachment. Most importantly, once it is determined that the exclusion of statements obtained in violation of *Massiah* is based on an analysis of its costs and benefits there is nothing in principle to prevent the Court from applying its balancing test to find statements obtained in violation of *Massiah* admissible in the prosecution's case in chief. Considering the importance of the issue, the Court's opinion in *Ventris* is remarkable for the curt and offhand manner in which it was decided. To say that the Sixth Amendment is violated when the defendant's statement is admitted at trial is "illogical", according to the Court, because "[a] defendant is not denied counsel merely because the prosecution has been permitted to introduce evidence of guilt—even evidence so overwhelming that the attorney's job of gaining an acquittal is rendered impossible". [137] Thus, the introduction of evidence obtained in violation of *Massiah* is not a violation of the right to counsel because "[i]n such circumstances the accused continues to enjoy the assistance of counsel; the assistance is simply not worth much."[138]

1.4 Conclusion

Kansas v. Ventris, the USSC's most recent statement on the exclusion of illegally obtained evidence, marks the final step in the nearly complete deconstitutionalization of the exclusionary rule. Exclusion of an involuntary confession obtained in violation of the Fifth Amendment right against compelled self incrimination and the Fourteenth Amendment due process clause is constitutionally required. The exclusionary rules for violations of the Fourth Amendment, the *Miranda* rule, and the *Massiah* right to counsel are applied to deter police misconduct based on a balancing of the deterrent benefits of exclusion against its costs in lost evidence.

---

[136] Ibid.

[137] Ibid.

[138] Ibid. To describe as merely disingenuous the Court's response to the argument that elicitation of statements from a charged defendant is not intrinsically unlawful would be overly generous. After making the irrelevant point that it works no violation of the right to counsel if the defendant is questioned about a crime for which he has not been charged, the Court writes that "[w]e have never said … that officers may badger counseled defendants about charged crimes so long as they do not use information they gain." Ibid. The question, of course, is not whether it violates the Sixth Amendment to "badger" defendants but whether it is a violation to elicit information from them. The Court in *Massiah* stated unequivocally that it is not.

The USSC's decisions deconstitutionalizing the exclusionary rules are, of course, based on its interpretation that the constitution does not require exclusion. Quite apart from the Court's constitutional exegesis, however, there is also apparent in recent exclusionary rule jurisprudence a distinct aversion on the part of some justices to excluding illegally obtained evidence. In *Herring v. United States*,[139] the other exclusionary rule decision in the Court's most recent term, the Court was at pains to emphasize that "exclusion 'has always been our last resort, not our first impulse'",[140] and that the exclusionary rule's "costly toll upon truth-seeking and law enforcement objectives presents a high obstacle for those urging [its] application".[141] These comments relate to the exclusion of evidence acquired as a result of a Fourth Amendment violation, but attitudes toward the use of the exclusionary rule in other contexts are much the same. It seems unlikely that the exclusion of illegally obtained evidence will be abolished entirely as a means of regulating the conduct of the police. But enthusiasm for the exclusionary rule on the USSC is at an all-time low, and the narrowing of the exclusionary rule that has occurred in recent decades is certain to continue.

Bibliography

Amsterdam, A. 1974. Perspectives on the fourth amendment. *Minnesota Law Review* 58: 349–478.

Tomkovicz, J.J. 2007. Saving Massiah from Elstad: The admissibility of successive confessions following a deprivation of counsel. *William & Mary Bill of Rights Journal* 15: 711–764.

[139] 555 U.S. 135 (2009).

[140] Ibid, 140 (quoting Hudson v. Michigan, 547 U.S. 586, 591 (2006)).

[141] Ibid, 141 (quoting Pennsylvania Bd of Prob. and Parole v. Scott, 524 U.S. 357, 364–365 (1998)).

Chapter 2
Ireland: A Move to Categorical Exclusion?

Arnaud Cras and Yvonne Marie Daly

2.1 The General Theory of Admissibility of Illegally Gathered Evidence

2.1.1 Introduction

The rules on the admissibility of improperly obtained evidence have developed and evolved in Ireland over many years, most vibrantly within the past 50 years. The rules have been almost entirely judicially constructed and have been set out and revisited in numerous cases in varying contexts including search and seizure, arrest and detention, interrogation, the right to silence and access to legal advice. This chapter attempts to describe the rules as developed and applied in the Irish courts, making, where appropriate, comparative remarks justified by the heritage of Irish jurisprudence in this area. We will be unable to account for all of the diverse judicial decisions made on the issue of the exclusion of improperly obtained evidence in Ireland, but will attempt to illustrate a number of the most controversial matters arising from the efforts to clarify the rules in this area.

To begin with, it is perhaps wise to outline the general approach to improperly obtained evidence which exists within this jurisdiction. The nuances and intricacies of this issue will be expanded upon throughout the rest of the chapter. Briefly, however,

A. Cras
College of Business and Law, School of Law, University College Dublin, 34 Upper Mount Pleasant Avenue, Ranelagh, Dublin 6, Ireland
e-mail: arnaud.cras@ucd.ie

Y.M. Daly (✉)
School of Law and Government, Dublin City University, Glasnevin, Dublin 9, Ireland
e-mail: yvonne.daly@dcu.ie

S.C. Thaman (ed.), *Exclusionary Rules in Comparative Law*, Ius Gentium: Comparative Perspectives on Law and Justice 20, DOI 10.1007/978-94-007-5348-8_2,

it can be stated that there is a dichotomy in Irish law between evidence which has been obtained in breach of the *legal* rights of an individual only and evidence which has been obtained in breach of such individual's *constitutional* rights.

In terms of *illegally obtained evidence*, the trial judge has discretion to admit or exclude the impugned evidence taking into account issues such as the nature and extent of the illegality, whether it was intentional or unintentional, whether it was an illegality of a trivial nature or otherwise, whether it was the result of an *ad hoc* decision or represented deliberate, settled policy, and whether the public interest would be best served by the admission or exclusion of the evidence in question.

There is a much stricter rule in place, however, in relation to *unconstitutionally obtained evidence*. Such evidence must be automatically excluded by the trial judge, who has no discretion to admit it, unless there are extraordinary excusing circumstances in place which justify its admission. If such circumstances exist, then the trial judge may, in his discretion, admit the evidence, once again taking into account the sort of concerns outlined above.

These two distinct rules were initially set out in the case of *People (A.G.) v. O'Brien*[1] though they have been revisited and modified in later cases. Before examining that seminal case in greater detail some comment on the Irish Constitution is required. Ireland's present Constitution was established in 1937 and it contains provisions similar to that of a Bill of Rights. Art. 38.1 Const., for example, creates the right to a fair trial: "No person shall be tried on any criminal charge save in due course of law." There is a general "substantive due process" type clause within Art. 40.3 Const., which guarantees the respect, defense and vindication of the personal rights of the citizen. This broad provision has led to the recognition of many unenumerated rights, including bodily integrity and privacy.[2] Of particular relevance to the development of the Irish exclusionary rule, Art. 40.4.1 Const. states that "No citizen shall be deprived of his personal liberty save in accordance with law" and Art. 40.5 Const. provides that "The dwelling of every citizen is inviolable and shall not be forcibly entered save in accordance with law."[3]

While the Irish courts have made a distinction between the consequences of evidence being illegally or unconstitutionally obtained, that distinction is problematic in a context where the Constitution guarantees "due course of law" and refers to the concept of particular matters being carried out "in accordance with law." Nonetheless, as outlined below, the courts in this jurisdiction have drawn a distinction between the two.

---

[1] [1965] I.R. 142.

[2] See, in particular, Ryan v. A.G. [1965] I.R. 294, McGee v. A.G. [1974] I.R. 284 and Norris v. A.G. [1984] I.R. 36.

[3] These provisions have been qualified by various Criminal Justice and Criminal Law Acts such as the Criminal Justice Acts 1984 and 2007, and the Criminal Law Act 1997.

2.1.2 The Landmark Decision of People (A.G.) v. O'Brien

In the 1965 case of *O'Brien,* a mistake was found on a search warrant issued with respect to Patrick and Gerald O'Brien, accused of stealing and receiving stolen property. The warrant wrongly described the premises to be searched as being located in Cashel Road as opposed to Captain's Road. The evidence obtained under the search warrant had been admitted at trial, and this was appealed by the O'Brien brothers. In the Court of Criminal Appeal it had been decided that Irish law should follow the traditional English inclusionary approach to improperly obtained evidence, whereby all relevant evidence would be admissible, unless there was some question of involuntariness.[4]

However, the Supreme Court took a different approach, with at least one member of the Bench clearly leaning towards the rather strict exclusionary rule which was in operation in the United States (US) at the time and had been set out in cases such as *Weeks v. United States*[5] and *Mapp v. Ohio.*[6] Walsh J., giving what was in fact the minority judgment of the Supreme Court, proposed an exclusionary rule with three components.

First, in order to protect constitutional rights, including the inviolability of the dwelling of every citizen,[7] the courts should not admit at trial evidence obtained in breach of those rights. This rule would not apply, however, if there were extraordinary excusing circumstances such as the "imminent destruction of vital evidence or the need to rescue a victim in peril."[8] In the absence of such circumstances, the evidence should be "absolutely inadmissible".

Second, exclusion should be reserved for breaches of constitutional rights. Evidence resulting from an *illegal* seizure should not become inadmissible by that reason only. There is a distinction made between mere illegality and illegality amounting to an infringement of a constitutional right.[9]

Finally, and most importantly, in order for exclusion to occur in the context of unconstitutionally obtained evidence, the breach of constitutional rights must be "deliberate and conscious".[10] This seemed to suggest that in order for evidence to be excluded the police must have been aware not only of what they were doing materially, but also of the fact that they were depriving the accused of a constitutional right: "...evidence obtained without a deliberate and conscious violation of the accused constitutional rights is not excludable by reason only of the violation of his constitutional right".[11]

---

[4] See cases such as R v. Sang [1979] 2 All ER 1222 and R v. Rennie [1982] 1 All ER 385.

[5] 232 U.S. 383 (1914).

[6] 367 U.S. 643 (1961).

[7] Protected under Art. 40.5 Const.

[8] [1965] I.R.142 at p.170.

[9] Ibid.

[10] Ibid.

[11] Ibid.

While Walsh J.'s three ingredients of an exclusionary rule contain a high level of subjectivity, which may seem to render it inimical to the traditional understanding of an exclusionary rule, it was presented as such and used in many later cases. Kingsmill Moore J., for the majority in *O'Brien*, agreed that under the conditions described by Walsh J., evidence should be excluded. However, he was reluctant to qualify the circumstances in which evidence should be admissible or not and preferred to leave the exclusion or admission of evidence to the discretion of the trial judge. He stated that: "It would not be in accordance with our system of jurisprudence for this Court to attempt to lay down rules to govern future hypothetical cases".[12] Also, referring to Walsh J.'s judgment, Kingsmill Moore J. stated that: "The views expressed in this judgment may seem to be a departure from what has hitherto been considered the law or the initiating of a principle in a field where up to now our law has been undefined. The further development of that principle should await clarification in the light of actual cases".[13] However, because Kingsmill Moore J. agreed to a large extent with Walsh J.'s judgment, albeit that he wished for a rule governed by judicial discretion in each case, subsequent judicial approaches focused essentially on the test developed by Walsh J., without perhaps questioning whether such test was the actual ratio of the *O'Brien* judgment.[14]

Concluding on the factual scenario in *O'Brien*, it was held by the Supreme Court that the evidence produced by the warrant was rightly admitted at trial as the violation was accidental and not "deliberate and conscious". Therefore, the violation was said to be outside of any issue of unconstitutionality, it was classed as a mere illegality and the Court held that in balancing such illegality against the public interest the trial judge had correctly exercised his discretion in admitting the evidence.

2.1.3 *Applying and Exploring the Exclusionary Rule After O'Brien*

While the exclusionary rule arose for examination and application in many cases post-*O'Brien*, space constraints allow only for a brief foray into the magnificent collection of uncertainties, controversies and difficulties which these cases exemplify.

---

[12] Ibid, 161.

[13] Ibid, 162.

[14] While there is some controversy as to the true *ratio decidendi* of the *O'Brien* case and as to which judgment delivered by the members of the Supreme Court ought to be regarded as the majority judgment, McGrath suggests that the matter is one of academic interest only at this juncture as the judgment of Walsh J. has generally come to be regarded as containing the *ratio* of the case: McGrath (2005, para. 7.07 fn.23). Although it is fair to say that this controversy has been concretized in more recent courts' decisions, including D.P.P. (Walsh) v. Cash [2007] IEHC 108; [2010] 1 I.R. 609, by renewed and varied judicial interpretations as to its true meaning.

One issue of major significance in the Irish incarnation of the exclusionary rule is the true meaning of the phrase "deliberate and conscious breach". This has stuck in the craw of the courts in applying the rule in many cases. In *D.P.P. v. Madden*,[15] the accused had been held under Section 30 of the Offences Against the State Act 1939 beyond the legal detention period of 48 h and he made a self-incriminating statement during that time. The Court of Criminal Appeal accepted that the confession was voluntarily made but they held that it had been made in circumstances which amounted to a "deliberate and conscious" breach of his constitutional right to liberty.[16] The Court adopted a narrower test of this concept than that which had been suggested by Walsh J. in *O'Brien* and held that the motives of the police or gardaí could not cure the fact that they had acted in breach of the accused's constitutional rights. The judgment in this case suggested that there was no requirement that the person who violated the constitutional rights of the suspect must have knowingly intended to cause harm to the suspect as a result of the breach in order for the evidence to later be excluded. O'Higgins C.J., purporting to clarify the rule set out by Walsh J. in *O'Brien*, stated that: "What was done or permitted by Inspector Butler and his colleagues may have been done or permitted for the best of motives and in the interests of the due investigation of the crime. However, it was done or permitted without regard to the right to liberty guaranteed to this defendant by Article 40 of the Constitution and to the State's obligation under that Article to defend and vindicate that right".[17] Thus, considering that there was no requirement of *mala fides* on the part of the violator of the Constitution in order to require exclusion of the impugned evidence, the Court of Criminal Appeal held that the evidence ought to have been excluded at trial.

While the judgment of Walsh J. in *O'Brien*, with specific reference to a "deliberate and conscious" breach of the constitutional rights of an individual, might have been thought to require intent on the part of the violator of the constitution to deprive an individual of his constitutional rights, or at least knowledge on the part of such violator that his actions would result in such deprivation, in the later case of *People (D.P.P.) v. Shaw*,[18] Walsh J. seemed to agree with the judgment of O'Higgins C.J. in *Madden* that such intent or knowledge was unnecessary.

John Shaw was accused and tried for the murder, rape and unlawful imprisonment of two women: Elizabeth Plunkett and Mary Duffy. The gardaí, believing that Mary Duffy may still be alive, extended his detention beyond the legal limits in the hope that they might obtain more information about her fate. During this time of unlawful detention, the accused confessed to her murder following which he volunteered to take them to a place of burial. In the Supreme Court, Walsh J. said that it was "immaterial whether the person carrying out the act may or may not have been conscious that what he was doing was illegal, that it amounted to a breach

---

[15] [1977] I.R. 336.

[16] Under Art. 40.4.1 Const.

[17] [1977] I.R. 336, 347

[18] [1982] I.R. 1.

of constitutional rights of the accused. It is the doing of the act which is the essential matter, not the actor's appreciation of the legal consequences or incidents of it".[19] Further to that, Walsh J. stated that: "there is nothing in *O'Brien's* to suggest that the admissibility of the evidence depends upon the state or degree of the violator's knowledge of constitutional law or, indeed, of the ordinary law. To attempt to import any such interpretation of the decision would be to put a premium on ignorance of the law".[20]

However, a judicial rift was becoming apparent in this case, with Griffin J. (Henchy, Kenny and Parke JJ. concurring) interpreting *O'Brien* differently and contradicting Walsh J.'s view that it was immaterial to be aware of breaching the constitutional rights of the accused. Griffin J. stated that: "it is the violation of the person's constitutional rights, and not the particular act complained of, that has to be deliberate and conscious for the purpose of ruling out a statement".[21]

The issue of the true meaning of "deliberate and conscious" continued to cause confusion in the Irish courts for some time,[22] until the 1990 case of *People (D.P.P.) v. Kenny*.[23] This case dropped a brick into the pond of the murky waters of the *O'Brien* rule and dramatically realigned the Irish exclusionary rule.

2.1.4 The Revolution of People (D.P.P.) v. Kenny

The *Kenny* revolution originated from a search conducted under the purported authority of a warrant issued pursuant to the Misuse of Drugs Act 1977. The warrant was issued by a Peace Commissioner on the ground that he was satisfied by information of a member of the gardaí, under Section 26 of the Act, that there was reasonable grounds to suspect that a controlled drug would be found on the premises. However, no evidence was given to the Peace Commissioner by the gardaí except their sworn statement that they suspected the presence of drugs. The Court of Criminal Appeal found the warrant invalid on the ground that no evidence was submitted. It was contended before the Supreme Court that the constitutional rights regarding the dwelling were deliberately infringed by the gardaí, despite the fact that they may have thought that they were acting under a valid search warrant. In other words, it was contended that "deliberate and conscious" should be interpreted as an awareness of one's own actions but not of the consequences of one's own actions on constitutional rights. So, unless the gardaí were sleepwalking into the property, or fell into the property, their action in entering the premises was deliberate and conscious.

---

[19] Ibid, 31–32.

[20] Ibid, 33.

[21] Ibid, 54–56.

[22] See cases such as People v. Lynch [1982] I.R. 64, People (D.P.P.) v. Lawless (unreported, Court of Criminal Appeal, November 28, 1985) and People (D.P.P.) v. McMahon, McMeel and Wright [1987] I.L.R.M. 87.

[23] [1990] 2 I.R. 110; [1990] I.L.R.M. 569.

The Court of Criminal Appeal adopted a subjective test of "deliberate and conscious" to excuse the action of the gardaí on the basis that they had taken all the necessary steps to obtain a valid warrant and were therefore not aware that they were breaching the constitutional rights of the accused. This was done by relying on the "good faith" exception to the US Fourth Amendment exclusionary rule pronounced by the US Supreme Court in *United States v. Leon*[24] and its exclusive emphasis on deterrence as the grounds for evidence exclusion. However, on appeal to the Irish Supreme Court in *Kenny*, a 3–2 decision led by Finlay C.J., redefined "deliberate and conscious" as being objective: so long as the actions of the gardaí were not accidental or unintentional, where there was a breach of constitutional rights the evidence resultantly obtained would have to be excluded, regardless of the gardaí's knowledge at the time that he was acting in breach of such rights.

This decision as to the "objective" nature of the concept of "deliberate and conscious" seems to constitute a departure from the original position taken by Walsh J. in *O'Brien* (though it seems to confirm Walsh J.'s views in *Shaw*). As Charleton J. said in the High Court in the later case of *D.P.P. (Walsh) v. Cash*: "this [*Kenny*] reversed the line of authority that had always been applied by the courts to the effect that a conscious and deliberate violation of someone's constitutional rights required that the act should be done deliberately with a consciousness that the effect of it would be to unlawfully invade someone's dwelling, or to deprive them of their liberty or whatever other constitutional right was infringed by the impugned action".[25]

The revolution went on in *Kenny* when the Court, rejecting any *Leon* deterrence-based approach to the protection of constitutional rights, chose to apply the "absolute protection rule of exclusion" without taking into account the subjective belief of the perpetrator of the violation that he or she was invading a constitutional right. Finlay C.J. declared that "[t]he detection of crime and the conviction of guilty persons, no matter how important they may be in relation to the ordering of society, cannot, however, in my view, outweigh the unambiguously expressed constitutional obligation 'as far as practicable to defend and vindicate the personal rights of the citizen'".[26]

Kenny radically altered the subjective approach to "deliberate and conscious" and resulted in a constitutional absorption of actions that were often deemed in the past to be merely illegal. It finally ruled that: "evidence obtained by invasion of the constitutional personal rights of a citizen must be excluded unless a court is satisfied that either the act constituting the breach of constitutional rights was committed unintentionally or accidentally, or is satisfied that there are extraordinary excusing circumstances which justify the admission of the evidence in its [the court's] discretion".[27] The

---

[24] 468 U.S. 897 (1983). For a detailed discussion of *Leon*, see Cammack, Ch. 1, pp. 19–20.

[25] [2007] IEHC 108, at para. 23.

[26] [1990] 2 I.R. 110, 134; [1990] I.L.R.M. 569, 579 quoting Art. 40.3.1 Const.

[27] Ibid.

action of the gardaí in this case was neither unintentional nor accidental. In other words, "deliberate and conscious" is to be applied to the act itself, not its constitutional implications.

There were two dissenters: Griffin and Lynch JJ. Griffin J. tried to assimilate *Kenny* with *O'Brien* in terms of the illegality affecting the warrant, and, as a true "O'Brienista," ruled that the act of the gardaí was not a deliberate and conscious violation of the constitutional rights of the applicant. Lynch J. concurred and referred to *O'Brien* as the true test that should apply in this case.

2.1.5 *The Exclusion of Unconstitutionally Obtained Evidence Since Kenny*

The dissenters in *Kenny* tried to identify the issues in that case with those in *O'Brien* and held that the same rule should apply. In *D.P.P. v. Balfe*,[28] Murphy J., in the High Court, did the same. In that case, a search warrant had been issued under the Larceny Act 1916 but with an incorrect name and address and description of goods and what was referred to as an "unsuitable and unlawful" attempted amendment of the address. Murphy J. referred to *O'Brien* and *Kenny* as the essential authorities in the case. Armed with those two cases, Murphy J. decided that, because there was no evidence of deliberate treachery and no policy to disregard the Constitution, this case should be distinguished from *Kenny*. In doing so he reconnected with *O'Brien's* original subjectivity, finding that: "the jurisprudence relating to the 'deliberate and conscious violation of constitutional rights' is still evolving, it is clear that a search warrant which innocently but vitally misdescribes premises which may be searched on foot thereof is not without operative effect".[29]

Thriving on his distinction between *O'Brien* and *Kenny*, Murphy J. held that the relevant garda had acted upon a warrant that allowed for the admission of the evidence seized, because the kind of defect in the warrant was more similar to that found in the *O'Brien* case than that in *Kenny*. One wonders whether the apparent triviality of the errors in *O'Brien* and the substantial flaw in *Kenny* do not share the same origin of basic carelessness that seem inimical to due process and the rights of the individual. Maybe one could question why they should be distinguished, and *O'Brien* given a separate identity to endure for generations. On the other hand, one can only admire the longevity of *O'Brien* in continuing to rule this issue.

Balfe can be contrasted with the later case of *D.P.P. v. Laide and Ryan*,[30] decided in 2005, in which the second-named accused was tried for manslaughter and violent disorder and where his house had been the subject of a search warrant that was held

---

[28] [1998] 4 I.R. 50.

[29] Ibid, 59. It is questionable whether the learned judge is correct in asserting that the jurisprudence in this area is still evolving and seems arguable that such evolution was stopped in its tracks in *Kenny* or perhaps even in *Shaw*.

[30] [2005] 1 I.R. 209.

to be invalid at trial. Having entered the accused's dwelling on foot of the search warrant the gardaí had then arrested him within his dwelling. It was held at the trial that his arrest was invalid by virtue of the defective warrant as the purpose of the warrant had not been to find evidence against the accused, but to allow the gardaí into the house to effect the arrest. There was, however, a power to arrest a person in a house without a warrant under Section 6(2) Criminal Law Act 1997. McCracken J. in the Court of Criminal Appeal disagreed with the trial judge on the subject of whether there was enough evidence to rule that the purpose of obtaining the search warrant was to operate an arrest but nonetheless held it was for the gardaí to bear the burden of establishing the lawfulness of their entry. The finding that the warrant was bad at the trial and the failure to invoke Section 6(2) Criminal Law Act 1997, resulted in an interference with the constitutional rights of the accused. Proper reasons must be given to breach the inviolability of the citizen's dwelling. The Court found that the circumstances of the *Kenny* case were very similar to those in the present case.[31] Quoting large extracts of Finlay C.J. in *Kenny* dealing with the "absolute protection rule", McCracken J. ruled that the gardaí acted intentionally and deliberately with no extraordinary excusing circumstances present, and that the evidence ought not to have been admitted at trial. The Court of Criminal Appeal therefore reasserted the *Kenny* majority ruling of absolute protection, departing from the position adopted in *Balfe*. The rule from *Kenny* has also been applied in many other cases, including *D.P.P. v Martin Joyce*[32] in the context of an invalid search warrant issued by a District Court judge sitting outside of the relevant district, and *D.P.P. (Lavelle) v. McCrea*[33] where there was a breach of the right of access to legal advice for a suspect arrested on suspicion of drunk-driving.

2.1.6 *Summary of the Doctrine in D.P.P. (Walsh) v. Cash*

A summary of the variations affecting the Irish exclusionary rule was provided in the High Court in 2007 by Charleton J. in *D.P.P. (Walsh) v. Cash*.[34] Previously, in an article written in 1980, Peter Charleton, then a barrister, had indicated his support for an absolute protection approach and an objective test of "deliberate and conscious" when he said that: "under no circumstances should a lack of knowledge of the law or Constitution provide an excuse for illegal action".[35] Charleton appeared

---

[31] There were also similarities with Freeman v. D.P.P. [1996] 3 I.R. 565 although that case was resolved by the application of the *O'Brien* rule.

[32] [2008] IECCA 53; unreported, Court of Criminal Appeal, April 21, 2008.

[33] [2009] IEHC 39; unreported, High Court, January 28, 2009, in which Edwards J, while applying the strict rule from *Kenny*, expressly endorsed Charleton J's criticism thereof in the High Court in D.P.P. (Walsh) v. Cash [2007] IEHC 108. See also the Supreme Court judgment in D.P.P. (Lavelle) v. McCrea [2010] IESC 60.

[34] [2007] IEHC 108; [2010] 1 I.R. 609.

[35] Charleton (1980, 175).

to support the view that the majority decision in *O'Brien* amounted to an exclusionary rule in the US tradition at the time. While it is arguable that the majority decision of the court in *O'Brien* presented a more subjective and flexible approach than that of the US courts at the time, Charleton considered that: "The absolute nature of the exclusionary rule for unconstitutionally obtained evidence means that the slightest infringement of a constitutional right is sufficient to render a statement inadmissible".[36] With great optimism he went on to say that "the Irish law on this topic is wholly logical and not easily criticized. It is also an advantage that the law can be stated with precision and certainty, the judgments referred to above being admirably clear".[37]

Interestingly, Charleton J.'s view from the bench in *Cash* was quite different to his 1980 rhetoric and in *Cash*, he referred to "the intractable question of improperly obtained evidence".[38] This case concerned a burglary where fingerprints had been found. The accused was arrested 2 months later on suspicion of having committed the burglary, as his fingerprints held in the Garda Technical Bureau matched those at the scene of the burglary. Upon arrest, the accused was requested to provide his fingerprints, which he did voluntarily. These matched the other two sets of prints. Consent was sought instead of invoking Section 6 Criminal Justice Act 1984. This Act provides that any record of fingerprints must be destroyed after 6 months if no prosecution occurs. The fingerprints on record were apparently taken by consent so there was no statutory requirement to destroy them, although the garda at trial refused to comment on their status. It was alleged by the defence that the gardaí had failed to discharge the burden of proof of their legality and that, accordingly, the evidence could not stand. These fingerprints resulted in the accused being arrested for the burglary.

Charleton J. embarked on a history of the Irish exclusionary rule, probably beyond what was required for disposing of the case. He referred to precedents that supported the discretionary approach to illegality, in a manner similar to that which prevailed in English law, at least until 1984. As was done in *Balfe*, but with a more lavish and dramatic presentation, the learned judge contrasted *O'Brien* with *Kenny* in a comprehensive manner, underlining the fact that the *O'Brien* rule had been applied for 25 years until *Kenny*, and implying that, regardless of the uncertainty of the ruling and its subsequent adaptation, it led to a subjective approach to the admission of evidence obtained illegally within the framework of the test in that case. He described *Kenny* as putting an end to the judicial discretion that was built into the *O'Brien* case, even though his views in 1980 were somewhat different on this matter. Furthermore, Charleton J. suggested that as a result of *Kenny* "it has become practically impossible to say when a constitutional right begins and when it ends".[39]

For Charleton J., the separation of powers requires that the courts be limited in their power to invent new rules. Although bound by the *Kenny* judgment, he expressed the unease which continues to affect the rule by regretting the fact that judges "are deprived,

---

[36] Ibid, 173.

[37] Ibid, 177.

[38] [2007] IEHC 108, para. 1.

[39] Ibid, para. 29.

on a non-discretionary basis, of considering evidence which is inherently reliable".[40] As an example, he suggested that fingerprints – unlike statements – are always reliable evidence, regardless of how they were obtained. From his point of view, *Kenny* "automatically requires the exclusion of any evidence obtained through a mistake which had the accidental, and therefore unintended, result of infringing any constitutional right of one individual, namely the accused".[41] Charleton J. squarely sided with the pragmatic approach to the admissibility of evidence of earlier times, and emphasized the public interest and the balance that needs to be achieved with the rights of the accused.

Ultimately, Charleton J. considered himself bound by the *Kenny* decision, despite his distaste for it. However, he did not allow the appeal against conviction as he held that "evidence resulting from a detention based upon a suspicion that cannot be proved as being founded entirely upon evidence lawfully obtained is not, for that reason, made unlawful" and that "[i]f a judge is satisfied that evidence has been obtained lawfully, the decision in *Kenny's* case does not apply and there is no judicial basis for the exclusion of evidence on the ground of the mistaken infringement of any constitutional right".[42]

A similar approach was adopted by the Supreme Court, on appeal. Fennelly J., giving the majority decision of the seven-judge court, held that the exclusionary rule is only relevant to evidence proffered at a criminal trial and is not concerned with the lawful provenance of evidence used to ground a suspicion. He suggested that the appellant in that case was seeking to extend the exclusionary rule beyond its correct boundaries and that doing so would blur the distinction between the arrest and the trial. Quoting from the High Court decision of Charleton J. in *Cash*, Fennelly J. observed that it has never been held that "what would found a reasonable suspicion in law, requires to be based on the kind of evidence that would be admissible under the rules of evidence during the hearing of a criminal trial".[43]

Fennelly J. further stated that "[t]he lawfulness of an arrest and the admissibility of evidence at trial are different matters which will normally be considered in distinct contexts"[44] and held that the appellant had not established that an onus rests on the prosecution to establish the lawfulness of material relied upon by a member of the Garda Síochána in order to form reasonable suspicion justifying an arrest, or that such material was obtained without breach of a constitutional right. Thus, the appeal was dismissed.

Given Charleton J's strongly stated views on the strict exclusionary rule in the High Court, it was thought that the Supreme Court might take the opportunity to renew or review the application of that rule within the *Cash* case. However, it chose not to do so. Whether this is to be taken as an endorsement of the exclusionary rule which emanated from the *Kenny* case and the manner in which it currently operates is unclear. Perhaps it is merely the case that the Court did not see it as being applicable

---

[40] Ibid, para. 65.

[41] Ibid para. 66.

[42] Ibid para. 68.

[43] [2010] 1 I.R. 609, 626, *per* Fennelly J., quoting [2007] IEHC 108 at para. 12, *per* Charleton J.

[44] Ibid, 634, *per* Fennelly J.

on the facts. However, it is possible to suggest that had the Court been minded to do so it could have examined the rule in some detail, as had Charleton J. in the High Court.

By side-stepping an analysis of the rule, the Supreme Court may, in fact, have done more harm than good. Its view that the exclusionary rule is not relevant to pre-arrest matters seems at variance with the general tenor of previous Irish case-law, and indeed the case-law of other jurisdictions, and provides a very weak basis for the protection of suspect rights.

Exclusionary rules have developed through the consideration of police activities and either their legality or constitutionality, depending on the legal system. Since *Weeks v. United States*,[45] which spoke of "unwarranted practices destructive of rights secured by the Federal Constitution" and used a language similar to the phrasing in *Kenny*,[46] the rule has been systematically applied to police procedures. One can refer to countless decisions of the Irish Supreme Court incorporating the concept of reasonable or articulable suspicion, as well as other prosecuting agencies' due process based behavior, into the decision to admit or exclude particular kinds of evidence.[47] The exclusionary rule does not mean that every irregularity of police behavior will lead to systematic inadmissibility of evidence, but that police behavior will be scrutinized and incorporated in the debate on the application of the rule. The consideration of the evidence supporting the suspicion is within the scope of the exclusionary rule.

The distinction between the suspicion required for an arrest and evidence admissible at trial, which was operated by Charleton J. in the High Court and relied upon by the Supreme Court, appears artificial in the context of both Irish and foreign practice and understanding of the exclusionary rule. In *Kenny* it was the behavior of the gardaí that was scrutinized, and the issue of suspicion is no different for the purpose of the exclusionary rule from the issue of the knowledge of the use of an improper warrant in that case. When the Court considered whether the rule in *Kenny* could "be extended to encompass the lawful provenance of facts", it would seem not to understand its own precedent, which criticized the rule in *United States v. Leon*[48] insofar as it accepted the principle of police good faith but was based on mere "deterrence" as opposed to "absolute protection". In *Cash*, the Supreme Court seems to have embarked on a trip of make-believe according to which police behavior should not be considered for the purpose of the exclusionary rule, although it has been considered in the past, and suspicion is artificially excluded as an element not covered by the broad ruling of *Kenny.* The case looks more like an exercise of restriction of the rule rather than one that refrains from extending it. The truth is that police behavior has always affected constitutional issues and can result in the breach of constitutional rights but the Court seems to want to deny this with the support of the High Court.

---

[45] 232 U.S. 383 (1914).

[46] [1990] 2 I.R. 110; [1990] I.L.R.M. 569.

[47] People (D.P.P.) v. Kenny [1990] 2 I.R. 110; [1990] I.L.R.M. 569., D.P.P. v. Fagan [1994] I.R. 555 or McCreesh [1992] 2 I.R. 239.

[48] 468 U.S. 897 (1983).

While it is correct to suggest that evidence which might ground an arrest would not always be acceptable under the evidentiary rules of the courts, it is arguable that there is a distinction between unlawfully or unconstitutionally obtained evidence and evidence lawfully obtained which would be excluded at trial for other reasons. One example of the type of evidence which might ground arrest but would not be admissible in evidence at trial, as outlined by Charleton J. in the High Court, is hearsay evidence. The rationales for the exclusion of hearsay evidence at trial center on the reliability of such evidence and the dangers inherent in not being able to adequately test that evidence in the courtroom. However, the rationale for the exclusion of unconstitutionally obtained evidence from trials in Ireland is based on the protection of constitutional rights. This was noted by Fennelly J. in the Supreme Court in *Cash* and he noted that in *Kenny* Finlay C.J., weighing up various options, sought to provide a positive encouragement to those in authority within the criminal process to consider in detail the constitutional rights of citizens and the effect of their powers of arrest, detention, search and questioning in relation to such rights.

If the earlier-obtained fingerprints in this case ought to have been destroyed then their retention could be seen as breaching the appellant's right to privacy, both under the Irish Constitution[49] and the ECHR, and their use to ground an arrest could be seen as a breach of the right to liberty.[50] It might have been thought that these matters would be of interest to the trial court, in order to ensure the protection of suspects' rights in the pre-trial period of the criminal process.[51]

While the Supreme Court may not have reviewed the general application of the exclusionary rule in *Cash*, it appears to have, somewhat worryingly, set pre-arrest investigative methods beyond its reach.[52]

2.1.7 Views Beyond the Case Law

Beyond the judicial benches there have been calls for change to the strict exclusionary rule on unconstitutionally obtained evidence from other quarters in Ireland too, most notably, the "Balance in the Criminal Law Review Group". This *ad hoc* group was established in November 2006 by then Minister for Justice, Michael McDowell, to consider and examine a number of specific issues including, *inter alia*, the right to silence, the rules on hearsay evidence, the admissibility of character

---

[49] The right to privacy has been recognized as a constitutionally protected right (within Art. 40.3.1 Const.) in a number of cases including: McGee v. A.G. [1974] IR 284; Norris v. A.G. [1984] IR 36; Kennedy v. Ireland [1987] IR 587.

[50] Expressly protected under Art. 40.4.1 Const. and under Art. 5 ECHR.

[51] Interestingly, Hardiman J gave a sensible judgment in the Supreme Court in *Cash*, lamenting the lack of evidence in relation to unconstitutionality in the retention of the first set of fingerprints and accordingly holding that the matter would have to be remitted to the District Court and none of the questions which appeared to be raised could be answered.

[52] For more on the *Cash* case see Daly (2011a, b).

evidence of an accused and the exclusionary rule of criminal evidence. In its Final Report, published in March 2007, a majority of the Group advocated a change in the exclusionary rule in relation to unconstitutionally obtained evidence: they recommended that trial courts ought not to be under a duty to automatically exclude evidence which has been obtained in breach of the constitutional rights of a suspect, but should have a discretion to admit such evidence or not, having regard to the totality of the circumstances with particular regard to the rights of the victim.[53] The majority of the Group suggested that it might be possible to bring about such a change by way of ordinary legislation, constitutional referendum, or a re-interpretation by the courts.[54] It is contended that the current rule is grounded in the protection of constitutional rights and thus may not be legislatively overruled.[55] A referendum then, or a re-interpretation by the Supreme Court seem to be the only plausible means of altering the current rule.

The Chairman of the Group, a well-respected Irish constitutional lawyer and scholar, Dr. Gerard Hogan S.C. (now a judge of the High Court), recorded his dissent to the recommendation of the majority that there ought to be a change in the formulation and application of the exclusionary rule in relation to unconstitutionally obtained evidence in Ireland. He stated that: "Our society has committed itself to abiding by the rule of law and to respect and vindicate the fundamental freedoms enshrined in the Constitution. It behoves us to take these rights and freedoms seriously and if the occasional exclusion of otherwise relevant evidence is the price of respecting these constitutional rights, then that is a price society should be prepared to pay in the interests of upholding the values solemnly enshrined in our highest law".[56] This clearly depicts the strict, protectionist stance of current Irish law on the exclusion of unconstitutionally obtained evidence and it remains to be seen whether there will be any decline from the heights of this position.

2.1.8 *Violations of Non-constitutional Legal Rules*

Some brief comment is necessary on the manner in which the Irish courts have exercised their discretion to admit or exclude evidence obtained in breach of legal rights only. First, it ought to be noted, as outlined by Charleton J. in the High Court in *Cash*, that the line between breaches of legal rights and breaches of constitutional rights is

---

[53] Balance in the Criminal Law Review Group (2007, 166). Part, though not all, of the reasoning of the Group was based on improvements in garda accountability outside of the courts which might supersede any argument that the current rule is necessary to insist on garda compliance with legal requirements. An argument similar to this was made by the US Supreme Court in Hudson v. Michigan, 547 US 586 (2006), to admit evidence obtained in breach of the knock-and-announce requirements of the Fourth Amendment. As the US rule generally proceeds on a deterrence rationale, however, this argument may be more relevant in that jurisdiction than in Ireland.

[54] Balance in the Criminal Law Review Group (2007, 161–166).

[55] A similar argument was made by the US Supreme Court in rejecting a challenge to the *Miranda* rule in Dickerson v. United States, 530 U.S. 428 (2000). See Cammack, Ch. 1, pp. 27–28.

[56] Balance in the Criminal Law Review Group (2007, 287–288).

a thin one. Of course, most of the interaction which a suspect will have with the gardaí in the pre-trial process will have some impact on constitutional rights such as the rights to liberty, silence, bodily integrity, privacy, inviolability of the dwelling and access to legal advice. Thus, it is not very often that improper garda actions within that period can be described as breaching legal rights only.

One example is the right of a suspect to consult in private with his solicitor in the pre-trial period. This is provided for under Regulation 11 of the Criminal Justice Act 1984 (Treatment of Persons in Custody in Garda Síochána Stations) Regulations, 1987 (the Custody Regulations 1987). While breach of this regulation *qua* regulation may not affect the admissibility in evidence at trial of any statement obtained from such a suspect, pursuant to Section 7(3) Criminal Justice Act 1984,[57] it may be held by the court that the statement was involuntary on grounds of oppression given that the gardaí were clearly listening to the consultation, or that the statement should be excluded from evidence because of a breach of the constitutional right of reasonable access to legal advice which includes a right to consult privately with one's solicitor in the pre-trial process.[58]

Generally, the courts appear very slow to exclude evidence on the basis of a breach of mere legal rights. As Hogan has suggested, in practice the courts almost never exclude evidence on the ground that there has been a breach of legal rights only as there is almost always a reason why such evidence should be admitted in the overall public interest.[59]

2.1.9 *Extraordinary Excusing Circumstances*

In *O'Brien*, Walsh J. gave examples of extraordinary excusing circumstances which might justify the admission of otherwise unconstitutionally obtained evidence, such as "the imminent destruction of vital evidence or the need to rescue a victim in peril".[60] Surprisingly this element of the Irish exclusionary rule has not been employed on very many occasions, possibly out of judicial concern for the integrity of the primary rule.[61]

One example of the operation of the extraordinary excusing circumstances element of the Irish rule on exclusion may be found in *D.P.P. v. John Lawless*.[62]

---

[57] Section 7(3) of the Criminal Justice Act, 1984 provides that a breach of the Custody Regulations 1987 does not provide grounds for an action, either civil or criminal, against a member of the Garda Síochána or of itself affect the lawfulness of a suspect's detention or the admissibility of any statement made by him.

[58] People (D.P.P.) v. Finnegan, unreported, Court of Criminal Appeal, July 15, 1997.

[59] Balance in the Criminal Law Review Group (2007, 289). This issue is discussed further below in the context of the law on private dwellings and other premises and on confession evidence.

[60] *Per* Walsh J. in People (A.G.) v. O'Brien [1965] 1 I.R. 142 at p.170.

[61] McGrath has suggested that the courts wish to avoid undermining the exclusionary rule in relation to unconstitutionally obtained evidence and will therefore adopt a restrictive approach to extending the list put forward by Walsh J.: McGrath (2005, para. 7.46).

[62] Unreported, Court of Criminal Appeal, 28th November, 1985.

Here a warrant was issued for the seizure of heroin. The validity of the warrant was challenged on the grounds that it did not comply with the wording requirements of Section 26 of the Misuse of Drugs Act, 1977, which requires that a garda provide information under oath that there is reasonable grounds to suspect possession before a warrant is issued. Furthermore, there were some errors in the description of the premises to be searched on the face of the warrant. The matter was complicated because the accused was not residing in the flat but merely a visitor there. The Court of Criminal Appeal accepted that the warrant was defective, and therefore the forced entry unlawful. However, the Court agreed that the evidence had nonetheless been properly admitted at trial. The Court based its decision on three issues. First, the defendant was not in fact a tenant in the flat where the evidence was found and therefore there was no violation of his right to inviolability of the dwelling. Secondly, there was no deliberate and conscious breach of any rights as the defective warrant was a mere oversight on the part of the gardaí (this case was decided prior to *Kenny*). Finally, even if any constitutional rights of the defendant had been breached, there were extraordinary circumstances in existence as the gardaí had heard the flush of a toilet and feared the imminent destruction of vital evidence.[63]

In the context of calls for change to what many perceive to be a very strict exclusionary rule in the aftermath of *Kenny*, it may be that the concept of extraordinary excusing circumstances may lessen the harsh effects of that rule. This may, however, allow for too much judicial subjectivity and undermine the protectionist stance adopted by the Supreme Court in *Kenny*.

2.2 Rules of Admissibility/Exclusion in Relation to Violations of the Right to Privacy

2.2.1 General Rights of Privacy

While the right to privacy has been recognized as an unenumerated constitutional right in Ireland,[64] it has not been relied upon in any notable manner in the context of the exclusion of improperly obtained evidence. This is most likely due to the existence of other constitutional and legal rights which are defined more clearly and more readily relied upon, for example, the specific constitutional protection of the inviolability of the dwelling under Art. 40.5 Const., whereas the Irish constitutional right to privacy remains somewhat ill-defined and fluid.

---

[63] The concept of extraordinary excusing circumstances has also been referred to in other cases such as People (D.P.P.) v. Shaw [1982] I.R. 1 and D.P.P. v. Michael Delaney [1997] 3 I.R. 453.

[64] A specific right to marital privacy was first recognised in McGee v. A.G. [1974] I.R. 284. A broader right to privacy was then recognized in Norris v. A.G. [1984] I.R. 36, in the context of a claim for the decriminalization of homosexual activity.

One case in which the right to privacy was successfully relied upon is *Kennedy v. Ireland*.[65] In that case, the Minister for Justice of the time had issued a warrant allowing for phone-tapping to be carried out on the phones of two political journalists.[66] When it became public knowledge that this had occurred, the minister accepted that it had been unjustified and went beyond anything that could be called an error of judgment. The plaintiff journalists sought damages, claiming a breach of their constitutional right to privacy and freedom from unlawful and unwarranted intrusion.

In the High Court, Hamilton P. held that the right to privacy is constitutionally protected and that it includes the right to hold private conversations without deliberate, conscious and unjustified intrusions by servants of the State. He held that the plaintiffs in this case were entitled to succeed in their claim for damages; however he also stated that the right to privacy is not absolute but is subject to the constitutional rights of others as well as the requirements of public order, public morality and the common good.

2.2.2 *Covert Surveillance*

Twenty-two years on from the *Kennedy* case the Irish legislature (the Oireachtas), has specifically provided, within the Criminal Justice (Surveillance) Act 2009, for the use of covert surveillance evidence at trial. This Act provides for the carrying out of covert surveillance by the gardaí, the defense forces, and the revenue commissioners in certain circumstances. Such surveillance is to include monitoring, observing, listening to or making a recording of a particular person or group of persons or their movements, activities and communications; or monitoring or making a recording of places or things, by or with the assistance of surveillance devices.[67]

Generally, under the legislation, a judge of the District Court may grant an authorization for surveillance upon the application of a superior officer (a garda, member of the defense forces or officer of the revenue commissioners of appropriate rank). In the context of the criminal justice system, an applicant garda must have reasonable grounds to believe that (a) as part of an operation or investigation being conducted by the Garda Síochána concerning an arrestable offense,[68] the surveillance being sought to be authorized is necessary for the purposes of obtaining information as to whether the offense has been committed or as to the circumstances relating to the commission of the offense, or obtaining evidence for the purposes of proceedings

[65] [1987] I.R. 587.

[66] Purportedly under the authority of Section 56 of the Post Office Act 1908.

[67] Section 1 Criminal Justice (Surveillance) Act 2009.

[68] An arrestable offense is any offense which is potentially punishable by at least 5 years imprisonment: Criminal Law Act 1997, Section 2 (1), as amended by the Criminal Justice Act 2006, Section 8.

in relation to the offense, (b) the surveillance is necessary for the purpose of preventing the commission of arrestable offenses, or (c) is necessary for the purpose of maintaining the security of the State. Once in possession of an authorization, the Act provides that certain members of the Garda Síochána may enter, if necessary by the use of reasonable force, any place for the purposes of initiating or carrying out the authorized surveillance, and withdrawing the authorized surveillance device, without the consent of a person who owns or is in charge of the place. The authorization is to last no longer than 3 months.[69]

In circumstances of urgency, provision is made for a member of the gardaí (in the criminal justice context) to carry out surveillance under the approval of a superior officer. Such approval is only to be issued by a superior officer upon application from a member or officer where the conditions for the grant of a judicial authorization are in place and before such judicial authorization could be obtained, one or more of a number of specifically listed difficulties exist, e.g. it is likely that a person would abscond for the purpose of avoiding justice. An urgent approval will last for 72 h at most.[70]

Tracking devices may be utilized by the gardaí under the Act without any recourse to the courts, under the approval of a superior officer only.[71]

The Act provides that evidence obtained as a result of surveillance carried out under a relevant authorization or approval may be admitted as evidence in criminal proceedings. More pertinently, the Act provides that information or documents obtained as a result of surveillance carried out thereunder may be admitted as evidence notwithstanding any error or omission on the face of the authorization or written record of approval concerned, if the court, decides that: (1) the error or omission concerned was inadvertent, and (2) the information or document ought to be admitted in the interests of justice. In making this decision the court should take the following into account: (1) whether the error or omission concerned was serious or merely technical in nature; (2) the nature of any right infringed by the obtaining of the information or document concerned; (3) whether there were circumstances of urgency; (4) the possible prejudicial effect of the information or document concerned; and (5) the probative value of the information or document concerned.[72]

Furthermore, the Act suggests that information or documents obtained as a result of surveillance may be admitted as evidence in criminal proceedings notwithstan ding any failure by any member of the Garda Síochána to comply with a requirement of the authorization or approval concerned, if the court decides that: (1) the member or officer concerned acted in good faith and that the failure was inadvertent, and (2) the information or document ought to be admitted in the interests of justice, again taking the above list into consideration.[73]

---

[69] Sections 4, 5 Criminal Justice (Surveillance) Act 2009.

[70] Section 7 Criminal Justice (Surveillance) Act 2009.

[71] Section 8 Criminal Justice (Surveillance) Act 2009.

[72] Section 14 Criminal Justice (Surveillance) Act 2009.

[73] Ibid.

Given that important constitutional rights, such as the right to privacy and the inviolability of the dwelling, will surely be affected by the provisions of this Act, the suggestion that evidence improperly obtained thereunder which is obtained nonetheless in "good faith" by the gardaí seems to undermine the strict exclusionary rule set out in *Kenny* and applied in Ireland for the past 20 years, and is perhaps likely to lead the courts back to a re-evaluation of the unwieldy concept of "deliberate and conscious" breach. It remains to be seen whether any constitutional challenge to the Act might arise in the future.

2.2.3 Powers of Search

There are a number of statutes in operation in Ireland which allow for the search of a person, premises, vehicle or vessel without the authority of a search warrant. The constitutionality of such powers has been tested on occasion, usually resulting in judicial approval of their existence and exercise.

In *O'Callaghan v. Ireland*,[74] the accused submitted that the powers, under Section 23 of the Misuse of Drugs Act 1977, to stop and search a person with reasonable cause and to detain for such time as is reasonably necessary for making the search, were unprecedented, independent of any decision to arrest and created such uncertainty that they ought to be declared invalid under the Constitution. It was held in the Supreme Court, upholding the decision of the High Court, that this power to search was an extension of the ordinary power of arrest on suspicion. In view of the potential damage to society from the possession of controlled drugs, the Supreme Court held that it was reasonable and proper to make such a procedure which, far from being oppressive, allows the suspect to avoid arrest and detention at the Garda station.[75]

In *D.P.P. v. Fagan*[76] the Supreme Court tackled the complex issue of general, as opposed to individual, suspicion. The case concerned the interpretation of Section 109(1) of the Road Traffic Act 1961 which provides that "a person driving a vehicle in a public place shall stop the vehicle on being so required by a member of the Garda Síochána and shall keep it stationary for such period as is reasonably necessary in order to enable such member to discharge his duties". The difficulty with this provision is that it does not mention "reasonable suspicion" as it is normally understood in the common law. Patrick Fagan was driving a motor vehicle in the city center after midnight when he was stopped. It is only then that the garda noticed a smell of alcohol on his breath and his slurred speech, which would create the reasonable suspicion

[74] [1994] 1 I.R. 555. See also D.P.P. v. Rooney [1992] 2 I.R. 7, where the High Court examined the police power under Section 29 of the Dublin Police Act 1842 to stop, search and detain any person who may be reasonably suspected of having or conveying in any manner any thing stolen or unlawfully obtained.

[75] Ibid, 563.

[76] [1994] 3 I.R. 265.

that he was driving while drunk. But should suspicion not be required in order to stop the car? Four justices of the Supreme Court held that it was not necessary. One dissenter, Justice Susan Denham, ruled that reasonable suspicion was always required and is implied under the Constitution.

The majority appeared to be particularly concerned about the horrific consequences of drunk driving and contended that there is a general common law power to stop vehicles and detect drunken drivers on the basis of a general suspicion as opposed to a specific suspicion about a particular driver. Blayney J., one of the majority in the Court, relied on the English case of *Chief Constable of Gwent v. Dash*[77] supporting random checks in similar circumstances under equivalent provisions of the English Road Traffic Act 1972. This case was, however, discredited by Michael Zander in a leading text book as not representing the general rule in England and Wales that individual suspicion is always required except in the case of public disturbances in anticipation of violence.[78]

Denham J., dissenting, held that the lack of individualized suspicion must be authorized by legislation in specific circumstances and that the requirement for same should be presumed otherwise. She added that there is no right to make an investigative stop and held: "Broadly, the garda is given powers, such as a right to stop, arrest, search, which are activated by the member's reasonable suspicion. That is the foundation of the constitutional protection of individual's rights and the rule of law".[79]

2.2.4 *Search of Private Dwellings and Other Premises*

There is specific constitutional protection in Ireland for the dwelling place, or home, of every citizen. The inviolability of the dwelling place is to be protected and may only be interfered with in accordance with law. As a result, the courts have afforded greater protection to the dwelling place, as opposed to other premises, in their application of the exclusionary rule.

In *People (D.P.P.) v. McMahon, McMeel and Wright*,[80] for example, two gardaí entered licensed premises without a search warrant and without identifying themselves as gardaí. Once on the premises, they obtained evidence of violation of the Gaming and Lotteries Act 1956. At the request of the Circuit Court, the Supreme Court ruled that the gardaí were unlawfully on the premises. Finlay C.J. emphasized that the gardaí in this case were trespassers only and were not involved in any criminal behavior or breach of constitutional rights. Thus, the question of admissibility should be left to the discretion of the court as provided for in *O'Brien*. In doing so, the court should bear in mind the public interest and balance it against the interest of the individual as was done by the majority in *O'Brien*.

---

[77] [1986] R.T.R. 41.
[78] Zander (1999, 164).
[79] [1994] 3 I.R. 265 at p. 286.
[80] [1987] I.L.R.M. 87.

The circumstances and, in particular, the public interest of avoiding grave social consequences could have, and did, lead the trial court to admit the evidence. Of course, if the property had been a dwelling, a question of unconstitutionally obtained evidence, rather than illegally obtained evidence, would have arisen pursuant to Art. 40.5 Const. and the stricter exclusionary rule would have applied.

Interestingly, there have been a number of cases which show that if the dwelling is not that of the accused himself then there is no breach of constitutional rights and the admissibility of any relevant evidence is to be decided at the discretion of the trial judge.[81] In *D.P.P. v. Forbes*,[82] the accused was arrested on the forecourt of the dwelling of a third party. When the lawfulness of the arrest was challenged, the Supreme Court held that there is no breach of the constitutional right to the inviolability of one's dwelling house when a garda goes on to the forecourt of a householder's premises with their permission. The Court further held that every householder gives an implied authority to members of the Garda Síochána to come onto the forecourt of his premises to see to the enforcement of the law or prevent a breach thereof.[83]

Therefore, the courts have held that the Gardaí have implied authority to enter the driveway of a dwelling belonging to the accused, unless the owner of the dwelling expressly withdraws such implied consent. Expanding upon cases such as *Forbes*, however, has led to a situation whereby "the Supreme Court appears to have extended the principles of implied authority to members of the Garda Síochána to come on to the curtilage of a private dwelling house to see to the enforcement of the law or prevent a breach thereof, from the case of a defendant pursued onto the driveway of the dwelling house of a third party to the case of a defendant pursued onto the driveway of his or her own dwelling house".[84]

If a householder then is confronted by the gardaí on the driveway of his/her own dwelling he/she may be lawfully and constitutionally arrested thereon unless he/she specifically asserts his/her constitutional right to the inviolability of the dwelling. There has been some dissatisfaction expressed by the judiciary in applying this rule,

[81] Notably, in D.P.P. v. Lynch [2010] 1 I.R. 543 it was held that a squatter/trespasser in a flat could claim a breach of constitutional rights when that flat was searched under the purported authority of what was in fact an invalid search warrant. Considering whether or not the applicant in this case could claim the protection of the constitutional right to the inviolability of the dwelling under Art. 40.5 Const., the Court of Criminal Appeal looked at the Irish-language version of the constitutional text, which refers to the English term "dwelling" as "ionad cónaithe" (living place). The Court held that the Irish version reinforced the view that it was a question of fact in each individual case as to whether a particular premises was someone's dwelling.

[82] [1994] 2 I.R. 542.

[83] See also Freeman v. D.P.P. [1996] 3 I.R. 565.

[84] *Per* Herbert J. in D.P.P. v. O'Sullivan [2007] IEHC 248; unreported, High Court, Herbert J., 31 July, 2007 examining the earlier case of D.P.P. (Riordan) v. Molloy [2004] 3 I.R. 321. This alters the position established in cases such as D.P.P. v. McCreesh [1992] 2 I.R. 239 wherein an unlawful arrest was held to have occurred due to the fact that the gardaí arrested the accused on the driveway of his home. In *McCreesh* this was held to amount to a violation of Art. 40.5 Const. and the evidence against the accused was therefore excluded from evidence under the strict exclusionary rule in relation to unconstitutionally obtained evidence.

however, and it remains to be seen whether the Supreme Court might alter or refine it in the future.[85] Such a rule has not, to date, been extended to the interior of a private dwelling and it is submitted that such extension is unlikely.

2.3 Rules of Admissibility/Exclusion in Relation to Illegal Interrogations

2.3.1 The General Right to Remain Silent/Privilege Against Self-Incrimination

The pre-trial privilege against self-incrimination, usually referred to in Irish jurisprudence as the right to silence, has been recognized by the courts in this jurisdiction as being of constitutional status. However, the constitutional protection of the right has not prevented legislative incursion upon it, and so long as such incursion can be seen to be proportionate, the courts have accepted that it is constitutionally allowable.

2.3.1.1 Offenses Based on Silence

The constitutional status of the right to silence was first accepted in the case of *Heaney and McGuinness v. Ireland*,[86] wherein a constitutional challenge was levied against Section 52 of the Offences Against the State Act 1939. That provision created an offense, punishable by a term of imprisonment not exceeding 6 months, based on the pre-trial silence of the accused in certain circumstances. Specifically, it provided that a person arrested and detained under the 1939 Act could be required by a member of the Garda Síochána to account for his movements and actions during a specified period and to give all the information which he possessed in regard to the commission or intended commission by another person of any offense under the Act or any scheduled offense.[87] The offense was committed where the individual failed or refused to provide the relevant account, or provided a false or misleading account.

---

[85] In D.P.P. v. O'Sullivan [2007] IEHC 248; unreported, High Court, Herbert J., 31 July, 2007 Herbert J. declared himself bound by the earlier Supreme Court decision of D.P.P. (Riordan) v. Molloy [2004] 3 I.R. 321 but declared that he thought the rule to be "an affront to commonsense."

[86] [1996] 1 I.R. 580, [1997] 1 I.L.R.M. 117, (2001) 33 E.H.R.R. 12, 264.

[87] In regard to the scheduling of offenses, Sections 35, 36 Offences Against the State Act 1939, provide that where "the Government is satisfied that the ordinary courts are inadequate to secure the effective administration of justice and the preservation of public peace and order in relation to offenses of any particular class or kind or under any particular enactment, the Government may by order declare that offenses of that particular class or kind or under that particular enactment shall be scheduled offenses".

This case was heard in both the High Court and the Supreme Court in Ireland, and ultimately in the ECtHR. In the High Court, it was held that, although not specifically stated within the text of the Constitution, the right to silence was constitutionally protected as an important element of the right to a fair trial, under Art. 38.1 Const. The Supreme Court agreed that the right to silence is of constitutional status, however, it chose to locate the right within Art. 40.6 Const., as a corollary of the expressed right to freedom of expression.[88] Art. 40.6 Const. contains a proviso allowing for curtailment of the right to freedom of expression where the exigencies of public order and morality so require. As a result, the Supreme Court held that the restriction on the right to silence within Section 52 of the 1939 Act could be deemed constitutionally sound as a proportionate interference with the right to silence in pursuit of the aim of assuring public order.

The *Heaney* case ultimately went on to be heard by the ECtHR, which noted, as it had previously done in the English case of *Murray v. United Kingdom*,[89] that the right to silence/privilege against self-incrimination is a generally recognized international standard which lies at the heart of the notion of a fair procedure under Art. 6 ECHR.[90] In relation to Section 52 of the Irish Act, the ECtHR came to the conclusion that the interference therein with the right to silence was not proportionate and, in fact, the degree of compulsion to provide information which was imposed on accused persons by virtue of the provision in effect destroyed the very essence of their right to remain silent. This amounted to a breach of Art. 6 ECHR.

Despite the judgment of the ECtHR, and the subsequent recommendation of the Irish Committee to Review the Offences Against the State Acts 1939–1998 that Section 52 be removed from the statute books,[91] the impugned provision remains in place.[92] Furthermore, a number of other provisions which create offenses based on the pre-trial silence of a suspect have also been promulgated by the Oireachtas and applied by the courts, though some such provisions compel only the utterance of an individual's name and address.[93]

---

[88] Art. 46.1.1 Const. provides: "The State guarantees liberty for the exercise of the following rights, subject to public order and morality: – The right of the citizens to express freely their convictions and opinions…"

[89] (2001) 33 E.H.R.R. 334.

[90] Heaney and McGuiness v. Ireland (2001, 33 E.H.R.R. 12, 264, 278, § 40). See also Saunders v. United Kingdom (1997) 23 E.H.R.R. 313.

[91] Committee to Review the Offences Against the State Acts 1939–1998 (1999, para. 8.57).

[92] See Quinn v. O'Leary [2004] 3 I.R. 128 where the High Court held that the judgment of the ECtHR in *Heaney* did not have the effect of requiring the State to repeal or otherwise nullify legislation. This position is somewhat altered now as the European Convention on Human Rights Act 2003 which integrates the ECHR into Irish law at a sub-constitutional level was not in force when the *Heaney* decision was made.

[93] These include Section 30 Offences Against the State Act 1939, Section 2 Offences Against the State (Amendment) Act 1972, Section 107 Road Traffic Act 1961, and Sections 4, 15,16 Criminal Justice Act 1984. Failure or refusal to provide the relevant information under each of these legislative provisions amounts to an offense punishable by imprisonment, fine, or both.

The level of interference with the right to silence which Section 52 and provisions like it entails may now be thought to be reduced by the effect of the Supreme Court ruling in *Re National Irish Bank (under investigation) (No.1)*.[94] This case, decided in relation to Section 18 of the Companies Act 1990, dealt with the use which can be made at trial of a statement obtained from the accused in the pre-trial process under the compulsion of a legislative provision which makes it an offense to refuse or fail to answer particular questions or provide particular information. The Supreme Court held that in such situations, the relevant constitutional provision was Art. 38.1 Const. which protects the right to a fair trial, and not Art. 40.6 Const. The Court suggested that a trial is either "in due course of law" (as provided for in Art. 38.1 Const.) or it is not; there is no middle ground or potential for interference in the fairness of a trial. Therefore, the main question for the court in situations involving pre-trial compulsion was whether statements of the accused tendered as evidence at trial were voluntary. Involuntary statements are inadmissible under the rules on confession evidence and the constitutional protection of the right to a fair trial. While this was held to be a question for each future court to decide on a case-by-case basis, the implication in reality seems to be that a statement obtained under the compulsion of a legislative provision creating a silence-based offense would be unlikely to pass muster.

2.3.1.2 Inferences Based on Silence

Perhaps because of the Supreme Court ruling in *Re National Irish Bank*, which diluted the impact of silence-based offenses, and also perhaps due to the ECtHR's' negative view of legislative provisions creating stand-alone silence-based offenses, the Irish legislature (the Oireachtas) has more recently adopted a new approach to the issue of silence and introduced provisions allowing for inferences to be drawn at trial from the pre-trial silence of the accused.

The first inference-drawing provisions in Ireland were promulgated in the Criminal Justice Act 1984. Since their promulgation they have been redrafted and substituted by virtue of the Criminal Justice Act 2007, but their basic premise and the inferences which may be drawn remain unchanged. Sections 18,19 of the 1984 Act provide that an adverse inference may properly be drawn at trial against a person, who has been arrested without warrant by a garda, due to his failure or refusal to account, on being requested to do so by a garda, for the presence of any object, substance or mark on his person, clothing or footwear, or in his possession, or in the place where he is arrested or for his presence at a particular place. The 2007 Act also inserted Section 19A into the 1984 Act. This applies to all arrestable offenses and provides that inferences may be drawn at trial from a suspect's failure in the pre-trial period to mention any fact, when he is being questioned, charged or informed that

[94] [1999] 3 I.R. 145; [1999] 1 I.L.R.M. 321. See also Saunders v. United Kingdom (1996) 23 E.H.R.R. 313.

he might be charged with a particular offense, which he later relies on in his defense at trial, being a fact which in the circumstances existing at the time "clearly called for an explanation".[95]

A number of statutory safeguards are provided for suspects under Section 19A and these are also applicable to Sections 18,19: (1) a person shall not be convicted solely or mainly on an inference drawn under this section, although, any inference drawn may amount to corroboration of any evidence in relation to which the failure is material; (2) inferences can only be drawn where the accused has been told in ordinary language that it may harm the credibility of his defense if he does not mention when questioned, charged or informed, something which he later relies on in court; (3) no inference ought to be drawn unless the accused was afforded a reasonable opportunity to consult a solicitor before his failure to account for the relevant matters or to mention the relevant fact; (4) the court or jury in deciding whether or not to draw inferences ought to consider when the account or fact concerned was first mentioned by the accused; and (5) no inference shall be drawn in relation to a question asked in an interview unless either the interview has been electronically recorded or the detained person has consented in writing to the non-recording of the interview.[96]

The constitutionality of inference-drawing provisions was tested in the Irish courts prior to the enactment of Section 19A. In *Rock v. Ireland*,[97] both the High Court and the Supreme Court held that Sections 18,19 Criminal Justice Act 1984 constituted proportionate restrictions on the right to silence protected under Art. 40.6 Const. It was held that the sections represented the necessary balance between the accused's right to silence and the duty of the State to defend and protect the life, person and property of all its citizens. Furthermore, it was noted that: (1) the inferences which might be drawn were evidential in nature only and they could not be the sole basis for the conviction of the accused; and (2) in deciding what inferences may be drawn from the accused's pre-trial silence, the court must have regard to an accused's right to a fair trial and is under a constitutional obligation to ensure that no improper or unfair inferences are drawn or permitted to be drawn.[98]

Section 19A Criminal Justice Act 1984 is the most broadly-applicable inference-drawing provision which has been introduced in this jurisdiction to date. It appears to be modelled almost directly on Section 34 Criminal Justice and Public Order Act 1994 which operates in England and Wales. That provision has caused some controversy and confusion in both the English courts and the ECtHR due to the difficulty of applying it in circumstances where an accused person claims that his only reason

---

[95] Section 19A of the 1984 Act as inserted by Section 30 of the 2007 Act. Similar provisions existed within the Criminal Justice (Drug Trafficking) Act 1996 (Section 7) and the Offences Against the State (Amendment) Act 1998 (Section 5) but they were confined to offenses specifically provided for under those statutes. Those provisions have now been repealed and replaced by Section 19A.

[96] Sections 18, 19, 19A Criminal Justice Act 1984 as inserted by ss 28, 29,30 Criminal Justice Act 2007.

[97] [1997] 3 I.R. 484; [1998] 2 I.L.R.M. 35.

[98] [1997] 3 I.R. 484, 501; [1998] 2 ILRM 35, 47 per Hamilton C.J.

for failing to mention particular facts in the pre-trial period was the legal advice which he was given to remain silent.[99] It remains to be seen whether such difficulties will arise in the Irish context.

In terms of any argument that Section 19A may be unconstitutional, it seems unlikely that this would be successful, despite the fact that the provision goes beyond inference-drawing provisions previously in existence or constitutionally tested in Ireland. In light of the Supreme Court decision in *Rock*, as well as the additional safeguards provided for suspects questioned under Sections 18, 19 and 19A (e.g. audio-visual recording of the interview), it is submitted that the incursion on the right to silence which Section 19A represents is likely to be accepted by the Irish courts as being proportionate and constitutional.

In 2009, another inference-drawing provision was introduced by the Oireachtas: Section 72A Criminal Justice Act 2006, as inserted by Section 9 Criminal Justice (Amendment) Act 2009 (an Act introduced with some level of controversy[100] in the wake of the murder of a man named Roy Collins in Limerick[101]). Section 72A applies to the rather broad concept of participating in or contributing to any activity of a "criminal organisation".[102] It provides that, in such "organised crime" cases, an inference may be drawn at trial from the pre-trial failure of a suspect to "answer a question material to the investigation of the offence".[103]

Under Section 72A, a person is not to be convicted solely or mainly on an inference drawn from the relevant pre-trial failure to answer. The suspect must have been told in ordinary language, when being questioned, what the effect of such a failure might be, he must have been afforded a reasonable opportunity to consult a solicitor before such a failure occurred, and the relevant interview must have been recorded by electronic or similar means unless the suspect consented in writing to it not being recorded.

"Any question material to the investigation of the offence" is defined within Section 72A(7) as including, *inter alia*: (1) a request that the suspect give a full account of his or her movements, actions, activities or associations during any specified period relevant to the offence being investigated; (2) questions related to

---

[99] See R v. Betts and Hall [2001] 2 Cr. App. R. 257; R v. Howell [2005] 1 Cr. App. R. 1, [2003] E.W.C.A. Crim. 1; R v. Hoare and Pierce [2005] 1 W.L.R. 1804, [2005] 1 Cr. App. R. 22, [2004] E.W.C.A. Crim. 784; Averill v. United Kingdom (2001) 31 E.H.R.R. 839; Condron v. United Kingdom (2001) 31 E.H.R.R. 1; and Beckles v. United Kingdom (2003) 36 E.H.R.R. 13.

[100] 133 lawyers objected to the introduction of the Criminal Justice (Amendment) Act 2009 by way of a letter to *The Irish Times* ("Criminal Justice (Amendment) Bill", *Irish Times*, July 8 2009) and the President considered referring the Bill to the Supreme Court under Art. 26 Const. However, following consultation with the Council of State, the President signed the Bill into law on July 23 2009.

[101] Mr Collins was related to a man who had given evidence in a "gangland crime" trial 5 years previously.

[102] "Criminal organisation" is currently defined under Section 70 Criminal Justice Act 2006 as "a structured group, however organised, that has as its main purpose or activity the commission or facilitation of a serious offence".

[103] Section 72A Criminal Justice Act 2006.

statements or conduct of the suspect implying or leading to a reasonable inference that he was at a material time directing the activities of a criminal organization; and (3) questions relating to any benefit which the suspect may have obtained from directing a criminal organization or committing a serious offense within a criminal organization. A question is not to be regarded as being material to the investigation of the offense unless the garda concerned reasonably believed that the question related to the participation of the defendant in the commission of the offense.[104]

Section 19A, discussed above, although applicable to all arrestable offenses, is confined to circumstances where the accused failed to mention a particular fact in the pre-trial period, which at that time "clearly called for an explanation" and which he then sought to rely on at trial as part of his defense. Sections 18 and 19 allow for inferences to be drawn from failure to account for very particular matters in the pre-trial investigatory stage, where such an account was, again "clearly called for". Section 72A involves a different concept which raises issues in relation to the presumption of innocence and the burden of proof in a criminal trial. The court may draw an inference against the accused basically on the grounds that he refused to co-operate with the garda investigation into his guilt. An inference, it seems, may be drawn whether or not an answer to the particular question was "clearly called for" or the failure to provide such an answer is a specifically relevant matter in the context of the later trial. Failure alone gives rise to the inference.

While, again, it seems likely that the Irish courts will consider Section 72A to be constitutionally proportionate, particularly given its "organised crime" criteria, the shifting of the goalposts in terms of its operation, as compared with other inference-drawing provisions, might be just enough to set it apart and have it deemed constitutionally unsound in an appropriate future case. Of course, the ECtHR has not disapproved of the use of adverse inferences at trial based on pre-trial silence per se. In *Murray v. United Kingdom*,[105] it was held that the right to silence within Art. 6 ECHR is not absolute and may be interfered with by way of inference-drawing provisions in appropriate circumstances.

It will be clear from the foregoing that the right to silence in the Irish pre-trial process is currently very restricted and carries with it hazardous consequences for a suspect.

2.3.2 *The Protection Against Involuntary Self-Incrimination: Torture, Coercion, Threats, Promises, etc.*

As noted above, the Irish courts will only accept a suspect's pre-trial statement, admission or confession in evidence if it can be shown to be voluntary. The traditional legal definition of voluntariness was laid out by Lord Sumner in the English

---

[104] Section 72A(7) Criminal Justice Act 2006.

[105] (1996) 22 E.H.R.R. 29.

case of *Ibrahim v. R*[106] and was adopted in Ireland in *A.G. v. McCabe*.[107] It prescribes that a voluntary statement is one which "has not been obtained … either by fear of prejudice or hope of advantage exercised or held out by a person in authority…"[108] Basically, a statement which is obtained on the basis of either a threat or an inducement will be seen as involuntary and deemed inadmissible at trial.

The concept of voluntariness is not merely a feature of the common law in Ireland, it in fact has constitutional status within the protection of the right to a fair trial under Art. 38.1 Const. This was set out clearly by the Supreme Court in *Re National Irish Bank Ltd. (No. 1)*.[109] Therefore, if a trial judge deems that a relevant statement was obtained due to a threat, or an inducement, or because of oppression, he *must* exclude it from evidence at trial under the voluntariness rule as to admit the statement would be in breach of the Constitution.

Importantly, the traditional voluntariness rule has been expanded in Ireland to apply in cases where a statement has been obtained in circumstances of "oppression". In the English case of *R v. Priestly*[110] oppression was defined as "something which tends to sap and has sapped the free will which must exist before a confession is voluntary". This definition was adopted into Irish law in *People (D.P.P.) v. Breathnach*.[111] In the later case of *People (D.P.P.) v. Pringle, McCann and O'Shea*[112] the more specific definition of oppressive questioning was adopted from the English case of *R v. Prager*[113] and consists in: "questioning which by its nature, duration or other attendant circumstances (including the fact of custody) excites hopes (such as the hope of release) or fears or so affects the mind of the subject that his will crumbles and he speaks when otherwise he would have stayed silent".[114] The test for oppression which has been adopted, and was applied in the *Pringle* case, is a subjective one. O'Higgins C.J. in the Court of Criminal Appeal in that case accepted that: "what may be oppressive to a child, an invalid, or an old man or somebody inexperienced in the ways of the world may turn out not to be oppressive when one finds that the accused person is of tough character and an experienced man of the world".[115]

Outside of the voluntariness rule, including the concept of "oppression", there are two other reasons that confession evidence might be excluded in Ireland: breach of constitutional rights and the absence of fundamental fairness. In relation to con-

---

[106] [1914] A.C. 599.

[107] [1927] I.R. 129; see also McCarrick v. Leavy [1964] I.R. 225.

[108] A.G. v. McCabe [1927] I.R. 129, 134 based on Ibrahim v. R [1914] A.C. 599, 609.

[109] [1999] 3 I.R. 145; [1999] 1 I.L.R.M. 321. See discussion above.

[110] (1965) 50 Cr. App. Rep. 183; [1966] Crim. L.R. 507.

[111] (1981) 2 Frewen 43 later affirmed in the Supreme Court in People (D.P.P.) v. Lynch [1982] I.R. 64; [1981] I.L.R.M. 389.

[112] (1981) 2 Frewen 57.

[113] [1972] 1 All E.R. 1114; [1972] 1 W.L.R. 260; 56 Cr. App. Rep. 151.

[114] [1972] 1 W.L.R. 260, 266 *per* Edmund Davies L.J.

[115] (1981) 2 Frewen 57, 82.

stitutional rights, the statement obtained will only be excluded if a causal link can be shown between the breach of the relevant right and the making of the impugned statement. This is clear from the case-law on the right of access to legal advice, discussed in detail below.

The concept of fundamental fairness as an issue which might influence the admissibility of confession evidence was first referred to by Griffin J. in the Supreme Court case of *People (D.P.P.) v Shaw*,[116] although it was not central to the decision in that case. Griffin J. proposed that two conditions must be satisfied in order to allow for the admission of a confession in evidence: (1) the statement must have been voluntarily made; and (2) the court must be satisfied that, besides voluntariness, no other circumstances existed to interfere with the fundamental fairness of the procedures adopted in the case. The notion of fundamental fairness is linked in some ways to the concept of oppression, however, it was held in *People (D.P.P.) v. C*[117] that there may be circumstances where the causal link necessary to exclude evidence on the basis of oppression may not be present, but the behavior and general circumstances of the case may be said to be so unfair as to necessitate the exclusion of the evidence obtained on broader public policy grounds or on grounds of a breach of fair procedures.[118]

It is clear that if a member of the Gardaí employed excessive physical force against a suspect such as to amount to a breach of his constitutional right to bodily integrity[119] it would automatically lead to the exclusion of any confession which could be causally linked to such use of physical force. If such excessive physical force was not seen by the court as enough to amount to a breach of the suspect's constitutional right to bodily integrity, it might yet amount to a breach of his legal rights such that he ought not to be assaulted, and a related confession may be excluded from evidence at trial in the exercise of the trial judge's discretion to exclude illegally though not unconstitutionally obtained evidence. Finally, if the excessive force employed was force of a psychological or emotional nature, rather than physical force, evidence may yet be excluded from trial on the basis of involuntariness due to threats or oppression or because of a lack of fundamental fairness.

2.3.3 The Protection Against Unknowing Self-Incrimination: The Miranda Paradigm

In Ireland, the right of access to pre-trial legal advice has to some extent been set out by the Oireachtas and has also been recognized by the courts as a right of constitutional status. The right to be informed of the right of access to legal advice is set out in legislation but its constitutional status is less clear.

---

[116] [1982] I.R. 1.

[117] [2001] 3 I.R. 345.

[118] See also People (D.P.P.) v. Breen, unreported, Court of Criminal Appeal, March 13, 1995; People (D.P.P.) v. Paul Ward, unreported, Special Criminal Court, November 27, 1998.

[119] Recognised in Ryan v A.G. [1965] I.R. 294 as an unenumerated constitutional right.

The first legislative provision to make reference to pre-trial legal advice was Section 5 Criminal Justice Act 1984 which required that persons arrested be informed of the right of access to legal advice in the pre-trial period. While this provision applies only to persons arrested and detained under Section 4 of that Act, the Custody Regulations 1987, which apply to all suspects held in garda custody, also refer to the possibility of consulting with a solicitor in the pre-trial period.

Recently, as noted above, the Oireachtas has made further provision for access to legal advice in the pre-trial process specifically where inference-drawing provisions are concerned. Under the newly substituted and inserted Sections 18, 19 and 19A Criminal Justice Act, 1984 and Section 72A Criminal Justice Act 2006, discussed above, unless a suspect in the pre-trial period has been afforded a reasonable opportunity to consult with a solicitor, inferences from his silence at that time cannot be drawn against him at trial. This is an interesting legislative recognition of the link between the right to silence and the right of access to pre-trial legal advice and the provision of this specific protection for the right to legal advice where inferences might later be drawn from pre-trial silence reflects the jurisprudence of the ECtHR under Art. 6 ECHR.[120]

The constitutional status of the right of access to pre-trial legal advice was declared in *People (D.P.P.) v. Healy*.[121] In that case, the suspect had been arrested and detained for questioning on suspicion of being in possession of unlawful firearms. He was questioned by gardaí for a number of hours in regard to an attempted armed robbery and eventually began to make an inculpatory statement. As he was making this statement, a solicitor who had been retained by the suspect's family arrived at the Garda station and sought to consult with him. The solicitor was refused immediate access to the suspect as the member in charge of the station at the time considered that it would be "bad manners" to interrupt the ongoing Garda interview.

At the suspect's trial, the only evidence against him was the inculpatory statement which he had made to gardaí. He was convicted on this evidence and appealed on grounds of breach of his right of access to legal advice in the pre-trial period. In the Supreme Court it was held that the right of reasonable access to a solicitor was derived from and protected by the Constitution. The Court stated that this right encompassed a right to be immediately informed of the arrival of one's solicitor at the place of detention and to be given immediate access to him if requested. Furthermore, it was held that if the denial of this right to a solicitor could be said to be the result of a deliberate and conscious act by a member or members of the Garda Síochána, then any admissions later obtained from the accused would be inadmissible against him at trial. The motives of the gardaí were irrelevant, so long as the act or acts which brought about the breach of the accused's constitutional right could be said to be "deliberate and conscious." It was held, on the facts, that the

120 See Murray v. United Kingdom (1996) 22 E.H.R.R. 29 and Averill v. United Kingdom (2001) 31 E.H.R.R. 839.

121 [1990] 2 I.R. 73; [1990] I.L.R.M. 313.

inculpatory statements made by the suspect following the breach of his constitutional right of access to pre-trial legal advice should have been excluded from evidence at trial.

Finlay C.J., giving the majority judgment of the court, did not specify the particular constitutional provision in which the court was locating the right of reasonable access to legal advice in the pre-trial period, however, he appeared to recognise a two-fold *raison d'être* for the right. First, he suggested that the right of access to pre-trial legal advice is necessary so that a suspect is made fully aware of all his legal rights so as to allow for any decision thereafter made by him as to whether or not to make a statement to be freely reached and therefore voluntary. Secondly, he suggested that the right was necessary to redress the imbalance which exists in the pre-trial period between the power and position of the detained suspect and that of the gardaí; he suggested that advice from a solicitor would contribute to some measure of equality of arms between these participants in the pre-trial process.[122]

The right of access to pre-trial legal advice, as defined by the Irish Supreme Court in *Healy*, is one of "reasonable access" only. The Supreme Court in *Healy* expressly reserved judgment as to whether or not that formulation of the right encompassed a right to have one's solicitor present throughout Garda interrogation, however later courts appear to have, rather bluntly, accepted that there is no such right.

One example of such a decision is the case of *Lavery v. Member-in-Charge, Carrickmacross Garda Station*,[123] which arose in the specific context of the inference-drawing provisions which predated Section 19A of the 1984 Act. The accused had been arrested on suspicion of membership in an unlawful organization and was detained for questioning at Carrickmacross Garda Station. One hour after his arrest, the detained suspect spoke with his solicitor on the telephone and received some general advice from him in relation to the law which allowed for inferences to be drawn at later trial from the failure of a suspect in the pre-trial process to mention particular facts or give particular information. The solicitor requested the gardaí to audio-visually record the interview with his client or to take a complete set of notes and to provide them to the suspect and his solicitor before the end of the detention period. Both of these requests were refused.

In the High Court, McGuinness J. granted an order of *habeas corpus*, holding that in light of the inference-drawing provisions then in force, persons in custody ought to have access to legal advice and to notes taken during Garda interviews. On appeal to the Supreme Court, however, this ruling was overturned. O'Flaherty J., giving the judgment of the Court, held that while blanket denial of access to legal advice would indeed render detention unlawful, there was no need for gardaí to give solicitors updates and running accounts of the progress of their investigations. He considered that the gardaí must be allowed to exercise their powers of interrogation

[122] [1990] 2 I.R. 73, 81; [1990] I.L.R.M. 313, 320.

[123] [1999] 2 I.R. 390.

as they see fit, provided that they act reasonably. O'Flaherty J. also made the blunt statement that "[t]he solicitor is not entitled to be present at the interviews".[124] No Irish case has arisen since *Lavery* to challenge the decision given therein and, accordingly, there is no right to have one's solicitor present throughout interrogation by gardaí within the contemporary pre-trial process in Ireland.

The ECtHR originally did not insist that the right of access to pre-trial legal advice should encompass a right to have one's legal adviser present throughout interrogation. More recently, however, in *Salduz v. Turkey*,[125] the Court stated: "in order for the right to a fair trial to remain sufficiently 'practical and effective' article 6(1) requires that, as a rule, access to a lawyer should be provided as from the first interrogation of a suspect by the police, unless it is demonstrated in the light of the particular circumstances of each case that there are compelling reasons to restrict this right".[126] This decision may require some rethinking of the definitional limits of the Irish right to legal advice.[127]

A matter of constitutional uncertainty is whether the questioning of a suspect must be suspended pending the arrival of a solicitor requested by him. The Custody Regulations, 1987 provide only that a suspect should not be asked to complete a written statement until a reasonable time has elapsed for the arrival of a requested solicitor, but they provide no legal obligation to refrain from questioning a suspect in such circumstances.[128] In the Supreme Court in *People (D.P.P.) v. Conroy*[129] Walsh J., in a dissenting judgment, suggested that the interrogation of a suspect by gardaí after he had requested a solicitor, but before the actual arrival of a solicitor, was a "constitutionally forbidden procedure".[130] However, the Court of Criminal Appeal suggested in *People (D.P.P.) v. Cullen*[131] that placing an obligation on gardaí to suspend questioning until such time as a solicitor has arrived and has consulted with the suspect would bring with it a duty on the State to provide a panel of solicitors who would be always available to attend at each Garda station where persons might be held if their presence was requested. Such a duty, it was suggested, did not exist and there was therefore no obligation on gardaí to cease questioning a detained suspect prior to the arrival of a requested solicitor. Other cases such as *People (D.P.P.) v. Buck*[132] and *People (D.P.P.) v. O'Brien*[133] seem to confirm this.

---

[124] [1999] 2 I.R. 390: see also McGrath (2000, 233–35). See also the *ex tempore* judgment of Carney J. in the High Court in Barry v. Waldron Unreported, High Court, *ex tempore*, May 23, 1996.

[125] (2008) 49 E.H.R.R. 19, 421.

[126] Ibid, 437, § 55. For more on the *Salduz* line of cases, see line of cases, see Ölçer, Ch. 16, pp. 395–397.

[127] It is notable, for example, that while the right to be advised of the right to legal advice exists at the statutory level in Ireland it has not been recognized as having constitutional status.

[128] Regulation 11 (6).

[129] [1986] I.R. 460.

[130] [1986] I.R. 460 at p. 479.

[131] Unreported, Court of Criminal Appeal, March 30, 1993.

[132] [2002] 2 I.R. 260; [2002] 2 I.L.R.M. 454.

[133] Unreported, Court of Criminal Appeal, June 17, 2002; [2005] 2 I.R. 206 (S.C.).

In *Buck*, while the gardaí continued to question the suspect while waiting for his solicitor to arrive, the court found that they made a good faith effort to contact the solicitor, and the suspect did not make a statement until after his solicitor had arrived. Therefore the court found no causal link which would make the statement inadmissible. Following *Buck*, the case of *O'Brien* arose wherein the gardaí were found to have acted *mala fides* in their efforts to secure a solicitor for the suspect to the extent that they had consciously and deliberately breached his constitutional right of access to legal advice in the pre-trial process. In this case, the suspect made statements to the gardaí both before and after consultation with his solicitor. It was held by both the Court of Criminal Appeal and the Supreme Court that the first set of statements made by the suspect while the breach of his right to pre-trial legal advice was ongoing had to be excluded from evidence at trial due to that breach, but that the second set of statements could be admitted in evidence as the breach was no longer ongoing at the time when those statements were made and there was no causal link between the breach and the making of the statements.[134]

These two relatively recent pronouncements on the constitutional right of access to pre-trial legal advice in Ireland show two things: (1) there must be a causal link between any conscious and deliberate breach of this right and the making of any statement in order for such statement to be excluded from evidence at trial and (2) there appears to be no constitutional prohibition on questioning a suspect prior to the arrival of his requested solicitor, so long as the gardaí have genuinely attempted to contact such solicitor. This approach, however, may now be at variance with the dictates of the ECtHR's decision in *Salduz v. Turkey*.[135]

As noted in *People (D.P.P.) v. Cullen*,[136] there are no duty solicitor schemes in place in Ireland. The only scheme which does exist to facilitate the provision of legal advice to detained suspects who cannot afford to retain their own solicitor is the Garda Station Legal Advice Scheme. This administrative, non-statutory scheme was established in February 2002. Only persons in receipt of Social Welfare payments or earning less than 20,316 per annum are entitled to free legal advice. As this is an administrative scheme only it creates no right to free legal advice for a detained suspect and places no specific obligation on gardaí to inform the detained suspect of the existence of the scheme or the possibility that he may be able to obtain legal advice free of charge if he is eligible under its terms.[137]

Another issue which ought to be briefly addressed is the audio-visual recording of Garda interrogations. Under the Criminal Justice Act, 1984 (Electronic Recording of Interviews) Regulations, 1997 interviews with persons arrested and detained

---

[134] For further analysis of this case see Daly (2006).

[135] (2008) 49 E.H.R.R. 421. For more on this see Heffernan (2011).

[136] Unreported, Court of Criminal Appeal, March 30, 1993; discussed in Butler and Ong (1995).

[137] A statutory scheme to provide legal aid to impecunious suspects at the trial stage operates separately, under the Criminal Justice (Legal Aid) Act 1962. The right to legal aid at the trial stage of the criminal process was placed on a constitutional footing in the case of State (Healy) v. Donoghue [1976] I.R. 325.

under Section 30 Offences Against the State Act, 1939, Section 4 Criminal Justice Act, 1984 or Section 2 Criminal Justice (Drug Trafficking) Act, 1996 shall be electronically recorded, "except where: (1) the equipment is unavailable due to a functional fault; (2) the equipment is already in use at the time the interview is to commence, and the member in charge considers on reasonable grounds that the interview should not be delayed until the fault is rectified or the equipment becomes available; or (3) where otherwise the electronic recording of the interview is not practicable".[138] As with the Custody Regulations, 1987, breach of these Electronic Recording Regulations does not of itself render a garda liable to civil or criminal proceedings or render inadmissible in evidence anything said during questioning, although a court may exclude evidence at its discretion.[139]

In interpreting and applying the Electronic Recording Regulations, 1997, the courts were originally somewhat lenient in relation to the absence of audio-visual recording,[140] but more recently they have become stricter in their approach, especially where inferences may later be drawn from the silence of a suspect during pre-trial Garda interview. In cases such as *People (D.P.P.) v. Connolly*,[141] *People (D.P.P.) v. Kelly*[142] and *People (D.P.P.) v. Diver*,[143] the superior courts observed the routine nature of audio-visual recording of pre-trial interrogations in most first world common law countries and criticized the failure of the Irish criminal justice system to bring the procedure to a similarly routine standing in this jurisdiction. As was noted above, however, since 2007 Sections 18, 19 and 19A Criminal Justice Act 1984, as amended, now require recording, otherwise no inferences from a suspect's silence may be drawn.

2.3.4 *Derivative Exclusion of an Otherwise Valid Confession as Fruit of an Unlawful Arrest/Seizure or Search*

Confessions may be excluded where there is a causal link between the breach of a constitutional right and the making of the confession. This is evidenced in cases such as *People (D.P.P.) v. Madden*[144] where the accused made a voluntary confession, but it was excluded from evidence as it had been obtained in breach of his

---

[138] Regulation 4. Audio-visual recording of interviews with suspects detained under Section 50 Criminal Justice Act 2007 does not seem to be specifically provided for in legislation or in the Regulations, though it does seem to be implied in Sections 56 and 57 of the 2007 Act and in Sections 18, 19 and 19A Criminal Justice Act 1984 as substituted by the 2007 Act..

[139] Section 27 Criminal Justice Act 1984.

[140] For example, People (D.P.P.) v. Holland, unreported, Court of Criminal Appeal, June 15, 1998.

[141] [2003] 2 I.R. 1.

[142] Unreported, Special Criminal Court, November 26, 2004 – see the *Irish Times*, "Basic fairness dictates that, where possible, interview of accused on IRA charge should be video-recorded", Monday 17 January 2005.

[143] [2005] 3 I.R. 270.

[144] [1977] I.R. 336. See discussion above.

constitutional right to liberty. Similarly, in *People (D.P.P.) v. Laide and Ryan*[145] it was held that statements made by the second-named accused ought not have been admitted at trial as they had been made while in unlawful detention, due to an unlawful arrest.

There must however be an ongoing causal link between the breach of constitutional rights and the making of the relevant confession in order for exclusion to occur. If the breach has been rectified or purged by the time the confession is made, the confession will be admissible. This is clear from the cases of *Buck* and *People (D.P.P.) v. O'Brien.* In the latter case, once the accused had had access to legal advice his second set of statements were deemed to be admissible, as the causal link between the earlier breach of his right to legal advice and the making of those statements was said to have been broken. However, there seemed to be little real consideration by the Court of Criminal Appeal or the Supreme Court as to whether or not there might be any ongoing affect of the earlier breach of the right to legal advice.

2.4 Conclusion

The Irish exclusionary rule is a complex one which has developed and evolved over many years and is, in fact, still in a state of flux. Much of the discussion in this chapter has focused on the operation of the rule where there has been a breach of constitutional rights, as this has been the most controversial issue in the Irish context. From the judgment in *O'Brien* through cases such as *Madden* and *Shaw* and the discussion on the meaning of "deliberate and conscious violation" on to the high protectionist stance adopted in *Kenny*, the Irish exclusionary rule has taken numerous twists and turns and has been considered from various angles by the judges of the Superior Courts. Even since *Kenny* the courts have vacillated in their application of the rule, circumventing it in cases such as *Balfe*, applying it in cases such as *Laide*, and strongly criticizing it, while endeavoring to avoid applying it, in *Cash*. The difficulty has often been that the rule was interpreted at different times and by different courts with a variable level of strictness and subjectivity, and with a variety of views as to its meaning when it was originated.

Recommendations for a relaxation of the strict rule in relation to unconstitutionally obtained evidence have come both from the judicial benches (e.g. Charleton J. in *Cash*) and from outside the courts (most notably from a majority of the Balance in the Criminal Law Review Group). Whether such change will come about, and how such change might be achieved, remains to be seen. While the Irish Supreme Court is generally slow to depart from its own precedents,[146] it has done so in exceptional circumstances in the past and might decide to do so in the context of the

[145] [2005] 1 I.R. 209. See discussion above.

[146] See State (Quinn) v. Ryan [1965] I.R. 110; Attorney General v Ryan's Car Hire Ltd [1965] I.R. 642; Mogul of Ireland Ltd v. Tipperary (North Riding) County Council [1976] I.R. 260.

exclusionary rule. The fact that the Court chose not to do so in *Cash* may be illustrative of a lack of Supreme Court appetite for change, or may simply reflect the facts of that case as viewed by the Court. If the Supreme Court does not review the rule, the majority of the Balance in the Criminal Law Review Group has suggested that a change could be brought about by legislation or by way of constitutional referendum. It is submitted that legislative change to a constitutional rule is not possible and therefore, a referendum may be the only way to alter the rule. Whether such referendum is warranted or wise is a question beyond the remit of this chapter, but it can certainly be said that there are interesting times ahead for the Irish exclusionary rule.

Bibliography

Balance in the Criminal Law Review Group. 2007. *Final Report*, Dublin: http://www.inis.gov.ie/en/JELR/BalanceRpt.pdf/Files/BalanceRpt.pdf.

Butler, A.S., and D.K. Ong. 1995. Breach of the constitutional right of access to a lawyer and the exclusion of evidence – The causative link. *Irish Criminal Law Journal* 5(2): 156–172.

Charleton, P. 1980. Improperly obtained evidence and the constitution. *Incorporated Law Society of Ireland Gazette* 74(8): 169–177.

Committee to Review the Offences Against the State Acts, 1939–1998. 1999. *Report*, (Hederman Report), Dublin: http://www.inis.gov.ie/en/JELR/hederman%20report.pdf/Files/hederman%20report.pdf.

Daly, Y.M. 2006. Does the buck stop here?: An examination of the pre-trial right to legal advice in light of O'Brien v. D.P.P. *Dublin University Law Journal* 28: 345–362.

Daly, Y.M. 2011a. Exclusion of evidence: DPP (Walsh) v. Cash. *International Journal of Evidence and Proof* 15: 62–69.

Daly, Y.M. 2011b. Judicial oversight of policing: Investigations, evidence and the exclusionary rule. *Crime, Law, and Societal Change* 55: 199–215.

Heffernan, L. 2011. The right to legal advice, reasonable access and the remedy of excluding evidence. *Criminal Law and Procedure Review* 1: 111–129.

McGrath, D. 2000. Evidence. In *Annual review of Irish Law 1999*, ed. R. Byrne and W. Binchy, 233–235. Dublin: Thomson Round Hall.

McGrath, D. 2005. *Evidence*. Dublin: Thomson Round Hall.

Zander, M. 1999. *Cases and materials on the English legal system*, 8th ed. London: Butterworths.

Chapter 3
Scotland: A Plea for Consistency

Findlay Stark and Fiona Leverick

3.1 The General Theory of Admissibility of Illegally Gathered Evidence

3.1.1 Introduction

The Scottish courts have taken an unsatisfactory approach to the question of whether illegally obtained evidence should be admitted in or excluded from criminal proceedings. The first part of this chapter discusses the incoherent development of the doctrine of illegally obtained evidence by the Scottish courts in criminal cases.[1] It should be noted from the outset that the judicial development of the criminal law and the attendant procedure is usual in Scotland. The substantive criminal law is not codified[2] and, although much of Scots criminal procedure has been legislated upon,[3] the law on illegally obtained evidence is one example of the courts' proactive approach.

---

[1] The approach of the Scottish courts with regard to illegally obtained evidence in civil cases is even less coherent than that adopted in criminal cases. For discussion, see Ross and Chalmers (2009, para. 1.7.8); and the cases cited there.

[2] A group of Scottish academics has created a draft criminal code, but this is unlikely to be adopted as the law: Clive et al. (2003).

[3] The most comprehensive piece of legislation is the Criminal Procedure (Scotland) Act 1995 (subsequently CP(S)A).

F. Stark (✉)
Faculty of Law, Downing College, University of Cambridge,
10 West Road, Cambridge CB3 9DZ, UK
e-mail: fgs23@cam.ac.uk

F. Leverick
School of Law, University of Glasgow,
Glasgow, G12 8QQ, UK
e-mail: Fiona.Leverick@glasgow.ac.uk; f.leverick@law.gla.ac.uk

S.C. Thaman (ed.), *Exclusionary Rules in Comparative Law*, Ius Gentium: Comparative Perspectives on Law and Justice 20, DOI 10.1007/978-94-007-5348-8_3,

The second part of the chapter then explores the relationship between privacy concerns (which have taken on renewed importance following the human rights legislation of the late 1990s)[4] and the doctrine of illegally obtained evidence in Scotland. The chapter concludes by discussing the need for reform of the law which has gone largely unaddressed for over 50 years.

It is sensible to begin by examining the leading case on illegally obtained evidence, before considering the law's later, inconsistent, refinement.

3.1.2 Balancing Competing Concerns

Historically, the Scottish courts adopted a similar approach to their English counterparts: in practice, it appears that illegally obtained evidence was usually (though not always)[5] admitted.[6] This changed, however, with the "watershed"[7] decision by a "Full Bench" of seven judges of the Court of Criminal Appeal (more commonly, "the Appeal Court") in *Lawrie v. Muir*[8] – the current leading case.[9] *Lawrie* removed the certainty of (what appeared, in the main, to be) a mandatory inclusionary rule and, in doing so, introduced an apparently principled balance of concerns of both due process and truth. In this respect, *Lawrie* was fairly revolutionary: Scots law is traditionally adversarial in nature, so ascertaining the "truth" is not mandated.[10]

In *Lawrie*, the Lord Justice-General (Cooper) opined that the court, in considering whether or not to admit illegally obtained evidence, must balance two competing interests:

> a) the interest of the citizen to be protected from illegal or irregular invasions of his liberties by the authorities, and b) the interest of the State to secure that evidence bearing upon the commission of crime and necessary to enable justice to be done shall not be withheld from Courts of law on any merely formal or technical ground.[11]

---

[4] See the discussion of the Human Rights Act 1998 and the Scotland Act 1998 below in Sect. 3.2.

[5] See, for example, HM Advocate v. Mahler (1857) 2 Irv 634, where a promise by the police not to prosecute the accused if he gave the police information about his cohorts (which was later broken) led to the exclusion of that evidence at trial.

[6] Gray (1966, 92), Macdonald (1948, 326), and Lewis (1925, 292).

[7] Davidson (2007, 349).

[8] 1950 JC 19.

[9] The doctrine of precedent means that consideration of an earlier decision is only possible by a larger court. Most appeals are heard by three judges, so a Full Bench is generally comprised of five judges. In *Lawrie*, the court had to consider a decision of five judges (Adair v. McGarry, 1933 JC 72), necessitating the formation of a larger court.

[10] It is widely recognised, however, that inquisitorial aspects are creeping into the Scots trial. See, for example: Duff (2004a, 29–50) and Gane (1999, 56–73).

[11] Lawrie v. Muir 1950 JC 19, at 26.

He continued that:

> Irregularities require to be excused, and infringements of the formalities of the law in relation to these matters are not lightly to be condoned. Whether any given irregularity ought to be excused depends upon the nature of the irregularity and the circumstances under which it was committed. In particular, the case may bring into play the discretionary principle of fairness to the accused.[12]

These two statements of the law make it clear that the Crown bears the burden of excusing any irregularity which is found to exist. Furthermore, the court must act to both vindicate the accused's right to a fair trial and to ensure that the State's interest in bringing criminals to justice is not thwarted.[13] This is the *only* approach taken towards illegally obtained evidence in criminal trials: no distinction is made in Scotland between different *types* of irregularity.[14] Furthermore, if an irregularity is excused, it is unusual for a civil action to be brought.[15] The court's discretion is thus, usually, absolute.

The position following *Lawrie* has been considered approvingly by English commentators[16] and Glanville Williams argued that the Appeal Court's decision had "much to commend it".[17] Despite this, the position is far from satisfactory. This is because *Lawrie* is unclear on exactly how the court is to assess "fairness". As Chalmers notes, the concept of fairness is "conspicuously malleable".[18] Regret tably, subsequent decisions served to obfuscate, rather than clarify, the issues at the core of the illegally obtained evidence doctrine in *Lawrie*. As Duff laments, "we are in a position where the leading text on evidence simply lists, without further explanation, a series of factors which the court may take into account in determining whether to excuse an irregularity and admit improperly obtained evidence".[19] In the following sections, these factors are examined.

---

[12] Ibid, 27.

[13] On the importance of representing both of these interests fairly, see Miln v. Cullen 1967 JC 21, 29–30, *per* Lord Wheatley.

[14] A distinction is, however, made between oral statements by the accused and real and documentary evidence, although the ultimate test (one of fairness) remains the same. See the discussion of interrogations below in Sect. 3.3.

[15] The Crown has, nevertheless, accepted that a civil action against the police is proper where there has been an irregularity: Lawrie v. Muir 1950 JC 19, 23.

[16] See, for example, Yeo (1982, 395) (arguing that adopting the Scottish approach in an English context would "go a long way to enhancing the proper administration of criminal justice"). Cross used to open his discussion of irregularly obtained evidence by citing extensively from *Lawrie*: Cross (1958, 259–68). More recent editions of Cross's text (now authored solely by Colin Tapper) argue that the Scottish approach could fall victim to an imagined "crude popular reaction": Tapper (2007, 562).

[17] Williams (1955, 349).

[18] Chalmers (2007, 102).

[19] Duff (2004b, 98), referring to Walker and Walker. Ross and Chalmers (2000, para. 1.7.5). The same approach is taken in the most recent edition: Ross and Chalmers (2009, para. 1.7.5).

3.1.3 Factors (Possibly) Bearing Upon the Admissibility/ Exclusion of Evidence

The most recent edition of Walker and Walker – the leading text on the Scots law of evidence – lists the following factors which *must* have a bearing upon the court's decision as to whether or not to admit illegally obtained evidence[20]: (1) the "gravity of the crime with which the accused is charged"; (2) the "seriousness or triviality of the irregularity"; (3) the "urgency of the investigation in the course of which the evidence was obtained … the likelihood of the evidence disappearing if time is taken to seek a warrant"; (4) the "authority and good faith of those who obtained the evidence"; and (5) the "fairness to the accused". It is useful to explore each of these points individually to demonstrate that the courts have not been consistent in their application.

3.1.3.1 Gravity of the Crime Charged

The first thing to note is that Walker and Walker's assertion that the court *must* take the above factors into account is misleading.[21] In fact, the considerations are rarely discussed expressly and the courts certainly do not consider *all* of them in each case.[22] A good example of this is consideration of the gravity of the offense, which has only been mentioned explicitly in a few reported cases.

It is clear that the courts are more willing to allow illegally obtained evidence to be admitted in particularly grave crimes, such as rape[23] and murder.[24] At the other extreme, the courts have been less willing to excuse irregularities (i.e. to admit evidence) in "trivial" crimes, such as selling milk in stolen bottles.[25] This position may appear perverse: the more serious the offense, the more likely it is that illegally obtained evidence will be admitted.[26] Nevertheless, as Gray explains, this is a tenable approach:

---

[20] The following points are all taken from Ross and Chalmers (2009, para. 1.7.5). Footnotes are omitted.

[21] Ibid.

[22] It is nevertheless *possible* that the court will consider a number of factors. For instance, in Edgley v. Barbour, 1995 SLT 711, the good faith of the police, the urgency of the situation and the public interest in prosecution were all expressly relied upon (see the Lord Justice-General (Hope)'s opinion at 715).

[23] HM Advocate v. Milford 1973 SLT 12, 13 *per* Temporary Sheriff Macphail. Milford had refused to give a blood sample for the purposes of finding out his blood group, so the case concerned whether or not the Crown could obtain one without consent. It is not, therefore, a case where a past irregularity had to be excused.

[24] HM Advocate v. Megrahi *(No 3)* 2000 SLT 1401 [13], *per* Lord Coulsfield.

[25] See Lawrie v. Muir, 1950 JC 19, 28 *per* the Lord Justice-General (Cooper).

[26] Gray (1966, 96).

> [S]ociety has nothing much to lose when people accused of trivialities are acquitted and can accordingly afford to take a more sporting attitude. Society is, however, not prepared to be quite so sporting to those accused of murder; a viewpoint which is understandable, though whether society is under any obligation to adopt such an attitude towards petty criminals and those charged with technical offences is extremely doubtful.[27]

Gray then notes that the relative "seriousness" or "triviality" of an offense is, nevertheless, an inherently subjective matter.[28] Between the two polarized positions (serious and trivial) there is, of course, significant middle ground. It is therefore unclear just *how* serious a crime must be before the courts will be minded to admit illegally obtained evidence.[29] In one case, for example, it was held that the public interest in prosecuting a driver who had radar detection equipment fitted to his car was great enough to excuse an illegal search of the car.[30] In another case, an armed robber was acquitted on the basis that the police had "tricked" him into making incriminating statements.[31] The severity of the offense did not sway the court in favor of admitting the evidence.[32] Admittedly, the irregularity was different in these two cases. In one, the police officer simply reached into an unlocked car; in the other, he manufactured a situation where the accused made self-incriminating statements. The question remains, however: just *how* serious must an irregularity or the crime charged be before the court will lean in a particular direction?

3.1.3.2 Seriousness or Triviality of the Irregularity

The seriousness or triviality of the irregularity is, then, a further factor that the courts may take into account. Nine months after the decision in *Lawrie*, the Appeal Court delivered its judgment in another illegally obtained evidence case: *McGovern v. HM Advocate*.[33] There, the police had taken scrapings from under a suspect's fingernails *before* he was arrested. The court held that this had, technically, been an assault and, in consequence, the irregularity was not to be excused.

---

[27] Ibid. Although see Ashworth (1977), for an argument that it is more important to exclude illegally obtained evidence in relation to serious crimes, as the need to protect the accused's rights is greater the more serious the potential consequences for him of a conviction. See, similarly, Ashworth (2003) and Choo (2008, 94).

[28] Gray (1966, 99). For an attempt at crafting a more objective account of offense seriousness, see Ashworth (2005, 102–50).

[29] Gray (1966, 103).

[30] Edgley v. Barbour 1995 SLT 711.

[31] HM Advocate v. Higgins 2006 SLT 946, discussed in more detail below.

[32] Ibid, [26] *per* Lord MacPhail.

[33] 1950 JC 33.

In Scots criminal procedure, the police may not search a person without her consent[34] before she is arrested.[35] Accordingly, the taking of scrapings from the suspect in *McGovern* was a flagrant breach of protocol. Had the police arrested McGovern before taking the scrapings, there would have been no irregularity. It is unclear, however, whether it was the ease with which the police *could* have followed the proper procedure that swayed the court, or rather that McGovern's rights had been infringed. This makes it difficult to discern what principle underlies the courts' concern with the seriousness or triviality of any irregularity. As Duff explains:

> Lord Cooper's initial comments about the 'prejudice' caused to the accused by the use of the evidence at trial suggest he was influenced by the need to protect the accused's rights because there was no question over its reliability. Thus, this comment seems to be founded in a vindicatory rationale but Lord Cooper concluded his opinion, with what appears to be a reference to a disciplinary rationale, by stating that the appeal had to be upheld because 'unless the principles under which police investigations are carried out are adhered to with reasonable strictness, the anchor of the entire system for the protection of the public will very soon begin to drag'.[36]

This lack of clarity is not limited to the discussion of whether the illegality was serious or trivial: the very basis of the discretion in *Lawrie* is, as noted above, rather abstract. This has meant that the confusion in *McGovern* has permeated other decisions which concern the nature of the irregularity. For example, in *Fairley v. Fishmongers of London*,[37] two inspectors of a private company collected evidence illegally. This was excused on appeal because "the appellant's assumption of the guise of a champion of the liberties of the subject failed to elicit [the court's] sympathies".[38]

As well as the seriousness or triviality of the illegality, then, it thus appears that the court's sympathies are a relevant factor. This is hardly a satisfactory criterion, given its extremely subjective nature.[39] Furthermore, the decisions in *McGovern* and *Fairley* seem to underplay the significance of the first criterion discussed above: the seriousness of the crime charged. McGovern was a safe-cracker, which is surely a more serious crime than possessing salmon out of season, the offense with which Fairley was charged.[40] Nevertheless, the illegally obtained evidence was admitted in relation to the less serious crime, but excluded in relation to the

---

[34] The accused can voluntarily be searched before this point: Davidson v. Brown 1990 JC 324. Merely ceasing to resist demands to be searched does not constitute consent to be searched: Lucas v. Lockhart (1980) SCCR (Supp) 256. As always, the over-arching principle is fairness to the accused: Brown v. Glen 1998 JC 4, 7 *per* Lord Sutherland.

[35] Adair v. McGarry 1933 JC 72, 89 *per* Lord Morison.

[36] Duff (2004b, 84). The quoted section is from McGovern v. HM Advocate 1950 JC 33, 37 *per* the Lord Justice-General (Cooper).

[37] 1951 JC 14.

[38] Ibid, 24, *per* the Lord Justice-General (Cooper).

[39] Gray (1966, 99) and Duff (2004b, 85).

[40] Duff (2004b, 85).

graver offense. This appears perverse. Nevertheless, the vagueness of the "balancing act" envisaged in *Lawrie* perhaps makes such unsatisfactory decisions inevitable.

The situation is further compounded by the courts' frequent reliance on whether the evidence was obviously incriminating[41] and whether it was discovered "accidentally" (yet irregularly) in a legal search for other evidence.[42] On the first point, the court has appeared confused as to whether evidence must be "plainly incriminating", or simply "very suspicious".[43] The second point led to a strange situation in *Drummond v. HM Advocate*[44] where the key question became – quite bizarrely – whether the police had opened a wardrobe to search for stolen furniture (which they had a warrant to do) or other stolen goods (which was not in terms of the warrant). The wardrobe contained stolen clothing, so the point appears to be that – if the search was for furniture – the irregularity would be trivial (and therefore excusable). If, however, the search was for any other incriminating evidence, it would be irregular.[45] For the sake of completeness, the court held that the police had been searching for furniture; the irregularity was excused.

Finally, it appears that, in some cases, the courts are not prepared to excuse irregularities in the execution of warrants,[46] whilst in other cases they are.[47] The reason for this distinction is not at all clear: the courts rarely articulate clearly whether (or why) they perceive some irregularities as *more* serious than others. All in all, it appears impossible to discern any consistent principle at the heart of the courts' assessment of whether an irregularity was serious or trivial. A similar situation exists with regard to whether or not the urgency of the situation justified (or excused) an illegal search.

3.1.3.3 Urgency

Urgency is one of the most frequently cited reasons for excusing an irregularity.[48] Unfortunately, this has not led to any consistency in the approach the courts adopt. A core consideration is clearly the likelihood that evidence will disappear if the

---

[41] On the importance of the obviousness of incriminating evidence, see Mowbray v. Valentine 1992 SLT 416.

[42] See, for example: HM Advocate v. Hepper 1958 JC 39; Burke v. Wilson 1988 SCCR 361; Tierney v. Allan 1990 SLT 178; Drummond v. HM Advocate 1992 JC 88.

[43] Both of these terms appear in HM Advocate v. Hepper 1958 JC 39, 40, *per* Lord Guthrie.

[44] 1992 JC 88.

[45] For examples of "fishing" for evidence, see: Jackson v. Stevenson (1897) 2 Adam 255; HM Advocate v. Turnbull 1951 JC 96; Leckie v. Miln 1982 SLT 177.

[46] Bulloch v. HM Advocate 1980 SLT (Notes) 5; McAvoy v. Jessop 1988 SLT 621; Hepburn v. Brown; 1998 JC 63; Singh v. HM Advocate 2001 JC 186.

[47] HM Advocate v. Foulis and Grant 2002 JC 262.

[48] Other than the cases discussed individually below, urgency appears to have been important in: HM Advocate v. McGuigan 1936 JC 16; HM Advocate v. Hepper 1958 JC 39; McHugh v. HM Advocate 1978 JC 12; Walsh v. MacPhai*l* 1978 SLT (Notes) 29; Webley v. Ritchie 1997 SLT 1241.

police take the time to seek a warrant. In some cases, this concession appears absolutely necessary. For example, in *Bell v. Hogg*,[49] the police took rubbings of the accused's hands in order to ascertain whether he had been in contact with copper wire. The police could hardly have prevented the accused from going to the bathroom and washing his hands (thus destroying the evidence), so there was a real urgency.[50] Other cases are, however, less convincing. For example, in *Hay v. HM Advocate*,[51] the Procurator Fiscal (public prosecutor) craved a warrant to take an impression of the suspect's teeth. The fear expressed was that, if this was delayed, the suspect could visit a dentist or damage his teeth. As Finnie notes, this is rather unconvincing: "it is unlikely that [the accused's teeth] would be destroyed accidentally and it would take a remarkably determined suspect to smash his own teeth deliberately, especially to the point of unrecognisability".[52] Again, then, it appears that there is room for argument over exactly what constitutes "urgency". The courts insist that urgency must be assessed objectively,[53] but this requirement has acted as a veil allowing the courts to act inconsistently. The courts have, for example, refused to excuse irregularities on the basis that there was no urgency,[54] or that the situation was not urgent *enough* to excuse an irregularity.[55] Again, the reasoning behind these decisions is usually unclear.

Further confusion appears to exist as to whether urgency justifies or excuses an illegal search. This question is important because the courts appear to assume that a justified search is not illegal, whilst an excused search is. In *Bell v. Hogg*,[56] however, Lord Migdale suggested that this distinction ought not to matter: "[w]hether one regards Sergeant Muirhead's actings as justified or holds them to be 'excused' … the question still remains whether it was 'fair' to the accused to allow this evidence to be used … against them".[57] Lord Migdale's statement appears to assume that urgency and fairness are both parts of one test, but this appears contrary to other authority. For example, in *HM Advocate v. McKay*,[58] Lord Wheatley opined that "the two tests of fairness and urgency fail to be applied".[59]

---

[49] 1967 JC 49.

[50] Another example of real urgency is where a breath sample is required from a driver in order to establish whether or not she is over the legal alcohol limit: Cairns v. Keane 1983 SCCR 277. Furthermore, where drugs are involved, the ease of destroying evidence clearly plays an important role in the courts' thinking: MacNeil v. HM Advocate 1986 SCCR 288.

[51] 1968 JC 40.

[52] Finnie (1982, 291).

[53] See: Bell v. Hogg 1967 JC 49, 61, *per* Lord Cameron.

[54] HM Advocate v. Turnbull 1951 JC 96.

[55] For example, where a warrant has been sought, urgency does not excuse errors in its form: HM Advocate v. Cumming 1983 SCCR 15.

[56] 1967 JC 49.

[57] Ibid, 59.

[58] 1961 JC 47.

[59] Ibid, 50.

3.1.3.4 Authority of Searcher

A further factor that the court may take into account in deciding whether to admit unlawfully obtained evidence is the authority of the person who carried out the search. Here, once again, the approach of the courts has been far from consistent. The person who uncovers evidence through illegal means will not always be a police officer. In comparison with other areas of the law on irregularly obtained evidence, however, the situation with regard to police officers appears to be relatively settled – the police must have reasonable grounds to exercise a statutory or common-law power of search. In other words, the police may not conduct "fishing" exercises, where they search a person or her property in the hope of finding evidence of illegal activity. This rule has been recognized for a long time,[60] but the question of what constitutes reasonable suspicion still gives rise to appeals. The consensus appears to be that the police must have objectively reasonable grounds for suspicion.[61] Without these, any evidence obtained from the search will be inadmissible.[62]

When the searcher is not a police officer, distinct issues are raised. Stewards in a nightclub, for example, have no authority to forcefully search a person for drugs.[63] Any evidence of illegal conduct gleaned from such a search is, thus, inadmissible.[64] Where a citizen's arrest has taken place, the citizen similarly has no right to search the accused. Nevertheless, as long as the police are contacted and they conduct their own search, evidence gleaned from such a search has, in the past, been admitted.[65] Furthermore, even if a citizen has acted illegally (for example, by performing an illegal eviction), evidence recovered as a result of the illegal act may be admissible if she acted in good faith.[66] Reconciling these conflicting opinions with regard to nightclub stewards and private citizens is difficult.

Whether the searcher acted in good faith is a wider concern in relation to both police officers and others. This factor has proved important in cases where the searcher misunderstood the scope of her authority, but – unfortunately – the courts have failed to decide cases consistently. Acting under an illegal warrant (or without warrant at all) has been excused in some cases,[67] but exceeding the terms of a warrant

---

[60] See, for example, Jackson v. Stevenson (1897) 2 Adam 255.

[61] Weir v. Jessop *(No 2)* 1991 SCCR 242; Cooper v. Buchanan 1997 SLT 54; Stark v. Brown 1997 JC 209; Houston v. Carnegie 1999 SCCR 605.

[62] See, for example, Ireland v. Russell 1995 JC 169.

[63] Where no force is used and the accused simply accedes to a request to hand over drugs to a steward, such evidence is, nevertheless, admissible: Mackintosh v. Stott 1999 SCCR 291. See, similarly, Devlin v. Normand 1992 SCCR 875.

[64] Wilson v. Brown 1996 JC 141.

[65] Wightman v. Lees 2000 SLT 111.

[66] Howard v. HM Advocate 2006 SCCR 321.

[67] Walsh v. MacPhail 1978 SLT (Notes) 29 (illegal warrant); Edgley v. Barbour 1995 SLT 711 (no warrant); Webley v. Ritchie 1997 SLT 1241 (no warrant); Hepburn v. Brown 1998 JC 63 (warrant's terms exceeded); Henderson v. HM Advocate 2005 1 JC 301 (information gathering not authorised in statutory terms).

has been held – despite the police officers' good faith – to be inexcusable in others.[68] (Again, this inconsistency is probably explained by the presence of other factors which the courts failed to explain fully.) Another circumstance where good faith has been held to excuse an irregularity is where the police are temporarily in charge of a suspect's possessions (for example, a car) and, while ensuring the possessions are secure from theft or damage, they uncover evidence of illegal activity.[69]

3.1.3.5 Fairness to the Accused

The final concern that the court should bear in mind when considering whether or not to admit illegally obtained evidence is fairness to the accused. It is unclear, however, whether fairness to the accused is part of the test which the court must consider, or is, in fact, *the* test. Certainly, from the parts of *Lawrie* cited above, it appears that the court envisaged the former scenario,[70] but other cases indicate otherwise. In *HM Advocate v. Turnbull*,[71] for example, the lack of urgency in the police's search combined with the fact that they were "fishing" for information meant that, in the court's opinion, a fair trial could not be conducted.[72] Other cases were decided on a similar basis.[73]

The notion of "fairness" has assumed renewed importance with the incorporation of the European Convention on Human Rights (ECHR) into Scots law[74] – an issue that will be discussed in more detail in the next section.[75] For now, it is sufficient to note that Art. 6 ECHR's right to a fair trial has been considered as equivalent to *Lawrie v. Muir*'s concern with "fairness".[76] As Art. 6 ECHR requires the circumstances of the trial to be looked at as a whole,[77] it is certainly plausible that fairness is the ultimate concern, not merely a constituent part of the test to be applied in deciding whether to excuse an irregularity.[78] Nevertheless, the matter remains to be settled definitively.

---

[68] McAvoy v. Jessop 1988 SLT 621; Morrison v. O'Donnell 2001 SCCR 272.

[69] See, for example, Baxter v. Scott 1992 SLT 1125.

[70] See, similarly: HM Advocate v. McKay 1961 JC 47; Miln v. Cullen 1967 JC 21.

[71] 1951 JC 96.

[72] See: HM Advocate v. Turnbull 1951 JC 96, *per* Lord Guthrie at 103–104.

[73] See, for example: Weir v. Jessop *(No 2)* 1991 SCCR 636; Namyslak v. HM Advocate 1995 SLT 528.

[74] Via the Human Rights Act 1998 and the Scotland Act 1998.

[75] See the discussion below of: HM Advocate v. Robb 2000 JC 127; Hoekstra v. HM Advocate (No 5) 2002 SLT 599; HM Advocate v. Higgins 2006 SLT 946. See, further, McGibbon v. HM Advocate 2004 JC 60.

[76] HM Advocate v. Higgins 2006 SLT 946.

[77] Holland v. HM Advocate 2005 1 SC (PC) 3, [41], *per* Lord Rodger.

[78] See Mowbray v. Valentine 1992 SLT 416, where the court held that, in order to establish whether proceedings were "fair," all circumstances must be known.

Now that the development of the doctrine of illegally obtained evidence in Scots law has been discussed, the paper moves on to consider the impact of human rights legislation upon it. The focus will be on Art. 8 ECHR, which deals with the right to privacy. As will become clear, however, the courts have also drawn upon the accused's Art. 6 ECHR right to a fair trial in their discussions of the law.

3.2 Rules of Admissibility/Exclusion in Relation to Violations of the Right to Privacy

This section discusses the impact of the right to privacy upon the Scots law on illegally obtained evidence. It begins by explaining the mechanism by which an alleged human rights violation can be heard before a Scottish court, before exploring the relevant jurisprudence.

3.2.1 The Right to Privacy in Scots Law

As Scotland does not have a written, legally-enforceable constitution, it is virtually meaningless to speak of a "right" to privacy before the introduction of the Human Rights Act 1998 (HRA). The HRA essentially incorporated the rights and protections of the ECHR into United Kingdom law.[79] Under Art. 8 ECHR, "[e]veryone has the right to respect for his private and family life, his home and his correspondence". Breaches of this right can, thus, now be complained about in the Scottish courts.

From the perspective of procedure, the accused in a Scottish criminal trial can now rely on the provisions of the HRA directly. This was not always the case. Initially, the accused had to rely on the Scotland Act 1998 (SA) because it came into force before the HRA.[80] The SA became relevant because members of the Scottish Executive have, under § 57(2), "no power to … do any … act, so far as the … act is incompatible with any of the Convention rights or with Community law". The Lord Advocate, the head of the public prosecutorial service in Scotland (the Crown Office and Procurator Fiscal Service (COPFS)), is a member of the Scottish Executive.[81] Accordingly, he has to act

[79] Art. 1 ECHR (the obligation upon contracting States to secure the rights under the Convention) and Art. 13 ECHR (the provision of an effective remedy for breaches of human rights) were excluded because it was felt that the HRA fulfilled the same roles.

[80] Since the HRA came into force, the courts have struggled with the question of whether the accused can still rely on the provisions of the SA. See: Jamieson (2007a, b). This has implications where the accused seeks damages, as such applications are time-restricted under the HRA, but not under the SA: Somerville v. Scottish Ministers 2007 SC (HL) 45. For claims arising after 2 November 2009, a time limit has been introduced into § 100(3B) of the SA.

[81] SA, § 44(1).

in accordance with the rights secured under the ECHR, including a suspect/accused's right to privacy.

In most trials[82] the accused can now also complain about the unfairness of her prosecution and trial in *general* (alleging a breach of her Art. 6 ECHR right to a fair trial). Accordingly, as will be seen in the next section, the Scottish courts have been asked to consider whether the submission of illegally obtained evidence – obtained through a breach of the accused's Art. 8 ECHR right to privacy – renders a trial unfair.

In the next section it will be argued that the incorporation of the rights protected under the ECHR has not resulted in any real change in the Scottish courts' approach towards illegally obtained evidence.

3.2.2 Interpreting the Right to Privacy When Considering Illegally Obtained Evidence

The starting point for discussion of the impact of the ECHR on the admissibility or otherwise of unlawfully obtained evidence is the case of *HM Advocate v. Robb*.[83] In *Robb* the accused argued that because his repeated requests to consult a solicitor during police questioning were ignored, the evidence obtained from the interview should not be tendered at his trial. Although there was, at the time, no right under Scots law to have a solicitor present during police questioning,[84] the accused relied on the Art. 6 ECHR right to a fair trial to argue that the act of the Lord Advocate, in tendering such evidence, would automatically render his trial unfair overall. The court held, however, that "in performing the 'act' of tendering evidence in a criminal trial, the Lord Advocate would [not] be infringing the Convention rights of the accused, even if there were a question of whether the evidence was obtained by means which themselves involved an infringement of such rights".[85] In other words, § 57(2) SA did not apply in relation to the presenting of evidence, so the accused could not complain that his human rights had been infringed before the close of the trial. Then, the ultimate test of "fairness" (under Art. 6 ECHR) would take the irregularity into account.

---

[82] There exists a limited right to private prosecution in solemn cases (i.e. proceedings before a jury), but not summary cases (where a judge sits alone): Criminal Justice (Scotland) Act 1995, § 63. This right requires the assent of the High Court and (at least) the acquiescence of the Lord Advocate. Accordingly, the right has been exercised twice in the last 100 years: J&P Coats Limited v. Brown 1909 JC 29; X v. Sweeney and Others 1983 SLT 48. It can thus be safely ignored for present purposes.

[83] 2000 JC 127.

[84] This has since changed: see Sect. 3.3.2.2 below.

[85] HM Advocate v. Robb 2000 JC 127, *per* Lord Penrose at 131.

From *Robb*, then, it appeared that Art. 6 ECHR's right to a fair trial was going to take on more importance than any other rights which might have been relevant to proceedings. This was confirmed in *Hoekstra v. HM Advocate (No 5)*.[86] There, Art. 8 ECHR was specifically relied upon by the accused, whose boat had been illegality "bugged" with a tracking device. Interestingly, however, the court decided to base its decision on *Lawrie*-esque reasoning. It considered whether the illegality could be excused and, given the limited role that the evidence from the "bug" played at trial, held that it could be. (This appears to be an example of a "trivial" irregularity, as discussed above.) The court then stated that, in its opinion, Art. 8 ECHR had been infringed but "it seems to … be impossible to state that the fairness of the proceedings has been affected by the introduction of [the tracking] evidence".[87] In other words, the ultimate test remained the fairness of proceedings: a breach of privacy was merely one piece of evidence to be considered in that assessment.

The decision in *Hoekstra* is in line with the European Court of Human Rights' (hereafter ECtHR) decision in *Khan v. United Kingdom*.[88] Khan was convicted of drugs offenses as a result of evidence obtained from a listening device unlawfully planted by the police. His appeals against conviction were rejected by the English courts. The ECtHR held that, irrespective of a breach of Art. 8 ECHR, "[t]he central question … is whether the proceedings as a whole were fair",[89] concluding that in Khan's case the proceedings were not rendered wholly unfair.

The decision in *Khan* did, nevertheless, lead to legislation regarding the covert surveillance of suspects in Scotland[90] – the Regulation of Investigatory Powers (Scotland) Act 2000 (RIPSA). This is because Art. 8 ECHR has an exception: privacy can be breached "in accordance with the law [where] necessary in a democratic society … for the prevention of disorder or crime".[91] In passing RIPSA, the devolved Scottish Parliament allowed breaches of Art. 8 ECHR to be authorized where necessary. The Scottish courts have, however, been rather inconsistent in their approach to breaches of RIPSA.

In *Gilchrist v. HM Advocate*,[92] for example, the police obtained invalid clearance to monitor a suspect. Nevertheless, by viewing the accused's acts as "public", the court bypassed Art. 8 ECHR and excused the irregularity in the police's approach. Similarly, in *Henderson v. HM Advocate*,[93] the court appears to have ignored Art.

---

[86] 2002 SLT 599.

[87] Ibid, 32, *per* the Lord Justice-General (Cullen).

[88] (2001) 31 E.H.R.R. 45.

[89] Ibid, 38.

[90] See, also, the Regulation of Investigatory Powers Act 2000, which regulates the procedure for covert surveillance in England and Wales. § 17 of RIPA applies to Scotland, and can result – in practice – in evidence of *intercepted* communications being declared inadmissible. This provision has not been explored meaningfully in any reported Scottish case, but see Spencer (2008).

[91] See Art 8(2) ECHR.

[92] 2005 JC 34.

[93] 2005 JC 301.

8 ECHR even where *no* authorization was sought in terms of RIPSA. The court applied the principles in *Lawrie*, noting that: RIPSA did not protect suspects (unlike, for example, the rules relating to the police's power of search)[94]; the evidence gleaned (a recording of the suspect's voice) was not "private"[95]; the police acted in good faith[96]; and the "phone tap" was installed with the consent of the owners of the telephone.[97] All of these factors conspired against the accused to render the proceedings against him "fair". Lord Marnoch relied upon *Lawrie* expressly: "I am further of the opinion that there is nothing so special or fundamental about a breach of Art 8 as to make it inappropriate to consider the effect of that breach on Art. 6 and the common law principle of 'fairness' within the context of *Lawrie v. Muir*".[98] Lord Hamilton agreed with this approach, suggesting that there was "no reason why in Scotland the admissibility of evidence obtained irregularly should not be addressed by reference to the common law principles set out definitively in *Lawrie v. Muir*".[99] In other words, the ECHR (via the HRA and the SA) added nothing new.

The provisions of the ECHR were discussed further in *HM Advocate v. Higgins*.[100] There, the court found that Arts. 6 and 8 ECHR were "entirely inseparable".[101] It was held that covertly listening to suspects strategically placed in adjacent cells was inexcusable as no explanation was given as to why RIPSA authorization was not sought. In consequence, police activities "must be regarded as a serious irregularity which not only cannot be condoned but also points strongly towards the transgression of the principle of fairness".[102] The decision in *Higgins* is noteworthy in two respects. First, although he referred to it, the judge thought it was unnecessary to address Art. 8 ECHR. He preferred to base his decision on the common law.[103] Second, the fact that importance was placed on the lack of an explanation for the irregularity suggests that transgressions of RIPSA might in some circumstances be explained away. In *Higgins*, the seriousness of the crime was offered as an "excuse" for the breach of RIPSA, but was not accepted. As the crime concerned was armed robbery, this suggests that breaches of RIPSA must have to be regarded as extremely "serious" irregularities (see above).

From *Gilchrist*, *Henderson* and *Higgins*, then, it is clear that even post-incorpo ration of the HRA, the Scottish courts have not departed markedly from the rather abstract principle of fairness set out in *Lawrie v. Muir*. An illegal breach of privacy is simply one factor which must be considered in determining the fairness of the

[94] Ibid, 9, *per* Lord Marnoch.
[95] Ibid, 10.
[96] Ibid, 11.
[97] Ibid, 12.
[98] Ibid, 16.
[99] Ibid, 36.
[100] 2006 SLT 946.
[101] Ibid, 13, *per* Lord MacPhail.
[102] Ibid, 25.
[103] Ibid, 29.

overall proceedings. Despite attempts by defense counsel to rely on it in illegally obtained evidence trials, the right to privacy in the HRA has not led the courts to adopt a more concrete and satisfactory approach.

One area concerning privacy which has only been addressed briefly by the Scottish courts concerns the "fruits of the poisoned tree" – real evidence which is obtained on the basis of a prior, illegally-obtained private statement by the accused. This issue has been, Raitt argues, "partially answered" in Scotland in the context of inadmissible confessions resulting from interrogation.[104] It is to this topic which the final part of the chapter now turns.

3.3 Rules of Admissibility/Exclusion in Relation to Illegal Interrogations

Interrogations clearly give rise to dual concerns about the accused's right to silence (or privilege against self-incrimination) and the reliability of any "confessions" elicited. This part of the chapter considers, first, the right to silence in Scots law. It then considers the Scots courts' approach to evidence gleaned from illegal interrogations.

3.3.1 The General Right to Silence/Privilege Against Self-Incrimination

The procedural provisions relating to police interrogations are contained in the CP(S)A, as amended by the Criminal Procedure (Legal Assistance, Detention and Appeals) (Scotland) Act 2010 ("the 2010 Act"). A suspect may be detained without charge for questioning at a police station for 12 h[105] and this period can be extended to 24 h under certain conditions.[106] Until 2010, detained suspects had no right to legal assistance during detention but this was rectified when the 2010 Act came into force and suspects now have the right to a "private consultation with a solicitor (a) before any questioning … begins, and (b) at any other time during such questioning".[107] This change, which was a momentous one for Scotland, came after the United Kingdom Supreme Court held in *Cadder v. HM Advocate*[108] that the failure to provide legal assistance during detention violated Article 6 of the ECHR, the right to a fair trial.[109]

---

[104] Raitt (2008, para. 10.19).

[105] CP(S)A, §14(2), as amended by the 2010 Act.

[106] CP(S)A, §14A, as inserted by the 2010 Act.

[107] CP(S)A, § 15A(3), as inserted by the 2010 Act.

[108] [2010] UKSC 43.

[109] For discussion, see Leverick (2011a, b) and Stark (2011).

Other than being obliged to give her name and address, the suspect has the right to remain silent during police questioning and must be informed of this right.[110] No adverse inferences may be drawn from silence either at the police questioning stage or at trial.[111]

The question of whether unlawfully obtained confessions can be admissible in evidence is considered in the next section. Three possible scenarios are examined: (1) confessions where the accused was not informed of her right to remain silent; (2) confessions obtained in the absence of legal advice; and (3) confessions obtained as a result of coercion or threats. The chapter then proceeds to consider the approach taken to the admissibility of "fruits of the poisoned tree".

3.3.2 *Case Law Regarding Illegally Obtained Confessions*

3.3.2.1 Confessions Obtained Where the Accused Was Not Informed of the Right to Remain Silent

It is important to note at the outset that, although a privilege against self-incrimi nation has been read into Art. 6 ECHR,[112] the position with regard to the admissibility of illegally obtained confessions has remained largely unchanged since the passing of the HRA. The starting point for any discussion of illegally obtained confessions is the case of *Chalmers v. HM Advocate*.[113] There, the accused had been subjected to "not merely … interrogation but … 'cross-examination'", and was "confronted with police information contradictory of the statement which he had already made".[114] This process continued until the accused broke down and confessed. A Full Bench of five judges decided that this confession had not been elicited voluntarily and, as such, was inadmissible. To argue for the contrary would be unfair to the accused.[115]

Thus, where the accused has not been advised of her right to remain silent, the test of whether any confession she makes thereafter can be admitted as evidence is whether it would be fair to her to do so.[116] It might have been thought at one time

---

[110] CP(S)A, §14(9).

[111] Larkin v. HM Advocate 2005 SLT 1087.

[112] Art. 6 ECHR itself provides only that everyone charged with a criminal offense shall be presumed innocent until proved guilty according to law, but see, for example, Condron v. United Kingdom (2001) 31 E.H.R.R. 1.

[113] 1954 JC 66.

[114] Ibid, 75, *per* the Lord Justice-General (Cooper).

[115] Ibid, 79.

[116] This test was confirmed in HM Advocate v. Aries [2009] HCJ 4, *per* Temporary Judge MacIver at [15]. See also Pennycuik v. Lees 1992 SLT 763; Williams v. Friel 1998 SCCR 649.

that it would never be considered fair to admit an admission obtained without the accused having been informed of her right to silence. In *HM Advocate v. Docherty*,[117] for example, a confession made by the accused after a defective caution had been administered (in which the right to remain silent was not mentioned) was held to be inadmissible because the accused "was not informed of one of his basic rights".[118]

Later cases do, however, suggest a relaxation of approach – if indeed this was ever a strict rule in the first place. In *Tonge v. HM Advocate*,[119] although the accused's confession was in fact deemed inadmissible after the police deliberately failed to caution him in the hope he would incriminate himself, the court noted that this need not always be the case where a caution has not been administered.[120] The court stressed that the significant factor in its decision was the fact that the police *deliberately* omitted to caution the accused. Likewise, in *Pennycuick v. Lees*,[121] the Lord Justice-General (Hope) stated that "[t]here is no rule of law which requires that a suspect must always be cautioned before any question can be put to him",[122] stressing once again that the ultimate test of the admissibility of any resulting confession is "whether what was done was unfair to the accused".[123] Thus, the admission by the accused in the case that he was falsely claiming state benefits was subsequently deemed to be admissible despite no caution having been administered. Likewise, in *Williams v. Friel*[124] incriminating statements made by the suspect to customs officers concerning his identity and nationality – in the absence of a caution – were also held to be admissible and the admission by the accused that he was in possession of a knife was treated similarly in *Custerson v. Westwater.*[125] All that can be stated with certainty, therefore, is that a failure to administer a caution will place the admissibility of any confession by the accused "in peril"[126] but will not necessarily result in its exclusion.

3.3.2.2 Confessions Obtained in the Absence of Access to Legal Advice

A related situation to that where a caution has not been administered is where the accused has confessed without having had access to legal advice. Until 2010, there was no right to legal assistance during detention in Scots law and, consequently, a confession obtained in the absence of legal assistance was not necessarily inadmissible

---

[117] 1981 JC 6.

[118] Ibid, 9, *per* Lord Cowie.

[119] 1982 JC 130.

[120] Ibid, 140, *per* the Lord Justice-General (Emslie).

[121] 1992 SLT 763.

[122] Ibid, 765. See also HM Advocate v. Aries [2009] HCJ 4, [11] *per* Temporary Judge MacIver.

[123] Pennycuick v. Lees 1992 SLT 764,765.

[124] 1999 JC 28.

[125] 1987 SCCR 389.

[126] Tonge v. HM Advocate 1982 JC 130, 145–146, *per* the Lord Justice-General (Emslie).

(presuming the general test of fairness was satisfied). The ECHR compatibility of this provision had been challenged unsuccessfully on a number of occasions following the incorporation of the ECHR into domestic law.[127] It became increasingly apparent, however, that this position was untenable. The catalyst for change was *Salduz v. Turkey*,[128] a unanimous decision of the Grand Chamber of the ECtHR, in which it was held that Article 6(1) requires that "as a rule, access to a lawyer should be provided as from the first interrogation of a suspect by the police, unless it is demonstrated in the light of the particular circumstances of the case that there are compelling reasons to restrict this right".[129] In *Cadder v. HM Advocate*,[130] the United Kingdom Supreme Court held that it would breach Article 6 of the ECHR for a confession obtained in the absence of legal assistance to be admitted as evidence. This led to the passing of emergency legislation, the Criminal Procedure (Legal Assistance, Detention and Appeals) (Scotland) Act 2010, which amended the CP(S)A to provide for a right to legal assistance during detention.[131] It can now be said with certainty that an admission made during detention where the accused was not offered legal assistance is inadmissible as evidence.

Various questions as to the scope of its applicability were left open by *Cadder* but at least some of these have been resolved. In *Ambrose v. Harris*,[132] the Supreme Court held that the *Cadder* ruling was not limited to detention under section 14 of the CP(S)A but applied to any situation where the accused was questioned as a suspect rather than as a potential witness.[133] However, the court did not go so far as to hold that any confession obtained in a non-custodial situation would always be inadmissible. Rather where a suspect was questioned without being detained in custody, the absence of legal assistance would simply be "one of the circumstances that should be taken into account in the assessment as to whether the accused was deprived of a fair hearing".[134] In *HM Advocate v. P*,[135] the Supreme Court held that incriminating evidence discovered as a result of questioning without legal assistance (the so-called "fruits of the poisoned tree") would not necessarily be inadmissible, but that this would depend on "whether the accused's right to a fair trial would be violated by the leading of the evidence".[136] In *McGowan v. B*,[137] it was held that

---

[127] See e.g. HM Advocate v. Robb 2000 JC 127; Paton v. Ritchie 2000 JC 271.

[128] (2009) 49 E.H.R.R. 19, 421.

[129] Ibid, 437, §55.

[130] [2010] UKSC 43.

[131] See Sect. 3.3.1 above.

[132] [2011] UKSC 43.

[133] Ibid. [63] *per* Lord Hope of Craighead. In *Ambrose*, for example, one accused was questioned by police in his car on suspicion of being in charge of a motor vehicle having consumed excess alcohol. Another was questioned in his house while it was being searched under a warrant relating to the possession of controlled drugs. Handcuffs had been applied to the suspect.

[134] Ibid, [64] *per* Lord Hope of Craighead.

[135] [2011] UKSC 44.

[136] Ibid, [27] *per* Lord Hope of Craighead. For further discussion, see Sect. 3.3.2.4 below.

[137] [2011] UKSC 54.

where the right to legal assistance had been validly waived, a confession made in these circumstances would be admissible, provided it met the overall test of fairness. Waiver is valid where the accused has "been told of his right, [where he] understands what the right is and that it is being waived and [where] waiver is made freely and voluntarily".[138]

3.3.2.3 Confessions Obtained as a Result of Coercion or Threats

Where a confession has been obtained as a result of coercion or threats, it will not be admitted in evidence unless it would be fair to the accused to do so.[139] Once again, the test is one of fairness to the accused. Following *Chalmers*, it will never be fair to the accused to admit a confession unless it was made "voluntarily".[140] Thus, as the Lord Justice-Clerk (Thomson) stated, evidence obtained by "bullying, pressure, third degree methods and so forth" is always inadmissible.[141]

Three points can be made about the decision in *Chalmers*. First, the court's concern was, very clearly, with the reliability of evidence obtained through interrogation. The Lord Justice-Clerk (Thomson) made specific reference to the "jury's problem" of discovering the truth of the matter and how an illegally obtained statement would be likely to hinder them in doing so.[142]

Second, the requirement for a *voluntary* confession in *Chalmers* has led to some difficulties in determining exactly what type or degree of police pressure would vitiate voluntariness. In *Lord Advocate's Reference (No 1 of 1983)*,[143] it was held that "improper forms of bullying or pressure designed to break [a suspect's] will" would render a confession inadmissible.[144] In *Brown v. HM Advocate*,[145] however, it was held that clarifying – rather than testing – the terms of a statement was not unreasonable. Where threats or inducements have been used, this will generally render a confession inadmissible. Thus in *Harley v. HM Advocate*,[146] the accused's confession was deemed inadmissible because the police had obtained it by threatening to tell of his affair with a married woman. Likewise, in *HM Advocate v. Aries*,[147] a threat to the accused that, unless he admitted certain things, he would be locked up for a long time without release would have rendered his confession inad-

---

[138] Ibid, [46] *per* Lord Hope of Craighead.

[139] Chalmers v. HM Advocate 1954 JC 66.

[140] Ibid, 82, *per* the Lord Justice-Clerk (Thomson). See also Manuel v. HM Advocate 1958 JC 41.

[141] Chalmers v. HM Advocate 1954 JC 66, 81–82, *per* the Lord Justice-Clerk (Thomson).

[142] Ibid, 83.

[143] 1984 JC 52.

[144] Ibid, 58, *per* the Lord Justice-General (Emslie).

[145] 1966 SLT 105.

[146] 1996 SLT 1075.

[147] [2009] HCJ 4.

missible.[148] This principle does, again, seem to have been applied rather inconsistently. In *Stewart v. Hingston*,[149] for example, the police arrived at the door of a woman who was suspected of theft and asked her to accompany them to the police station for an interview. She was at home with her young children at the time and no one else was available to look after them. She was told that they could be taken into the care of a social worker, and she could be forcibly detained, but that this could be avoided if she made a statement immediately. Immediately after being told this, she confessed. This was held not to be an inducement and her confession was admissible evidence at her subsequent trial.[150]

Third, *Chalmers* concerned not only the admissibility of the accused's confession, but also that of real evidence gleaned from it ("fruit of the poisoned tree"). This point is considered below.

3.3.2.4 Fruits of the Poisoned Tree

In *Chalmers*, after he had confessed, the accused took police officers to where he had hidden the deceased's purse. The court held that this evidence should not have been admitted at trial because it was "part and parcel of the same transaction as the interrogation and if the interrogation and the 'statement' which emerged from it are inadmissible as 'unfair,' the same criticism must attach to the conducted visit to the [locus]".[151]

Until recently this was the only reported case in which the courts had considered the question of the fruits of the poisoned tree but, in *HM Advocate v. P*,[152] the issue arose again, this time in relation to evidence obtained as a result of an interview conducted with a suspect who had not been offered legal assistance. In *P*, the accused was charged with rape, but claimed that he had not had sexual intercourse with the complainer. Whilst being questioned by police, he claimed to have ingested mind altering drugs at the time of the incident and told police that a friend of his could speak to this. When the police questioned the friend, the friend told of a telephone call between himself and the accused in which the accused admitted (consensual) sexual intercourse with the complainer. The United Kingdom Supreme Court was asked to rule on the question of whether evidence obtained in this way would, in principle, be admissible. The court drew a clear distinction between evidence "created by answers given in reply to … impermissible questioning" and evidence that "existed independently of those answers, so that those answers do not have to be relied upon to show how it bears upon the question whether the accused is guilty

---

[148] Ibid, 4, *per* Temporary Judge MacIver. In the event his confession was admissible as it was not proved that such a threat had, in fact, been made by the police.

[149] 1997 SLT 442.

[150] Ibid, 444, *per* the Lord Justice-General (Hope).

[151] Chalmers v. HM Advocate 1954 JC 66, 76 *per* the Lord Justice-General (Cooper).

[152] [2011] UKSC 44.

of the offence with which he has been charged".[153] The evidence in *Chalmers* fell into the first category and this was rightly excluded. The evidence in *P* fell into the second category as it could have equally been discovered independently, without the assistance provided by the accused. In this case, the question to be considered is "whether the accused's right to a fair trial would be violated by the leading of the evidence".[154] This determination is in line with earlier recommendations made by MacPhail,[155] the Thomson Committee[156] and the Scottish Law Commission[157] – all of whom proposed that, provided the "fruit of the poisoned tree" was appropriated legally, it should be admissible.

3.4 Conclusion

In this chapter we have tried to demonstrate the confused nature of Scots law's approach to illegally obtained evidence. It is submitted that this is symptomatic of a wider problem in Scots criminal procedure: uncertainty.[158] The problem with the term "fairness" is, as Chalmers notes, its malleability.[159] Basing Scots law's approach upon the test of fairness has thus led to, in one commentator's opinion, distinctions of "dubious validity and sometimes ... to rather absurd results".[160] There is little doubt that, although at one point lauded elsewhere, the Scots approach to illegally obtained evidence is in need of a more concrete basis.[161] It is regrettable (yet perhaps unsurprising) that aside from the issue of confessions obtained in the absence of legal assistance, the ECHR has failed to have much of an impact in this regard, itself focussing on the fairness test, albeit in a different guise: that of what constitutes a "fair" trial.

None of the above is new: reform has long been argued for. A particularly stinging article by Professor Peter Duff argues that the court must have a clear rationale at the heart of its approach, and he discusses various possible options.[162] Rather than the current "fairness" approach, Duff proposes that a firmer basis would be the

---

[153] Ibid,[27], *per* Lord Hope of Craighead.

[154] Ibid.

[155] MacPhail (1987, para. 21.04).

[156] *Criminal Procedure in Scotland: Second Report* (Cmnd 6218, 1975), para. 7.27.

[157] *The Law of Evidence* (Scot Law Com Memo No 46, 1980), at para. U.02. Nb: this memorandum was meant to be read in conjunction with MacPhail (1987).

[158] Another example is the Crown's duty to disclose "material" evidence to the accused. See: Criminal Justice and Licensing (Scotland) Act 2010, pt 6.

[159] Chalmers (2007, 102).

[160] JTC (1969, 64). The use of initials indicates that the author was probably an advocate (a lawyer with right of audience in the High Court of Justiciary and the Court of Session).

[161] Chalmers (2007, 102).

[162] Duff (2004c).

"moral legitimacy" of the trial. The advantage of this approach, he argues, is that the courts explicitly have to consider a number of factors "which would lead not only to fewer 'rogue' decisions but also to greater clarity and consistency in the law in future".[163] This approach certainly sounds sensible: rather than picking and choosing which factors to consider (as seen above in part I), the courts would be required to elucidate the principles at the heart of their judgments. Unfortunately, it is unlikely that the courts will wish to depart from the veil of "fairness". In fact, a review of the law of criminal procedure set up in the wake of *Cadder*[164] has recommended that Scotland move towards a position of free evaluation of evidence constrained only by the principle that the accused's right to a fair trial under Article 6 should not be breached:

> In the modern world, the courts, including juries, must be trusted to be sufficiently sophisticated to be able to assess the quality and significance of testimony without the need for intricate exclusionary rules. [This] would move Scotland towards a system in which-evidence is freely considered by judge or jury on its own merits, and with an emphasis on its relevancy to the crime charged, rather than its admissibility in terms of exclusionary rules drafted in and for a bygone age.[165]

To date, there is no indication whether the Scottish government will implement the proposals of the review, which include abandonment of the fairness test in *Chalmers* (to be replaced by test of whether or not to admit the evidence would breach the accused's fair trial rights under Article 6)[166] and abolition of the requirement in Scots law for corroboration of evidence in criminal trials.[167] Either way, it seems that the Scots approach to illegally obtained evidence is likely to continue to be vague and, inevitably, arbitrary for some time yet.

Bibliography

Ashworth, A. 1977. Excluding evidence as protecting rights. *Criminal Law Review* 3: 723–735.

Ashworth, A. 2003. Exploring the integrity principle in evidence and procedure. In *Essays for Colin Tapper*, ed. P. Mirfield and R. Smith, 107–125. London: LexisNexis UK.

Ashworth, A. 2005. *Sentencing and criminal justice*. Cambridge: Cambridge University Press.

Chalmers, J. 2007. More fair play for suspects: *HM Advocate v Higgins*. *Edinburgh Law Review* 11(1): 100–104.

[163] Ibid, 176.

[164] The Carloway Review (2011 para 7.0.10). For discussion of *Cadder* – the landmark case in which it was held that admitting confessions obtained where the suspect had not been offered legal assistance breached Article 6 of the ECHR – see Sect. 3.3.2.2 above.

[165] Ibid, para. 7.0.10.

[166] Ibid, para. 6.2.64.

[167] Ibid, para. 4.0.14.

Choo, A. 2008. *Abuse of process and judicial stays of criminal proceedings*, 2nd ed. Oxford: Oxford University Press.

Clive, E., P. Ferguson, C. Gane, and A.M. Smith. 2003. *A draft criminal code for Scotland with commentary*. Edinburgh: HMSO.

Cross, R. 1958. *Evidence*. London: Butterworths.

Davidson, F.P. 2007. *Evidence*. Edinburgh: Thomson/W. Green/SULI.

Duff, P. 2004a. Changing conceptions of the Scottish criminal trial: The duty to agree uncontroversial evidence. In *The trial on trial: Vol I – Truth and due process*, ed. A. Duff, L. Farmer, S. Marshall, and V. Tadros, 29–50. Oxford: Hart.

Duff, P. 2004b. Irregularly obtained real evidence: The Scottish solution. *International Journal of Evidence and Proof* 8(2): 77–99.

Duff, P. 2004c. Admissibility of improperly obtained physical evidence in the Scottish criminal trial: The search for principle. *Edinburgh Law Review* 8(2): 152–176.

Finnie, W. 1982. Police powers of search in the light of *Leckie v. Miln*. *Scots Law Times (News)* 289–295.

Gane, C.H.W. 1999. Classifying criminal procedure. In *Criminal justice in Scotland*, ed. P. Duff and N. Hutton, 56–73. Aldershot: Ashgate.

Gray, J.W.R. 1966. The admissibility of evidence illegally obtained in Scotland. 1966 *Juridical Review* 89–114.

Jamieson, I. 2007a. The *Somerville* case. *Scots Law Times (News)* 111–116.

Jamieson, I. 2007b. Remedies under the Scotland Act: Implications of *Somerville*. *Scots Law Times (News)* 289–294.

JTC. 1969. Evidence obtained by means considered irregular. *Juridical Review* 55–77.

Leverick, F. 2011a. The right to legal assistance during detention. *Edinburgh Law Review* 15(3): 352–380.

Leverick, F. 2011b. The Supreme Court strikes back. *Edinburgh Law Review* 15(2): 287–292.

Lewis, W.J. 1925. *Manual of the law of evidence in Scotland*. Edinburgh: W Hodge & Co.

Macdonald, J.H.A. 1948. *A practical treatise on the criminal law of Scotland*, 5th ed. Edinburgh: W. Green.

MacPhail, I.D. 1987. *Evidence: A revised version of a research paper on the law of evidence in Scotland*, 2nd ed. Edinburgh: Law Society of Scotland.

Raitt, F.E. 2008. *Evidence – Principles, policy and practice*, 4th ed. Edinburgh: W. Green.

Renton, R.W., and H.H. Brown. 1996. *Criminal procedure*, 6th ed. Edinburgh: W. Green.

Ross, M.L., and J. Chalmers (eds.). 2000. *Walker and walker: The law of evidence in Scotland*, 2nd ed. Edinburgh: T&T Clark.

Ross, M.L., and J. Chalmers (eds.). 2009. *Walker and walker: The law of evidence in Scotland*, 3rd ed. Haywards Heath: Tottel.

Spencer, J.R. 2008. Intercept evidence: the case for change. *Justice of the Peace & Local Government Law* 651–655.

Stark, F. 2011. The consequences of *Cadder*. *Edinburgh Law Review* 15(2): 293–298.

Tapper, C. 2007. *Cross and tapper on evidence*, 11th ed. Oxford: Oxford University Press.

The Carloway Review. 2011. *Report and Recommendations*, 17 Nov 2011, available at http://www.scotland.gov.uk/Resource/Doc/925/0122808.pdf. Last visited 28 Feb 2012.

Williams, G. 1955. Evidence obtained by illegal means. *Criminal Law Review* 339–349.

Yeo, M.H. 1982. Inclusionary discretion over unfairly obtained evidence. *International and Comparative Law Quarterly* 31: 392–395.

Chapter 4
Israel: The Supreme Court's New, Cautious Exclusionary Rule

Rinat Kitai Sangero and Yuval Merin

4.1 The General Theory of Admissibility of Illegally Gathered Evidence Under Israeli Law

4.1.1 Traditional Approach

Israeli law lacks a general statutory provision concerning illegally gathered evidence. Until recently, the basic concept of Israeli evidence law, as expressed by the Supreme Court, was that unlawfully obtained evidence is admissible, subject to three specific statutory exceptions.

The first exception if found in § 12(a) Evidence Ordinance [New Version] (1971), which mandates the exclusion of involuntary confessions, leaving the court no discretion to admit the evidence.

The second exception derives from § 13 of the Secret Monitoring Law (1979), which provides for the exclusion of statements obtained through unlawful wiretapping, subject to two exceptions: (1) such statements are admissible in criminal proceedings, when the defendant is charged with performing the unlawful wiretapping; (2) statements obtained through unlawful wiretapping could be deemed admissible in criminal cases where the police acted in good faith, believing it had lawful authority to perform the wiretapping, and the defendant is charged with a serious felony. If these

---

R.K. Sangero (✉)
The Academic Center of Law and Business, 16 Givat Canada Street, Jerusalem, Israel 93890
e-mail: sangero-kitai@bezeqint.net

Y. Merin
Senior Lecturer, College of Management School of Law, 82 Hagefen St., Ramat-Hasharon, Israel 47287
e-mail: ymerin@yahoo.com

S.C. Thaman (ed.), *Exclusionary Rules in Comparative Law*, Ius Gentium: Comparative Perspectives on Law and Justice 20, DOI 10.1007/978-94-007-5348-8_4,

conditions are met, the court has to apply a balancing test and determine whether, in the circumstances of the case, the need to ascertain the truth outweighs the need to protect the right to privacy.

The third exception is found in § 32 of the Protection of Privacy Law (1981), which provides for the exclusion of materials obtained through the infringement of the right to privacy, subject to the court's general discretion to admit such evidence on special grounds. The Supreme Court ruled that in applying the general discretion to admit evidence obtained through the breach of the right to privacy, courts should balance the seriousness of the violation against the importance of the evidence.[1] § 2 of the Protection of Privacy Law defines the infringement of the right to privacy as including, *inter alia*, spying on a person or otherwise harassing them, photographing or filming a person in their private domain, and publicizing any matter relating to a person's intimate life, health condition or conduct in the private domain. The Protection of Privacy Law was interpreted as limited to the informational type of privacy, which made it inapplicable to police misconduct and illegal searches.[2]

Subject to these three exceptions, it has been a matter of established case law for many years that improper measures do not affect the admissibility of the evidence (but may only affect its weight), as the goal of ascertaining the truth was conceived of as having priority over the protection of the rights of the accused. Accordingly, the Supreme Court had continuously refused to apply a general exclusionary rule, deeming inadmissible only evidence obtained in breach of the three aforementioned statutes.[3]

As a result of this approach, despite various legislative provisions intended to protect against unreasonable searches of the body, premises and personal effects,[4] and the fact that the right to be protected against unreasonable searches is also enshrined in the Basic Law: Human Dignity and Liberty of 1992,[5] instances of unlawful searches have scarcely been discussed in Israeli case law since the illegality of the search was perceived as irrelevant to the outcome of the criminal proceedings.

4.1.2 The Issacharov Case of 2006

However, in the landmark case of *Issacharov*, decided in 2006, the Israeli Supreme Court departed from this long held concept, and recognized that protecting the rights of the defendant is not only a means for ascertaining the truth, but also an important end in and of itself, which could potentially outweigh the duty to ascertain the truth.[6]

---

[1] X v. The Rabbinical District Court (May 14, 2006; not published).

[2] Military Court of Appeal v. Va'aknin (1988) 42(iii) P.D. 837. See also Harnon (1999, 709).

[3] See, for example, Military Court of Appeal v. Va'aknin, Ibid.

[4] E.g., The Criminal Procedure (Powers of Enforcement – Body Search and Methods of Identification) Law, 1996 (setting limits on the power to search the body of a suspect).

[5] § 7 Basic Law: Human Dignity and Liberty (1992)

[6] Chief Military Prosecutor v. Issacharov, 61(1) P.D. 461 (2006), §§ 45–46.

Accordingly, the Court re-evaluated its prior holdings regarding the scope and interpretation of § 12(a) of the Evidence Ordinance (i.e., the requirement of voluntariness of the confession), and more importantly, adopted a new exclusionary rule.

The *Issacharov* case involved a soldier in the Israeli Defense Forces, who was accused of using and possessing illicit drugs. The evidence against him for possession of the drugs was very compelling. A package of drugs fell from his underwear when he was asked to undress during the process of admission into the military prison. Moreover, during his interrogation by a military police officer, Issacharov confessed to the offenses and mentioned other occasions on which he had used drugs. Although the interrogator informed Issacharov of his right to remain silent, he failed to inform him – at the beginning of the interrogation – of his right to consult with an attorney. Only after taking the statement did the interrogator inform Issacharov that he was under arrest and that he had the right to counsel. In response to the charges brought against him, Issacharov confessed to the possession count, but denied the use of illicit drugs. There was no dispute that the interrogator had acted unlawfully when failing to inform Issacharov, prior to taking his statement, that he was under arrest and that he had the right to consult with an attorney. There was also no dispute that Issacharov was in fact unaware of that right. Moreover, the district military court determined that the interrogator, acting in bad faith, had deliberately refrained from informing Issacharov of the right to counsel. Other than that, the interrogation was quite standard, as no external pressures were used in order to break Issacharov's free will.

Issacharov's conviction, thus, depended on the admissibility of his initial confession. In order to decide this matter, the Supreme Court considered two main questions: (1) whether Issacharov's confession was voluntary; and (2) whether it was appropriate to exclude the confession based on a new exclusionary doctrine, a doctrine not yet recognized under Israeli law. After long deliberation, the Supreme Court answered both questions in the affirmative, holding that Issacharov's confession was voluntary, despite the failure to notify him of his right to counsel, but excluding the confession on the basis of the newly adopted doctrine. In doing so, the Supreme Court recognized its general authority to exclude improperly gathered evidence, notwithstanding the lack of an explicit statutory provision to that effect. The Court held that in light of Basic Law: Human Dignity and Liberty – which elevated the human rights entrenched therein to a constitutional level – courts should be accorded wide discretion to exclude unlawfully obtained evidence, considering the circumstances of each specific case, and balancing between the conflicting values and interests involved.

4.2 The Judicial Exclusionary Rule

The *Issacharov* case was the first opportunity for the Israeli Supreme Court to determine whether Basic Law: Human Dignity and Freedom requires the adoption of a general exclusionary rule as the proper remedy for breach of the defendant's constitutional rights. In light of the Basic Law, and since none of the proposed bills for enacting a general rule for the exclusion of illegally gathered evidence have passed into law,[7] the Court saw fit to adopt a judicial exclusionary doctrine. The Court held that in light of the Basic Law, the balance between the conflicting interests had shifted, so that the interest in protecting the rights of the accused may occasionally gain priority over the interest in ascertaining the factual truth. The Court ruled that along with the established, clear and overriding objective of the criminal process – ascertaining the factual truth in order to determine guilt or innocence – more weight should now be given to the extra evidential value of protecting the rights of the accused to dignity and liberty and protecting the fairness and integrity of the criminal trial.[8] In order to provide due protection to the rights of the accused and to give effect to the shift in the balance between the conflicting interests, the Court decided to adopt a general and relative exclusionary rule, leaving the courts wide discretion in deciding on the admissibility of unlawfully gathered evidence on a case-by-case basis.[9]

According to the newly adopted doctrine, unlawfully gathered evidence could be excluded if two cumulative conditions are met: (1) it should be established that the law enforcement agencies acted unlawfully in obtaining the evidence; and (2) that the admission of the evidence in trial will substantially and unduly harm the defendant's right to a fair trial.[10] The second condition is a balancing formula that seeks to achieve a proper compromise between all of the rights and interests that are relevant to the question of the admissibility of illegally obtained evidence. If both conditions are met, the court should exclude the evidence, as its admission at trial would unlawfully harm the defendant's constitutional right to dignity and liberty.[11]

The social value inherent in the newly adopted exclusionary rule is the right to due process, which is part of the constitutional right to dignity and liberty stipulated in the Basic Law. The Court determined that the most appropriate theoretical model for the exclusion of unlawfully gathered evidence under Israeli law is the "preventative model", practiced in most of the common law countries (including Canada, England, South Africa and Australia).[12] According to this model, as defined by the *Issacharov* Court, the exclusion of the evidence is a relief the purpose of which is to prevent a future violation of a protected value when the evidence is admitted in trial, and not a remedial relief for the initial harm to the accused that was completed when the evidence was obtained.[13] The Court rejected the "deterrent-educational approach" practiced in the U.S., which is based on the "remedial model" (including the doctrine of the fruit of the poisonous tree that characterizes this model), according to which

[7] It should be noted that Issacharov's appeal before the Supreme Court was filed in 1998, and the Court handed down its decision only in 2006, allowing the legislature more than enough time to act on the matter.

[8] Issacharov, 61(1) P.D. 461 (2006), §§ 46–47.

[9] Ibid.

[10] Ibid.

[11] Ibid, §60.

[12] Ibid, §60.

[13] Ibid, §§ 56, 60.

the exclusion of evidence that was obtained in an improper manner is intended mainly to educate the investigation authorities and deter them from adopting similar methods in the future, by making it impossible for the prosecution to benefit from the fruits of the illegality that was involved in obtaining the evidence.[14]

The Supreme Court stressed that the primary objective of the exclusionary rule is protecting the fairness and integrity of the criminal process and not the need to deter and educate the police. The purpose of the Israeli exclusionary rule is to prevent substantial harm to the integrity and propriety of the administration of the justice system if the evidence is admitted in the trial.[15] According to this approach, the main emphasis in excluding illegally obtained evidence is placed on the moral aspect of the criminal proceeding. As the Court put it, making use of evidence that was obtained improperly by the law enforcement authorities may, in certain circumstances, taint the criminal conviction and undermine its legitimacy. The court may thus be regarded as sanctioning the defect and being a party, after the fact, to the illegality in the behavior of the law enforcement authorities.[16] Moreover, since the police investigation stage is a part of the complete system of the administration of justice, the admissibility of evidence which was obtained by means of illegal interrogation methods may undermine the integrity of the judicial process and public confidence therein.[17] However, the right to a fair trial is not an absolute right and it must be balanced, on a case-by-case basis, against conflicting values, including the duty to ascertain the factual truth, the fight against crime and the protection of public safety and the rights of victims of the offense.[18] Therefore, as aforementioned, the doctrine adopted is a relative one, leaving wide discretion to the court.

Finally, the Court set out guidelines for exercising the discretion within the framework of the balancing formula. The criteria were designed to guide the courts in the application of the new exclusionary rule on a case-by-case basis, depending on the circumstances. Based on the Canadian model,[19] the Court identified three main groups of relevant considerations with regard to the question of when admitting illegally obtained evidence will inflict a substantial violation on the right of the accused to a fair trial.

The first relevant group of considerations for deciding the question of the admissibility of illegally obtained evidence pertains to the character and seriousness of the illegality that was involved in gathering the evidence, and focuses on the improper conduct of the investigative authorities.[20] In this context, the Court held that admitting evidence that was obtained by means of technical and marginal defects does not substantially violate the right of the accused to a fair trial, and therefore there

---

[14] Ibid.

[15] Ibid, § 60. cf.: R. v. Collins [1987] 1S.CR. 265, 275, 280–281.

[16] Isacharov, 61(1) P.D. 461 (2006), § 55.

[17] Ibid.

[18] Ibid, § 67.

[19] See Collins, [1987] 1S.CR. 265.

[20] Issacharov, 61(1) P.D. 461 (2006), § 70.

will be no reason to exclude it. However, in cases where the evidence was obtained by means of a major violation of an express statutory provision that was intended to protect the rights of defendants during interrogations, or in circumstances where obtaining the evidence involved a serious violation of one of the main basic rights of the person under investigation, the weight of the values that support inadmissibility of the evidence will increase.[21] The court should also examine: whether the law enforcement authorities made use of the improper investigation methods intentionally and deliberately or in good faith[22]; whether in the case before it there are "mitigating circumstances" that are capable of reducing the seriousness of the illegality that was involved in obtaining the evidence[23]; and the ease with which it would have been possible to obtain the evidence lawfully.[24] Finally, the court may consider whether the evidence would have been discovered or obtained by the law enforcement authorities even without making use of the improper investigative methods.[25]

The second relevant group of considerations for exercising the judicial discretion within the doctrine of inadmissibility concerns the degree to which the improper investigation method influenced the evidence that was obtained. In this context, the court should consider the degree to which the illegality that was involved in obtaining the evidence is likely to affect its credibility and probative value.[26] The Court did not limit itself to holding that a flaw in the credibility of the evidence due to the inappropriate means used to obtain it was a factor that supported its exclusion, but also held that whenever the inappropriate means do not negatively impact on the credibility of the evidence (as its existence is separate and independent of the unlawfulness) – the weight of the considerations that support its admission increases.[27] The Court further ruled that there may be great importance in the character of the evidence (tangible, verbal, etc.) that is being considered,

---

[21] Ibid.

[22] Ibid. The Court clarified that in circumstances where the defect that occurred in the manner of obtaining the evidence was serious and involved a substantial violation of the protected rights of the person under investigation, then the mere fact that the authority acted in good faith will not prevent the evidence being excluded.

[23] This is the case, for example, when the illegality committed by the investigation authorities was intended to prevent the disappearance or destruction of essential evidence by the accused, when the accused contributed to the illegality in conducting the investigation, by abusing his rights, or when the illegality was the result of an urgent need to protect public security. Ibid.

[24] If obtaining the evidence in permitted ways was possible and easy, then the violation of the rules of proper investigation should be considered more serious, in such a way that it will support the conclusion that admitting the evidence in the trial will create a serious and disproportionate violation of the right of the accused to a fair trial. Ibid. In this context, in Canada it has been ruled that when the police had no legal option for gathering the evidence – this does not mitigate the seriousness of the violation; under such circumstances and lacking alternative investigative means that do not violate the Charter, the police must leave the suspect alone. See: R. v. Kokesch [1990] 3S.C.R. 3, 29.

[25] Issacharov, 61(1) P.D. 461 (2006), § 70.

[26] Ibid, § 71.

[27] Ibid.

and that tangible evidence, such as firearms, drugs or stolen property, having an independent and distinct existence from the illegality that was involved in obtaining them, should generally not be excluded.[28]

In our view, the credibility of the evidence should not have been regarded as a factor which supports its admission in trial, as it is an inappropriate consideration within the exclusionary framework. The Court's determination that evidence, the credibility of which was not adversely affected by the unlawful means should generally be admissible is irreconcilable with the stated purpose of the new exclusionary rule, and it clearly tips the balance between the conflicting interests in favor of the value of ascertaining the truth. Considerations relating to the credibility of the evidence should be regarded as external to the exclusionary doctrine. The declared purpose of the exclusionary doctrine adopted in the *Issacharov* case was, as aforementioned, to give more weight than in the past to the value of protecting the rights of the accused and the fairness and integrity of the criminal trial (while re-balancing it against the value of ascertaining the truth),[29] and in doing so, to depart from the "presumption of admissibility" which characterized preceding Israeli case law regarding the exclusion of unlawfully obtained evidence. A constitutional exclusionary rule should allow for the exclusion of evidence despite its credibility and potential contribution to the establishment of the truth. The degree of protection provided to the rights of the accused is not measured according to the compatibility of the factual truth with the legal truth. Rather, it should be measured according to the willingness of the legal system to recognize, under the appropriate circumstances, the existence of a discrepancy between the two. The adoption of an exclusionary rule indicates the Court's internalization of the perception that in certain cases, the rights of the accused and the fairness of the judicial system should take priority over considerations of credibility. However, the *Issacharov* Court seemed reluctant to extend the protection of the rights of the accused to instances where the evidence is credible and of probative value. In our opinion, even when the unlawful means did not affect the credibility of the evidence, its admissibility could still harm the fairness of the proceedings. By allowing the admission of unlawfully gathered evidence, the Court is condoning the violation of the rights of the accused. In this regard, the admission of the evidence is no more "legitimate" simply because it is credible.

Take, for example, the *Va'aknin* case of 1983.[30] Va'aknin, an inmate in a military prison, was suspected of smuggling drugs into the prison by swallowing them. Va'aknin agreed to the suggestion of his interrogators to drink saltwater in order to induce vomiting. As a result of drinking the saltwater, Va'aknin regurgitated a packet. Va'aknin then tried to convince the interrogators that he had nothing more on him. At this stage, the interrogators forcibly made him drink and swallow more saltwater. As a result of this coerced drinking, Va'aknin regurgitated two more

---

[28] Ibid.

[29] Ibid, § 48.

[30] Military Court of Appeal v. Va'aknin (1988) 42(iii) P.D. 837.

packets of illicit drugs. Stressing the importance of ascertaining the factual truth, the Supreme Court ruled that the Protection of Privacy Law did not apply in such circumstances and that the drugs should be admitted as evidence. The Court further reasoned that it had no authority to exclude evidence obtained in violation of a legal prohibition that is not expressly enumerated in the Protection of Privacy Law (in this case, the penal prohibition against assault).

Would the court's holding in the *Va'aknin* case have been any different had it been decided today, after the adoption of the exclusionary rule? Not necessarily. The packets of illicit drugs removed from Va'aknin's body against his will were tangible evidence, which had an "independent and distinct" existence from the illegality that was involved in obtaining them.[31] But should these attributes render it appropriate to determine that the "weight of the considerations in favor of their admissibility is significant", as the *Issacharov* court noted with respect to this type of evidence? Does the classification of the evidence as "tangible" (and credible) necessarily mitigate the degree of infringement of the accused right to a fair trial or lessen the harm to the integrity of the legal proceeding? If the answer to these questions is in the affirmative, then it would seem that the level of protection afforded to the accused under the new exclusionary doctrine does not exceed the protection given to him in the past.

The third and final group of considerations for deciding the question of the admissibility of illegally obtained evidence pertains to the social damage, as compared with the social benefit, in excluding the evidence, i.e., the effect that the exclusion of the evidence will have on the administration of justice in its broad sense.[32] The court should determine whether the social price involved in excluding the evidence is higher than the potential benefit that will arise from admitting it. The main parameters in this regard are the importance of the evidence for proving guilt, the nature of the offense attributed to the accused and its degree of severity.[33] The Court noted that in cases where the evidence is important and decisive for the prosecution and the offenses attributed to the accused are very serious, the exclusion of the evidence may cause excessive harm to the public interests of fighting crime and protecting public safety and the victims of crime. The Court reasoned that in these circumstances, the interest in ascertaining the truth may exceed the weight of the interest in protecting the rights of the accused, since the acquittal of the accused

---

[31] In Issacharov, 61(1) P.D. 461 (2006), § 48, the Court ruled that when evidence has a separate and independent existence from the unlawfulness, "the unlawful means of investigation do not impact on the content of the evidence". Therefore, it appears that the Court interpreted the concept of "separate and independent" to mean that the evidence existed prior to the violation and with no connection to it, even if it would not have been discovered or obtained without the violation. We believe that it would have been proper to rule that there may be circumstances under which tangible evidence does not have a "separate and independent existence". Thus, for example, wherever the evidence would not have been obtained without the violation, and thus could not have been admitted in court, then it should not be viewed as having and independent existence.

[32] Issacharov, 61(1) P.D. 461 (2006), § 72.

[33] Ibid.

in such cases may in itself undermine the administration of justice and public confidence in the courts.[34] However, since the Court recognized that the foregoing considerations involve certain difficulties,[35] it opted to leave the question of the degree to which the courts in Israel should take into account the importance of the evidence and the seriousness of the offense to be decided in the future.[36] That being said, the Court did apply the aforesaid considerations in the case of *Issacharov* itself, indicating – as part of the considerations supporting the exclusion of Issacharov's confession – that the offenses attributed to him were not among the most serious ones in the statute book.[37]

The Court concluded that given the circumstances of the case, admission of Issacharov's confession would result in a substantial and disproportionate violation of his right to a fair criminal trial. Accordingly, the Court decided to declare the confession inadmissible by virtue of the new exclusionary doctrine.[38] The main and decisive consideration for the exclusion of Issacharov's confession was the seriousness of the violation by the military police investigator, who intentionally refrained from informing Issacharov of his right to counsel and deliberately violated this basic right. The Supreme Court based its decision on the importance of the right to consult with an attorney and its contribution to the proper course of investigative and trial proceedings.

The case of *Issacharov* was an "easy" one. All the considerations given by the Court (except for the credibility of the confession) supported the exclusion of the evidence (the deliberate violation and the ease with which it was possible to obtain the confession lawfully) and, at the same time, there was no social price involved in excluding the evidence: the offense with which the defendant was charged was not a serious one, and he had completed serving his sentence several years prior to the handing down of the Supreme Court's decision. Under these circumstances, the significance of the exclusion of Issacharov's confession (or its admission) was merely declarative.

Moreover, the Court emphasized that Issacharov's confession was to be excluded in light of "the unique circumstances of the case".[39] It is possible to think of many situations different from the "unique" circumstances of the *Issacharov* case – situations in which it is unclear whether the court would have still excluded the evidence. Thus, for example, what would have happened had the illegality involved in the conduct of the investigator not been so severe? What would have happened

---

34 Ibid.

35 As the Court noted, taking into account the aforesaid considerations may lead to a situation in which precisely in investigations of serious felonies in which the constitutional right of the accused to dignity and liberty deserves substantial protection, the compliance with the rules of conducting a fair and proper investigation will decrease. Ibid, § 73.

36 Ibid.

37 Ibid, § 81.

38 Ibid.

39 Ibid.

had the offense involved been a much more serious one? What would have happened had the case dealt with physical evidence rather than a statement? What if the defendant were still incarcerated, a more common situation than in the *Issacharov* case?

The manner in which the *Issacharov* Court delineated the criteria for exercising the discretion within the framework of the balancing formula makes it impossible to predict the outcome in other circumstances, since the Court limited itself to outlining all the relevant criteria, without providing any guidelines for their implementation. The Court held that none of the considerations outlined for deciding the question of the admissibility of illegally obtained evidence has an exclusive or decisive status, and refused to take a position regarding their relative weight, leaving this matter to be determined in light of the circumstances of each case on its own merits.[40] This flaw may lead to the inappropriate result of courts ruling as they see fit and reaching different outcomes in similar situations.[41]

4.3 The Right to Remain Silent and the Exclusion of Involuntary Confessions

4.3.1 The Right to Silence and the Duty to Hand Over Documents and Submit to a Search

Israeli law recognizes the suspect's right to remain silent as a basic and fundamental right. However, the Israeli Supreme Court has held that the silence of an accused person at the police station may, under certain circumstances, add weight to the evidence against him.[42] In a similar vein, and although a defendant is entitled to refrain from testifying at his own trial,[43] his silence at trial could be regarded as corroborating the prosecution's evidence.[44]

An accused person, however, must cooperate with the interrogating officers in other spheres of the investigation. The question whether (and if so, to what extent) a suspect has a duty to hand over documents in his possession to the investigative authorities arose in the case of Gilad Sharon, the son of the former Israeli Prime Minister Ariel Sharon, who was suspected of having committed the offense of offering and accepting a bribe, as well as violating the Political Parties (Financing) Law.[45]

---

[40] Ibid, § 74.

[41] For general critique of leaving wide discretion in the hands of the courts regarding the admissibility of evidence, Stein (2005, 11).

[42] Attorney General v. Keynan, 7 P.D. 619, 637–649 (1952).

[43] § 161 Criminal Procedure Law [Consolidated Version] (1982).

[44] Ibid, § 162.

[45] State of Israel v. Sharon, 58(1) P.D. 748 (2003).

The police refrained from conducting a search in the house of the suspect, who had lived in his father's home, since they preferred to avoid having to request the lifting of the prime minister's immunity in order to search his residence. Instead, the police petitioned the magistrate's court to compel Gilad Sharon to hand over various documents in his possession, in particular, documents related to transfers of funds to his bank account and documents regarding the activities of a company that he had established. The magistrate's court granted the motion and the defendant appealed to the Supreme Court.

The Supreme Court ruled that a suspect cannot invoke the right to remain silent in response to a court order requiring him to hand over documents, but can only invoke the privilege against self-incrimination. Thus, a suspect must hand over the requested documents. However, he may invoke the privilege against self-incrimination by submitting the documents to the court in a closed envelope and requesting the court to release him from the duty to hand them over to the police. The hearing on the suspect's motion is held in the presence of the suspect alone. The Supreme Court had earlier ruled that a distinction should be drawn between "public documents" produced by an impartial entity such as a bank, which do not benefit from the privilege against self-incrimination, and "personal documents" produced by the suspect – such as a personal diary, personal letter or appointment calendar – which would generally be regarded as privileged as they essentially bear the nature of testimony. This distinction is problematic since the main factor that should have been considered is the inherent potential of the document to lead to the criminal conviction of the suspect. In this respect, the nature of the document should not have been regarded as relevant. The decision of the Supreme Court in the case of *Gilad Sharon* thus infringes on the right of a suspect to detach himself from the process being conducted against him and to refrain from cooperating with his interrogators under compulsion.

Additionally, an accused person must submit to a lawful search. When the suspect refuses to do so, reasonable force may be used to conduct a search entailing the examination and photography of the naked body, taking imprints of a part of the body, extracting material from under the fingernails, taking a hair sample, taking material from the surface of the body and examining the skin.[46] Reasonable force may not be used, however, to perform an internal search or to take hair from concealed parts of the body, due to the violation of dignity entailed in such a search. Furthermore, due to the danger of suffocation as a result of forcibly opening the mouth, reasonable force may not be used for the purpose of taking a saliva sample, a dental imprint, a breath sample and cells from the inner part of the cheek. And, for obvious reasons, it is physically impossible to compel a person to provide a urine sample.[47]

A refusal to submit to a lawful search that results in the search not being performed may add weight to the prosecution's evidence.[48] The refusal of a murder

---

[46] § 3(b) Criminal Procedure (Powers of Enforcement – Body Search and Methods of Identification) Law (1996).

[47] Ibid.

[48] Ibid, § 11.

suspect, or a person suspected of having committed a drug or a sex offense with a prison sentence of 10 years or more, to submit to a lawful search, constitutes a separate criminal offense with a maximum prison sentence of 2 years.[49] Notwithstanding the case law stating that the privilege against self-incrimination does not apply to the search and examination of a person's body,[50] it seems that the existence of a criminal offense for refusal to submit to a search is far-reaching in that it treats the individual as an instrument for supplying self-incriminating evidence.

4.3.2 *Interrogation*

One of the main effects of the right to remain silent relates to the voluntariness of the confession, as the right to remain silent cannot be reconciled with permission to force a person to make a statement. §12(a) of the Evidence Ordinance (1971), stipulates that testimony regarding the confession of an accused to committing an offense shall be admissible only if the prosecutor brings testimony regarding the circumstances under which the confession was given, and the court establishes that the confession was free and voluntary. The requirement of voluntariness stipulated in §12 of the Evidence Ordinance is not subject to balancing. If the court finds that a confession given outside the courtroom was involuntary, it is required to exclude the evidence without considering the reasons that motivated those taking the statement to break the free will of the interrogee. However, Israeli case law has consistently interpreted the requirement of voluntariness narrowly.

A condition for the exclusion of the confession is that unlawful behavior by the police investigators is proven. Israeli case law has recognized five groups of factors that could indicate unlawful conduct and thus lead to the exclusion of a confession as involuntary.[51] The first is violence or threat of violence.[52] The second is use of unfair methods of interrogation, designed to wear down or break the will of the interrogee. The parameters in this regard include the time, length and manner of the interrogation.[53] The third group pertains to the infliction of unfair psychological pressures that could break the interrogee's will or humiliate him, such as curses and insults, threats to harm others and the withholding of medication. The fourth is the use of unfair techniques of deceit.[54] The fifth is temptation, i.e., rewarding or promising a reward in exchange for a confession, as well as promising to release the suspect from detention or to ease his punishment or to waive a count in the indictment.[55]

---

[49] Ibid, § 12.

[50] Khoury v. State of Israel, 36(2) P.D. 85 (1981).

[51] Kedmi (1999, 42).

[52] The Public Committee against Torture v. State of Israel, P.D. 43(4) 817 (1999).

[53] J. Doe v. the Public Attorney, P.D. 13 1205, 1213–1214 (1959).

[54] Bitter v. State of Israel, P.D. 41(1) 52, 56 (1987).

[55] Twaig v. Attorney General, P.D. 10 1083, 1089 (1956).

However, use of unlawful means does not necessarily entail the exclusion of a confession as involuntary. Case law has held that the use of an illegitimate method during an interrogation is not sufficient to exclude a suspect's confession as involuntary, stressing the importance of establishing the truth, as well as the enforcement of the law and the protection of the public.[56] The prevailing approach, followed by Justice Goldberg in the *Muadi* case, holds that the illegality in itself does not render a confession inadmissible under § 12 of the Evidence Ordinance. Rather, the court should examine each case from a factual perspective, on its merits, in order to determine whether the improper interrogation method in fact deprived the accused of his free will in making his confession; if it did, the confession will be inadmissible.[57] However, Justice Goldberg also noted that in cases where the level of impropriety amounted to a violation of the accused's "humanity", then the confession should automatically be declared inadmissible, without considering the *de facto* effect of the improper interrogation method on the free will of the accused.[58] According to Justice Goldberg, this type of judicial policy was in line with the interest of fighting crime, but did not put the value of credibility above any consideration of protection of the individual.[59]

In the case of *Issacharov*, the Supreme Court adopted and expanded Justice Goldberg's approach in the *Muadi* decision, holding that the rule of inadmissibility enshrined in § 12 of the Evidence Ordinance should be interpreted in such a way that improper interrogation methods that illegally violate the right of the person under interrogation to physical integrity or humiliate and degrade him beyond what is required as a result of conducting the interrogation, will automatically lead to the inadmissibility of the confession notwithstanding the truth of the confession made in the interrogation.[60] The Court further held that in view of the purpose concerning the protection of defendants' rights in interrogations and the spirit of the Basic Law, the nature and scope of the improper interrogation methods that will be included within the scope of "a violation of the humanity of the person under interrogation" are likely to be wider than in the past.[61] The illegality in Issacharov's interrogation (i.e., the failure to inform him of his right to counsel) did not involve improper interrogation methods of the kind that are capable of humiliating and degrading the person under interrogation or of harming his physical or emotional well-being.[62]

According to the case law that preceded the *Issacharov* ruling, failure to inform a suspect of his right to remain silent and the right to consult with an attorney was only a circumstance that should be considered in examining voluntariness, but could

---

[56] Abu Midjam v. State of Israel, P.D. 34(4) 533, 546 (1980) (Justice Chaim Cohen).

[57] Muadi v. State of Israel, 38(1) P.D. 197, 222–224 (1982).

[58] Ibid.

[59] Ibid, 225.

[60] Issacharov, 61(1) P.D. 461 (2006), § 33.

[61] Ibid.

[62] Ibid.

not, in itself, render the confession inadmissible as involuntary.[63] The Court in *Issacharov* held that an illegal violation of the right to remain silent and the right to counsel within the framework of the interrogation process will constitute a weighty consideration when examining the admissibility of a confession under § 12 of the Evidence Ordinance, given that infringement of these rights may significantly violate the freedom of will and choice of the person under interrogation when making his confession.[64] However, the Court rejected the argument according to which § 12 of the Evidence Ordinance was intended to protect the full scope of the right to remain silent and the right to consult a lawyer, so that a violation thereof would necessarily lead to the inadmissibility of a confession under § 12. §12 was rather designed to protect the interrogee solely from material harm to his autonomy and body.[65] Therefore, a confession will be excluded as involuntary when an interrogee who was not informed of his rights was actually unaware of the right to remain silent, and as such, his autonomy of will and freedom to decide whether or not to cooperate with the interrogators was seriously violated.[66] In contrast, a confession will not be excluded if the interrogee was, in fact, aware of his right to remain silent.[67] In this respect, the Court did not deviate from its prior holdings in the matter.

The Court further held that following the enactment of the Basic Law: Human Dignity and Liberty, the status of the right to autonomy of free will has been strengthened, since it is derived directly from the conception of man as an end and not merely a means, and in view of the possible inclusion of the aforesaid right in the inner circle of the constitutional right to dignity and liberty.[68] Furthermore, the Court ruled that the purpose concerning the protection of the rights of the person under interrogation should be strengthened today, giving them independent protection, in order to render confessions inadmissible, both under § 12 of the Evidence Ordinance, and in appropriate circumstances, even when there is no concern with regard to the truth of the confession.[69] The basic rights of the person under interrogation deserve independent protection: these are the right to be protected against physical and emotional harm, and the right to autonomy of free will.[70] However, when implementing these, the Court ruled that only material and serious violations of the autonomy of the accused's will and freedom of choice in confessing would lead to exclusion of the confession under § 12.[71] According to the Court, this interpretation is attributable to the need not to unnecessarily undermine the

---

[63] Abed Alhadi v. Attorney General, P.D. 3, 13, 33–34 (1950); 747/86 Eisenman v. State of Israel, P.D. 42(3) 447, 454 (1988).

[64] Issacharov, 61(1) P.D. 461 (2006), § 35.

[65] Ibid.

[66] Ibid.

[67] Ibid.

[68] Ibid, § 34.

[69] Ibid, §§ 32, 34.

[70] Ibid, § 32.

[71] Ibid.

values of establishing the truth, fighting crime and protecting the public welfare.[72] The *Issacharov* Court held that in the circumstances of the case, the deliberate violation of the suspect's right (i.e., the failure to inform him of his right to counsel) did not amount to a material and serious violation of the autonomy of will and freedom of choice in making his confession.[73]

Despite the *Issacharov* Court's awareness of the fact that custodial interrogation could entail emotional pressure or physical discomfort for the suspect, which are inherent in the situation, it was determined that this fact alone does not materially impact on the voluntariness of the confession.[74] The Israeli Supreme Court has flatly rejected the *Miranda* rule, which requires the mandatory exclusion of a confession obtained during custodial interrogation absent warnings of the right to remain silent and the right to consult with an attorney.[75] As previously noted, under Israeli case law, failure to inform a suspect of the right to remain silent or the right to counsel is only one factor to be considered among the overall circumstances relevant to the admissibility of the confession. However, it is insufficient on its own to automatically render the suspect's confession involuntary. This approach of the Israeli Supreme Court does not give adequate weight to the distress of the suspect interrogated while in custody and, as a result, to the risk of breaking his will. Additionally, it does not properly reflect the strong connection between the right to an attorney and the voluntariness of the confession.

The Israeli Supreme Court has consistently insisted that the right of a suspect held in detention to consult with his attorney is an integral aspect of the right to remain silent.[76] Furthermore, the Criminal Procedure (Enforcement Powers – Detention) Law (1996) (hereinafter – Detention Law) anchors the right of the detainee to meet and consult with his lawyer.[77] However, according to the position taken by the Supreme Court and the wording of the detention law, the right of access to counsel is not an absolute one. Thus, the Court has held that there was no obligation to cease interrogation when the detainee expresses a desire to consult with a defense attorney until the attorney arrives at the police station.[78]

The Detention Law does not grant the detainee a right to have an attorney present during the interrogation, as opposed to the possibility to meet with the attorney prior to or during breaks in the interrogation. Moreover, notwithstanding the recognition

---

[72] Ibid.

[73] Ibid, § 37. The Court reasoned that not only had the suspect been informed of the right to remain silent, but he had also chosen to respond to the interrogator's questions when his second statement was taken, after having been informed of his right to consult with an attorney.

[74] Ibid, § 23.

[75] Miranda v. Arizona, 384 U.S. 436, 457 (1966). See also Dickerson v. United States, 530 U.S. 428 (2000) (Confirming the *Miranda* rule).

[76] Tao v. Attorney General, P.D. 20(2) 539, 545–546 (1966); Muadi v. State of Israel, 38(1) P.D. 197, 231 (1982); Sufian v. Commander of IDF Forces in the Gaza Strip, P.D. 47(2) 843, 847 (1993); Issacharov, 61(1) P.D. 461 (2006), section 14.

[77] § 34(a) Detention Law.

[78] Zakai v. State of Israel, 38(3) P.D. 57 (1982); Hason v. State of Israel, 56(3) P.D. 274 (1998).

of the fundamental right of a detainee to meet with counsel, the Detention Law permits delay of this meeting for various reasons. When a detainee is in the midst of interrogation proceedings, or other activities related to the investigation, and his presence is necessary for their completion (such as a re-enactment of the commission of the crime), and if the interruption of the investigation or its delay, for the purpose of meeting with an attorney, is liable to substantially hinder its progress, then an officer with the rank of superintendent or higher who is in charge of the investigation may, in writing, order the postponement of the meeting for several hours.[79] Furthermore, the meeting between the detainee and the attorney may be delayed for up to 24 h from the time of the arrest, if the officer in charge believes that the meeting is liable to frustrate or hinder the arrest of additional suspects in the same matter, or prevent the discovery of evidence or the seizure of something obtained in connection with said offense.[80] It may be delayed for a period of 48 h if the officer in charge is convinced that this is necessary to protect human life or to frustrate a crime.[81] The period of delay permitted regarding suspects detained for security offenses is much longer. For these detainees, the meeting may be delayed for up to 21 days if it is liable to interfere with the arrest of other suspects, disrupt the discovery or seizure of evidence, hinder the investigation in some other manner, or if the prevention of the meeting is necessary to frustrate an offense or to protect human life.[82] With respect to these detainees, the power to delay the meeting is exercised almost automatically.[83]

In light of the aforementioned statutory and case law limitations on the right of suspects to meet and consult with an attorney, Israeli detainees are in fact unable to speak with their counsel prior to the taking of their statements.[84] Even if Issacharov had known of his right to meet and consult with an attorney, he would not have been able to exercise this right prior to the taking of his statement, as the interrogator would not have been obligated to wait for the attorney's arrival. Moreover, when the attorney would have arrived at the police station, Issacharov would have been in the middle of the interrogation. Therefore, if the Supreme Court had decided to exclude Issacharov's confession due to his inability to exercise his right to an attorney prior to the taking of his statement, nearly all confessions taken by the Israeli police would be inadmissible due to involuntariness.

---

[79] § 34(d) Detention Law.

[80] § 34(e) Detention Law.

[81] § 34(f) Detention Law. Nevertheless, according to the last part of this section, the postponement of the meeting does not derogate from the right of a detainee, who has requested it, to be given a reasonable opportunity to meet with an attorney before being brought to court in regard to the arrest.

[82] § 35(a) Detention Law. An officer in charge may postpone the meeting by 10 days: §35(c) Detention Law. The President of the district court may postpone it for 21 days: § 35(d) Detention Law.

[83] Jarjura (1984, 95).

[84] See the findings of a field study conducted by the Public Defense Office presented to the Supreme Court in Issacharov, 61(1) P.D. 461 (2006), § 11.

The fact that Israeli law allows for sweeping postponements of meetings between detainees and attorneys provides the basis for assuming that postponement of the meeting between the two is designed to "overcome" the strong connection between the right to an attorney and the right to remain silent, as described in the *Miranda* Rule. Although the Supreme Court does not – at least rhetorically – view the fear that the suspect will exercise his right to remain silent after consulting with a defense attorney as a valid argument for delaying the meeting between them,[85] this rhetoric is neither in line with the sweeping prevention of such a meeting nor with the Court's own ruling.[86] In the case of *Sharitakh*, not only did the court approve the prevention of a meeting between the detainee and his lawyer, but also denied the request of the lawyer to inform the detainee that his family had appointed him an attorney and that he had the right to remain silent. The Supreme Court ruled on this case as follows:

> Petitioner is aware that a meeting between himself and an attorney was, and still is, prohibited. However, Advocate Rozental ... requests that petitioner be informed that people on the outside have appointed an attorney – Advocate Rozental – to represent him. We put the question to the respondent and his representatives, and we are satisfied that informing the petitioner of this, in addition to informing him of the prohibition on his meeting with an advocate – will harm the advancement of the investigation. Advocate Rozental further requests that he be permitted to convey a letter to the petitioner, informing him of his right to remain silent during interrogation and not to incriminate himself. Here, too, we have listened to the respondent and his representatives, and in this matter as well are satisfied that the advancement of the investigation and the security of the region prevent us from assenting to Advocate Rozental's request.[87]

This decision reflects a perception according to which the effectiveness of the investigation justifies allowing the police time to interrogate the suspect without interruption and without giving him the opportunity to consult with an attorney. Indeed, given that the attorney usually informs the suspect of the right to remain silent granted to him (and frequently even advises him to exercise this right) and, by his very presence, assists him in coping with the pressures exerted on him to give a statement, it is no wonder that a defense attorney is frequently viewed by the police investigators as an obstacle in their investigative efforts.

Despite the obligation to notify a person being interrogated as a suspect of his right to remain silent when his statement is being taken (regardless of whether or not he is under arrest), the Supreme Court (in the *Smirk* case) distinguished between an interrogation conducted by the General Security Service (GSS), which is designed to extract information in order to prevent the commission of a future offense against national security, and an interrogation intended to link the suspect to an offense that had already been committed, by gathering evidence for the purpose of conducting a trial.[88] In this case, the Court ruled that the first type of interrogation did not entail

---

[85] Rumchia v. Israeli Police, 47(1) P.D. 209 (1992).

[86] Osama Ali Sharitakh v. General Security Services (2001) (not published).

[87] Ibid.

[88] Smirk v. State of Israel, 56(3) P.D. 529, 545–46 (1999) (dealing with the appeal of a German citizen, who, after converting to Islam and joining the ranks of the Hezbollah (Party of God) terrorist organization in Lebanon, came to Israel on behalf of the organization to photograph potential targets for suicide attacks).

an obligation to apprise the suspect of the right to remain silent, whereas, in the second type of interrogation, a duty of notification does arise. This distinction may explain the ruling of the Supreme Court in the matter of *Sharitakh*: if there is no duty to inform the interrogee of his right to remain silent (although he is allowed to remain silent, in the sense that silence during interrogation does not constitute a criminal offense), then there is also no need for the defense attorney to inform him of such. The Supreme Court did not, however, rule that a confession extracted during interrogation, which was intended to prevent a future offense, would not be admissible against the interrogee in his trial due to its involuntary nature.

That said, even when dealing with detainees for crimes that are not security related, the right to consult with an attorney under Israeli law, despite the rhetoric regarding its importance, is limited in scope as compared to the right to an attorney under American law. Even after the *Issacharov* ruling, the Court continued to recognize the voluntariness of confessions given without prior notice of the right to counsel. An exceptional ruling in this regard is the case of *Alzam*.[89] In that case, the Court ruled that the defendant's confession of murder was to be excluded both due to its involuntariness and by virtue of the exclusionary rule, given the fact that the acts of the undercover agents who entered the detainee's cell deviated from legitimate tactics and deteriorated into a variety of unlawful actions that undermined the right to remain silent and the right to consult with an attorney. In that case, the undercover agents advised the suspect not to exercise his right to remain silent and convinced him that his attorney was not representing him properly and that he should replace him.[90] The ruling ostensibly expresses the willingness to balance the interests in favor of safeguarding the rights of accused persons and the fairness of the proceedings even in serious offenses. However, even in this ruling, the Supreme Court was not required to pay the actual price of acquitting criminals of serious offenses. Alzam was found dead in his cell in jail after his conviction by the district court, and prior to the hearing of his appeal by the Supreme Court. The circumstances of his death remain unknown. Under such circumstances, the acquittal of a dead person did not prejudice the enforcement of the law and did not risk the public's safety.

4.4 Conclusion

The Israeli Supreme Court has made significant progress in bringing the rules of procedure and evidence in line with the basic rights of suspects and defendants. However, and despite the impressive rhetoric of the *Issacharov* ruling, it seems that the Court is reluctant to pay the price required for the adequate protection of these

[89] Estate of the late Alzam v. State of Israel (delivered on June 22, 2009 and not yet published).
[90] Ibid, §§ 5, 9.

rights. As opposed to the position of the United States Supreme Court in the *Miranda* case, the Israeli Supreme Court did not recognize the inherent pressures of custodial interrogation as a factor that works to materially break the will of the suspect, and thus sustained the narrow interpretation of the voluntariness requirement. The Court did not give proper weight to the right to consult with an attorney as an essential means for enabling the suspect to make an informed decision as to whether he should give a statement or remain silent.

As far as the judicial exclusionary doctrine is concerned, despite the much welcome result of the adoption and application of the rule in the matter of *Issacharov* itself, the manner of interpreting the criteria for its application in future cases could clearly tilt the balance towards the value of ascertaining the truth, thus negating the declared purpose of the new rule. Although the *Issacharov* ruling has left the courts wide discretion to exclude unlawfully gathered evidence, the determination that the seriousness of the offense, the credibility of the evidence and its classification are all relevant considerations, may unduly restrict the rule's scope of applicability. The adoption of an exclusionary rule conveys the message that the moral legitimacy of the judgment is generally dependent upon the manner in which the evidence was obtained and the extent to which the basic human rights of the accused were respected. The true test of an exclusionary rule is expressed in the willingness of society to pay the price of exclusion of credible evidence and of the acquittal of factually guilty persons. In light of the *Issacharov* ruling, it would seem that the goal of safeguarding the dignity of defendants and their right to a fair trial will only be achieved when society is not required to pay the social price involved in their acquittal.

Time will tell how the relatively new exclusionary rule influences the activities of law enforcement officials and the willingness of the courts to exclude evidence obtained illegally. To date, courts have tended not to exclude unlawfully obtained evidence as part of the overall balance of interests.

Bibliography

Harnon, E. 1999. The impact of the basic law: Human dignity and liberty on the law of criminal procedure and evidence. *Israel Law Review* 33: 678–719.

Jarjura, R. 1984. The excessive rights of the Israel police regarding detainment of suspects and meetings with attorneys. *Hapraklit* 36: 92–96.

Kedmi, J. 1999. *On evidence*, vol. 1. Tel Aviv: Dyunon Publishing.

Stein, A. 2005. *Foundations of evidence law*. Oxford/New York: Oxford University Press.

Chapter 5
Germany: Balancing Truth Against Protected Constitutional Interests

Sabine Gless

Abbreviations – For Case Citations

BGH	Bundesgerichtshof, Federal Court of Appeal/German High Court
BGHSt	Entscheidungen des Bundesgerichtshofs für Strafsachen; Decisions of the German Supreme Court-in Criminal Cases
BVerfG	Bundesverfassungsgericht, German Constitutional Court
BVerfGE	Entscheidungssammlung des Bundesverfassungsgerichts, Decisions of the Constitutional Court
BvR	Bundesverfassungsgericht ?
ECtHR	European Court of Human Rights
E.H.R.R.	European Human Rights Reporter
EuGRZ	Europäische Grundrechts-Zeitschrift
GA	Goltdammer's Archiv für Strafrecht
JR	Juristische Rundschau
LG	Landgericht
NJW	Neue Juristische Wochenschrift
NStZ	Neue Zeitschrift für Strafrecht
NVwZ	Neue Zeitschrift für Verwaltungsrecht
OLG	Oberlandesgericht
StV	Der Strafverteidiger

S. Gless (✉)
Faculty of Law, University of Basel,
Postfach/Peter Merian-Weg 8, CH-4002, Basel, Switzerland
e-mail: Sabine.Gless@unibas.ch

S.C. Thaman (ed.), *Exclusionary Rules in Comparative Law*, Ius Gentium: Comparative Perspectives on Law and Justice 20, DOI 10.1007/978-94-007-5348-8_5,

5.1 The General Theory of Admissibility of Illegally Gathered Evidence

The general theory of admissibility of illegally gathered evidence in German law is complex, sometimes even confusing, since it tries to serve both: the establishment of truth and the commitment to due process.

It is often said that the German doctrine on exclusionary rules has its origins in a lecture given by Ernst Beling in 1903 entitled: "Exclusionary Rules – Limits for the Truth-Finding Process in Criminal Proceedings".[1] Advocating a doctrine on the exclusion of certain evidence, Beling, a visionary of his time, focused on how important it was that law enforcement was exercised in accordance with the Code of Criminal Procedure (CCP) introduced in 1871 (Strafprozessordnung, StPO); furthermore he touched on issues concerning due process with regard to a general respect for the rights of individuals.[2] After more than a century of political, economic and social upheavals as well as a technological revolution in (secret) surveillance, the German theory on admissibility of evidence is, on the one hand, still committed to Beling's teachings. On the other hand, the post-war constitution (Basic Law/Grundgesetz, GG), implemented by an alert and ambitious Federal Constitutional Court (Bundesverfassungsgericht, BVerfG), offers a new foundation with another reference system more concerned with human rights in general. Lately new influences and concepts, especially the idea of a fair trial and the watching eye of the European Court of Human Rights (ECtHR), have started to influence the theory on exclusionary rules as well. Today the different frameworks form a rather complex system for monitoring the use of illegally gathered evidence. Overall, however, two patterns recur constantly: (1) An allusion to Beling's vision of staying clean-handed while adhering to the rule of law, which mingles with the more modern concept of "fair trial", and (2) a focus on the protection of the individual's right to privacy – may it concern a suspect, a victim or a witness. When it comes to the violations of statutes regulating evidence collection and use, the "clean-handed"-approach and "fair trial"-test both follow the doctrine on exclusionary rules (Beweisverwertungsverbote) handed down from the early twentieth century. Although they might form the basis for a coherent modern theory of admissibility of evidence considering due process in the future, for the moment the traditional doctrine prevails. The reasons for this are manifold. First of all, as is well known, jurisprudence naturally holds on to traditional concepts and absorbs more modern approaches only reluctantly. Second, in the German system the question of admissibility is confronted with the fact that professional criminal court judges decide, themselves, in delivering the final judgment, whether a piece of evidence presented before the court may be used as such or not.[3] Third, the question whether certain evidence illegally obtained is used for the fact-finding process is traditionally confronted

[1] Beling (1903).

[2] See also, Beling (1928, 284).

[3] Weigend (2007, 254).

with the inherent paradox that you have the choice of either including potentially valuable information or to fuel doubt about this very evidence as it might be unreliable or illegally gathered information and thus not suitable to support the establishment of truth.

5.1.1 Constitutional or Statutory Rules

German law knows no constitutional provisions and only few statutes which explicitly impose exclusionary rules. Furthermore there is no general exclusionary rule which, for example, would render illegally obtained evidence inadmissible as such.

One of the few statutory exclusionary rules ("gesetzliche Beweisverwertungsverbote", literally "prohibitions on using evidence") in the CCP, § 136(1) StPO, explicitly requires exclusion under certain circumstances.[4] According to this provision the accused "shall be advised that the law grants him/her the right to respond to the accusation, or not to make any statements on the charges and, even prior to his/her examination, to consult with [a] defense counsel of his/her choice". A violation of this duty to instruct the suspect adequately leads to an exclusion of evidence.[5] Thus, in most cases, the courts have to decide without statutory guidance whether illegally gathered evidence triggers an exclusionary rule or not (*non-standardized exclusionary rules* – "nicht normierte Beweisverwertungsverbote"); they do so mainly if the breach of rights is so grave that it taints the evidence (*exclusionary rules on the basis of grave breach*, see Sect. 5.1.2.2). Such cases form the main body on which the German doctrine on admissibility is based. According to this approach, exclusionary rules are triggered by violations of the codified rules for the collections of evidence. These rules, however, are not only found in the CCP, but also are derived from superior principles, such as those from constitutional law.

The most prominent example for a violation of a constitutional right, which gives rise to exclusion of evidence – but based not in the statute, but in the case law – is the infringement of the right to privacy based on a broad concept of personal rights including the right to the free development of personality (allgemeines Persönlichkeitsrecht), located in Arts. 2 (1), 1(1) GG.[6]

5.1.1.1 General Exclusionary Rules/Rules Relating to Procedural "Nullities"

German law does not know the concept of nullity. Neither in the constitution, nor in the codes, can one find a general rule for prohibitions on the use of evidence.

---

[4] All StPO quotations in English are available on http://www.iuscomp.org/gla/statutes/StPO.htm.

[5] BGHSt 38, 214 (2.27.1992).

[6] See Sect. 5.2.1.1.

However, German scholars and courts have developed numerous approaches for deciding on the exclusion of different types of illegal evidence.

In order to understand the German doctrine it may help to know some of the basic terminology in this context. Apart from distinguishing between those exclusionary rules explicitly laid down in statutes (*statutory exclusionary rules*) and those not expressly stated therein (*non-standardized exclusionary rules*), jurisprudence and legal scholars use different – partly overlapping – categories, such as (1) *independent exclusionary rules* ("selbständige Beweisverwertungsverbote"), which, in general, lead to a strict exclusion of evidence, and are also called *obligatory exclusionary rules* ("absolute Verwertungsverbote"); and (2) *dependent exclusionary rules* ("unselbständige Beweisverwertungsverbote") based on a grave breach of a rule regulating the collection of evidence, which include cases of strict, absolute or so-called *obligatory exclusionary rules*, which always lead to an evidentiary prohibition, as well as *relative exclusionary rules*, in which the judges weigh the pros and cons for an exclusion ("relative Verwertungsverbote").[7]

The first category excludes evidence irrespective of the activities of the law enforcement agency, or rather regardless of misconduct, i.e. the violation of provisions regulating evidence collection. A typical example for an "independent exclusionary rule" is the prohibition directly deduced from the right to privacy, which is part of a more general constitutional "right to free development of [one's] personality" based mainly on Arts. 2 (1), 1(2) GG. The same applies to the violation of other specific constitutional rights, such as the right to "privacy of correspondence, mail and telecommunications" in Art. 10 GG as well as the "inviolability of the home" in Art. 13 GG[8] etc. Both, the Supreme Court (Bundesgerichtshof, BGH), in its early decisions in the Tape Recording Case,[9] the first Diary Cases[10] as well as recently in the Hospital Room Case,[11] and the BVerfG in the decision on electronic bugging of homes[12] and online searches,[13] excluded evidence on the ground that privacy was violated.

Thus it is mainly the second category, the "dependent exclusionary rules", which relates to the exclusion of evidence based on its illegal collection or rather due to the violation of statutory rule regulating the collection of evidence by law enforcement agencies or even by private citizens.

---

[7] Koriath (1994, 15–16). Theoretically oblig atory exclusionary rules can be both, dependent or independent. The obligatory aspect refers to the *effect*, i.e. legal consequence, that an exclusion of evidence entails; whereas the *cause* of the obligatory exclusionary rules can be either called "dependent" when the violation of a rule is not considered due to overriding aspects like privacy etc or regarded as "independent" as soon as rules on evidence gathering get violated.

[8] All GG quotations in English based on http://www.iuscomp.org/gla/statutes/GG.htm or http://www.geocities.com/iturks/html/documents12.html.

[9] BGHSt 14, 358 (6.14.1960), (Recording Tape Case).

[10] BGHSt 19, 325 (2.21.1964), (First Diary Case); other diary case: BGHSt 34, 397 (7.9.1987), in which a murderer elaborates his wish to kill in his diary.

[11] BGH NJW 2005, 3295 (8.10.2005).

[12] BVerfGE 109, 279 (3.3.2004).

[13] BVerfGE (2.27.2008) (1 BvR 370/07 -1 BvR 595/07).

Furthermore, the case law is controlling, as a sort of last resort, in deciding whether an investigation measure was used arbitrarily against somebody[14] and in so doing applies the "principle of proportionality" ("Grundsatz der Verhältnismässigkeit")[15] to balance an individual's constitutional right of privacy and the state's interest in fighting crimes.[16] The BVerfG, for example, declared the search for and seizure of the records of clients of a drug counselling agency unconstitutional, because in that case the intrusiveness of the search was disproportionate to the legitimate interests of law enforcement.[17]

Only recently, the courts have discussed the question of whether the accused may waive an exclusionary rule, if he/she wants to introduce exonerating evidence that would otherwise be subject to exclusion according to the statutory rules.[18] The question has not yet been resolved.

5.1.1.2 General Duty to Determine the Truth

German courts, traditionally, are obligated to ascertain the truth. Thus a justification for the exclusion of evidence is necessary, because a court must consult all relevant evidence in searching for the truth.[19] § 244(2) StPO explicitly commits the deciding court to unearth substantive truth: "In order to establish the truth, the court shall, *proprio motu* [of its own accord], extend the taking of evidence to all facts and means of proof relevant to the decision". The statute points to the inquisitorial origin of German criminal procedure[20]: the duty of the judge, and the trust in the judge – and law enforcement agencies[21] – to find the truth has been an essential feature for centuries. The duty to establish the truth is not absolute, however, or – as the BGH puts it in a famous dictum: "It is not a principle of criminal procedure to arrive at the truth at any cost".[22] The duty to search out the truth, thus, has its limits, in particular as soon as human and constitutional rights of individuals are derogated.[23] The BGH justified the exclusion of evidence balancing constitutional principles: although the task of solving and punishing crimes is extremely important, it must

---

[14] BGHSt 41, 30, 34 (2.16.1995); BGHSt 47, 362 (8.1.2002).

[15] The German Federal Constitutional Court established this principle of proportionality for cases dealing with compulsory measures in criminal processes. See BVerfGE 209, 7 (1.15.1958); BVerfG, NJW 1962, 2243 (11.9.1962); BVerfG NJW 1963, 147 (12.18.1962).

[16] BGHSt 19, 325 at 332 (2.21.1964).

[17] BVerfGE 44, 353 (5.24.1977).

[18] See: BGH NStZ 2008, 706; Rogall (1996, 944) and Godenzi (2008, 500).

[19] For the traditional approach see: BVerfGE 57, 275 (predominant principle of German law); Spencer (2002, 25 ff, 624 ff); for further analysis see Gless (2006, 84–89) and Weigend (2003, 159).

[20] For further information on the "accusatorial" and "inquisitorial" models, see Spencer (2002, 20–21).

[21] § 160 (2) StPO obliges the prosecution also to "ascertain not only incriminating but also exonerating circumstances," and to "ensure that such evidence is taken which is at risk of being lost."

[22] BGHSt 14, 361, 364–365 (6.14.1960), translated paraphrase of German original.

[23] "Keine Wahrheitserforschung um jeden Preis", BGHSt 14, 358, 365 (6.14.1960); Beulke (2008, 279,); Weigend (2003, 162).

be stressed that the purpose thereof is not and cannot always be the predominant interest of a state. Rather such an important public interest has to fit the overall context of broader more general interests. The provisions of the constitution express its *corrective effect* in the sphere of existing laws, as well as in criminal procedure law, which is understood as *applied constitutional law*.[24]

In German law the decision to limit the pool of information available, i.e. to exclude evidence, is left to the professional judges in the trial court.[25] Because of this, a particular situation arises: by establishing the facts through "free evaluation of the evidence" ("freie Beweiswürdigung"), the professional judges[26] must erase their knowledge gained from excluded evidence and thus reject proof that might support the reasons for the judgment. This dilemma brings about a strong risk of diluting the impact of exclusionary rules.[27]

On the whole, however, the mission to establish truth in criminal proceedings has been modified in recent years. Especially the practice of "plea bargaining" ("Absprachen"), which was recently codified, introduced a paradigm shift with regard to the traditional assignment of a court to find out the true facts of a case.[28]

5.1.2 General Rules of Admissibility/Exclusion of Illegally Gathered Evidence in High Court Jurisprudence

5.1.2.1 Statutory Exclusionary Rules

As already explained, the case law distinguishes between the exclusion of evidence, because a statute expressly requires it (statutory exclusionary rules, see Sect. 5.1.1.1), and the judges' non-evaluation of evidence, because it is gained by a breach of rule which is sufficiently grave to justify this exclusion (non-standardized exclusionary rules, see Sect. 5.1.1.1).

It took the German legislator roughly 50 years after Beling's famous lecture before the first statutory exclusionary rule banning illegally gathered evidence was introduced. § 136a StPO requires a court to exclude involuntary confessions. The statute, which will be discussed below,[29] expressly forbids the use of statements obtained during the questioning of suspects or witnesses by the use of improper

---

[24] BGHSt 19, 325, 329–330 (2.21.1964), emphasis added and translated summary of German original; see also: BGHSt 38, 214 (2.27.1992).

[25] The non-admission of evidence is not a discretionary decision, but a question of applying the law, which may be challenged by appeal to a higher court.

[26] The situation is different for lay judges ("Schöffen") who sit in judgment on special cases of severe criminality and have no knowledge of the contents of the investigative file.

[27] Frase, Weigend (1995, 334).

[28] On *Absprachen*, see Altenhein (2010, 157–179).

[29] See Sects. 5.3.2.2 and 5.3.2.3.

methods such as ill-treatment, fatigue, physical violence, forced drugs application, deception, hypnosis, unlawful threats and the use of measures which interfere with the accused's memory or his/her ability to understand. The provision is seen as a tribute to Art. 1 GG, which protects human dignity and signals a renunciation of the law enforcement methods commonly used during the Nazi regime.[30]

The application of such statutory exclusionary rules appears to be rather easy at first view. However, numerous questions regarding the scope of the provisions have to be considered, for example, it has to be discussed how tainted derivative evidence should be handled.

5.1.2.2 Non-standardized Exclusionary Rules: Exclusionary Rules Because of Grave Breaches

Apart from an explicit statutory rule, irregularities during the collection of evidence or other encroachments may trigger a prohibition on the use of evidence. In general, the infringement of a right or the breach of a statute which is too important to ignore brings about the exclusion of information. Since no statute deals with this kind of non-standardized exclusionary rule (because of grave breach etc.), courts and academia have developed various approaches to guide the decision on whether to exclude.[31] Two disparate approaches to exclusion are relevant in prevailing case law[32]: (1) a doctrine of "clean hands", which relates to the "rule of law" in criminal proceedings and basically focuses on the illegal gathering of evidence in violation of a rule designed to safeguard the defendant's basic procedural rights leads to the exclusion of evidence (see Sect. 5.1.2.2.1); and (2) a constitutional approach which basically protects the right to privacy so that any infringement of the sacrosanct private sphere leads to an exclusion of evidence (see Sect. 5.1.2.2.2).

Theory: Exclusion Due to Illegal Gathering of Evidence

Without a statutory exclusionary rule it is always difficult to decide whether the violation of a *rule for gathering evidence* triggers an exclusionary rule, i.e. brings about a prohibition on the use of the evidence collected. In Germany, three predominant theories about exclusionary rules have to be considered in this context.

The first is the "balancing approach" ("Abwägungstheorie"), a doctrine applied by courts and supported by some academics.[33] Whenever procedural rules are

---

[30] BGHSt 1, 387 (10.30.1951).

[31] BGHSt 42, 170, 172 (5.21.1996); BGHSt 47, 172, 179 (11.22.2001); for a critical analysis see Roxin (2007, 452); see also: BVerfG NVwZ 2005, 1175 (6.30.2005): "Aus dem Prozessgrundrecht auf ein faires, rechtsstaatliches Verfahren ergibt sich *nicht*, dass die Verwertung fehlerhaft gewonnener Beweise stets unzulässig ist".

[32] There are, however, many other theories and approaches that justify the exclusion of evidence.

[33] BGHSt 42, 170, 172, 179 (5.21.1996); for a critical view see Grünwald (1993, 143).

violated by law enforcement agencies, the courts, in determining the truth, weigh the seriousness of the violation against the public interest as well as against the legal interests of the aggrieved party (victim).[34] Illegally obtained evidence shall be excluded only if the interests of law enforcement cannot outweigh those of the defendant, i.e. if the severity of the offense investigated significantly outweighs the seriousness of the violation.[35] Circumstances considered include the severity of police misconduct, the importance of the violated legal interest, the seriousness of the crime committed by the defendant and the relevance of the piece of evidence for the resolution of the case. Although jurisprudence has refused to establish strict rules on the exclusion of illegally obtained evidence so far, it emphasizes that the violation of a rule securing the defendant's basic procedural rights normally leads to the exclusion of the evidence obtained. Thus, according to case law, for example, if the suspect is not informed of his/her right to "respond to the accusation, or not to make any statements on the charges and, even prior to his/her examination, to consult with a defense counsel of his/her choice", this omission leads to an exclusion of any statement the suspect makes during this interrogation,[36] unless the accused was aware of the rights, and nevertheless made a statement. Then the statement may be admitted .

The second approach is that of the "theory of protective purpose" ("Schutzzwecktheorie"), which in its pure version does not permit of balancing the competing interests of state and defendant, and instead advocates a uniform framework for exclusionary rules.[37] This theory maintains that any balancing which had to be done was already done by the legislator in the legislation relating to the norm which was violated, and that the courts should therefore not engage in any further balancing, but must exclude the evidence resulting from the violated rule. Today this doctrine, however, has been diluted by many modifications which have taken place.

Finally, the third approach, developed in academia, is entitled the "theory of the right to control information" ("Lehre von den Informationsbeherrschungsrechten"), and focuses on the protection of the right to privacy and the confidentiality of one's communications, and also to maintaining these protections in the public sphere.[38] A defendant, whose right to keep protected confidential information private has been violated by illegal police misconduct, may move to exclude, and/or return the illegally obtained evidence.[39]

Despite their differences all three theories agree that the primary task of exclusionary rules in Germany – in contrast to the US doctrine – is not to exercise discipline

[34] See e.g. BGHSt 47, 172, 179–180 (11.22.2001); BGH NJW 2003, 2034.

[35] For a comparison with US Law see Thaman (2001, 608)

[36] BGHSt 38, 372 (10.29.1992).

[37] See Grünwald (1993, 155) and Rudolphi (1970, 97).

[38] Amelung (1990a, 24, 30).

[39] Ibid, 52.

over law enforcement authorities. The case law applies a combination of elements from the balancing approach along with some variations of the theory of protective purpose.[40]

Theory: Exclusion Based in Protection of the Right to Privacy

The approach of the German high courts for protecting the privacy of individuals involved in criminal proceedings, such as suspects, does *not* predominantly focus on the issue of *illegally collected evidence.* Basically it differentiates three spheres relating to information gathering. According to the "three-sphere-approach" ("Drei-Sphärentheorie")[41] law enforcement agencies may gather information about a person and his/her private life in three situations.

In the first sphere, that of public life, photographs may be taken, visual recordings made, movements observed, speeches in front of an audience like a business club, etc., recorded and all such material may be used as evidence.[42] On the other hand, information gathered secretly *without meeting the legal requirements* may most likely not be used.[43]

The second sphere involves otherwise private activity which is, however, exposed in public, such as a private conversation being overheard in a restaurant. Such information may only be used if law enforcement interests outweigh individual privacy interests, taking into account the severity of the charge, the importance of the privacy right, the relevance of the evidence, etc.[44]

There is finally a sacrosanct private sphere, such as a diary entry never meant for other eyes or a soliloquy uttered in a hospital room. Such strictly off-the-record information may not be seized nor used as evidence in a criminal proceeding,[45] since it would violate the human dignity.[46]

Although the "three-sphere-approach" has been criticized from the beginning,[47] it is still a relevant guideline for decisions today.[48]

---

[40] BGHSt 46, 189, 195 (11.3.2000).

[41] BVerfGE 34, 238, 245–247 (1.31.1973); BVerfGE 109, 279 (3.3.2004) (electronic tapping of private residences, "grosser Lauschangriff").

[42] Beulke (2008, 288).

[43] BGHSt 31, 304 (3.17.1983); BGHSt 31, 309 (4.6.1983); BGHSt 32, 68, 70 (8.24.1983); Beulke (2008, 288).

[44] See BGH JR 1994, 430.

[45] See e.g. BVerfGE 80, 367 (9.14.1990) (Diary Case of 1990); BVerfG 109, 279, 281 (3.3.2004) (electronic bugging of homes); BGHSt 50, 206 (8.10.2005), BGH NStZ 2005, 700 (Hospital Room Case); Baldus (2008, 219) and Baum and Schantz (2008, 137).

[46] As protected by Art. 1 (1) GG, see BVerfGE 109, 279 (3.3.2004) as well as BVerfGE 80, 367 (9.14.1990) (Diary Case of 1990); BGH NStZ 2005, 700 (Hospital Room Case); Jahn (2000, 384).

[47] See e.g. Wolter (1993, 1) and Lindemann (2006, 191).

[48] See BGHSt 33, 217 (9.5.1985) and § 100f StPO as an example of corresponding legislation; see also: Hohmann-Dennhardt (2006, 545) and Beulke (2008, 288).

5.1.2.3 Restrictions on the Enforcement of Exclusionary Rules

Despite the development of a rather broad application of doctrines of inadmissibility, German jurisprudence has recognized three important restrictions on the enforcement of exclusionary rules.

Standing in Relation to the Legally Protected Sphere – "Rechtskreistheorie"

According to established case law a person may only challenge the admissibility of illegally obtained evidence, if the violated rule on evidence gathering protects his or her acknowledged interests and thus forms part of his or her legally protected rights ("Rechtskreistheorie"). This approach, similar to the American notion of "standing", creates a general obstacle to enforcement of an exclusionary rule otherwise triggered by an illegality in the gathering of criminal evidence. The BGH first introduced it in a case involving exclusion of evidence due to the violation of a witness's privilege against self-incrimination.[49] The court held that the witness's statement was admissible against the defendant because the violation had not infringed upon the defendant's legally protected rights.

Requirement of an Objection to Admission of the Evidence – "Widerspruchslösung"

Only recently the German courts have introduced another exception to the exclusion of otherwise inadmissible evidence. Only if the person whose rights have been violated during the gathering of evidence explicitly objects to the admission of the illegally obtained evidence in a timely fashion, will the exclusionary rule will be enforced.[50] If, for example, a defendant is not cautioned properly, she or her defense counsel must object to the use of such evidence as soon as possible, otherwise the claim is lost. This "Widerspruchslösung" is heavily criticized by various scholars.[51]

Hypothetical Clean Path

In some cases courts apply the "hypothetical clean path" analysis ("hypothetischer Ermittlungsverlauf") to justify the admission of evidence *directly* obtained by illegal means. This is similar to the US doctrine of "inevitable discovery" in some

---

[49] BGHSt 11, 213 (1.21.1958); see also: BGHSt 38, 214, 220 (2.27.1992).

[50] BGHSt 38, 214, 225 (2.27.1992); BGHSt 39, 349, 352 (10.12.1993); BGH NStZ 1997, 502; BGH JR 2005, 385, 386, in favor: Basdorf (1997, 491) and Hamm (1996, 2188). "Widerspruchslösung" does not apply in cases of § 136a StPO, see BGH StV 1996, 360.

[51] See Gless (2007, 567 f.), Grünwald (1993, 149 ff), and Wohlers (1995, 46).

of its applications. The courts argue that relevant evidence should not be excluded because of a mere "technical fault", if the evidence could otherwise have been obtained by legal means.[52]

For example, in the case of an illegal, i.e. unauthorized, search of the suspect's apartment, the BGH argued that the evidence found in the apartment should not be excluded, since under different circumstances judicial authorization could have been granted and thus would have converted the seized objects into admissible evidence.

In another case, the BGH, although confronted with the fact that the inside of a car is reckoned to belong to the protected private sphere, still considered admissible the tape of a "live" conversation in a suspect's car which was accidentally recorded through a procedure designed only to record conversations on the suspect's cell phone. The court argued that the installation of a hidden microphone in the suspect's car could have been granted legally on the basis of another provision of the CCP. According to its view the use of the wrong legal provision alone was no reason to exclude the evidence.

In a case decided more recently by the High Regional Court of Celle/Lower Saxony (Oberlandesgericht, OLG), a police officer acquired a blood sample of a suspect from a nurse after the suspect had undergone emergency surgery. Despite the fact that the police officer had acted illegally, the court admitted the blood sample, arguing that it would be formalistic to exclude it, since the officer could have obtained *another* blood sample by immediately ordering a physical examination of the suspect in accordance with § 81a StPO.[53]

Although the "hypothetical clean path"-approach has been criticized from the beginning, it is still predominant[54] in case law.[55]

5.1.3 Effect of International Human Rights Jurisprudence

After a period of reluctance the German courts have over the years finally recognized the jurisprudence of the European Court of Human Rights (hereinafter: ECtHR) and its impact on, and even priority over, German law. Meanwhile, German jurisprudence has absorbed several approaches introduced by the ECtHR, especially

---

[52] BGHSt 24, 125 (3.17.1971); BGH NStZ 1989, 375 (2.15.1989); Roxin (1989, 376 f.) and Meurer (1990, 388 f.); for a comparative perspective see Thaman (2001, 611–612).

[53] OLG Celle NStZ 1989 (3.14.1989). If, however, the police *deliberately* circumvents legal requirements, the evidence will be excluded, see OLG Dresden NJW 2009, 2149 (5.11.2009).

[54] In some cases the BGH refrained from applying a "hypothetical clean path doctrine", see BGHSt 25, 168 (3.28.1973).

[55] BGH NJW 2003, 2034, for a critical analysis see: Rogall (1998, 385), Wesslau (2003, 483), and Jahn and Dallmeyer (2005, 304).

the test of a "fair trial" which requires an examination of whether the proceedings have been fair, using an "overall approach".[56]

5.2 Rules of Admissibility/Exclusion in Relations to Violations of the Right to Privacy

5.2.1 General Provisions Protecting the Right to Privacy and Personality Development

German law does not have an explicit provision protecting the right to privacy. But after the Second World War German courts have – after the experience of a totalitarian regime – invented a multi-faceted approach to privacy protection. This approach is chiefly based on constitutional provisions, in particular Art. 2 (1) GG which grants the "right to free development of [one's] personality".

In 1954, roughly 50 years after Beling's lecture on the exclusion of certain kinds of evidence, the BGH, for the first time, embarked on a new doctrine for excluding evidence in a case in which it prohibited the use of a polygraph, declaring it to be a violation of an individual's personality rights. In the 1960s, the BGH issued two landmark decisions, the Tape-Recording Case (Tonbandentscheidung)[57] and the First Diary Case (Erste Tagebuchentscheidung),[58] and thus the concept of excluding evidence primarily for privacy reasons got introduced. Before these precedents, the courts had refrained from the suppression of illegally obtained, but reliable evidence. From these two decisions, German high court jurisprudence deduced several constitutional personality rights, among them being a right protecting the individual's spoken word.[59]

Unlike in the US, German jurisprudence grants suspects privacy rights not only in private locations, but also in public spaces. The issue of privacy is not attached to location alone, but to the private nature of the information.[60] This derives from the right to personality and human dignity, which includes the right to "informational self-determination", which transcends the mere expectation "to be left alone".[61] In the Hospital Room Case, for example, a murder suspect was admitted to a rehabilitation hospital, where police bugged his room with the consent of the hospital

---

[56] For further information see Gaede (2007) and Simon (1998).

[57] BGHSt 14, 358 (6.14.1960), (Recording Tape Case).

[58] BGHSt 19, 325 (2.21.1964), (First Diary Case).

[59] See also right to privacy of correspondence, posts and telecommunications as protected by Art. 10 GG.

[60] For a comparative perspective see Ross (2005).

[61] See BVerfGE 65, 1 (12.15.1983); Amelung (1990b, 1755) and Kutscha (2007, 1169).

administration. Talking to himself he muttered: "... very aggressive! I should have shot him in his head". The BGH excluded the evidence, since it detected an infringement of the suspect's private sphere.[62]

5.2.1.1 Constitutional Provisions

The German constitution guarantees in its Art. 2 (1) GG the "right to the free development of personality" as long as a person does not violate the rights of others or offend against the constitutional order or the moral code. The right of free self-determination of personality is acknowledged as a basic value of the German legal order which, as a consequence, protects the (sacrosanct) private sphere from investigations by law enforcement agencies.

Various other constitutional provisions protect the right to privacy as well. For example, Art. 13 GG guarantees the sanctity of the home, Art. 10 secures the secrecy of the correspondence by mail or telephone, thus protecting the individual's right to be left alone; and Art. 104 GG ensures the right of free movement.[63]

5.2.1.2 Statutory Provisions

There is no explicit provision in the StPO protecting the "right to privacy" as such. However, the StPO retains the right to privacy in various provisions safeguarding traditional civil rights and liberties, thus, in part, implementing constitutional protections, while also regulating in a differentiated manner, particular types of investigative measures. The right of free movement, for example, which is also guaranteed in Art. 104 GG, is implicitly secured in §§ 112–13 StPO.

Many statutory provisions relate to privacy, with several relating to the right of individuals to their own spoken words. For example, § 477(2)(2) StPO covers the use of information inadvertently discovered during a wiretap ("Zufallsfunde bei Telefonüberwachungen"), § 100c (5)(3) StPO deals with recordings of intimate communications during electronic eavesdropping operations in private residences ("Intimaufzeichnungen beim grossen Lauschangriff"), § 100d (5)(1) StPO deals with information inadvertently discovered during the electronic bugging of private residences ("Zufallsfunde beim grossen Lauschangriff") or § 100h (2)(2) StPO deal with information inadvertently discovered while recording private conversations in public ("Zufallsfunde beim Einsatz technischer Hilfsmittel und beim kleinen Lauschangriff").

---

[62] For example: BGH NStZ 2005, 700 (Hospital Room Case).

[63] See e.g. BVerfGE 32, 54 (10.13.1971).

5.2.1.3 Interpretations of the Constitution by the BGH

German courts focused on the right to privacy in many of their early judgments. A very prominent decision in this respect, was that of the BGH in 1964 in the First Diary Case.[64] This judgment not only focused on privacy rights, but prepared the groundwork for a new important doctrine. The BGH had to decide whether a defendant's diary was admissible as evidence in a perjury trial. The defendant was called to be a witness in the adultery trial of her former lover. She denied any involvement with him. The wife of another former lover of the defendant found the defendant's diary in her home and handed it over to the police. The trial court admitted the diary as evidence and convicted the defendant of perjury. However, the BGH reversed the defendant's conviction on the ground that the use of the defendant's private diary against her in court decisively violated her "right of free self-determination of personality" under Arts. 1 and 2 of the GG.[65] Even before this diary decision, the BGH considered the admissibility of privately recorded tapes in a criminal case, in the so-called 1960 Tape-Recording Case.[66] The defendant, an attorney of a rape victim, proceeded with negotiations with a female friend of the defendant in the rape case during the trial phase. The female friend secretly tape-recorded the conversation between herself and the attorney who was accused of attempting to press his client to perjure herself. The BGH eventually excluded the tape on the basis that tape-recording of words without the speaker's consent violates his sphere of personality and right to his spoken word, and as a consequence the defendant was acquitted.[67] In later cases, the Court reaffirmed this theory and continued to refine it.

It was, however, the BVerfG that went beyond mere interpretation, and further elaborated the right to privacy by extending it to the protection of individual autonomy and "informational self-determination" as aspects of privacy and dignity.[68] In the Census Case[69] it stressed that it is "a right of every citizen to know what information the government has collected about him and to limit the government's use, storage, and transmission of the data".[70] More recently the court developed this reasoning further in the GPS Case and argued that, given the progress in surveillance technology, the German piecemeal regulation on secret information gathering will, in the end, not be able to protect privacy as established by case law. One reason for this failure is the fact that rules on information gathering only cover one law enforcement tool at a time, but never the whole picture that might, for instance, include a combination of telephone tapping, data mining in financial matters, GPS surveillance etc.[71]

[64] BGHSt 19, 325 (2.21.1964), (First Diary Case).

[65] Ibid, 326–327; BGHSt 19, 329, 330 (2.21.1964) (emphasis added).

[66] BGHSt 14, 358 (6.14.1960), (Tape-Recording Case).

[67] BGHSt 14, 358, 359 (6.14.1960).

[68] BVerfGE 65, 1 (12.15.1983); for further information see: Ross (2005).

[69] BVerfGE 65, 1 (12.15.1983) ("Volkszählungsurteil").

[70] Ibid.

[71] BVerfGE 112, 304 (4.12.2005).

5.2.2 Protection of Privacy in Private Residences and Other Private Buildings

5.2.2.1 Constitutional Provisions

People are entitled to privacy and to enjoy the sanctity of the home. Art. 13 GG declares that "(1) The home is inviolable. (2) Searches may be authorized only by a judge or, when time is of the essence, by other authorities designated by the laws, and may be carried out only in the manner therein prescribed".

Intimate information uttered inside one's home is also protected and is generally immune to any government interference.[72] The exception, however, is when the authorities get judicial authorization to bug a domicile.

5.2.2.2 Statutory Provisions

Several provisions of the StPO which are based on Art. 13 GG establish a series of exceptions, allowing the gathering of information in peoples' homes. According to §§ 102, 105 StPO, a judge may order a search of a defendant's premises, private or otherwise, if it is suspected that a crime has been committed or is being committed, and "it may be presumed that the search will lead to the discovery of evidence". However, when there is "danger in delay", the public prosecutor and his auxiliary police officials are authorized to order such searches according to §§ 98, 105 StPO. A "danger in delay" exists whenever the delay involved in acquiring a judicial warrant endangers the success of the search, because the object in question could be destroyed or concealed.[73] In 1998 the parliament introduced the law that allows electronic tapping of private residences (grosser Lauschangriff) in cases of severe crimes. In doing so it was, inevitably, facilitating the recording of intimate communication. As a consequence of the judicial doctrine on protection of privacy, § 100c (5)(3) StPO rules that such tapping has to be stopped as soon as statements belonging to the core area of privacy are recorded. Accidental recordings of such material have to be deleted immediately and potential insight gained from such recordings in the meantime must not be used as evidence.

5.2.2.3 High Court Jurisprudence Interpreting the Effect of Violations of the Above Provisions on the Admissibility of Illegally Seized Evidence

The German high courts have been inconsistent in interpreting when a violation of the laws governing wiretapping or bugging will lead to inadmissibility of the

[72] See exclusionary rule in § 100c StPO.

[73] See Frase and Weigend (1995, 332).

evidence, and when they will not. For example, German courts were called upon to decide whether information gathered by law enforcement agencies by bugging the inside of an apartment could still be used, when authorization was only valid for evidence gathering outside of the house. The BGH ruled that the evidence could not be used.[74]

However, in another case in which law enforcement agencies violated the three-month limitation on electronic eavesdropping, the court admitted the seized information as evidence nevertheless.[75] These examples show that the exclusionary rules which protect privacy still lack a doctrine that makes the outcome of such particular cases more predictable.

5.2.2.4 Admissibility of Indirect Evidence (Fruits of the Poisonous Tree)

According to case law and the prevalent view in the literature, the inadmissibility of illegally obtained evidence does not extend to derivative evidence.[76] The doctrine of "fruits of the poisonous tree" is recognized neither in the case law, nor by a majority of scholars.[77] As a result, the BGH has held that statements by witnesses obtained as a result of an illegal wiretap[78] or entrapment[79] are nonetheless admissible. The same is true for a confession by the defendant to an expert witness a few days after he had been confronted with an illegally recorded tape revealing his self-incriminating remarks.[80] The fruits of illegal searches are also usually held to be admissible.[81]

However, in one instance the BGH excluded derivative evidence gained by violating provisions of the wiretap law.[82] In this particular case the court held that the police had disregarded statutory requirements relating to the confidentiality of press sources, and that this violation tainted the indirect evidence.

A majority of academics, however, is of the opinion that a failure to advise the accused of his/her rights, as required by § 136 StPO, must always lead to the exclusion of leads gathered on the basis of the inadmissible statements.[83] However,

[74] BGHSt 42, 372, 377 (1.15.1997).

[75] BGHSt 44, 243, 248 (11.11.1998) (Verletzung der Dreimonatsfrist); Wolters (1999, 524).

[76] See e.g. BGHSt 29, 244, 247 (4.18.1980); BGHSt 32, 68 (8.24.1983); BGHSt 34, 362 (4.28.1987); BGHSt 35, 32 (8.6.1987).

[77] However there are strong critical dissenting voices, among them: Otto (1970, 284).

[78] BGHSt 32, 68 (8.24.1983).

[79] BGHSt 34, 362 (4.28.1987).

[80] BGHSt 35, 32 (8.6.1987).

[81] BVerfGE 2 BvR 2225/08 (7.2.2009); BGHSt 27, 355, 358 (2.22.1978); BGHSt 32, 68, 71 (8.24.1983).

[82] BGHSt 29, 244, 247 (4.18.1980)("Spiegel case").

[83] Gless (2007, 578) and Grünwald (1966, 489).

even if information may not be used as evidence, case law still allows its use to further the investigation ("Spurenansatz").[84] Thus, according to the critics, even tainted evidence may turn into untainted evidence.[85]

The rejection of any "fruit of the poisonous tree" doctrine and the acceptance of the "hypothetical clean path"[86] is probably best explained by the fact that in Germany evidence is not excluded in order to deter police misconduct, but basically on the "clean hands" rationale.[87] Indirect evidence itself is not tainted by the violation of procedural rules so that the interests of justice outweigh any remaining reservations with regard to possible defects in the process of seizure.

5.3 Rules of Admissibility/Exclusion in Relation to Illegal Interrogations

Broadly speaking German law does not recognize any type of "illegal interrogation" which would taint all subsequently gathered evidence. Compared with the approach of the English Police and Criminal Evidence Act (PACE)[88] or the US courts, the German StPO has a less detailed system when it comes to regulations limiting the investigative power of the police, the safeguard of the individual's procedural rights at each step of the investigation, and the sanctions against police misconduct. Particularly, the procedural rights during pre-trial interrogations is treated less extensively. However, §§ 136 StPO and 136a StPO do address illegal interrogation techniques and the consequences for evidence collected by such means.

5.3.1 The General Right to Remain Silent and the Privilege Against Self-Incrimination

5.3.1.1 Constitutional Provisions

No constitutional provision explicitly addresses the right to remain silent. However, the BGH, in emphasizing human dignity as a basic value of the German legal system and principle of a criminal procedure based on the rule of law, issued the following famous *obiter dictum*[89]:

> The instructions [of §§ 136 (1) and 136 a StPO] are not isolated rules for their own sake, but rather they express the constitutional stance of a criminal procedure which does not permit

---

[84] See BGHSt 27, 355, 358 (2.22.1978).

[85] See Beulke (2008, 292).

[86] See Sect. 5.2.2.4.

[87] See Weigend (2007, 253).

[88] See Choo, Ch. 14, p. 345.

[89] BGHSt 14, 358, 361 (6.14.1960).

> degrading proceedings against the defendant…Under the same circumstances it must not be allowed that the defendant's utterances illegally obtained by tape recordings can be used against him/her…This interpretation entails that important or even the only evidence available in order to solve a crime has to be discarded. However, this dilemma has to be accepted. Besides, it is not a principle of criminal procedure to arrive at the truth at any cost.[90]

5.3.1.2 Statutory Provisions

The defendant's right to silence derives from the *nemo tenetur*-principle introduced by the Code Napoleon.[91] However, this principle is not explicitly articulated in a special provision of the German code, but is acknowledged as a basic maxim in order to protect an individual from being forced to accuse him-/herself.[92]

5.3.1.3 High Court Interpretation of the Scope and Protected Interests Covered by the General Right

In addition to excluding evidence due to violation of a provision of the code, the case law has also recognized manifold other implications to the principle of *nemo tenetur*[93]: Each accused has the right to refuse to answer questions and may not be punished for exercising this right in any way.[94] According to the principle of *nemo tenetur* the court must not regard or treat silence as an inferior strategy of defense.[95] As a consequence an accused who remains silent in all respects and during the entirety of the proceedings, may not be regarded as worse off compared to the one who testifies.[96] The silent defendant, however, risks paying a (high) price, since a confession could lead to a mitigation of punishment.[97]

---

[90] Ibid, 364–365.

[91] See Spencer (2002, 610–611).

[92] Vgl. etwa BVerfGE 38, 105, 113 (10.8.1974); BVerfGE 56, 37, 43 (1.13.1981); BGHSt 37, 340, 343 (3.19.1991); BGHSt 38, 214, 220 (2.27.1992) and BGHSt 38, 302, 305 (5.26.1992); Rogall (2004, §136) and Bosch (1998, 24 f.)

[93] See Grünwald (1981, 428), Rogall (1998, 67 f.), Weßlau (1997, 343), on the one hand, and Hackethal (2005, 137), Neumann (1998, 376), and Verrel (2001, 223), on the other hand.

[94] BGHSt 38, 214, 218 (2.27.1992); Beulke (2008, 287), Böse (2002, 99 ff.), and Weßlau (1998, 1f.).

[95] Torka (2000, 74) and Böse (2002, 119).

[96] BGHSt 32, 140, 144 (10.26.1983); BGH StV 1989, 90; Miebach (2000, 235).

[97] See Bosch (1998, 197 f.) and Hönig (2004, 78f). One could, however, claim, that it is possible in Germany to draw from the accused's silence a legal inference of guilt. Because a court may use a stubborn denial by the accused as evidence of the fact that the accused is lacking in remorse, thus justifying the imposition of a more severe sentence.

5.3.2 The Protection Against Involuntary Self-Incrimination: Torture, Coercion, Threats, Promises, etc.

5.3.2.1 Constitutional Provisions

The German constitution does not contain an explicit provision banning torture or comparable mistreatment. However, according to Art. 1 GG: "Human dignity shall be inviolable. To respect and protect it shall be the duty of all state authority". This has been interpreted to prohibit any kind of ill-treatment. Art. 104 (1) GG, also provides that: "Persons in custody may not be subjected to mental or physical mistreatment".

The decision of the BGH in the Tape-Recording case illustrates post-war reasoning when it stresses that the prohibitions listed in § 136a StPO are not isolated rules, but have to be seen in the constitutional context of a criminal procedure based on the rule of law that protects human dignity.[98]

Nevertheless, the *Gäfgen* case in Germany, at the beginning of this millennium, launched a discussion about the legitimacy of "torture for rescue" ("Rettungsfolter").[99] Gäfgen had abducted a boy and killed him. Subsequently he deposited a letter at the victim's parents' home asking for money. The police secretly observed him picking up the ransom and arrested him. Believing that the victim was still alive, the police officers dutifully informed the defendant that he was suspected of being a kidnaper, that he had the right to remain silent and that he could consult a lawyer. The ensuing interrogation was conducted with a view to finding the boy's whereabouts, but this undertaking was of no avail. The next day a police officer, following the orders of the deputy chief, threatened the defendant, that he would be subjected to a considerably painful treatment by a specially trained person, if he did not disclose the child's whereabouts, whereupon he revealed the truth and led the police to the location of the victim's body. In subsequent interviews the defendant reiterated his confession. Furthermore the police confirmed that the defendant had left other evidence, such as DNA traces on the ransom and corpse. The lower courts excluded the confession, but decided to admit this derivative evidence. Gäfgen appealed to the Constitutional Court, which upheld the lower court's refusal to exclude the evidence obtained as a result of the confession extorted from him by threats.[100]

---

[98] BGHSt 14, 358, 365 (6.14.1960).

[99] Hamm (2003, 946), Hecker (2003, 210), Jerouscheck and Kölbel (2003, 613), Kinzig (2003, 799 f.), Saliger (2004, 48 f.), and Hilgendorf (2004, 331 ff.).

[100] BVerfGE NJW 2005, 656. The applicant had failed to raise this issue in the proceedings before the Federal Court of Justice.

5.3.2.2 Statutory Provisions

§ 136a StPO explicitly prohibits confessions obtained by improper measures which impair the ability to freely decide whether to make a statement:

(1) The accused's freedom to make up his/her mind and to manifest his/her will shall not be impaired by ill-treatment, induced fatigue, physical interference, forced administration of drugs, deception or hypnosis. Coercion may be used only as far as this is permitted by criminal procedure law. Threatening the accused with measures not permitted under its provisions or holding out the prospect of an advantage not envisaged by statute shall be prohibited.
(2) Measures which impair the accused's memory or his/her ability to understand shall not be permitted.
(3) The prohibitions under subsections (1) and (2) shall apply irrespective of the accused's consent [to the proposed measure]. Statements which were obtained in breach of this prohibition shall not be used [as evidence], even if the accused agrees to their use.

5.3.2.3 High Court Jurisprudence Interpreting the Effect of Violations of the Above Provisions on Admissibility of Illegally Seized Evidence

There has been much discussion in the case law as to when a confession or statement must be excluded pursuant to § 136a StPO, which prohibits improper interrogation methods. The conclusion reached is based on a doctrine that regards any interrogation techniques which improperly affect the suspect's free will as illegal. For instance, fatigue must be avoided by granting any suspect sufficient sleep. However, if the suspect cannot go to sleep because of restlessness, he/she may be questioned nevertheless.[101] Administering analeptics may qualify as a forceful drugging, whereas coffee may be served.[102] It is prohibited to administer emetics pursuant to § 136a StPO, even in cases in which drug dealers have swallowed packages of drugs, whether for purposes of transportation, or after a police bust in order to suppress evidence.[103] It is treated as illegal deception and not a mere ruse, if the police tells a person bone-crushing evidence of guilt is at hand, when, in fact, law enforcement agencies are in the dark.[104] To threaten to arrest a person who refuses to cooperate is illegal,[105] if the threat is only made to compel the person to co-operate. The same holds true in the case of a promise of exemption from punishment, if a suspect incriminates an accomplice.[106]

---

[101] BGH NStZ 1999, 630.

[102] BGHSt 11, 211 (3.4.1958).

[103] Jalloh v. Germany (2007), 44 E.H.R.R. 32, 667. Cf. BVerfG StV 2000, 1; KG Berlin NStZ-RR 2001 204; Eisenberg (2002, 654).

[104] BGHSt 35, 328 (8.24.1988).

[105] BGH GA 1955, 246; StV 2005, 201;see also: BGH StV 1996, 76.

[106] OLG Hamm StV 1984, 456.

A breach of § 136a StPO brings about an automatic exclusion of evidence, which is applied without any restrictions to all suspects or co-defendants involved in the case, whether or not they were subject to coercion or ill-treatment.[107]

Cases of ill-treatment have led to heated discussions twice recently in Germany: (1) in relation to the admissibility of indirect evidence obtained by illegal questioning, as in the *Gäfgen* case; and (2) in relation to evidence received from a third country where "rough interrogation" methods or torture are still considered to be permissible in questioning suspects, such as in the *Motassadeq* case.[108] The admissibility of evidence in the *Gäfgen* case has been discussed above.[109] The *Motassadeq* case has not been discussed as intensely by academics, although it raises an important question with regard to international law enforcement: may a court use statements which have been allegedly obtained under torture in a third country? Although German courts acknowledge the exclusionary rule of Art. 15 of the United Nations Convention Against Torture in general (and would thus prohibit such tainted evidence),[110] they only suppress the statements, if inhuman ill-treatment during the overseas interrogation has actually been proved.[111]

5.3.2.4 Admissibility of Indirect Evidence (Fruits of the Poisonous Tree)

There is a heated discussion in Germany as to whether indirect evidence gained by forbidden treatment of a suspect is admissible.[112] Three positions can be distinguished. The first, reflecting a prevailing view in the case law, points to the silence in § 136a StPO with respect to exclusion of derivative evidence,[113] and thus considers it to be admissible, in particular if law enforcement agencies can point out a "hypothetical clean path" which would have eventually led to it.[114] However, not all courts follow this doctrine.[115] The second, opposing standpoint,[116] would clearly adopt

---

[107] For instance, in the *Gäfgen* case, the Frankfurt-on-Main regional court, in a decision of April 9, 2003, found that the threat to cause Gäfgen pain was illegal under § 136a StPO, Arts. 1, 104(1) GG, and Art. 3 ECHR, and required exclusion of the statements. But it refused to dismiss the case in its entirety, see furthermore: LG Stuttgart NStZ 1985 569; Eisenberg (2002, 712); but also: OLG Köln NJW 1979 1218.

[108] OLG Hamburg NJW 2005, 2326; Salditt (2008, 595).

[109] See Sect. 5.3.2.1.

[110] BVerfGE EuGRZ 1996, 328; BVerfG NJW 2004, 1858; OLG Hamburg NJW 2005, 2328; Schomburg et al. (2012, 430 f.).

[111] OLG Hamburg NJW 2005, 2326 (6.14.2005); BGH NStZ 2004, 343 (3.4. 2004); BGH NStZ 2008, 643–644.

[112] See Gless (2007, 626 f.), Eisenberg (2002, 714 f.), and Müssig (1999, 136 f.).

[113] BGHSt 34, 362 (28.04.1987), considering the hypothetical clean path OLG Hamburg MDR 1976, 601; OLG Stuttgart NJW 1973, 1941.

[114] See Sect. 5.1.2.3.3.

[115] See for example, LG Hannover StV 1986, 522.

[116] Eisenberg (2002, 714 f.), Grünwald (1993, 158), and Beulke (1991, 669).

the doctrine of the "fruit of the poisonous tree" and prohibit the use of any indirect evidence,[117] hoping that such an approach may deter police from using illegal questioning techniques.[118] Finally, a third, conciliatory approach both in court jurisprudence and the literature,[119] would require case-by-case balancing before a decision was made.

In the *Gäfgen* Case, the question was whether the continuous effect of the threat of violence against the defendant as well as the finding of the victim's body, which had become known to the investigation authorities through the statements extracted from Magnus Gäfgen, tainted all further statements, making them inadmissible in the on-going criminal proceedings. The Frankfurt am Main Regional Court took the conciliatory approach, mentioned above, and, after balancing under the particular circumstances of the case the flagrant violation of the fundamental rights of the defendant against the seriousness of the offense being investigated, decided not to exclude the subsequently obtained evidence.[120] Thus the Court ruled that the defendant's testimony at the trial could be taken into account by the court, since the defendant had been instructed anew about his right as a defendant to remain silent and nevertheless decided to confess in court.

5.3.2.5 Effect of International Human Rights Jurisprudence

Art. 3 ECHR provides: "No one shall be subjected to torture or to inhuman or degrading treatment or punishment". Whether and when this provision triggers an exclusion of evidence in German criminal proceedings was discussed recently in the *Gäfgen* Case. Gäfgen petitioned the ECtHR claiming a violation of Art. 6 ECHR of his right to a fair trial, and, among other rights, his right not to incriminate himself.[121]

In its judgment the ECtHR stresses that Art. 3 ECHR enshrines one of the most fundamental values of democratic societies. The said article does not make any provision for exceptions and prohibits inhuman treatment such as Gäfgen was subjected to. Consistent with its previous case law, however, the ECtHR conceded

---

[117] From a U.S. and comparative perspective: Thaman (2001, 581); on U.S. doctrine, see Forbes (1987, 1221).

[118] For a comparative view (from a German perspective) see: Harris (1991, 313) and Salditt (1992, 59); on the consideration of hypothetical investigative paths in German criminal procedure: Jahn and Dallmeyer (2005, 297 f.)

[119] BGHSt 27, 329 (12.21.1977); BGHSt 29, 244, 249 (18.04.1980); BGHSt 34, 362, 364 (8.28.1987); OLG Stuttgart NJW 1973, 1942.

[120] LG Frankfurt StV 2003, 325: "Balancing the severity of the interference with the defendant's fundamental rights – in the present case the threat of physical violence – and the seriousness of the offense he was charged with and which had to be investigated – the completed murder of a child – makes the exclusion of evidence which has become known as a result of the defendant's statement – in particular the discovery of the dead child and the results of the autopsy – appear disproportionate".

[121] Gäfgen v. Germany (2009), 48 E.H.R.R. 13, 253.

that it would not decide on the admissibility of a particular type of evidence, but only whether the proceedings as a whole, including the way in which the evidence was obtained, had been fair.[122] It pointed out that evidence recovered by measures found to be in breach of Art. 3 ECHR, such as Gäfgen's confessions obtained by means of torture or other ill-treatment, always raises serious questions as to the fairness of the proceedings[123] and most probably renders the proceedings as a whole unfair, irrespective of whether the admission of the evidence was decisive in securing the applicant's conviction.[124]

Nevertheless, dissecting the details of the case, the Court eventually concluded that the use of the specific items of indirect evidence in the *Gäfgen* Case did not fall within the category of cases in which such use automatically renders the trial unfair under all circumstances. It emphasized that the German courts had excluded not only the coerced statements as such, but also all other statements that might have been made as a result of the continuous effect of the ill-treatment in violation of Art. 3 ECHR. However, there were enough "reliable" items of evidence left in order to uphold Gäfgen's conviction, like the defendant's DNA found on the ransom and at the location where the corpse was found.[125]

5.3.3 The Protection Against Unknowing Self-Incrimination: The Miranda Paradigm

5.3.3.1 Constitutional Provisions Requiring Admonititions as to the Right to Silence/Counsel

The constitution does not offer an explicit provision protecting the defendant from unknowing self-incrimination. But the BGH held in an early judgment, that the *Miranda*-type[126] warning of § 136 (1) StPO expresses a foundational principle in a criminal procedure based on the rule of law, which is designed to uphold the respect for human dignity.[127]

---

[122] Ibid, 279.

[123] Ibid, 279–280. with reference to İçöz v. Turkey, no. 54919/00, ECHR, 9 January 2003; Jalloh v. Germany (G.C.), 44 E.H.R.R. 32, 667, 693 §§ 99, 104; Göçmen v. Turkey, no. 72000/01, ECHR, 17 October 2006, § 73; and Harutyunyan v. Armenia (2009) 49 E.H.R.R. 9, 202, 218, § 63.

[124] Gäfgen v. Germany, 48 E.H.R.R. 13, 253, 280, with reference to Harutyunyan v. Armenia, 49 E.H.R.R., 202, 218–219, §§ 63, 66 and *Göçmen*, §§ 74–75.

[125] Gäfgen v. Germany, 48 E.H.R.R. 13, 253, 283.

[126] Unlike Miranda, however, this warning does not require the suspect to be in custody. For further information see: Thaman (2001, 584).

[127] BGHSt 14, 361, 364–365 (6.14.1960); see Sect. 5.1.1.

5.3.3.2 Statutory Provisions on Admonition of Right to Silence/Counsel

§§136 (1), 163a(3,4) StPO oblige all law enforcement agencies to instruct a defendant[128]: "At the commencement of the first examination the accused shall be informed of the offense with which he[/she] is charged and of the applicable penal provisions. He[/she] shall be advised that the law grants him[/her] the right to respond to the accusation", or to remain silent, and at all times "to consult with a defense counsel of his/her choice".

5.3.3.3 High Court Jurisprudence Interpreting the Effects of Violations of the Above Provisions on the Admissibility of Illegally Seized Evidence

In previous case law interpreting § 136 (1) StPO, advising the accused of his/her rights was not mandatory, but "advisory" and in case of default did not automatically result in the exclusion of confessions or self-incriminating statements.[129] In its recent jurisprudence, however, the BGH now requires the exclusion of statements, if the law enforcement agencies interrogate a person without giving prior and adequate information about his/her right to remain silent or to consult with a defense attorney.[130] In 1993, the BGH finally rejected a predominant feature of the inquisitorial model of criminal procedure and emphasized, that the defendant was a party not merely an object of criminal proceedings. Legal scholars have embraced this decision.[131] The admonitions required by § 136 (1) StPO must be given "when the suspicion already present at the beginning of the interrogation has so thickened that the suspect can seriously be considered a perpetrator of the investigated crime".[132] The duty to admonish arises regardless of who is doing the questioning, be it the police, the prosecutor or a judge. If the extraction of information, however, is not carried out during a *formal* interview, the approach to giving the admonitions is different.

Official Interrogations by Law Enforcement Agencies

German courts oblige law enforcement agencies to give qualified instructions to the suspect before an interrogation is conducted. It is essential that the suspect's right to remain silent is not undermined and that the accused is aware of the privilege.

---

[128] The duty to caution was introduced in 1964, albeit in a different mode; Gless (2010, 79–90).

[129] See BGHSt 22, 129 (4.30.1968). See also BGHSt 22, 170 (5.31.1968); BGHSt 31, 395 (6.7.1983). In 1974, the BGH held that the administration of the required warning in the judicial phase was mandatory.

[130] BGHSt 39, 349, 352 (10.12.1993).

[131] Rieß (1993, 334).

[132] BGH NStZ 2007, 653, 654; BGHSt 37, 48 (5.31.1990); BGHSt 38, 214, 228 (2.27.1992); BGHSt 40, 211 (7.21.1994).

The admonition has to be repeated should there be any doubts about whether the suspect understood it.[133] However, if an interrogator only finds out during the questioning that a person examined as a witness actually turns out to be a suspect, he/she must not only inform the person of his/her right to refuse to give evidence, but also of the fact that nothing which had been said so far may be used as evidence in the subsequent proceedings ("qualifizierte Belehrung").[134]

Although the case law has been rather defendant-friendly, courts do acknowledge exceptions to the exclusionary rule and admit statements gained during an interview without proper cautioning, if the accused knew his rights (e.g. from earlier proceedings).[135]

Unofficial/Undercover Extraction of Information from the Defendant

The case law struggles to handle situations where information is gathered during *informal* interview situations, in particular in the context of secret surveillance and undercover investigations. In these situations, the duty to give qualified admonitions is neglected, and the suspect is exposed to overreaching. For example, if an undercover agent is placed in the cell of an incarcerated suspect, the evidence obtained may not be used at trial, but the courts leave open the possibility of its use as a lead to find further untainted evidence.[136]

In general the courts tend to admit information gathered by undercover police officers and in doing so roughly follow the rules of admissibility applied in wiretapping. According to this approach, evidence would be inadmissible, if the measure would have been illegal from the outset, but would be admissible, if only minor formal regulations have been violated.[137] Statements are inadmissible, if an undercover agent purposely questions a defendant in order to circumvent the privilege against self-incrimination.[138] In doing so he dirties his hands and taints the evidence.

The admission of information obtained by private persons, including police informants, is governed by different rules, the focus being on the protection of privacy and a minimum standard of what is a "fair trial", rather than the "clean hands" approach. An illustrative example is offered by the case law on telephone entrapment ("Hörfallen"), where a private person induces a suspect to talk on the

---

[133] BGHSt 39, 349 (10.12.1993).

[134] BGH (12.18.2008) – 4 StR 455/08 mit Anmerkung: Gless and Wennekers (2009, 380–385); BGHSt 51, 367 (7.3.2007).

[135] BGHSt 47, 172 (11.22.2001) (Pizzeria Murder Case): defendant knew from other criminal proceedings about his right to consult a lawyer and asked for one.

[136] BGHSt 34, 362 (4.28.1987); Schneider (2001, 8).

[137] For further information see: Beulke (2008, 295).

[138] BGHSt 31, 304 (3.17.1983); BGH NJW 2007, 3138; see also BGHSt 33, 217 (5.9.1985).

phone while police officers are overhearing the conversation.[139] Such information is admissible as evidence, if used in the prosecution of a serious crime, and if the lack of the information would significantly jeopardize the investigation.[140] However, information gathered with the help of private persons may be used as evidence in criminal proceedings, but with restrictions which guarantee a minimum of "fair trial" and privacy.[141] If, for example, the police plant an informant into the cell of an incarcerated person, who cannot retreat into his/her own sphere of privacy, the information obtained may not be used as evidence, because law enforcement agents have intentionally avoided a formal interrogation preceded by warnings, advising the suspect of the right to silence, and counsel, etc.[142]

The courts justify the different rules for handling evidence gained in informal undercover police questionings on the one hand, and formal questionings on the other, on the grounds that only during official interrogations is the accused confronted with the authority of law enforcement and must respond to an accusation.[143] During informal interviews or private conversations, on the other hand, he/she is free to reveal some knowledge or keep silent. Such a formalistic approach, however, has been criticized, because it fails to take into consideration that both situations – formal and informal interrogations – serve law enforcement and thus must trigger respect for the defendants' rights.[144]

5.3.3.4 Admissibility of Indirect Evidence (Fruits of the Poisonous Tree)[145]

As was explained above, the prevailing view in Germany recognizes neither the doctrine of "fruits of the poisonous tree" nor a strict rule against hearsay. Information gathered by undercover agents may, in principle, be funneled into the trial by questioning the contact officer, since hearsay evidence is admissible under certain circumstances and may also be used to further the investigation.[146]

---

[139] BGHSt 39, 335, 348 (10.8.1993); BGH NStZ 1995, 410; BGH NStZ 1996, 200; see further: BVerfG NStZ 2000, 489.

[140] BGHSt 42, 139–145 (5.13.1996).

[141] BGHSt 44, 129 (7.21.1998).

[142] BGHSt 34, 362 (4.28.1987).

[143] BGHSt 42, 139–145 (5.13.1996); BGHSt 44, 129 (7.21.1998); Lesch (1999, 638); Müssig (1999,126 f.); compare with. BVerfG NStZ 2000, 489.

[144] Gless (2007, 539), Roxin (1995, 18), and Weßlau (1998, 20 f.).

[145] As with coerced or involuntary confessions, here the question is whether physical evidence found (weapon, drugs, etc.) may be used, even where the statement itself is not usable. A more sophisticated question is whether a subsequent confession preceded by the proper admonitions, may be used following a confession taken without the proper admonitions.

[146] BGHSt 34, 362 (4.28.1987).

5.4 Conclusion

In summing up this report on German law and its approach to the use of illegally obtained evidence in criminal proceedings, one must state that the doctrine presents no clear-cut image, but rather gives the impression of an emerging mosaic without a plan for completion.

However, two basic patterns constantly recur. The first is based on Beling's doctrine of "clean hands", which more recently has been often combined with a "fair trial" approach. Following this doctrine, the courts exclude evidence obtained in breach of procedural rules, not only where statutes like § 136a StPO explicitly require it, but also in other cases of grave breach of defendants' rights.

In the latter situations, statements obtained through interrogation are excluded where the *Miranda*-like admonitions have been neglected. However, in certain situations German courts will weigh the interests of the defendant against broader law enforcement interests, and often reject the remedy of exclusion. This "balancing theory" has been consistently criticized in academia. Nevertheless it must be noted that the approach of the German case law is rather similar to that of French or English judges when it comes to deciding whether to exercise the discretion to exclude evidence. In those countries, the following aspects are considered: (1) the severity of the violation in relation to the gravity of the offense under investigation; (2) the effect of the violation breach on the credibility of the evidence; (3) the "technical" nature of the breach, in the sense that, had the proper procedure been followed, the evidence would have been lawfully obtained.

The second basic pattern concerns the protection of privacy. Following this doctrine, courts exclude evidence which was obtained or used in a manner which violated the defendant's basic right to privacy, derived from the constitutionally protected "universal personality rights" ("allgemeines Persönlichkeitsrecht"). The underlying theory is that, in view of the constitution, there is an absolute sphere of privacy which bans the use of evidence obviously stemming from a person's private life, such as diaries, tape-recordings of conversations in intimate/private surroundings, etc., which if not protected would impair free development of the personality.

There are different possible explanations for the way the law is developing, as well as for the lack of a master plan. First, in a changing society with ever new technological inventions we are constantly faced with new questions and challenges in this area. Secondly, we are dealing with different legal frameworks. Like other European jurisdictions, today's German criminal justice system is shaped by a code of criminal procedure dating from the nineteenth century, while, at the same time, based on a rather modern constitution, interpreted by ambitious courts. The German doctrine on exclusionary rules reflects the patchwork combination of those two basic regimes, and German jurisprudence strives to reconcile law enforcement interests and the inquisitorial search for truth with basic rights.

German courts have handed down a complex and complicated body of case law with regard to the admission or exclusion of illegally obtained evidence. In spite of some struggle and warranted critique from academia, it is important to acknowledge that

German jurisprudence has achieved a high standard when it comes to guaranteeing "due process" and has consented to limiting the types of evidence which can be used to ascertain the truth in order to protect the rights of defendants. Thus, while it has traditionally been assumed that exclusionary rules are more prevalent in systems adhering to the adversarial system,[147] Germany, coming from an inquisitorial regime, has moved towards the protection of the criminal suspects' right to a fair trial and right to privacy and human dignity by enforcing exclusionary rules.

Bibliography

Altenhain, K. 2010. Absprachen in German criminal trials. In *World plea bargaining*, ed. S.C. Thaman, 157–179. Durham: Carolina Academic Press.

Amelung, K. 1990a. *Informationsbeherrschungsrechte im Strafprozess*, Schriften zum Prozessrecht, Berlin: Duncker & Humblot.

Amelung, K. 1990b. Die zweite Tagebuchentscheidung des BVerfG. *Neue Juristische Wochenschrift* 1755–1760.

Baldus, C. 2008. Der Kernbereich privater Lebensgestaltung – absolut geschützt, aber abwägungsoffen. *JuristenZeitung* 218–227.

Basdorf, C. 1997. Formellee und informelle Präklusion im Strafverfahren – Mitwirkungspflichten und gesteigerte Verantwortung des Verteidigers. *Der Strafverteidiger* 488–493.

Baum, G.R., and P. Schantz. 2008. Die Novelle des BKA-Gesetzes – Eine rechtspolitische und verfassungsrechtliche Kritik. *Zeitschrift für Rechtspolitik* 137–140.

Beling, E. 1903. *Die Beweisverbote als Grenzen der Wahrheitsfindung im Strafprozess*. Breslau: Schletter'sche Buchhandlung.

Beling, E. 1928. *Deutsches Reichsstrafprozessrecht mit Einschluss des Strafgerichtsverfassungsrechts*. Berlin/Leipzig: W. de Gruyter & Co.

Beulke, W. 1991. Hypothetische Kausalverläufe im Strafverfahren bei rechtswidrigem Vorgehen von Ermittlungsorganen, *Zeitschrift für die gesamte Strafrechtswissenschaft* 657–680.

Beulke, W. 2008. *Strafprozessrecht*, 10th ed. Heidelberg: C.F. Müller.

Bosch, N. 1998. *Aspekte des nemo tenetur-Grundsatzes aus verfassungsrechtlicher und strafprozessualer Sicht*. Berlin: Duncker & Humblot.

Böse, M. 2002. Die verfassungsrechtlichen Grundlagen des Satzes Nemo tenetur se ipsum accusare. *Goltdammer's Archiv für Strafrecht* 98–128.

Eisenberg, U. 2002. *Beweisrecht der StPO, Spezialkommentar*, 4th ed. Munich: C.H. Beck.

Forbes, J. 1987. The inevitable discovery exception, primary evidence, and the emasculation of the fourth amendment. *Fordham Law Review* 55: 1221–1238.

Frase, R., and T. Weigend. 1995. German Criminal Justice as a Guide to American Law Reform: Similar Problems, Better Solution? *Boston College International and Comparative Law Review* 18: 317–360.

Gaede, K. 2007. *Fairness als Teilhabe: Das Recht auf konkrete und wirksame Verteidigung gemäß Art. 6 EMRK*. Berlin: Duncker und Humblot.

Gless, S. 2006. *Beweisrechtsgrundsätze einer grenzüberschreitenden Strafverfolgung*. Baden-Baden: Nomos.

Gless, S. 2007. *Löwe/Rosenberg-Kommentar zur Strafprozessordnung*, vol. 4, 26th ed. Berlin: De Gruyter Recht.

[147] Weigend (2003, 168–169).

Gless, S. 2010. Der Nemo tenetur-Grundsatz: ein Erbe Napoleons im deutschen, französischen und europäischen Recht. In *200 Jahre Code d'Instruction Criminelle*, ed. H. Jung, J. Leblois-Happe, and C. Witz, 79–90. Baden-Baden: Nomos.

Gless, S., and J. Wennekers. 2009. Anmerkungen zum Urteil vom 18.12.2008 – 4 StR 455/08 (BGHSt 51 367). *Juristische Rundschau* 380–385.

Godenzi, G. 2008. Das strafprozessuale Verbot staatlicher Beweismittelhehlerei: Königsweg oder Luftschloss?. *Goltdammer's Archiv für Strafrecht* 500–515.

Grünwald, G. 1966. Beweisverbote und Verwertungsverbote im Strafverfahren. *JuristenZeitung* 489–501.

Grünwald, G. 1993. *Beweisrecht der Strafprozessordnung*. Baden-Baden: Nomos.

Grünwald, G. 1981. Probleme der Gegenüberstellung zum Zwecke der Wiedererkennung. *JuristenZeitung* 423–428.

Hackethal, A. 2005. *Der Einsatz von Vomitivmitteln zur Beweissicherung im Strafverfahren*. Berlin: Duncker und Humblot.

Hamm, R. 1996. Staatliche Hilfe bei der Suche nach Verteidigern – Verteidigerhilfe zur Begründung von Verwertungsverboten. *Neue Juristische Wochenschrift* 2185–2190.

Hamm, R. 2003. Schluss der Debatte über Ausnahmen vom Folterverbot!. *Neue Juristische Wochenschau* 946–947.

Harris, K. 1991. Verwertungsverbot für mittelbar erlangte Beweismittel: Die Fernwirkungsdoktrin in der Rechtsprechung im deutschen und amerikanischen Recht. *Der Strafverteidiger* 313–322.

Hecker, W. 2003. Relativierung des Folterverbots in der BRD?. *Kritische Justiz* 210–218.

Hilgendorf, E. 2004. Folter im Rechtsstaat?. *JuristenZeitung* 331–339.

Hohmann-Dennhardt, C. 2006. Freiräume – Zum Schutz der Privatheit. *Neue Juristische Wochenschrift* 545–549.

Hönig, S. 2004. *Die strafmildernden Wirkung eines Geständnisses im Lichte der Strafzwecke*. Frankfurt am Main: Peter Lang.

Jahn, M. 2000. Zu BHG, Beschl. V. 13.10.1999 (2 BJs 112/97-2 – StB 10 und 11/99) – Beschlagnahme von Notiz- und Taschenkalendern. *Neue Zeitschrift für Strafrecht* 383–385.

Jahn, M., and J. Dallmeyer. 2005. Zum heutigen Stand der beweisrechtlichen Berücksichtigung hypothetischer Ermittlungsverläufe im deutschen Strafverfahrensrecht. *Neue Zeitschrift für Strafrecht* 297–304.

Jerouschek, G., and R. Kölbel. 2003. Folter von Staats wegen. *JuristenZeitung* 613–620.

Kinzig, J. 2003. Not kennt kein Gebot?: Die strafrechtlichen Konsequenzen von Folterhandlungen an Tatverdächtigen durch Polizeibeamte mit präventiver Zielsetzung. *Zeitschrift für die gesamte Strafrechtswissenschaft* 791–814.

Koriath, H. 1994. *Über Beweisverbote im Strafprozess*. Frankfurt am Main/New York: P. Lang.

Kutscha, M. 2007. Verdeckte 'On-line' Durchsuchung und Unverletzlichkeit der Wohnung. *Neue Juristische Wochenschrift* 1169–1172.

Lesch, H. 1999. Inquisition und rechtliches Gehör in der Beschuldigtenvernehmung. *Zeitschrift für die gesamte Strafrechtswissenschaft* 624–646.

Lindemann, M. 2006. Der Schutz des ‚Kernbereichs privater Lebensgestaltung' im Strafverfahren. *Juristische Rundschau* 191–198.

Meurer, D. 1990. Anmerkung zum BGH Urteil vom 17.2.1989 – 2StR 402/88 (BGHSt 36, 119). *Juristische Rundschau* 389–392.

Miebach, K. 2000. Der teilschweigende Angeklagte – materiell-rechtliche und prozessuale Fragen anhand der BGH-Rechtsprechung. *Neue Zeitschrift für Strafrecht* 234–242.

Müssig, B. 1999. Beweisverbote im Legitimationszusammenhang von Strafrechtstheorie und Strafverfahren. *Goltdammer's Archiv für Strafrecht* 119–142.

Neumann, U. 1998. Mitwirkungs- und Duldungspflichten des Beschuldigten bei körperlichen Eingriffen im Strafverfahren. In *Festschrift für E.A. Wolff*, ed. R. Zaczyk, M. Köhler, and M. Kahlo, 373–393. Berlin/New York: Springer.

Otto, H. 1970. Grenzen und Tragweite der Beweisverbote im Strafverfahren. *Goltdammer's Archiv für Strafrecht* 289–305.

Rieß, P. 1993. Anmerkung zum BGH Urteil vom 29.10.1992 – 4 StR 126/92 (BGHSt 38, 372). *Juristische Rundschau* 334–335.

Rogall, K. 1996. Über die Folgen der rechtswidrigen Beschaffung des Zeugenbeweises im Strafprozess, *JuristenZeitung* 944–955.

Rogall, K. 1998. Hypothetische Ermittlungsverläufe im Strafprozess. *Neue Zeitschrift für Strafrecht* 66–68.

Rogall, K. 2004. Vernehmung des Beschuldigten – §136 Erste Vernehmung. In *Systematischer Kommentar zur Strafprozessordnung und zum Gerichtsverfassungsgesetz*, ed. H.J. Rudolphi, W. Frisch, K. Rogall, E. Schlüchter, J. Wolter, and H.U. Paeffgen. Cologne: Carl Heymanns Verlag.

Ross, J. 2005. Germany's Federal constitutional court and the regulation of GPS surveillance. *German Law Journal* 6(12): 1805–1812. http://www.germanlawjournal.com/.

Roxin, C. 1989. Anmerkung zum BGH Urteil vom 15.2.1989. *Neue Zeitschrift für Strafrecht* 375–379.

Roxin, C. 1995. Nemo tenetur: die Rechtsprechung am Scheideweg. *Neue Zeitschrift für Strafrecht* 465–469.

Roxin, C. 2007. Anmerkung zum BGH Urteil vom 3.7.2007. *Der Strafverteidiger* 450–452.

Rudolphi, H-J. 1970. Die Revisibilität von Verfahrensmängeln im Strafprozess. *Monatsschrift für Deutsches Recht* 93–99.

Salditt, F. 1992. 25 Jahre Miranda – Rückblick auf ein höchstrichterliches Experiment. *Goltdammer's Archiv für Strafrecht* 51–75.

Salditt, F. 2008. Bruchstellen eines Menschenrechts, Schweigen gefährdet. In *Festschrift für Rainer Hamm*, ed. R. Michalka and W. Köberer. Berlin: De Gruyter.

Saliger, F. 2004. Absolutes im Strafprozess? Über Das Folterverbot, seine Verletzung und die Folgen seiner Verletzung. *Zeitschrift für die gesamte Strafrechtswissenschaft* 35–65.

Schneider, H. 2001. Verdeckte Ermittlungen in Haftanstalten. *Neue Zeitschrift für Strafrecht* 8–15.

Schomburg, W., O. Lagodny, S. Gless, and T. Hackner. 2012. *Internationale Rechtshilfe in Strafsachen*. Munich: C.H. Beck.

Simon, O. 1998. *Die Beschuldigtenrechte nach Art. 6 Abs. 3 EMRK*. Tübingen: Köhler Druck.

Spencer, J.R. 2002. Evidence. In *European criminal procedures*, ed. M. Delmas-Marty and J.R. Spencer, 594–640. Cambridge: Cambridge University Press.

Thaman, S.C. 2001. Miranda in comparative law. *Saint Louis University Law Journal* 45: 581–622.

Torka, R. 2000. *Nachtatverhalten und Nemo tenetur*. Berlin: Duncker und Humblot.

Verrel, T. 2001. *Die Selbstbelastungsfreiheit im Strafverfahren*. Munich: C.H. Beck.

Weigend, T. 2003. Is the criminal process about truth?: A German perspective. *Harvard Journal of Law and Public Policy* 26: 157–173.

Weigend, T. 2007. Germany. In *Criminal procedure. A worldwide study*, 2nd ed, ed. C.M. Bradley, 243–272. Durham: Carolina Academic Press.

Weßlau, E. 1997. Anmerkung zu OLG Frankfurt/M. 1Ss 28/96 vom 11.10.1996 Beweisverwertungsverbot infolge Zwangsvergabe von Brechmitteln; kurzfristige Freiheitsstrafe. *Der Strafverteidiger* 341–344.

Weßlau, E. 1998. Zwang, Täuschung und Heimlichkeit im Strafverfahren. *Zeitschrift für die gesamte Strafrechtswissenschaft* 1–35.

Weßlau, E. 2003. Das Konsensprinzip im Strafverfahren. *Der Strafverteidiger* 483–484.

Wohlers, W. 1995. BGH, Urteil vom 10.8.1994 – 3 StR 53/94. *Neue Zeitschrift für Strafrecht* 45–46.

Wolter, J. 1993. Verfassungsrecht im Strafprozess- und Strafrechtssystem. *Neue Zeitschrift für Strafrecht* 1–10.

Wolters, G. 1999. Anmerkung zum BGH Urteil vom 11.11.1998 – 3 StR 181/98 (BGHSt 44, 243). *Juristische Rundschau* 524–525.

Part II
From Nullities to Statutory Exclusionary Rules in Continental Europe

Chapter 6
France: Procedural Nullities and Exclusion

Jean Pradel

6.1 The General Theory of Admissibility of Illegally Obtained Evidence

6.1.1 Introduction

Evidence – "that which persuades the mind of the truth" according to Domat – is at the heart of the criminal justice system[1]: indeed, taking into consideration the principle of the presumption of innocence, a guilty verdict cannot survive unless proof of the guilt of the accused is established. Additionally, the proof of the facts must be done properly, that is, established by legally correct means. If all evidence is theoretically admissible (the rule of the freedom of evidence), its administration is nevertheless subject to conditions (rule of legality in the administration of evidence). In France there is a general theory about the admissibility of illegally gathered evidence, in connection with which we will emphasize two of its applications, one regarding the right to privacy and the other regulating interrogations.

In the French Code of Criminal Procedure (CCP) no general law exists (no title, chapter, or section) governing evidence. Instead, the material is scattered throughout the rules governing investigations by the judicial police, preparatory

---

Translated from the French by Josuha Walker and Stephen C. Thaman.

[1] According to H. Lévy-Bruhl, "evidence is the process by which a fact or a right in controversy and in doubt acquires by means of a judgment in which it is implicated, the value of truth" Lévy-Bruhl (1964, 7).

J. Pradel (✉)
Professor Emeritus, University of Poitiers, 33, rue des Couronneries, 86000 Poitiers, France
e-mail: isabelle.michaud@univ-poitiers.fr

S.C. Thaman (ed.), *Exclusionary Rules in Comparative Law*, Ius Gentium: Comparative Perspectives on Law and Justice 20, DOI 10.1007/978-94-007-5348-8_6,

examinations by investigating magistrates, or trial court jurisdiction. We must also keep in mind the European Court of Human Rights (hereinafter ECtHR) and the *Cour de cassation* (in its Criminal Chambers). We will look one by one into the decisions of the Constitutional Council,[2] the ECtHR,[3] and into the law, including the CCP and case law of the Criminal Chambers which deals with the CCP's application.

6.1.2 Decisions of the Constitutional Council

In policing the conformity of the law to the "block of constitutionality", the nine judges of the Constitutional Council have rendered decisions concerning the rules of evidence as intended by the legislature. These decisions are based upon the Declaration of Human Rights and Rights of Citizens of August 1789 and the preamble to the constitution of October 1958 (which itself references the preamble to the 1946 constitution, which lays out the famous "fundamental principles recognized by the laws of the Republic").

Some decisions have affirmed the principle of respect for the *rights of the defense*. Although undefined, this principle "results from the fundamental principles recognized by the laws of the Republic".[4] Included among these rights of the defense is "the right of the subject to meet with a lawyer while being detained even if the exercise of this right may give rise to differences depending on the nature of the offense".[5] The Constitutional Council has also recognized the equality of arms in challenging the evidence (*principe du contradictoire*). According to this principle, the suspect must have access to the procedural material and be allowed to respond to the accusations against her.[6]

Other decisions have enshrined the principle of human dignity (or the respect thereof). The concept is rather vague and it rests, according to the nine council members, upon a passage of the preamble to the Constitution of 1946 according to which "all human beings… possess certain sacred and inalienable rights".[7] This principle of dignity could lead to a declaration of unconstitutionality of any violation of the law during investigations and searches. There has never been a case that has done so, at least not yet.

---

[2] Pradel (2003, 84) and Sciortino-Bayart (2000).

[3] Pradel et al. (2009, no. 250, 231).

[4] CC decision no. 76–70 DC, Dec. 2, 1976; Jan. 19–20, 1981; Jan. 23, 1999.

[5] CC decision no. 93-326 DC, Aug. 11, 1993, JCP 1993 II no. 66355; CC decision no. 04-492 DC, Mar. 2, 2004. There has been talk of the constitutionalization of the role of the lawyer.

[6] CC decision no. 99-416 DC, July 23, 1999; CC decision no. 92-307 DC, Feb. 25, 1992; Julien-Laferrière, 1992 AJDA 656.

[7] CC decision no. 94-343-344 DC, July 27, 1994, RJC I 592.

So we see, the gathering of evidence is limited by the constitution. Can the same be said for decisions of the ECtHR?[8]

6.1.3 *Decisions of the ECtHR*

A small number of texts touch our subject.[9] We shall cite the two main ones.[10] The basic text is Art. 6 European Convention of Human Rights (hereinafter ECHR) on the right to a fair trial. Subsection § 3 establishes: "Everyone charged with a criminal offense has the following minimum rights:

(a) to be informed…of the nature and cause of the accusation against him;
(b) to have adequate time and facilities for the preparation of his defense;
(c) to defend himself in person or through legal assistance of his own choosing or, if he has not sufficient means to pay for legal assistance, to be given it free…;
(d) to examine or have examined witnesses against him and to obtain the attendance and examination of witnesses on his behalf under the same conditions as witnesses against him;
(e) to have the free assistance of an interpreter…"

The judges of the ECtHR construe these rights liberally, even more so because it is not an exhaustive list as seen by the adjective "minimum". Cases have addressed in a clear manner the question of the value of illegally obtained evidence. These decisions do not necessarily involve France, but they do interest France because it is understood that decisions of the ECtHR apply throughout the 47 member states of the Council of Europe. The principle the ECtHR has decided upon when ruling on evidence gathered in violation of national law, is that: "the convention…does not lay down any rules on the admissibility of evidence as such, which is therefore primarily a matter for regulation under national law".[11] European judges would not in principle rule *in abstracto* on the admissibility of evidence gathered in an illegal manner. Their duty only involves looking into whether the petitioner's trial comes across in its totality as being "fair".[12] In a case where the guilt of the accused was established by means of a wiretap, the Swiss avoided condemnation by the court for

---

[8] It should be remembered that they affect both the legislature and national judges. Indeed, according to Art. 46 ECHR "Any of the High Contracting Parties may at any time declare that it recognizes as compulsory 'ipso facto' and without special agreement the jurisdiction of the Court in all matters concerning the interpretation and application of the present Convention." In practice, condemnations of states lead them inevitably to modify their laws and/or their jurisprudence.

[9] For a recent detailed general study, see Renucci (2007).

[10] We could also include Art. 3 ECHR on torture and inhumane and degrading treatment, which we will save until the third section.

[11] Schenk v. Switzerland, (1991), 13 E.H.R.R. 242, 265–266, § 46; for a very similar formulation Barberà, Messegué & Jabardo v. Spain (1989), 11 E.H.R.R. 360, 384–385, § 68.

[12] Schenk v. Switzerland, 13 E.H.R.R. 242, 265–266.

two reasons: the accused had the opportunity to challenge the authenticity of the recordings in question and the recordings were not the only means of proof used as the foundation of the guilty verdict.[13] The ECtHR approaches this principle with caution for two reasons. First, the administration of criminal evidence is a question of national law according to the doctrine recognizing a "margin of appreciation". Second, the condemnation of a state is impossible unless the procedure, in its entirety, was unfair and/or there was an express violation of the ECHR, such as Art. 3 ECHR on torture and inhuman or degrading treatment or punishment.

The same spirit is found in Article 8 ECHR: "Everyone has the right to respect for his private and family life, his home and his correspondence. There shall be no interference by a public authority with the exercise of this right except such as is in accordance with the law and is necessary in a democratic society in the interests of…the prevention of disorder or crime".

Many decisions by the ECtHR have found proceedings to be fair for the purposes of Art. 6 ECHR where the guilt of the accused was established in violation of Art. 8 ECHR.[14] We would be looking in vain however for a general theory of penalties for the illegal gathering of evidence. Here again, the ECtHR essentially tosses the issue back to national law.

6.1.4 National Law and Its Jurisprudence

French law, like many of its continental European counterparts, speaks of evidentiary nullities and not of exclusion of evidence as does the common law.[15] Generally, French law follows a policy of restricting nullities: the legislature has multiplied the hurdles to declaring nullities and judges follow this same paradigm.[16] The doctrine is far-reaching.[17]

Dealing first with cases of nullities, French law has two categories. First, there are textual (or formal) nullities, established by the legislature: these lay down rules that end with the words "under penalty of nullity" or some analogous expression. Textual nullities are for irregularities concerning searches and seizures (§§ 56, 56-1, 57, 59, 76, 95, and 96 CCP) or wiretapping a lawyer without informing the president of the bar association (§100-7 CCP). Next are substantive (or virtual) irregularities as

---

[13] Ibid, 266, § 47.

[14] Khan v. United Kingdom (2001), 31 E.H.R.R. 45; P.G. v. United Kingdom (2008), 46 E.H.R.R. 51; Allan v. United Kingdom (2003), 36 E.H.R.R. 12.

[15] For a general comparison, see Pradel (2008, 240).

[16] The president of the criminal chamber is the renowned Maurice Patin, who in the 1960's wrote many notes defending his theory founded on the trust due to the judge and regarding the disasters resulting from nullities, including in relation to public opinion.

[17] Guinchard and Buisson (2011, 1293), Desportes and Lazerges-Cousquer (2009, 1230), and Pradel (2011, 684).

provided by § 171 CCP, which are not established by statute, but were invented by case law in two areas: (1) rules concerning public order, which means that they deal with the greatest concerns of the judicial system, such as judicial incompetence, the absence of a date on a document, the failure of an expert witness to swear an oath or a failure to question the accused; (2) the rights of the defense, but only if the violation of a rule causes prejudice to a party, essentially meaning prejudice to the accused.

This last rule was enshrined by a statute that extended it to textual nullities. A 1975 law introduced § 802 CCP, which provides: "In the event of a violation of formalities prescribed by law under penalty of nullity or in the event of a non-observance of substantive formalities, any court, the Court of cassation included, which is seised of an application for annulment, or which raises such an irregularity on its own motion, may pronounce the nullity only where this has had the effect of damaging the interests of the party concerned". Thus, and as if by retrenchment, only substantive nullities affecting public policy fall outside § 802 CCP and must, therefore, bring about the nullity of the act.

This expression, "the effect of damaging the interests", is vital. The purpose of this was to "strangle" nullities. It requires some sort of harm, some grievance suffered by the pleading party in order for him to triumph in his motion for a nullity. This grievance is taken into consideration *in concreto*: there must have been real prejudice, which actually harmed the defense. What matters is the gravity of the prejudice suffered by the pleading party, not the procedural error committed by the judge or the investigators.[18] For example, a grievance has been suffered if the investigating judge fails to provide his client (the accused) with an attorney during the first interrogation, or an expert's report that led to the indictment.[19] In practice, judges presented with a request for nullity usually reject it, largely by applying § 802 CCP.[20]

The implementation of nullities falls to two jurisdictions: (1) the *chambre de l'instruction*, a section of the court of appeals (with three judges) which rules on nullities committed by *juges d'instruction* (investigating magistrates) and the judicial police and; (2) the trial judge, who cannot rule on nullities, unless seised by a means other than that of the decision of the investigating magistrate. Indeed, when an investigation is opened, the investigating magistrate "purges" the nullities, and they may not be raised before the trial judge. Because all crimes and serious misdemeanors are the object of an investigation, the *Cour d'assises* (jury court) and certain criminal courts may not annul prior procedures. This system generally sterilizes nullities before they reach the trial judge. The legislature thought that raising a nullity before the trial court risked sabotaging the proceedings when they were on the verge of being completed. The party requesting that a nullity be declared, therefore, should do so in all haste, before the trial court is seised.

---

[18] Which leaves a large amount of discretion to the judge of nullities.

[19] Cass. crim., Jan. 29, 2003, Bull. crim., No. 22.

[20] Statistically, for each decision to nullify there are three decisions refusing to do so.

What are the effects of a nullity? Should they be limited to the nullified act or should they extend to subsequent acts, as would the American theory of the "fruit of the poisonous tree"? According to §§ 147 paragraph 2 and 206 CCP, the judge "decides if the nullity should be limited to all or part of the acts or pieces of evidence of the vitiated proceedings or should extend to all or part of subsequent proceedings". These texts apply only to the investigating magistrate's chambers, but the rule is the same for the trial court when it is competent to rule on nullities.

To make their decision, judges deciding a nullity use the criteria of whether there is a causal nexus between the vitiated act and subsequent acts. For example, a confession following an illegal search will be nullified.[21] But on the other hand, the nullification of an act does not affect a subsequent search so long as the expert did not refer to any of the nullified acts.[22] Similarly, acts following an illegal wiretap are not nullified if the contents of the illegal wiretaps were not exploited in any of those acts.[23]

6.2 The Right to Privacy and the Exclusion of Evidence

6.2.1 General Provisions on the Right to Privacy and the Right to Develop One's Personality

The protection of the individual's "secret garden" is safeguarded. A French publicist, Royer-Collard, wrote at the beginning of the nineteenth century that "one's private life should be walled off". Nevertheless, under French law, material on the issue is scattered.

There is no express reference in the constitution to any protection of private life. However, several different times the Constitutional Council has been called upon to decide the conformity to the constitution of pieces of legislation capable of affecting privacy. Nevertheless, for quite a while the means were lacking in law. The Constitutional Council waited several years before identifying a principle of constitutional magnitude in the protection of privacy, stating that it was the petitioners who ascribed to it this nature in their petition.[24] And it is in returning to the precedent of "personal liberty," based in the general principle of liberty laid out in the Declaration of 1789 that the Council seems to punish violations that potentially

[21] Cass. crim., Jan. 22, 1953, JCP 1955 II no. 7456, note J. Brouchot.

[22] Cass. crim., July 13, 1971, Bull. crim., No. 230.

[23] Cass. crim., Apr. 15, 1991, Bull. crim., No. 179; JCP 1992 II no. 21795, note W. Jeandidier.

[24] CC decision no. 93-325 DC, Aug. 13, 1993, Rec. 224.

could undermine the protection of privacy.[25] More precisely, given the decision of January 20, 1993, if the court's power to protect individual liberty remains the governing principle, it is only in cases of serious violations of private life (breach of the inviolability of one's domicile or of the secrecy of correspondence resulting from searches or seizures) where there is a violation of individual liberty in the sense of Art. 66 Const. Its text provides: "No one shall be arbitrarily detained. The judicial authority protecting individual liberty, ensures respect of this principle under conditions established by law". Shortly after the decision of January 20, 1993, the Constitutional Council would proclaim in a more general way that the "disregard of the right to respect for private life may be of a kind so as to interfere with individual liberty". In that case, the constitutional judges held that the installation of a video surveillance system is compatible with respect due to individual liberty subject to compliance with the safeguards established by the legislature.[26]

In short, the Constitutional Council distinguishes private life as protected under Article 66 Const.(secrecy of private life) and private life protected as part of one's personal life, enshrined in Arts. 2 and 4 of the Declaration of 1789, the protection of which rests in the hands of two court jurisdictions.[27]

Leaving the constitutional terrain to take on ordinary law, we discover several texts specific to particular situations (*see infra*). Indeed there does not exist in French law any general law governing the protection of privacy in the Penal Code. But case law has developed the following principle: "Criminal courts may not set aside evidence produced by the parties for the sole reason of it being obtained in an illegal or unfair manner". Their only task is to weigh probative value: disregarding the provisions of § 427 CCP (according to which the judge may use any mode of evidence and decide according to his innermost conviction so long as the evidence was adversarially discussed before him). "The Court of Appeals declares inadmissible as evidence a document produced by the civil plaintiff where it could not have been obtained except by illegal means".[28]

We must nevertheless keep in mind § 9 Civil Code (law of July 17, 1970), which reads, "Everyone has the right to respect for his private life. Without prejudice to compensation for injury suffered, the court may prescribe any measures, such as sequestration, seizure and others, appropriate to prevent or put an end to an invasion

---

[25] CC decision no. 92316 DC, Jan. 20, 1993, RFDA 902, note F. Pouyaud; Renoux and De Villiers (2005, 590). In this case an administrative agency (le Service Central de Prévention de la Corruption) was given by law a right to disclose any documents they got their hands on, without cause or restrictions, which allowed them to withhold documents without limitation and summon anyone, with no respect given to the right to a defense or the adversarial principle. The general principle of liberty was violated and therefore so too was the constitutional principle of personal liberty.

[26] CC decision no. 94-352 DC, Jan. 18, 1995, Rec. 170.

[27] Renoux and de Villiers (2005, 591).

[28] Cass. crim., June 15, 1995, Bull. crim., No. 210; Recueil Dalloz 1994, 613, note C. Mascala; Cass. crim., Apr. 6, 1994, Bull. crim., No. 136.

of personal privacy; in case of emergency those measures may be provided for by interim order." The Constitutional Council confers the nature of a constitutional principle to the right to privacy and it does so based on Art. 2 of the Declaration of 1789: the liberty proclaimed by that Article (which covers the rights to freedom, security and the resistance to oppression) implies the right to privacy.[29] Once again, respect for the right to privacy is affirmed as a fundamental principle and is seen as an aspect of liberty. Nevertheless, § 9 Civil Code is not of a criminal nature. No penalty is established.

6.2.2 *Protection of the Home*

Because the home is a part of one's private life, it is protected as a constitutional value. Moreover, in support of this idea, when applying Article 8 ECHR,[30] the ECtHR adopts an expansive definition of private life.[31] For European judges, not only must the right to secrecy of one's private life be protected, but also the right to respect for privacy in relations with others as expressed in the *Niemietz*[32] and *Burghartz*[33] cases. More precisely, the Constitutional Council previously decided that the right to individual liberty as used in Art. 66 Const. includes protection of the home and private localities.[34] In a similar way, the ECtHR condemned home visits by the French Customs Administration, as constituting an interference with the private lives and the correspondence of the applicants, as well as with their privacy in their homes.[35] Beginning from the principle that the home should be protected because it is a constitutional value, we shall make two complementary remarks coming out of constitutional jurisprudence.

First, the requirements of justice lead authorities to search for a balance between the home as an inviolable space and the fight against crime. According to the Constitutional Council, "the search for the perpetrators of crimes is necessary for safeguarding the principles and rights of constitutional value. It is up to the legislature

[29] CC decision no. 99-416 DC, July 23, 1999, Recueil Dalloz 2000, Somm. 265, obs. Marino; RTD civ. 1999, 725, obs. Molfessis.

[30] Whose first section reads: "Everyone has the right to respect for his private and family life, his home and his correspondence."

[31] Guerra v. Italy (1998), 26 E.H.R.R. 357.

[32] Niemietz v. Germany (1993), 16 E.H.R.R. 97.

[33] Burghartz v. Switzerland (1994), 18 E.H.R.R. 101.

[34] CC decision no. 83-164 DC, Dec. 29, 1983, Rec. 67, JCP 1984 II no. 20160, note R. Drago & A. Decocq: decision safeguarding individual freedom in all respects, in particular the inviolability of the home. *See also* CC decision no. 93-325 DC, Aug. 13, 1993, Rec. 224.

[35] Funke v. France (1993), 16 E.H.R.R. 297, 326, § 48; Crémieux v. France (1993), 16 E.H.R.R. 357, 373, § 31; Miailhe v. France (1993), 16 E.H.R.R. 332, 351, § 28.

to assure the reconciliation of this goal with its constitutional value and, on the other hand, the necessary protection of private property and the exercise of personal liberty, specifically the inviolability of the home".[36] Thus, the Constitutional Council declared constitutional a law permitting police agents acting under the order and the responsibility of judicial police officers, who themselves are acting under authority of a warrant by the prosecutor of the Republic, to enter into localities used for business, unless they constitute a home. Under these conditions, and notably by reason of the role of the prosecutor, who is responsible for monitoring the implementation of the measure and may stop it at any time, such an intrusion is in conformity with the constitution.[37] Similarly, the prohibition on visits and searches between 9 p.m. and 6 a.m. is a "fundamental principle recognized by the laws of the Republic", meaning that such measures are not possible except in situations of flagrancy[38] or involving organized crime.[39]

Next, the Constitutional Council wanted judges to exercise rigorous control over the methods of searches. Specifically, the Council establishes three guarantees: (1) the right to do a search must be confined to a particular time and place; (2) the rights of the defense must be assured and the search must guarantee, according to the Council, "the sincerity of the findings and the clear identification of pieces of evidence seized during visits"; and (3) judicial authorities must exert effective control over the entirety of the search, just as they would over any measure affecting personal liberty.[40] The *Cour de cassation* also oversees the effectiveness of the control of the trial judge.[41]

The Code of Criminal Procedure contains various provisions on searches of the home. We must distinguish between two types of searches according to the nature of the underlying crime.

Under the *droit commun* the investigator may only enter the domicile of persons who "appear to be involved in a felony or to be in possession of documents, information or articles pertaining to the criminal offense".[42] The operation may only commence between 6:00 a.m. and 9:00 p.m. Special measures are taken to ensure the protection of the rights of the defense and the attorney-client privilege. For example, a search must be done in the presence of a representative of the Bar, or the Order of Medical Doctors. All these provisions are required under penalty of nullity according to § 59 CCP, and a violation will constitute a textual nullity unless the party that the rule favors did not suffer from the violation.

---

[36] CC decision no. 94-352 DC, Jan. 18, 1995, Rec. 170; CC decision no. 96-377 DC, July 16, 1996, Rec. 87; CC decision no. 97-389 DC, Apr. 22, 1997, Rec. 45.

[37] CC decision no. 97-389 DC, Apr. 22, 1997, Rec. 45.

[38] CC decision no. 96-377 DC, July 16, 1996, Rec. 87.

[39] CC decision no. 2004-492 DC, Mar. 2, 2004, étude J. C. Schoettl, Gaz. Pal. 2004, doctrine, p. 3.

[40] CC decision no. 89-268 DC, Dec. 29, 1989, Rec. 110.

[41] Cass. ch. mixte, Dec. 15, 1988, JCP 1989 II no. 21263, obs. Dugrip; Hatoux (1988).

[42] (§§ 56 para. 1, 76 para. 3 CCP).

On the issue of organized crime, a law of March 9, 2004, which introduced §§ 706-89 through 706-94 CCP, established a less protective regime for personal liberties. Searches may begin at night if the needs of the investigation "justify this", leaving a certain margin of discretion to the investigator. They may also take place at any location. Still, searches of the home are not possible unless charges have been filed (which means that an investigating magistrate is seized). Other conditions must likewise be met: (1) the existence of a flagrant felony or misdemeanor; (2) the existence of an immediate risk that evidence or clues will disappear; and (3) the existence of a plausible reason to suspect that a person or persons within the premises where the search is to be carried out are in the process of committing felonies or misdemeanors which fall within the scope of the law against organized crime.[43] Ultimately, only a judge may order a search. And the search must, under penalty of nullity, have no other purpose than investigating and establishing the offenses mentioned in the warrant.[44]

The case law faithfully applies the above rules, following the general principles laid out above. Overall, the *Cour de cassation* will try to keep evidence in unless the violation of the rules relative to obtaining the evidence harmed the defense. Nevertheless, for the rights of the defense the case law is very strict. But this does not prevent the investigating magistrate from authorizing a search of a home or a lawyer's offices.

6.2.3 *Protection of Communications*

In France there are no constitutional provisions that regulate the protection of written or oral communications. The CCP, however, is more verbose. First, seizures of communications between lawyer and client (generally a suspect) are prohibited. Indeed, according to § 432 CCP: "Written evidence may not be derived from the correspondence exchanged between the defendant and his lawyer". There are also certain restrictions on intercepting telephone communications: (1) no interception may be made from the telephone line of a member of parliament or senator unless the president of the assembly he belongs to is informed of the interception by the investigating judge; (2) before making an interception from the telephone line of a lawyer, the judge must inform the president of the bar association[45]; (3) before making an interception from the telephone line of the chambers or domicile of a judge

[43] § 706-91 para. 2 CCP.

[44] § 706-93 para. 1 CCP; de Lamy (2004, 1910), Vergès (2004, 184), and Pradel (2004, no. 134), AJ pénale, 2004, 184; J. Pradel, JCP 2004 I no. 134.

[45] Cass crim., Jan. 15, 1997, Bull. crim., No. 14. Wiretapping a lawyer may take place "only in exceptional cases", if there is evidence the lawyer participated in a crime, and in the absence thereof, the report recounting the conversations constitutes a nullity.

or prosecutor, the president or the prosecutor general of the court with jurisdiction over the area in question must be informed.[46]

As for other situations involving persons who do not enjoy special protection, intercepting communications is regulated. France once had no rules in this particular area and was condemned by the ECtHR.[47] This caused the legislature to intervene. It did so with a law of July 10, 1991, which introduced § 100 et seq. CCP. Intercepting communications is only possible "where the requirements of the investigation call for it", that is to say only if no other (less intrusive) means of proof would suffice to obtain the evidence. This is an example of the principle of subsidiarity. Only a judge (an investigating magistrate or other) may order a wiretap. A wiretap may last 4 months with the possibility of renewal for another 4 months. Finally, the recordings of the intercepted conversations must be destroyed if they are not used, or after they have been used.

The ECtHR has established some rules in this area. In the case of *Klass v. Germany*, telephone wiretaps were held to be in conformity with the ECHR, but on the condition that adequate protections were established against abuse, notably the presence of a judge to govern the process. An equilibrium must be reached between the right to privacy (Art. 8(1) ECHR) and public safety which may require secret surveillance (Art. 8(2) ECHR).[48] On the other hand, the procedure regulating the interference with privacy through wiretapping must be established in a law as required by Art. 8(2) ECHR. The absence of such a law brought about the condemnation of the United Kingdom, which had no law governing the area.[49]

6.2.4 *Other Attacks on Private Life*

Two situations should be mentioned without hiding the fact that other possible situations exist. Searches of automobiles pose a challenge. A distinction should, however, be made. In cases of known crimes, if it is clear that evidence of the crime could be uncovered by the search of a vehicle, the investigators may go forward with the search either upon judicial approval by an investigating magistrate, or based in their authority for situations of flagrance.[50]

In cases where there is only a possible suspicion that a crime has been or is being committed, we hesitate more before authorizing investigators to search vehicles

---

[46] (§ 100-7 CPP).

[47] Huvig v. France (1990), 12 E.H.R.R. 528, 545, § 35; Kruslin v. France (1990), 12 E.H.R.R. 547, 565, § 36. RUDH 1990, 18, obs. G. Cohen-Jonathan; Dalloz 1990, 353, note J. Pradel.

[48] Klass v. Germany (1979–1980), 2 E.H.R.R. 214.

[49] Malone v. United Kingdom (1985), 7. E.H.R.R. 14.

[50] As it does not involve a search, the formalities of searches laid out in §§ 56 *et seq.* CCP do not apply (presence of attesting witnesses and prohibiting searches between 9:00 p.m. and 6:00 a.m.), Cass. crim., Dec. 8, 1979, JCP 1980 II no. 19337, note Davia.

which may be able to provide them proof of the crime they suspect. Yet, faced with a rise in delinquency, the legislature has taken strides. With a law of March 18, 2003, which introduced § 78-2-2 CCP, police may now proceed with searching vehicles "upon the written request of the district prosecutor, for the purpose of investigating and prosecuting acts of terrorism…offenses relating to weapons and explosives…or acts of drug trafficking". The magistrate must specify the time and place in which the operation will take place.

The law of March 9, 2004, which introduced §§ 706-96 to 706-12 CCP, allowed recording the words or the image of a person in a private location. This is a particularly intrusive measure requiring strict regulation. Only the investigating magistrate may order such a measure. And if it must be carried out in a home and at night, the magistrate must seise the liberty and custody judge who also may give authorization: in sum the measure requires the permission of two judges. The order must be reasoned and indicate the premises concerned. Finally, law and medical offices, notaries and bailiffs are all excluded. But a prison visiting room may contain a recording device.[51]

6.3 Illegal Interrogations and Exclusion of Evidence

6.3.1 Right to Remain Silent and the Privilege Against Self-Incrimination

The constitution is silent on this issue, and the CCP speaks neither of the right to silence nor of the privilege against self-incrimination. However, the right to remain silent works in two ways: (1) the person has the right to remain silent before police without incurring any penalty and (2) a judge may not draw any conclusions from the silence of the accused. It is the first meaning which is the more important and which should hold our attention in two respects. During the investigation, a law of March 4, 2002 required that a detainee must be "informed that she has the right to make a statement, respond to questions posed or remain silent" (§ 63-1 CCP). But under pressure by police, the legislature changed its mind in 2003. Today, the suspect is not required to speak, but the police officer no longer has the duty to advise him of the right to remain silent. Thus, no nullity can result because the police officer did not advise someone of the right to remain silent. During the investigation, the investigating judge must, upon the first appearance of the accused, advise him of the right to remain silent (§ 116 para. 4 CCP). He understands that the person is coming from detention and must be accorded some time to "relax".[52]

---

[51] Cass. crim., Mar. 1, 2006, Bull. crim., No. 59; Dalloz 2007, 1504, note J. Pradel; *See also* Verny (2004, 777).

[52] Pradel (2008, 468).

The ECHR does not enshrine the right to remain silent,[53] but has recognized it in its case law.[54]

The privilege against self-incrimination is tied to the right to remain silent. But because French law says nothing about the right to remain silent, it does not take into account the privilege against self-incrimination. An old case even forbade a witness from invoking this privilege.[55] Rare legislative exceptions exist nevertheless. For example, while §434-11 Penal Code criminalizes not testifying in favor of a convicted innocent person, a person who is actually guilty is not required to testify and this privilege extends even to his or her spouse, partner and direct relatives.[56]

6.3.2 *Protection Against Involuntary Self-Incrimination (Torture, Coercion, Threats, Promises)*

Neither the Constitution, nor the CCP contains provisions on this issue. But in the case law two penalties apply in situations involving confessions induced by means counteracting the will.

First, there is the possibility of pursuing investigators criminally when they use violence. These acts of violence are punished by §§ 222-7 *et seq.* Penal Code. And the fact that the person having used violence is a "person holding public authority or discharging a public service duty in the exercise or on account of his functions or duty" constitutes an aggravating factor. For example, if the perpetrator is a person holding public authority and the injury results in an inability to work for more than 8 days, the crime is punished by 5 years instead of the normal punishment of 3 years of imprisonment.[57] Convictions are extremely rare and certain procedures for bringing charges drag on very long.[58] The ECtHR condemned France for torture in a case where officers exercised violence against a person in custody, saying the violent act "caused 'severe' pain and suffering and was particularly serious and cruel".[59]

The second penalty is obviously the nullity of statements made by the suspect. It is a substantive nullity with no textual support, which prevents the application

[53] Contrary to the International Covenant on Civil and Political Rights, Art. 14 §3(g).

[54] Saunders v. United Kingdom (1996), 23 E.H.R.R. 313, 337, §§ 68–69: "The right not to incriminate oneself lies at the heart of a fair procedure ... It is primarily concerned with respecting the will of an accused person to remain silent"; See also Pradel et al. (2009, 389).

[55] Cass. crim., Dec. 23, 1847, D. 1848 I no. 29, a decision invoking the risk of disturbing social order and the "sacred duty the oath imposes".

[56] Pradel (2008, 280–281).

[57] §§ 222-11, 222-12 Penal Code. Of course disciplinary measures and civil liability are also imposed upon the perpetrator.

[58] See the Grange case, which lasted ten years for procedural reasons. Couvrat (1989, 409).

[59] Selmouni v. France (2000), 29 E.H.R.R. 403, 442, § 101; RTDH 2000, 138 obs. Lambert; Recueil Dalloz 2000, Somm. 179, obs. J. F. Renucci; Recueil Dalloz 2000, Somm. 31, obs. Y. Mayaud.

of textual nullities. Investigatory acts following statements by the suspect are also nullified. But nullifying a procedure for violence committed by the investigators is extremely rare. Some cases should be mentioned relating to Art. 3 ECHR.[60] One case did not see it as inhumane treatment where detention was carried out in a tense atmosphere.[61] But another nullified a detention where the person involved was forced to wear handcuffs or restraints, and the judge did not limit the duration of the measure, nor refer to any circumstances that could have justified it.[62]

On the fringes of coercion, threats and promises, we can cite some captious cases. Interrogators traditionally would record responses of the suspect by preceding them with the initials SI ("sur interpellation" or "under interrogation"), thereby not indicating what the question actually was. This procedure today is prohibited by a law of June 15, 2000, which introduced §429 para. 2 CCP, which provides that every official record of an interrogation or a hearing must contain the questions that were answered therein. It is true nevertheless that the *Cour de cassation* opposes nullities where there was no harm done to the rights of the defense.[63]

6.3.3 *Protection Against Involuntary Declarations and the Right to Counsel*

Neither the Constitution nor the CCP say anything about incriminating statements made under torture, coercion, threats or promises. Indirectly, such declarations are kept out. We may cite the legally recognized right of a suspect to not speak to the investigating magistrate until his first appearance. We can especially mention the presence of counsel, which is currently becoming more important. Since 1897, counsel may assist his client while before the investigating magistrate and correspondingly see the dossier before any interrogations. Today, the right to counsel extends upstream from charging, which is to say throughout the investigation. In this respect, three stages can be distinguished:

First, counsel traditionally did not appear during the interrogation, at least not if the suspect is in custody. Only suspects not deprived of their liberty could consult a lawyer after (or before) being heard by a police officer.

Second, with the laws of January 4 and August 24, 1993, as modified by the laws of June 15, 2000 and May 9, 2004, counsel could appear, but in the form of a 30 min

---

[60] Art. 3 ECHR: "No one shall be subjected to torture or to inhuman or degrading treatment or punishment".

[61] Cass. crim., Feb. 26, 1991, Bull. crim., No. 97.

[62] Cass. crim., May 4, 2008, RSC 2008, 930, obs. Finielz.

[63] Cass. crim., Sept. 21, 2005, AJ pénal 2006, 127; Cass. crim., May 27, 2008, Bull. crim., No. 132.

interview at the beginning of the custody period.[64] The attorney, however, could not sit in on the entire interrogation and is not allowed to see the dossier.

Finally, the decisions of the ECtHR, beginning in 2008, further enshrined the presence of counsel during the police interrogation. In a decision of November 27, 2008, the court held:

> In order for the right to a fair trial to remain sufficiently 'practical and effective' Article 6(1) requires that, as a rule, access to a lawyer should be provided as from the first interrogation of a suspect by the police, unless it is demonstrated in the light of the particular circumstances of each case that there are compelling reasons to restrict this right. Even where compelling reasons may exceptionally justify denial of access to a lawyer, such restriction – whatever its justification – must not unduly prejudice the rights of the accused under Article 6. The rights of the defense will, in principle, be irretrievably prejudiced when incriminating statements made during police interrogation without access to a lawyer are used for a conviction. [65]

The attorney therefore should be present during a police interrogation. But the court did not appear to require that he be allowed to see the dossier. It is not impossible, nevertheless, that one day, because of the dynamic nature of defense rights, counsel may be allowed to see the dossier. Yet there is no hiding the fact that this "sneak peek" could harm the police investigation. It would be especially dangerous in cases of organized crime. The mere presence of counsel in this matter could hurt the investigation, and indeed following the ECtHR's formula, which states a general rule that the attorney should be present, could allow for their exclusion in situations involving organized crime.

6.4 Conclusion

In sum, the Constitution is of little help because it is old (1959) and at the time constitutional drafters paid little attention to criminal matters. In contrast, the CCP and case law (European, constitutional and judicial) have provided, case by case, a theory of illegal criminal evidence. Custom and practice however bear little weight. Remember nevertheless that the *Cour de cassation* is handing down decisions and the authors of these decisions are themselves practitioners, which leads to a restriction on nullities.[66] Remember too that national jurisprudence can easily integrate foreign law, which can then be applied to national laws.[67]

---

[64] § 63-4 CCP

[65] Salduz v. Turkey [GC], (2009), 49 E.H.R.R. 19, 421, 437, § 55. *See also*, Pishchalnikov v. Russia, No. 7025/04, ECHR, 24 Sept. 2009; Dayanan v. Turkey, No. 7377/03, ECHR, 13 October 2009, Gaz. Pal. Dec. 3, 2009, note H. Matsopoulou.

[66] There is, admittedly, a part of the doctrine which fights back against this strangling of nullities, but that is not our opinion. See Pradel (2008–2009, 780).

[67] We especially think of the ECHR, most notably Art. 3 (on torture), Art. 6 (on fair trials) and Art. 8 (on privacy).

Bibliography

Couvrat, P. 1989. Le Contrôle Pénal de la Police. *Droits de L'individu et Police, Revue Themis, Faculté de droit de Montréal*, Canada, 409–418.

de Lamy, B. 2004. La lutte contre la criminalité organisée. *Dalloz chron*, 1918–1990

Desportes, F., and L. Lazerges-Cousquer. 2009. *Traité de Procédure Pénale*. Paris: Economica.

Guinchard, S., and J. Buisson. 2011. *Procédure Pénale*, 7th ed. Paris: Litec.

Hatoux, B. 1988. *Le droit de visite et de saisie des agents des administrations en matière fiscale, douanière et de concurrence*. Paris: Librairie de la Cour de cassation.

Lévy-Brulh, H. 1964. *La Preuve Judiciaire*. Paris: Rivière.

Pradel, J. 2003. Les Principes Constitutionnels du Proces Penal, no. 14. *Les Cahiers du Conseil constitutionnel, Paris* 84–92.

Pradel, J. 2004. Vers un aggiornamento des réponses de la procédure pénale à la criminalité. Apports de la loi du 9 mars 2004. La Semaine juridique, I, n°132, 134, 821–828, 881–887.

Pradel, J. 2008. *Droit Pénal Comparé*, 3rd ed. Paris: Dalloz.

Pradel, J. 2011. *Procédure Pénale*, 16th ed. Paris: Cujas.

Pradel, J., G. Corstens, and G. Vermeulen. 2009. *Droit Penal Européen*, 3rd ed. Paris: Dalloz.

Renoux, T., and M. De Villiers. 2005. *Code constitutionnel*. Paris: Litec.

Renucci, J.F. 2007. *Traité de Droit Européen des Droits de L'homme*. Paris: LGDJ.

Sciortino-Bayart, S. 2000. *Recherches sur le Droit Constitutionnel de la Sanction Pénale*, Doctoral Thesis, Aix-Marseille 3 (digital copy, not published).

Vergès, E. 2004. La notion de criminalité organisée après la loi du 9 mars 2004. *AJ pénal*, 181–186.

Verny, E. 2004. Les Sonorisations et Fixations D'images Décidées par le Juge D'Instruction. *Revue Pénitentiaire et de Droit Pénal* 4: 777–786.

Chapter 7
Belgium: From Categorical Nullities to a Judicially Created Balancing Test

Marie-Aude Beernaert and Philip Traest

7.1 The General Theory Concerning the Admissibility of Illegally Gathered Evidence

7.1.1 Constitutional and Legal Rules

Any means of achieving certainty may be considered a type of evidence.[1] Under Belgian law, there is no general theory concerning evidence in criminal matters, neither in the Constitution, nor in the Belgian Penal Code or any other law.

True, Art. 6 of the European Convention on Human Rights (hereafter ECHR) lays out a foundational rule that touches upon evidence and more specifically the burden of proof, namely, the presumption of innocence. Art. 14.2 of the International Covenant on Civil and Political Rights (hereafter ICCPR) takes up the same principle. It follows that it is up to the prosecution and the civil party to bring proof of the offense. This principle is important, but it says nothing in terms of the fate that should be reserved for evidence where it appears to the judge that it was obtained irregularly or illegally. In the jurisprudence of the European Court of Human Rights (hereafter ECtHR) it appears that the ECHR does not require the national judge to automatically set aside means of proof that were irregularly obtained. The court

---

Translated from the French by Joshua Walker and Stephen C. Thaman.

[1] Franchimont et al. (2009, 1033)

M.-A. Beernaert (✉)
Professor of Law, Université Catholique de Louvain, Place Montesquieu, 2 bte L2.07.01, 1348 Louvain-la-Neuve, Belgium
e-mail: Marie-Aude.Beernaert@uclouvain.be

P. Traest
Professor of Law, University of Ghent, Universiteitstraat 4, 9000 Ghent, Belgium
e-mail: Philip.Traest@UGent.be

S.C. Thaman (ed.), *Exclusionary Rules in Comparative Law*, Ius Gentium: Comparative Perspectives on Law and Justice 20, DOI 10.1007/978-94-007-5348-8_7,

only reviews whether the procedure followed in the national court, taken in its entirety, reflects a character of fairness within the meaning of the convention. Art. 6 ECHR does not actually regulate the admissibility of evidence in itself, as this is primarily a matter of national law.[2]

The Belgian Constitution, for its part, contains an expression of some fundamental rights, such as the inviolability of the home (Art. 15) and the right to respect for private life (Art. 22). Additionally, Art.12 Const. guarantees the right to personal liberty. The second paragraph of Art. 12 states, "No one can be prosecuted except in the cases provided for by law, and in the form prescribed by law". But, even if that phrase could be interpreted as an expression of the principle of legality of the prosecution (and thereby containing a requirement of the regularity of the evidence obtained), the Belgian Supreme Court (*Cour de Cassation*) has never ruled that Art. 12 Const. requires the trial judge to exclude from trial any irregularly obtained evidence.

Thus, there is no general theory of evidence in Belgian law, neither in the Constitution nor in the codes. The only exception to this is found in Art. 13 of the law of December 9, 2004 on international assistance in criminal matters which modifies § 90*ter* of the Code of Criminal Procedure (hereafter CCP).[3] That article is a literal transposition – concerning elements of proof obtained abroad – of the jurisprudence of the *Cour de Cassation* laid down in a case dating October 14, 2003, discussed below.

There are no other legal texts in Belgium that explicitly and generally regulate the admissibility of evidence in criminal matters. The theory of evidence in criminal matters may, therefore, be considered to be a judicial construction, in which the academic literature has also played a fairly important role.

No constitutional or legal rules exist – the only exception is a rule concerning jury trials in the Assizes Court – which expressly requires that the criminal judge has the mission of searching for the truth. In the literature it is generally accepted that the goal of every criminal trial is to search for the truth regarding an event constituting a crime or misdemeanor. This same literature warns that the search for the truth may not be undertaken at any price. The search for truth may not be done to the detriment of the respect of the fundamental rights of citizens and in particular the rights and liberties found in the ECHR. On the other hand, even though the principle of the criminal judge's search for the truth is not expressly mentioned in the CCP, that same code gives the criminal judge the right to order on his own initiative measures which he deems useful for revealing the truth. The judge may, for example, appoint *sua sponte* an expert during a criminal trial.

The procedure before the Assizes Court is of an exceptional nature. Not only is the decision regarding criminal responsibility made by a popular jury, but also the procedure to be followed before that jurisdiction is, contrary to procedures of courts

[2] This is the established case law of the ECHR; *See,* e.g., Eur. Ct. H.R. decisions of Schenk v. Switzerland (1991), 13 E.H.R.R. 1342 and Ramanauskas v. Lithuania (2010), 51 E.H.R.R. 11.

[3] Moniteur Belge [Official Journal of Belgium], 24 Dec. 2004.

and tribunals staffed by professional judges, the object of fairly detailed legislation. Thus, § Art. 281 (formerly 268) CCP describes the discretionary right of the president of the Assizes Court in the following terms, "[t]he president is vested with a discretionary power, by virtue of which he may take into account anything he believes to be useful for finding the truth; the law charges him with employing in honor and conscience all efforts for bringing the truth to light". The same article (§ 269 CCP) further states that with regard to that power, the presiding judge may hear any witness or introduce any new evidence that seems to him to be "able to shed more light on the disputed fact". This list is merely demonstrative and the discretionary power is not limited to the mentioned acts.[4]

Although these articles are only related to procedures before the Assizes Court, we can say that the duties of the president of the Assizes Court apply by analogy to professional judges. There is no reason to believe that the search for truth would be less important for professional judges in the normal courts than it is for the Assizes Court. That there is an express mention of truth only when referring to the Assizes Court could very well be explained by the fact that when the CCP was promulgated in 1808, the Assizes Court played a far more important role than it does in our time.

We can, thus, conclude that the search for truth occupies as important a place in the normal courts staffed by professional judges as it does in the Assizes Court, but it may not be pursued to the detriment of the fundamental rights of citizens.

7.2 Jurisprudence of the Cour de Cassation Concerning the Admissibility of Illegally Obtained Evidence

As was indicated above, the rules governing the possible exclusion of illegally gathered evidence were to be found exclusively in the jurisprudence of the *Cour de Cassation*. The classical theory of the exclusion of illegal evidence was formulated in a decision by the *Cour de Cassation* of December 10, 1923.[5] In that landmark decision the court held that evidence illegally obtained was void and without any effect. The *Cour de Cassation* made no distinction, at that time, between an illegality caused by a government agent or a private citizen. If either a government agent or a private citizen was only able to prove a fact in court by virtue of exploiting an illegal act, then the proof was deemed to be contrary to law.[6] It is therefore clear that, beginning in 1923, the theory of excluding illegal evidence was applied by the *Cour de Cassation* without admitting of any exceptions.

Beginning in 1986, the principle of excluding illegally obtained evidence was extended to evidence obtained in an "irregular" manner. Indeed, in a decision of

---

[4] Braas (1925, 324).

[5] Pasicrisie 66 (1924, I); See also, Cass., 12 Mar. 1923, Pasicrisie 233 (1923, I). Except in the case of older decisions, the decisions of the *Cour de Cassation* that we cite in the present report may be consulted online on the site www.cass.be.

[6] Kuty (2005a, 350).

May 13, 1986, the *Cour de Cassation* found that the exclusion of evidence should apply even if the evidence was gathered "by an act not reconcilable with the substantive rules of criminal procedure or with the general principles of law, and more specifically with respect for the right to a defense".[7]

Since this landmark decision, one customarily distinguishes, among different types of illegally gathered evidence, between evidence obtained by means of a crime or at least an act expressly prohibited by law, and "irregular" evidence obtained by means of an act which, without being illegal, was contrary to the basic requirements of a good administration of justice or to certain general principles of law.[8] Under this second category fall, for example, confessions obtained by means of a false promise of impunity or a hearing of the accused under oath, in violation of his right to silence.

In reality, it would have been possible to distinguish a third category of illicit evidence, which would include evidence obtained by means of an act which did not comply with all the formalities prescribed by law. In this case, the evidence results from an act which indeed was permissible to do by the judicial authorities but which should have been legally performed by investigating authorities. It violated the law because certain formalities were not respected. And the answer to the question of what lot should be reserved to this last type of evidence would depend then on the type of formalities at issue: if they are established under penalty of nullity or were considered by case law as essential formalities, the evidence would be inadmissible; but in the opposite situation, the non-compliance with the formality would have, to the contrary, no repercussions upon the validity and the admissibility of the evidence at issue.

Beginning in 1990, the *Cour de Cassation* introduced the first step in softening the exclusionary rule for illegal and irregular evidence. Indeed, in two decisions handed down on January 19, 1990[9] and April 17, 1991,[10] the *Cour de Cassation* decided that an illegal act committed by an individual in the gathering of evidence does not render that evidence inadmissible if the illicit act was not the work of either the investigator or a police informant but of a third party, and if it was not committed with the goal of reporting the facts to the authorities. According to this decision, evidence, even where obtained illegally, could contribute to the conviction of the accused under the double condition that the illegality was not committed by a public official, but by a private citizen, and that the private citizen in question did not act in coordination with a public official. Some in the literature criticized this decision[11] on the grounds that, henceforth, the source (legal or not) of the evidence no longer constitutes the only criterion for deciding the admissibility of the evidence in question.

---

[7] See Cass., 13 May 1986, I Pasicrisie 1107 (1986), and the conclusions of the Procureur général Dujardin in conformity with this.

[8] Beernaert (2005, 1095) (note on Cass., 2 Mar. 2005).

[9] *Rechtskundig Weekblad* 463 (1990–1991). Note of L. Huybrechts

[10] *Revue de droit pénal et de criminologie* 94 (1992), note of C. De Valkeneer.

[11] Traest (1994, 72–75).

A second evolution in the softening of the principle of exclusion of illegally obtained evidence was set in motion by the *Cour de Cassation* in its decision of May 30, 1995. A decision by the Court of Appeal of Ghent had found evidence to be inadmissible where it was gathered in Belgium on the basis of information sent by the French Gendarmerie, since this information was obtained from wiretaps at a time when France did not have legislation compatible with the requirements of Art. 8 ECHR. The *Cour de Cassation* quashed the ruling by the Ghent Court of Appeal on the grounds that "evidence of an offense is different than the disclosure of a crime" and, even if the person reporting an offense obtained that information in an illegal manner, this does not affect the validity of evidence later obtained without an illegal act.[12] In other words, the *Cour de Cassation* refused to apply the principle of exclusion of illegally or irregularly obtained evidence to a mere tip or a report of a crime. In its opinion, a crime report or a disclosure could not be treated as if it did not exist. If a report or a tip was illegally obtained, it is up to the judicial authorities to try to put together evidence of that offense in a valid manner. The illegal or irregular character of the crime report or the reception of the tip in question does not render it impossible, according to the *Cour de Cassation*, to gather evidence of that offense in a completely valid manner.[13]

Following these two decisions softening the principle of exclusion of illicitly gathered evidence, one could have anticipated a fundamental shift in the jurisprudence of the *Cour de Cassation* on this issue. This fundamental shift took place in a decision by the *Cour de Cassation* of October 14, 2003.

Even accounting for some fine tuning done to the classical theory of exclusion of illicit evidence, one principle remained still intact: that of the inadmissibility of evidence obtained by means of an illegal action committed by investigating or prosecuting authorities. This principle was fundamentally modified by the October 14, 2003 decision of the *Cour de Cassation*.

It is worth explaining the circumstances of that case. During a police operation in Antwerp (operation "Antigone"), the appellant was subjected to a pat-down search. Car keys were found in his jacket pocket and the police used them to open his vehicle, where a loaded revolver was found with the serial number filed off. The search of the vehicle was illegal because it was done in violation of Art. 29 of the law of August 5, 1992, on the function of police. The Antwerp Court of Appeals refused to exclude the evidence gathered from this illegal search. The *Cour de Cassation* dismissed the appeal of that decision, deciding, in clear terms, that "the fact that a piece of evidence was obtained irregularly only has, as a rule, the result that the judge in forming his decision may not take that evidence into consideration either directly or indirectly where either: (1) the respect of certain formal conditions is required under penalty of nullity; (2) the irregularity has hurt the trustworthiness of the evidence, or; (3) the use of the evidence is contrary to the right to a fair trial".[14]

---

[12] Cass., 30 May 1995; Kuty (1998, 489) and Traest (1996, 151).

[13] The question remained whether this theory should also apply where the report of the crime itself was a crime (for example where it constituted a violation of professional secrecy).

[14] Cass., 14 Oct. 2003; Kuty (2004, 405).

This landmark decision of the *Cour de Cassation* in October 2003 signaled the beginning of a new Belgian judicial theory in matters of excluding illicitly gathered evidence. In the place of a *prima facie* prohibition on the use of illicit evidence, this decision of the *Cour de Cassation* substituted a *prima facie* authorization of its use, only limited by a few exceptions specified by the court. It follows that the discretion to consider evidence given to the judiciary is now quite considerable.[15]

In the years following the landmark decision of October 14, 2003 (which is today commonly referred to as the "Antigone case"), the *Cour de Cassation* has had several opportunities to explain the criteria put forth in that decision. Namely, the prohibition on using illegally obtained evidence where the use of that evidence would be contrary to the right to a fair trial, which begged for further explanation. These clarifications have come about through the jurisprudence of the *Cour de Cassation* from 2003 until the present. The first two criteria for their part, called for less explanation. The practice of criminal law since 2003 clearly shows that the debates before Belgian courts on the exclusion of an illegally or irregularly obtained piece of evidence have to do for the most part with the interpretation of the third criterion, that of fair trial. This does not come as much of a surprise, considering that the first two criteria are more clearly described by the *Cour de Cassation* than the third criterion on fair trial which is a clear reference to the decisions of the ECHR, that the notion of a fair trial must be analyzed on the basis of the specific facts of each case.

Going back to the first scenario where evidence would be excluded – that of a violation of a formality required under penalty of nullity – it must be said that this is rarely applied in Belgium.[16] In the current version of the Belgian CCP, very few formalities are actually prescribed under penalty of nullity. This would apply for example in relation to certain formalities required for hearing witnesses who are under a complete cloak of anonymity or for wiretaps (governed respectively by §§ 86*bis*, 86*ter*, and 90*quater* of the Belgian Penal Code).

There exist other formalities not established under penalty of nullity by law but which are considered in the case law and the literature as substantive formalities. According to the classical doctrine of evidence in criminal matters, violation of a substantive formality, although not established under penalty of nullity by law, should equally result in the declaration of a nullity. The question was raised, after the *Antigone* decision of October 14, 2003, whether violation of a substantive formality, not established by law under penalty of nullity, could still lead to the exclusion of evidence thus obtained. The answer to this question would appear to be no. Indeed, in two decisions on November 16, 2004, the *Cour de Cassation* addressed the problem of the possible exclusion of evidence obtained through an illegal search. In one of these cases,[17] an accused's home was entered without him

---

[15] Kuty (2005a, 352).

[16] Beernaert (2005, 1103).

[17] Cass., 16 Nov. 2004, R.G. P.04.1127.N, *Revue de droit pénal et de criminologie* 665 (2005). On the consequences of an irregular search warrant, we also refer to the decision of November 15, 2005. Pasicrisie 2254 (2005).

having consented to it in writing, in spite of the fact that Art. 1*bis* of the law of June 7, 1969 makes the legality of a consensual search – one without a warrant by a magistrate – dependent upon there being a document signed by the person who has lawful enjoyment of the premises. Although not established under penalty of nullity, the requirement of a written consent to search signed by the person in question before beginning a search is considered to be a substantive formality in the literature. The *Cour de Cassation* nevertheless decided that the failure to abide by this formality did not bring about the exclusion of the evidence obtained in the search. The *Cour de Cassation* argued: "it does not follow from Art. 6 ECHR that guarantees a fair trial, nor from Art. 8 ECHR which guarantees the right to respect for one's private and family life, his home and his correspondence, nor from any constitutional or legal provision that evidence obtained in violation of one of the fundamental rights guaranteed by the Convention or by the Constitution is always inadmissible". And the court continued: "Except in cases where a treaty or statutory provision itself establishes the legal consequences of the failure to follow a legally established formality relating to obtaining evidence, the judge shall decide what the consequences of that irregularity are to be". For the court, this rule also applies where the formality that was disregarded concerns one of the fundamental rights guaranteed by Arts. 6, 8(2) ECHR and by Arts. 12 (2), 15 Const. Following this precedent, it seems clear that the *Cour de Cassation* is no longer interested in finding that the failure to follow a substantive rule of criminal procedure would require the nullification of evidence which stems from it.[18]

The *Antigone* jurisprudence of the *Cour de Cassation* does not seem to apply to cases where strict formalities that the legislature enacted to guarantee the intrinsic quality of evidence were not followed (such as in matters requiring expert testimony relating to DNA[19] or measuring the concentration of alcohol in a breathalyzer test[20]): even if they are not established under penalty of nullity but "merely" by statute, the evidence obtained in violation of these rules is intrinsically flawed and may not be admitted.[21]

The second factor put forth by the *Antigone* decision of October 14, 2003 concerns cases where an irregularity has hurt the trustworthiness of the evidence. Opportunities for applying this option may themselves prove to be exceedingly rare. This option is likewise of little help to the extent that a piece of evidence which is not trustworthy would not be taken into account by the criminal judge anyway, regardless of the cause of its lack of trustworthiness.

---

[18] Kuty (2005a, 353). See also, more recently, Cass., 26 Jan. 2011, R.G. P.10.1321.F, *Revue de droit pénal et de criminology* 82 (2012), note of D. Dillenbourg.

[19] Cass., 25 May 2005, R.G. P.05.0672.F, *Revue de Jurisprudence de Liège-Mons-Bruxelles* 1408 (2005).

[20] Cass., 26 Nov. 2008, R.G. P.08.1293.F, *Journal des Tribunaux* 741 (2008) (and the conclusions of D. Vandermeersch).

[21] Franchimont et al. (2009, 1045).

As mentioned above, the third factor in the *Antigone* decision, namely the respect of the right to a fair trial, is what has given rise to the greatest amount of discussion in the literature and in case law developments. Since 2003, the *Cour de Cassation* has actually identified in its jurisprudence four additional criteria[22] that the criminal judge should take into account when deciding whether taking an irregularly obtained piece of evidence into account would or would not impair the right to a fair trial.

In a decision of March 23, 2004,[23] the *Cour de Cassation* held for the first time that a criminal judge may, in determining if there was or was not a violation of the right to a fair trial, take into account one or several of the following factors: (1) whether the authority in charge of an inquiry, an investigation, or the prosecution of an offense did or did not intentionally commit the illicit act; (2) whether the gravity of the underlying offense significantly eclipses the illicit act committed; and (3)whether the evidence illicitly obtained concerns only one of the material elements required to prove the offense. The literature has raised fundamental questions about these additional criteria.

First, the intentional nature of the illegality committed by the authorities can certainly play an important and even decisive role in any potential disciplinary or criminal proceedings against the officials involved, but it is not clear that this fact should also play a role in the decision of the criminal courts whether or not to accept the evidence in question in the original criminal proceedings.[24]

The reference to the relative seriousness of the illegality committed and the underlying offense being investigated introduces, for its part, a certain criterion of proportionality in the decision of the judge on the admissibility of evidence. Although proportionality tests are certainly not unknown in criminal law or in criminal procedure, the introduction of this criterion in the decision regarding the possible exclusion of an illegally obtained piece of evidence still raises some questions. On the one hand, it is understandable that the extreme seriousness of an offense committed by the accused could go against excluding an illegally obtained piece of evidence where the act in question only involved a "minor" illegality. But on the other hand, we could just as easily argue that a guilty verdict involving a particularly serious offense will typically bring with it a very heavy punishment and it is therefore particularly important that the verdict be the result of a procedure conducted in conformity with existing law. There exists a paradox in saying that the rules governing admissibility of evidence in cases involving a serious offense should be more flexible than those which apply in the trial of less serious offenses with lesser punishments.[25]

The third factor, namely whether the illicitly obtained evidence concerns only one of the material elements required to prove the offense, seems at first glance to be fairly obscure. This third factor should probably be understood in relation to cases

---

[22] Criteria which are nevertheless neither exhaustive nor cumulative. Ibid, 1052.

[23] Pasicrisie 500 (2004); *Revue de droit pénal et de criminologie* 661 (2005).

[24] Bosly et al. (2010, 1015–1016).

[25] Ibid.

where the illicit evidence would establish the guilt of the accused all by itself.[26] We could use the example of an illegal entry of a place used for selling narcotics, during which the police discover the corpse of a murder victim. In such a case, the discovery only relates to the substance of the crime of homicide. It is therefore logical and appropriate that this circumstance would justify opening an investigation, independent of the illegal nature of the search of the home.

In a decision on March 2, 2005,[27] the *Cour de Cassation* added a fourth factor to the three already cited. The *Cour de Cassation* decided that the criminal court, when deciding on the possible exclusion of an illegally obtained piece of evidence, may also take into account the fact that the illegality committed had no impact upon the rights or liberties protected by the standard violated. The case in question concerned the existence of a security camera focused upon the cash register of a store, which made it possible to show that one of the cashiers had not registered the totality of purchases made by clients and had fraudulently appropriated the difference between the registered sales and the actual sales. The recordings were made without the knowledge of the cashier, which constituted an illegal practice, contrary to Art. 9 of Collective Labor Agreement No. 68 of June 16, 1998. The appellate judges nevertheless argued that the camera, focused on the store's cash register, was only watching this and not the cashier herself. And the *Cour de Cassation* decided that, in such circumstances, the illegality did not have any impact upon the right to privacy protected by the standard violated, and that the criminal judge could therefore have accepted the evidence, although irregularly obtained.

The *Cour de Cassation* has, since 2003, held, that it is up to the judge to decide the admissibility of illegally obtained evidence that is not expressly excluded by statute, in light of Art. 6 ECHR and Art. 14 ICCPR taking into account all facts of the case, including the means used to obtain the evidence and the circumstances surrounding the illegal act. The three aforementioned criteria—whether the authority in charge of the investigation intentionally committed the illicit act, the extent to which the gravity of the illicit act eclipses that of the underlying offense, and whether the evidence illicitly obtained concerns only one of the material elements of the offense—all must be taken into consideration.[28]

In case law since 2003, the *Cour de Cassation* has also specified that the three factors, put forth in the *Antigone* case of October 14, 2003, and interpreted in decisions on March 23, 2004, November 16, 2004, and March 2, 2005, are the only criteria that can lead to the exclusion of an illegally obtained piece of evidence. The judge excluding a piece of evidence following the violation of a rule not established under penalty of nullity may therefore not do so without examining in what way that illegal act compromises the right to a fair trial or harms the trustworthiness of the evidence.[29]

---

[26] De Valkeneer (2005, 688).

[27] *Journal des Tribunaux* 211 (Kuty 2005a).

[28] Cass., 31 Oct. 2006, Pasicrisie 2239 (2006); Cass., 21 Nov. 2006, Pasicrisie 2437 (2006); Cass., 4 Dec. 2007, *Rechtskundig Weekblad* 110 (2008–2009).

[29] Cass., 12 Oct. 2005, *Revue de Jurisprudence de Liège-Mons-Bruxelles* 585 (2006).

The jurisprudence of the Belgian *Cour de Cassation*, which commenced with the *Antigone* decision of October 14, 2003 has since then been the object of a decision by the ECtHR. Indeed, one of the two decisions given by the *Cour de Cassation* on November 16, 2004, concerning an illegal act during a search, was subjected to the scrutiny of the Strasbourg court. In its decision of July 28, 2009, that court repeated that it does not in principle decide on the admissibility of certain categories of evidence, for example evidence obtained illegally according to national law. The Court held that, in order to determine if the procedure in its entirety was fair, the court must ask itself if the rights of the defense were respected and it must specifically look into whether the accused was given the possibility to challenge the authenticity of the evidence and to oppose its use. The European court held that, in the case in question, the evidence gathered in violation of internal law was not in violation of *any* article of the convention. It was clear that the national law violated in the case in question, did not coincide with Art. 8 ECHR[30] or any other article dealing with certain rights considered to be among the most fundamental of the Convention. The court noted that before the Belgian court of appeals the judges engaged in a thorough examination of the configuration of the premises in order to rule on the question of whether there was or was not a trespass.

The ECtHR concluded: "In this case, the circumstances in which the impugned evidence was obtained shed no doubt whatsoever on its reliability or accuracy. Furthermore, the applicant had an opportunity to challenge the evidence at three levels of jurisdiction and to object to its use and to the resulting findings, in conformity with the jurisprudence cited by the court. Thus, the Court finds the merits of the criminal charges against the applicant were examined fairly, in keeping with the requirements of Article 6(1), and there has been no violation of that provision of the Convention".[31]

From this decision of the ECtHR, we can infer that the jurisprudence of the *Cour de Cassation* developed in the *Antigone* case and subsequent cases was not itself contrary to the European Convention, certainly not if the legal provision of internal law that was violated in obtaining the evidence did not constitute a fundamental right guaranteed by the Convention.

The jurisprudence of the *Antigone* case of the *Cour de Cassation* also poses the question regarding the fate that will meet the exclusionary rule of the "fruits of the poisonous tree".

The jurisprudence of the *Cour de Cassation* since the *Antigone* case of 2003 has not expressly challenged the rule according to which the nullity of an act extends also to subsequent evidence to the extent that, without the act that was done irregularly, that evidence would not have been obtained.[32] The so-called *Antigone*

---

[30] Illegally searched premises were certainly not publicly accessible but they were not a "home" within the meaning of Art. 8 of ECHR.

[31] Lee Davies v. Belgium, No. 18704/05, ECHR, 28 July 2009.

[32] Cass., 12 May 2004, R.G. P.04.0572.F.

jurisprudence has to do with the question of whether or not to exclude an illegally obtained piece of evidence. The fundamental shift in the jurisprudence of the *Cour de Cassation* since 2003 does not necessarily mean that the rule of the "fruits of the poisonous tree" should be abandoned or marginalized.

We can say that the fundamental principle of the "domino" theory remains valid, in the sense that pieces of evidence that are the direct or indirect result of illegal or irregular evidence are tainted by the same vices as the original evidence.[33] However, if the judge decides that illegal evidence should not be excluded from trial because its exclusion could not be justified by one of the factors arising from cases of the *Cour de Cassation*, it seems clear that the subsequent piece of evidence should not be kept from trial either, even if it is the result of the first, illegally obtained piece of evidence. These pieces of evidence are all just as illicit, but their exclusion from trial would no longer be automatic: it would depend on the fate of the piece of evidence from which they arose.

Conversely, if the judge decides to exclude the evidence based upon the *Antigone* cases and the factors described above, it seems that pieces of evidence that are the result of the evidence in question should be excluded from trial for the same reason because they are the product of it. We believe the jurisprudence of the *Antigone* case should not be applied to each piece of subsequent evidence. If a piece of evidence is excluded because it is the result of an act of investigation contrary to a statutory provision established under penalty of nullity, the evidence resulting from it should be kept out of trial in the same way because it is the direct consequence. The same answer applies where said evidence was gathered or introduced into court in violation of the right to a fair trial. In this situation, it is enough that the criminal judge decides first that a piece of evidence was illegally obtained and that its use would be in violation of the right to a fair trial, then notes that the subsequent evidence is the direct result of the first piece of evidence, itself illegally obtained and without which the subsequent evidence would not have been obtained. Indeed these circumstances corrupt the subsequent procedural acts that follow.[34]

According to one theory, we could still allow an exception to the "domino" theory where a piece of evidence is the result of another piece of evidence obtained through an illegal or irregular act which stains its trustworthiness. We could indeed argue that the simple fact that the illegality or the irregularity stains the trustworthiness of evidence resulting from it does not necessarily extend to other evidence which result from that and which, itself, may prove to be completely reliable.[35]

---

[33] Kuty (2005b, 95).

[34] Ibid.

[35] Ibid, 96.

7.3 Admissibility of Evidence and Protection of Privacy

7.3.1 The General Framework of the Protection of Privacy

Many provisions guarantee, in Belgian law, a general protection of privacy. This is the case of Art. 22 Const. but also Art. 8 ECHR and Art. 17 ICCPR, which are both considered to have a direct effect upon national law.[36] Regarding the treatment of personal information, Belgium moreover has an organic law with a date of December 8, 1992,[37] which establishes an exception for the treatment of information of a personal nature, administered by public authorities as part of the exercise of their duties as judicial police.

Following the lead of the ECtHR, the Belgian *Cour de Cassation* holds that the right to the protection of one's private life guaranteed by Art. 8 ECHR is not absolute and may be subject to restrictions. The restrictions are listed in Art. 8(2) ECHR: the restriction must be established by law (legality principle); must work towards one of the enumerated goals of Art. 8(2) (principle of finality); and must be necessary in a democratic society for the realization of that goal (principle of proportionality).[38] Regarding the first condition, the legality principle, the *Cour de Cassation* again aligns itself with the jurisprudence of the European Court in recognizing that, for the purposes of applying Art. 8 ECHR, "the term 'law' means any rule of internal law, written or otherwise, provided that it is accessible to the persons concerned and is stated in a precise manner."[39]

7.3.2 Protection of the Private Home

Art. 15 Const. contains the principle of the inviolability of the private home. §§ 87 and 88 of the Belgian Penal Code confer upon the investigating magistrate the right to issue a search warrant and, thus, impair the right of a citizen to the inviolability of his home. Indeed, these provisions allow the investigating magistrate, where he deems it useful, to enter into the home of the accused or in any other place where he might believe that objects helpful for revealing the truth might be hidden.[40]

---

[36] Particularly in this sense *see* the decision of the Constitutional Court (at the time the *Cour d'arbitrage*) No. 14/93 of 18 Feb. 1993, point B.2.7.

[37] Supplemented by a royal decree of February 13, 2001.

[38] For an illustration, see e.g. Cass., 8 Jan. 2003, RG P.02.0694.F.

[39] See in particular Cass., 2 May 1990, RG 8168.

[40] §§ 46*quinquies* and 89*ter* of the Criminal Code go even further because they allow an investigating magistrate to put a home under a "discrete visual inspection". This measure allows for entry into a private space to inspect it, not only without the consent of the owner, but even without knowledge of it. Bosly et al. (2010, 404). This is nevertheless subject to strict conditions and may not, in particular, be authorized other than for certain offenses (those for which wiretaps may be authorized or those committed in the context of a criminal organization).

The search warrant issued by the investigating magistrate must always mention the police officer's desire to search, the reason for the search, the person whose place will be searched, the exact location where it is to take place, the goal of the search, and the offense to which it is related.[41] In a decision of December 9, 2004, the ECtHR decided that information provided in the search warrant should, among other things allow the interested person to have control over the limits of the warrant by identifying, preventing and denouncing abuses committed upon execution of the search and, where that fails, to be able to seek remedies either at that time or retrospectively.[42]

Belgian law recognizes several exceptions to the need for approval from a magistrate. Thus, a search warrant is not necessary in cases of consent by the person who has lawful enjoyment of the premises, provided that the consent is established in writing (Art. 1 *bis* of the law of June 7, 1969).

Any possible illegality committed during the execution of a search warrant could bring about the exclusion of the pieces of evidence resulting therefrom. In practice, this exclusion could result in those things found as a result of a search and seizure not being usable as the basis for convicting the accused. However, exclusion of evidence obtained during an illegal search is not automatic. The rules and criteria coming from the *Antigone* decision of the *Cour de Cassation* must also apply when the judge decides whether or not to exclude any evidence obtained during a search deemed illegal. At this point we may return to the decision of the *Cour de Cassation* of November 16, 2004, concerning a search done without the approval of a magistrate and without the written consent of the person having lawful enjoyment of the premises. The Belgian *Cour de Cassation* applied the criteria of the *Antigone* decision plain and simple. The decision by the ECtHR of July 28, 2009, in the case of *Lee Davies v. Belgium* supports applying these rules to evidence resulting from an illegal search. It remains to be seen if the *Cour de Cassation* and/or the ECtHR will be so "permissive" in a case where a search is done in flagrant violation of the principle of the inviolability of the home guaranteed by the constitution and the Convention, without any authorization by the magistrate and without the consent, even oral, of the person having lawful enjoyment of the premises in question.

7.3.3 Protection of Private Communications

The secrecy of private communications is not specifically protected by the Constitution apart from the protections accorded to written correspondence. Indeed, Art. 29 Const. effectively guarantees the secrecy of letters. All other forms of private communication fall under the scope of the general protection of privacy, guaranteed by Art. 22 Const., Art. 8 ECHR and Art.17 ICCPR.

---

[41] Franchimont et al. (2009, 460–461).

[42] Van Rossem v. Belgium, No. 41872/98, ECHR, 9 December 2004.

These provisions are supplemented by a law of June 30, 1994, "relating to the protection of private life against wiretaps, surveillance and recording of communication and private telecommunications", which implemented the general principle of prohibiting wiretaps, surveillance and recording of communications and private telecommunications during their transmission and with the assistance of any sort of device. These prohibitions are set up as crimes, punished heavily with fines and imprisonment (§§ 259*bis*, 314*bis* Penal Code).

The Belgian CCP regulates three types of investigative measures which affect the secrecy of private communications: the identification of the user of a means of telecommunications (§ 46 *bis* CCP[43]), the identification and location of telecommunications (§ 88*bis* CCP[44]) and, finally, wiretaps and the recording of private communications or telecommunications (§ 90*ter et seq.* CCP[45]).

The first measure allows for contacting phone service providers and/or internet access providers, either to know to which means of communication a given person subscribes, or, conversely, to obtain the identity of the person using a given means of communication. This is allowed equally during a preliminary investigation, done by the prosecution, or during a judicial investigation, supervised by an investigating magistrate, and for all crimes or misdemeanors.

The second measure of identifying and determining the location of telecommunications is an even more intrusive search technique into private life, because it allows identification of the means of communications used on both ends of a conversation: the apparatus used for incoming communications and that used for outgoing communications. It also permits the determination of the time and the length of the call or communication. It further allows discovery of the origin or the destination of a call or a communication,[46] but never allows for intercepting the content of such communications. An investigating magistrate may authorize the identification and localization of telecommunications in the investigation of all offenses, whether felonies or misdemeanors. As an exception, the prosecutor may prescribe the measure in two very specific situations: in cases of phone or electronic harassment, under the condition that the complainant requests it, or in cases of flagrant crimes or misdemeanors, but only where it involves an offense listed under § 90*ter* (2–4) CCP[47] and only for a maximum of 24 h.[48]

---

[43] Inserted by a law dating June 10, 1998, becoming effective on October 2, 1998.

[44] Inserted by a law dating February 11, 1991, becoming effective on March 26, 1991.

[45] Inserted by a law dating June 30, 1994, becoming effective on February 3, 1995.

[46] Which, in the case of mobile phones, involves identifying the antennae that relayed the telecommunication.

[47] These are different offenses which can, among other things, give rise to wiretaps and recording private (tele)communication (see infra).

[48] Beyond this duration, the intervention of an investigating magistrate will be necessary.

The last investigative measure consists of intercepting, or alternatively recording, private words or messages exchanged between people,[49] either directly,[50] or via a means of telecommunication. Because it is particularly intrusive into one's private life, this surveillance measure is subject to very strict conditions: it is reserved for a number of serious offenses, exhaustively enumerated in the code (§ 90*ter* (2,4) CCP),[51] and it is not allowed where other means of investigation could suffice for discovering the truth[52] (§ 90*ter*(1) CCP); it is strictly limited in time[53]; and finally, in theory only the investigating magistrate may authorize this,[54] by a reasoned order subject to a series of formal conditions, the violation of which is punished by nullity (§ 90*quater*(1) CCP).

The *Cour de Cassation* has issued opinions relating to the various investigative measures. It has held that telephone communications constitute aspects of one's private life and correspondence, which are protected by Art. 8(1) ECHR,[55] but that both § 88*bis* CCP (authorizing tracking) and § 90*ter* CCP (governing wiretaps) are standards which, because they are accessible to the persons concerned and articulated in a sufficiently precise manner, are interferences in private life by public authorities in conformity with Art. 8(2) ECHR.[56]

The *Cour de Cassation* also applies *Antigone* case law relating to the admissibility of evidence, whereby the judge may no longer exclude illegally gathered evidence except in three situations: where a formal rule established under penalty of nullity

---

[49] To fall within the scope of the measure, the interception must occur during the transmission of the speech or message, that is to say, on the trajectory between transmitter and receiver. The *Cour de Cassation* has held, however, that the discovery of the contents of a recording from a telephone answering machine and its seizure, done in the context of a search executed in a regular manner by the investigating magistrate or under his order, do not fall under § 90*ter* CCP (and further do not violate Art. 8 ECHR). (Cass., 27 Oct. 1999, RG P.99.0715.F).

[50] This type of eavesdropping, called direct, may be done with the assistance of technical means placed *outside* the private space where the intercepted conversations are taking place (in which case, the *Cour de Cassation* believes there hasn't been an affront to the inviolability of the home; Cass., 26 Mar. 2003, RG P.03.0412.F), or *inside* that space and without the knowledge of its occupants (it is then a special type of discrete visual inspection; see § 90*ter* (2) C.C.P.).

[51] Under § 90ter(1)(para. 3) CCP, the measure may not be ordered except in respect, either to persons suspected, on the basis of specific evidence, of having committed one of the infractions listed in the law, or regarding (tele)communications regularly used by these suspects, places thought to be frequented by them, or people presumed, on the basis of specific evidence, to be in communication with them.

[52] However this requirement is considered *in abstracto*, and does not assume that all other means of investigation have actually been attempted before the measure is ordered.

[53] It may not exceed 1 month after the decision ordering it (§ 90*quater*(1)(4) CCP), unless renewed for a new term not permitted to exceed 1 month, with a maximum limit of 6 months (§ 90*quinquies*(1) CCP).

[54] Except in flagrant cases of hostage taking or extortion for which the prosecutor may authorize the measure exceptionally for a duration not lasting more than 24 h (§ 90*ter*(5) CCP).

[55] Cass., 10 Apr. 1990, RG 4346.

[56] Cass., 11 Oct. 2000, RG P.00.1245.F; Cass., 26 Mar. 2003, RG P. 03.0412.F; Cass., 10 Oct. 2007, RG P.07.0864.F.

was disregarded, where the irregularity harms the trustworthiness of the evidence, or where use of the evidence would compromise the right to a fair trial. Although § 90*quater*(1) CCP is one of the rare provisions established under penalty of nullity in matters of evidence, the Court has recently interpreted this nullity provision in rather restrictive terms, because it felt that it did not apply except in relation to defects affecting the warrant itself, but not its execution: thus, even though § 90*quater*(1)(paras. 2,5) CCP provide that the order by which the magistrate authorizes a wiretap must indicate, under penalty of nullity, the name and rank of the officer of the judicial police who will execute the measure, a violation of this requirement would not lead to the declaration of a nullity and exclusion of the evidence thus gathered if the surveillance measure was actually executed by a different agent. According to the court, this only concerns the execution of the measure and does not involve the regularity of the order itself.[57]

7.3.4 Searches of Vehicles or Other Means of Transportation

Art. 29 of the law of August 5, 1992, on the role of the police, allows the search of a vehicle if police officers have reasonable grounds for believing, on the basis of physical evidence, the behavior of the driver or passengers, or the circumstances of time and location, that the vehicle or the means of transportation was, is or could be used to commit an offense, to hide or transport wanted persons, to avoid an identity check or to store or transport objects dangerous to public order, evidentiary exhibits from a trial or general evidence of a crime.[58]

If the vehicle is in a private garage or is parked on private land, the judicial authorities must abide by the requirements relating to dwelling searches. The search of a vehicle converted in a permanent manner into housing and which is actually used to this effect at the time of the search is treated as a search of a dwelling. Such a vehicle, therefore, benefits from the protection tied to the inviolability of the home. In this case, the rules governing the legality of a dwelling search must also be applied.

It thus follows that a search of a vehicle, which is neither being used as a home nor found in a private garage or on private property, is governed by Art. 29 of the law on the role of the police, not by the legal provisions concerning the legality of a dwelling search. An irregularity or an illegality committed during a search of a vehicle based on the law of August 5, 1992, must also be judged according to the so-called *Antigone* criteria. The landmark decision of the *Cour de Cassation* of October 14, 2003, also specifically addressed searches of vehicles that did not serve as a home which were done contrary to the provisions of Art. 29 of the law on the role of the police.

---

[57] Cass., 19 Jun. 2007, RG P.07.0311.N.

[58] On this question, *see* Franchimont et al. (2009, 308–310).

Searches of computers, for their part, are governed by §§ 88*ter*, 88*quater* CCP. The magistrate has the power to authorize a search of a computer system. In this case, also, any possible illegality or irregularity must be judged on the basis of the *Antigone* jurisprudence of the *Cour de Cassation*. There is indeed no reason to suppose that this new jurisprudence of the *Cour de Cassation* on the exclusion of illegally obtained evidence would not apply to evidence obtained in violation of §§ 88*ter*, 88*quater* CCP.

7.4 Admisibility of Evidence and the Legality of Interrogations

7.4.1 The Right to Silence and the Principle of nemo tenetur

The Belgian Constitution does not guarantee persons accused of an offense the right to remain silent and to not contribute to their self-incrimination. For some time,[59] on the other hand, the *Cour de Cassation* has held that the right to silence is part of the right to a defense and that under this rubric, it constitutes a general principle of law.[60] Since then, it has been expressly guaranteed by § 47bis CPP, as modified by the law of August 13, 2011.[61]

There exists, as well, an obligation imposed by international standards, which are given direct effect in the Belgian legal order. While the right to silence is formally guaranteed by Art. 14 (3)(g) ICCPR, it is not expressly mentioned in the ECHR. However, the ECtHR has, since 1993, recognized that it is included in the right to a fair trial, guaranteed by Art. 6 of the Convention.[62]

In the opinion of the ECtHR, the reason for this right has to do with protecting the accused from abusive coercion on the part of the authorities and the acquisition of pieces of evidence through duress or pressure, without regard to the will of the accused, and, thus, helps to avoid judicial error and makes it possible to achieve the goals of a fair trial under Art. 6 ECHR.[63] But the court also sees a corollary to the presumption of innocence enshrined in Art. 6(2) ECHR,[64] which implies that the prosecution has the burden of proving its case, while the defense may carry on in a purely passive role.

---

[59] Cass., 13 May 1986, I Pasicrisie 1107 (1986), and the conclusions of the Procureur général Dujardin in conformity with this.

[60] Traditionally, the Belgian Cour de Cassation evokes, on this topic, the respect of the rights of the defense "which the right to silence is a part of" (*see* notably Cass., 13 May 1986, RG 9136 and Cass., 13 Jan. 1999, RG P 98.0412.F). More recently, it has specified that there "does not exist a general principle of a right to silence *separate* from the general principle of law concerning the rights of the defense" (Cass., 16 June 2004, RG P.04.0671.F).

[61] Usually referred to as the "Salduz law".

[62] Funke v. France (1993), 16 E.H.R.R. 297, 326, § 44.

[63] Murray v. United Kingdom (1996), 22 E.H.R.R. 29, 60, § 45.

[64] Saunders v. United Kingdom (1996), 23 E.H.R.R. 313, 337, § 68.

The right to not contribute to your own incrimination can be undermined in two different ways, neither of which excludes the other: it can be violated through extracting statements from a suspect against his will, by means of ill treatment, pressure or threats but also in cases where an accused makes uninformed statements, and in particular if he is not fully informed of the fact that he has the right to remain silent throughout the interrogations to which he is subjected, and that he is entirely free to decide how to deal with the charges brought against him.[65]

7.4.2 *Protection Against "Extracted" Statements*

There are different ways to extract statements from an accused against his will. The most characteristic ways, obviously, include the use of ill treatment (torture or inhumane and degrading treatment). But more subtle forms of pressure can also be exercised, such as interrogating a suspect, as if he were a mere witness, where he is obliged to answer and tell the truth.

7.4.2.1 Torture and Inhumane and Degrading Treatment

The law of June 14, 2002, brought Belgian law into conformity with the Convention against Torture and other Cruel, Inhuman or Degrading Treatment or Punishment (CAT), which was adopted in New York on December 10, 1984. It added §§ 417*bis* and 417*quinquies* to the Penal Code, which penalize torture and the use of inhumane or degrading treatment and establish heightened penalties for public officials when acting within the scope of their duties. This law did not expressly include the prohibition contained in Art. 15 of the New York Convention against using as evidence a statement that was obtained through torture. Such a ban should result from the application of the combined jurisprudence of the Belgian *Cour de Cassation* and the ECtHR. For according to Belgian precedent, exclusion will ensue if there was a violation of the right to a fair trial (so-called *Antigone* jurisprudence), and according to the ECtHR, the use of statements as evidence in criminal proceedings or other material collected by means of acts that qualify as torture automatically taints as unfair the entirety of the proceedings.[66] It is difficult to see how such evidence could be admitted in criminal proceedings in Belgium.

Things are less clear when dealing with evidence gathered by means of acts no longer qualifying as torture, but "merely" inhumane or degrading treatment. When dealing with these, the jurisprudence of the ECtHR[67] is indeed less clear-cut: although

[65] In other words, confessions or other self-incriminating statements must be both free and made in full knowledge of the facts.

[66] Gäfgen v. Germany (G.C.) (2011) , 52 E.H.R.R. 1, 42, § 166 and the case law cited therein.

[67] Which, indirectly, also sets the standards applicable in Belgian law regarding the case law of the *Cour de Cassation* and the benchmarks made therein for the criteria of a fair trial.

the Court believes that there absolutely has been a violation of Art. 6 ECHR in cases involving the use of *statements* obtained by means of treatment contrary to Art. 3 ECHR, but not considered torture, it is not as categorical when dealing with the use of physical evidence that was found as a result of such treatment. On the contrary, in this second situation the possible violation of Art. 6 will depend, according to the Court, upon the circumstances of the case and, in particular, on whether there has been "a break in the causal chain leading from the prohibited methods of investigation to the [accused] conviction and sentence in respect of the impugned real evidence".[68]

It remains, in any case, for the defendant to prove the existence of any possible bad treatment he may have been subjected to during interrogations and, on this point, the protection offered by Belgian law has recently been increased, since suspects interrogated while being taken into police custody do now receive the right to be assisted by counsel during all the interrogations conducted before they're placed in pre-trial detention.[69]

7.4.2.2 Testimony Under Oath

For the *Cour de Cassation*, the right to silence prohibits questioning an accused under oath during his own trial.[70] This does not mean, however, that the right to a fair trial will thereby be irreparably compromised. In the view of the Court, an appropriate solution would be to exclude from the trial any evidence found to be null and any evidence derived there from.[71] In contrast an accused who was not himself heard under oath may not move to exclude from the trial a statement made against him by another suspect under oath, which would be inadmissible against that suspect.[72]

7.4.3 *Protection Against "Uninformed" Statements*

If we wish to ensure that an accused who makes self-incriminating statements is doing so with full understanding of the facts and is duly informed of the right to silence which he is waiving, two minimum guarantees seem necessary: an express

---

[68] Ibid, 42, § 180.

[69] This right has been guaranteed by the *Salduz* law of August 13, 2011, which entered into force on January 1, 2012.

[70] Cass., 16 Feb. 1996, RG A.84.0002.F.

[71] Cass., 16 Sept. 1998, RG A.94.0001.F. This decision is older than the new *Antigone* jurisprudence of the *Cour de Cassation*, but its teachings remain, for our purposes, valid, because in cases of violations of the right to silence, we find ourselves in one of the three situations where the *Cour de Cassation* still allows setting aside illicit evidence, namely where the use of the evidence would compromise the right to a fair trial.

[72] Cass., 27 June 2007, RG P.07.0333.F.

warning regarding the existence of this right and the assistance of an attorney who could clarify the exact extent of that right. On both these points, Belgian law which offered insufficient protection in light of the *Salduz* jurisprudence of the ECtHR, has recently been reformed.

Respect for the right to silence would, in principle, prohibit the use of any unfair procedures for obtaining confessions, but would not lead to exclusion of statements obtained through the use of surprise and secret information.

7.4.3.1 The Duty to Warn the Accused of His Right to Silence and the Right to Assistance by an Attorney

Since January 1, 2012, §§ 47*bis* and 70*bis* CCP expressly provide that any person interrogated as a suspect must be informed of his/her right to remain silent. Besides, if the suspect is interrogated in relation to "serious" offenses (i.e. offenses punished with a maximum sentence of at least one year imprisonment, and not related to road traffic), he/she has the right to a private consultation with a lawyer prior to being interrogated. The first interrogation can be delayed at the suspect's explicit request in order to allow such consultation. However, if the interrogation takes place upon written invitation informing the suspect of his/her rights as well as of the facts and events he/she will be questioned on, the prior consultation with a lawyer is presumed.

In addition, and as already mentioned, the suspect taken into police custody also receives the right to be assisted by counsel during the interrogations conducted before he/she is placed in pretrial detention.

7.4.3.2 Prohibition on Unfair or Deceptive Practices

Statements obtained with the help of false promises have been declared illegal for being acquired in violation of the right to silence.[73] This should also be the case where confessions are obtained because of lies by those preparing a report, which reflect an unfair attitude on the part of the person in charge.[74]

7.4.3.3 Right to Silence and the Effect of Surprise

It goes without saying that, to be effective, investigative measures such as wiretaps are done without the knowledge of the persons being listened to, who may during that time – and this is of course the goal of the measure – provide the authorities

---

[73] Cass., 13 May 1986, RG 9136. In this case, agents of the *Inspection spéciale des impôts* had obtained statements from suspects by guaranteeing them they would not be prosecuted criminally, even though they did not have the authority to make such a promise.

[74] On this issue, *see* De Valkeneer (2006, 171–174) and the case law cited therein.

with information that they would not have agreed to provide in a classic interrogation. However, these methods do not imply a violation of the right to silence, so long as, of course, they are not accompanied by illegal or unfair means. The *Cour de Cassation* has held that "neither Arts. 6(1) and 6(2) of the ECHR, nor the general principle of law relating to the rights of the defense prohibit listening and recording the communications of a suspect, made pursuant to § 90*ter* (1) CCP, even if this act of investigation makes it possible to obtain statements the declarant would not have made in the presence of a judicial authority or the police".[75]

7.5 Conclusion

For years it was said in Belgian law that the criminal judge could not take into consideration, as the basis for a conviction, any evidence that was gathered in an illicit manner. Following the new teaching of the *Cour de Cassation* – beginning with the *Antigone* decision of October 14, 2003 – this is no longer the case. In lieu of a *prima facie* prohibition on the use of illicit evidence, the Court substituted a *prima facie* authorization, except in three narrow cases: violations of a formality established under penalty of nullity, where the reliability of the evidence has suffered, or the right to a fair trial has been undermined.

This reversal of the traditional rule was received rather poorly in the literature. It was argued that it was apparent nonsense for the legislature to incorporate a series of evidentiary rules into law that fix strict limits and conditions on when evidence can be used, and afterwards to admit evidence that was gathered in disregard of the rules thus adopted. Such a form of "legal schizophrenia", consisting of taking from one hand and giving to the other, deprives the law of evidence of a good part of its effectiveness: if illicitly gathered evidence can contribute to forming the opinion of the judge, it is hard to see how it would be possible to effectively dissuade the investigating authorities from again resorting to illegal conduct.

It is also painful to admit that the question of the fate reserved for illegal evidence has up to the present essentially been left to the courts. It seems to us that it would be more in line with the principle of legality of the prosecution if it were decided by the legislature itself.

While waiting for this legislative intervention, it is left to the *Cour de Cassation* to continue fashioning Belgian evidentiary law in criminal matters.

Bibliography

Beernaert, M.-A. 2005. La fin du régime d'exclusion systématique des preuves illicitement recueillies par les organes chargées de l'enquête et des poursuites. *Revue de Jurisprudence de Liège, Mons et Bruxelles* 1094–1109.

[75] Cass., 10 Oct. 2007, RG P.07.0864.F.

Bosly, H.-D., D. Vandermeersch, and M.-A. Beernaert. 2010. *Droit de la procédure pénale*, 6th ed. Brussels: La Charte.

Braas, A. 1925. *Traité élémentaire de l'instruction criminelle*. Brussels: Bruylant.

De Valkeneer, C. 2005. Que reste-t-il du principe de la légalité de la preuve? Variations autour de quelques arrêts récents de la Cour de cassation. *Revue de droit pénal et de criminologie* 685–695

De Valkeneer, C. 2006. *Manuel de l'enquête pénale*, 3rd ed. Brussels: Larcier.

Franchimont, M., A. Jacobs, and A. Masset. 2009. *Manuel de procédure pénale*, 3rd ed. Brussels: Larcier.

Kuty, F. 1998. Doit-on admettre avec la Cour de cassation, que la circonstance que le dénonciateur d'une infraction en a eu connaissance en raison d'une illégalité n'affecte pas la regularité de la preuve qui a été obtenu ultérieurement sans aucune illegalité. *Revue de Jurisprudence de Liège-Mons-Bruxelles* 489–501.

Kuty, F. 2004. La règle de l'exclusion de la preuve illégale ou irrégulière : de la précision au bouleversement. *Revue critique de jurisprudence belge* 408–438.

Kuty, F. 2005a. Le droit de la preuve à l'épreuve des juges. *Journal des Tribunaux* 349–355.

Kuty, F. 2005b. Le droit de la preuve au regard de la jurisprudence récente de la Cour de cassation. In *Questions d'actualité de droit pénal et de procédure pénale*, ed. J. Messinne, 53–107. Brussels: Bruylant.

Traest, P. 1994. Wanneer is door een derde verkregen bewijs ontoelaatbaar? (note on Cass., 4 Jan. 1994) *Recente cassatie* 72–75.

Traest, P. 1996. De internationalisering van het bewijsrecht: Over telefoontap en de eisen die aan het in het buitenland verworven bewijs moeten gestead Worden. *Recente cassatie* 142–150.

Chapter 8
The Netherlands: Statutory Balancing and a Choice of Remedies

Matthias J. Borgers and Lonneke Stevens

8.1 The General Theory of Admissibility and Exclusion of Illegally Gathered Evidence

8.1.1 An Introduction to Dutch Criminal Evidence Law

This chapter will give an overview of the way in which the Dutch law of criminal procedure deals with illegally gathered evidence, in particular when the suspect's right to privacy or privilege against self-incrimination is violated.[1] For a proper understanding of this aspect of the Dutch law of criminal procedure, it is important to outline several basic principles of Dutch evidentiary law in criminal cases.

First, the evidentiary system in criminal cases is based on the principle of establishing the substantive truth. This is expressed in the Dutch Code of Criminal Procedure (CCP) (*Nederlandse Wetboek van Strafvordering (Sv)*) in the requirement that a judge may assume that the offense charged is proven only if he "is convinced of it".[2] This means that a high degree of certainty must exist that the accused has committed the offense.

The judge must also be convinced by the contents of legal evidence. This is the evidence that the CCP considers admissible in criminal proceedings. It may include: the judge's own perception, statements by the defendant, statements by witnesses,

[1] For literature on this subject, see: Embregts (2003, 2010), Van Woensel (2004, 119–171), Nijboer (2008, 138–156), Kuiper (2009, 35–59), and Corstens and Borgers (2011, 724–740).

[2] There is no constitutional provision articulating the same principle.

M.J. Borgers (✉) • L. Stevens
Faculty of Law, VU University Amsterdam,
De Boelelaan 1105, 1081 HV Amsterdam, The Netherlands
e-mail: m.j.borgers@vu.nl; l.stevens@rechten.vu.nl

S.C. Thaman (ed.), *Exclusionary Rules in Comparative Law*, Ius Gentium: Comparative Perspectives on Law and Justice 20, DOI 10.1007/978-94-007-5348-8_8,

statements by experts and written documents (§ 339 CCP). In reality, there is scarcely any evidence that the law does not consider admissible.[3]

The statutory provisions on admissible evidence also contain a few so-called minimum evidence rules. These minimum evidence rules limit the free evaluation of the evidence by the judge for the purpose of facilitating establishment of the substantive truth.[4] An example of a minimum evidence rule is the rule that proof that the accused has committed the offense charged may not be presumed (in principle)[5] only on the basis of a statement by one witness or by the accused. Because there is always a chance that the witness or the accused will not tell the truth, the law requires a second statement to be used as evidence in these cases. In the judicial system, minimum evidence rules tend to have minimum explanations as well.

Apart from the aforementioned minimum evidence rules, the provisions on admissible evidence do not contain any rules on the reliability of the evidence or how it is gathered. Consequently, unreliable or illegally gathered evidence is admissible in itself as legal evidence. Evidence can, however, be excluded and otherwise admissible evidence may be excluded because of its unreliability or the way it was gathered. In such a case, the judge does not use that evidence as a basis for his opinion on whether the offense charged was committed.

The above-mentioned reasons for excluding evidence – unreliability and illegalities in its collection – should be distinguished. If evidence is unreliable, its exclusion is required because of the principle that the trial should consist in a pursuit of the substantive truth. The exclusion of illegally gathered evidence has a separate legal basis in § 359a CCP. Gathering evidence illegally does not automatically result in exclusion of the evidence. As discussed in more detail below, other sanctions are also possible. In some cases, evidence is unreliable because certain legal rules on gathering evidence have been violated. In such cases, where unreliability coincides with the illegalities in the gathering of the evidence, the evidence will already be excluded on the basis of unreliability. In principle, the rule of § 359a CCP need not be applied.[6]

8.1.2 *Sanctions on Illegal Gathering of Evidence*

8.1.2.1 The Legal Framework

The Dutch Code of Criminal Procedure gives rules in § 359a CCP which regulate the assessment of illegally gathered evidence. The text of § 359a CCP reads as follows:

---

[3] An exception would be statements made by lawyers during closing arguments at trial or otherwise during the proceedings.

[4] de Wilde (2008, 269–294), and Corstens and Borgers (2011, 712–716).

[5] An important exception is contained in the rule that evidence that the accused has committed the offense charged *can* – not *must* – be assumed by the judge on the basis of an official report by an investigating officer. See § 344(2) CCP.

[6] For a detailed explanation of the distinction between unreliable and illegally gathered evidence, see Dubelaar (2009, 93–105).

1. If procedural rules prove to have been breached during the preliminary investigation, which breach can no longer be remedied, and the legal consequences of the breach are not apparent from statutory law, the court may rule that:
   a. the severity of the punishment will be decreased in proportion to the gravity of the breach if the harm caused by the breach can be compensated in this way;
   b. the results of the investigation obtained through the breach may not contribute to the evidence of the offense charged;
   c. the Public Prosecution Service will be barred from prosecuting if the breach makes it impossible to hear the case in compliance with the principles of due process.
2. In applying the first subsection, the court must take account of the interest that the breached rule serves, the gravity of the breach and the harm it causes.
3. The judgment must contain the decisions referred to in the first subsection. These must be reasoned.

Before discussing the way in which the rule in § 359a CCP has developed in the case law of the Dutch Supreme Court (Hoge Raad), two parts of this provision require further attention for the purpose of a comparison with other legal systems.

The first subsection of § 359a CCP refers to the court. By "court", the law means the judicial authority that handles the substance of the case. In all cases, this is a professional court. Lay judges do not exist in the Netherlands. The judge who rules on the attachment of consequences to the illegal gathering of evidence also rules on the guilt or innocence of the accused. Owing to this, the situation can occur that the judge takes cognizance of the contents of an article of evidence and then decides that this evidence must be excluded because it was gathered illegally. The consequence is that the judge, even though he has knowledge of the contents of the evidence, may not use those contents as a basis for his opinion on whether the offense charged has been proven. This has not gone without criticism: there is a risk that the judge – consciously or unconsciously – will nevertheless be guided by the contents of the excluded evidence. Nevertheless, that criticism did not result in the introduction of separate proceedings in which a judge other than the judge hearing the case (exclusively) decides whether or not to remove the evidence from the file because it was gathered illegally. In the Dutch law of criminal procedure, there is trust that the (professional) judge will ignore the contents of the excluded evidence in forming his or her opinion.

The first subsection of § 359a CCP also mentions the breach of procedural rules during the preliminary investigation. This means failure to observe written and unwritten rules that apply to gathering evidence. No distinction is made between the different types of rules. They can be rules on respecting fundamental rights, such as the right to remain silent. But they can also be rules that pertain "only" to the contents of certain documents that have to be shown to the suspect when means of coercion are used. § 359a CCP is intended to be a provision that applies to all these rules. No distinction is made between violations of constitutional and non-constitutional rights. The reason for this is partly that the Dutch Constitution only regulates the manner of gathering evidence to a limited extent. Such regulation ensues rather from "ordinary" legislation and also from the European Convention for the Protection of Human Rights (ECHR). Violations of the ECHR that take place in the context of gathering evidence also count as breaches of procedural rules within the meaning of § 359a CCP.

8.1.2.2 Further Development in the Case Law of the Dutch Supreme Court

§ 359a was introduced into the CCP in 1996. To a great extent, it codified the applicable case law up to then on illegal gathering of evidence. After 1996, the rule of § 359a CCP was further developed in the case law of the Dutch Supreme Court. A very important judgment is that of March 30, 2004, in which the Dutch Supreme Court gave a summary of the case law which up to then had applied § 359a CCP.[7] The lines the Dutch Supreme Court set out in this judgment can still be considered a representation of the prevailing law. The standard judgment of March 30, 2004 is discussed point-by-point below and explained in more detail where necessary.

Basic Principles of the Application of § 359a CCP

Based on the text of § 359a CCP and its explanation by the legislature, the Supreme Court formulated some basic principles for the application of § 359a CCP. These include two preconditions that have to be met.

First of all, § 359a CCP pertains only to breaches of procedural rules committed during the preliminary investigation, in so far as that preliminary investigation relates to the offense with which the accused is charged and thus on which the judge has to decide.[8] This means that no legal consequences are attached to breaches of procedural rules committed in the context of an investigation aimed at someone other than the accused. An example: in the investigation of accused A, and in violation of the rules, a telephone tap is conducted. During the monitoring of the calls, incriminating material is collected on B. This material can be used in the criminal case against B, because the breach of procedural rules did not take place in the context of the investigation relating to the offense with which B is charged.[9]

Secondly, §359a CCP only applies to *irremediable* breaches of procedural rules. If the breach has been or can still be remedied, there is no reason to attach a legal consequence to it. An example is a failure to inform the accused of the results of a

---

[7] *Dutch Law Reports (Nederlandse Jurisprudentie)* 2004, 376 annotated by Buruma.

[8] In principle, breaches of procedural rules relating to custodial means of coercion, which the accused could have put before the investigating magistrate (the judge in the preliminary investigation) at an earlier stage, are not assessed again by the session judge on the basis of § 359a CCP.

[9] HR (Supreme Court) October 18, 1988, *Dutch Law Reports (NJ)* 1989, 306.

DNA test, thereby depriving the accused of the opportunity to request a second opinion.[10] The trial judge then needs to examine whether it is still possible to obtain a second opinion. If that is the case, the accused must still be given the opportunity to obtain it. This, of course, has to be a remediable breach of procedural rules. If a search of a home has been conducted without the required authorization, no remedy is possible. Such authorization must be granted prior to the search.

The Supreme Court stated further that in deciding whether a legal consequence will be attached to a breach of procedural rules, and what particular consequence that would be, the judge must take account of the points of view formulated in the second subsection of § 359a CCP: (1) the interest that the breached rule serves; (2) the gravity of the breach, and (3) the harm caused by the breach. These points of view deserve some further explanation.

The interest that the breached rule serves. Here, the law refers to the so-called relativity requirement, referred to at times using the Gerrman term: *Schutznorm.* One must see what interest the breached rule is intended to protect, and to what extent this interest relates to the accused. The rules relating to searches of homes are intended to protect the privacy interests of the occupant. So only the interests of the occupant are harmed if these rules are breached. An example is a situation in which someone uses a room in a house only as a storage place (for drugs), while not being an occupant of that house. In such a case, no consequences need be attached to a breach of the rules on searches of homes.[11] Apart from that, the Supreme Court leaves some room to attach a sanction nevertheless to the illegal gathering of evidence in cases in which the relativity requirement is not met. This gives the judge a certain margin in responding to breaches of procedural rules that do not harm the accused's interests, but regarding which he nevertheless considers it inappropriate not to respond. These are, however, exceptional situations.[12]

The gravity of the breach. This point of view is especially important for the choice of the sanction. In the event of very grave breaches of procedural rules, the most severe sanction – barring the Public Prosecution Service from prosecuting – is likely, while the most minor breaches are settled by some reduction of the sentence or by the mere determination of illegality. Under certain circumstances, the good faith of the investigating officers who caused the breach of procedural rules can play a part. For example: an investigating officer enters premises which he presumes to be vacant. After he enters, the premises prove to be occupied. In that case, the absence of the written authorization required to enter the premises does not have to

---

[10] Cf. HR June 3, 2001, *Dutch Law Reports* 2001, 536.

[11] Cf. HR March 26, 2002, *Dutch Law Reports* 2002, 343.

[12] See for example HR January 12, 1999, *Dutch Law Reports* 1999, 290, in which evidence is excluded because a telephone call between a co-suspect and his lawyer was tapped. Tapping calls with professionals entitled to privilege constitutes a serious breach of procedural rules.

result in exclusion of the evidence if the judge is of the opinion that this investigating officer could and was entitled to assume that the premises were unoccupied.[13]

The harm caused by the breach. If a rule is breached that was written in the interest of a suspect, this is as a rule harmful to the suspect. Under certain circumstances, however, no harm is done. An example is not informing a suspect his right to remain silent. This is in itself harmful to the suspect, unless the suspect is a lawyer. The suspect then knows, after all, without being told, that he has the right to remain silent.

The Supreme Court finally held that not every breach of procedural rules necessarily results in one of the legal consequences referred to in § 359a (1) CCP. § 359a CCP formulates a power, not an obligation. The rationale of § 359a CCP is not that a breach of procedural rules has to result in some advantage for the accused, no matter what. The point is rather to see whether attaching a sanction to a breach of procedural rules is called for in light of the aforementioned points of view. It is possible, therefore, for a judge to find that procedural rules have been breached without attaching a legal consequence to the breach.

If the judge is of the opinion that a legal consequence should be attached to a breach of procedural rules, the judge will have a choice of the sanctions referred to in § 359a (1) CCP: barring the Public Prosecution Service from prosecuting, excluding evidence and sentence reduction. The Supreme Court formulates the conditions to be met for each of these sanctions before the relevant sanction can be imposed.

Barring Prosecution

The Supreme Court has repeatedly ruled that barring prosecution is an option only in exceptional cases. There is room for this sanction only if investigating officers or the Public Prosecution Service has seriously breached principles of due process, through which, either on purpose or with gross disregard for the interests of the accused, his right to a fair trial has been breached to a considerable extent.[14] To date, this sanction has been imposed mainly in cases where the possibilities of judicial monitoring of the gathering of evidence were deliberately thwarted.[15] Another instance is when an unacceptable agreement is made with a witness for the prosecution that, in exchange for acting as such, any prison sentence imposed would not be enforced.[16]

---

[13] Cf. HR June19, 2001, *Dutch Law Reports* 2001, 574, annotated by Reijntjes.

[14] See in particular HR December 19, 1995, *Dutch Law Reports* 1996, 249 annotated by Schalken.

[15] HR February 4, 1997, *Dutch Law Reports* 1997, 308, annotated by Schalken and HR September 8, 1998, *Dutch Law Reports* 1998, 879, annotated by Schalken.

[16] HR June 1, 1999, *Dutch Law Reports* 1999, 567, annotated by Schalken and HR June 8, 1999, *Dutch Law Reports* 1999, 773, annotated by Reijntjes.

Exclusion of Evidence

According to the Supreme Court, exclusion of evidence can be up for discussion only if the evidence was obtained through the breach, and is considered when a rule or legal principle (of criminal procedure) has been seriously breached by the illegal gathering of evidence. The Supreme Court thus actually sets two requirements. Firstly, a (sufficient) causal connection must exist between the breach of procedural rules and gathering of the evidence. Secondly, an important rule or legal principle must have been breached to a considerable extent.

It is not usually problematic to determine a causal connection between a breach of procedural rules and evidence. If, for example, a search of premises was not conducted in accordance with the applicable rules, evidence gathered during the search may be considered illegal. Nevertheless, it is a fact that relatively high requirements are set in the case law on the requisite causal connection. For instance, a temporal connection is not necessarily a causal connection. If, for example, a statement is made during unlawful detention, that statement will not necessarily count as a result of the unlawful detention.[17] The causal connection can also be broken. An example of this is the situation in which a suspect is unlawfully arrested, while subsequently, when asked, the suspect gives permission for a search of his home. Giving such permission breaks, as it were, the causal connection between the arrest and the search.[18]

The Supreme Court does not explain when a rule is important and under what conditions such a rule is breached to a considerable extent. In a certain sense, the Supreme Court refers to the viewpoints provided by § 359a (2) CCP.[19] After all, a rule that is not intended to protect essential interests of the suspect could generally be considered an unimportant or less important rule. The element of a breach "to a considerable extent" indicates that there must have been a relatively serious breach and that harm has demonstrably been suffered as well. Exclusion of evidence will generally follow, for instance from a breach of rules pertaining to the suspect's privilege against self-incrimination.[20] This also holds if an illegal body search is conducted during which drugs are found in a natural cavity of the suspect's body.[21]

More generally speaking, the Supreme Court lets it be known that exclusion of evidence is a sanction that should be used with restraint. The Supreme Court emphasizes, for example, that exclusion of evidence is a power, not an obligation, of the court. The Supreme Court points out further that account must be taken not only of the points of view referred to in § 359a (2) CCP, but also of the circumstances of the case. This leaves room to make allowance for the gravity of the offense, in the sense that evidence is less likely to be excluded if the offense is serious than if the offense is minor.

---

[17] See for example HR January 19, 1999, *Dutch Law Reports* 1999, 251.

[18] Cf. HR February 8, 2000, *Dutch Law Reports* 2000, 316.

[19] Cf. Embregts (2010, note 10.11 to § 359a).

[20] See Sect. 8.3.

[21] HR May 29, 2007, *Dutch Law Reports* 2008, 14, annotated by Reijntjes.

Sentence Reduction

The Supreme Court formulates four conditions for the use of sentence reduction as a sanction for a breach of procedural rules: (1) the suspect has actually been harmed; (2) the harm was due to the breach; (3) the harm is suitable for compensation by sentence reduction; and (4) sentence reduction is justified in light of the importance of the breached rule and the gravity of the breach. The first and last requirements reflect the viewpoints referred to in § 359a (2) CCP, while the second requirement pertains to the requisite causal connection. It is especially interesting to pay attention to the third requirement: the harm is suitable for compensation by reducing the sentence. It is important that "compensation" is involved. Where exclusion of evidence can be considered to have *remedied* the illegal gathering of evidence, sentence reduction does not go as far. Nothing is remedied, but something is given in return for the breach. For that reason, sentence reduction is mainly an appropriate sanction for less serious breaches of procedural rules. Examples are a search which observes the main, but not all legal requirements,[22] or systematic surveillance of a home from the public road without permission from the public prosecutor.[23] In addition, sentence reduction is also a sanction that can be imposed if unlawful actions do not result in evidence and evidence cannot be excluded for that reason. If such unlawful actions are not so serious that they must be followed by barring prosecution, sentence reduction is an appropriate sanction. An example is an arrest lawful in itself that is accompanied by unnecessary force.[24]

Fruits of the Poisonous Tree

The Supreme Court does not pay specific attention to the doctrine of "fruits of the poisonous tree", i.e. evidence indirectly obtained through a violation of the rules. The reason is that, on closer analysis, this issue is covered by the causality test, which is already contained in the conditions for application of the above-mentioned sanctions. There must be a *direct connection* each time between the breach of procedural rules and the deliberate or grossly negligent failure to consider the accused's interest in fair treatment on the one hand and, on the other, the obtaining of evidence or the harm actually suffered by the accused.[25] In the discussion of the exclusion of evidence, it was already noted that a temporal connection does not suffice and that a causal connection can also be broken. This means that fruit of the poisonous tree

[22] Cf. HR July 2, 2002, *Dutch Law Reports* 2002, 624.

[23] HR March 21, 2000, LJN AA5254.

[24] Cf. HR December 21, 2004, *Dutch Law Reports* 2005, 172, annotated by JR.

[25] Such a direct connection means that the fruit of the poisonous tree must *exclusively* be the result of the unlawful actions. It is not sufficient (any more) that the fruit of the poisonous tree is *largely* the result of those actions. The recent case law of the Supreme Court is at any rate interpreted in this way.

will not easily be involved.[26] Example: a man was arrested, and asked whether he had burglar's tools on him. The man threw his bag and jacket on the ground and yelled: "See for yourself!" Burglar's tools were then found in the bag and jacket. It was argued in the criminal proceeding that the man had been arrested unlawfully (because there was no suspicion) and that finding the burglar's tools had to be considered fruit of the poisonous tree of that arrest. The Supreme Court held that, insofar as the arrest should have to be considered unlawful, it cannot be said that this evidence was the direct result of the arrest.[27] The discovery of burglar's tools was primarily the result of throwing the jacket and bag on the ground and yelling: "See for yourself!" The fact that he did so after the arrest did not affect this.

Examples can also be found in the case law in which fruit of the poisonous tree is indeed excluded from the evidence. An example is a case where, in conflict with the applicable rules, a telephone conversation between the accused and a doctor was tapped. At the hearing, the accused was confronted with the report of the wiretap. The Supreme Court held that the way in which the accused reacted when confronted with the wiretap report could not be used as evidence.[28] The reaction could be considered a direct result of the breach of procedural rules.

8.2 Violations of the Right to Privacy

8.2.1 The Right to Privacy in Dutch Law

Art. 10(1) of the Dutch Constitution provides that everyone has a right to respect of his privacy, barring restrictions to be set by or pursuant to the law. This gives the right to privacy the status of a constitutional right. In addition, the right to privacy is guaranteed by Art. 8 ECHR. This convention provision has direct effect in Dutch law. This is very important because the Dutch courts are not at liberty to declare laws unconstitutional. But they make rulings which declare laws to be in accordance with or in violation of the ECHR.

In addition to the right to privacy, the Dutch Constitution also protects the right to inviolability of the home. Under Art. 12(1) Const., entering a home without permission is allowed only in the cases specified by or pursuant to the law, and by those designated to do so by or pursuant to the law. Art. 12 Const. prescribes further that prior identification and notification of the purpose of the entry are required.

---

[26] Other possible reasons not to assume a causal connection can be based on alternative causality (evidence arising from an unlawful act, but at the same time also from an independent source) or due to the "inevitable discovery" exception (the evidence could most likely have been gathered legally as well). These reasons are put forth relatively rarely in the case law. See Embregts (2010, note 5.10 to § 359a).

[27] Cf. HR February 24, 2004, *Dutch Law Reports* 2004, 226.

[28] HR October 2, 2007, *Dutch Law Reports* 2008, 374, annotated by Legemaate.

Moreover, a written report of the entry must be provided to the occupant as soon as possible. The right of inviolability of the home can be construed as a right partly for the purpose of protecting privacy. Protection of the inviolability of the home enables people to enjoy their privacy in their own homes as far as possible without interruption.

8.2.2 Violation of Privacy in the Context of a Criminal Investigation

The exercise of various powers of criminal procedure violates privacy. One can particularly think of searches of homes and telecommunication taps. The violation of privacy is justified by the existence of specific statutory provisions setting the conditions under which the powers in question may be exercised. Those conditions are for the purpose of ensuring that privacy is not needlessly violated. The law defines the offenses with respect to which the relevant powers may be used, while providing for judicial review of the need to use these powers.[29] In principle, as long as the statutory conditions are observed, there is no question of illegally gathered evidence. Disregarding these conditions constitutes a breach of procedural rules. Sanctions are imposed on such a breach under the provisions of § 359a CCP. To that extent, breaches of procedural rules that constitute an unacceptable violation of the right to privacy are not treated differently than other breaches of procedural rules. For that reason, this section will be limited to a few comments on the Dutch provisions on searches of homes and telecommunication taps.

8.2.3 Searches of Homes

The CCP contains comprehensive rules on searches of homes. The central point is that the search must be conducted as far as possible by the investigating magistrate.[30] The (acting) public prosecutor conducts the search only if it is not possible to wait for the investigating magistrate to arrive. In that case, authorization from the investigating magistrate is required. Such authorization can be obtained by telephone if necessary. The fact that the investigating magistrate plays an important part here is connected with the rights to privacy and inviolability of the home. If a home is searched without authorization from the investigating magistrate, an important rule of criminal procedure will have been breached. As a rule, this is followed by exclusion of evidence.

---

[29] See Corstens and Borgers (2011, 433–446, 473–501).

[30] §§ 97, 110 CCP.

Besides the rules in the CCP, the Act on Entry into Dwellings (*Algemene Wet op het Binnentreden*) is also important. The latter Act can be considered to be an elaboration of Art. 12 Const., in which the right to inviolability of the home is guaranteed. The General Act on Entry into Dwellings is especially important to the situation in which investigating officers enter a home without searching it. Investigating officers are authorized to do so if an offender is caught in the act or in case a more serious offense is suspected. The purpose of the entry is to seize objects that can be found without a search. If necessary, the situation on site can be frozen with a view to the arrival of the investigating magistrate to conduct a search. The General Act on Entry into Dwellings provides for this situation (among other situations) in a series of rules, such as the obligation to identify oneself and an obligation to report. Especially important is the fact, that this Act also sets the requirement that on entering a home without the occupant's permission, investigating officers must have written authorization from the public prosecutor or acting public prosecutor. The General Act on Entry into Dwellings entails rather a lot of paperwork for those involved in the practice. Because of this, things sometimes go wrong in filling out the required forms. Although this constitutes a breach of procedural rules, consequences need not always follow in light of § 359a CCP. For instance, the Supreme Court ruled that the lack of a signature on an authorization form did not result in exclusion of evidence, because it was plausible that such authorization had also been given orally.[31]

8.2.4 *Tapping Telecommunications*

The CCP also contains detailed rules for intercepting telecommunications (including wiretaps).[32] Telecommunications may be intercepted upon an order of the public prosecutor. Before this order is given, however, the public prosecutor has to demand an authorization from the investigating magistrate. The investigating magistrate will issue such an authorization only if the relevant statutory conditions are met. Wiretapping is allowed only in the event of (1) suspicion of an offense that constitutes a serious breach of the legal order; (2) a suspicion that an organization is plotting or committing serious crimes; or (3) indications of a terrorist crime. There must also be real urgency for a wiretap to be approved. This means that no other, less radical means of investigation could be used to establish the truth. Within this framework, the investigaing magistrate is the most important authority. Without previous authorization of the investigating magistrate, the interception of telecommunications

[31] HR 16 June 2009, *Dutch Law Reports* 2009, 294.

[32] §§ 126la–126nb, 126t–126ub and 126zg-zja CCP.

is not allowed. Here, too, the lack of an authorization will in principle result in exclusion of evidence.

It is also worthy of note that the trial judge is also authorized to exercise the power to intercept telecommunications. In doing so, the trial judge checks whether "the investigating magistrate could reasonably have made the decision for authorization", while also judging "whether the subsequent use by the public prosecutor of his authority to order the interception of telecommunications by technical means is in accordance with such authorization and lawful as well".[33]

8.3 Illegal Interrogations

8.3.1 § 29 of the Code of Criminal Procedure: The Right to Remain Silent and the Protection Against Giving Involuntary Statements

The suspect's right to remain silent and the protection against involuntary statements are laid out in § 29 CCP. Subsections 1 and 2 of that section read:

> [1] In all cases in which someone is interrogated as a suspect, the interrogating judge or official must refrain from doing anything for the purpose of obtaining a statement that cannot to be said to have been made freely. The suspect is not required to answer.
> [2] Prior to the interrogation, the suspect must be told that he is not required to answer.

The protection against giving involuntary statements contained in § 29(1) CCP (the phrase "(...) that cannot be said to have been made freely") and the right to remain silent ("the suspect is not required to answer") are considered the core values that give shape to the position of the suspect in a criminal proceeding.[34] A right to remain silent is effective only if the suspect is aware of it. For that reason, § 29(2) CCP contains the obligation for the interrogating official to inform the suspect of his right to remain silent, the so-called caution (reading the suspect his rights).

Much more than the right to privacy, the suspect's right to remain silent has been the subject of debate within Dutch criminal procedure. Because of the importance of the right to remain silent and some interesting recent developments, the suspect's right to remain silent and the application of § 359a CCP to violation of the right to remain silent will be discussed in detail below.

[33] HR October 11, 2005, *Dutch Law Reports* 2006, 625.

[34] See among others Groenhuijsen and Knigge (1999, 33). See also Prakken and Spronken (2001, 57–63).

8.3.2 The Principles on Which § 29 CCP is Based and Their Influence on the Scope of the Provision

8.3.2.1 Prohibition of Compulsion

§ 29 CCP was introduced in 1926 because of the need for protection against improper interrogation methods.[35] § 29 CCP guarantees, not just in a general sense, that the authorities will act appropriately towards the suspect. The fact that a statement was made freely also enhances the reliability of the establishment of the truth. Initially, the suspect's right to remain silent – the phrase "the suspect is not required to answer" – was not included in the text of §29 CCP. The point was that the suspect could make a statement freely, not that he should not make any statement at all. The right to remain silent ultimately ended up in the text of the provision, not because the legislature held that suspects were indeed allowed to keep their mouth shut, but because not having to answer was viewed as the strongest guarantee for not having to make a statement under duress.[36] That the accent in later years remained on the viewpoint of preventing duress is evident from the fact that the obligation to read a person his rights was dropped for almost 40 years (between 1935 and 1974). Informing the suspect of a right to remain silent was, as was reasoned at the time, confusing, and above all inefficient.[37]

8.3.2.2 The *nemo tenetur* Principle and the Autonomy of the Accused During the Trial

Although the regulation of government actions had traditionally been the dominant aim of the law, in the course of time the accused's position at trial has become more visible and has been strengthened. This was initially inspired by the English accusatorial system. Later, particularly as of 1993, when the European Court of Human Rights (ECtHR) recognized the right to remain silent and the privilege against self-incrimination in its case law as essential elements of a fair trial, § 29 CCP was interpreted more and more in line with the idea that the accused must be treated as an autonomous party in the fair trial, as guaranteed by Art. 6 ECHR. The accused is not (merely) an object of investigation, but has the freedom to determine his position and defend himself from that position. The accused has no set role in the trial under public law; he does not have to account for his attitude to the other participants in the trial. The expression and realization of that position is found particularly in § 29 CCP.[38] The accused has the freedom to state what he wants and even the freedom to make no statement at all. The accused should also be aware of that position.

---

[35] Stevens (2005, Chapter 4).

[36] *Parliamentary Papers II* 1913/14, 286, no. 3, 71. Cf. also the Explanatory Memorandum to the Draft-*Staatscommissie* (Government Committee) 1913, 67–70; Lindenberg (2002, 436–437).

[37] *Parliamentary Papers II* 1935/36, 309, no. 3, 1–2.

[38] This development is described by Stevens (2005, 51–53).

Reintroduction of the reading of rights in 1974 was therefore typical of the development in relation to § 29 CCP outlined here.

The autonomy of the accused under § 29 CCP is sometimes expressed by saying that the accused cannot be compelled to incriminate himself or herself,[39] or, as articulated in the Latin adage *nemo tenetur prodere se ipsum*. As already noted, § 29 CCP is not based only on the prohibition of pressure but also on the *nemo tenetur* principle.

The accused's freedom to determine his attitude toward the trial is not unlimited. The right to remain silent, for example, does not extend to giving answers to questions about personal details, although such information can indeed be incriminating for the accused under certain circumstances.[40] Nor does the right to remain silent apply to a reply card that the driver of an illegally parked car has to fill out.[41] Interrogating an accused by way of a so-called jail plant – an undercover investigating officer in the jail – is allowed as well. Whether or not the right to remain silent is violated in that situation depends on the pressure exerted and the attitude taken by the accused to the trial up to that time in the criminal case.[42]

In the court decision-making stage, the accused's position is assessed in the context of the incriminating evidence available. A statement made by the accused may be considered "false" by the judge and as such become part of the evidence against the accused.[43] The judge can also, for example, reject a defense, if the accused does not want to answer further questions regarding that defense.[44] Remaining silent, however, cannot as such contribute to the evidence.

8.3.3 Exclusion of Statements from Evidence Due to Violation of the Right to Remain Silent and Related Rights and Principles

8.3.3.1 Reading a Suspect His Rights

Pursuant to § 29(2) CCP, a suspect must be informed of the fact that he is not required to answer. Neither in § 29 CCP nor elsewhere in the law are sanctions imposed on failure to observe the rule on reading suspects their rights. In somewhat

---

[39] Cf. also HR January 16, 1928, *Dutch Law Reports* 1928, 233.

[40] See among many others HR September 18, 1989, *Dutch Law Reports* 1990, 531, annotated by Van Veen. Asking for a telephone number can under certain circumstances come under the protection of § 29 CCP, and in that case must be preceded by reading the suspect his rights. This does not apply, however, if the suspect has already given permission to investigate his telephone traffic. See HR April 3, 2007, *Dutch Law Reports* 2007, 209.

[41] HR October 1, 1985, *Dutch Law Reports* 1986, 405 and 406.

[42] HR March 29, 2004, *Dutch Law Reports* 2004, 263. In this case, the Supreme Court relies on European case law. See ECHR, November 5, 2002, *Dutch Law Reports* 2004, 262 (Allan), annotated by Schalken. Even though the ECHR seems to dislike sneaky undercover practices somewhat more than the Supreme Court.

[43] See e.g. HR November 12, 1974, *Dutch Law Reports* 1975, 41, annotated by Van Veen.

[44] HR March 19, 1996, *Dutch Law Reports* 1996, 540, annotated by Schalken.

older case law, it is nevertheless recognized that failure to read a suspect his rights can result in exclusion of evidence. The point of departure in these judgments is that § 29(2) CCP is for the purpose of protecting the suspect against compelled self-incrimination and that, if he was not read his rights during the preliminary investigation or at the trial, the statement may not as a rule be used as evidence unless the suspect's interests or defense is not harmed.[45] The subjective approach and relativity requirement of § 359a CCP can be recognized in this.

Starting from the principle of autonomy during criminal proceedings as a background of the right to remain silent, accused persons must have a real possibility to choose the position they will take in relation to the prosecution as they see fit.[46] Whether an accused's defense has been harmed depends for example on the way in which and the circumstances under which the accused's statement was obtained. If the accused's lawyer was present during the interrogation, the judge will not easily assume that the accused was harmed by the lack of notification. The same holds if the accused knows or is expected to know that he is not required to answer. This can be the case, for example if in a series of interrogations, rights were not read to the accused in the second or third interrogation, but were in the first interrogation.[47] Whether the accused's defense is harmed, however, depends particularly on the procedural position the accused takes in court. If the accused makes a different statement in court than in the preliminary investigation, his interests may have been infringed. If the accused says that he has no objection to the fact that his rights were not read to him, or if he is assisted in court by a lawyer and does not rely on such omission, his interests will not have been harmed. Even if the accused makes the same statement in court as in the preliminary investigation after having been read his rights, or if the accused confesses again in a second lawful interrogation during the preliminary investigation, he is deemed to have had a real freedom of choice. The reservation can be made to all this that it is sometimes difficult to determine how real the accused's freedom of choice actually was. Once the accused has made a detailed statement during the interrogation, it will presumably not be easy for him to keep his mouth shut at the next interrogation.[48]

The case in which, after a statement was obtained unlawfully, the suspect still makes a statement under lawful circumstances was "resolved" in older case law by way of relativity. Regarding the statements made later, it may be more accurate to

---

[45] See for example HR January 17, 1978, *Dutch Law Reports* 1978, 341 and HR January 26, 1982, *Dutch Law Reports* 1982, 353.

[46] Stevens (2005, 57).

[47] For an overview of this case law, see Lensing (1988, 205–207). See also Jörg (2010, note 16 to § 29). Cf. also HR June 14, 2005, LJN AS8854.

[48] Jörg (2010, note 16 to § 29).

speak of broken causality. The reading of rights in the second instance prevents the lawfully obtained statement from being viewed as fruit of the earlier omission of the reading of rights.[49]

8.3.3.2 Improper Compulsion and Improper Methods During the Interrogation at the Investigation Stage

What Is Improper Compulsion?

Besides a right to remain silent for the suspect, § 29 CCP contains an instruction for the interrogating officials: they may not use any unacceptable pressure or duress during the interrogation. This instruction rule is the necessary counterpart of the right to remain silent,[50] and is intended also to guarantee the appropriateness of government actions. The boundary between appropriate and inappropriate is difficult to determine. The difficulty in applying § 359a CCP lies first of all in determining the unlawfulness itself.

There is no debate in this context over the unlawfulness of physical abuse.[51] Such compulsion is not allowed under any circumstances, as well, by Art. 3 ECHR, the ban on torture and inhuman and degrading treatment. But duress can also be psychological. Exerting a certain degree of psychological pressure is allowed and is considered necessary to get a suspect to talk.[52] There are no problems, for instance, in confronting a suspect with incriminating evidence. His attention may also be drawn to contradictions in his own story and the weakness of his position. It is allowed as well to tell a suspect that he can go home if he cooperates and stops remaining silent. Case law, however, stipulates that various interrogation methods must be considered unlawful. These methods are usually categorized as "threat and intimidation", such as making shooting movements next to the suspect's head, suggesting that the police could see to it that the suspect gets sentenced to 20 years imprisonment, that it was possible to have the suspect's face match the composite drawing in the file, as well as suggesting that the suspect's lawyer did not serve the suspect's interests but those of the criminal organization.[53] The most well-known unlawful method is the so-called Zaandam interrogation method. With this method, suspects were interrogated intensively and for a long time with the aid of a

---

[49] HR March 25, 1980, *Dutch Law Reports* 1980, 437 and HR January 26, 1988, *Dutch Law Reports* 1988, 818. In this case, the judge did not use previous statements taken without rights being read, so the Supreme Court only had to deliberate on the question of the use of later statements that were lawful in themselves. Cf. also Embregts (2003, 148).

[50] See Jörg (2010, note 9 to § 29).

[51] Cf. on the historic background of § 29 CCP, Stevens (2005, 40–46).

[52] See Lensing (1988, 39 et seq.), and Jörg (2010, note 9 to § 29).

[53] For a detailed overview of the case law, see Jörg (2010, note 10 to § 29). See also Gerritsen (2000, 228–238).

communications expert, while surrounded by photos of both his family and that of the victim.[54]

Exclusion of Statements Obtained Through Improper Compulsion

Once the unlawfulness of the interrogation method is established, a decision must be made on the consequences to be attached on the basis of § 359a CCP as interpreted by the Supreme Court in its seminal judgment of 2004. If exclusion of evidence is to be considered, the unlawful interrogation method must constitute a serious breach of § 29 CCP, meaning that the actions taken were unacceptable beyond any doubt, the suspect actually made an incriminating statement harming his own position in the trial (relativity requirement), and that statement, as well as the fruits thereof, must have resulted exclusively from the improper interrogation (causality requirement).

Exclusion of evidence due to an unlawful manner of interrogation does not often occur in judicial practice. It is also important in this context that motions to exclude evidence must meet rather stringent requirements if the judge is to hear them. Defense counsel cannot simply rely on § 29 CCP. He must also state specifically why the interrogation method was unlawful, what consequence should be attached to this, and why.[55] Even if the defense meets these requirements, exclusion of evidence will not readily take place. In some cases, exclusion of evidence is not considered because there is simply nothing to exclude. This can be the case because the suspect did not make a statement despite the pressure exerted on him,[56] the lower court did not rely on the questionable statements in its judgment reasons, and based its guilt decision on other evidence,[57] or on statements made by the suspect before the police started using the unacceptable methods.[58] The debate, in such cases, is then limited to the question of whether the Public Prosecution Service should be barred from prosecuting at all, which occurs very rarely, or whether the sanction of sentence reduction should be applied.

In cases where exclusion of evidence is possible in principle, because the statement allegedly obtained under duress was indeed used as evidence, there may still be reasons within the assessment framework of § 359a CCP for not excluding that

[54] HR May 13, 1997, *Dutch Law Reports* 1998, 152. The complaint to the ECHR that the method was in conflict with Art. 3 ECHR due to inhuman and degrading treatment was rejected by the ECtHR. Ebbinge v. Netherlands, No. 47240/99, ECHR, 14 March 2000.

[55] HR June 10, 1980, *Dutch Law Reports* 1980, 591, HR 21 February 1989, *Dutch Law Reports* 1989, 668 and HR November 4, 2008, *Dutch Law Reports* 2008, 581.

[56] HR September 22, 1998, *Dutch Law Reports* 1998, 104.

[57] HR May 13, 1997, *Dutch Law Reports* 1998, 152. The central issue was whether the methods were so unlawful that the Public Prosecution Service should have been barred from prosecuting. According to the Supreme Court, that was not the case.

[58] HR May 9, 2000, *Dutch Law Reports* 2000, 521.

evidence. In a case from 2002, for instance, the Supreme Court held that occasional unlawful actions can be compensated by the fact that the interrogation or interrogations were predominantly calm and without illegal conduct (this would fall under the "gravity of the breach" factor of § 359a(2) CCP). Where there exists a multiplicity of interrogations and statements, the Supreme Court will at times find that the causal nexus between violation and statement has been broken, i.e., the statements used as evidence were not made as a *direct* result of the unlawful actions and therefore there was no need to exclude them according to the Supreme Court.[59]

All in all, it is difficult to achieve the exclusion of a confession or statements by alleging the use of unlawful interrogation methods. In our view, this is connected with the fact that the unlawful interrogation methods have remained relatively innocuous to date. Difficult issues regarding torture have simply not occurred yet in the Netherlands. Moreover, the consequences of the unlawful actions for the accused are usually limited because most judges are able to circumvent the contaminated statements. The case law of the lower courts does, however, show that there has been more willingness in recent years to attach consequences to unreliable interrogation methods.[60] Although strictly speaking, judges should not have to apply the rules of § 359a CCP in such a case, in practice, reliability seems often to be addressed in the context of the unlawfulness issue.

An interesting question is the extent to which all of the ramifications of § 359a CCP would apply if it were determined that the suspect had been tortured. It seems obvious that this would be a severe breach of an important principle of procedural law that protects the suspect. After all, this follows not only from the prohibition of pressure but also from the absolute prohibition of torture under Art. 3 ECHR that applies in the Netherlands. According to the ECHR, the use of statements obtained by torture as evidence comes down to a violation of the right to a fair trial under Art. 6 ECHR, regardless of the circumstances of the case. On the basis of that case law, fruits of such statements could not be used in the Netherlands, either. The strict causality requirement does not apply in this case.[61] Where the illegal conduct which induced the confession amounts to inhuman and degrading treatment, rather than torture,[62] the ECHR nevertheless allows for a weighing of interests.[63] Since it is very difficult to determine where the boundary lies between inhuman treatment and torture – and especially since the Court took account of the

---

[59] HR March 12, 2002, LJN AD8906. An interesting question is the extent to which an accused is still free to choose his position and remain silent during lawful interrogations once he has confessed as a result of unlawful methods. See in that connection, Gäfgen v. Germany (G.C.)(2011), 52 E.H.R.R. 1, 37–38, §§ 147–149.

[60] See Dubelaar (2009, 93). A good example of such a judgment is the judgment of the Breda District Court of March 2, 2009, LJN BH4358. Cf. Duker and Stevens (2009).

[61] Jalloh v. Germany (G.C.)(2007), 44 E.H.R.R. 32, 667, 676, 679–680, §§ 40, 50, 51; Gäfgen v. Germany, 52 E.H.R.R. 1, 42, § 166.

[62] Article 3 ECHR prohibits both torture and inhuman and degrading treatment.

[63] Gäfgen v. Germany, 52 E.H.R.R. 1, 45, § 178.

pressure on the interrogating officials due to the urgency of the situation in its ruling[64] – the obligation to exclude evidence formulated by the ECHR ultimately seems less categorical.[65]

8.3.3.3 Right to Consult with an Attorney and to Have an Attorney Present During Police Interrogation

Recent Developments

The debate over the question whether suspects are entitled to be assisted by a lawyer during the first police interrogation has been going on in the Netherlands for about 40 years. Since 2007, developments have been in progress that compel a detailed discussion of this subject.

The CCP has several provisions pertaining to the suspect's right to free access to a lawyer.[66] It is also provides that the suspect has a right to be visited by a duty attorney during detention.[67] The Supreme Court, however, does not interpret these rights so broadly that they entail a right to assistance by a lawyer during police interrogation, or that the suspect has a right to consultation prior to that interrogation.[68]

This restrictive interpretation is part of the Dutch tradition to place the accent in criminal proceedings on the interest of establishing the truth and the central role the suspect's statement obtained during the police interrogation plays in this. A lawyer who advises his client to remain silent thwarts that interest in a certain sense. Furthermore, the interrogation can be regulated by requiring its audiovisual recording. Proponents of the right to a lawyer during the interrogation assert on the other hand that in this way, the autonomous position of the accused to which he should be entitled under § 29 CCP is not sufficiently taken into account. The right to remain silent and the freedom to make statements are effective rights only if the accused has been fully informed of the consequences of talking and remaining silent. Only then does the accused have a real option to choose his procedural position during the proceedings.[69]

As a result of several interesting recent developments, a change will soon be made in the situation described above. An initial development came in the wake of the so-called Schiedam Park murder case. In this case, a man was convicted,

---

[64] Ibid.

[65] The question whether the *Schutznorm* applies in cases of torture has not yet been brought up in European case law, nor, in general, has it been answered by the Court of Justice. Van Kempen is critical of this. See the annotation by P.H.P.H.M.C. van Kempen, *Dutch Law Reports CM Bulletin* 2007, p. 367.

[66] See §§ 28(2), 50(1) CCP.

[67] See § 40(2) CCP.

[68] See in detail, Spronken (2001, 112–114, 223–235). See e.g. the conclusion of deputy A–G Bleichrodt for HR November 13, 2007, *Dutch Law Reports* 2008, 116.

[69] About this debate, also for literature references, see, Stevens (2005, 62–64).

wrongly, as was later determined, partly on the basis of his own false confession. As part of a set of measures intended to prevent such miscarriages of justice in the future, the Minister of Justice started an experiment called "Lawyer during Interrogation" ("*raadsman bij verhoor*"). For a period of 2 years, in two regions, lawyers will be admitted to the first police interrogation in murder and manslaughter cases under strict conditions.[70] Based on the results of the research on that experiment, the Minister will decide if and to what extent there will be a future right for lawyers to attend certain interrogations.[71] A second development is the debate over the consequences that should be attached to the judgments of the ECtHR in the *Salduz* and *Panovits* cases. In these cases dating from 2008, the ECtHR held that "access to a lawyer should be provided as from the first interrogation of a suspect by the police".[72] The meaning of these words is not immediately clear. The bar in particular states that the judgments should be interpreted to mean that lawyers have a right to be present during police interrogations, which would be a reversal of the existing case law of the ECtHR in which this right is not explicitly recognized.[73] The Dutch Minister of Justice and Supreme Court, however, do not want to go that far. Both the Supreme Court and the Minister of Justice recognize the right of a suspect to consult with a lawyer before the interrogation by the police, as well as the obligation of the police to point this out to the suspect.[74] Regarding underage suspects, the Supreme Court does recognize a right to be assisted during an interrogation, but such assistance can be provided by a lawyer as well as a trusted representative.[75]

Exclusion of Evidence Following a Violation of the Right to Counsel

A suspect has a right to assistance from his lawyer from the time he is taken into custody. According to the case law in the pre-*Salduz* situation, that right does not

---

[70] For instance, the lawyer must sit a small distance behind his client. The lawyer may not have eye contact with his client, may not say anything and will be removed from the interrogation room as soon as he interrupts the interrogation after being warned not to do so. See the protocol of the experiment on http://www.advocatenorde.nl/newsarchive/Protocol_Raadsman_politieverhoor.def.pdf.

[71] See the Letter from the Minister of Justice, *Parliamentary Papers II* 2006–07, 30 800, VI, no. 86, section 4.

[72] Salduz v. Turkey (G.C.) (2009), 49 E.H.R.R. 19, 421, 437, § 55; Panovits v. Cyprus, no. 4268/04, ECHR, 11 December 2008, § 76.

[73] See for example, Spronken (2009, 94–100). See also Braanker (2009, 276–282). See also for a less far-reaching interpretation, also followed by the Minister and Supreme Court: Borgers (2009, 88–93).

[74] See the letter from the Minister of April 15, 2009 on the presence of a lawyer during police interrogation, sections 4.3 and 5 (*Parliamentary Papers II* 2008/09, 31700 VI, no. 117) and HR June 30, 2009, *Dutch Law Reports* 2009, 349, 350, 351, with note by Schalken.

[75] See e.g. HR June 30, 2009, LJN BH3081, legal ground 2.6.

include a right for the lawyer to be present during the first interrogation by the police, or even that the suspect has a right to speak to his lawyer before the first interrogation. Totally in line with this approach is the case law relating to exclusion of evidence under § 359a CCP, which seldom rules for defendants who base their motion to exclude on the fact that they were denied a visit with defense counsel while in police custody. Even a suspect who initially makes incriminating statements and remains silent after the (late) visit by his lawyer cannot expect to benefit very much from § 359a CCP because of the relativity requirement, because, as long as he has been read his rights and other guarantees relating to the interrogation have been fulfilled, his interests will not have been harmed. The right to a lawyer during police custody does not, after all, necessarily guarantee a suspect's right to speak to his lawyer prior to the interrogation.[76]

Things have changed since the *Salduz* judgment and its interpretation by the Dutch Supreme Court. In its judgment of June 30, 2009, the Supreme Court not only recognized the right to consultation, but also held that if this right is violated, *as a rule*, the statement obtained during the police interrogation will be excluded from the evidence – except for situations in which the suspect voluntarily waived his right to consultation and there are urgent reasons in a specific case to restrict the right.[77] In reasoning this way, the Supreme Court almost literally embraces the words of the ECtHR in *Salduz* and *Panovits* and holds, in addition, that if the right to consultation has been violated, a grave breach of an important principle of criminal procedure has taken place.[78] The right to consultation with counsel now protects, of itself, the suspect's freedom to determine his procedural position in relation to the making of a statement, which makes the relativity requirement, of great importance before *Salduz,* largely irrelevant.[79] Nevertheless, the requirement of direct causation still applies. According to the Supreme Court, exclusion of statements made by a suspect will not even be considered, if they were made by the suspect after he was able to consult a lawyer and his rights were read to him.[80]

---

[76] Cf. HR November 13, 2007, *Dutch Law Reports* 2008, 116, in particular the note by Borgers. See also HR May 29, 1990, *Dutch Law Reports* 1990, 754 and HR 13 May 2006, *Dutch Law Reports* 2006, 369, in which the statement already did not qualify for exclusion because it was not plausible that the lack of legal assistance by a duty attorney influenced the contents of the statements made by the suspect. Because the suspect persisted in his confession, no causal connection could be shown.

[77] HR June 30, 2009, *Dutch Law Reports* 2009, 349, 350, 351, legal ground 2.7.2.

[78] The ECtHR also mentioned exclusion of evidence "as a rule". Salduz v. Turkey (G.C.), 49 E.H.R.R. 19, 421, 437, § 55.

[79] See for example HR January 17, 2012, National Case Law Number (LJN) BU4227, at www.rechtspraak.nl.

[80] HR June 30, 2009, *Dutch Law Reports* 2009, 349, 350, 351, legal ground 2.7.3.

8.3.4 Exclusion of a Lawfully Obtained Statement After an Unlawful Investigative Act?

In principle, an unlawful detention does not prevent the use of a statement taken from the person who was unlawfully detained or arrested, if the statement was otherwise taken in accordance with the rules outlined above. In that case, there is a temporal and not a causal connection ("afterwards but not because").[81] Exclusion of evidence enters into the picture as an option (naturally with all the corresponding preconditions already explained above) only if the defense can demonstrate that, for example, unacceptable pressure was also exerted during the unlawful detention or the suspect was not read his rights. There is also no problem in using an otherwise lawfully taken statement following an unlawful search (followed perhaps by an arrest), for there is a lack of a causal connection with the unlawful search.

The situation is somewhat different if the suspect is confronted during a lawful interrogation with results of an unlawful search and then confesses. If it is plausible that the statement is only the result of the unlawful confrontation, it should be excluded from the evidence.[82] That this does not readily occur is evident from a Supreme Court judgment in which the suspect was confronted during the interrogation with DNA material found at the crime scene that came from him. This material should, however, never have been linked to the suspect because the match was made on the basis of material taken earlier from the suspect that should already have been removed from the DNA database. The Supreme Court ruled that the confession may well have been made after a suggestion that DNA material from the suspect was available, but it was made before the suspect was confronted with the actual DNA match. For that reason, exclusion of evidence was not considered to be appropriate.[83]

8.4 Conclusions

It is evident from the above description of § 359a CCP and its elaboration in the case law, that the Supreme Court of the Netherlands applies a differentiated balancing test when dealing with illegally gathered evidence and the sanctions potentially applicable thereto. As is also evident from the description of the treatment of violations of privacy and the right to silence/protection against involuntary

---

[81] See for example HR January 26, 1988, *Dutch Law Reports* 1988, 818.

[82] See HR October 22, 1991, *Dutch Law Reports* 1992, 218, legal ground 6.2, in which the Supreme Court used a broader causality requirement ("largely"). This is deemed to be restricted by the seminal judgment of 2004.

[83] HR January 27, 2009, *Dutch Law Reports* 2009, 86 (retrial).

self-incrimination, there are numerous criteria and approaches that the judge may take into consideration in assessing breaches of procedural rules and choosing the appropriate sanctions to apply. Because of that balance, the system of § 359a CCP is not always easy to fathom. The interrelationship among the sanctions also not easy to characterize. It can nevertheless be said that a bar to prosecution by the Public Prosecution Service is pronounced only in exceptional cases, and that Dutch courts tend to be relatively restrained in excluding evidence. Breaches of procedural rules are disposed of fairly regularly by sentence reduction or by a mere finding of unlawfulness.

Criticism is voiced in the Dutch literature, particularly of the restrained manner of dealing with the exclusion of evidence. In many cases, this criticism is based on constitutional arguments.[84] According to this viewpoint, the government should be first and foremost bound by its own laws. Only by excluding evidence does the government demonstrate that it obeys its own rules (the demonstration argument), that it refuses to benefit from illegally gathered evidence (the reparations argument) and, only by such exclusion can future breaches of procedural rules be prevented (the prevention argument).[85] If one chooses this approach, it is not very logical, for example, to place a lot of emphasis on the relativity requirement. Whether or not the suspect's interests have been harmed is not particularly relevant if the focus is on the government's behavior.

There are, however, other approaches, which differ from this constitutional point of view.[86] One can, for instance, take as the point of departure the protection of the suspect's subjective rights. In that case, a response to unlawful government actions is appropriate only if those rights have been undermined. When this approach is applied, there is every reason to apply the relativity requirement. There are other arguments as well for exercising restraint in excluding illegally gathered evidence. Paramount in this respect, of course, is the goal of establishing the substantive truth. Moreover, the exclusion of evidence can result in social unrest, for instance, if it leads to acquittal. The impression is quickly aroused that an accused is benefitting from exclusion of evidence, while the victim of the crime in question is left out in the cold.

§ 359a CCP and the related case law of the Supreme Court are not based on a fundamental choice of one approach or another. The case law of the Supreme Court tends to take a course in which the constitutional viewpoint outlined above, which focuses on the appropriateness of Government actions in a general sense, is pushed to the background, while the question of imposing sanctions for breaches of procedural rules focuses primarily on the specific interest of an individual suspect in a fair trial.[87] But not exclusively, for the Supreme Court allows a certain discretion in deciding whether or not to apply the relativity requirement in certain cases.

---

[84] See e.g. Embregts (2003), and Van Woensel (2004).

[85] One can, for that matter, put forth the same arguments to a certain extent for sentence reduction as a sanction, also the repercussions are less radical for the government.

[86] See e.g. Corstens and Borgers (2011, 725–727), and Kuijper (2009).

[87] Cf. Kuiper (2009, 52–53).

While the Supreme Court recognizes the importance of establishing the substantive truth and the (perceived) social need for satisfaction, these interests are not automatically deemed to be decisive in all cases. To this extent, the court applies a test based on the totality of the circumstances, in which the various arguments and viewpoints all play a part, and in which a moderate response to breaches of procedural rules is preferred. The result is a balanced, but not always easy to fathom system of rules for imposing sanctions following illegalities in the gathering of criminal evidence.

Bibliography

Borgers, M.J. 2009. Een nieuwe dageraad voor de raadsman bij het politieverhoor? *Dutch Law Reports* 88–93.

Braanker, M.B. 2009. Risicomanagement of Russische Roulette aan de Nederlandse verhoortafel? *Strafblad* 276–282.

Corstens, G.J.M., and M.J. Borgers. 2011. *Het Nederlands strafprocesrecht*. Deventer: Kluwer.

de Wilde, B. 2008. Bewijsminimumregels als waarborgen voor de waarheidsvinding in strafzaken? In *De waarde vaan Waarheid: Opstellen over waarheid en waarheidsvinding en het strafrecht*, ed. J.H. Crijns, P.P.J. van der Meij, and J.M. ten Voorde, 269–294. The Hague: Boom Juridische uitgevers.

Dubelaar, M.J. 2009. Betrouwbaarheid versus rechtmatigheid in strafzaken. *Rechtsgeleerd Magazijn Themis* 3: 93–105.

Duker, M.J.A., and L. Stevens. 2009. *Het politiële verdachtenverhoor: meer aandacht gewenst voor de totstandkoming van een betrouwbare verdachtenverklaring*. Nijmegen: Wolf Legal Publishers.

Embregts, M.C.D. 2003. *Uitsluitsel over bewijsuitsluiting*. Deventer: Kluwer.

Embregts, M.C.D. 2010. Notes on Section 359a. In *Het Wetboek van Strafvordering*, ed. A.L. Melai, M.S. Groenhuijsen, et al. Deventer: Kluwer (loose-leaf), notes 5.10 to 10.11 to sec. 359a.

Gerritsen, K. 2000. (On)duidelijkheden.rondom ongeoorloofde pressie in het verdachtenverhoor. Verdacht mistig, *Ars Aqui* 228–238.

Groenhuijsen, M.S., and G. Knigge. 1999. Algemeen Deel. In *Het onderzoek ter zitting. Eerste interimrapport onderzoeksproject Strafvordering 2001*, ed. M.S. Groenhuijsen and G. Knigge, 1–55. Groningen: Rijksuniversiteit.

Jörg, N. 2010. Notes on section 29. In *Het Wetboek van Strafvordering*, ed. A.L. Melai, M.S. Groenhuijsen, et al. Deventer: Kluwer (loose-leaf). note 16 to § 29.

Kuijper, R. 2009. Strafvermindering als reactie op vormverzuimen. In *WelBeraden*, ed. M.J.A. Duker et al., 35–59. Nijmegen: WLP.

Lensing, J.A.W. 1988. *Het verhoor van de verdachte en strafzakken: een rechtsvergeleijkende studie*. Arnhem: Gouda Quint.

Lindenberg, K. 2002. *Van Ort tot ORO. Een verzameling van de werken die hebben geleid tot het Oorspronkelijk Regeringsontwerp van een nieuw Wetboek van Strafvordering (1914)*, 436–437. Groningen: University of Groningen.

Nijboer, J.F. 2008. *Strafrechtelijk bewijsrecht*. Nijmegen: Ars Aequi Libri.

Prakken, E., and T. Spronken. 2001. Grondslagen van het recht op verdediging. In *Legitieme strafvordering Rechten van de mens als inspiratie in de 21ste eeuw*, ed. C.H. Brants, P.A.M. Mevis, and E. Prakken, 57–63. Antwerp/Groningen: Intersentia Rechtswetenschappen.

Spronken, T. 2001. *Verdediging*. Deventer: Gouda Quint.

Spronken, T. 2009. Ja, de zon komt op voor de raadsman bij het politieverhoor!. *Dutch Law Reports* 94–100.

Stevens, L. 2005. *Het nemo-teneturbeginsel: van zwijgrecht tot containerbegrip* (diss. Tilburg), Nijmegen: Wolf Legal Publishers.

Van Woensel, A.M. 2004. Sanctionering van onrechtmatig verkregen bewijsmateriaal. *Delikt & Delinkwent* 119–171.

Chapter 9
Spain: The Constitutional Court's Move from Categorical Exclusion to Limited Balancing

Lorena Bachmaier Winter

9.1 The General Theory of Admissibility of Illegally Gathered Evidence

9.1.1 Introduction

The scope of the exclusionary rule for illegally obtained evidence impacts directly on the difficult balance between prosecutorial efficiency in protecting the security of citizens, and respecting the fundamental rights of those same citizens, and particularly the rights of the accused. This issue is still hotly debated in the Spanish legal literature and in the case law, as the limits of the exclusionary rules and the exceptions that could apply in each case are anything but clearly defined. Particularly controversial is the issue of excluding indirect evidence, as its limits are not easy to define and the position of the courts has undergone significant non-lineal changes.

Despite the unquestionable importance of the historical evolution of evidentiary exclusionary rules in Spanish criminal procedure, this study will focus mainly on the treatment of illegally obtained evidence in criminal proceedings by the Spanish courts,[1] since the enactment of the 1978 Constitution, without entering into lengthy academic discussions.

[1] For a general legal comparative view see Armenta Deu (2007, 544–575; 2009)

L.B. Winter (✉)
Facultad de Derecho, Universidad Complutense, E-28040 Madrid, Spain
e-mail: l.bachmaier@der.ucm.es

S.C. Thaman (ed.), *Exclusionary Rules in Comparative Law*, Ius Gentium: Comparative Perspectives on Law and Justice 20, DOI 10.1007/978-94-007-5348-8_9,

9.1.2 The Legal Framework

Before the enactment of the Spanish Constitution on December 6, 1978, there was a general position in favor of the admissibility of any kind of relevant evidence that could help to ascertain the truth of the facts alleged in a criminal trial. Truth-finding was the central concern, and courts did not worry about how the evidence was gathered, as long as it was relevant in proving the alleged facts.[2]

This general stance toward the admissibility of evidence, contrasted strongly with the progressive character of the Spanish Code of Criminal Procedure of 1882 (*Ley de Enjuiciamiento Criminal*, hereinafter CCP), which is still in force although it has undergone numerous piecemeal reforms. The Code of 1882 was surprisingly liberal, considering the time it was enacted, and was strongly influenced by a view of criminal procedure as an instrument for guaranteeing the defendant's rights. In its outstanding Explanatory Memorandum, the CCP states that one of the aims of the new Code was "to correct the chronic defects of our traditional system of doing justice and surround the citizen with all necessary safeguards so that under no circumstances his individual rights will are sacrificed for a wrongly conceived interest of the State". [3]

The CCP designed a quite advanced criminal procedure in which the oral trial gained pre-eminence, the impartiality of the trial court was guaranteed, equality of arms between prosecution and defense was elevated to a procedural principle, and time limits were set for the investigative stage. Within this move towards more safeguards, the Code already showed some concern with regard to the gathering of evidence, thus indicating, although still in a flimsy way, that not everything was admissible in order to determine the truth and punish the guilty. The Code in 1882 already prohibited obtaining confessions through threats or compulsion, and provided for exclusion of statements of the accused obtained in violation of the free will or dignity of the defendant.[4] § 416.1 CCP is another example of an exclusionary rule of evidence. This rule exempts a spouse and other relatives from the obligation to testify as witnesses. The judge, before interviewing them, has to inform them of this exemption, and a failure to do so would often—although not always—lead to the inadmissibility of any statements they had made.[5]

In addition, since the enactment of the CCP in 1882, judicial authorization based on well-founded suspicion was required for the entry and search of dwellings, and any search required the presence of the court clerk, functioning as "judicial notary", who was required to bear witness that every act was performed in a lawful manner.

---

[2] Guasp Delgado, (1947, 583–584), Muñoz Sabaté (1993,74), and Fernández Entralgo (1996, 121); quoting the same authors, see also Miranda Estrampes (2004, 54).

[3] Explanatory Memorandum, VI. Also in XIX: "Sacred is the interest of society (to punish the infringement of the criminal law); but no less sacred are individual rights".

[4] Gómez Colomer (2008, 108 ff.).

[5] Ibid, 109–110.

9.1.3 The General Duty to Determine the Truth

The search for truth has always been viewed as one of the main aims of Continental European criminal procedure. Nonetheless, the Spanish Constitution makes no mention of it. Nor is any specific reference thereto made in the CCP. Nonetheless, the goal of searching for the truth may be deduced from several of its provisions, as well as from the whole structure of Spanish criminal procedure. According to the CCP, the preliminary investigation is carried out by an investigating magistrate under the supervision of the public prosecutor (§ 306 CCP). § 299 CCP specifically states that the purpose of the pre-trial investigative stage is to prepare the trial and to perform all acts aimed at determining the facts and proving the relevant circumstances of the crime committed.

Several code provisions also refer expressly or implicitly to the search of the truth. For instance, § 406 CCP indicates that the confession of the accused will not exempt the investigating magistrate from performing all investigative acts necessary to confirm the truth of the facts confessed and the existence of the crime. In addition, § 729 CCP allows the trial judge to *sua sponte* order the taking of any evidence so as to better ascertain the facts alleged in the accusatory pleadings. § 336 CCP, which narrowly deals with investigation of the crime scene, calls on the investigating magistrate or other official to gather not just incriminating evidence, but also evidence which could go to exonerate the suspect—that is all the evidence related to the truth, or lack of truth of the alleged criminal violation.

The ancient conception of criminal procedure as an instrument to obtain the truth at any price, in which even the most cruel and abominable measures, such as torture, were acceptable, has, of course, long been abandoned and the search for truth is no longer an absolute value. It finds its limits in the respect of the moral and legal values of the rule of law.[6] It is generally accepted that the criminal process should reach a "correct" decision, which does not necessarily mean one comporting with the material truth, if that truth can only be approximated by violating fundamental rights of the citizens.[7]

9.1.3.1 General Exclusionary Rules and Rules Relating to Procedural "Nullities"

Constitutional Rules

The Spanish Constitution of 1978 does not contain any rule establishing evidentiary prohibitions or exclusionary rules. However, from Arts. 10,15 Const., which accord protection to human dignity, the right to life and physical integrity, and specifically

[6] Fernández Entralgo (1996, 219).

[7] Vives Antón, (1987, 125–126).

prohibit torture and any kind of degrading or inhuman treatment, one could deduce a rule excluding evidence obtained in violation of fundamental rights.[8] But the Spanish Constitutional Court, in a decision handed down on November 29, 1984,[9] expressly declared that there is no rule that recognizes an autonomous constitutional right to the exclusion of illegally obtained evidence. It held, that in the case before the Court, the admission of illegally gathered evidence did not necessarily cause the breach of a fundamental right.[10]

However, this decision did not necessarily mean that exclusionary rules did not have a solid basis in constitutional rules.[11] When it addressed the issue of exclusion or admissibility of the illegally obtained evidence, the Court recalls that it was confronted with conflicting interests: that of finding the truth and that of respect for fundamental rights. The citizens' rights may have to give way in order to successfully prosecute a case, but only where the violation was of an infra-constitutional right, "but not when the fundamental rights violated are recognized at the constitutional level".[12] A criminal conviction based on evidence gathered in violation of fundamental constitutional rights would further undermine the following three important constitutional protections.

The first is the fundamental right to a fair trial guaranteed by Art. 24 Const. The second, is the principle of equality of arms, because one of the parties, the prosecution, would be able to use illegally obtained evidence and benefit from the violation of the constitutional rights of the other, the defendant.[13] Finally, the admission of unconstitutionally gathered evidence would undermine the presumption of innocence, guaranteed by Art. 24(2) Const. The presumption of innocence in the Spanish legal order not only implies the right to be treated as innocent until a judgment of conviction becomes final, but has a wider scope. It also encompasses the right not to be condemned if there been insufficient lawfully gathered evidence to prove the defendant's guilt.

Statutory Rules

Art. 11.1 Law on the Judicial Power

The key statutory provision regarding the exclusion of evidence is § 11.1 of the Law on the Judicial Power (Ley Orgánica del Poder Judicial, hereinafter LOPJ).[14]

---

[8] See Moreno Catena (1987, 134).

[9] STC 114/1984, of 29 November.

[10] STC 114/1984, FJ 2.

[11] Aguilera Morales (2009, 83), who considers that the STC 114/1984, of 29 November, has granted the exclusionary rule the status of a constitutional right. Of a different opinion Del Moral García (2001, 138).

[12] STC 114/1984, FJ 4. On this decision of the Constitutional Court see also, Gómez Colomer (2008, 114).

[13] STC 114/1984, FJ 5. After this judgment, the close relation between the exclusionary rule and the right to a fair trial has been recognized in numerous Constitutional Court decisions.

[14] For a detailed study of this rule see Asencio Mellado (1989, 80–91), Díaz Cabiale (1991, 120 ff.), Urbano del Castillo (1996, 228–237).

The LOPJ was enacted in 1985, 1 year after the Constitutional Court's landmark decision in STC 114/184, and this decision clearly influenced the wording of § 11.1 LOPJ, which, after declaring that in all court proceedings the principles of good faith shall be respected, reads as follows: "Evidence obtained, directly or indirectly, in violation of fundamental rights or liberties, shall have no effect".

This short rule was welcomed by practitioners and scholars, to give teeth to the Constitutional Court's decision and the use of exclusion to bolster respect for fundamental rights. However, the concise wording of the rule has left open a number of questions, and thus prevented the rule from ensuring sufficient legal security in the area of admissibility of illegally obtained evidence. We will parse the language of the provision to illustrate this.

The expression, "*they shall have no effect*", can be interpreted as either a prohibition on admitting the evidence, or as a prohibition on evaluating it. Most scholars at present assert that the lack of effect applies to admissibility as such during the criminal proceedings, but add, that if the evidence were erroneously admitted, the prohibition would not allow its evaluation and use as a basis for a criminal conviction. This interpretation has also been adopted, by and large, in the case law.

Regarding the words "*the evidence obtained*", it was at first thought that § 11.1 LOPJ was only applicable when the violation of a fundamental right took place during the preliminary investigation when the evidence was gathered. This was the stance of the Constitutional Court in a decision in 1986,[15] in which it construed § 11.1 LOPJ in a restrictive way, so that infringements that occurred either at the moment of procedural introduction or testing the evidence would not fall under its provisions, but under those which regulate procedural nullities. This initial interpretation, which was followed by some legal scholars,[16] did not prevail in the end. At present the exclusionary rule of §11.1 LOPJ is applied to all evidence obtained in violation of fundamental rights, regardless of the moment the violation occurred, be it pre-trial or at trial.

As to the interpretation of the words, "*directly or indirectly*", the general opinion in the literature, as well as in Supreme Court and Constitutional Court jurisprudence, is that by this expression the law recognizes the doctrine of "fruits of the poisonous tree" and mandates exclusion not only of evidence directly resulting from the constitutional violation, but indirect evidence derived from the violation as well. The courts originally were strict in excluding the "fruits of the poisonous tree", but more recently they have been allowing exceptions to its application.[17]

Finally, the phrase, "*violating fundamental rights and liberties*",[18] refers to any infringement of essential procedural rules which restricts the right to defense

---

[15] STS 64/1986 of 21 May.

[16] For example, Díaz Cabiale (1991, 121). For the different opinions in the literature see, Miranda Estrampes (2004, 69).

[17] On the evolution of the jurisprudence see Sect. 9.1.2.

[18] The Spanish text uses the word "violentar" which literally means to force, but, more broadly, it is equivalent to breach or violation, in this case, of a fundamental right.

(*derecho de defensa*), or other fundamental rights which cannot be purged or corrected. Here again arises the question as to which rights, if violated, would result in exclusion per §11.1 LOPJ. The view in literature and case law is unanimous, that this would apply to the violation of any of the fundamental rights that enjoy special constitutional protection, and may be the subject of a constitutional appeal (*recurso de amparo*), namely, the fundamental rights recognized in Arts. 15–29 Const., the right to equality (Art. 14 Const.) and the right to be a conscientious objector (Art. 30 Const.).[19] However in individual decisions the Constitutional Court has extended the application of § 11.1 LOPJ to violations of fundamental rights, which cannot give rise to a constitutional appeal, such as the right to private property, right to form labor unions, to set up foundations, or to engage in free enterprise.[20]

Art. 238 Law on the Judicial Power

§ 238 LOPJ is the main provision dealing with the nullity of procedural acts. This provision has been amended several times since first introduced in 1985. Leaving aside the controversial amendments of this article,[21] we will focus on its current formulation, which reads:

> "Procedural acts will be fully void in the following cases:
> 1. When the court lacks subject-matter jurisdiction.
> 2. When the act has been performed under violence or compulsion.
> 3. When the essential rules of procedure are not respected and this may have caused an actual restriction of the right of defense.
> 4. When the act is done without the assistance of lawyer, in the cases where the law prescribes it as mandatory.
> 5. When an oral hearing is held without the mandatory presence of the court clerk.
> 6. In all other cases where the procedural rules so state."

With regard to exclusion of evidence in criminal cases, paragraph 3 of this provision is of interest. In reference to it, the Supreme Court has asserted, that evidence obtained or admitted attrial in violation of a procedural rule which restricts the right to defense, will be null. In doing so, it differentiated between a constitutional inadmissibility of evidence on the one hand, which would cause inadmissibility under § 11.1 LOPJ, and evidence obtained through infringement of statutory procedural rules, on the other, which would be treated as nullities under § 238 LOPJ.[22]

---

[19] See for example, González García (2007, 31–54).

[20] For example, STC 85/1994.

[21] On the tortuous regulation of procedural nullities, see, among others, Vergé Grau (1982), Martín de la Leona (1996), Garcimartín Montero (2002), Lourido Rico (2004), Serra Domínguez (1981, 43 et seq.), Borrajo Iniesta (1993, 265 ff.), Bachmaier Winter (1994, 243 ff.), and Bachmaier Winter (1996, 1676 ff.).

[22] See STS 4 April 1994 (RJ 2867); STS 2096/1996 of 9 April; 4859/1997, of 8 July; STS of 11 February 2000 (RJ 743), among many others.

9.1.4 General Rules of Admissibility or Exclusion of Illegally Gathered Evidence in High Court Jurisprudence

9.1.4.1 The Importance of the 1984 Constitutional Court Decision

Before explaining the doctrine of the Spanish high courts on this topic, it bears remembering, that international human rights treaties are directly binding on the Spanish courts[23] and thus the doctrine of the European Convention of Human Rights (ECHR) has had a significant influence on Constitutional Court jurisprudence.

As we have already noted, the Constitutional Court has held since 1984 that respect of fundamental rights constitutes a limit to the pursuit of material truth and the accomplishment of the state interest in the prosecution of crime. Since then, the courts have applied the rule laid down in STC 114/1984, and in its 1985 statutory embodiment, § 11.1 LOPJ.[24]

In STC 114/1984, the Constitutional Court did not seek to elaborate a complete doctrine on illegally gathered evidence in its judgment,[25] but it nonetheless became a bench-mark decision setting up a seemingly absolute exclusionary rule when evidence is obtained in violation of fundamental rights.

It is important to note, however, that the exclusionary rule will not apply in those cases where the illegally gathered evidence is exculpatory, and proves the innocence of the defendant. For example, if during an unlawful search a firearm with the fingerprints of a murderer is found, this physical evidence may not be used to incriminate the defendant, but should be admitted to prove the innocence of a person who has been unjustly accused of the same crime.[26]

9.1.4.2 Strict Application of the Doctrine of "Fruits of the Poisonous Tree"

According to the Constitutional Court case law of the early 1980s, the invalidity caused by the violation of fundamental rights extended to derivative evidence, and this inspired the language of § 11.1 LOPJ. In a decision of March 14, 1994, the Constitutional Court explicitly adopted the "doctrine of the fruit of the poisonous tree",[27] also called the doctrine of "reflex effects" in Spain. STC 84/1994 dealt with

---

[23] Art. 10.2 Const.: "The principles relating to the fundamental rights and liberties recognized by the Constitution shall be interpreted in conformity with the Universal Declaration of Human Rights and the international treaties and agreements thereon ratified by Spain".

[24] See Sect. 9.1.3.1 and subsections, above.

[25] This can be deduced from FJ 4°, where the Court indicates it is not establishing a general doctrine on exclusion of illegally obtained evidence, but is just deciding the issue as it applies to the case before it.

[26] However, this question is still a subject of controversy in the legal literature. See among others, Fernández Entralgo (1996, 157) or Díaz Cabiale and Martín Morales (2001, 197).

[27] STC 84/1994 of 14 March.

an illegal wiretap, which led to an arrest and seizure of a package containing drugs. The Constitutional Court reasoned, that the package with the drugs could not have been seized without the information obtained through the illegal wiretap, a direct causal nexus existed between them, "tainting" them with illegality, which required their suppression.[28]

9.1.4.3 Limitation of the Doctrine of "Fruits of the Poisonous Tree"

Since 1998, the Constitutional Court has mitigated the reach of the doctrine of "reflex effects, and introduced exceptions to the earlier categorical rule, which have followed exceptions allowed in the case law of the US Supreme Court.

The Constitutional Court has held that the exclusion of "fruits of the poisonous tree" is absolute only if the following circumstances are met: (1) the interference with a fundamental right must be of a *certain intensity* and; (2) there must be a "causal nexus of illegality". These terms are vague and will require explanation.

In applying this test, the courts have determined, for instance, that evidence against a third party fortuitously found following a violation of a fundamental right of another, will not necessarily be excluded against the third party due to the weaker causal link with the violation. This is similar to the German *Rechtskreistheorie* which is in turn similar to the "standing" limitations in American exclusionary doctrine.

Both the Spanish Supreme and Constitutional Courts have also recognized the "independent source" exception, for instance, in cases where a defendant pleads guilty to a drug charge, where his detention with the drugs was the fruit of an illegal wiretap. In such a case, the causal nexus between illegal wiretap, arrest and search, was broken, and the guilty plea was entered independently while defendant was represented by counsel.[29]

Another exception, also recognized in US law, is that of "inevitable discovery". This doctrine allows the use of illegally obtained evidence if law enforcement agents would have eventually discovered it by legal means independent of the evidence illegally obtained. For example, in a Constitutional Court decision of April 2, 1998, the police learn of a visit planned by a drug trafficker through an illegal wiretap and arrested him and discovered drugs. The Court ruled that the evidence need not be suppressed, because the suspect was already under legal police surveillance prior to the illegal wiretap, and the information obtained through the wiretap was neither indispensable nor determinative for the discovery and seizure of the drugs.[30]

---

[28] Ibid, FJ 4.

[29] SSTC 6/1995 of 6 June; 54/1996 of 26 March.

[30] STC 81/1998 of 2 April; STS 4 July 1997. On this decision see the study of Martínez García (2003, 191).

In describing the fact that the discovery of drugs was not inextricably linked to the illegal wiretap, however, the Court did not use the term "inevitable source" but coined the term "nexus of illegality" (*nexo de antijuridicidad*), requiring that the link between the violation and the discovery of the disputed evidence had to be legal rather than merely factual.[31] The Court, without denying that there was a factual link between the unlawful wiretap and the subsequent seizure of the drugs, found that there was no "illegality connection", i.e., the illegality of the wiretap did not transfer to the seizure of the drugs.

A useful summary of this loosened doctrine related to indirect evidence can be found in a decision of the Supreme Court of January 19, 2004. There the court indicated that there was a presumption that both direct and indirect evidence gained from a constitutional violation would be suppressed, unless there was no "illegality connection" between the two. To determine whether or not there was such "illegality connection" the following elements would be weighed: (1) the significance of the constitutional infringement; (2) the importance and relevance of the evidence obtained; (3) whether there was a hypothetical clean path ("inevitable discovery") to discover the evidence; (4) whether the fundamental right violated requires special protection due to its vulnerability; (5) whether the officers acted in good faith, or in blatant disregard of the law, so as to evaluate the potential deterrent effect of ordering exclusion.[32]

One can see here, that most of the limitations on the doctrine of the "fruit of the poisonous tree" established by the US Supreme Court are taken into account in this evaluation of the "illegality connection", namely, the doctrines of "independent source", "inevitable discovery", "good faith" and "attenuation of the taint". An additional balancing factor is that of the seriousness of the infringement. These restrictions on the exclusion of "fruits of the poisonous tree" have been justified for the sake of avoiding impunity and ensuring an effective administration of justice, but it is still a very controversial issue, and academic[33] as well as judicial opinions are divided.

This loosening of the previously categorical rule excluding derivative evidence could lead to courts finding a way to admit all such evidence. Aware of this situation the Supreme Court has warned of these risks and indicated that the exceptions are to be applied with caution and in a way that does not eliminate the safeguards and aims of the exclusionary rule as stated in § 11.1 LOPJ.[34]

---

[31] STC 81/1998 of 2 April. This doctrine has been followed in numerous cases. See, Sect. 9.2.3.4, below, for examples relating to illegal wiretaps. On the relation between the concept of "illegality connection" within the evidentiary exclusionary rules and the dogmatic German theory of the "objective accountability" (teoría de la imputación objetiva), see González Cusac (2008, 279).

[32] STS 127/2004 of 19 January.

[33] For criticism of the limitations, see, Gómez Colomer (2008, 145), and Aguilera Morales (2009, 105–106).

[34] See STS 1203/2002, of 18 July.

9.1.4.4 Jurisprudence Dealing with the Distinction Between Exclusion Under § 11.1 LOPJ and Nullity Under § 238 LOPJ

In the Spanish jurisprudence, one distinguishes between "irregular" evidence and "illegal" evidence depending on the seriousness of the violation.[35] "Irregular" evidence is that which is obtained in violation of a statutory procedural rule, whereas "illegal" evidence is gathered in violation of a fundamental right. However some authors contend that irregular evidence is a type of illegal evidence, because a violation of a procedural rule brings with it the violation of the constitutional right to a fair trial with all guarantees recognized in Art. 24 Const.

There is a lack of clarity in the jurisprudence, however. While a mere statutory violation which does not impact fundamental rights would clearly be dealt with under § 238 LOPJ and not § 11.1 LOPJ, some of the protections afforded by § 238 LOPJ appear to be directed at fundamental rights, such as violations of the right to defense and to assistance of a lawyer. In such a case, the issue would, however, be handled under § 238 LOPJ as a nullity and not under § 11.1 LOPJ.

The Supreme Court has also made some interesting distinctions, for instance, in a decision of November 2, 1993. There it distinguished between a dwelling search performed without judicial warrant, which violates a constitutional rule and leads to exclusion under § 11.1 LOPJ and a dwelling search done with a warrant, but in violation of some other procedural rule, which would be treated as a nullity.[36] Yet in an earlier case from March 29, 1990, the Supreme Court left open that some violations of sub-constitutional rules could also lead to exclusion, and opted for a case-by-case approach to exclusion in such cases.[37]

The distinction would be of no importance if the consequences for a finding of nullity were the same as for exclusion under § 11.1 LOPJ. But, in the case of a finding of a nullity, any possible exclusion would not extend to derivative evidence.

9.2 Rules of Admissibility/Exclusion in Relation to Violations of the Right to Privacy

9.2.1 General Provisions Protecting the Right to Privacy and to Develop One's Personality

9.2.1.1 Constitutional Provisions

Art.18.1 Const. states:

> The right to honor, to personal and family privacy and to one's own image is guaranteed.

[35] See Armenta Deu (2009, 47–48).

[36] STS 7310/1993, of 2 November.

[37] STS 2943/1990, of 29 March.

These rights are enshrined in the framework of the so called *status libertatis* and grant the individual person a space of liberty and privacy against interferences from third persons, be it from public authorities, other citizens or private entities.[38] They are rights linked to the individual personality and thus derived from the human dignity recognized in Art.10 Const. Art. 18 Const. grants protection to an individual private sphere to be enjoyed by each person, and from which they may exclude all others.[39] The rights recognized in Art. 18 Const.—inviolability of the domicile, secrecy of communications, limits on data processing, etc.—seek to protect the general right to privacy.

The right to personal privacy (intimacy according to the wording of the Spanish Constitution) encompasses the protection against intrusions into the human body. Body examinations or tests can only be undertaken it the affected person consents or if an adequately reasoned judicial warrant authorizes it. Furthermore, any physical examination has to be performed by medical personnel, and any body search that affects the right to intimacy has to be done with respect for human dignity and without any degrading treatment.[40]

9.2.1.2 Statutory Provisions

The CCP does not regulate searches of the body or clothing. However, the Organic Law on Citizen's Protection of February 21, 1992 (*Ley Orgánica de Protección Ciudadana*), gives police the power to frisk (*cacheo*) a person suspected of committing an offense without a previous judicial order. A suspect may also be frisked for safety reasons, to check if he is carrying a weapon or other dangerous object. The search of clothing made without a serious suspicion is considered to be an infringement of the constitutional right to privacy.

9.2.1.3 High Court Jurisprudence Interpreting the General Right

The lack of statutory regulation has led the Supreme Court to identify the conditions under which an external search of the body will be constitutional: (1) the search must be conducted by a person of the same sex as the frisked suspect; (2) it must be done in a non-public place, if possible; and (3) degrading or humiliating positions must be avoided.[41] If a more intrusive searching is considered necessary, a reasoned judicial warrant is required, which must take into account the lawfulness, necessity and proportionality of the measure.[42] A search of the suspect's body may include

[38] STC 231/1988, of 1 December.

[39] See Serrano Alberca (1980, 233).

[40] STC 37/1989, of 15 February.

[41] STS 2623/2000, of 31 March.

[42] See Moreno Catena (2005, 230), Gil Hernández (1995, 60).

body cavities. When a legal body search uncovers evidence of crime other than what it was aimed at discovering, such evidence will not be considered to be illegally obtained evidence.[43]

In a decision of May 11, 1996, the Supreme Court found that narcotics evidence gathered during a body search, in which the defendant was forced to undress and, while nude, make squat exercises with the aim of expelling a drug out of his body, was inadmissible. It was considered to be the result of humiliating and degrading treatment in violation of Arts. 18(1), 15 Const.

9.2.2 Protection of Privacy in the Home

9.2.2.1 Constitutional Provisions

Art. 18(3) Const. provides: "The home is inviolable. No entry or search may take place without the consent of the occupant or a judicial warrant, except in cases of flagrant crime (*flagrante delicto*)".

9.2.2.2 Statutory Provision

Searches of the home are widely regulated in the CCP but the majority of the provisions date from the nineteenth Century and should be brought up to date. For instance, public buildings (§ 546 CCP) and dwellings (§ 550 CCP) may be entered and searched during a criminal investigation, where consent is lacking, pursuant to a reasoned order of the investigating magistrate. The CCP has separate sections for different kinds of buildings, but, in general, the notion of "home" should today be understood in a broad sense: any closed space that is used as a dwelling on a temporary or permanent basis, as well as spaces used as professional rooms fall under the meaning of "home" in the context of privacy protection according to the case law of the European Court of Human Rights (ECtHR).[44]

According to § 558 CCP, the search warrant must be well-founded and particularly describe the place to be searched. Any object that may be relevant for the investigation of the offense may be seized (§ 574 CCP), but books and papers may only be examined during a home entry if there is grave suspicion that they will contain evidence of criminality (§ 573 CCP).

---

[43] SSTS 4064/2003, of 12 June and 1470/2003, of 4 March.

[44] In Niemietz v. Germany (1993), 16 E.H.R.R. 97, 111, § 29, the ECtHR said it would be too restrictive "to limit the notion of private life to an 'inner circle.'" *See* also Veeber v. Estonia (2004), 39 E.H.R.R. 6, 125.

9.2.2.3 High Court Jurisprudence Concerning the Admissibility of Evidence Seized in Violation of the Right to Privacy in the Home

How Extensive Is the Protection of the "Home"?

The general rule is that the constitutional protection of home privacy refers to all those closed spaces with minimum living conditions to allow the development of one's personality. The CCP regulates the entry and search of dwellings and other premises, either private or public. Following the case-law of the ECtHR, the concept of domicile has been interpreted by the courts in a broad sense and encompasses also a hotel room,[45] tents pitched lawfully on private or public land, a trailer or a mobile-home, where a person lives and has a reasonable expectation of privacy.[46] The constitutional safeguards applicable to the home also apply to parts of the home like the garage or a store room.[47] However the courts have refused to consider as a "home" for the purposes of entry and search places open fields, a corral, a shed or an elevator. An industrial storehouse open to the public also does not have the constitutional protection accorded to the "home".[48]

Admissibility of the Immediate Fruits of the Search

Pursuant to Constitutional Court doctrine, which closely follows the case law of the ECtHR, the protection of the inviolability of the domicile has an instrumental character as it serves to protect the right to personal and family privacy and intimacy by recognizing a protected space to develop one's own private life.[49] This notwithstanding, the Constitutional Court has extended the constitutional protection to the domiciles of legal entities (juridical persons) as well.[50]

According to the case law, the consent which may make a judicial warrant unnecessary may be given by any person living in the dwelling, unless there are conflicting interests between them and the defendant.[51]

The judicial warrant authorizing the entry and search has to specify clearly the premises to be searched, the names of the occupants, the day when it is going to take place, the offense under investigation, as well as the reasons that justify the

---

[45] STC 10/2002, of 17 January.

[46] See SSTS 13585/1994, of 19 September; 503/2001, of 29 January; 705/2003, of 5 February. In general see, Hinojosa Segovia (1996), and Cabezudo Bajo (2004).

[47] See STC 171/1999, of 27 September.

[48] ATC 290/2004, of 19 July.

[49] See STC 22/1984, of 17 February; 137/198, of 17 October; 95/1999, of 31 May or 161/1999, of 19 July.

[50] ATC 171/1989, of 3 April.

[51] STC 22/2003, of 10 February.

search. In the reasons, the magistrate must balance the right to be infringed, with the importance of the evidence sought and justify the proportionality of the measure.[52]

If during a lawful search of premises the police find evidence of the commission of an offense different from the one which justified the search, such evidence is normally admissible. Only if there were indications that the police abused its powers, using deception to obtain the warrant, or exceeded the scope of the warrant in a kind of *inquisitio generalis*, would the evidence be inadmissible.[53]

If the entry and search are in violation of the aforementioned requirements, the evidence obtained is indamissible at trial. This exclusionary rule applies to illegal contraband seized, such as drugs as well as to the testimony of the officers who conducted the illegal search.[54]

Admissibility of Indirect Evidence

The Spanish courts have often had to decide, whether a statement made by a suspect or defendant after a privacy violation would be suppressible as a fruit of the privacy violation. [55] In a decision of July 22, 1999, for instance, involving a search warrant which lacked probable cause, the Constitutional Court refused to extend the exclusionary rule beyond the drugs and gun found in the search (and the testimony of the serving officers), to an incriminating statement later made by the defendant before the investigating magistrate and subsequently ratified at trial.[56]

Later, the same year, the Constitutional Court reached a similar decision.[57] The defense argued that, without the illegal search which discovered the drugs, the subsequent statement would not have been made, and had the defendant known the search were illegal, he would not have voluntarily admitted guilt. However, the statement was made at trial, when represented by a lawyer, after he had challenged the legality of the search, and had been previously advised of the right to remain silent and privilege against self-incrimination. The Court found no legal causation in the case due to the time which elapsed between the illegality and the otherwise proper admissions at trial.[58]

---

[52] SSTC 290/1994, of 27 October; 50/1995, of 23 February, 136/2000, of 29 May; 56/2003, of 24 March. The Spanish case law has definitely been influenced by the jurisprudence of the ECtHR in this area, especially in relation to the requirement of proportionality.

[53] See STC 41/1998, of 24 February.

[54] STC 94/1999.

[55] For a discussion of this issue, *see* Vegas Torres (1996, 367–370).

[56] STC 139/1999 of July 22. This doctrine has been reiterated in subsequent decisions: SSTC 161/1999, of 27 September, 136/2000, of 29 May, or 149/2001, of 27 June.

[57] STC 161/1999 of September 27.

[58] In the same sense STC 8/2000, of 17 January; STS 422/2002, of 28 January; 7995/2002, of 29 November.

The courts will suppress admissions made directly after an illegal search finds incriminating evidence,[59] but if the statements are reiterated at trial, the taint will be deemed to have been attenuated, i.e. with no legal causation.[60]

9.2.3 *Protection of Privacy in One's Communications*

9.2.3.1 Constitutional Provisions

Art.18(3) Const. provides: "The confidentiality of communications, especially postal, telegraphic and telephone communications, is guaranteed, unless there is judicial authorization".

9.2.3.2 Statutory Provisions

§ 579 CCP provides:

1. A court may authorize the seizure, opening and examination of private postal and telegraphic correspondence sent or received by a person charged if there is reason to believe that facts or circumstances material to the case may thereby be uncovered or verified.
2. A court may also authorize, in a reasoned decision, the monitoring of the telephone calls of a person charged if there is evidence to show that facts or circumstances material to the case may thereby be uncovered or verified.
3. Likewise, a court may, in a reasoned decision, authorize for a maximum renewable period of three months the monitoring of the postal, telegraphic and telephonic communications of persons reasonably believed to have committed an offense and of communications made for criminal purposes.[61]

The CCP provides for detailed regulation in the area of postal and telegraphic communications (§§ 579–88 CCP), which encompass the opening of letters and packages, in both of which there is a protected right to privacy, or delaying their delivery.[62] A judicial warrant is required to open mail or packages, unless one is dealing with a type of mail as to which the sender consents to its opening.[63] Interception

---

[59] STS 1055/2004, of 18 February.

[60] ATC 123/2002, of 15 July. In an isolated decision, however, the Supreme Court ruled that a subsequent court confession should be suppressed if the court erroneously admitted the illegally seized physical evidence which preceded it, STS 13 March 1999 (RJ 2105).

[61] § 579(4) CCP also provides, that in urgent cases involving offenses committed by armed bands or terrorist groups, the interception of telephone calls may be authorized by the Ministry of Home Affairs or the Director for the State Security, but the order must be ratified, or revoked, by a judge within 72 h in a reasoned decision.

[62] See the guidelines set by the Criminal Chamber of the Supreme Court on April 4, 1995 in favor of this broad interpretation. Since then, see SSTS 308/1999, of 25 January; 6051/1994, of 26 September; 5195/2000, of 26 June.

[63] See Moreno Catena (2005, 248).

of postal communications has been non-controversial in Spain, but the same cannot be said for wiretapping or the interception of electronic communications.

Art. 18(3) Const. was only statutorily implemented in 1988, when Sect. 9.3 was added to § 579 CCP. But the language of § 579(3) CCP insufficiently regulates wiretapping, so further procedural rules had to be added by the Spanish high courts in order to bring the code in line with requirements of the ECtHR. Nonetheless, the Spanish arrangement has been criticized by the ECtHR because of the failure of the legislature to incorporate the further protections into the CCP.[64]

9.2.3.3 High Court Jurisprudence Interpreting the Wiretap Statute and the Admissibility of Evidence in Case of Its Violation

On June 18, 1992, the Spanish Supreme Court decided the landmark *Naseiro* case in which, for the first time, it laid out the requirements for legal wiretaps in Spain, which if violated, would lead to exclusion of the conversations intercepted and any indirect evidence derived therefrom. These requirements are: (1) wiretap warrants must be based on a kind of "probable cause" which would not be fulfilled by "mere suspicion", which was all the police had in the case before the court; (2) the judge, in issuing the warrant, must make a finding of proportionality as well, based on the circumstances of the crime investigated, and determine whether the legitimate law enforcement interests outweigh the privacy interests of the affected parties, and must determine the means of carrying out the intervention which will least harm the rights of the affected parties; (3) there must be judicial supervision of the measure, to make sure it does not go on for an unreasonable period or further than the suspicion merits; (4) the investigating magistrate must review the content of all of the recordings in order to determine whether the content is related to the investigation and also whether the measure should be continued or terminated and, if terminated, the affected parties must be notified; (5) if the police who carry out the wiretap discover evidence of commission of a crime or crimes different than those for which the warrant was obtained, they must immediately inform the investigating magistrate who ordered the measure, so he or she may determine whether further interception of conversations related to these new crimes would be justified on grounds of proportionality.[65]

After the *Naseiro* case, the Constitutional Court rendered a judgment on April 5, 1999, reiterating the requirements laid down by the Supreme Court in its 1992 opinion.[66]

---

[64] In general, on the telephone tapping in Spain see, López Barja de Quiroga (1989), López-Fragoso Álvarez (1991), Martín Morales (1995), Montero Aroca (1999), and Gómez Colomer (1998, 145–167).

[65] See Montón Redondo (1995, 1043–1052), Gimeno Sendra (1996, 1617–1624).

[66] STC 49/1999, of 5 April.

Unlike the decisions of the Supreme Court, those of the Constitutional Court are binding precedent for all courts in the Spanish legal system.[67]

9.2.3.4 Admissibility of Fruits of the Poisonous Tree (Indirect Evidence)

As was stated in Sect. 9.1.4, above, Spanish courts are required to exclude indirect evidence gathered from violations of fundamental (constitutional rights), unless the connection is attenuated (no "legal causal nexus"), or a situation of inevitable discovery or independent source would apply. For instance, the Constitutional Court in 1995 ruled that drugs seized during an arrest, the time and place of which was only discoverable by virtue of an illegal wiretap, had to be suppressed.[68] Testimony of a witness who was found through an illegal wiretap was declared inadmissible by the Supreme Court in a 1996 case.[69]

However, in the seminal case of the Constitutional Court which developed the test of "legal nexus" involved an illegal wiretap which led to discovery of a drug sale, which would have otherwise been "inevitably" discovered due to pre-existing surveillance of the suspect, thus attenuating the "taint" of the illegal wiretap.[70] The Court reached a similar result in 1999, where it admitted, that though the illegal wiretap might have opened up new lines of investigation, the information on the route the suspect took when delivering the subsequently seized drugs was discovered through police surveillance unrelated to the wiretap.[71]

The Constitutional Court also admitted a voluntary confession, which was taken in compliance with all procedural rules relating to interrogations, though it came on the heels of an unlawful wiretap, finding that there was no "nexus of illegality", i.e., the taint was attenuated.[72]

---

[67] For subsequent decisions of the Constitutional Court applying the requirements: STC 239/1999, of 20 December; STC 47/2000, of 17 February; STC 126/2000, of 16 May; STC 299/2000, of 11 December; STC 202/2001, of 15 October; STC 87/2002, of 22 April; STC 167/2002, of 18 September; STC 184/2003, of 23 October; STC 165/2005, of 20 June; STC 205/2005, of 18 July; and STC 26/2006, of 30 January. For subsequent decisions of the Supreme Court: STS 310/2000, of 24 January; STS 1683/2000, 3 March; STS 879/2001, 10 February; STS 5207/2001, of 18 June; STS 5466/2001, of 25 June; STS 2417/2002, of 4 April; STS 2912/2002, of 24 April; STS 4707/2003, of 4 July.

[68] STC 86/1995 of 6 June. The Supreme Court reached a similar result after an illegal interception of a cell phone conversation, STS 734/1999, 8 February.

[69] STS 4 October 1996 (RJ 7564).

[70] See Sect. 9.1.4.3 above, with discussion of STC 81/1998, of 2 April.

[71] STC 238/1999 of 20 December. See STC 26/2006 of 30 January and STC 70/2007 of 16 April, for similar decisions.

[72] STC 136/2006, of 8 May. The Supreme Court reached a similar decision in the so-called *Al Qaeda Case* of May 31, 2006 (STS 7464/2006).

9.2.3.5 Effect of International Human Rights Jurisprudence

Despite Spain's vigorous exclusionary rule applicable to illegal wiretaps, § 579 CCP was found by the ECtHR in 1999 to be in violation of Art. 8 ECHR, which protects the right to privacy in one's communications, because, despite the meticulous attempts by the Spanish courts to interpret so that it conformed to modern standards, it still provided an insufficient legal basis to put citizens on notice, as to when and according to what procedures the authorities may intercept private conversations.[73] In 2003 the ECtHR reached a similar decision,[74] and it wasn't until 2006 that the ECtHR finally found that § 579 CCP, in conjunction with the case law of the high courts, finally provided sufficient guarantees to be in compliance with Art. 8 ECHR.[75]

9.2.4 *Other Actions Invasive of Privacy Which Could Lead to Suppression of Evidence*

9.2.4.1 Rules Relating to Search of Personal Effects: Automobiles, Private Containers, etc.

There are no statutory provisions that specifically regulate the entry and search of automobiles or other effects. The Supreme Court, however, has ruled that the constitutional protection accorded a home cannot be extended to vehicles that are used as a means of transportation.[76]

9.2.4.2 Rules Relating to Data Mining and the Collection of Semi-private Information and Related Jurisprudence

According to a European Union Directive aimed at harmonizing member states' handling of electronically stored data,[77] the Spanish legislator enacted a 2007 law which regulates the obligation of communication service providers to retain data

---

[73] Valenzuela-Contreras v. Spain (1999), 28 E.H.R.R. 483, 506–107, §§ 58–61.

[74] Prado Bugallo v. Spain, no. 58796/00, ECHR, 18 Feb. 2003.

[75] Abdulkadir Coban v. Spain, ECHR, Decison of inadmissibility, 25 Sept. 2006.

[76] SSTS 1011/2001, of 14 February; 3687/2001, of 7 May; 1303/2003, of 26 February or 6395/2003, of 17 October.

[77] Directive 2006/24/EC of the European Parliament and of the Council of 15 March 2006, on the retention of data generated or processed in connection with the provision of publicly available electronic communications services or of public communications networks. As stated in its Art. 1, this Directive aims to harmonize Member States' provisions concerning the obligations of the providers of publicly available electronic communications services or of public communications networks with respect to the retention of certain data which are generated or processed by them, in order to ensure that the data are available for the purpose of the investigation, detection and prosecution of serious crime, as defined by each Member State in its national law.

concerning the origin and destination of all telephone or internet communications, but not the content.[78] The law requires that the data be retained for a minimum period of 12 months. In theory, access to this data is only possible for the investigation of serious crimes and must be authorized by a judicial warrant, which heeds the requirements of legality, necessity and proportionality. There is an explicit exception, however, for cases affecting national security. We are not aware of any Spanish cases dealing with access to this data, or its suppression, but the general principles discussed above would clearly apply if such case arises.

9.3 Rules of Admissibility/Exclusion in Relation to Illegal Interrogations

9.3.1 The General Right to Remain Silent/Privilege Against Self-Incrimination

9.3.1.1 Constitutional Provisions

Art. 17.3 Const. provides: "Any person in custody must be informed immediately, and in a manner understandable to him or her, of his or her rights and of the grounds for his or her arrest, and may not be compelled to make a statement. The arrested person shall be guaranteed the assistance of a lawyer during police and judicial proceedings, under the terms established by the law".

Furthermore, Art. 24(2) Const. provides, in pertinent part: "[A]ll persons have the right [...] to the defense and assistance of a lawyer; to be informed of the charges brought against them" [...] as well as the right "to not make self-incriminating statements; to not admit guilt; and to be presumed innocent".

9.3.1.2 Statutory Provisions

The most important statutory provisions relate to protection against coerced or unknowing statements and will be dealt with in Sects. 9.3.2.2 and 9.3.3.2 below.

9.3.1.3 High Court Interpretations of Scope of the Right to Silence

The Spanish Constitutional Court, relying on the clear enunciation of the right to silence and privilege against self-incrimination incorporated in Art. 24(2) Const., as components of the right to a defense and the presumption of innocence, as well as on the jurisprudence of the ECtHR, has held that law enforcement authorities

[78] Spanish Law 25/2007 of 18 October.

must prove guilt without inducing the suspect/accused to incriminate himself. The presumption of innocence, thus, forbids any attempt to shift the burden of proof from the prosecution to the defense.[79]

This is a great change from the ancient inquisitorial procedure where the defendant was considered to be the object of the procedure, from whom the truth should be obtained, with no subjective procedural rights. As a party in criminal proceedings, the defendant has the right to freely choose his defense strategy, with one such choice being that of remaining silent. Whether he decides to make a statement and the content thereof are his choice, and not that of law enforcement authorities.[80]

The right to silence and privilege against self-incrimination extend only to testimonial evidence, and not to the gathering of other material evidence. For example, the privilege against self-incrimination does not allow the defendant to refuse to be examined by a physician or to refuse to perform an alcohol breath-test.[81]

9.3.2 *The Protection Against Involuntary Self-Incrimination*

9.3.2.1 Constitutional Provisions

Art. 15 Const. guarantees the right to "life and to physical and moral integrity" and prohibits torture or inhuman or degrading punishments or treatment. Any method or technique used to coerce a statement from a suspect/accused would be also contrary to Art. 10(1) Const., which declares that the "human dignity and the inviolable rights inherent therein" as well as "the free development of the personality" are "foundations of the political order and social peace". As mentioned above, Art. 17(3) Const. also prohibits compelling an accused to make a statement.

9.3.2.2 Statutory Provisions

§ 389 CCP requires that questions be posed to the accused in a direct manner, avoiding tricky or leading questions.[82] It further states that "no compulsion or threats shall be used against the accused". This rule, which was mentioned earlier as an example of the statutory limits on the search for truth in Spanish criminal procedure, is supplemented by § 393 CCP, which requires that the accused be allowed to rest and regain his calm, especially in cases of lengthy interrogations.

---

[79] STC 18/2005, of 1 February.

[80] See STC 161/1997, of 2 October; 61/2005, of 14 March; 127/1992, of 28 September; 197/1995, of 21 December.

[81] In this sense, SSTC 37/1989 of 15 February and 161/1997, of 2 October.

[82] On the interrogation of the defendant and the consequences of its unlawfulness, see Asencio Mellado (1989, 127).

The prohibition of § 389 CCP includes, of course, the prohibition of using torture or inhuman or degrading treatment, or other methods or techniques which might undermine the free will of the person under interrogation.[83] The scientific literature is very clear on this issue: an involuntary confession is not even considered to be a confession, not to speak of evidence.[84] A narcoanalysis test is prohibited, even if requested by the defendant to prove his own innocence.[85]

9.3.2.3 High Court Jurisprudence Regarding the Admissibility of Involuntary Statements or Their Fruits

This issue has seldom presented itself to the Spanish courts. In a decision of 1987, however, the Constitutional Court stated the obvious, that evidence obtained through torture is void and clearly inadmissible.[86]

Although there is no Spanish case dealing with the indirect fruits of a confession induced through torture or cruel, inhuman or degrading treatment, such fruits, such as the discovery of physical evidence, would clearly be inadmissible under the general Constitutional Court case law and § 11.1 LOPJ. The ECtHR recently decided that physical evidence found as a result of torture would clearly be inadmissible, though evidence found following cruel, inhuman or degrading treatment, might be admissible if there was sufficient attenuation.[87]

9.3.3 The Protection Against Unknowing Self-Incrimination

9.3.3.1 Constitutional Provisions on Admonition of the Right to Silence/Counsel

As mentioned above in Sect. 9.3.1.1, Arts. 17(3), 24(2) Const. clearly require that criminal suspects/defendants be advised of the right to silence and to the assistance of counsel before being interrogated.

9.3.3.2 Statutory Provisions on Admonition of the Right to Silence/Counsel

According to § 118 CCP, from the moment a person is suspected or charged with a crime the right to defense must be guaranteed, whether or not the person is

---

[83] STS 6635/1991, of 26 November.

[84] See, for example, Silva Melero, *La prueba procesal* (1963, 193–195).

[85] On the discussion of the use of narco-analysis to obtain confessions, from a psychological point of view, see Romero Coloma (1989, 45–56).

[86] ATC 970/1987.

[87] Gäfgen v. Germany (G.C.) (2011) 52 E.H.R.R. 1, 42, §§ 166–167.

in custody. This right to defense includes the right to be assisted by a lawyer. The suspect-accused must be advised of the right to counsel. In Spain this includes the right to hire one's counsel of his choice, or, if the accused is not able to, or refuses to do so, a duty lawyer will be appointed by the Bar Association.

§ 520(2) CCP provides that law enforcement organs advise detained persons of their basic rights, yet the courts have extended this duty also to suspects-accused who are not in custody.[88] Thus, suspects and defendants must be informed of the following immediately upon detention or charge: (1) the nature of the charges (and, if detained, the reasons for imposing pretrial detention; (2) the right to remain silent and not answer any and all questions, or to do so only in front of the investigating magistrate; (3) the privilege against self-incrimination; (4) the right to consult with and be assisted by a lawyer; (5) the right to communicate with a relative (in case of arrest); (6) the right to be assisted by an interpreter at no cost, if he does not understand the Spanish language; and (7) the right to be examined by a physician (in case of arrest).

Furthermore, § 767 CCP requires mandatory representation by counsel of all defendants from the moment of their arrest and the police, public prosecutor, or investigating magistrate must immediately notify the Bar Association so that counsel may be appointed in those situations where the arrestee does not have retained counsel.

§ 387 CCP, which has not been amended since enacted in 1882, lays out the procedure for interrogating criminal suspects in classic inquisitorial fashion, requiring that the suspect be informed of his obligation to answer all the questions truthfully and in a clear manner. The courts have, however, declared this rule to be unconstitutional, because it is inconsistent with the constitutional right to remain silent which is expressly guaranteed in Arts. 17, 24 Const.[89]

9.3.3.3 High Court Jurisprudence Relating to Admissibility of Confessions or Indirect Evidence Following the Failure to Advise of the Right to Silence/Counsel

The Supreme Court has held that the failure to advise suspects of their constitutional rights constitutes a violation of the right to a defense guaranteed by Art. 24(2) Const. and any evidence thus obtained is inadmissible at trial.[90] This doctrine was explicitly applied in 1991 to statements taken from the defendants who were interrogated

---

[88] In this sense STC 37/1989, of 15 February, quoted by Vegas Torres (1993, 83).

[89] See SSTS 3155/1995, of 2 June and 6296/1996, of 12 November. Of another opinion, however, is, Vegas Torres (1993, 82), who considers that the right to remain silent and the privilege against self-incrimination are compatible with the admonition of the accused to declare according to the truth.

[90] STS 3843/1990, of May 19.

as witnesses, and thus, without having been informed of the right to silence and the right to counsel.[91] The tactic of interviewing a suspect as a "witness" and thus circumventing the requirement of admonitions has been roundly condemned by the courts and the ensuing statements are never admissible. If, however, the court finds that the defendant did know his rights and was represented by counsel, and counsel was present during the interrogation, a failure to formally advise the defendant of the right to counsel or to silence will not result in exclusion of any ensuing statement.[92]

The Constitutional Court has repeatedly declared that statements made without legal assistance are inadmissible under Arts. 17(3), 24(2) Const. and the "the fruits of the poisonous tree" are equally inadmissible per § 11.1 LOPJ. In this case, in which the accused was interrogated without legal assistance and revealed information about a hiding place where physical evidence was discovered, the Court ruled that all information obtained through the inadmissible declaration could not be used as evidence. [93]

Attention must be drawn to the fact that the Spanish legal system attaches no evidentiary value to incriminating statements given before the police or the public prosecutor, if the accused retracts those statements before a judicial authority. A judgment of conviction cannot be based alone on such statements. However, the statements lawfully made at the pretrial stage can, under certain circumstances, be repeated at trial by reading them aloud, for the purpose of impeaching the credibility of statements made at trial. They may also be used to further the investigation.

However, the Supreme Court has held that the inadmissibility of statements made at the pretrial stage do not affect the validity of statements thereafter made before the investigating magistrate, as long as the accused was informed properly of his rights before the subsequent statement. The nullity of a pretrial statement also does not carry over to a confession or admission made at trial, as they are considered to be independent of the earlier inadmissible statements.[94]

Statements made by a detained person to the police in the absence of counsel and/or without being advised of the right to remain silent, are not admissible as evidence, and the prohibition also extends to the "fruits of the poisonous tree". This also holds true, if the statements were made "spontaneously, freely and voluntarily" after proper admonition of rights, but without counsel.[95] Yet in these situations, the information gleaned from the unlawful confessions may be used as leads to further the investigation.

---

[91] STS of April 11, 1991 (RJ 2606).

[92] STS 621/1992, of January 30.

[93] See SSTC 128 y 129/1993 both of 19 April. For a similar decision, see STS 8120/ 1991, of October 25.

[94] SSTS 1430/1995, of 10 March; 4739/1995, of 28 September; or 1199/1996, of 26 February.

[95] STS 879/1998, of February 11; STS 740/1996, of February 7.

9.3.4 *Exclusion of Confessions as Fruits of an Unlawful Arrest, Search or Seizure*

This situation seldom arises in Spain, but would seem not to require exclusion under the general doctrine of the Constitutional Court in interpreting § 11.1 LOPJ. We have seen that lawfully conducted interrogations are considered to attenuate the taint of unlawful violations of privacy and unlawful detentions. There would be no "illegality nexus", to use the expression of the Constitutional Court.

On the other hand, if the confession was obtained in violation of the law, either due to involuntariness or failure to administer the proper warnings, it would be excluded of itself, without having to resort to the prior illegality. In this analysis, of course, the illegal arrest could be a coercive factor that would contribute to finding the confession to have been made involuntarily.

9.4 Conclusion

Although the 1882 Spanish CCP established certain limits on the gathering of evidence, the general practice was to accept at trial any evidence which could contribute to the determination of the truth of the facts contained in the accusatory pleadings, regardless of how the evidence was gathered.

The 1978 Constitution, however, placed the protection of human rights at the heart of the constitutional order, and this led to an increasing awareness of the importance of due process and the recognition of an exclusionary rule in relation to evidence gathered in violation of fundamental constitutional rights. This shift began with the landmark decision of the Constitutional Court in 1984 (STC 114/1984), which required exclusion of evidence following violations of fundamental rights. The enactment in 1985 of § 11.1 LOPJ then statutorily anchored a broad exclusionary rule extending to indirect as well as direct evidence gathered in violation of fundamental rights. The Constitutional Court then explicitly recognized the American doctrine of "fruits of the poisonous tree" in 1994 (STC 84/1994).

Over the years, however, the high courts have introduced more flexibility into what once was a nearly absolute rule excluding derivative evidence. The Supreme Court, for instance, began suggesting the use of a balancing test before excluding the derivative evidence. This gradually led to the Constitutional Court's adoption of the test requiring a "nexus of illegality" in order to suppress the fruits of a violation of fundamental constitutional rights in STC 81/1998. The vagueness of the notion of "illegality nexus", however, opens up the possibility of courts balancing their way around the exclusion of the "fruits of the poisonous tree".

A second problem is the lack of a clear distinction between infringements that cause a procedural nullity of the act and infringements which affect constitutional rights, and thus render the evidence clearly inadmissible. It is neither clear in the doctrine nor in the jurisprudence, whether the breach of procedural rules, which also violate fundamental rights, should be treated as procedural nullities (§ 238 LOPJ) or as inadmissible illegally obtained evidence (§ 11.1 LOPJ).

Bibliography

Aguilera Morales, E. 2009. Regla de exclusión y acusatorio. In *Proceso penal y sistemas acusatorios*, ed. L. Bachmaier Winter, 73–108. Marcial Pons: Madrid-Barcelona.

Armenta Deu, T. 2007. Nuevas tendencias en materia de prueba ilícita. In *XIII World Congress of Procedural Law,* Rio de Janeiro: Editorial Forense, 544–575.

Armenta Deu, T. 2009. *La prueba ilícita. Un estudio comparado*. Madrid- Barcelona: Marcial Pons.

Asencio Mellado, J.M. 1989. *Prueba prohibida y prueba preconstituida*. Madrid: Lince INPECCP.

Bachmaier Winter, L. 1994. *La rebeldía en el proceso civil norteamericano y español*. Madrid: Publicaciones UCM.

Bachmaier Winter, L. 1996. Nulidad de actuaciones y agotamiento de la vía judicial previa al recurso de amparo. A propósito de la STC 271/1994, de 17 de octubre. *La Ley* 1996–1: 1676–1688.

Barja, López, and J. de Quiroga. 1989. *Las escuchas telefónicas y la prueba ilegalmente obtenida*. Madrid: Akal.

Borrajo Iniesta, I. 1993 La nulidad de actuaciones según la Ley Orgánica del Poder Judicial. *Principios constitucionales en el proceso civil Cuadernos de derecho Judicial*, Madrid: CGPJ, 265–286.

Cabezudo Bajo, M.J. 2004. *La inviolabilidad del domicilio y el proceso penal*. Madrid: Iustel.

Del Moral García, A. 2001. Tratamiento de la prueba ilícita por vulneración de los derechos fundamentales. *Estudios Jurídicos, Ministerio Fiscal* V-2001: 137–174.

Díaz Cabiale, J.A. 1991. *La admisión y práctica de la prueba en el proceso penal*. Madrid: CGPJ.

Díaz Cabiale, J.A., and R. Martín Morales. 2001. *La garantía constitucional de la inadmisión de la prueba ilícitamente obtenida*. Madrid: Civitas.

Fernández Entralgo, J. 1996. Las reglas del juego. Prohibido hacer trampas: prueba ilegítimamente obtenida. In *La prueba en el proceso penal*. Madrid: Consejo General del Poder Judicial, 57–210.

Garcimartín Montero, R. 2002. *El incidente de nulidad de actuaciones en el proceso civil*. Madrid: Civitas.

Gil Hernández, A. 1995. *Intervenciones corporales y derechos fundamentales*. Madrid: Colex.

Gimeno Sendra, V. 1996. Las intervenciones telefónicas en la jurisprudencia del Tribunal Constitucional y del Tribunal Supremo. *La Ley* 1996–2: 1617–1624.

Gómez Colomer, J.L. 1998. La intervención judicial de las comunicaciones telefónicas a la luz de la jurisprudencia. *Revista Jurídica de Catalunya* 1: 145–167.

Gómez Colomer, J.L. 2008. La evolución de las teorías sobre la prueba prohibida aplicadas al proceso penal español. In *Prueba y proceso penal*, ed. J.L. Gómez-Colomer, 107–147. Valencia: Tirant lo Blanch.

González Cusac, J.L. 2008. La conexión de antijuridicidad en la prueba prohibida. In *Prueba y proceso penal*, ed. J.L. Gómez-Colomer, 279–322. Valencia: Tirant lo Blanch.

González García, J. 2007. El proceso penal español y la prueba ilícita. In *La prueba ilícita en el procedimiento penal México-España-Argentina-Brasil*, ed. Alfredo Delgadillo Aguirre, 31–54. México: INESD División editorial.

Guasp Delgado, J. 1947. *Comentarios a la Ley de Enjuiciamiento Civil*, vol. 2. Madrid: Aguilar.

Hinojosa Segovia, R. 1996. *La diligencia de entrada y registro en lugar cerrado en el proceso penal*. Madrid: Edersa.

López-Fragoso Álvarez, T. 1991. *Las intervenciones telefónicas en el proceso penal*. Madrid: Colex.

Lourido Rico, A. 2004. *La nulidad de actuaciones: Una perspectiva procesal*. Granada: Comares.

Martín de la Leona, J.M. 1996. *La nulidad de actuaciones en el proceso civil*. Madrid: Colex.

Martín Morales, R. 1995. *El régimen constitucional del secreto de las comunicaciones*. Madrid: Civitas.

Martínez García, E. 2003. *Eficacia de la prueba ilícita en el proceso penal (a la luz de la STC 81/98, de 2 de abril)*. Valencia: Tirant lo Blanch.

Miranda Estampes, M. 2004. *El concepto de prueba ilícita y su tratamiento en el proceso penal*, 2nd ed. Barcelona: Bosch.
Montero Aroca, J. 1999. *La intervención de las comunicaciones telefónicas en el proceso penal. Un estudio jurisprudencial*. Valencia: Tirant lo Blanch.
Montón Redondo, A. 1995. Las interceptaciones telefónicas constitucionalmente correctas. *La Ley* 1043–1052.
Moreno Catena, V. 1987. Garantía de los derechos fundamentales en la investigación penal. *Revista del Poder Judicial*, special issue, 131–172.
Moreno Catena, V., et al. 2005. *Derecho Procesal Penal*. Valencia: Tirant lo Blanch.
Muñoz Sabaté, L. 1993. *Técnica probatoria (Estudios sobre las dificultades de la prueba en el proceso*. Barcelona: Praxis.
Romero Coloma, A. 1989. *La prueba de confesión y el interrogatorio del acusado. Una visión psicológica*. Barcelona: Serlipost.
Serra Domínguez, M. 1981. El incidente de nulidad de actuaciones. *Justicia* 43–73.
Serrano Alberca, M. 1980. Comentario al Artículo 18 de la Constitución. In *Comentarios a la Constitución*, ed. F. Garrido Falla, 233–248. Madrid: Civitas.
Silva Melero, V. 1963. *La prueba procesal*. Madrid: Editorial Revista de Derecho Privado.
Urbano del Castillo, E. 1996. Prueba ilícita en particular (I). In *La prueba en el proceso penal,* Madrid: Consejo General del Poder Judicial, 228–237.
Vegas Torres, J. 1993. *Presunción de inocencia y prueba en el proceso penal*. Madrid: La Ley.
Vegas Torres, J. 1996. Prueba ilícita en particular (II). La ilicitud de la diligencia de entrada y registro en lugar cerrado y sus consecuencias. In *La prueba en el proceso penal*. Madrid: Consejo General del Poder Judicial, 293–372.
Vergér Grau, J. 1982. *El incidente de nulidad de actuaciones*. Barcelona: Bosch.
Vives Antón, T.S. 1987. Doctrina constitucional y reforma del proceso penal. In *Revista Poder Judicial*, special issue, Consejo General Poder Judicial, 2, 93–128.

Chapter 10
Italy: Statutory Nullities and Non-usability

Giulio Illuminati

10.1 General Rule

The general rule excluding illegally obtained evidence was introduced in the Italian criminal justice system with the reform of 1988. According to § 191 of the Code of Criminal Procedure (hereinafter CCP): "1. Evidence obtained in violation of prohibitions established by law may not be used. 2. The non-usability (*inutilizzabilità*) may be declared on the judge's own motion at any stage or level of the proceedings". Non-usability represents a legal limitation on judicial knowledge of the prohibited evidence; it prevents the judge from basing a ruling on the merits of the case upon pieces of evidence which were the result of violations of the rules which govern the collection of evidence.[1]

10.1.1 Non-usability and Procedural Models

Non-usability is tied to the principle of legality of the evidence, on which mode of adjudication the code of 1998 is programatically based.[2] The adjudicative power of the judge is a legally regulated activity subject to the limits set by law, as it is a given that the search for the truth may not be done by using any means deemed suitable in the discretion of the judge.

Translated from the Italian by Stephen C. Thaman, with the help of Joshua Walker.

[1] Grifantini (1993, 243).

[2] Nobili (1990a, 381).

G. Illuminati (✉)
Dipartimento di Scienze Giudidiche, Università di Bologna,
Via Zamboni 27/29, 40126, Bologna, Italy
e-mail: giulio.illuminati@unibo.it

S.C. Thaman (ed.), *Exclusionary Rules in Comparative Law*, Ius Gentium: Comparative Perspectives on Law and Justice 20, DOI 10.1007/978-94-007-5348-8_10,

For this reason it is believed that non-usability, as a type of exclusionary rule, forms part of the adversarial procedural model, upon which the reformed CCP is based. The requirement is that evidence be submitted by the parties and be put before the judge in a manner consistent with adversarial principles; that being said, it is necessary nevertheless that the evidence be admitted beforehand in accordance with rules established by law.

In contrast, the logic behind inquisitorial procedure requires that the introduction of evidence is done by the judge, according to his own admissibility criteria for the establishment of the truth. In this way, the judge's free evaluation of evidence translates into freedom to adduce evidence which goes not only to the weight given the evidence, but also to whether the evidence will even be admitted in the first place. Accordingly, the adversarial dialectic between the parties is reduced to nothing more than an *a posteriori* supervision over the judge's ruling, and checking the legality of evidence occurs mainly through a system of nullities and appeals.[3]

10.1.2 Precedents

Non-usability of evidence was not unknown under the now-repealed code,[4] but it was not understood to be a general rule of exclusion of evidence; because of the absence of a specific provision, it would be absorbed into the rules for nullities. A clear example of this may be found in relation to wiretapping done beyond the cases authorized by the law (§ 226-*quinquies* of the repealed code), where it was forbidden to "take into account" this evidence "under penalty of absolute nullity".[5] However, from time to time the law provided only for the non-usability of evidence, as in the case of incriminating statements by the accused during interrogation in the absence of counsel (§ 304 para. 4 of the repealed code), but in these cases, the procedural effects of such a violation were in dispute.[6]

It must be remembered that, in the case of illegal wiretapping, the Constitutional Court, though upholding the constitutionality of the measure, once delivered a decision, which, articulated a guiding principle which is still current, whereby "activities in violation of the fundamental rights of a citizen may not be used to justify, or be made the foundation of a procedural decision which is contrary to the interests of those who have suffered from the unlawful activities".[7] In other words, evidence may not be used against the defendant which was obtained in violation of those individual rights which the constitution declares are inviolable. Given this assertion, the doctrine assumes the possibility of recognizing a category of "unconstitutional"[8] evidence, which becomes subject to an exclusionary rule.

---

[3] For this observation, Grifantini (1993, 243–244).

[4] For this reference, Scella (2000, 96–105).

[5] On this point, See Illuminati (1983, 144–147).

[6] See Grevi (1972, 181–188).

[7] Corte cost.. April 6, 1973, n 34, in *Giur. Cost.*, 316 (1973), note of Grevi.

[8] Grevi (1972, 341).

§ 191 CCP refers in general terms to "prohibitions established by law". However, it does not define the concept of non-usability and its procedural implications.

10.2 Features of Non-usability

Non-usability is mostly considered to be a type of invalidity,[9] which can be deduced from § 606(c) CCP, which treats it as a reason for appeal in cassation for violation of the law, alongside other "traditional" violations, including nullities. Nevertheless, it is a form of invalidity which applies exclusively to criminal evidence,[10] not being applicable to acts which do not have an evidentiary function. Accordingly, it becomes a cause of invalidity only to the extent that it is reflected in a decision which took into account the evidence which could not be used.[11]

The doctrine and case law have distinguished between "general" and "special" non-usability.[12] The first refers to cases where the law establishes a prohibition on the use of evidence without saying anything about the consequences of the underlying violation. Such cases fall under §191 CCP, which in a general manner governs violations of the prescriptions relating to the admissibility of evidence. "Special" non-usability, in contrast, is that which is expressly provided in a norm related to a specific means of proof, as a sanction for violating rules relating to its admissibility or the mode of its acquisition.

10.2.1 Prohibitions on the Use of Evidence

In relation to the identification of the "prohibitions" referred to in § 191 CCP, it must be emphasized that, dealing with violations of norms concerning the acquisition of evidence, they may only be established by procedural law, which must fix the criteria for admissibility.[13] From this angle, the prohibitions which could be implicitly deduced from the substantive elements of penal offenses, or those which arise from provisions of another genre (civil or administrative) are not important. Procedural laws, in any case, are not only those contained in the CPP, because norms of this type are also found elsewhere, for example, in other statutory laws. In particular, the constitutional norms are considered to be procedural, which are promulgated to protect

[9] Grifantini (2005a, 543); See also Pierro (1992, 7–9), Scella (2000, 138–141), and Daniele (2009, 19).

[10] Galantini (1997, 690), and Ruggieri (2010, 1835).

[11] Nappi (2007, 189) and Grifantini (2001, 272).

[12] Grifantini (1993, 246), Grifantini (2005a, 545), and Ruggieri (2010, 1837); Cass. ss. un. 20 November 1996, Glicora, in *Giust. pen.*, III, 217 (1998); Cass. 12 October 1998, Aliu, in *Arch. n. proc. pen.*, 47 (1999).

[13] Cordero (1963, 149) and Grevi (2010, 314). See also Galantini (1992, 205), Scella (2008, 490–491), and Grifantini (2001, 278–279).

inviolable rights (such as personal liberty, privacy in one's home and communications) which can be put at risk during the acquisition of certain means of proof and those which lay down particular guarantees concerning criminal proceedings.[14]

The irrelevance of violations of substantive norms implies that there is no *per se* non-usability of so-called "illicit" evidence, that is, evidence which is formed or gathered by public officials or private persons through acts which violate a penal norm.[15] That is, it is necessary that the latter is decked by a procedural rule of exclusion. For example, to reveal for no reason a piece of information protected by the attorney-client privilege represents a crime and for that reason § 200 CCP prohibits those in possession of the privileged information from being forced to divulge its contents in their testimony. But should a witness, in violation of the law, spontaneously reveal the privileged information, his testimony is admissible and may be taken into consideration (without prejudice to an eventual application of a penal sanction). In contrast, the testimony may not be used if, notwithstanding the prohibition, the witness is forced to testify. Similarly, any statement obtained through use of violence may not be used, not by virtue of being the result of a crime, but based upon § 188 CPP, which prevents the use of "methods…capable of influencing the freedom of self-determination".

It is maintained in the literature, that the existence of a specific prohibition does not depend on the literal formulation of the norm: prohibitions can be those enunciated explicitly ("it is prohibited", "it is not permitted", "may not be used"), as well as those expressed in indirect form, such as a power subject to obligatory presuppositions or conditions.[16] It must nevertheless be emphasized, that not every failure to observe the rules established by law for a legitimate acquisition of evidence is *per se* sufficient to render it non-usable.[17] It must however be ascertained, through interpretation, whether in the particular case, a violation of an evidentiary prohibition can be recognized, either by verifying the existence or not of the investigative power of the judiciary,[18] or rather by having recourse to the nature of the interest protected by the respective provision,[19] an interest which can be internal (i.e., the protection of the right to confront witnesses) or external to the criminal process (i.e., the freedom of communications). Either way, according to case law, the use of evidence acquired in violation of fundamental rights protected by the Constitution is prohibited, given that these rights may be encroached upon only in the cases and according to the conditions established by law.[20]

---

[14] Grifantini (1993, 249–250), Ruggieri (2001, 63–70), *contra* Cordero (1963, 154), and Galantini (1997, 699).

[15] On this issue, *contra*, Nobili (1990b, 413), Siracusano (2003, 11), and Dinacci (2008, 62–65).

[16] Nobili (1990b, 411), Grifantini (1993, 246; 2005a, 546), and Ruggieri (2010, 1837).

[17] Scella (2008, 484).

[18] Cordero (1963, 70–73), and Scella (2000, 159–160).

[19] Galantini (1992, 139–148), and Galantini (1997, 694–695).

[20] Cass. ss. un. 13 July 1998, Gallieri, in *Cass. pen.*, 465 (1999); Cass. ss. un. 23 February 2000, D'Amuri, in 27 *Guida al dir.* 58 (2000); Cass. ss. un. May 28, 2003, Torcasio, in *Cass. pen.*, 21 (2004).

10.2.2 Non-usability of the Acts of the Preliminary Investigation

The approach, which deemed that non-usability referred exclusively to the trial phase, because § 191 CPP mentions "evidence", which, strictly speaking, is only formed in front of the judge, and not also to the preliminary investigation, is now outdated.[21]

It should in fact be acknowledged, that the term "evidence" is often used in the CPP in an atechnical manner, according to its generic meaning as an object of knowledge, also applicable during the investigative phase. It must also be taken into account, that the text of the preliminary draft of the CPP, in which one spoke of "evidence admitted by the judge", was replaced in the final version of § 191 with "evidence obtained", precisely with the aim of encompassing the acts of the public prosecutor's investigation. In addition, § 191(2) declares that non-usability may be raised "in any stage or level of the proceedings" and the "proceedings" includes the preliminary investigation phase (which otherwise is excluded when the law speaks of "process".)

Thus, the public prosecutor is also required to respect the general prohibitions and the rules of gathering evidence laid out for the investigative phase and may not consider material which was illegally obtained.

10.2.3 Evidence Favorable to the Accused

The question of the non-usability of prohibited evidence in favor of the accused is primarily of theoretical interest, for, in truth, there are no jurisprudential precedents in this area. It must be determined, whether non-usability, being generally a principle which is independent of the will of the parties, could be derogated when the evidence shows the innocence of the accused.

There are some provisions in the CPP which limit the prohibitions exclusively to use against the accused (§ 63(1)), or to proof of guilt (§ 526-*bis*), but one cannot deduce a general rule from this (and, moreover, the prohibition of use against a particular person does not necessarily imply its use in his favor).[22]

The requirements of substantive justice would certainly privilege a flexible use of the evidentiary prohibition.[23] However, it is difficult to find such an indication in the text of the law. In this regard, it has been suggested to resort to the general norm which provides, at any stage or level of the trial, for an immediate declaration in the form of a judgment, of the reasons which exclude punishment (§ 129 CPP). This is based on the notion that the ascertainment of innocence should also have precedence in relation to the correct application of procedural rules.[24] This argument is, however,

[21] See, Grifantini (2005a, 545) and Ruggieri (2010, 1835).

[22] Galantini (1992, 76).

[23] Lozzi (2008, 197).

[24] Cordero (1963, 143–144).

not conclusive, given that the probative value of a single piece of evidence is almost never apparent without a comprehensive evaluation of all the evidence gathered, which should take place at the time, and in the form prescribed. Moreover, the not improbable case would still remain unresolved, in which the demonstration of the innocence of one accused would consist in the proof of the guilt of others, even in the same trial. Separating the two aspects does not seem proper without a normative reference, whereas allowing a discretionary application of non-usability could also undermine the efficacy of the sanction in cases different from the one referred to.

10.3 Effects

As was just noted, a claim of non-usability may be raised "at any stage or level of the proceedings", that is, during the entire course of the preliminary investigation, the trial in the first instance and those on appeal, all the way to the Court of Cassation.[25] It may be raised by the judge *sua sponte,* that is, without a need for a motion by a party, and without it even being necessary to specifically mention it in the grounds for an appeal. In theory, therefore, a violation which occurs in the first instance could also be recognized for the first time at the hearing before the Court of Cassation, even if the question had never been previously raised. Usually, however, an initiative of a party is not lacking, and, in practice, is necessary to seize the Court of Cassation, inasmuch as the reasons upon which such a recourse may be based are only those which are exclusively listed in the law: among which is, quite to the point, "the failure to observe procedural norms established upon penalty of non-usability" (§ 606(c) CPP).

10.3.1 Prohibitions on Admitting and Evaluating Evidence

Non-usability may be linked to a prohibition on admitting evidence or a prohibition on taking it into account. Inadmissibility of evidence and a prohibition on evaluating it are two sides of the same coin, in the sense that if evidence cannot be admitted, neither may it be evaluated and, vice versa, if it may not be used for the decision, it should not be admitted.[26]

The different legislative techniques depend on the diverse moments in which the prohibition operates. Admission is prohibited when the evidence should be excluded from the beginning, but a prohibition on evaluation exists when, given the characteristics of a particular means of proof, its effect can only be eliminated after it has

[25] Grifantini (2005a, 555).

[26] Galantini (1992, 106–110).

been introduced.[27] For example, testimony about public opinion is inadmissible (§ 194(3) CPP), and questions soliciting it are prohibited; however if, while being questioned, the witness makes statements in this regard, they may not be considered by the judge. The same may be said regarding statements made in the absence of counsel by a person who has not yet been accused, and therefore not protected by the rights of defense. It is impossible to prevent him anticipatorily from making a statement; but if such a statement includes any self-incriminating declarations, they may not be used (§ 63 CPP).

Looking at the question from another angle, if the prohibited evidence is erroneously admitted, or the judge's decision on admissibility is reversed on appeal, the prohibition on admitting the evidence is transformed into a prohibition on use, which can only be declared *a posteriori*.

10.3.2 Findings of Non-usability

In both the hypotheses mentioned above (prohibition of admissibility and prohibition of evaluation), non-usability results in exclusion of the evidence from the materials of which the judge can officially take cognizance. The judge who makes a finding of non-usability of evidence, must declare it, and if called upon to adopt a decision he may not take it into account.

10.3.2.1 The Preliminary Investigation

During the preliminary investigation, the prosecutor is required to acknowledge prohibitions on the use of evidence and he may not base his decisions on such evidence. Nevertheless, the public prosecutor may not declare an exclusion, a power held exclusively by the judge.[28] An analogous treatment should be applied to investigative acts of the defense, permitted by the CPP but subject to specific rules (§§ 391*bis*-391*decies* CCP) which define the methods, forms and rules of exclusion.

In this phase, the competence to declare non-usability is with the judge of the preliminary investigation, who is called to intervene before the beginning of the trial upon the request of the public prosecutor or the suspect, when it is necessary to adopt a measure with jurisdictional character (for example, a measure impacting on the liberty of the person). Among the pieces of evidence furnished by the parties, the judge may not, in reaching his decision, utilize those which are expressly or implicitly prohibited for investigative purposes, nor may he use those which would not be admissible as evidence during the trial.

[27] Grifantini (1993, 246).

[28] Grifantini (2005a, 555).

It took some trouble to get this principle affirmed in the jurisprudence of the Court of Cassation, which at an earlier time had considered that non-usability would be implicated only in a final judgment on the merits as to the guilt or innocence of the defendant, and would thus exclusively have an effect in the trial court. The question assumes particular relevance with reference to the procedure to apply coercive measures (such as pretrial detention). Such measures can only be adopted by the judge of the preliminary investigation upon petition of the public prosecutor, which must be based on evidence gathered by the public prosecutor himself, which demonstrates the probable guilt of the accused.

The problem was principally posed in relation to the use, for the purpose of imposing pretrial detention, of wiretaps executed in violation of the procedures established by law. In this respect, the Court of Cassation finally affirmed, that non-usability is applicable "also in the decision to impose pretrial detention because it affects the results of an investigative measure regardless of the stage of the proceedings".[29] The issue was then expressly resolved by the legislator with the modification of § 273 CPP, according to which one must consider non-usability provided by the law regulating wiretaps when evaluating the evidence of guilt for the purpose of imposing pretrial detention.[30]

According to the Court of Cassation, however, the fact that non-usability has been declared within the procedure concerning the deprivation of personal liberty decided during the preliminary investigation, does not preclude the use of the evidence at trial, for evaluations made in imposing coercive measures cannot bind the trial judge.[31]

In addition, the judge, who in the preliminary hearing, must decide on the basis of the acts in the preliminary investigation file whether to accept the petition of the public prosecutor and set the case for trial, or to acquit the accused, is compelled to exclude the evidence he deems to be non-usable in his decision.

10.3.2.2 Trial in the First Instance and Appeal

At the trial in the first instance before the normal court or the assizes court (court composed of two professional judges and six lay "popular judges"), the parties must indicate the evidence they intend to introduce and request its admission. The judge decrees the admission of all evidence, except that which is cumulative or irrelevant, or is "prohibited by law" (§ 190(1) CPP). If, on the other hand, the non-usability of a piece of evidence arises during the trial, the judge makes a declaration to that effect *sua sponte*, applying § 191(2) CPP. In any case the judge must decide on objections raised by the parties in this respect (§ 495 CPP).

---

[29] Cass. ss. un. 20 November 1996, Glicora, *supra* note 13; Cass. ss. un. March 27, 1996, Monteleone, in *Cass. pen.*, 2913 (1996).

[30] Law of March 1st 2001, which introduced paragraph 1-*bis* into § 273 CCP

[31] Cass. December 12, 1995, Falsone, in C.E.D. CASS. 205649; Cass. February 11, 1998, Seseri, in *Arch. n. proc. pen.* 759 (1998); Cass. February 8, 2007, Firenze, in *Arch. n. proc. pen.* 369 (2008).

Non-usable evidence may not form the basis of a decision. One can observe that this is true above all for the judgment on the merits of the charge, but the rule is also applicable to any procedural decisions based on facts which need to be proved, which are adopted during the proceedings, including, as was noted, during the preliminary investigation stage. If the judge considers non-usable evidence in the decision, his ruling is invalid.

The invalidity of the decision translates into a ground for appeal. When the decision is appealed, its effects depend on the powers attributed to the judge in the second instance.

The judge on appeal has full competence to decide on the merits. He can thus re-evaluate the facts, after having, where necessary, again heard the evidence, and may confirm or modify the judgment under appeal. However, if the court ascertains, that in the trial in the first instance evidence was not excluded which was either inadmissible or should not have been evaulated, it should simply decide anew on the merits without taking that evidence into account. In other words, in the trial on appeal, non-usability operates directly: the decision on the merits should be made independently of the use of evidence made by the judge in first instance.[32]

On appeal, in the case of non-usability (unlike with certain types of nullity), the remedy is not automatically the reversal of the judgment and a remand to the judge of first instance for the celebration of a new trial. If the evidence taken, after elimination of that which may not be considered, results in being insufficient to confirm the conviction, the defendant is acquitted. Nevertheless, the judge, where he deems it absolutely necessary, can also adduce new evidence not taken in the trial in the first instance (§ 603 CCP), as long as the prohibited evidence remains excluded.

10.3.2.3 Non-usability in Cassation

The trial in cassation, which is limited to violations of the law, does not, however, permit a new decision on the merits. If the decision appealed in cassation is invalid, the Court of Cassation must annul it, and if a new evaluation of the evidence is necessary, it remands the case to a different judge than that which pronounced the judgment. Here we assume that non-usability was not declared in the trial on appeal, or that the Court of Cassation was directly seized in relation to the judgment in the first instance, without it having been heard at the appeal stage (a procedure which is, however, practically obsolete).

To reverse a judgment it must therefore be established that the trial judge considered non-usable evidence. This finding can only be made through the control of the reasons for the appealed judgment, in which the judge who pronounced it had to indicate, among other things, "the evidence upon which the decision was based" (§ 546(1)(e) CPP). Therefore, to "use" evidence, is equivalent, on the formal plane, to employing it as an argument in justification of the judgment reasons.

---

[32] Grifantini (1993, 254; 2005a, 555).

It follows, that in order to establish a violation (in the sense of § 606(c) CCP), it is not sufficient that the evidence was not excluded, as it should have been, but it must have been the basis for the decision,[33] as evidenced from the text of the decision under appeal. There is no need to say that it is not possible to measure the effective influence which non-usable evidence, even if not mentioned in the judgment reasons, could have had in practice on the decision of the judge who was conscious of it. But at base, we are dealing with a juridically irrelevant fact if it is not reflected in the written arguments which sustain the judgment.

In practice, according to the prevailing view in the jurisprudence, one must verify whether the reasons, deprived of the argumentative contribution offered by the non-usable evidence, are still able to justify the decision. The judgment, that is, will be reversed only if the illegitimately used evidence is shown to have had a determinative influence on the conviction of the judge, such that the decision would have been different without the use of that evidence.[34]

According to a more rigorous approach, on the other hand, reversal should take place any time the lack of influence of the illegitimate evidence does not emerge from the reasons of the court in first instance. That is, the reasoning itself should demonstrate the legitimacy of the evidence used and the irrelevance for the decision of that which is non-usable.[35]

The Court of Cassation, once it has determined invalidity, should simply reverse the challenged judgment, if once the reference to non-usable evidence is eliminated from the judgment reasons, the acquittal of the defendant is required (lack, insufficiency, or contradictory nature of the evidence of guilt: § 530 CPP). It reverses, on the other hand, and remands if it is necessary to evaluate the impact of the non-usable evidence on the other legitimately adduced evidence and to pronounce a new decision on the merits. The judge on remand, as is logical, should not take into account the evidence declared to be non-usable.

10.4 Non-usability and Nullities

Non-usability is considered to be different from a nullity, though they overlap on occasion. The CCP of 1988, as a methodological choice, proposed to institute two separate regimes: "non-usability" should refer to prohibited evidence and "nullity" to violations of prescribed formalities. From a theoretical point of view, in fact, non-usability presumes that the evidence was gathered in the absence of or in abuse of the power attributed to the judge: it should therefore be reserved for all violations

[33] Galantini (1992,265).

[34] Cass. ss. un. June 21, 2000, Tammaro, in *Cass. pen.*, 3259 (2000).

[35] Cordero (1963, 181, 188). See also Illuminati (1983, 151), Grifantini (1993, 255), Scella (2000, 203), and Daniele (2009, 187–188).

concerning the admission of evidence, rendering it without effect, without considering the mode of acquisition. A nullity, on the other hand, is a defect in the act, hypothetically, where a legitimate power to gather the evidence was exercised in a way that did not conform to the law. These are regarded as violations committed during a procedure which is directed at acquisition of evidence which is *per se* admissible.[36]

The law provides a panoply of procedural sanctions, differentiated according to the type and gravity of the violation, to the end of more efficiently securing respect for the rules. Not all formal violations of the legal model necessarily provoke a procedural sanction: in certain cases the law prescribes certain behavior, but does not react by rendering invalid the act which was performed without adherence to the prescription. If the error was harmless, and if the failure to observe the rule does not produce consequences relevant to the course of the trial or the violation of the rights of the parties, it is treated as a mere irregularity, to which the law attaches no effect. In other words, the act is considered to be invalid only when the sanction (non-usability or nullity) is expressly provided in the law, either directly or indirectly.

10.4.1 The Differing Characteristics of the Remedies

It must first be said, that non-usability, though limited to acts with an evidentiary content, represents the gravest sanction provided in the CPP. Besides the fact that it may be raised by the judge *sua sponte* at any stage and level of the procedure, in fact, the taint may not be purged, because it applies, except in special cases, regardless of the will and conduct of the parties.[37] In addition, once a violation has been established, the act may not be performed anew, for it is the object of a prohibition.

There are three levels of nullities, which each receive different procedural treatment.[38] Only those nullities defined as being "absolute" may not be purged and may be raised by the judge *sua sponte* at any stage and level of the proceedings. The others ("intemediate" and "relative") may be purged and are subject to a discipline which is progressively less rigorous, and must actually be raised through objection by a party and within a short period of time, which is the case with relative nullities. The effects of absolute nullities, therefore, coincide, in part, with those of non-usability. However, the law provides that a nullified act should be performed anew if necessary and possible by, as a rule, returning the procedure to the stage or level at which the irregularity occurred (§ 185(2,3) CPP). A finding of non-usability, on the other hand, results in the definitive elimination of the act and therefore also of its evidentiary content, from the materials upon which the decision is to be based, and implies no regression to earlier procedural stages.

[36] Grifantini (2005a, 546).

[37] See Cass. ss. un. May 23, 2003, Torcasio, in *Cass. pen.*, 21 (2004).

[38] For the system of nullities, see generally, Rafaraci (1998, 597).

10.4.2 *Reciprocal Interference*

The CPP of 1988 was not able to fully realize the aforementioned methodological premises, thus allowing the creation of overlaps and intereferences between the two categories of invalidity.[39] On the one hand, nullities are not limited to "formal" defects in the acts, but are recognized as a remedy for any type of violation. On the other hand—as a result of the modification of § 191 in the final text of the CPP which we have mentioned—,[40] non-usability refers to evidence "obtained" in violation of prohibitions, such that it includes not only evidence which is inadmissible, but, according to the most widely accepted interpretation, also evidence introduced in violation of the legally established rules.[41] The evidence, that is, may be prohibited and therefore non-usable, either due to its intrinsic illegitimacy, or as a result of a manifestly illegitimate mode of acquisition which places it completely outside of the system of legal evidence.[42]

The establishment of a general rule of non-usability,[43] that is, which refers to an indeterminate series of hypothesis, multiplies the cases in which this sanction may be applied. And one may say the same in relation to nullities of a general order, that is, those which are provided for all violations of the same type: to give just one example, failure to observe the norms relating to the defense of the accused are always considered to be a cause for a nullity (§ 178(c) CPP), which is often accompanied by an evidentiary prohibition.

For these reasons, it can easily happen that both non-usability and a nullity will converge upon a single violation. As a consequence, the choice of one or the other type of sanction in a given case is not always clearly defined. It is therefore necessary to be aware of the possibility of an overlap and, in the absence of specific normative indications, to identify the criteria for resolving the question on a case-by-case basis.

As a matter of fact, and notwithstanding that the law is silent on the matter, nullified evidence may also not be used.[44] But it does not become non-usable in a technical sense, for the applicable regime remains that of the nullity. And, without taking into consideration the cases in which there is the possibility of purging the taint, there may always be a renewed acquisition of the evidence.

According to some writers, we should apply the principle of particularity: that is to say, if the sanction is provided expressly for a specific case, the applicable rule should be the corresponding one.[45] In particular, the *ad hoc* threat of a special nullity

---

[39] Grifantini (1993, 245).

[40] Section 10.2.2.

[41] Nobili (1990b, 412); Grifantini (1993, 247); Galantini (1997, 696). See also Dinacci (2008, 54–60).

[42] Cass. ss. un. March 27, 1996, Sala, in *Cass. pen.*, 3268 (1996).

[43] Section 10.1, above.

[44] Daniele (2009, 6–7).

[45] Nobili (1990b, 412) and Conti (2007, 72).

for a violation of the modality for acquiring a certain means of proof should prevail over an eventual finding of non-usability: but in such way, except when one is dealing with an absolute nullity, the less rigorous rule should prevail. It would be better, however, to impose the effects of the more severe sanction and hold, that when non-usability concurs with a purgeable nullity, the former should prevail.[46]

10.5 The Problem of "Derivative" Non-usability

For years there has been a discussion as to whether non-usability can be transmitted from invalid evidence to subsequently gathered evidence, according to the North American doctrine of the "*fruits of the poisonous tree*". The issue is still controversial in the absence of a pertinent rule corresponding to that relating to nullities, according to which "the nullity of an act renders invalid the subsequent acts which depend on the act declared null" (§ 185 CCP).

The issue has also been presented to the Constitutional Court, which, however, declared it to be inadmissible,[47] affirming, among other things, that it is not possible to transfer the concept of a derivative taint, which the system regulates exclusively in relation to nullities, into the discipline of non-usability, because the theme itself of dependence between evidentiary acts encompasses, already on the logical plane, a wide variety of possible configurations and alternatives.

Indeed, the problem is susceptible to opposing conclusions, to the extent that the nexus of dependency between the evidence is considered to be exclusively fortuitous, and thus of a mere psychological type, or rather of a legal and functional nature, that is, in the sense of a necessary precondition for the subsequent act.[48] This second hypothesis surely occurs when the illegitimate evidence is made the basis of a reasoned decision, aimed at the acquisition of other pieces of evidence (for example, a search warrant or wiretap order), which therefore, in turn, end up being invalid. It is important to establish, however, what happens if the illegally acquired evidence would be determinative only factually in the discovery of the subsequent evidence, which would not have been obtained without the prior evidence.

The case law does not speak with one voice. The Court of Cassation has dealt with the problem specifically in relation to the legitimacy of a seizure executed as a result of an illegal search. To one approach, which deems a seizure to be legitimate independent of the invalidity of the operation which gave rise to it,[49] is contraposed

---

[46] Grifantini (1993, 245–246; 2001, 303–304). See also Cass. March 25, 1991, D'Errico, in *Giur. it.*, II, 130 (1992), referring to the unusable results of a judicially authorized wiretap declared to be a nullity due to insufficient justification.

[47] Corte cost. September 24, 2001, n. 332.

[48] Grifantini (1993, 253); See also Galantini (1992, 83–89), Ruggieri (2001, 137–141), and Conti (2007, 254–267).

[49] Cass. April 24, 1991, Lionetti, in *Cass. pen.*, 1879 (1992).

another, according to which there is a functional nexus between the act of looking for the evidence and the material acquisition thereof, which results in the evidentiary non-usability of the things seized.[50] Ultimately the Court of Cassation sitting *en banc*, intervened with a decision, the conclusion of which did not perfectly correspond to its premises. After affirming that the inviolability of the home prevents use of evidence obtained as a result of a search which was carried out illegally, it nevertheless admitted that the *corpus delicti* and evidence related to the crime may be seized and used as evidence.[51]

A case-by-case approach, is, however, emerging from the jurisprudence of the Court of Cassation. For example, declarations of the accused and of witnesses who were questioned on the basis of non-usable wiretaps have been deemed admissible.[52] The same is true as to declarations made by victims of extortion who confirmed the content of conversations they had with the extortionists following a reading of transcriptions of non-usable wiretaps,[53] testimony of a police officer as to the results of an investigation conducted on the basis of a confession which could not be used as evidence,[54] and otherwise legal wiretaps which were executed in relation to a telephone number which was discovered by virtue of a preceding wiretap which was already declared to be non-usable.[55] On the other hand, evidence of child pornography was held to be non-usable, which was seized on the basis of non-usable information resulting from the activity of an *agent provocateur*.[56] A search and subsequent seizure effectuated as a result of an anonymous tip were also rendered invalid[57] and, finally, the testimony of persons who executed illegal wiretaps as to their contents was declared to be inadmissible.[58]

10.6 The "Pathological" and "Physiological" Prohibition on Using Evidence

§ 526(1) CCP, referring to the trial judgment, establishes that "the judge may not use for the purposes of the deliberations, any evidence other than that which was legitimately introduced at trial." This provision, other than anchoring the principle of the legality of the evidence, represents the cornerstone of the adversarial system introduced by the CCP of 1988.[59]

---

[50] Cass. April 13, 1992, Casini, in *Cass. pen.*, 339 (1993).

[51] Cass. ss. un. March 27, 1996, Sala, , in *Cass. pen.*, 3268 (1996).

[52] Cass. December 22, 1997, Nikolic in *Cass. pen.*, 1569 (1999).

[53] Cass. November 141997, Meriani, in *Cass. pen.*, 1897 (1999).

[54] Cass. November 4, 1997, Lugano, in *Giust. pen.*, III, 660 (1998).

[55] Cass. February 10, 2004, Mache, in *Cass. pen.*, 3945 (2005).

[56] Cass. April 29, 2004, Bonaiuti, in *Riv. pen.*, 636 (2005).

[57] Cass. March 8, 1995, Ceroni, in *Cass. pen.*, 1876 (1996).

[58] Cass. June 21, 1996, Sindoni, in *Gazz. giur.*, 42, 28 (1996).

[59] Illuminati (2010, 749–756).

The introduction of an adversarial system of presenting evidence and the principles of orality and immediacy, fundamental characteristics of the new system, were accomplished by tracing a clear line between the phases of the preliminary investigation and the trial: consequently, as a general rule, the acts of the preliminary investigation may not be used as evidence and may be evaluated only for decisions to be adopted within that phase (decisions of the judges of the preliminary investigation and the preliminary hearing). The reports of the public prosecutor and the judicial police (or of defense counsel who has conducted investigations) may be read at trial only in exceptional cases, when the evidence may not be correctly articulated in adversarial form. Otherwise they may only be read by parties to impeach the declarations of witnesses and others before the court during their cross-examination.

The violation of this type of prohibition is also subject to the sanctions of the general provision on non-usability of § 191 CCP. But here must be considered, that the exclusion touches on items which were acquired according to the rules, and which can be legitimately used during the phase of the preliminary investigation, even if they are not admissible as evidence at trial. Thus, we are dealing with a prohibition which is not absolute, but limited to a certain type of use, for it is operative only during the phase of the trial and only for the proof of facts, with use only being permitted to evaluate the creditibility of the witnesses.

Speaking in more general terms, it can be affirmed that non-usability, as a technical instrument, is characterized precisely by its adaptability to the various necessities which from time to time are presented to the legislator. There is, for instance, evidence which may be used only in certain procedural phases, only for certain ends, against certain persons and not others, or, indeed, only within a specific period of time. In this regard one also speaks of relative non-usability, an instrument in keeping with the accusatory system, which, with the turn to the adversarial confrontation between the parties presupposes, as one is accustomed to say, a relativistic conception of evidence,[60] according to which the evidentiary result is determined by the context in which the evidence is formed.

The difference is evident between the absolute prohbitions which prevent any effect whatsoever of non-usable evidence and which have the function of protecting interests which are external to the procedure (such as inviolable rights) or of eliminating means of proof due to their inherent untrustworthiness.[61] On the other hand, in the cases examined above, non-usability is posited primarily in order to safeguard a method of forming the evidence and one is dealing with knowledge, which is not excludable as such, but only according to the modality used to acquire it.

The case law has come to distinguish effectively between pathological non-usability and physiological non-usability,[62] with the former referring to evidence

---

[60] Grifantini (1993, 249) and Nappi (2007, 193, 196).

[61] Grifantini (1993, 249).

[62] Cass. ss. un. June 21, 2000, Tammaro, in *Cass. pen.*, 3259 (2000). For the doctrine, see Galantini (1992, 5), Ruggieri (2010, 1833), and Conti (2007, 18–25); the distinction is criticized by Scella (2008, 481–482).

which is unconditionally prohibited, and the latter referring to exclusion from the trial of elements of proof which were gathered in violation of the right to confrontation. Pathological non-usability is applicable in all the phases of the procedure, including the preliminary investigation and the preliminary hearing. Physiological non-usability is applied only in relation to trial, and in derogation of the general rule, may also be conditioned on the will of the parties, who have the option of waiving in advance the right to confront the witnesses at an adversarial trial.

10.6.1 Non-usability in Special Procedures

It is on the basis of the distinctions just discussed, that the problem of non-usability is resolved in those special procedures which involve a waiver of the trial on the part of the defendant, or provide for an agreement between the defendant and the public prosecutor. We are referring to the abbreviated trial (*giudizio abbreviato*) and the application of punishment upon request of the parties, which are carried out as a rule during the preliminary hearing and are decided by the judge on the basis of the investigative file.

Initially, the case law held that a request for an abbreviated trial was equivalent to a waiver by the defendant of the application of the doctrine of non-usability.[63] Subsequently, this approach was partially abandoned, and it was held that in the abbreviated trial only the following are irrelevant: physiological non-usability, because this procedure is based on documents in the file which would be non-usable as evidence at trial, and relative non-usability, solely with reference to the trial phase. On the contrary, pathological non-usability survives, because it is posited on the protection of interests which may not be waived by the parties.[64]

In relation to the application of punishment upon request of the parties, as well, one should recall that § 191 CCP is in principle applicable, and that, as a consequence, limits may not be imposed in relation to the possibility that illegally acquired evidence would be declared to be non-usable. It is not plausible that an agreement between prosecution and defense could imply a waiver of any and all issues[65] and therefore constitute a purging of non-usability. Nevertheless, the violation of evidentiary prohibitions will be difficult to raise in the concrete, due to the fact that the judgment reasons in this type of procedure are very synthetic, and are limited to excluding the existence of the basis for pronouncing a judgment of acquittal.[66]

---

[63] Cass. April 20, 1994, Mazzaraco, in *Riv. pen.*, 337 (1995); Cass. April 1, 1996, Toth, in *Dir. pen. proc.*, 454 (1997).

[64] Cass. ss. un. June 21, 2000, Tammaro, in *Cass. pen.*, 3259 (2000). See Grifantini (2005a, 553) and Scella (2000, 194–196).

[65] Grifantini (2005a, 553–554). *Contra*, Cass. February 11, 1992, Maradona in *Giur. it.*, II, 283 (1993).

[66] See generally, Cass. ss. un. March 27, 1992, Di Benedetto, in *Cass. pen.*, 2060 (1992); Cass. ss. un. September 27, 1995, Serafino, in *Cass. pen.*, 67 (1996).

10.7 Cases of Non-usability

For the reasons explained above, it is not possible to formulate a complete list of the types of non-usability, given that non-usability is not always mentioned in the law in reference to a specific means of proof. This does not exclude, nonetheless, that a violation of a prohibition established directly or indirectly by the law is required, and therefore, the existence of a rule excluding the evidence. In other words, the general formulation of § 191 CCP singles out an indeterminate, but determinable number of cases of non-usability.[67]

A few examples, relating to the main causes of exclusion and to the most common means of proof, are nevertheless useful for clarifying the practical relevance of non-usability.

10.7.1 The Protection of the Freedom of Will of the Individual

§ 188 CCP, mentioned above, establishes a general rule in reference to all means of proof: the use of "methods or techniques designed to exert influence over the freedom of self-determination or to alter the capacity to remember or evaluate the facts" is prohibited, notwithstanding the consent of the interested party. This prohibition relates both to the defendant as well as to witnesses.

The code rejects any instrument used to manipulate or coerce the psyche, because, regardless of the credibility of the result, it would constitute an injury to the dignity of the person, and truth may not be obtained at any cost. The irrelevance of the consent of the interested party means that this protection is non-waivable, and at the same time serves to impede any psychological conditioning, even indirectly of those who refuse to consent and could be suspected of wanting to hide the truth.[68]

In the first place, evidence is excluded which results from physical or moral violence, such as an extorted confession. In addition, instruments like the lie detector, narcoanalysis and hypnosis are banned.[69] The CCP does not exclude the admissibility of evidence not specifically enumerated in the code, but emphasizes, with reference to § 188 CCP, that such evidence can be adduced only if does not prejudice "the moral liberty of the person"(§ 189 CPP).

On the other hand, those means are not considered to be prohibited which condition the self-determination of the subject through the holding out of an award for collaboration (if permitted by law) or which are aimed at obtaining information even if against his will, such as, for example, a body search, a forced identification procedure, a genetic investigation or a wiretap.[70]

---

[67] Grifantini (1993, 248; 2005a, 547).

[68] Cordero (1963, 70) and Grifantini (2005b, 529).

[69] Grevi (2010, 310).

[70] Grifantini (2005b, 530–531).

10.7.2 Interrogations of the Accused and the Right to Silence

The prohibition contained in § 188 CPP is reproduced verbatim in § 64(2) CCP among the general rules applying to the interrogation of the accused. Thus, an interrogation conducted in a manner which violates the moral liberty of the person is prohibited and may not be used.

One should add, that according to § 141-bis CCP, the interrogation of a person in custody "must be documented in its entirety, upon penalty of non-usability, by phonographic or audiovisual means of reproduction". This obligatory comprehensive documentation also serves to verify the absence of possible abuses tending to coerce the will of the subject or psychological pressures aimed at inducing him to confess. The special protection reserved for the accused who is deprived of liberty is justified by the situation of peculiar subjection in front of the judicial authority which conducts the interrogation.[71]

But the main guarantee during an interrogation consists in the right to not respond to the questions. The suspect must be advised of the right to remain silent, otherwise the declarations made are non-usable. He must be advised, at the outset that: "(a)his declarations can always be used agains him" and that "(b)..he has a right to not respond to any question" (§ 64(3) CPP).

The applicability of the right to silence extends to the case in which a person not suspected of crime or not under investigation (for instance during a police questioning of a witness), makes declarations from which emerge evidence of his guilt of a crime, such as would require his prosecution. In order to assure respect for the guarantees which should be immediately made known to him upon such a change of procedural position, the investigating authority should interrupt the examination, advise him that he can be the subject of an investigation, and invite him to designate defense counsel. As a consequence, the preceding declarations—without the assistance of defense counsel and without the admonitions required for interrogations—cannot be used against the person who made them (§ 63(1) CPP).

This procedure also has the goal of dissuading the interrogator from possible circumventions of the rules of interrogation, interrogating as a witness, and therefore under an obligation to answer truthfully, a person who immediately after his declarations could be transformed into a suspect or accused.[72] The punitive effect is even more pronounced in cases where the interrogators were required from the very beginning to adopt the forms and guarantees provided for the interrogation, but abusively circumvented them. In such a case the declarations are neither usable against the person who made them, nor against others (§ 63(2) CPP).

The first case, therefore, is a case of relative non-usability, and the second, of absolute non-usability.[73] The case law, however, has not been firm enough in drawing the distinction, given that it allows for usability against third parties even in the

[71] Voena (2010, 218).

[72] Grosso (2005, 192).

[73] See Sect. 10.6, above.

second hypothesis,[74] or, limits the prohibition to declarations regarding offenses connected or linked to the offense charged.[75]

Independently of this specific guarantee, the privilege against self-incrimination is also recognized in relation to witnesses. § 198 CPP provides, that "a witness may not be compelled to make declarations as to facts, which could expose him to criminal responsibility". The violation of this prohibition leads to non-usability of the eventual declarations.

10.7.3 Limitations on Witness Testimony

With reference to witness testimony, there are prohibitions regarding the admissibility of evidence as such, and prohibitions concerning its object, which therefore impede the formulation of certain questions and render the eventual responses non-usable.

In principle, all have the capacity to testify as a witness, independent of their age and mental conditions. There are, however, cases of incompatibility with the status of being a witness, such as with codefendants charged with the same crime until judgment is final, or those who have acted as a judge, public prosecutor or defense investigator in the same proceeding (§ 197 CPP). An incompatible witness may not be sworn to testify, and if this happens illegally, his testimony may not be used.[76]

The case of a witness who is the depositary of a professional secret (the priest, lawyer or doctor) is completely different. The protection of the secret is a tool required for the free exercise of professional activity, and, as such, designed to protect values guaranteed by the Constitution. § 200 CPP does not allow the judge (and the norm also applies to the public prosecutor during the preliminary investigation) to compel the witness to reveal the secret, even if he retains the power to evaluate the merits of the claim of privilege. If the privilege was in effect, a coerced deposition may not be used; but if the witness reveals it spontaneously, then the evidence is valid.[77]

Testimony "on the character of the defendant" is always prohibited (§ 194(1) CPP) as is that based on "public opinion" (§ 194(3) CPP). The latter prohibition is linked to the fundamental principle that information from anonymous sources is excluded from the trial.[78] Besides the symmetrical prohibition of the use of documents which contain public opinion, provided in § 234(3) CPP, § 240(1) CPP more generally establishes that "documents which contain anonymous declarations may neither be acquired nor used", while § 333(3) CCP prohibits any use of anonymous reports of crime or denunciations.

---

[74] Cass. August 10, 1995, Calabrese Violetta, in *Cass. pen.*, 2644 (1996), Critical comments by Fabio Grifantini, "Sulla inutilizzabilità contra alios delle dichiarazioni indizianti di cui all'art. 63 comma 2 c.p.p."

[75] Cass. ss. un. October 9, 2009, Carpanelli, in *Cass. pen.*, 2428 (1997). For a criticism, see Orlandi (2002, 182).

[76] Di Bitonto (2005a, 610).

[77] See Sect. 10.2.1, above. See also Triggiani (2010, 2048).

[78] Valentini (2005, 588).

In principle, however, hearsay is admissible, but also in this case the law provides for non-usability if the source of the information is not revealed, that is, if the witness refuses or is not capable of identifying the person from whom he heard the information (§ 195(7) CPP, and, in relation to police informants, § 203 CPP). Indirect testimony, however, may be used within strict limitations, and this is not so much because it is considered to be unreliable, but rather in order to protect the adversary taking of evidence and in particular the right to cross-examine.[79] Indeed, if a party requests, the judge should order that the hearsay declarant also be examined, unless this is impossible. If the judge ignores such duty, the indirect testimony becomes non-usable (§ 195(1,3) CPP).

It is always for the purpose of guaranteeing the adversary presentation of evidence at trial that § 195(4) CPP is invoked, according to which the judicial police may not testify "as to the contents of declarations acquired from witnesses" during the preliminary investigation. This is an example of a rule of exclusion which is logical in a system in which evidence must be formed at trial and the reports which constitute the preliminary investigation file may not be used as evidence.[80] It would not make sense to prohibit the reading of the report of testimony and at the same time allow its content to be narrated by the person who compiled it.

Nevertheless, the Constitutional Court initially declared the provision to be unconstitutional,[81] giving thus the go-ahead to a series of decisions which in practice frustrated the 1998 code's turn to an accusatory and adversarial procedure. After the constitutional reform of 1999, which introduced in Art. 111(4) Const. the recognition in criminal procedure of the "principle of confrontation in the formation of the evidence",[82] and the subsequent law modifying the CPP which put the aforementioned prohibition back into operation,[83] the Constitutional Court recognized its legitimacy,[84] and finally declared the interpretation to be unconstitutional, according to which the testimony would be nevertheless admissible whenever the police omitted to record the statements they had taken, if they were obliged to do so.[85]

10.7.3.1 Testimony of the Defendant

In derogation of the right to silence, the defendant may be called to testify and be required to tell the truth in a trial of another person charged with the same crime, a related crime or one linked for evidentiary reasons.

---

[79] Santini (2005, 594).

[80] Ibid, 600.

[81] Corte cost., January 31, 1992, n. 24.

[82] Constitutional Law, November 23, 1999 n. 2.

[83] Law of March 1, 2001, n. 63.

[84] Corte cost. February 26, 2002, n. 32.

[85] Corte cost. July 30, 2008, n. 305; previously, Cass. ss. un. May 28, 2003, Torcasio, in *Cass. pen.*, 21 (2004).

According to § 197-bis CPP, the defendant's testimony is always admissible after his trial has concluded with a final irrevocable judgment. Before this time, except in cases of co-defendants charged with the same crime, a defendant could become a witness where he had previously made voluntarily declarations as to facts concerning the responsability of others after having been advised pursuant to § 64(c) CPP, that as a consequence of his declarations he would, in relation to those facts, be treated as a witness.

Outside of these cases, the incompatibility provided in § 197 CPP prevails, and the defendant can not testify, but may only be questioned, maintaining the right to not answer the questions (§ 210 CPP) and any eventual testimony would not be usable.[86]

Objective limits to the testimony of the defendant have nevertheless been established. First of all, if he has been convicted and the judgment is final, "he may not be compelled to testify" as to facts upon which the final judgment of guilt was based "if during the criminal proceedings he denied personal responsability or made no statemeents". If, on the other hand, his trial is still going on, the defendant "may not be compelled to testify to facts which concern his own responsibility in relation to the crime before the court" (§ 197-bis(4) CPP). In these cases, as well, any eventual statements which were not made spontaneously, may not be used.[87]

In any case, statements nevertheless made by defendants called to testify may not be used against them in any proceeding, including a proceeding to review the conviction due to judicial error (§ 197-bis(5) CPP).

10.7.4 Interceptions of Communications

The freedom and confidentiality of communications are recognized as inviolable by Art. 15 Const. From this, the Constitutional Court, as we have seen, deduced the non-usability of evidence acquired by a means which violate fundamental rights.[88] The current regulation of wiretaps establishes mandatory conditions and determinate forms, accompanied, in case of their violation, by the non-usability of the results.

§ 271(1) CPP provides that wiretaps may not be used if they are executed in relation to crimes, for the investigation of which wiretaps are expressly prohibited by the statute. The same applies to wiretaps executed by private individuals,[89] which, due to their lack of authorization in this regard, are considered to directly violate Art. 15 Const. Non-usable, as well, are wiretaps which were not authorized by a judge by an order conforming to the requirements of the law, those which were conducted under a claim of exigent circumstances by the public prosecutor, which

[86] See Sect. 10.7.3, above.

[87] Di Bitonto (2005b, 617).

[88] Corte cost. April 6, 1973, n. 34, in *Giur. Cost.*, 316 (1973), note of Grevi.

[89] Camon (2005, 815–816).

was not validated by a judge within the required time, or those which were executed using other than the required equipment (which has as its aim avoiding a possible circumvention of control by the judicial authority).

The prohibition on use also affects the interception of communications which are covered by a professional privilege, unless the protected communication was in some way revealed by persons who are themselves covered by the privilege (§ 271(2) CPP). A particular type of protection applies to communications of defense counsel during criminal proceedings, the interception of which are not even subject to judicial authorization (§ 103(5) CPP). Naturally, if such communications are accidentally intercepted during a legitimately authorized wiretap, the prohibition on ordering the measure is transformed into a prohibition on utilizing the results.

A peculiar feature of the current rules consists in the duty of the judge to order the destruction of the documentation relating to the non-usable wiretaps (§ 271(3) CPP). The aim of this provision is to reinforce the non-usability, neutralizing any consequence, even if indirect, which might result from the excluded evidence and at the same time more effectively protecting the right to confidentiality,[90] and thus avoiding that the confidential information gained by the illegal violation of the privilege, could be divulged in any way.

The Court of Cassation has resolved, by a finding of non-usability, the problem relating to the secret recording by a police agent participating in a conversation (the so-called secret agent "equipped for sound").[91] Though excluding that this was a case of non-authorized interception (an interception presupposes the interference of an outside third person), the Court concluded, that in this case that either the prohibition concerning the interrogation of the accused was violated (§ 63(2) CPP),[92] or, alternatively, the prohibition concerning indirect testimony by the police (§ 195(4) CPP).[93]

Finally, in the absence of a specific norm permitting it, video recordings of the goings-on in another's dwelling, without the affected person's knowledge are considered to be non-usable. The prevailing view in the case law distinguishes between "communicative behavior", that is, conversations or exchange of messages, and "mere conduct", that is, images of persons or their movements. The former can be recorded with previous judicial authorization, dealing as they do with the interception of communications, which are subject to the normal rules. The latter may not, however, be authorized, and are therefore non-usable, as they are not authorized by law.[94] This interpretation has been confirmed by the Constitutional Court.[95]

---

[90] Ibid, 819.

[91] Cass. ss. un., May 28, 2003, Torcasio, in *Cass. pen.*, 21 (2004).

[92] See Sect. 10.7.2, above.

[93] See Sect. 10.7.3, above.

[94] Cass. November 10, 1997, Greco, in *Cass. pen.*, 1188 (1999).

[95] Corte cost., April 24, 2002, n. 135.

10.7.5 Statements by Defendants Cooperating with the Authorities

A singular form of non-usability has to do with delayed statements by those who collaborate with the authorities. A special statute[96] provides that those who manifest their desire to collaborate with the authorities[97] in prosecutions for crimes involved with terrorism, subversion, the mafia and child pornography—and who for this reason can also, if the conditions are met, be eligible for protective measures—must, within 180 days from the commencement of the collaboration, turn over to the public prosecutor all the information in their possession which is useful in the reconstruction of the facts, the discovery and capture of the perpetrators and the confiscation of their assets.[98]

The limit of 180 days was imposed to avoid that statements, if too diluted over time, could be used for obtaining undeserved benefits, would otherwise not be trustworthy, or would expressly be aimed at obstructing the course of justice.[99] In a provision subject to much criticism, the law establishes that statements made to the public prosecutor or the police beyond the fixed time limit, "may not be evaluated in order to prove the facts affirmed therein against persons other than the declarant, except in cases where they cannot be reproduced".

This formulation is not very clear, given that, in any case, the statements acquired by the public prosecutor and the police during the preliminary investigation would not be, pursuant to a general rule, usable as evidence at trial (physiological non-usability).[100] As a result, the prohibition, if it is related exclusively to the trial, would in the end only apply in those exceptional cases in which it is provided that the contents of the investigative dossier can be transformed into evidence, thus preventing any use whatsoever.

The prevalent view in the case law, however, excludes any operation of the rule of non-usability other than at trial: thus, declarations made beyond the prescribed time limits may be used to impose coercive measures during the preliminary investigations and in both the preliminary hearing and the abbreviated trial.[101]

---

[96] D.l. January 15, 1991, n. 8, changed to law of March 15, 1991, n. 82, as modified by law of February 13, 2001, n. 45, "Nuove norme in materia di sequestri di persona e per la protezione dei testimoni di giustizia, nonché per la protezione e il trattamento sanzionatorio di coloro che collaborano con la giustizia" (Art. 16-*quater*).

[97] Following Cass. 21 November 2002, Bertuca, in *Cass. pen.*, 2963 (2004), the rule does not apply to witnesses.

[98] Art. 16-*quater* of the special statute cited in f.n. 97, *supra*.

[99] D'Ambrosio (2002, 119).

[100] See Sect. 10.6, above.

[101] Cass. ss. un. September 25, 2008, in *Cass. pen.*, 2278 (2009) critical commentary by R.A. Ruggiero, "I discutibili confini dell'inutilizzabilità delle dichiarazioni tardive dei 'collaboratori di giustizia'".

10.8 Conclusions

Non-usability is the most effective tool to guarantee respect for evidentiary exclusionary rules. Rules relating to nullities, however, are not sufficient to insure that evidence is effectively excluded. In addition, non-usability is very flexible because it might apply, if necessary, only for certain uses of the evidence and not for others.

Some problems remain, however. The main one regards the difficulty of identifying with precision the prohibitions which are not accompanied by a specific provision for non-usability. The case law tends to recognize non-usability only where it is specifically mentioned in the law, or where the law points to a means of proof solely for the purpose of prohibiting it. It thus overlooks prohibitions depending on the mode of acquiring evidence, at times degrading them to a relative nullity which may therefore be purged.

The issue relating to derivative non-usability also remains controversial. The Court of Cassation has not given a conclusive answer, but it seems to be difficult to apply the doctrine of the "fruits of the poisonous tree" in the Italian system with its exceptions, given that the law provides for no way to ascertain the sources of the public prosecutor's information except when a reasoned ruling is required.

The fact remains, that the introduction of non-usability and its recognition in general terms has represented an appropriate reinforcement of the principle of legality of the evidence, given that the free conviction of the judge may be exercised only in relation to evidence which was lawfully acquired. The duty of uncovering crimes and defending society, while being constitutionally relevant values, should stand aside with respect to the method of doing so, when it is a matter of the protection of inviolable rights.

Bibliography

Camon, A. 2005. Art. 271. In *Commentario breve al codice di procedura penale*, ed. G. Conso and V. Grevi, 814–21. Padua: Cedam.
Conti, C. 2007. *Accertamento del fatto e inutilizzabilità nel processo penale*. Padua: Cedam.
Cordero, F. 1963. *Tre studi sulle prove penali*. Milan: Giuffré.
D'Ambrosio, L. 2002. *Testimoni e collaboratori di giustizia*. Padua: Cedam.
Daniele, M. 2009. *Regole di esclusione e regole di valutazione della prova*. Turin: Giappichelli.
Di Bitonto, M.L. 2005a. Art. 197. In *Commentario breve al codice di procedura penale*, ed. G. Conso and V. Grevi, 609–14. Padua: Cedam.
Di Bitonto, M.L. 2005b. Art. 197-bis. In *Commentario breve al codice di procedura penale*, ed. G. Conso and V. Grevi, 614–18. Padua: Cedam.
Dinacci, F.R. 2008. *L'inutilizzabilità nel processo penale*. Milan: Giuffré.
Galantini, N. 1992. *L'inutilizzabilità della prova nel processo penale*. Padua: Cedam.
Galantini, N. 1997. Inutilizzabilità (diritto processuale penale). In *Enciclopedia del diritto, I Aggiornamento*, Milan: Giuffré, 690–709.
Grevi, V. 1972. *Nemo tenetur se detegere. Interrogatorio dell'imputato e diritto al silenzio nel processo penale italiano*. Milan: Giuffré.
Grevi, V. 2010. Prove. In *Compendio di procedura penale*, 5th ed, ed. G. Conso and V. Grevi, 293–385. Padua: Cedam.

Grifantini, F. 1993. Inutilizzabilità. In *Digesto delle discipline penalistiche*, Vol. VII, Turin: Utet, 242–255.

Grifantini, F. 2001. *Il segreto difensivo nel processo penale*. Turin: Giappichelli.

Grifantini, F. 2005a. Art. 191. In *Commentario breve al codice di procedura penale*, ed. G. Conso and V. Grevi, 543–55. Padua: Cedam.

Grifantini, F. 2005b. Art. 188. In *Commentario breve al codice di procedura penale*, ed. G. Conso and V. Grevi, 528–35. Padua: Cedam.

Grosso, D. 2005. Art. 63. In *Commentario breve al codice di procedura penale*, ed. G. Conso and V. Grevi, 192–95. Padua: Cedam.

Illuminati, G. 1983. *La disciplina processuale delle intercettazioni*. Milan: Giuffré.

Illuminati, G. 2010. Giudizio. In *Compendio di procedura penale*, 5th ed, ed. G. Conso and V. Grevi, 747–830. Padua: Cedam.

Lozzi, G. 2008. *Lezioni di procedura penale*. Turin: Giappichelli.

Nappi, A. 2007. *Guida al codice di procedura penale*, 10th ed. Milan: Giuffré.

Nobili, M. 1990a. Il 'diritto delle prove' e un rinnovato concetto di prova. In *Commento al nuovo codice di procedura penale*, vol. II, ed. M. Chiavario, 381–88. Turin: UTET.

Nobili, M. 1990b. Art. 191. In *Commento al nuovo codice di procedura penale*, vol. II, ed. M. Chiavario, 408–14. Turin: Utet.

Orlandi, R. 2002. Dichiarazioni dell'imputato su responsabilità altrui: Nuovo statuto del diritto al silenzio e restrizioni in tema d'incompatibilità a testimoniare. In *Il giusto processo*, ed. R.E. Kostoris, 153–95. Turin: Giappichelli.

Pierro, G. 1992. *Una nuova specie di invalidità: l'inutilizzabilità degli atti processuali penali.* Naples: ESI.

Rafaraci, T. 1998. Nullità (diritto processuale penale). In *Enciclopedia del diritto, II Aggiornamento*, Milan: Giuffré, Milan, 597–627.

Ruggieri, F. 2001. *Divieti probatori e inutilizzabilità nella disciplina delle intercettazioni telefoniche.* Milan: Giuffrè.

Ruggieri, F. 2010. Art. 191. In *Codice di procedura penale commentato*, 4th ed, ed. A. Giarda and G. Spangher, 1832–53. Milan: IPSOA.

Santini, S. 2005. Art. 195. In *Commentario breve al codice di procedura penale*, ed. G. Conso and V. Grevi, 590–606. Padua: Cedam.

Scella, A. 2000. *Prove penali e inutilizzabilità. Uno studio introduttivo*. Turin: Giappichelli.

Scella, A. 2008. Inutilizzabilità della prova (diritto processuale penale). In *Enciclopedia del diritto, Annali.* Milan: Giuffré, 479–496.

Siracusano, D. 2003. Prova: (III) nel nuovo codice di procedura penale. In *Enciclopedia giuridica*, Vol. XV, Rome: Treccani, 1–14.

Triggiani, N. 2010. Art. 200. In *Codice di procedura penale commentato*, 4th ed, ed. A. Giarda and G. Spangher, 2038–52. Milan: IPSOA.

Valentini, E. 2005. Art. 194. In *Commentario breve al codice di procedura penale*, ed. G. Conso and V. Grevi, 584–91. Padua: Cedam.

Voena, G.P. 2010. Atti. In *Compendio di procedura penale*, 5th ed, ed. G. Conso and V. Grevi, 169–291. Padua: Cedam.

Chapter 11
Greece: From Statutory Nullities to a Categorical Statutory Exclusionary Rule

Georgios Triantafyllou

11.1 The General Theory of Admissibility of Illegally-Gathered Evidence

11.1.1 The Principle of Discovery of the Material Truth

The basic source of Greek criminal procedure law is the Code of Criminal Procedure (CCP), a statute which has been in force since January 1, 1951. Criminal procedural issues are also regulated in other ordinary statutes, such as Law 2225/1994, which protects the freedom of communications and sets out the conditions under which the State may legally infringe upon the general rule on the inviolability of communications.

Some norms are also included in other legal sources which have priority over ordinary statutes, such as the Constitution of Greece (hereafter Const.) which came into force in 1975 and was last amended in 2001, or international conventions, such as the European Convention on Human Rights (ECHR), which are incorporated in domestic law when implemented by statute pursuant to Art. 28(1) Const.

As is true in many other continental European legal systems, the Greek procedural model is a mixed one, combining elements taken from both the inquisitorial and the accusatorial systems. The pre-trial investigation is quite inquisitorial in character, while the trial is marked to a great extent by features of the adversary type of procedure.

The *principle of discovery of the material truth* applies typically to both phases of this mixed procedural model. As far as Greek law is concerned, this

---

G. Triantafyllou (✉)
Faculty of Law, University of Athens, Patission 119, GR-112 51, Athens, Greece
e-mail: getrianlaw@otenet.gr

S.C. Thaman (ed.), *Exclusionary Rules in Comparative Law*, Ius Gentium: Comparative Perspectives on Law and Justice 20, DOI 10.1007/978-94-007-5348-8_11,

principle is derived from several provisions of the CCP, the most basic of which is § 239(2) CCP, which states that during the pretrial stage of the proceedings state officials must do everything *ex officio* to determine the truth of the charge, whether it lead to the guilt or innocence of the accused. This basic principle imposes a duty on the prosecutor[1] and the judge to investigate any criminal case with all the means at their disposal. Material truth, as the goal of any judicial activity in the field of criminal procedure, is differentiated from the "formal truth", i.e. the truth arising from the evidence adduced in court by the parties. Judges and prosecutors in Greece do not restrict themselves to examining the evidence produced by the parties, but are obliged to look for any evidence which could help them in discovery of the truth "*Probatio fit non solum judici, sed etiam per judicem*".[2]

One view expressed in the literature as well as in one line of case-law[3] states that the discovery of truth is not just a principle derived from different provisions of the CCP, but is a principle of superior importance, having, as it does, an origin in the Constitution. Although there is no explicit constitutional provision to this effect, this view is based on other constitutional guarantees, such as the duty of the state to punish crimes, which is established in Arts. 25(1), 96(1) Const.[4] or the personal and functional independence of judges, protected by Art. 87(1) Const.[5]

As extremely important as this principle may be, it has also been acknowledged, both in doctrine and case law to an equal extent, that the material truth may not by searched for by any means.[6] Other contradictory interests, mainly the constitutional rights of the parties in criminal proceedings, may prevail over the interest of the state in determining the truth and punishing the perpetrators of criminal acts. It is for this reason that various norms are established, either prohibiting the search for the material truth in order to safeguard these competing interests, or providing that specific protective formalities for crime detection and examination of evidence must be complied with. For example, § 212 CCP prohibits witnesses from making depositions on matters falling within the scope of professional secrecy. Similarly, Art. 9(1) Const. requires, as a protective formality relating to the inviolability of one's home, that a judge be present during any search of the premises.

---

[1] Prosecutors in Greece are not parties to the procedure, but independent judicial officials obliged to search for the material truth.

[2] See Androulakis (2007, 187).

[3] Cf. Court of Appeal of Patras, Judgment No. 26-27/1997, *Poinika Chronika Law Review* (1997), 118, (1997), comment, Agnastopoulous, 118–120.

[4] See Androulakis (2007, 214) and Spinellis (1986, 865 ff.).

[5] See Triantafyllou (1993a, 1083).

[6] Androulakis (2007, 207).

11.1.2 General Constitutional Rules for Exclusion of Illegally Gathered Evidence

Violations of prohibitions or procedural formalities concerning the collection of evidence, may lead to it becoming inadmissible. This happens when an exclusionary rule is in force, prohibiting the admission of the illegal piece of evidence. Such rules are to be found in all sources of criminal procedure law.

As far as the Constitution is concerned, there is no general rule providing for the exclusion of evidence collected in breach of other constitutional provisions. Most of the latter, although prohibiting certain methods of criminal investigation, do not provide for the exclusion of evidence if prohibited methods are used. For instance, Art. 7(2) Const., while prohibiting torture and any other abuse of human dignity, does not contain any exclusionary rule relating to evidence discovered as a result of using these illegal investigative methods.[7]

Constitutional prohibitions of this type, which are not reinforced by an explicit exclusionary rule, allow for a general *ad hoc* balancing test. In this sense, the question of whether evidence is excluded or not depends on the result of weighing the seriousness of the violation against the importance of the evidence, the seriousness of the crime alleged, the probative value of the illegal piece of evidence, and so on. The prevailing view in legal theory advocates such a balancing test,[8] except for cases of serious infringements of human dignity, such as torture.[9] Another view favors a more radical approach, arguing that any evidence obtained by violating constitutional rights must not be admissible under any circumstances.[10]

A major change to this constitutional regime was brought about in the last constitutional reform which took place in 2001, in which a new Art. 19(3) Const. provided for exclusion of evidence gathered in violation of the right to privacy (See discussion, below, at Sect. 11.2.2.1).

11.1.3 Exclusionary Rules Derived from International Conventions

Some exclusionary rules are also included in international conventions, which have become part of domestic law. See Sect. 11.3.2.2, below, for a discussion of exclusonary rules for torture-induced confessions derived from international conventions.

---

[7] In any event, as will be shown below, the lack of any explicit exclusionary rule at constitutional level, is covered by other rules in inferior legal sources which prohibit the use of statements obtained by torture.

[8] See Kostaras (1984, 169 ff), Spinellis (1986, 865 ff.), Dimitratos (1992, 47 ff.), and Dalakouras (1996, 337 ff.).

[9] See Sect. 11.3.2.1 below for discussion of exclusion of fruits of torture.

[10] See Karras (2006, 742 ff.) and Triantafyllou (1993b, 425 ff.).

11.1.4 Statutory Rules of Exclusion

11.1.4.1 Statutory Nullities and the Exclusion of Evidence

At the level of statutory law, the CCP, the basic source of criminal procedure law, provides for two types of sanctions against procedural violations, which may lead to the inadmissibility of illegally gathered evidence.

The first, which dates from the initial version of the Code, is the nullity of the whole procedure or of a specific procedural act. In the situations laid down in the CCP, the sanction of nullity, which is the usual sanction against irregular procedural acts, may apply also in the case of illegally-obtained evidence. A finding of "nullity" strips illegally gathered evidence of its probative value, thus constituting, for all practical purposes, a type of exclusionary rule. Nullities are divided into absolute nullities and relative nullities.

"Absolute nullities" are regulated by § 171CCP, and may be invoked at any stage of the procedure, even *sua sponte* by the Supreme Court (*Areios Pagos*), without having to be invoked by a party. Pursuant to § 171(1)(d) CCP, an absolute nullity is caused when a provision formally regulating the defendant's exercise of his right to a defense or right to counsel has been violated. It is especially important when this violation takes place during the gathering of, or examination of evidence. The pieces of evidence which were obtained or examined in disregard of defense rights are null, and may not serve as a basis of the court's decision. In the event that such illegally obtained pieces of evidence are used against the defendant, the judgment may be reversed on appeal in cassation. A few examples from the case law are set out below.

For instance, § 192(1)CCP provides that if a forensic expert is appointed by the investigating magistrate during the pre-trial judicial investigation of a felony, the judge has to notify the defendant of that appointment. This notification is designed to allow the defendant to challenge the expert, or to permit forensic counsel to be appointed. If the investigating magistrate fails to notify the defendant, the forensic expertise provided is invalid and may not serve as evidence because it was produced in disregard of a defense right. The judgment which relied on this inadmissible expert evidence, is subject to reversal upon appeal in cassation by the defendant.[11]

Another example is provided by §§ 364–65 CCP, which stipulate that documents submitted to the court to be used in evidence, must be read out publicly in court. Furthermore, § 358 CCP guarantees the right of the parties to comment and provide explanations in relation to the evidence admitted at trial. If a document is admitted into evidence and considered by the court, though not read aloud in public sessions, the procedure is null, because the defendant could not exercise his right to comment and explain the evidence.[12] As a result, documents that were not read out publicly are inadmissible pieces of evidence.

[11] See for example Hellenic Supreme Court Judgments Nos. 1267/1985 and 2176/2007.

[12] See for example Hellenic Supreme Court Judgment No. 993/2008.

§ 170 CCP, on the other hand, regulates "relative nullities". Its first paragraph establishes that the relative nullity of a procedural act or document results only in cases expressly provided by law. § 170(2) CCP provides for a "relative nullity" upon denial of the right to a hearing (the so-called "lack of hearing" nullity). That is, when the defendant, his lawyer or the prosecutor petition to exercise a right accorded them by law and the court denies or refuses to respond to the petition, a "relative nullity" exists. In contrast to absolute nullities, relative nullities only occur when invoked by the prosecutor or the party with an interest in the annulment (§ 173(1) CCP).

The sanction of relative nullity may be relevant in relation to the collection and examination of evidence. This occurs when the law expressly sanctions a violation of a rule of criminal evidence with the nullity the piece of evidence or the procedure as a whole. For example, § 218(1)CCP provides for a nullity when a witness is not administered an oath before testifying in court. Similarly § 212 CCP recognizes a nullity, where certain categories of professionals, such as lawyers, doctors etc., are examined as witnesses in violation of their duty of professional secrecy. In both examples, invocation of the relative nullity leads to the exclusion of the testimony as evidence or to the reversal of a judgment that was based on that piece of evidence. If the prosecutor or the interested party does not invoke the nullity, this constitutes a waiver and the illegal evidence may be used by the court.[13]

Both absolute and relative nullities are statutory grounds for reversing criminal judgments in cassation (§ 510(1)(A,B)CCP). Thus, if the court ignores a rule which pronounces the nullity of an act or the taking of evidence, the judgment of that court is subject to appeal in cassation by either the prosecutor or the defendant and may be reversed by the Supreme Court.

Nullities, as a specific type of exclusionary rule, leave no room for *ad hoc* balancing in relation to the specific circumstances of each case. Once a nullity has occurred, it inexorably leads to the exclusion of the illegal evidence and/or to the reversal of the judgment.

11.1.4.2 Modern Statutory Exclusionary Rules

While nullities were the only type of procedural sanction in the original version of the CCP, and also served as a means for excluding illegal evidence, nowadays there is a second type of sanction which leads to a similar result. These sanctions apply specifically in the area of criminal evidence, unlike nullities, and function as genuine exclusionary rules, i.e., they prohibit the use of evidence if a particular irregularity has occurred in the process of collecting it or examining in court.

---

[13] See e.g. Hellenic Supreme Court Judgment No. 1473/2002 in regard to testimony in court by a police investigator who had participated in the investigation of the case. Pursuant to § 211A CCP these persons are not competent witnesses.

The first exclusionary rule of this type was introduced in 1996 by Law 2408/1996, which inserted a second paragraph into § 177 CCP, which now stipulates that evidence is of no probative value in criminal proceedings if it was obtained by or through criminal acts. A similar type of exclusionary rule relating to hearsay evidence, is included in § 224(2) CCP, also introduced by Law 2408/1996, which provides that testimony is of no probative value if the witness does not reveal the source of his information.

This new generation of exclusionary rules expands the cases where irregularities in procedure lead to the inadmissibility of evidence. In the two examples mentioned above, however, the legislator did not provide for a nullity of the entire procedure, even where criminal acts were committed. Thus, reversal of judgments based on failure to exclude these types of evidence is not automatic.[14] The Supreme Court has so ruled in relation to a violation of § 224(2) CCP.

Under this regime, the rules relevant to the exclusion of evidence present a rather confusing picture. On the one hand, there are genuine exclusionary rules included in the Constitution, in international conventions and in ordinary statutory law, mainly the CCP. In spite of their great importance, those rules are not expressly established as grounds for the reversal of judgments. On the other hand, there are exclusionary rules which take the traditional form of nullities, which constitute explicit grounds for reversal, especially upon appeal in Cassation before the Supreme Court. The inconsistency of this regime calls for immediate reform. The legislator should take the necessary steps to unify the different types into a single form of exclusionary rule, which should always constitute a ground for appeal.

11.1.5 General Rules of Admissibility/Exclusion of Illegally-Gathered Evidence in Supreme Court Case Law

Final criminal judgments are subject to appeal in cassation to the Supreme Court (*Areios Pagos*). Most criminal cases are brought before the Criminal Divisions of the Supreme Court upon petitions for review in cassation filed by the defendant following conviction in the trial court. Only occasionally does the public prosecutor appeal acquittals using this procedure.

The Supreme Court has handed down judgments regarding both nullities and the recently introduced modern exclusionary rules. The vast majority of these judgments concern issues connected with nullities, since they were for a long time the only type of sanction available to contest the breach of procedural rights or procedural formalities related to the gathering of evidence.

[14] It has been argued in the literature that § 177(2) CCP establishes a new case of absolute nullity. See Karras (2006, 742).

Until recently the Supreme Court adhered to the principle that a nullity, which could lead to reversal of a judgment, could only be found in the explicit cases provided for by law. In all other cases of procedural irregularities, where no specific provision for a nullity or other exclusionary rule existed, the Supreme Court has consistently ruled that evidence gathered in violation of the law is admissible. This view reflects the idea (although the latter is not clearly expressed in most of these judgments) that exclusion of evidence is an exception to the principle of discovery of the material truth.

Taking an approach consistent with this view, the Supreme Court ruled in an old judgment handed down before the enactment of the 1975 Constitution that a statement of the defendant induced by violence was admissible as evidence against him since no rule existed to the contrary.[15] In another judgment handed down in 1989, the Supreme Court ruled that illegal wiretappings were admissible as the law did not provide for any nullity or other exclusionary rule.[16] The same view was shared in other judgments, which dealt with the admissibility of hearsay evidence in cases where the witness, in violation of the obligation established in § 224 CCP, did not reveal his sources. In well-established case-law handed down before the enactment of the exclusionary rule for such types of testimony, the Supreme Court ruled that this evidence was admissible as no rule existed to the contrary. But even after the enactment of the exclusionary rule in 1996, the Supreme Court continued to hold that the violation of the exclusionary rule is not reviewable on appeal, because the law does not provide for exclusion of the testimony as to the otherwise illegal act.[17]

Nowadays, this traditional view is on the wane, and the prevailing view is that violation of a prohibition on the collection of evidence or an exclusionary rule produces an absolute nullity pursuant to § 171(1)(d) CCP. The Supreme Court adopted this view, for example, in a judgment which found a nullity in a case of an illegal search of a premises without there being a specific provision for this in the CCP (see Sect. 11.2.2.2 below).[18] This case-law is based on the argument that a violation of an exclusionary rule is itself equivalent to a violation of defense rights, in other words, that the defense has an innate right to exclude illegally gathered evidence. This is not always true, however. An absolute nullity, according to § 171(1)(d),

---

[15] Hellenic Supreme Court, Judgment No. 761/1973, *Poinika Chronika Law Review* (1973), 806 ff, comment, Benakis.

[16] Hellenic Supreme Court, Judgment No. 1150/1989.

[17] See, for example, Hellenic Supreme Court Judgments Nos. 783/2001, 71/2007 and 316/2007.

[18] See also Hellenic Supreme Court Judgments Nos. 9/1994, 589/94 and more recently 297/2002 regarding illegal wiretappings, 1568/2004 regarding illegal overhearing of a private conversation with an acoustic device, 622/2003 and 2035/2005 regarding a recording of a private discussion and 1713/2006 regarding secret bank documents. The same view has been supported with several arguments in legal theory. See Karras (2006, 737 ff), Papageorgiou-Gonatas (1989, 564), Konstantinides (1995, 1183), and Dimitratos (2001, 13).

presupposes the violation of norms relating to the right to counsel and the exercise of defense rights, the latter being perceived as active rights, which secure the accused's participation in the process. This is not the case when, for example, an illegal wiretapping has taken place.

As far as absolute nullities are concerned, the Supreme Court has ruled that they also arise when rights guaranteed in international conventions have been violated. Thus, in its Judgment No. 23/2001, which was confirmed later by other judgments,[19] the Supreme Court ruled on the admissibility of transcripts of pretrial witness statements that were made in the absence of the accused and in violation of the right to confront and cross-examine the witness. In contrast with previous judgments on this point, the Supreme Court adopted the position that such records were admissible as evidence against the accused only if the witness were unavailable to be called before the court due to death, serious illness, unknown whereabouts, living abroad, etc. In any other case, such written pretrial testimony is inadmissible, if the defendant objects to its use. This judgment referred expressly to the defendant's right guaranteed in Art. 6(3)(d) ECHR, to cross-examine the witnesses against him.

In contrast with these recent judgments, which are ready to attach a nullity to any exclusionary rule, other Supreme Court judgments have gone in the opposite direction, loosening rigid exclusionary rules so as to facilitate the ascertainment of truth. This disregard of a constitutional exclusionary rule relating to illegal wiretaps will be discussed below in Sect. 11.2.3.3. The reasoning behind these exceptions to seemingly ironclad constitutional exclusionary rules, is that the admission of such illegal evidence would ensure a fair balance in the examination of evidence. This balance respects a basic value of law, which is the "proportional protection of all conflicting interests". This line of reasoning reveals that the Supreme Court does not respect absolute exclusionary rules, even if contained in the constitution itself, when they sacrifice discovery of truth in the interest of human rights.

In order to define the circle of persons who may take advantage of an absolute or relative nullity, the Supreme Court examines the reasons for the prohibition that was violated. For example, in a case involving lawyer-client privilege, the violation of which leads to a relative nullity, it has ruled that the defendant may not benefit from a violation committed by his own lawyer.[20] This criterion also applies, although to a lesser degree, where absolute nullities are concerned. The violation of a defense right may thus not lead to the reversal of a judgment finding the defendant not guilty.[21]

[19] See recent Judgments Nos. 1628/2006 and 416/2007.

[20] Hellenic Supreme Court, Judgment No. 2433/2003.

[21] See for example Hellenic Supreme Court, Judgment No. 1375/2004.

11.2 Rules of Admissibility/Exclusion in Relation to Violations of the Right to Privacy

11.2.1 General Provisions Protecting the Right to Privacy and the Right to Develop One's Personality

11.2.1.1 Constitutional Provisions

The 1975 Greek Constitution has undergone three revisions so far. The last took place in 2001. The original version included a full list of human rights (Arts. 4-25), some of which are of great importance for criminal procedure. The subsequent revisions to the text, especially the last one, have added some new rights which were already protected in statutory law or were acknowledged in doctrine.

The right to develop one's personality and the right to privacy were included in the human rights list contained in the original version of the Constitution. Art. 5(1) Const. guarantees the right to develop one's personality and to participate in social, economic and political life, provided that one does not harm others' rights and does not violate the Constitution and morality. The right to privacy is guaranteed in Art. 9(1) Const. along with the inviolability of one's home and the right to family life.

Although the general right to develop one's personality and the general right to privacy have little effect in the field of criminal evidence, the specific right to inviolability of the home, which is also protected in Art. 9(1) Const., the right to privacy in one's telecommunications (Art. 19(1) Const.) and the right to privacy in one's personal data (Art. 9A Const.), are of much greater significance when it comes to the question of admissibility of evidence.

11.2.1.2 Statutory Provisions

The general right to privacy is not protected as such in statutory law. There are, however, specific statutes regulating particular aspects of this general right, such as personal data, the inviolability of one's telecommunications or bank secrecy (see Sect. 11.2.4.2 below). Enactment of these statutes is expressly required by the Constitution so as to establish the terms under which these constitutional rights may be limited.

11.2.1.3 Supreme Court Jurisprudence Interpreting the General Right

Due to the protection of special aspects of the general right to privacy, as well as to the lack of statutory provisions referring to this matter and to the right to develop one's personality, there is no Supreme Court jurisprudence relating to the general right to privacy. However, some judgments do refer to these general rights in the interpretation of some regulations which indirectly influence the application of exclusionary rules. In two judgments concerning the use of videotapes recorded by individuals which showed the defendants at the very moment they were embezzling funds, the Supreme Court examined whether these recordings were inadmissible, as they were obtained as a result of criminal acts (§ 177(2) CCP).[22] In order to answer this question, the court had to interpret § 370(a) of the Penal Code (PC), which punishes the recording of acts performed *in private* without the consent of the persons being recorded. Although it recognized that this criminal provision aimed, *inter alia*, at protecting these general rights, the Court held that the defendants' acts were not of a private nature. Consequently, it reached the conclusion that since the recording was not a criminal offense it could not trigger the exclusionary rule contained in §177(2) CCP.

11.2.2 Protection of Privacy in One's Home or Other Private Premises

11.2.2.1 Constitutional Provisions

Privacy in one's home is protected as a special constitutional right along with the general right to privacy. Art. 9(1) Const., which protects this general right, also states that everyone's home is inviolable (in the sense that it constitutes "asylum") and that a search of a home may only be carried out in the presence of a representative of the judicial authorities, when and where this is provided for by law. The second paragraph of this Article states that any person who does not comply with the first paragraph is to be punished for a violation of the sanctity of the home and for abuse of power, and in addition is liable to pay full compensation to the victim as specified by law.

The wording of the present version of Art. 9(1) Const. is different than the original text of the provision, in that it includes the requirement of a judge being present at the search. This requirement arose from an effort to protect the right from abuse of police power of the type which was usual during the 7-year dictatorship which preceded the enactment of the Constitution.

The term 'home' in Art. 9 Const. is used in its broader sense, comprising not only the premises where one lives on a permanent basis but also other places not open to the public, such as offices or workplaces in general, as well as caravans or other automobiles used as homes.[23]

---

[22] Hellenic Supreme Court, Judgments Nos. 1317/2001, *Poinika Chronika* (2002), 435 ff., comment, Anagnostopoulos and 874/2004.

[23] See Triantafyllou (1993b, 96 ff.).

A new paragraph was inserted into Art. 19(3) Const., explicitly providing for the exclusion of evidence obtained in violation of Arts. 9 Const. (as well as of Arts. 9A and 19 Const., which will be discussed below). This new exclusionary rule appears to eliminate any possibility of a balancing test. The wording of Art. 19(3) Const. clearly states that the products of a violation of the inviolability of the dwelling, *inter alia*, may not be used in court, even if necessary to prove the innocence of the defendant. It is for that reason, that this provision was sharply criticized by legal scholars.[24] In any case it is unclear if this rule applies to evidence gathered illegally by private individuals (see Sect. 11.2.3.3, text and fn. 36).

11.2.2.2 Statutory Provisions

The CCP contains a special section regulating searches as a specific type of investigative act (§ 253-259 CCP). § 253 CCP sets out the general terms and conditions under which any type of such investigative act may be conducted, and also applies to searches of one's home in the broader sense. Pursuant to this provision, which is considered to be the epitome of the principles of proportionality and necessity, a search may be conducted during a judicial or summary investigation of a felony or a misdemeanor, only if there is reasonable ground for believing that this is the only means to confirm the crime, detect or arrest the offender, or, lastly to confirm the quantum of damage caused by the crime or assess the compensation payable for such damage.

§ 254(1) CCP enumerates the circumstances when night searches (which are otherwise not permitted) may be conducted (i.e. to arrest a person for a crime committed in the home, when people are congregating in a home for the purposes of gambling or debauchery, or when the home is otherwise accessible to the public at night). § 255 CCP specifies those officers who may conduct a house search and § 256 CPP describes the way in which the search should be executed. Finally, § 258 CCP requires preparation of an inventory of the items seized.

Since illegal searches are criminal acts pursuant to § 241 PC, they fall within the scope of § 177(2) CPP, which provides for the inadmissibility of evidence obtained by or through criminal acts. This exclusionary rule co-exists with the constitutional rule contained in Art. 19(3) Const. Both of them lead to the same result, which is to say the inadmissibility of the products of the illegal search, although they do have different objectives: the first rule contributes to the prevention of criminal acts during criminal investigation, while the second aims to protect human rights.

[24] See Iliopoulos-Strangas (2003) and Triantafyllou (2007, 295 ff).

11.2.2.3 Supreme Court Jurisprudence Interpreting the Rules of Admissibility in Relation to Searches of the Home

Notwithstanding the importance of the right to privacy in one's home, the Supreme Court jurisprudence in this area is comparatively poor. This phenomenon is explained by the lack of any provision requiring the nullity of illegal searches. Another factor, leading to the same result, seems to be the difficulty of proving that an irregularity occurred during the process of the search.[25]

The only Supreme Court judgment referring to the admissibility of evidence collected during illegal searches at a premises is Judgment No 1338/2003. The issue raised by the defendants in their cassational appeal, was the absolute nullity of a search performed during the stage of the investigation conducted by the public prosecutor, before the case is turned over to the investigating magistrate for the formal preliminary investigation. § 253 CCP does not allow searches of premises during this stage of the procedure. Consequently the Supreme Court confirmed that searches at this stage are illegal. Despite the absence of a specific nullity rule for such searches, the Supreme Court ruled that this was a situation which triggered an "absolute" nullity, thus making all the evidence collected inadmissible. This judgment followed the line taken in other cases, by expanding the scope of absolute nullities to areas not specifically provided in the law (see Sect. 11.1.4.1 above).

Admissibility of Indirect Evidence (Fruits of the Poisonous Tree)

Admissibility of indirect evidence has always been a controversial issue in the legal theory of exclusionary rules. Some authors support the view that indirect evidence should be excluded only on the occasion of grave violations of human rights, such as torture or other offenses against human dignity.[26] According to this view, the admissibility of indirect evidence produced by an illegal search of one's home would remain intact. Others, referring specifically to illegal searches, hold that the fruits of the poisonous tree should always be excluded.[27] A third view believes that the admissibility of indirect evidence should be decided in each separate case on the basis of an ad hoc balancing test[28] and a fourth view rejects in general the exclusion of indirect evidence, notwithstanding the rule of "dependence"[29] (see next paragraph).

---

[25] See Triantafyllou (1993b, 23 ff).

[26] Androulakis (2007, 215) and Tzannetis (1995, 12 ff). With special emphasis on violations of the defendants' rights, Dalakouras (1996, 344 ff).

[27] See Triantafyllou (1993b, 429 ff), where I express the opinion that, regardless of the nullity produced, by virtue of article 175 CCP, an illegal search renders inadmissible all indirect evidence derived from it, such as the results of seizures, other searches, confessions etc.

[28] See Papageorgiou-Gonatas (1989, 561 ff) and Dimitratos (2001, 9 ff).

[29] Karras (2006, 2006, 744).

As far as the Supreme Court jurisprudence is concerned, Judgment No 1338/2003, which ruled that the consequence of an illegal search is an absolute nullity, was not asked to rule on the question of whether the nullity should lead to the exclusion of indirect evidence. Nonetheless, this ruling favors the doctrine of the "fruits of the poisonous tree", as § 175 CCP provides that the nullity of a procedural act renders any subsequent act which depends on it invalid. The concept of "dependence" in § 175 CCP has not been sufficiently addressed in legal theory and Supreme Court case-law, at least with regard to the exclusion of evidence.[30] In another judgment, dealing with an invalid autopsy, the Supreme Court ruled that the nullity affected the judgment only to the extent that it had taken the autopsy into account in its reasons. The court did not refer to the consequences of the invalid act on other acts.[31] In my opinion, § 175 CCP suggests that illegal searches may contaminate indirect evidence.[32]

In addition to the dependence rule, which applies in the case of nullities, inadmissibility of indirect evidence also arises from § 177(2) CCP, the main statutory provision on exclusion of illegally obtained evidence, which provides that any piece of evidence obtained by criminal acts or *through them* is not admissible. This wording supports the view that the exclusionary rule applies not only to the direct, but also to the indirect products of criminal acts.[33] Since illegal searches normally constitute a criminal act under § 241 PC, one reaches the conclusion that the indirect products of an illegal search are not admissible as evidence in criminal proceedings.

11.2.2.4 Effect of International Human Rights Jurisprudence

Greece has ratified the ECHR. Consequently, final judgments of Greek courts may undergo a further review by the European Court of Human Rights (ECtHR) in regard to alleged violations of the Convention. § 525(1)(5) CCP also provides for further review of cases where Greece is convicted of violating the ECHR.

Although the jurisprudence of Greek courts in criminal matters is thus influenced by the jurisprudence of the ECtHR, its case law in relation to Art. 8 ECHR, which guarantees everyone's right to respect for his private life, including the privacy in one's home, and in the privacy of one's communications is of little importance in the

---

[30] In a plenary judgment (No. 2/1996), not referring to the exclusion of evidence, the Hellenic Supreme Court has ruled that such dependence has to be "real and exclusive". The court defined dependent acts as only those which are produced because of the initial invalid act, which is, legally and logically, a prerequisite for them.

[31] Hellenic Supreme Court Judgment No. 1610/2000.

[32] See more details in Triantafyllou (1993b,401 ff), where I adopt a broad interpretation of the concept of dependence resulting in the exclusion of evidence produced by a wide range of procedural acts and statements, including seizures, other searches, confessions etc.

[33] See Karras (2006, 740), Tzannetis (1998, 107), and Dimitratos (2001, 11).

area of exclusion of evidence found by means of illegal searches or wiretaps. This is because Greek constitutional and statutory law offer a stronger level of protection than the ECtHR which has seldom, if ever, found that the use of evidence gathered in violation of Art. 8 ECHR has violated the right to a fair trial under Art. 6 ECHR.

11.2.3 Protection of Privacy in One's Communications

11.2.3.1 Constitutional Provisions

Art. 19(1) Const. protects privacy in one's communications, pronouncing the inviolability of postal and any other type of communication. The same paragraph also requires that a statute lay down the preconditions, according to which judicial authorities may issue a warrant allowing a breach of this inviolability for reasons of national security or the detection of particular serious crimes. Art. 19(3) Const. prohibits the use of any information gathered in violation of Art. 19(1) Const.

11.2.3.2 Statutory Provisions

Statutory regulation of the privacy of communications is covered by a wide range of provisions referring to different types and different aspects of communications. In addition to the CCP, relevant provisions are to be found in the Penal Code and other ordinary statutes. Most of these provisions have been repeatedly amended, especially those dealing with wiretapping and secret recordings. It is thus difficult to present anything but a provisional analysis of the state of the law in this area.

The most significant statute in this area is Law 2225/1994 on the protection of the freedom of correspondence and communications, which has been amended several times. This statute lays out the conditions which must exist, before a judge may order the lifting of the secrecy of communications for the purpose of crime detection. §4(1) of this law sets out a list of felonies and misdemeanors during the investigation of which a judicial order permitting invasion of the secrecy of communications will be allowed. The power to lift the secrecy of communications lies with the investigating chamber, a court which is empowered to decide, *in camera*, on the infringement of constitutionally protected rights during the preliminary investigation. In very urgent cases, the measure may be ordered by the public prosecutor or the investigating magistrate, who then have 3 days to seek ratification of the measure by the investigating chamber.

Non-compliance with the conditions laid out in § 4(1) of Law 2225/1994 leads to a prohibition of use of the evidence obtained by an unlawful interception of confidential communications. Exclusion is required by both Art. 19(3) Const.[34] as

---

[34] Cf. Piraeus Multi-Member Court of First Instance, Judgment No, 7056/2004, *Poinika Chronika Law Review* (2006), 459, comment, Tsolias, which excluded illegally seized mail, based on the norm contained in Art. 19(3) Const.

well as § 177(2) CCP, since an illegal breach of the secrecy of one's communications constitutes a crime punishable under § 370A PC.

Furthermore, §4(10) of Law 2225/1994 establishes an additional exclusionary rule relating to the fruits of unlawful interception of communications, by imposing a sanction of nullity which also extends to the use of the fruits for any purpose even in trials against third parties. An exception exists, however, which would allow use of the fruits in another trial if permission is obtained from the authority which ordered the measure and it relates either to the detection of a crime which is included in § 4(1) of the law or is to be used in defense of the accused.

11.2.3.3 Supreme Court Jurisprudence Relating to Admissibility of Evidence Gathered as a Result of Unlawful Interceptions of Confidential Communications

Due to the repeated amendments of the relevant legislation, mainly regarding wiretaps, it is quite difficult to present what one could call well-established case-law on the consequences of an illegal intrusion into the privacy of communications. In addition to changes in the case-law occasioned by legislative reforms, the Supreme Court jurisprudence in this area is characterized by inconsistencies, attributable to different approaches as to the scope of nullities and the applicability of exclusionary rules.

However, recent judgments do adhere to some basic principles as to the admissibility of evidence seized in consequence of a violation of this right. First, it is accepted that Art. 19(3) Const. and § 177(2) CCP prohibit the use of illegal recordings or interceptions. It is remarkable, however, that courts do not fully comply with the new exclusionary rule in Article 19(3) Const. which was introduced in 2001. In disregard of the absolute character of this rule of exclusion, the Supreme Court has ruled that illegal wiretappings or recordings of private communications may be used as evidence when they are the only means for proving innocence, or even guilt, in the case of a very serious crime. The court has repeatedly stressed the need for a balance between conflicting interests in the criminal process, which necessitates some exceptions to the constitutional rule.[35] This case-law reflects objections expressed in the literature to the absolute character of the constitutional exclusionary rule.[36]

---

[35] Hellenic Supreme Court, Judgments Nos. 42/2004, 1622/2005, 611/2006, 1537/2007, 813/2008 and 2617/2008.

[36] One could reach the same conclusion, i.e. that the exclusionary rule of Art. 19(3) did not apply in the cases examined by the Supreme Court, arguing that the Constitution regulates only the cases, where illegal wiretappings were obtained in the exercise of state powers. Consequently, any illegal evidence gathered by individuals does not fall within the scope of the provision. See on this controversial issue, Triantafyllou (2007). However, the Supreme Court decisions do not seem to adopt this view.

In some rulings, such as that in Judgment No. 297/2002, the Supreme Court has looked only to § 177(2) CCP, which requires exclusion of evidence gathered as a result of a criminal offense, and has ignored the constitutional exclusionary rule, in declaring the inadmissibility of private communications evidence, in that case, in the form of illegal wiretaps. Similarly, in its Judgment No. 1568/2004, the Supreme Court declared inadmissible per § 177(2) CCP evidence of a private conversation, gathered by a private citizen who used a special recording device to record the conversation from a distance of 100 m. The reason for the exclusion was that the act of recording was a criminal offense punishable under § 370(2) (a) PC.

Admissibility of Indirect Evidence (Fruits of the Poisonous Tree)

Regarding indirect evidence, or "fruits of the poisonous tree" there are no cases decided by the Supreme Court directly relating to the interception of confidential communications. However, the views expressed above (Sect. 11.2.2.3) would apply in this area as well. The "dependence" rule in § 175 CCP and the clear requirement of exclusion of indirect evidence in § 177(2) CCP should require exclusion of "fruits of the poisonous tree".

11.2.4 Other Invasions of Privacy Which Could Lead to Suppression of Evidence

11.2.4.1 Rules Relating to Body Searches and Searches of Automobiles and Other Personal Effects

A search of personal effects, such as automobiles and private containers, is a type of investigative act regulated by § 253 CCP, which contains a general provision, requiring that all searches be conducted only if they are absolutely necessary for the achievement of certain procedural goals. § 257 CCP regulates body searches. It differentiates between the accused and third persons, the former being liable to a search of his body, when there are serious grounds to believe that it will help in the discovery of truth, while the latter may be searched only when there is serious and probable cause or it is an absolute necessity. § 257(2) CCP provides that a search of a woman must be conducted in private and only by a female official. The prevailing view in legal theory suggests that Article 257 CCP also applies to personal effects being carried by a person, such as bags, wallets, etc.[37]

[37] See on this issue Triantafyllou (1993b, 112 ff.).

A rather controversial question, which has raised difficulties in police practice, is the legal status of automobiles.[38] While automobiles used for a residence are unanimously considered to be homes, minds are divided as to the status of those used primarily for transportation. The controversy is linked to practical considerations, insofar as the law requires that a judge be present during the search of a home (Art. 9(1) Const.). Although the Constitution and the CCP do not explicitly resolve this question, other statutory provisions, such as § 96(3)(a,b) of Presidential Decree No 141/1991, which regulates police searches in the field of crime prevention, differentiate between homes and automobiles, placing them under different regimes. Relying on this Decree, police officials usually search automobiles without asking a judge to be present during the search.[39]

11.2.4.2 Rules Relating to Data Mining and the Gathering of Other Types of Semi-private Information

The right to confidentiality of one's personal data is guaranteed in Art. 9A Const., which accords everyone protection against the collection, processing and use of his of her personal data, especially through electronic means. An independent state agency has been established for the purpose of guaranteeing data protection, and the law sets out when the state may use private data and how the agency ensures that the law is adhered to.

This special statute, Law 2472/1997, regulates in detail the issues relating to protection of private data, yet its relationship to the provisions of the CCP has long been in dispute. In the face of opposing views both in legal theory and case law, the Supreme Court has finally decided, in Judgment No. 1945/2002, that the provisions of the CCP prevail, as specific ones, over the more general provisions of Law 2472/1997. In that case, the Supreme Court ruled that the accused and his lawyers, when exercising their right to subpoena documents and impeach the credibility of the prosecution's witnesses, may use documents revealing sensitive personal data reflecting on the character of the witness. In doing so, they do not have to comply with the special provisions of Law 2472/1997.[40]

This view has been partially implemented by Law 3625/2007 which amended § 3(2)(b) of Law 2472/1997, so that the law no longer applies to the use of personal data in criminal proceedings, either in the investigative or trial stages. This area would thenceforth be exclusively regulated by the CCP and the Penal Code.

It can be inferred *a contrario* that the general legislation on personal data applies nonetheless in relation to the prosecution of less serious crimes. But the precise

---

[38] Ibid, 106 ff.

[39] Cf. the opinion of the Public Prosecutor by Hellenic Supreme Court, Judgment No. 13/2004, who regards searches of automobiles as body searches contributing thus to the confusion which exists on this point.

[40] See also Hellenic Supreme Court, Judgment No. 1561/2005.

relationship between the principle of the material truth and the right to protect one's personal data is still unclear in this area. However, due to the silence in § 3 of Law 2472/1997 with respect to this question, I believe that one should still apply the language of Judgment No. 1945/2002 and insist that less serious crimes also be investigated in conformance with the dictates of the CCP, which specifically regulate the relationship between the right to personal data and the mandate to discover the material truth and limit the application of the stricter provisions of Law 2472/1997 to non-criminal use of protected material.

Apart from the general Law 2472/1997, personal data are also protected by fairly recent amendments to the CCP, added to that Code by recent reforms. The most important of these provisions were added by Law 2928/2001, which was aimed at combating organized crime, and later amended by Law 3251/2004, which was aimed at combating terrorism.

The first of these sections is § 200A CCP regulating the testing of DNA, which may be conducted in order to discover the perpetrators of offenses connected with organized crime and terrorism. DNA testing is considered to be an intrusive investigative method, which places sensitive personal data at considerable risk. In the original version of § 200A CCP, DNA samples could not be taken unless the investigating chamber ordered otherwise in the interests of investigating organized crime and terrorism cases. However, amendments in 2009 to § 200A(2) CCP have now made it possible to preserve genetic material in normal cases to the end of creating a DNA bank in the interests of future crime detection.

The other important recently added sections are § 253A(1)(d) CCP, which regulates the recording of public activities using special technical devices, and § 253(4) CCP, which regulates data mining in relation to the same recorded activity. Pursuant to § 253(4) CCP, evidence produced by these special investigative acts may only be used for the initial purpose of their collection, unless the investigating chamber authorizes their use for the detection of other organized criminality or terrorist crimes.

The Supreme Court has not yet ruled on whether violations of the above statutes will lead to exclusion of evidence.

11.2.5 Treatment of Invasions of Privacy Which Are Fruits of the Violation of a Different Constitutional Right

As already mentioned (see Sect. 11.2.2.3), the question of admissibility of indirect evidence is expressly addressed in § 177(2) CCP, which requires that the fruits of criminal offenses be excluded. This means that pieces of evidence found by searches, data mining, wiretapping etc. are not admissible, if these investigative acts are the result of another act, which itself constitutes a criminal offense. This would be the case if a statement, which led to a search or a wiretap, was a result of torture, since torture is punishable under §§ 137A PC. The same would happen if a search was conducted, based on a prior illegal dwelling search which violated § 241 PC. In all these cases it is not the violation of a constitutional right, but its criminal character, which contaminates indirect evidence. Therefore, if an unlawful arrest is itself a crime, a statement or evidence found following it would be suppressed.

11.3 Rules of Admissibility/Exclusion in Relation to Unlawful Interrogations

11.3.1 The General Right to Remain Silent and Privilege Against Self-Incrimination

11.3.1.1 Constitutional Provisions

A general right to remain silent and the privilege against self-incrimination are not expressly articulated in the Greek Constitution. Nevertheless academics try to establish a basis for these rights in various constitutional rights, such as the right to human dignity or to develop one's personality (Art. 5(1) Const.) or the right to be heard by a court (Art. 20(1) Const.).[41]

11.3.1.2 Statutory Provisions

The right to silence/privilege against self-incrimination are guaranteed by statute to the extent that Greece has passed laws implementing international human rights conventions which guarantee these rights, which then, pursuant to Art. 28(1) Const., have priority over domestic law. Thus, Law 2462/1997 implemented the United Nations International Covenant on Civil and Political Rights (ICCPR), Art. 14(3)(g) of which guarantees the right not to be compelled to testify against oneself or to confess guilt. As a result, defendants may exercise this right at every stage of the procedure, even where not expressly acknowledged in domestic law. The same right has been acknowledged in the case-law of the ECtHR, which has ruled on several occasions that, although not expressly protected in the ECHR, the right to silence is part of the general right to a fair trial protected under Art. 6(1) ECHR.[42]

The CCP does, however, contain specific provisions which set out the right to silence or certain aspects thereof. Pursuant to § 273(2)CCP, the accused, for instance, has a right to refuse to answer questions during pretrial interrogation before the

---

[41] See a critical presentation of these opinions in Tsolka (2002, 85 ff.).

[42] See e.g., Funke v. France (1993), 16 E.H.R.R. 297; Murray v. United Kingdom, (1996) 22 E.H.R.R. 29, Saunders v. United Kingdom (1996) 23 E.H.R.R. 313.

investigating magistrate. § 105 CCP also allows the accused to refuse to answer during interrogations conducted in urgent cases before police inspectors. Furthermore, pursuant to § 31(2) CCP, the suspect may refuse, in whole or in part, to give explanations relating to the charges during all preliminary interrogations.

In relation to the trial itself, § 366(3) CCP allows the defendant to refuse to take the witness stand and answer questions. This provision is interpreted as guaranteeing the right to silence, although in a rather indirect manner.[43] As a complement to these provisions, § 223(4) CCP allows a witness to refuse to answer questions which may contribute to proof of his guilt.

11.3.1.3 Supreme Court Case Law Interpreting the Scope of the Right to Silence

The Supreme Court has ascertained the significance of the right to silence and more generally the privilege against self-incrimination in two remarkable plenary judgments. Neither bothered to search for constitutional origins of these rights in Greek law, but they looked, instead, directly to the international conventions ratified by Greece which guarantee these rights.

The first decision, handed down in 1999, addressed the privilege against self-incrimination as a right of the accused and held that violation thereof leads to the absolute nullity of the procedure.[44] In this judgment the court noted that the right to silence and the privilege against self-incrimination are part of the general right to a fair trial established in Art. 6(1) ECHR, citing directly to the ECtHR's seminal judgment of *Murray v. United Kingdom.*

In the second judgment, handed down in 2004, the Supreme Court ruled that the privilege against self-incrimination constitutes not only a defense right, but also a basic principle of criminal procedure.[45] This decision went one step further in clarifying the relationship between the general right and the right to a fair trial, noting that the right to a defense, which includes the right to silence, constitutes part of the right to a fair trial. Furthermore this judgment referred to the priority of Art. 14 (3) (g) ICCPR over domestic legal provisions.

Both judgments, which have been affirmed nearly unanimously in subsequent case law, confirm that the violation of the right to silence leads to the absolute nullity of the procedure, and the resulting inadmissibility of the statements thus

[43] See Tsolka (2002, 100).

[44] Hellenic Supreme Court, Judgment No. 2/1999 (Plen.), *Poinika Chronika Law Review* (1999), 811 ff, comment, Anagnostopoulos.

[45] See Hellenic Supreme Court, Judgment No. 1/2004 (Plen), in *Poinika Chronika Law Review* (2005), 113 ff., note, Anagnostopoulos, *and in Poiniki Diki Law Review* (2004), 917, comment, Papadamakis. See also Judgment 1731/2007. In his written opinion as to the latter case, the public prosecutor confirmed that this right applies to all interrogations of the accused at any stage of the proceedings. Violation of the right would thus render any act related thereto invalid.

obtained. To the extent these decisions dealt with certain aspects of unknowing self-incrimination, they will be examined below in Sect. 11.3.3.2.

11.3.2 Protection Against Involuntary Self-Incrimination

11.3.2.1 Constitutional Provisions

The Greek Constitution prohibits torture and any other offense against human dignity (Art. 7(1) Const.). Greece also ratified by Law 1782/1988, the United Nations Convention against Torture and Other Cruel, Inhuman or Degrading Treatment or Punishment (hereafter CAT). Art. 15 CAT provides: "Each State Party shall ensure that any statement which is established to have been made as a result of torture shall not be invoked as evidence in any proceedings, except against a person accused of torture as evidence that the statement was made".

This provision prohibits the use of any statement made as result of torture, without allowing for any ad hoc balancing test of the kind stated above, even though the Constitution does not expressly provide for a similar exclusionary rule.[46] Greece is also bound by Art. 3 ECHR, which prohibits torture or inhuman or degrading treatment.

11.3.2.2 Statutory Provisions

§ 137 PC punishes as a felony any torture committed by officials commissioned to investigate criminal acts for the purpose of obtaining a confession, statement or other information. Pursuant to § 137(2) PC, torture is defined so as to include any illegal use of chemical, physical and technical means or drugs, with a view to undermining the victim's will. § 137(3) PC punishes less serious abuses, such as physical or psychological violence, not amounting to torture, and any other offense to human dignity, such as the use of lie detectors.

The violation of these norms constitute crimes and would thus lead to the exclusion of evidence pursuant to §177(2) CCP, which provides for the exclusion of evidence obtained by or through criminal acts.

11.3.2.3 Supreme Court Case Law Addressing Admissibility of Fruits of Involuntary Confessions

It has already been mentioned, that the Supreme Court in 1973 allowed use of statements resulting from the use of violence during the interrogation of a suspect, because no rule of nullity said otherwise.[47] This ruling came under fierce criticism,

---

[46] See previous footnote and Androulakis (2007, 214) and Dalakouras (1996, 340).

[47] Hellenic Supreme Court, Judgment No. 761/1973, *Poinika Chronika Law Review* (1973), 806 ff, comment, Benakis.

which emphasized that the search for truth was limited by the need to protect human rights.[48] The Supreme Court, nowadays, however, has consistently ruled that statements made as result of torture are inadmissible, among other reasons, because they violate the rule of law or due process.[49]

The prevailing view in legal doctrine also holds that indirect evidence seized as a result of torture or other violations of human dignity is not inadmissible. This view is in harmony with the wording of § 177(2) CCP, which prohibits the use of any evidence obtained *through* criminal acts. The issue has not yet been raised in case-law.

11.3.3 *The Protection Against Unknowing Self-Incrimination: The Miranda Paradigm*

11.3.3.1 Statutory Provisions Relating to Right to Silence and Counsel During Interrogations

§ 100(1) CCP provides that the accused has a right to the presence of a lawyer during his interrogation. He should be informed of this right by the investigating magistrate who should record the fact of the admonition in the record (§ 103 CCP). The same right applies during either the summary or full preliminary investigation (§§ 31(2)(2), 104 CCP).

Similarly, the defendant must be advised of the right not to answer questions or give explanations, whether during the formal preliminary investigation, conducted by an investigating magistrate, or summary investigations carried out by the police in urgent cases (§§ 31(2)(2), 105 CCP). § 105 CCP also requires police to advise suspects of the right to counsel and the right not to answer questions when they investigate on their own without an order of the public prosecutor. The last subparagraph of § 105 CCP also provides for the nullity of any statement made in the absence of the required admonitions. Thus, Greek *Miranda* rights must be communicated to suspects during the investigation and defendants at the trial stage and the practice is overwhelmingly welcomed in the literature.[50]

The accused is also protected against use of statements made by him when obligated to testify as a witness, if he is later charged with a crime. More specifically, § 31(2)(3) CCP provides that any prior testimony of the suspect, which was given as a witness under oath or otherwise without him being able to have counsel present,

---

[48] Ibid. See also, Androulakis (1974, 1352), Kostaras (1984, 169 ff), Charalampakis (1995, 345), and Dalakouras (1996, 345).

[49] Hellenic Supreme Court, Judgment No. 611/2006.

[50] See Dalakouras (1989, 319 ff); Hellenic Supreme Court, Judgment No. 556/1993, *Poinika Chronika Law Review* (1993), 387, comment, Livos. Karras (2006, 424) and Tsolka (2002, 150ff).

may not be included in the investigative file, and thus may not be introduced at trial.

The provisions contained in §§ 31(2)(3), 105 CCP are aimed at eliminating the long illegal practice of police investigators, who used to interrogate suspects as witnesses, in order to circumscribe the rights to counsel and silence.

11.3.3.2 Supreme Court Case Law Relating to Admissibility of Evidence Following Violations Relating to Admonitions or the Right to Counsel

Both of the seminal judgments discussed in Sect. 11.3.1.3 above, which recognized the privilege against self-incrimination as part of the right to a fair trial and an absolute nullity upon violation of such right, involved cases of defendants who were first interrogated as witnesses before being charged and prosecuted. In Judgment 2/1999, the accused was interrogated as a witness during the police investigation, whereas in Judgment 1/2004, the accused had testified as a witness in an administrative inquiry regarding the criminal act for which he was later prosecuted. In both cases the testimony was used by the Court of Appeal as evidence against the accused. The Supreme Court overturned both convictions, determining that the statements were taken in violation of §§ 31(2)(3), 105 CCP, and criticized the police practice of interrogating suspects as witnesses.[51]

Despite these rulings, the Supreme Court has not gone so far as to accept that a nullity is also caused when the investigators fail to advise the defendant about his general right to silence. The court accepted that advice as to the right "not to answer", explicitly required by § 273(2) CCP, is tantamount to an admonition of the right to silence.[52] This view is far from convincing, for the right to remain silent is of a much more universal character than a mere right not to answer. On the other hand, the failure to advise of the right to counsel results in an absolute nullity.[53]

The failure of investigators to advise the defendant of either the right to counsel or the right to silence is not punishable as a criminal act. Therefore, § 177(2) CPP is inapplicable when assessing whether fruits of the poisonous tree would be admissible following Greek *Miranda* violations. However, inadmissibility of indirect evidence could result from § 175 CCP, which establishes the "dependence" principle in relation to absolute nullities discussed in Sect. 11.2.2.3 above. Insofar as a

[51] See also Judgments Nos. 1750/2008, concerning testimony taken by police authorities and 90/2006, 2521/2008 and 133/2009, concerning testimony before officials of the Financial Crime Authority. Surprisingly Hellenic Supreme Court, Judgment No. 377/2008 has ruled recently that testimony given by the accused in the course of administrative enquiries is not excludable in the criminal process.

[52] Hellenic Supreme Court, Judgment No. 1724/2007.

[53] Hellenic Supreme Court, Judgment No. 105/1998, which finally dismissed the appeal in cassation, holding that the admonition had taken place in that case.

statement of the accused is null, due to the violation of his right to silence or counsel or his right to be informed thereof, a search which relied upon that statement would be equally invalid.

The Supreme Court has, however, ruled that, notwithstanding the invalidity of a statement as such, it can still be used when the defendant refers to it during a subsequent statement given with proper admonitions and without any other violations of the right to silence or counsel.[54]

11.4 Exclusion of a Confession as Fruit of Another Constitutional Violation

The Supreme Court has not yet handled a case in which an otherwise valid confession was challenged as having been the fruit of, for instance, an unlawful arrest. However, as was mentioned in Sect. 11.2.5, above, one could easily argue that, since an unlawful arrest is a criminal violation, that the "fruits of the poisonous tree" doctrine of § 177(2) CCP would apply. The same would apply under the "dependence" rule, unless the correct application of *Miranda* rights would break the confessions dependence on the unlawful arrest.

11.5 Conclusion

The evolution of Greek written law, as well as the jurisprudence of the Supreme Court, reveal the significance of material truth and due process as the main foundational principles of criminal procedure. In many ways, these principles have a force which transcends written statutory provisions.

This can be illustrated by the approach to exclusionary rules in Greek law and in its interpretation by the Supreme Court. Greek law recognizes both nullities and modern exclusonary rules. Nullities have a long history in Greece, existed in the original version of the CCP and have always served as means to exclude evidence. Genuine exclusionary rules have been enacted in the last two decades in response to the need for more adequate protection of constitutional rights. Nevertheless, these new rules did not have the desired effect, as the law did not explicitly provide that violation of those rules was a cause for the reversal of judgements.

The Supreme Court, complementing the legislative reforms, has ruled on several occasions that the use of illegal evidence is a cause for nullity of the procedure. In doing so, the Supreme Court has attempted to reach a fair balance between the principles of material truth and due process. However, the inconsistency of its case law

[54] Hellenic Supreme Court Judgment, No. 1370/2007.

has prevented it from actually accomplishing this task. Consequently a total reform of the law of exclusionary rules is necessary in order to achieve clear and coherent regulation of this issue.

Regarding the relationship between the principles of due process and the search for material truth, it is also remarkable that the judiciary is not willing to accept norms, even of constitutional rank, which exclusively favor one of these principles over the other. The judgments which recognize nullities in cases of serious violations of constitutional rights, despite the absence of statutory privisions, clearly show that the Supreme Court is not attached to discovering of truth at any cost. On the other hand, the case law relating to violations of the right to privacy in communications implies that discovery of truth, as a principal goal of the procedure, is considered to have a constitutional standing and may not be ignored, despite the fact that it is never mentioned in the Constitution.

The Greek Supreme Court is thus still struggling to accomodate the principle of discovery of the material truth with due process and the protection of constitutional rights, but still has a way to go. This is especially true in co-ordinating the relationship of nullities to modern exclusionary rules and their application to derivative evidence.

Bibliography

Androulakis, N. 1974. The problem of confessions during the preliminary investigation. *Nomiko Vima Law Review* 22: 1345–1356.

Androulakis, N. 2007. *Fundamental concepts of criminal procedure*, 3rd ed. Athens: Law & Economy-P.N. Sakkoulas S.A.

Charalampakis, A. 1995. The Greek law on torture. *Yperaspisi Law Review* 5: 660–672.

Dalakouras, T. 1989. The Defendant's silence in criminal procedure. *Armenopoulos Law Review* 72: 319–333.

Dalakouras, T. 1996. Illegal evidence. *Poinika Chronika Law Review* 46: 321–347.

Dimitratos, N. 1992. *Exclusionary rules in criminal procedure*. Athens: Ant. N. Sakkoulas Publishers.

Dimitratos, N. 2001. The evolution of the regulation of exclusionary rules in Greek law of criminal procedure. *Poinika Chronika Law Review* 51: 9–13.

Iliopoulous-Strangas, J. 2003. *The use of illegally-obtained evidence and the right to defense – The evidentiary prohibition in Article 19 paragraph 3 of the revised [Greek] Constitution*. Athens: Ant. N. Sakkoulas Publishers.

Karras, A. 2006. *Criminal procedure law*, 3rd ed. Athens: Ant. N. Sakkoulas Publishers.

Konstantinides, A. 1995. Remarks on the regulation of evidence in the draft Code of Criminal Procedure. *Poinika Chronika Law Review* 45: 1179–1188.

Kostaras, A. 1984. The admission of illegally gathered or illegally used evidence. *Ephimeris Ellinon Nomikon Law Review* 51: 169–185.

Papageorgiou-Gonatas, S. 1989. Illegal indirect evidence in criminal process. *Poinika Chronika Law Review* 39: 545–565.

Spinellis, D. 1986. Exclusionary rules in criminal procedure. *Poinika Chronika Law Review* 46: 865–886.

Triantafyllou, G. 1993a. The position of the co-defendant in the present evidentiary system. *Poinika Chronika Law Review* 43: 1076–1104.

Triantafyllou, G. 1993b. *Regulation and function of searches in the Code of Criminal Procedure*. Athens: Ant. N. Sakkoulas Publishers.

Triantafyllou, G. 2007. Exclusionary rules and the principle of proportionality. *Poinika Chronika Law Review* 57: 295–310.

Tsolka, O. 2002. *The principle nemo tenetur se ipsum prodere/accusare in criminal procedure*. Athens: Law & Economy-P.N. Sakkoulas S.A.

Tzannetis, Aristomenis. 1995. Exclusionary rules and alternative legal collection of evidence. *Poinika Chronika Law Review* 45: 5–36.

Tzannetis, A. 1998. Punishable collection of evidence. *Poinika Chronika Law Review* 48: 105–109.

Chapter 12
Turkey: The Move to Categorical Exclusion of Illegally Gathered Evidence

Adem Sözüer and Öznur Sevdiren

12.1 The General Theory of Admissibility of Illegally Gathered Evidence

12.1.1 Introduction

If one accepts Herbert Packer's famous distinction between two types of criminal process, due process and crime control,[1] a review of Turkish law on evidentiary exclusionary rules convincingly shows that Turkey has long since made a choice in favor of the due process model in this regard. Tensions and problems do exist, as will be explained below. Nevertheless, to our knowledge, in no other civil law jurisdiction are exclusionary rules so extensively covered and strictly delineated as in Turkish law. After a brief consideration of the history which led up to the current legal regulations in this area, this chapter will go on to outline the existing constitutional and legislative bases for evidence exclusion and case law in this respect, within the parameters we set for this study.

[1] Packer (1968, 149–173).

A. Sözüer (✉)
Hukuk Fakültesi, Istanbul Üniversitesi, Ceyave Ceya Usul Hukuku Anabilim dali,
Beyazit-Istanbul, 34116, Turkey
e-mail: adam1@superonline.com

Ö. Sevdiren
Hukuk Fakültesi, Uludag Üniversitesi, Uludag Üniversitesi Gemlik Sungipek Yerleskesi,
16600, Gemlik/Bursa, Turkey
e-mail: oznur.sevdiren@googlemail.com

S.C. Thaman (ed.), *Exclusionary Rules in Comparative Law*, Ius Gentium: Comparative Perspectives on Law and Justice 20, DOI 10.1007/978-94-007-5348-8_12,

12.1.2 Historical Development of Exclusionary Rules

Prior to 1992, Turkish law did not provide for exclusionary rules or prohibitions on the use of unlawfully obtained evidence (*delil yasakları*).[2] Nonetheless, even then, it was generally agreed that confessions obtained through illegal interrogation methods such as torture, were not admissible, regardless of their probative value.[3] In practice, however, although a conviction could not be based solely on a confession obtained through illegal interrogations, the Turkish Court of Cassation did allow for use of such evidence if other supportive evidence was available.[4] Hence, it would be correct to conclude that in a small, but important number of decisions, the Turkish Court of Cassation found that such unlawfully procured evidence could be admissible under certain circumstances.

In the 1980s, the use of unlawful evidence gained increasingly more attention in public discussion. On the one hand, the state's failure to prevent serious human rights violations, particularly with regard to ill-treatment of suspects during police custody after the coup d'état on September 12, 1980, was particularly subjected to vigorous criticism by both domestic and international human rights authorities.[5] On the other hand, Turkey's desire to become a fully-fledged member of the European Union

---

[2] For studies on the theme see e.g., Tosun (1976), Öztürk (1995), Toroslu (1995, 55–58), Şahin (1994, 169–236), Yenisey (1995), Istanbul Barosu, Marmara Üniversitesi Rektörlüğü (1995), Demirbaş (1996, 247–305), Şahin (1998, 343–354), İçel (1998, 121–127), Şen (1998), Yurtcan (1998, 519–22), Koca (2000, 105–146)), Soyaslan (2003, 9–26), Çınar (2004), Kunter et al. (2006, 986–1027), and Öztürk and Erdem (2007, 476–525). See also the relevant sections of the following commentaries: Yasar (2007), Tasdemir and Özkepir (2007), and Yurtcan (2008). In foreign languages, Öztürk (1992, 667–687) and Bıçak (1996).

[3] See eg., the Decision of the Court of Cassation, the Assembly of Criminal Divisions (hereafter CGK) *CGK*, Judgment March 24, 1980, 1/121 and 1 CD, Judgment August 9, 1977, 2261/2580 cited in Erem (1996, 291). (It is rare in Turkey to refer to a case by the names of the parties. Citations normally include the court, date and registration number of the cases in the court). The Court of Cassation ruled that "…taking the confession, which was clearly made under pressure and which did not reveal consistency, as a basis for the judgment is unlawful." *Yargıtay Kararları Dergisi*, vol. 12 (March 1991) no.3., p. 420, "For a confession to be accepted as evidence, it should result from the individual's free will and be made before the judge, and should not be withdrawn in a further stage of criminal proceeding and finally it must be supported by corroborative evidence", *CGK*, Judgement February 16, 1987, 6–271/50, cited in Erem (1996, 293). See also Judgment December 12, 1991, 1–301/334, *Yargıtay Kararları Dergisi* (1992), Vol. 13, 1108–1111.

[4] CGK, Judgment December 10, 1990, 6–257/335 "Without support of other evidence, if a confession is withdrawn on the grounds that it was made under pressure, a confession made during the police interrogation cannot be the sole basis for a conviction" see also, CGK Judgment, March 7, 1983, 3–104, *CGK* Judgment April 1, 1985, 6/511–182, cited in Yasar (2007, 748–755).

[5] In 1996, the European Committee for the Prevention of Torture observed that "resort to torture and other forms of severe ill-treatment remains a common occurrence in police establishments in Turkey". CPT, Public Statement on Turkey, CPT/Inf(96)34, 6 December 1993, para.38. On the legal implications of the coup d'état in English, see Gemalmaz (1989).

required a broader acceptance of supranational rules in the field of human rights.[6] The fact that Turkey recognized the competence of the European Court of Human Rights (ECtHR) to receive applications from individuals,[7] ratified the European Convention for the Prevention of Torture and Inhuman or Degrading Treatment or Punishment[8] and the United Nations Convention Against Torture and Other Cruel, Inhuman or Degrading Treatment or Punishment (CAT),[9] and committed itself to join the European Union reflected the country's aspirations to consolidate the rule of law and ensure protection of fundamental rights and freedoms, with due regard to the European Convention on Human Rights (ECHR) and the case law of the ECtHR.[10]

One of the early and significant steps in this respect was the reform of criminal procedure law in 1992.[11] Among other provisions, Law no 3842[12] added two important provisions to the Code of Criminal Procedure of 1929, which was originally based on the German Code of Criminal Procedure of 1877 (hereafter CCP (1929)), both requiring the exclusion of improperly obtained evidence.[13] Significantly, the incorporation of these provisions was justified by adherence to the principle of due process and the principle of a state under the rule of law (*hukuk devleti*).[14]

The first provision, that of § 135A CCP (1929), was a *specific* exclusionary rule relating to unlawful interrogations. It was laid down that:

> The freedom of the suspect or the accused to determine and exercise her/his free will shall not be impaired by ill-treatment, torture, administering drugs, fatigue, deception, physical force and violence or by using different devices. Promising an *unlawful* benefit is prohibited. Statements obtained in violation of these prohibitions cannot be used as evidence even if the accused consents to their use.

The second, and more significant general exclusionary rule, added as § 254(2) CCP (1929), provided that: "Evidence obtained *unlawfully* by investigative authorities (*soruşturma ve kovuşturma organları*) cannot be used as a basis for the judgment".

---

[6] Hafızogulları (1993, 37–47) and Sokullu-Akinci (1998, 253–269). See also Toroslu (1995) and Tezcan et al. (2004, 414–417).

[7] Turkey ratified the ECHR with Law no. 6366, 10 March 1954. *Official Gazette*, 1567. Since then, the Convention has been a part of national law. See Gölcüklü and Gözübüyük (1998).

[8] Law no 3411, 25 February 1988, *Official Gazette* 25.02.1988, no. 19737.

[9] Law no 3441, date: 21.04.1988, *Official Gazette*, 29.04.1988, no, 19799.

[10] Ünal (2000, 63–85), and Gözlügöl (2002, 435–454).

[11] For an American view on the subject, see Calhoun (2000, 61–68).

[12] Law no 3842, *Official Gazette*, 01.12.1992, no. 21422.

[13] The reformed procedural rules were not applicable to persons suspected of offenses such as terrorism, drug smuggling, membership in illegal organizations and espousing or disseminating ideas prohibited by law as damaging the indivisible unity of the State. For a discussion see Calhoun (2000, 61–68).

[14] The principle of a state under the rule of law in Turkey has constitutional footing. Art.2 of the Turkish Constitution (hereafter Const.) states that "The Republic of Turkey is a democratic, secular and social *state governed by the rule of law*…." Art. 125 Const. furthermore states that "Recourse to judicial review shall be available against all actions and acts of administration". See on the implications of the principle of the *Rechtsstaat* with regards to criminal procedural law, Öztürk and Erdem (2007, 163).

The legislature's preference, in particular, for a mandatory exclusionary rule, was met with certain resistance in both professional and academic circles.[15] Indeed, in spite of the relatively clear phraseology of both provisions, the nature and boundaries that they created were (and have been) subject to heavy discussion. The essential point of the debate was the meaning given to the notion of "unlawfulness" as it appeared in the wording of both provisions. Emphasizing the difference between the notions of "unlawfulness" and "illegality", it was argued that the meaning of the former concept would go far beyond a mere infringement of positive law, because the meaning of "unlawfulness" cannot always be equated with "illegality". From this perspective, any breach of positive law in obtaining evidence should not trigger automatic exclusion of evidence. Many held that criteria should be established according to which a distinction could be made between cases that do and do not warrant suppression of evidence.

Inspired by German doctrine, some scholars resorted in this regard to the German limitations on exclusion of evidence (the so-called *Rechtskreistheorie*[16]), which postulates that any unlawfulness (and/or illegality) in the gathering of evidence that does not infringe on the fundamental rights of the defendants before the court should not be grounds for exclusion of evidence. For example, when a search, which must be conducted in the day time, is executed in the night time, the unlawfulness is rather of a technical nature. Again, failure to provide all required information in a search warrant should not lead to exclusion of the evidence derived from this search, if there is no violation of fundamental rights in the strict sense. According to this view, recourse to absolute (mandatory) exclusion of evidence, without making any distinction between violations impacting fundamental rights and "mere" infringements of law would impede an effective criminal policy, particularly with regard to organized criminality. It is thus argued that obtaining evidence illegally ought not to lead to suppression of the resulting evidence, unless there is a violation of: (1) the privilege against self-incrimination; (2) the privilege not to testify against close relatives; (3) the right to remain silent and consult with defense counsel; or (4) the right to privacy.

In other cases involving less significant legal violations, according to this view, a public interest test linked to the principle of "proportionality" should be applied. Under such a test, resulting evidence would not have to be excluded where the public interest outweighs the prejudicial effect of an unlawful or illegal investigative act, due to the probative value of the evidence and the gravity of the charged offense.

Advocating a similar, but nonetheless distinct approach, other critics were of the opinion that not all unlawful conduct in obtaining evidence should lead to its exclusion, unless the *constitutionally protected sphere of fundamental rights* of the suspect or

---

[15] Most vocally, see Savaş and Mollamahmutoğlu (1995, 1155–1214). Demirbaş argues that "Acting with the intention to go far beyond European provisions and discovering 'America' again was unfortunate for the Turkish system". Demirbaş (1996, 303).

[16] Öztürk (1995, 11); See Gless, Chap. 5, Sect. 5.1.2.3.

the accused is violated.[17] In this sense, only a substantive and significant breach violating such constitutionally protected rights as the right to legal assistance and other fair trial rights of the suspect/accused (in the context of Art. 36 Const.) should lead to suppression of the evidence. Therefore, the judge must consider whether the unlawfulness and illegality in question amounted to the violation of the right to fair trial in the light of the circumstances of the case as a whole.[18] Again, where the law explicitly provides for a specific exclusionary rule when certain prohibited methods are used, evidence so obtained must be excluded.[19]

Finally, in opposition to these views, others, with whom the present authors agree, have argued that once it is determined that a piece of evidence was obtained in breach of any rule, it must be excluded without any further consideration, because the regulation of exclusionary rules in Turkish law does not permit the balancing of criminal policy considerations under the rubric of proportionality.[20] The rule of law requires mandatory exclusion of such evidence and the state should not benefit from its own unlawful activities. The organs and agents of the State are bound by the law and no gradual distinctions should be made between different types of unlawfulness. By enacting such absolute exclusionary rules, the legislature decided in favor of maximum assurance and protection of the rights and freedoms of individuals. Undoubtedly, truth-finding is the essential purpose of the criminal process, but neither human dignity nor the rights of the defense should be sacrificed to attain it.

This doctrinal debate reverberated in the decisions of the Court of Cassation, as will be seen below. In principle, the Court has recognized that: "...in a democratic society, procuring evidence is the fundamental purpose of the criminal process and the duty of security forces,[21] [however] this purpose and duty cannot be an excuse for legitimatizing human rights violations and unlawful conduct; security forces must fulfill their duties by respecting human rights and by acting lawfully".[22]

Yet, in practice, the Court has tended to restrict the scope of exclusionary rules, by applying a cause/effect criterion. Even the amendment to Art. 38 Const., which will be dealt with in the next section, appears not to have resolved the controversy on the scope of the regulations regarding exclusionary rules.

---

[17] Yenisey (1995, 218–219); See also Şahin (1998, 353–354). Sokullu-Akıncı observes that "This solution is taken from American law where many procedural rules are in the American Constitution and violations of these rights of the individual are hence "unconstitutional". But this is not true for Continental Europe and Turkey where only a few of the procedural rules are in the Constitution but the majority of procedural rules are in separate Codes. So all illegal evidence is not "unconstitutional". This proposition seems to be one of the unfortunate efforts to limit the application of § 254(2) CCP (1929). If we respect the rule of law, all illegal evidence must be considered within said article". Sokullu- Akıncı (1998, 267).

[18] Kunter et al. (2006, 986–992).

[19] Ibid, 986.

[20] Koca (2000, 105–146), Yurtcan (1998, 519–522), Toroslu (1995, 55–58), and Şen (1998, 159–161).

[21] Security forces in Turkey are composed of police and gendarmerie.

[22] CGK, Judgment October 15, 2002, 8–191/362, cited in Çınar (2004, 52).

12.1.3 The Present Legislative Framework: An Overview

Currently, the Turkish Constitution provides a solid foundation for the exclusion of unlawfully obtained evidence. The amended version of Art.38(7) Const. prescribes that "Findings obtained through *illegal* methods shall not be considered to be evidence". Two conclusions can be drawn from this provision. First, not only does illegally obtained evidence fall under the scope of this provision, but also *findings* which may not be technically categorized as evidence. Second, any breach of the standards as established in law may result in the exclusion of the evidence, regardless of the gravity of the illegality in question. This follows from the legislative choice to use the term *findings* in Art. 38 Const., thereby apparently also opting for the assurance of a firmer constitutional base for exclusionary rules.

In the new Code of Criminal Procedure, which was passed in 2004 and went into effect on June 1, 2005 (hereafter CCP), as part of a package of reforms that went into effect in 2005, the constitutional mandate for exclusion of illegally gathered evidence found clear implementation. The new CCP contains various measures, which reveal the legislature's intention to attach crucial importance to evidentiary prohibition rules. Before proceeding to outline the pertinent statutory framework currently in place in Turkish law, it should be noted that both the notions of "illegality" and "unlawfulness" are used almost interchangeably in the related provisions.

Bearing that in mind, the outline will begin with § 206(2)(a) CCP, which requires the suppression of any evidence which is *illegally* obtained. This prohibition also applies at the pretrial stage, such that an accusatory pleading based on unlawfully obtained evidence would be without effect.[23] This can be logically deduced from a combined reading of § 170(5) CCP, which requires that the accusatory pleading include points which are both unfavorable and favorable to the suspect, and § 160(2) CCP, which stipulates that in seeking the material truth (*maddi gercek*), public prosecutors are obliged to collect and secure evidence which may be favorable to the suspect.

Furthermore, § 217 CCP, while giving the judge discretionary power to form her/his own opinion on the reliability and credibility of evidence, emphasizes in its second subsection that the offense charged may be proven only with *lawfully obtained* evidence. Hence, as distinct from the previous regulation, according to which unlawfully obtained evidence could not be used as the basis for the *judgment*,[24] the new CCP goes further and implies that illegally obtained evidence is not considered to be evidence at all. This means, in our opinion, that under Turkish law evidence gathered in contravention of law is not only inadmissible in court, but may also not be used as a basis for imposing pretrial detention or for authorizing any investigative measure designed to secure evidence (such as a seizure, search or wiretap).

In order to assure conformity with the aforesaid provisions, § 230(b) CCP provides that the judgment must include not only a description of the evidence upon which it

---

[23] According to § 174 CCP (2004). See Öztürk and Erdem (2007, 487).

[24] See § 254(2) CCP (1929), in Sect. 12.1.2, above.

is predicated, but also, in a separate section, a description of the suppressed unlawfully obtained evidence. §289(i) CCP explicitly states that use of evidence obtained through unlawful methods as a basis for a judgment violate the law, are of no effect and will be reversed on appeal.

Clearly, what is substantively to be considered "unlawful" or "illegal" is laid out in the constitution and in the CCP in the sections dealing with the procedure for gathering evidence (e.g. of arrest, search, seizure, interception of communication, etc.). In evaluating the admissibility of evidence, the judge must base her/his judgment on those specific legal requirements. Needless to say, judges are not solely bound by domestic law. Under Art. 90 Const., they are also required to apply supranational rules.[25] Among others, those provided in the ECHR have proven to be of special importance in legislation and case law. It is a welcome development that since Turkey recognized the right to individual complaint, Turkish courts make frequent references to the ECHR and the case law of the ECtHR in Strasbourg in support of their reasoning.

It is still too early to make a confident judgment about the way in which these provisions will be interpreted and applied by the courts. Since the CCP went into effect in 2005, the Court of Cassation has only occasionally addressed the suppression of unlawfully obtained evidence. It remains to be seen, therefore, to what extent the Court will limit the suppression of evidence. Nevertheless, as will be pointed out below, a well-disseminated decision on the inclusion of evidence that was illegally seized as a result of a search without a warrant, does indicate that the Court's hitherto restrictive approach is unlikely to change in the near future.

12.2 Rules of Admissibility/Exclusion in Relation to Violations of the Right to Privacy

12.2.1 General Provisions Protecting the Right to Privacy and/or to Develop One's Personality

12.2.1.1 Constitutional Provisions

A number of provisions in the Turkish Constitution aim to secure the right to privacy and the right to develop one's personality. Art. 20 Const. (as amended) affirms as a fundamental principle that "everyone has the right to demand respect for her/his

[25] Art. 90 Const. provides: "International agreements duly put into effect bear the force of law. No appeal to the Constitutional Court shall be made with regard to these agreements, on the grounds that they are unconstitutional. In the case of a conflict between international agreements in the area of fundamental rights and freedoms duly put into effect and the domestic laws due to differences in provisions on the same matter, the provisions of international agreements shall prevail".

private and family life. Privacy of an individual or family is inviolable". Pursuant to this section restrictions of this right may only be based on one or several of the grounds of national security, public order, prevention of crime, protection of public health and public morals, or protection of the rights and freedoms of others. The second paragraph of Art. 20 Const. provides that the power to issue a search warrant belongs only to a judge of the competent jurisdiction, yet that searches and seizures may also be conducted by other authorized law enforcement agencies when "delay is prejudicial". In the latter case, the authorized agency must seek retroactive approval of the measure by a judge within 24 h, and the judge must make a ruling within 48 h of the time of the emergency search or seizure. The seizure or search is deemed to be unlawful if this procedure is not followed, or if the judge, of course, refuses to ratify the legality of the measure.

It is important to note, that the Preamble of the Constitution states that every Turkish citizen has the (birth)right "to develop her/his material and spiritual assets under the aegis of national culture, civilization and the rule of law, through the exercise of the fundamental rights and freedoms set forth in the Constitution in conformity with the requirements of equality and social justice". This objective finds further expression in Art. 5 Const., which provides, that one of the State's fundamental aims and duties, is to guarantee "the conditions required for the development of the individual's material and spiritual existence". The other side of this state duty is established in Art. 17 Const., which declares that "everyone has the right to life and the right to protect and develop her/his material and spiritual existence".

12.2.1.2 Statutory Provisions

In order to protect the constitutional right to privacy and to develop one's material and spiritual existence, the law provides both criminal and civil remedies in case of their violation. § 24 of the Civil Code, for example, recognizes that an individual whose personal rights are unjustly violated may bring a civil action to prevent the continuation of the violation and/or to be compensated for damages arising from it. The new Criminal Code (CC), which entered into force on June 1, 2005, includes a number of provisions dealing with the right to privacy. Under § 134 CC the violation of another person's privacy is punishable by a penalty of imprisonment for a term of 6 months to 2 years or a fine. In cases in which the violation of privacy occurs "as a result of recording images or sound" the mandatory minimum penalty is 1 year imprisonment (§ 134(2) CC). § 135 CC provides that unlawful storage of personal data is subject to a penalty of imprisonment from 6 months to 3 years. Unlawful transmission or reception of personal data is punishable by a term of imprisonment from 1 to 4 years (§ 136 CC). Where such crime is committed by public officials through misuse of their discretionary power or in order to benefit a profession or trade, the punishment must be increased by half (§ 137 CC). Furthermore, those who do not delete or destroy personal data upon the expiration of a statutory time period, must be punished by imprisonment from 6 months to 1 year (§ 138 CC).[26]

Under the rubric, "unlawful search", § 120 CC provides that "a public official who performs an unlawful search on a person, or of her/his personal belongings, must be sentenced to a penalty of imprisonment for a term of three months to one year".

12.2.2 *Protection of Privacy in One's Home and Other Private Premises*

12.2.2.1 Constitutional Provisions

Art. 21 Const. proclaims that "the domicile of an individual is inviolable". It further provides that searches may be ordered only by a judge for reasons of national security, public order, prevention of crime, protection of public health and morals, or protection of the rights and freedoms of others. It also provides for the emergency competence of law enforcement agencies to issue a written order when there is danger in delay, which must be submitted to a judge for ratification within 24 h of the search. Any seizure is invalidated if this procedure is not followed, or if the judge does not ratify the measure within 48 h from the time it was conducted.

12.2.2.2 Statutory Provisions

§ 116 CCP provides that the search of a domicile, a place of business or other premises of the suspect or accused, requires a *reasonable suspicion* that the suspect or the accused is guilty of a crime and subject to arrest, and/ or that a search of the premises may lead to the discovery of evidence.

§ 118 CCP provides that domiciles and business premises, as well as other properties that are not open to public access, shall not be searched during the nighttime, unless the suspect has been caught *in flagrante delicto*, there is danger in delay, or the search is conducted for the purpose of recapturing escaped persons, suspects or convicted persons.

§ 119 CCP confirms the constitutional principle that a search warrant may be issued only by a judge. This requirement can be waived only if delay is prejudicial, in which case a search can be conducted upon a written order of the public prosecutor.

---

[26] There are also provisions in §§ 73, 159 of the Banking Law (Law no. 5411). §§ 23, 29 of the Bank Cards and Credit Cards Law (Law no. 5464), which entered into force on March 1, 2006, also includes certain provisions aimed to protect the personal data of bank card and credit card holders.

Significantly, in Turkish law no search in domiciles, business or other premises that are not open to public access can be conducted upon a written order of a superior official of the security forces. Accordingly, § 119 (4) CCP stipulates that two municipal officials or two neighbors must be present at a search that is conducted in the absence of the public prosecutor. The owner of the premises or the possessor of the items is entitled to be present at the search. If s/he is not present, her/his representative, a competent relative, or a person living in her/his household, or a neighbor may be called. It is also significant, that § 120(3) CCP recognizes that the lawyer of the affected party cannot be prevented from attending the search.

A search warrant must include a description of the offense under investigation, the person with respect to whom the search will be conducted, the address of the domicile or the place to be searched, the material that is sought, and the duration of the validity of the warrant. A report must also be made which includes identities of those who have conducted the search (§ 119(2) CCP).

There are also detailed provisions with regard to the seizure of private papers. In this context, §138 CCP provides, that if a search or seizure reveals evidence, which is not related to the alleged offense under investigation or prosecution, but provides reasonable grounds for suspicion that another offense was committed, those items must be immediately secured and the public prosecutor must be notified.

12.2.2.3 Court of Cassation Jurisprudence Interpreting the Effect of Violations of the Above Provisions on the Admissibility of Illegally Seized Evidence

There are two cases from 2007 which are quite indicative of the approach of the Court of Cassation with regard to admissibility of illegally seized evidence. In one decision, the Court of Cassation considered whether the breach of the statutory requirement that two persons from the municipality or two neighbors must be present during searches carried out in the public prosecutor's absence should in itself lead to the suppression of evidence derived from the search.[27] The Court held that such a violation is of a minor and technical nature; there was consequently no violation of the rights of the individual, who confessed to the offense, and whose confession was deemed reliable by expert testimony. In the second case, the Court of Cassation ruled that a search warrant must be issued by the judge of competent jurisdiction unless a delay would have a prejudicial effect. Recourses to searches based on a decision of the public prosecutor or the written order of a high official of security forces must be the exception. The Court found that a search in that case did not comply with this condition, thus was unlawful, so that evidence so obtained could not be used to support a conviction.[28] Consequently, the Court of Cassation reversed

[27] CGK, Judgment June 26, 2007, 7–147/159, *İstanbul Barosu Dergisi* (2008), 82(no.1), 451–466.

[28] CGK Judgment February 22, 2007, 5671/1111, accessible from: www.hukukturk.com.

the conviction because, other than the unlawfully acquired evidence, there was nothing to support the judgment of conviction.

As these two examples show, the Court of Cassation does not favor "automatic" exclusion when a departure from the standards established by law occurs. It further considers whether or not other evidence exists which may support a judgment of conviction.

In a 2005 decision, the Court of Cassation addressed the issue of the "fruits of the poisonous tree". By applying the provisions of the CCP 1929, the Court discussed whether or not evidence seized as a result of a warrantless search of the domicile could be admitted, given that the suspect had also confessed.[29] Although the accused's wife had consented to the search, there had been neither a judicial order, nor a written order of the public prosecutor or a superior police official. As a result of the search, a certain amount of marijuana was seized. The Court of Cassation ruled that the conviction could be based on such evidence, even though it recognized that the search in question did not conform "strictly" to the criteria as specified in the law.

12.2.3 Protection of Privacy in One's Communications

12.2.3.1 Constitutional Provisions

Art. 22 Const. guarantees the freedom of communication, proclaiming that "the confidentiality of communication is fundamental". As with searches, the protections may be set aside only upon judicial warrant, and based on reasons of national security, public order, prevention of crime, protection of public health and public morals, or protection of the rights and freedoms of others. Written emergency orders may also be issued by the public prosecutor or other law enforcement officials in emergency situations. These officials must, again, seek ratification from a judge within 24 h, which ratification must ensue within 48 h of the measure, or it is without legal effect.

12.2.3.2 Statutory Provisions

According to §129 CCP, communications in the forms of letters or packages transmitted by the postal services, may be seized upon judicial order if there is suspicion that they constitute evidence of an offense and that the seizure is necessary for the purposes of truth-finding. Where there is danger in delay, the public prosecutor also possesses the power to order seizure of such materials. Seized items must be sealed in the presence of postal officials and delivered immediately to the judge or to the public prosecutor. The concerned person should be notified where there is no risk of

[29] CGK, Judgment November 29, 2005, 7–144/150, accessible from: www.kazanci.com.

endangering the investigation and prosecution. Provided that the judge finds it unnecessary to open the items or considers further administrative custody unnecessary after their inspection, the items must be immediately returned to the addressee.

In the CCP (1929) which was in force prior to 2005, there was no regulation of the interception of telecommunications.[30] The first provision in this respect was enacted by Law no. 4422, on Combating Profit-Making Criminal Organizations, in 1999. An interesting case before the ECtHR had exerted far-reaching influence in Turkish law in this respect. In that case, the applicant, Agagoglu, complained that the proceedings that led to his conviction had been unfair, maintaining that he was convicted on the basis of illegally intercepted telephone calls, an argument which was based on Art. 6 ECHR (right to fair trial) and Art. 8 ECHR (right to respect for private life). After this judgment the gap in the law in this respect was frequently discussed and eventually the new CCP incorporated a detailed provision in this regard.

Pursuant to § 135 CCP, an order to intercept and record telecommunications as an investigative measure can be issued if two conditions are met. First, there must be *strong suspicion* to believe that one of a catalogue of crimes has been committed. Examples of such crimes are human trafficking, intentional homicide, torture, sexual assaults, drug trafficking, creating or participating in a criminal organization, counterfeiting, prostitution, securities fraud, bribery, money laundering and crimes against the state (§ 135(6) CCP). Secondly, there must be no other possibility of obtaining the evidence, such as through a search or seizure. However, it is not necessary for an interception order that other measures have actually already been used. A reasoned expectation that they would not bring about the desired result is sufficient.[31]

The interception and recording of telecommunications can in principle only be ordered by a judge. The public prosecutor may order the interception and recording of telecommunications without prior judicial authorization only in cases where there is danger in delay. The public prosecutor is required to submit her/his decision immediately for judicial approval. The judge is then obliged to render a decision within 24 h. In cases, where this time period expires or the judge does not approve the decision of the prosecutor, the measure must be terminated by the public prosecutor without delay.

It is also significant, that under the current law a wiretapping order may not be issued to intercept communications between the suspect/accused and those who have a privilege not to testify against the defendant, such as close family members (§ 135(2) CCP). If it is only discovered after the interception that such a privileged individual was involved in the recorded conversations, then the recording must be immediately destroyed. In addition, the law explicitly prohibits the implantation of telecommunications devices in the office or domicile of the suspect's defense counsel in relation to the offense under investigation (§ 136 CCP).

A wiretap order is valid for up to 3 months and can be extended, once, for an additional 3 months, if the prerequisites therefore still exist (§ 135(3) CCP). After

---

[30] See Sözüer (1997, 76).

[31] Öztürk and Erdem (2007, 632).

6 months, however, no other extensions are allowed. An exception, however, exist for offenses related to organized crime, when a judge may order further extensions for 1 month at a time, when necessary.

Once a decision has been made no longer to proceed with the investigation or prosecution of the case, or the judge has refused to ratify an emergency wiretap or extend an ongoing one, the public prosecutor must immediately terminate the interception and the recordings must be destroyed within 10 days[32] (§ 137(3) CCP).

§ 138(2) CCP regulates what has been called "coincidental evidence", that is, the situation where evidence is obtained during a wiretap that was not within the scope of the judicial authorization which gave rise to the measure, but which also gives rise to a suspicion that a catalogue offense listed in § 135(6) CCP has been committed. When this happens, the evidence should be secured and the public prosecutor should be immediately notified.

Finally, it is also important to emphasize that the external aspects of private communication, what in the U.S. is sometimes called the "envelope information", is not protected by § 135 CCP. Such information, such as the fact of a telephone call between certain phones, the date and time, the person to whom the telephone is registered, etc., may be obtained in relation to the investigation of all crimes and is governed by another law, the Regulation on the Interception of Telecommunications.[33]

12.2.3.3 High Court Jurisprudence Interpreting the Effect of Violations of the Above Provisions on the Admissibility of Evidence

Already before the enactment of the new CCP, the Court of Cassation had adopted a more stringent approach towards of the privacy of telecommunications that it had in relation to illegal searches. In 2003, the Court of Cassation ruled that evidence obtained by a wiretap without prior judicial authorization could not be used in evidence.[34]

In 2007, the Court of Cassation issued a judgment dealing with the admissibility of "coincidental evidence" arising from an otherwise legal wiretap. It held that such evidence may only be used if the crime revealed by the accidentally discovered evidence was also included in the catalogue of crimes contained in § 135(6) CCP.

---

[32] The office of the public prosecution is required to inform the individual in question in writing within 15 days of the completion of the investigation about the reasons, context, duration and outcome of the wiretapping if the recordings related to the measure have been destroyed.

[33] Telekomünikasyon Yoluyla Yapılan İletişimin Tespiti, Dinlenmesi, Sinyal Bilgilerinin Değerlendirilmesi ve Kayda Alınmasina Dair Usul ve Esaslar ve Telekomünikasyon İletişim Başkanlığı'nin Kuruluş, Görev ve Yetkileri Hakkinda Yönetmelik, *Official Gazette* 10.11.2005, 25989, Section 3-f. Yargitay 4 CD, Judgment November 29, 2006 4669/17007, 5CD, Judgment October 3, 2005, 14969/20489, accessible from www.hukukturk.com.

[34] *CGK,* Judgment April 8, 2003, 9–30/98 accessible from www.kazanci.com. See also, 8CD, Judgment June 9, 1999, 9021/9538 and 9CD Judgment October 26, 1995, 4186/5414, cited in Çınar (2004, 55).

In that case, the wiretap was authorized to investigate a violation of Law no. 4422 "On Profit-Making Criminal Organizations" but the inadvertently discovered new offense, was that of "abuse of public trust" which is not among the crimes for which wiretapping could legally be authorized. As a result, the evidence was deemed to be inadmissible.[35]

12.2.4 Other Violations of the Right to Privacy Which Could Lead to Suppression of Evidence

12.2.4.1 Search of the Person, Automobiles, Private Containers and Related Jurisprudence

§ 116 CCP, which authorizes searches of dwellings and other premises upon reasonable suspicion, also allows searches of the person based on the same suspicion. But once the search amounts to an *internal physical examination* of the suspect/accused, then the stricter regulations apply.[36] According to § 75 CCP, such search is possible, as long as it does not create a danger of harm to the health of the suspect/accused. It must be authorized by a judge, or by the public prosecutor upon danger in delay, and the examination must be undertaken by a member of the medical profession. As with other emergency orders by the public prosecutor, the prosecutor must request ratification of the order by a judge within 24 h, and the judge must decide on the legality of the measure within another 24 h. The evidence is inadmissible if the judge fails to ratify the measure.

12.2.4.2 Rules Relating to Data Mining, Collection of Other Semi-private Information and Related Jurisprudence

The new CCP provides for a comprehensive regulation of digital data mining. § 134(1) CCP allows the public prosecutor during a criminal investigation to petition the judge for an order to search computers, computer programs and computer records used by the suspect as well as to copy, analyze and textualize those records, provided that it is not possible to obtain the evidence by other means.

In cases where computers, computer programs and computer records are inaccessible, because passwords are not known or concealed data is unreachable for other reasons, the computers and other necessary equipment may be temporarily seized in order to retrieve data and make the necessary copies (§ 134(2) CCP). Seized equipment

---

[35] CGK, Judgment July, 3, 2007, 5–23/167, www.kazanci.com.Cited in Öztürk and Erdem (2007, 670).

[36] Generally, it is accepted that a body search may include stripping the suspect or the accused without actually conducting an internal physical examination. Öztürk and Erdem (2007, 582).

must be returned as soon as passwords have been discovered and the necessary copies have been made.

While executing the order to seize computers or computer records, the data included in the system may be copied in whole or in part also without seizing the computer or the computer records (§ 135(3) CCP).

12.2.4.3 Surveillance by Technical Means

Another relevant provision in this context is § 140 CCP, which regulates surveillance by technical means. According to this provision, if there is *strong suspicion* that one of the specifically enumerated offenses in this provision has been committed, and if there are no other available means of obtaining the evidence, activities of the suspect or the accused in public places, automobiles, or business premises may be subjected to surveillance by technical means, including voice and image recording. The surveillance does not extend to homes or other private premises, however. Technical surveillance means may be used to investigate the following catalogue of offenses: human trafficking, intentional homicide, drug trafficking, counterfeiting, creating a criminal organization, prostitution, securities fraud, bribery, money laundering, participation in an armed band, or contributing arms thereto, offenses against state security, and weapons smuggling (§ 140(1)(a) CCP).

Surveillance with technical means must be ordered by a judge, or in cases of danger in delay, by the public prosecutor, who must then get the decision ratified by a judge within 24 h (§ 140(2) CCP). A technical surveillance order may last for up to 4 weeks (§ 140(3) CCP). This period may be extended once, for another 4 weeks, but then must end. An exception is made for investigations of criminal organizations, where the judge may order further extensions of 1 week each.

12.3 Rules of Admissibility/Exclusion in Relation to Illegal Interrogations

12.3.1 The General Right to Remain Silent/Privilege Against Self-Incrimination

12.3.1.1 Constitutional Provisions

No provision in the Turkish Constitution explicitly guarantees the right to remain silent. Nonetheless, the existence of this right can be inferred from Art. 25 Const. which states: "No one shall be compelled to reveal her/his thoughts and opinions for any reason or purpose, nor shall anyone be blamed or accused on account of his thoughts and opinions". Furthermore, Art. 38(5) Const. includes an articulation of the principle of *nemo tenetur*, when it provides: "No one shall be compelled to make a statement that would incriminate himself/herself or her/his legal next of kin, or to present such incriminating evidence".

12.4 Statutory Provisions

Pursuant to § 147(1)(c,e) CCP, a suspect/accused who is summoned to be interrogated must be advised of her/his right to counsel and right not to make a statement before interrogation commences.

12.4.1 The Protection Against Involuntary Self-Incrimination

12.4.1.1 Constitutional Provisions

Art. 17 Const. states that "No one shall be subjected to torture or ill-treatment; no one shall be subjected to penalties or treatment incompatible with human dignity". This provision is based on the constitutional principles that "the dignity of man is inviolable" and that "everyone has the right to the free development of her/his personality".

12.4.1.2 Statutory Provisions

§ 148(1–3) CCP deal with forbidden examination methods that are very likely to cause involuntary incriminating statements and is phrased as follows:

(1) The statements of the suspect or the accused shall reflect her/his free will. The freedom of the accused to determine and exercise her/his free will shall not be impaired by bodily or mental intervention such as ill-treatment, torture, forceful administration of drugs, fatigue, deception, the use of physical force, threats or any other devices which distort the will.
(2) No illegal advantage shall be promised.
(3) Statements obtained through violation of this provision shall not be used as evidence, even if the individual has consented.

As is clear from the wording of this provision, the enumeration of forbidden methods is not meant exhaustively, but rather, illustratively.

Furthermore, § 94 CC protects the right to remain silent by defining torture and recognizing it as a crime. Accordingly, any act conducted by a public officer against a person that is incompatible with human dignity, and which causes physical or mental suffering, affects the person's capacity to decide, or her/his ability to act in pursuit of her/his own will, or insults her/him, is punishable by a penalty of imprisonment for a term of 3–12 years. Where the offense is committed against a child, a pregnant woman, a public officer or a lawyer in the exercise of her/his duties or where the act constitutes sexual harassment the punishment is aggravated (8–15 years of imprisonment).

It goes without saying that alleged perpetrators of torture may also be subject to disciplinary sanctions. According to § 125 of Law no. 657 "On Public Servants",[37] these sanctions include condemnation, blocking promotion, a fine, suspension or dismissal from office. Sanctions are imposed in accordance with the gravity of the misconduct. Although as a rule, such sanctions may be imposed irrespective of the result of criminal proceedings, the outcome of those proceedings must be awaited before a disciplinary sanction is imposed.

12.4.1.3 High Court Jurisprudence Interpreting the Effect of Violations of the Above Provisions on the Admissibility of Illegally Seized Evidence

Where it appears that a confession was given under physical coercion during police interrogation (this is often corroborated by medical reports), and the confession is not repeated before the court of first instance, the Court of Cassation has tended to doubt the reliability of such evidence, irrespective of its evidentiary value. In so doing, unless there is other evidence that reveals that the offense under investigation was committed beyond doubt, the Court overturns convictions based on evidence obtained through such forbidden interrogation methods.[38]

The Court of Cassation reached an interesting decision in 2004 which is illustrative of its approach. In that case, the suspect refrained from giving a statement during police interrogation. Nonetheless, without informing the suspect, the police recorded an informal conversation with the suspect by using a video camera. The Court held that the statement was obtained by deception in violation of § 135(a) CCP (1929) and that such evidence cannot be made the foundation for a judgment of conviction.[39]

Since the 1992 Amendment of the CCP (1929), the issue of the admissibility of indirect evidence has been the subject of a heated debate. For those who have given an absolute meaning to the exclusionary rule and the principle underlying its use, namely, the rule of law and human dignity, evidence obtained through illegal interrogation methods is not admissible. Recognizing the doctrine of the "fruits of the

[37] *Official Gazette*, 23.7.1965, no.12056.

[38] See eg. *CGK*, Judgment, October 4, 1993, 6/192–217, cited in Yasar (2007). See also CGK Judgement December 2, 1991, 301/334, YKD, 1992/7 cited in Erem (1996, 1108). See also, CGK, Judgment October, 18, 1993, 236/255, YKD, 1994/5, p. 804, cited in Erem (1996, 297), CGK Judgment December 5, 1988, 6/424–506 cited in Yasar (2007, 748), CGK Judgment April 5, 1985, 6/511–182, cited in Yasar (2007, 749), 8CD, Judgment March, 20.1985, 583–1390 cited in Yasar (2007,756).

[39] Judgment February 16, 2004, 1CD, 3819/299, cited in Çınar (2004, 52).

poisonous tree", they argue that such evidence derived indirectly through illegal interrogations should also be suppressed,[40] for accepting the use of evidence ultimately derived from illegal interrogation methods would be paving the way for the use of "deceit" by law enforcement agents. The prohibition on torture and inhumane treatment is of an absolute character. Recognizing exceptions would undermine the very *raison d'être* of the prohibition while giving positive incentive to police officials to torture or threaten to torture in the near future. Others assert that even if it based in an illegal interrogation, crucial evidence seized as an indirect result of such interrogation (e.g. a weapon, the body found in a search and so on), cannot be disregarded. Otherwise, suppressing such important evidence would have formidable consequences for the administration of criminal justice. Going even further, some scholars resort to a two-tiered criterion. For them, only such illegal methods as torture should lead to absolute exclusion of evidence. Any other methods, such as deceit should be seen merely as "unlawful" evidence and when determining the admissibility of evidence courts should take the gravity of the violation of the rights of the suspect or the accused into account.[41] In a somewhat distinct vein, others argue that although evidence obtained through involuntary confessions cannot be the sole basis for a conviction, it can be admissible if other probative evidence such as witness testimony is available.[42]

12.4.1.4 Effect of International Human Rights Jurisprudence

In a number of decisions against Turkey involving offenses falling within the boundaries of the Anti-Terrorism Law, the ECtHR has found violations of the prohibition against torture contained in Art. 3 ECHR.[43] While acknowledging that combating terrorism and the damage it causes to society poses undeniable difficulties for criminal justice, the Strasbourg Court emphasized, that even in these circumstances the prohibition in Art. 3 ECHR against torture or inhuman or degrading treatment or punishment remains firm. In this context, the Court has found violations of the fair trial right of Art. 6 ECHR because of the use of statements obtained through physical force as the basis for a judgment of conviction, where the trial court conducted no proper inquiries into the allegations of torture which were made in the case.[44]

The impact of the judgments of the ECtHR in this regard upon Turkish law has been substantial. As early as 2001, in a letter, the Ministry of Foreign Affairs, urged the judiciary to comply with the international obligations of the state.[45] A circular

---

[40] Toroslu (1995, 58), Öztürk (1995, 135), and Koca (2000, 131).

[41] Feridun Yenisey advocated this approach at a symposium on unlawful evidence in1995, see Istanbul Barosu, Marmara Üniversitesi Rektörlüğü (1995, 45); see also Yenisey (1995, 1235).

[42] İçel (1998, 124).

[43] Gemalmaz (1997), and Doğru (2004).

[44] See also, İnceoğlu (2005).

[45] For the document see Alexander et al. (2008, 463).

issued by the Ministry of Interior underlined the accumulating case law against Turkey and others, with regard to be breaches of the prohibition against the use of torture. Besides these governmental actions, a series of legislative initiatives were undertaken in order to prevent ill-treatment of suspects in police custody.[46]

12.4.2 *The Protection Against Unknowing Self-Incrimination: The Miranda Paradigm*

12.4.2.1 Statutory Provisions Requiring Admonitions as to the Right to Silence and Counsel

Though the Turkish Constitution contains no explicit language concerning the *Miranda* paradigm, § 90(4) CCP requires that a person arrested should be immediately advised of her/his rights. The suspect or accused must be informed about her/his rights also before every interrogation, whether it takes place in the police station or in court (§ 147 CCP).

As far as the right to legal advice is concerned, § 147(1)(c) CCP expressly states that, prior to being interrogated, the suspect or accused must be advised of the right to counsel, and the right to have counsel present during the course of the police and judicial interrogations. If the suspect or accused is not financially able to retain counsel, but desires the assistance of counsel, the suspect must be advised that defense counsel will be appointed by the Bar Association. Furthermore, for those suspects or accused persons who do not have defense counsel and who have not yet attained the age of 18, or have hearing and speaking impairments lacking the ability to defend themselves, state appointment of defense counsel is obligatory. Under § 150(2) CCP, appointment of defense counsel by the State is also mandatory where the offense being investigated or prosecute is punishable by more than 5 years imprisonment.

In order to demonstrate the significance attached to the right to legal assistance, § 148(4) CCP provides for a very specific exclusionary rule. Under that provision, statements obtained by the police in the absence of defense counsel, cannot not be used as a basis for a conviction, unless the content of the statement is confirmed by the suspect or the accused before the court. If such a statement is used in evidence without such consent, that judgment must be overturned by the Court of Cassation.[47]

Furthermore, § 147(1)(e) CCP requires that a suspect/accused, prior to interrogation, be advised of the right to make no statements in relation to the charges. A similar admonition of the right to silence is made the beginning of the trial (§ 191(3)(c))CCP.

---

[46] See in English e.g., Smith (2007, 262–274).

[47] Öztürk and Erdem (2007, 482).

12.4.2.2 High Court Jurisprudence Interpreting the Effect of Violations of the Above Provisions on the Admissibility of Statements and Other Evidence

In various decisions, the Court of Cassation has reversed judgments based on illegal interrogations even in cases where defective interrogations led to acquittal.[48] A judgment of the General Assembly of Criminal Divisions of the Court of Cassation on December 19, 1993, is noteworthy in this regard. In this case, the breach of the requirements that the trial must commence with the identification of the accused and the presentation of the indictment was held to be reversible error. In substantiating its decision, the Court held that the requirement of notification of the suspect or the accused of her/his rights prior to interrogation is a constitutive rule rather than a regulative rule and that any breach in this regard must automatically result in suppression of the evidence derived from such interrogations.[49]

The Court of Cassation, however, has been much less categorical, when it comes to excluding statements made, or evidence gathered as a result, during the preliminary investigation following a failure to advise the suspect/accused of the right to silence or counsel, holding that automatic exclusion would impede the administration of criminal justice.[50] The Court has rejected automatic exclusion, and asserted that evidence should only be suppressed in cases where a causal nexus can be established between the judgment and the breach of the interrogation procedures.[51] For example, the Court of Cassation held that notwithstanding the violation of the interrogation procedure, no confession was actually made, meaning that no link existed between the judgment and the unlawful interrogation. There was therefore no reversible error.

12.5 Conclusion

After examining the law governing the exclusion of evidence obtained as a result of illegal methods in Turkey, it is clear, that the principal focus of Turkish exclusionary rules in criminal proceedings lies in protecting the rights of the suspect and the

---

[48] CGK. Judgment December 19, 1994, 6–322/343, *Yargıtay Kararları Dergisi* (July 1995), 21, no. 6, 1119ff; CGK Judgment October 24, 1995, 6–238/305, *Yargıtay Kararları Dergisi* (December 1995),21, no.12, 1884; Judgment December 17, 1996, 6–263/282, *Yargıtay Kararları Dergisi* (March 1997), 434; see also 4CD Judgment October 4, 1994, 7351/7693, *Yargıtay Kararları Dergisi* (September 1995), 1476–1478; CGK Judgment October 24, 1995, 6–238/305, *Yargıtay Kararları Dergisi*, (December 1995), 21, no.12, 1888.

[49] 2CD, 9.6.2004, 2003/4094, 2004/11538, 4CD, 21.1.2004, 2003/891, 2004/433. cited in Çınar (2004, 53–54); see also CGK Judgment October 24, 1995, 7–165/302, cited in Demirbaş (1996, 261); (YKD 1996, S. 1, s.103), CGK, Judgment (March 26, 1996), 6–63/66 (unpublished, cited in Demirbaş (1996, 263–264).

[50] Judgment September 26, 1994, 7114/7264, cited in Yurtcan (1998, 521); for a similar case: 4CD Judgment October 4, 1994, 7351/7693, *Yargıtay Kararları Dergisi* (September 1995), 1476–1478, 4CD, Judgment October, 1994, 7351/7693, cited in Savaş and Mollamahmutoğlu, *op. cit.*, p. 741.

[51] See for a positive evaluation of this decision, İçel (1998, 127).

accused. Undoubtedly, the historical and constitutional developments in Turkey gave stimulus to the incorporation of exclusionary rules in criminal procedure. The contribution of the ECtHR, which has been of particular significance in dealing with pervasive use of forbidden methods of interrogation, must be acknowledged in this regard.

As early as 1992, exclusionary rules were incorporated into Turkish law through amendments of the CCP (1929). The new CCP has laid down further new rules, while clarifying the scope of existing regulations with regards to investigative measures. So far, the Court of Cassation has taken a narrow view of exclusionary rules and has disregarded the "fruits-of-poisonous-tree" doctrine in determining the admissibility of indirect evidence secured from illegal searches. Nevertheless, the growing body of academic opinion is critical of the Court's approach and it may be hoped therefore that the Court will modify its position in the near future.

Bıblıography

Alexander, Y., E.H. Brenner, and S. Tutuncuoglu Krause. 2008. *Turkey, terrorism, civil rights and the European Union*. London: Routledge.

Bıçak, V. 1996. *Improperly obtained evidence (a comparison of Turkish and English Law)*. Ankara: Yardımcı.

Calhoun, R.K. 2000. Confessions and the right to counsel: Reflections on recent changes in Turkish Criminal Procedure. *Annual Survey of International and Comparative Law* 6: 61–69.

Çınar, A.R. 2004. Hukuka Aykırı Kanıtlar. *Türkiye Barolar Birliği Dergisi* 55: 31–64.

Demirbaş, T. 1996. *Sanığın Hazırlık Soruşturmasında. İfadesinin Alınması*. Izmir: DEÜ.

Doğru, O. 2004. *İnsan Hakları Avrupa Mahkemesi İçtihatları*, vol. 1, 2. Istanbul: Legal Yayıncılık.

Erem, F. 1996. *Ceza Muhakemeleri Usulü Kanunu (Şerhi)*. Ankara: Dayınlarlı.

Gemalmaz, S. 1989. *The ınstitutionalization process of the Turkish type of democracy: A politico-juridical analysis of human rights*. Istanbul: Amaç Yayıncılık.

Gemalmaz, S. 1997. *Avrupa İnsan Hakları Komisyonu Önünde Türkiye-1: Kabuledilebilirlik Kararları*. Istanbul: Beta.

Gölcüklü, A.F., and A.Ş. Gözübüyük. 1998. *Avrupa İnsan Hakları Sözleşmesi ve Uygulaması*, 2nd ed. Ankara: Turhan Kitabevi.

Gözlügöl, S.V. 2002. *Avrupa İnsan Hakları Sözleşmesi ve İç Hukukumuzdaki Etkisi*, 2nd ed. Ankara: Yetkin.

Hafızogulları, Z. 1993. Ceza Muhakemeleri Usul Hukukunda Yapılan Değişiklikler Üzerine. *Ankara Üniversitesi Hukuk Fakültesi Dergisi* 43(1–4): 37–47.

İçel, K. 1998. *Sorgulamada Hukuka Aykırılık ve Sonuçları in Nurullah Kunter Armağanı*, 121–127. Istanbul: İHF yayını.

İnceoğlu, S. 2005. *nsan Hakları Avrupa Mahkemesi Kararlarında Adil Yargılanma Hakkı*, 2nd ed. İstanbul: Beta.

İstanbul Barosu, Marmara Üniversitesi Rektörlüğü. 1995. *Hukuka Aykırı Deliller Sempozyumu*. Istanbul: Istanbul Barosu Yayınları.

Koca, M. 2000. Ceza Muhakemesinde Hukuka Aykırı Delilleri Değerlendirme Yasağı. *Atatürk Üniversitesi Erzincan Hukuk Fakültesi Dergisi* 4(1–2): 105–146.

Kunter, N., F. Yenisey, and A. Nuhoğlu. 2006. *Muhakeme Hukuku Dalı Olarak Ceza Muhakemesi Hukuku*, 15th ed. Istanbul: Beta.

Öztürk, B. 1992. Beweisverbote im türkischen Recht. *Zeitschrift für die gesamte Strafrechtswissenschaft* 104: 667–687.

Öztürk, B. 1995. *Yeni Yargıtay Kararları Işığında Delil Yasakları*. Ankara: AÜ SBF İnsan Hakları Merkezi Yayınları.

Öztürk, B., and M.R. Erdem. 2007. *Uygulamalı Ceza Muhakemesi Hukuku*, 11th ed. Ankara: Seçkin.

Packer, H. 1968. *The limits of the criminal sanction*. Stanford: Stanford University Press.

Şahin, C. 1994. *Sanığın Kolluk Tarafından Sorgulanması*. Ankara: Yetkin.

Şahin, C. 1998. *"Yargıtay Kararları Işığında Hukuka Aykırı Deliller ve Değerlendirme Sorunu" in Nurullah Kunter Armağanı*, 343–354. Istanbul: İHF yayını.

Savaş, S., and S. Mollamahmutoğlu (eds.). 1995. *Ceza Muhakemeleri Usulü Kanunun Yorumu*, vol. 1, 2. Ankara: Seçkin.

Şen, E. 1998. *Türk Ceza Yargilamasi Hukuku'nda Hukuka Aykırı Deliller Sorunu*. Istanbul: Beta.

Smith, T.W. 2007. Leveraging norms: The ECHR and Turkey's human rights reforms. In *Human rights in Turkey*, ed. Z.F. Arat-Kabasakal, 262–274. Philadelphia: University of Pennsylvania Press.

Sokullu-Akinci, F. 1998. Recent attempts to guarantee human rights in the Turkish Penal Procedure Law. *Annales de la Faculté de droit d'Istanbul* XXXII(48): 253–269.

Soyaslan, D. 2003. Hukuka Aykırı Deliller. *Atatürk Üniversitesi Erzincan Hukuk Fakültesi Dergisi* 7(3–4): 9–26.

Sözüer, A. 1997. Türkiye'de ve Karşılaştırmalı Hukukta Telefon, Teleks, Faks ve Benzeri Araçlarla Yapılan Özel Haberleşmenin Ceza Yargılaması Önlemi Olarak Denetlenmesi. *İstanbul Üniversitesi Hukuk Fakültesi Mecmuası* 55(3): 6, 66–110.

Tasdemir, K., and R. Özkepir. 2007. *Ceza Muhakemesi Kanunu Şerhi*, vol. I, 3rd ed. Ankara: Turhan Kitabevi.

Tezcan, D., M.R. Erdem, and O. Sancakdar. 2004. *Avrupa İnsan Hakları Sözleşmesi Işığında Türkiye'nin İnsan Hakları Sorunu*. Ankara: Seçkin.

Toroslu, N. 1995. *Hukuka Aykırı Deliller Sorunu, Hamide Topçuoğlu Armağanı*. Ankara: AÜHF yayınları.

Tosun, Ö. 1976. *Ceza ve Medeni Muhakeme Hukuku Açısından Hukuka Aykırı Yollarla Elde Edilen Delillerin İspat Kuvveti*. Istanbul: İHF Yayınları.

Ünal, S. 2000. Avrupa İnsan Hakları Mahkemesi Kararlarının Türk İç Hukukuna Etkileri. *Anayasa Yargısı* 17: 63–85.

Yasar, O. 2007. *Uygulamalı ve Yorumlu Ceza Muhakemesi Kanunu*, 2nd ed. Ankara: Seçkin.

Yenisey, F. 1995. Yasak Yöntemlerle ve Hukuka Aykırı Şekilde Elde Edilen Deliller. In *Ceza Muhakemeleri Usulü Kanunun Yorumu*, vol. 1, ed. S. Savaş and S. Mollamahmutoğlu, 1214–1239. Ankara: Seçkin.

Yurtcan, E. 1998. Yargıtay Kararları Işığında Hukuka Aykırı Delile Dayanma Yasağı. In *Armağanı*, ed. Nurullah Kunter, 519–522. İstanbul: İstanbul Üniversitesi Yayınları.

Yurtcan, E. 2008. *CMK Şerhi*, 5th ed. İstanbul: Beta.

Chapter 13
Serbia: Courts Struggle with a New Categorical Statutory Exclusionary Rule

Snežana Brkić

13.1 The General Theory of Admissibility of Illegally Gathered Evidence

13.1.1 General Constitutional or Statutory Exclusionary Rules

13.1.1.1 The Relationship of Specific Statutory "Nullities" to the General Exclusionary Rule

The Constitution of the Republic of Serbia of 2006[1] does not contain any explicit provisions with regard to nullities or exclusion of evidence, giving the Serbian legislator the ability to write on a clean slate.

A bit of history is in order, however, in order to understand the Serbian approach to nullities. On March 28, 2002, the federal Yugoslav Code of Criminal Procedure of 1976 (hereafter, CCP-Yugoslavia (1976)) went into force as the new Code of Criminal Procedure of the Union of Serbia and Montenegro (hereafter CCP (2001)) after the code was adopted by the legislature in 2001.[2] This was the result of Art. 64(2) of the Constitutional Charter of the State Union of Serbia and Montenegro which provided that Serbia was to enforce the CCP-Yugoslavia (1976) as its own legislation pending the adoption of a new code. The CCP (2001) was amended several times[3] and was actually considered to be a modern and successful code, when Serbia finally adopted its new CCP on May 25, 2006 (hereafter, CCP (2006)).[4]

---

[1] *Official Gazette of the Republic of Serbia* (Off. Gaz. RS) 98/06 (hereafter Const.)

[2] *Off. Gaz. FRY* No. 70/01.

[3] *Off. Gaz. RS* No. 58/04; 85/05; 115/05; 49/07; 122/08; 20/09; 72/09 and 76/10.

[4] *Off. Gaz. RS* No. 46/06.

S. Brkić (✉)
University of Novi Sad, Bulevar cara Lazara 71/64, 21000, Novi Sad, Serbia
e-mail: brksne@uns.ns.ac.rs; sbrkic@pf.uns.ac.rs

S.C. Thaman (ed.), *Exclusionary Rules in Comparative Law*, Ius Gentium: Comparative Perspectives on Law and Justice 20, DOI 10.1007/978-94-007-5348-8_13,

The implementation of the code, however, was delayed several times, with the explanation that material-technical conditions were not yet ready for the transfer of the preliminary investigation from the investigating magistrate to the public prosecutor. Actually, the substance of the new Code was met with wide and strong criticism by expert and scientific circles who found that its adoption was uncalled for, considering that it would have been sufficient enough if the existing Code was merely changed and modified. It seems as if the Ministry of Justice itself did not have a clear concept about this issue, considering the guidelines given to the previous work group and the next-to-last amendments of the 2001 CCP, adopted on September 2009.[5] Once the amendments came into force on 11 September 2009, the CCP (2006) ceased to be in force.

By the end of 2008, a new working group was formed to prepare the text of the new Code of Criminal Procedure of Serbia, which would be based on the prosecutor's investigation. This Code (hereafter CCP (2011)) was adopted on 26 September 2011, while its application is to commence from 15 January 2013.[6] This means that the CCP (2001), which was last amended in 2010, is still in force until the CCP (2011) goes into effect in 2013. Therefore, this article will primarily offer an insight into the solutions currently in force, with reference to those provisions of the new CCP (2011), where they differ. Of necessity, judicial practice will be in reference to the CCP (2001) as it developed over the years.

The attitude of our jurisprudence towards the issue of illegally gathered evidence is evidenced by four groups of rules. The legislator not only prohibits certain methods of gathering and presenting evidence, it also explicitly prohibits the foundation of any court decision on certain types of illegal evidence, and judgments based on a violation of this rule are subject to appeal. When a court decides to exclude evidence, it must immediately remove the evidence physically from the case file and put it in a separate folder, which is then sealed and deposited with the investigating magistrate, so that such evidence cannot be seen or used in the further course of the trial. This prevents the trial court from knowing about such illegal evidence, and either consciously or unconsciously taking it into account even when it is prevented from basing the decision thereon. This is the core approach to exclusion in Serbia, which exists alongside general rules on nullities, and specific evidentiary nullities, which might lead to exclusion of records, procedural sanctions, or even effects on derivative evidence.

The CCP (2001), which is now in force, extends the scope for exclusion of evidence resulting from illegal investigative methods beyond that which existed in the CCP-Yugoslavia (1976).[7] Provisions relate to exclusion of confessions (§ 89(10)

---

[5] *Off. Gaz. RS* No. 72/09.

[6] An exception exists for provisions dealing with organized crime or war crimes, to be heard before a special court, which have been in force since 15 January 2012 (*Off. Gaz. RS* 72/11)

[7] For example, under the CCP-Yugoslavia (1976), a judgment could not be based on a defendant's statement only if it was given under duress, or in the absence of counsel. §89(10) CCP (2001), on the other hand, prohibits not only the use of force or threats, but also the use of deceit, promises, duress, fatigue or other similar methods.

CCP (2001)), witness testimony (§ 99 CCP (2011)), expert testimony (§ 116(1) CCP (2001)), and wiretapping and other eavesdropping (§ 233(4) CCP (2001)). There are no provisions for excluding evidence based on illegal searches or seizures of objects.

It should also be noted, that the new CCP (2011) widens the scope of inadmissible evidence to include all evidence gathered as a result of investigative measures which violate the CCP, or which violate an order given by the public prosecutor (§ 163(3) CCP (2011)). In particular, the code focuses on violations in the area of interception of confidential communications, secret monitoring and recording, "stings" or other feigned criminal conduct, computer data searches, controlled narcotics buys, etc. This goes beyond the exclusionary provisions of the CCP (2001), which refer only to secret monitoring and undercover investigations.

Under the CCP (2001), any information gathered by police in investigating crime may only serve as cognitive leads for furthering the investigation, and is not admissible without more in court. This extends to statements given the police by citizens, presumptive witnesses and even suspects. This changes the widely criticized § 84 CCP-Yugoslavia (1976), which made exceptions and allowed use of such statements either upon the request of the defendant, or by court decision if the charged crime was punishable by 20 years imprisonment.

The CCP (2011) has changed the procedure used in dealing with evidence deemed to be inadmissible prior to trial. First, the special sealed envelope with such evidence is no longer kept with the investigating magistrate since this function no longer exists. The envelope is kept with the pretrial judge, who no longer carries out investigative duties, but also does not act as trial judge. Second, this evidence must be preserved until the case has been appealed and the judgment is final, unless criminal proceedings have been initiated against the official or other person who violated the law in gathering the evidence. In such case, the evidence is preserved to be used in a trial against that person.

Until the enactment of the CCP (2001), the law precisely laid out the rules for gathering and presenting evidence in court and determined when violations of these rules would lead to a sanction, or a "nullity". However, in those days, legal theory and court jurisprudence did not restrictively interpret these provisions. Distinctions were made between explicitly admissible evidence, explicitly inadmissible evidence, and something in between, evidence which was neither explicitly admissible nor inadmissible.[8] For example, it has long been held in the literature that the use of polygraph evidence would constitute a nullity, though the law itself says nothing about this.

In addition to the explicit provisions in the CCP (2001) which prevent use of certain types of evidence, § 18(2) CCP (2001) originally provided that judgments may not be based on evidence gathered in violation of the code, the constitution or

[8] According to one view, any evidence gathered in violation of any constitutional or procedural rule would be inadmissible, even though the evidence was otherwise suitable for establishing a relevant fact. Grubač (2006, 70).

international law. A question arose, as to whether this general exclusionary rule went beyond the specific evidentiary exclusionary rules contained in other sections of the code, or was only of declaratory nature and ceded priority to the more specific rules. The prevailing view, was that it provided a broader exclusionary rule, though dissenting voices wanted to limit it to a mere declaratory provision.[9]

By and large, the case law would occasionally tolerate some irregularities in the gathering of evidence but saw errors in gathering evidence as being absolute, as opposed to errors only relating to its presentation in court.[10] Other voices, however, insisted that there be an explicit legal provision requiring exclusion of the particular type of evidence, otherwise the violations would be treated as a "relative" violation and be subject to balancing.[11] However, the general language used in § 18(2) CCP (2001), which is similar to § CCP (2006), can be criticized, because even the slightest violation of a CCP provision committed in the process of gathering evidence is sanctioned as an absolute violation and would require exclusion. Such an interpretation would render the explicit exclusionary provisions of the CCP meaningless.

I am of the opinion that, other than the specific exclusionary provisions, only violations which affect fundamental human rights under the Constitution or international law, should be treated as "absolute" and lead to non-use of the evidence. I believe that the new formulation of § 18(2) CCP (2001), from September 2009 is better and eliminates some of the ambiguities. It provides: "Court decisions cannot be grounded on such evidence that, due to its essence or method of gathering is in conflict with the Constitution or international law, or is explicitly prohibited by this Code or any other law". A step back in this sense comes with the provision of § 16(1) CCP (2011), which reads: "Court decisions cannot be grounded on such evidence that is, directly or indirectly, due to its essence or its method of collection, contrary to the Constitution, this Code, other laws or generally accepted regulations of international law and ratified international agreements, except in proceedings carried out for the purpose of collecting such evidence". This provision is similar to the original formulation of § 18(2) CCP (2001), and thus reopens the old dilemma about whether any violation of the rules of the CCP, however slight, would render evidence inadmissible at trial and in the court's judgment reasons.

Under the CCP-Yugoslavia (1976), the use of impermissible evidence to justify a criminal judgment, was absolute reversible error unless it was harmless, i.e., there was other admissible evidence which could sustain the judgment. This approach was grounded in the principle of material truth, according to which the general interest in criminal prosecution should not be jeopardized by violation of the rules, if the legally obtained evidence itself would support a conviction. However, this approach tacitly permitted state bodies to abuse procedural rules. Therefore, it was frequently met with bitter criticism in the literature. This relative approach was

---

[9] Such as the judgment HCS Kž. I ok 7/05.

[10] Subotić (2007, 69).

[11] Ibid, 70.

eliminated in the current version of the CCP (2001), which no longer permits such "harmless error" analysis.[12] This should lead to higher discipline of law enforcement organs. Unfortunately, however, the CCP (2011), will return to the old relativist approach. According to § 438(2)(1) CCP (2011), basing a judgment on illegally obtained evidence no longer constitutes an absolute violation, leading to reversal, if other properly admissible evidence will sustain the judgment. This reversion to the old harmless error standard was done in the interests of procedural economy, but I consider it to be an unfortunate step backwards.

13.1.1.2 Indirect Evidence or "Fruits of the Poisonous Tree"

Until 2011, there were no explicit provisions relating to the indirect use of otherwise inadmissible evidence and a controversy existed in Serbian theory and practice in relation to applying the doctrine of the "fruits of poisonous tree". Due to the statutory lacuna, it was left to the courts to improvise solutions in such cases, and they were reluctant to do so.[13] The academic community was divided. Those who advocated in favor of extending exclusion to derivative evidence, relied on moral-ethical arguments, deterrence, improving the discipline of law enforcement, etc. Some reached the same conclusion by interpreting other provisions of the CCP in force at the time.[14] Others pointed to the widespread acceptance of the doctrine in foreign legislation.[15] Some advocated a compromise, balancing approach, which would take into consideration interests of criminal policy.[16]

Those who are against excluding derivative evidence emphasize its unacceptability from a social-ethical point of view. "A dangerous delinquent is set free, society is unprotected and the injured party's family is left without satisfaction".[17] Besides this, strong skepticism has been expressed as to whether a strong exclusionary rule will have a deterrent effect in relation to law enforcement organs.[18] According to this view, excluding fruits of the poisonous tree would not lead to punishment of the organs who violated the law. Others would never exclude derivative evidence if it was to the benefit of the defendant.[19] Finally, still others believe it

---

[12] There are still some cases in which first instance courts simply continue the old practices, although the new law proscribes otherwise.

[13] One of the few cases involved the exclusion by the High Court of Croatia of a photograph taken by the police, which was based on an inadmissible statement by the suspect (HCC Kž. 447/82, 26 May 1982).

[14] Trajković (1978, 6) and Bayer (1978, 18).

[15] Šimatović (1981, 31).

[16] Feješ (1990, 230).

[17] Damaška (1960, 229).

[18] Damaška (1962, 212).

[19] Kobe (1985, 1280).

is too difficult to investigate the causal link between an illegality and the evidence sought to be admitted at trial. Two authors claim the current formulation of § 18(2) CCP (2001), which emphasizes the illegality of the "method of gathering" evidence, would extend to fruits of the poisonous tree,[20] whereas others do not think that formulation signalled a change in the doctrine and treat exclusion of "fruits" as excessive "puritanism" unacceptable in Serbian law.[21] The majority thus take a narrow view when interpreting the illegality of the collection of the evidence. The case law also contains decisions which break the link between an illegal "search" and the seizure of evidence during such a search,[22] and others which would exclude such evidence.[23]

§ 16(1) CCP (2011) is finally unequivocal in extending the exclusionary rule to the fruits of the poisonous tree by providing that court decisions cannot be grounded on evidence which is, *directly or indirectly*, collected in violation of the Constitution, the CCP, or international treaties. When the CCP (2011) goes into effect, there should no longer be any disputes as to whether a violation of fundamental rights will affect the admissibility of evidence seized indirectly as a result.

13.1.2 General Duty to Determine the Truth

The Const.-Serbia makes no mention of any duty of courts or judges to ascertain the truth. This duty, however, is laid out in § 17 CCP (2001), and is referred to as the principle of material truth. It is frequently pointed out that the "truth" in criminal cases is not the same as that sought in civil cases. One differentiates between "material" and "formal" truth, and often sees the adversarial system as one which seeks the "formal" truth, and the mixed inquisitorial system, as that which endeavors to ascertain the "material" truth. Philosophically, however, truth either exists or not, and thus the syntagma of "material truth" is meaningless, and sows confusion.

Although the notion of criminal procedure as a search for truth permeates Serbian legal literature, there has been a certain shift in the attitude toward the principle in criminal procedure theory. It has been transformed from being the ultimate goal of the trial, to a more relative position, where the principle of due process or fair trial, taken from Anglo-American law, now has priority.

One of the most important changes in the CCP (2011), and which gave rise to the most controversy during the legislative process, concerns the role of the court in the proof of facts. According to the new code, the court and other law enforcement

[20] Such interpretation is offered by Škulić (2007, 223) as well as Ilić (2006, 123).

[21] For example, Grubač (2006, 251) and Vasiljević and Grubač (2003, 334).

[22] District Court in Belgrade, Kž. 2333/02 (19 December 2002) and the Third Municipal Court in Belgrade K. 582/02 (18 June 2002).

[23] HCS, Kž. I 1964/2004 (29 December 2004).

bodies, no longer have an obligation to ensure the complete and truthful determination of the facts upon which the judgment is based. The burden of proof is on the public prosecutor, and the court is relegated to only adducing the evidence which is suggested by the parties and has limited powers to, *sua sponte*, intervene in the evidence taking. In defense of the new duties of the court in evidentiary procedure it is often stressed that the principle of truth formulated in § 17 CCP (2001) reflects effort rather than result, ethics more than logic. Thus, court proceedings are not an arena for the epistemological determination of absolute truth—the most that can be achieved is a relative, empirical or subjective truth. As a consequence, the principle of § 17 CCP (2001), could never guarantee the truth value of the ultimate result of criminal proceedings. Besides, the presumption of innocence and the principle of *in dubio pro reo* have made it clear enough upon whom the burden of proof rests. Thus, articulation of the burden of proof in the new CCP (2011) does not merely proclaim the removing of an evidentiary burden from the court, but is a logical consequence of the presumption of innocence and the notion of *in dubio pro reo*.[24]

Therefore, neither the principle of material truth, nor the prohibition against use of illegally gathered evidence are anchored in the constitution, yet both are regulated by the CCP (2001) as basic procedural principles. There is also no doubt that the prohibition on use of illegally gathered evidence works against the determination of truth.[25] To determine which of these two principles should have priority, the underlying values they serve should be taken into account. In the case of evidence exclusion, these are, of course, the protection of fundamental human rights, which should be given priority over the search for truth.

The new CCP (2011) is clear in this respect. It no longer proclaims the court's duty to determine the truth. On the other hand, it recognizies the notion of legally invalid evidence and now undoubtedly embraces the theory of the fruit of the poisonous tree. This leads to the conclusion that the principle of material truth no longer stands in the way of a consistent disqualification of legally invalid evidence.

13.1.3 General Exclusionary Rules Developed in the Case Law of the High Courts of Serbia

It has already been mentioned in Sect. 13.1.1.1 above, that evidence gathered by the police during its preliminary investigation, including statements it has taken from witnesses, is not as such admissible at trial. The high courts of Serbia have been fairly strict in preventing any circumnavigation of this rule, for instance, by calling a police officer as a witness at trial to testify about investigative acts he or she con-

---

[24] Beljanski et al. (2011, 14–15).

[25] The case will only be different in rare instances. For example, if a false confession is made under duress by means of torture, it will not undermine truth in the proceedings.

ducted. A statement given to the police during the pretrial investigation may also not be used as the basis for an expert opinion.[26] In general, inclusion of evidence given to the police as a basis for a judgment is grounds for appeal.[27]

Courts also exclude indirect evidence gained from inadmissible police investigative activity. Thus, photographs of a defendant made while re-enacting the crime at the behest of the police is considered to be an inadmissible statement of the defendant per § 225(1) CCP (2001).[28] Similarly, a photo of a defendant handcuffed is considered to be a "statement" of the defendant made in the absence of defense counsel, and thus inadmissible at trial.[29] On the contrary, one court determined that a photograph of a defendant at the crime scene was not tantamount to being a "statement" and did not exclude it as evidence.[30] A defendant's signature on a receipt for temporarily seized items is a "statement" which must be excluded if taken in violation of the appropriate CCP provisions.[31]

13.2 Rules of Admissibility/Exclusion of Evidence in Relation to Violations of the Right to Privacy

13.2.1 Protection of the Privacy of One's Home

13.2.1.1 Constitutional Provisions

The right to privacy of one's home[32] is guaranteed in Art. 40 Const. Nobody can enter one's home or other premises nor carry out a search therein against the occupant's will without a written court order. The owner or occupant has the right to be present during a search, either personally or through a proxy, and in the company of two adult civilian witnesses. If the owner, occupant or proxy is not present, the search can be carried out in the presence of two adult witnesses. An exception is allowed to the above rules in urgent situations, in order to arrest a criminal or avoid an immediate and serious threat to people or property.

---

[26] In a concrete case, however, a court expert in forensic medicine partially quoted defendants statement given to the police, but he gave his expertise based on material traces found on the spot and the inflicted injuries (HCS, Kž. 154/02, 2 March 2004 and the Municipal Court of Belgrade, K. 5/00 (7 September 2002)).

[27] HCS, Kž. I 2317/05, 7 September 2006 and Municipal Court of Čačak, K. 66/05 (15 September 2009).

[28] HCS, Kž I 698/87(13 October 1987).

[29] HCS, Kž. I 305/2005 (14 September 2005).

[30] HCS, Kž. 510/01(27 December 2001) and the District Court of Belgrade K. 365/99 (7 December 1999).

[31] HCS, Kž. I 4/2004 (3 February 2004).

[32] Serbian law does not recognize a general right to privacy in either the constitution or the CCP, nor do high court decisions recognize such a right.

13.2.1.2 Statutory Provisions

The provisions of the CCP (2001) relating to house searches are by and large echoed in the new CCP (2011). I will note, however, where there are differences.

A search of a dwelling or other premises may be carried out if it is likely that a criminal suspect, evidence of criminal activity, or evidence useful to prove guilt of criminal activity may be found therein. The search must be authorized by a court in the form of a written warrant stating the reason for the search. Unless there are exigent circumstances, in the form of a threat of violence or imminent destruction of evidence, the search warrant must be handed to the person whose premises or whose person is to be subjected to the search before the search is carried out. That person is also asked to volunteer information about the whereabouts of the person or items sought, and is also told he or she has a right to have a lawyer present at the search and, if presence of a lawyer is requested, the commencement of the search must be delayed for up to 3 h to await the lawyer's arrival. Normally searches must commence during the daytime, unless exigent circumstances obviate the necessity for a search warrant. Forced entry is possible if the occupant is not present or refuses to open the door voluntarily, though unnecessary damage should be avoided.

The CCP repeats the constitutional requirements that the defendant or a proxy be present, and that two adult civilian witnesses be present in the capacity of witnesses. These witnesses must be instructed to carefully observe the course of the search before it starts, and to note their objections if the record does not reflect how the search actually transpired. The affected party (or proxy) and the civilian witnesses are asked to sign the report of the search, verifying its accuracy. During the search only such objects and documents may be seized which are linked to the purpose of the search. These items must be truthfully reflected in the report as well as in the receipt given to the affected party.

If a search reveals evidence related to a public criminal offense different from that for which the search was ordered, such objects may also be seized and the public prosecutor must be immediately informed for the purpose of initiating criminal proceedings. If no prosecution is initiated, the items must be returned.

§ 81(1) CCP authorizes police to enter a dwelling or other premises and search without judicial authorization, if the occupant consents, asks for help, or when it is necessary to arrest a fleeing criminal, prevent a serious threat to life or health of a person, or serious damage to property. The homeowner must be advised of the right to refuse consent before his or consent is valid, however. The requirement of civilian witnesses can be ignored in emergency situations. Any warrantless search must be immediately reported to the investigating magistrate, or, if charges have not yet been brought, to the public prosecutor who is in charge.

The CCP (2001) nowhere states that a violation of these provisions will lead to exclusion of evidence.

The CCP (2011) contains only a few changes. § 155 CCP (2011) specifically prescribes the requirements for a search and the public prosecutor must submit a reasoned affidavit comporting with these requirements. The warrant is no longer issued by the investigating magistrate, but by the new pretrial judge, upon motion of the public prosecutor, which reflects the new organization of pretrial criminal proceedings which will go into effect with the new code (§ 153(3) CCP (2011)). The search must be commenced within 8 days of the issuance of the warrant (§155(2) CCP (2011)). Search warrants may now be issued to search automatic data processing equipment and equipment which is used or can be used for storing electronic data. The search of such equipment can be conducted only with judicial authorization, and, if need be, with the assistance of an expert (§ 152(3) CCP (2011)). Finally, searches conducted in the absence of civilian witnesses must be recorded using audio and video equipment or still photography (§ 157 CCP (2011)).

13.2.1.3 Jurisprudence of the High Court of Serbia

The High Court of Serbia has been reluctant to suppress narcotics seized by police without judicial authorization and without the presence of civilian witnesses, if the police claim that the narcotics would have been destroyed if action was not taken promptly.[33] A similar decision was reached in a case where police conducted the search of a yard belonging to a suspect who had already started pulling out cannabis plants, although the search was conducted without a search warrant, civilian witnesses or the usual admonitions.[34] In the aforementioned cases, the conditions for a search of the home without a court order were not met, though the presence of civilian witnesses could be properly waived under the circumstances. Courts are more likely to allow the use of evidence gathered in violation of the requirement of two civilian witnesses.[35] The courts have also correctly ruled that no warrant or witnesses are needed when a car or a person is searched upon reasonable suspicion that they are carrying narcotics.[36]

Evidence has been considered to be inadmissible, however when other provisions of the CCP were violated. For instance, in one case a search was carried out at night and without the presence of civilian witnesses, though no reason therefore was included in the record.[37] In another, the search was without judicial authorization, no urgent reasons were stated and there was no indication the homeowner consented, and the case was not brought immediately thereafter to the investigating magistrate.[38] Finally, in one case, the Serbian High Court ruled that evidence seized in a search conducted with only one of the two required civilian witnesses could not

---

[33] HCS, Kž. 1309/06 (11 September 2006).

[34] HCS, Kž. – I – 2243/2003 (13 September 2004).

[35] HCS, Kž. 1491/04 (4 November 2004) and District Court in Subotica, K. 45/03 (17 March 2004).

[36] HCS, Kž. I 2627/2006 (23 January 2007); HCS, Kž. 2301/05 (26 January 2006) and Distric Court in Prokuplje, K. 6/05 (26 October 2006).

[37] HCS, Kž. 2064/05 (21 December 2005) and District Court in Sombor, K. 72/04 (23 May 2005).

[38] HCS, Kž. 264/2004 (25 March 2004).

be the basis for a judgment of guilt,[39] yet in another case refused to overturn a conviction based on similar facts by resorting to the harmless error analysis which was purportedly prohibited many years ago.[40]

13.2.1.4 Admissibility of Indirect Evidence

As stated previously, the Serbian courts rarely apply the theory of the fruits of the poisonous tree. The courts have, however, refused to admit evidence which was the fruit of an unlawful search of a dwelling or other premises. In explaining their decisions, the courts do not consider the evidence to be "fruits of the poisonous tree" but simply state that the evidence was gathered in a manner prohibited by law.[41]

In my opinion, the acceptance of the theory of the fruits of poisonous tree in search cases is more logical and natural for our courts, than in some other situations, such as for example when a defendant's involuntary confession yields the information about the place where the corpse of a victim is hidden. This increased willingness to accept the doctrine in search cases stems from the fact that the acts of search and seizure have a direct and rigid nexus that can be easily proven.

13.2.2 Protection of Privacy in One's Communications

13.2.2.1 Constitutional Provisions

Art. 41 Const. guarantees the confidentiality of letters and other means of communication. It also provides for exceptions in criminal cases when there is judicial authorization, or for temporary exceptions to protect the security of the state as provided by law. Contrary to Art. 8 European Convention of Human Rights (ECHR), the Serbian constitution does not allow exceptions based on the "economic well-being of the state", "the protection of health and morals", or the "protection of the rights and freedoms of others".

13.2.2.2 Statutory Provisions

Pursuant to § 85 CCP (2001), the investigating magistrate may, *sua sponte* or on request of the public prosecutor, order the seizure of postal or telegraphic

---

[39] HCS, Kž. 1849/03 (29 December 2003) and verdict of the District Court in Belgrade K. 228/03 (24 June 2003).

[40] HCS, Kž. I 57/2005(1)(21 February 2005).

[41] For example HCS Kž. I 1964/2004 (29 December 2004); HCS Kž. 264/2004 (25 March 2004); HCS Kž. I 2064/2005 (21 December 2005).

communications, if such communications could serve as evidence in a criminal investigation. Once seized, these communications are opened by the investigating magistrate in the presence of two civilian witnesses. Such interceptions must be re-examined every 3 months, may be in effect no longer than 9 months, and must be terminated as soon as the reasons which justified them cease to exist.

The CCP (2001), introduced the possibility of intercepting telephone and other confidential conversations, as well as covert video-surveillance. Prior to reforms in 2009, this was a generally applicable measure, but it is now limited by § 504 CCP (2001), to the investigation of cases involving organized crime, corruption and other grave felonies listed in the provision. Judicial orders to intercept oral communications are limited by the principle of necessity, and may only be used if evidence sought cannot be obtained by any other means or its collection would be much more difficult, or would be dangerous.

The interception order is issued in writing by the investigating magistrate, upon request of the public prosecutor, and must contain a statement of reasons. The order must contain the name of the person targeted, the grounds of suspicion, the method of execution, and the scope and duration of the measure. These orders may not extend longer than 6 months, but may be extended twice for periods of 3 months each. The interception must terminate when the reasons which justified it cease to exist.

Postal, telegraphic and other communications service providers are obliged to aid in the execution of such measures. The records of interceptions must be turned over to the investigating magistrate and if, after consultation with the public prosecutor, it is decided the information contained therein will not be needed in the prosecution, the records of the wiretaps or other surveillance must be destroyed. The code explicitly provides for exclusion of information gathered in violation of the statutory rules. After amendments to the CCP (2001) in 2009, § 504z(5) CCP (2001), now allows "accidental findings" related to crimes which were not a subject of the interception order, to be used, but only if they pertain to one of the crimes catalogued in § 504a CCP (2001).

The CCP (2011) has two separate provisions, one for wiretaps and other secret surveillance of communications and the other for secret monitoring and recording. Under the new code, the orders will be issued by the pretrial judge, and not the investigating magistrate, which will be abolished. Regarding wiretapping, there have been few changes, other than the order is originally only good for 3 months, though three extensions, up to a maximum of 1 year are permissible.

The pretrial judge will be able to issue a monitoring and recording order to track suspects in public in order to reveal the activities of the suspect and his or her contacts, as long as the monitoring is limited to public places. Monitoring may also be conducted in relation to a particular place or vehicle, where it is believed the suspect will engage in criminal activity.

Despite the improvements in the law found in the amendments of 2009 and the CCP (2011), another law dealing with state security is still on the books, which contradicts the provisions in the CCP and which contains provisions similar to those of an earlier law which was declared to be unconstitutional. This Law on the Security

Information Agency also does not clearly limit the types of criminal offenses, for which communications may be intercepted. The Military Security Service can also issue orders to wiretap or intercept other communications, but only to the extent provided in the CCP (2001).[42] Finally, the Law on Amendments to the Law on Organization and Jurisdiction of State Bodies in War Crimes Trials,[43] has amended the CCP (2001), to allow wiretaps and other surveillance in relation to persons who are accessories after the fact to war crimes. Orders for such wiretaps may remain in force for up to 6 months, with the law allowing two further 3 month extensions.

13.2.2.3 Jurisprudence of the High Court of Serbia

The High Court of Serbia has ruled that the constitution and CCP do not require judicial authorization to use pen registers or trap-and-trace devices to discover incoming and outgoing telephone activity (i.e., the telephone numbers involved) as long as there is no revelation of the content of the calls.[44] The High Court has also ruled that law enforcement organs may inspect the information contained in a mobile phone, such as reading the contents of SMS communications, without violating the wiretap or search and seizure regulations.[45]

13.2.3 Other Actions Invasive of Privacy Which Could Lead to Suppression of Evidence

13.2.3.1 Searches of the Person, Effects, or Vehicles

Clearly, persons may be searched when arrested or when being committed to jail or prison. Search incident to arrest is allowed, if the person is suspected of bearing arms or tools which can be used for attack, or if there is a suspicion that such person might throw away, hide or destroy evidence.

§ 64 Law on Police allows for police to stop and search a person, his or her personal effects and vehicle, when necessary to find weapons. A search of a person is defined as an inspection of the contents of clothes and shoes. A search of a vehicle is defined as an inspection of all open and closed spaces in a vehicle and transported objects. A search of personal effects is defined as an inspection of objects found on one's person or in one's immediate vicinity or objects belonging to a person who

---

[42] The Law on Security Services of SRY (Off. Gaz. of SRY 37/02, *Off. Gaz. of Serbia and Montenegro* 17/04).

[43] *Off. Gaz. RS* 101/07.

[44] HCS Kž. I 1274/2004 (23 September 2004).

[45] HCS Kž. I 2678/2007 (18 February 2008).

has entrusted them for transport. Technical means and trained dogs can be used when conducting such inspections. An official is authorized to forcefully open a closed vehicle or an object found with the person subject to search. If there are grounds to suspect that a person carries on their person, in the vehicle or transported objects such objects that can serve as evidence in criminal or misdemeanor proceedings, the official is authorized to hold such person until acquiring a search warrant for not longer than 6 h.

13.2.3.2 Protection of Private Data

The Constitution protects private personal data. Gathering, holding, processing and use of personal information is regulated by law.[46] It is prohibited and punishable to use personal information for any other purpose other than that for which it was legally gathered, unless it is needed for the purpose of prosecuting a crime or protecting the security of the Republic of Serbia. Everyone is entitled to be notified about data gathered about them in conformity with the law, and to protection from misuse thereof.

13.2.3.3 Protection of Financial Information

The UN Convention Against Transnational Organized Crime requires that participating states allow courts to order inspections into the banking, financial and commercial transactions of persons suspected of committing crimes. Such authorization was first introduced in Serbia in § 234 CCP (2001), which provides, that when there is a suspicion that a crime punishable by 4 or more years deprivation of liberty has been committed, the investigating magistrate can, upon a written, reasoned petition by the public prosecutor, order a bank, financial or other organization to provide data on the state of a suspect's business or private accounts. The investigating magistrate can also order the said organization to temporarily interrupt financial transactions which are suspected of constituting a criminal offense, or of otherwise constituting money laundering. The public prosecutor has similar authority under § 504k CCP (2001) in cases involving organized crime.

§ 143 CCP (2011) includes similar provisions, but is not limited to crimes punishable in excess of 4 years. The pretrial judge may order an audit of bank and other accounts for up to 3 months, with the possibility of another 3-month extension. The pretrial judge may also order that a transaction be suspended or delayed for up to 72 h.

---

[46] See Law on Protection of Personal Data (*Off. Gaz. RS* 97/2008).

13.2.3.4 Computer Searches and Data Mining

In 2009 the CCP (2001) was amended to introduce a new measure allowing computer data searches, if there are grounds for a suspicion that a crime related to organized crime or corruption or an otherwise serious criminal offense has been committed. Such a search may be ordered only upon a showing of necessity, i.e., that other measures have been or will be ineffective in finding the evidence, or would be excessively dangerous.

The measure involves the automatic search of the stored personal and other related data and their automatic comparison to data referring to the crimes under investigation and the suspect, to confirm or rebut the suspicions. It is ordered by the investigating magistrate upon request of the public prosecutor. The order must clearly specify the data to be searched. The order can remain in effect for a maximum of 6 months, but may be extended once for an additional 3 months. § 178 CCP (2011) reduces the length of such data mining orders to 3 months, but allows two more 3-month extensions.

13.3 Rules on Admissibility/Exclusion of Evidence in Relation to Illegal Interrogations

13.3.1 The General Right to Remain Silent/Privilege Against Self-Incrimination

13.3.1.1 Constitutional Provisions

Art. 23(7) Const. provides that "any person charged or prosecuted for a criminal offense shall not be obliged to provide self-incriminating evidence…nor be obliged to confess guilt". Some consider the privilege against self-incrimination to be an expression of the inviolability of one's human dignity or a consequence of the presumption of innocence.

13.3.1.2 Statutory Provisions

§ 89(2) CCP (2001) provides that a defendant may not be obliged to present a defense or to answer any questions, and that he or she must be advised of these rights before any interrogation. It is a clear statutory anchoring of the right to remain silent as a means to protect against self-incrimination. The practice has thus been abolished, where law enforcement organs advised a defendant that the failure to give a statement could undermine his or her defense. Now, the defendant is cautioned that everything said can be used against him/her as evidence. A judgment of conviction cannot, thus, be based on the defendant's statement, if he/she was not advised of the right to remain silent. §§ 85(5), 68(1) CCP (2011), reaffirm these rights, and prevent the use of statements both where the person has not been advised of the right to silence, but also where the person has not been allowed to exercise this right freely.

13.3.2 Protection Against Involuntary Self-Incrimination

13.3.2.1 Constitutional Provisions

According to Art. 23 Const., human dignity is inviolable, and everyone is obligated to protect it. Everyone has the right to free development of the personality, if this does not violate the rights of others as guaranteed by the Constitution. Art. 24 Const. guarantees the inviolability of human life and Art. 25 Const. guarantees the inviolability of physical and mental integrity, and prohibits torture, or any cruel, inhuman or degrading treatment. According to Art. 28 Const., imprisoned persons must be treated humanely and with respect for human dignity, and any form of violence towards an imprisoned person is prohibited. Art. 28 Const. also explicitly prohibits the extortion of statements from persons deprived of liberty.

13.3.2.2 Statutory Provisions

§ 89(8) CCP (2001) states that a defendant may not be subjected to force, threats, deceit, coercion, exhaustion or other similar means to obtain a statement or confession or any other form of behavior which could be used against him/her as evidence. A judgment of guilt may not be based on evidence gathered in violation of these prohibitions.

The prohibition of self-incrimination also implies that a defendant cannot be coerced to give a statement through use of medical interventions, narco-analysis, lobotomy, or other practices which would affect the consciousness and will of the defendant thus preventing a voluntary choice between giving a statement or remaining silent. The use of hypnosis has also been held to fall within the prohibitions and would render any ensuing statement inadmissible.

The CCP (2011) makes it clear, as did the CCP (2001), that the privilege against self-incrimination does not prevent law enforcement organs from taking fingerprints, photographs, blood samples, urine samples, unless the procedure would affect the defendant's health. § 142 CCP (2011) will also allow the taking of samples for forensic-genetic analysis upon order of either the public prosecutor or the court.

13.3.3 The Miranda Paradigm

13.3.3.1 Constitutional Provisions

Art. 27(2) Const. stipulates that a person, upon arrest, must be immediately informed of his or her rights in a language this person understands, as well as of the reasons for their arrest and the charges brought against them. Art. 29 Const. provides that a person arrested without a judicial warrant, must be immediately informed of the right to remain silent and not to be interrogated without the presence of a defense attorney of their own choice or counsel appointed free-of-charge by the state if the arrested person is unable to afford counsel.

13.3.3.2 Statutory Provisions

According to § 5 CCP (2001), an arrested person must immediately be informed of the reasons for the arrest and all the charges brought against them as well as the following rights, *inter alia*: (1) to remain silent, and that anything and everything they say can be used as evidence against them; (2) to the assistance of an attorney of their own choice; (3) to consult with a lawyer without being interrupted; (4) to have counsel present when questioned. Pursuant to § 13(3) CCP (2001), law enforcement interrogators must advise a suspect before the first interrogation that he or she has the right to consult with an attorney and to have the attorney present at questioning, and that anything they say can be used against them as evidence. § 89(2) CCP (2001) provides that any statement taken from a person who was not advised of his/her rights may not be used as evidence in a criminal trial.

13.3.3.3 Jurisprudence of the High Court of Serbia

The position of the High Court of Serbia is that if the investigating magistrate fails to *caution* a person charged with a crime that everything she says may be used as evidence against her, this does not make an ensuing statement inadmissible evidence, if the defendant has been *instructed* as to their rights as provided for under the CCP. The High Court explains this decision by distinguishing between the mandatory *instruction* required by §§ 89(2), 13(3) CCP (2001), that they are under no obligation to give a statement, that they have a right to speak to an attorney before the first interrogation and to have the attorney present during any questioning, and the later *caution*, required by the same sections, that everything they say may be used against them as evidence. According to the court, a clear distinction is made between the rights a person charged with a crime must be advised of before the first questioning and the caution they are given, if they do choose to speak.

Since § 89(10) CCP (2001) only mandates exclusion when a person has not been informed of their rights per § 89(2) CCP (2001), then the failure to *caution* would not trigger the same sanction.[47] From a formal-logical point of view, this interpretation by the High Court of Serbia is correct. However, I am not so sure that the legislature's intent was to make a terminological and legal distinction between instruction as to rights and cautions.

13.4 Conclusion

There are two fundamental theoretical approaches to excluding evidence: the prohibition against using certain types of evidence to prove guilt in a criminal case and the notion of inadmissible, legally invalid evidence or "nullities". The latter notion of inadmissible evidence would, of course, extend to evidence which it is unlawful to use to prove guilt. There is considerable confusion in the use of this theoretical terminology.

Many writers do not use the notion of prohibitions on proof (*Beweisverwertungsverbot*), imported into the doctrine by Beling in the early twentieth century.[48] In the former Yugoslavia, this term was introduced by Munda, followed by Damaška, Kobe and Krapac. In today's Serbia, the term is still used, for example, by Grubač, Feješ and Škulić. In the most general sense, prohibitions on proof place limitations on evidence in order to protect other legal interests. Krapac understands them to be legal rules which: (1) prohibit either obtaining and using certain kinds of evidence, or obtaining and using it in particular ways; or (2) prohibit using certain evidentiary procedures for proving facts in a criminal case. He distinguishes between *preventive* prohibitions and *exclusionary* prohibitions.[49] Preventive prohibitions play their role during the investigative stage, when law enforcement organs collect evidence. The exclusionary prohibitions aim at impeding the use of evidence that has already been obtained. It might take effect either during the presentation of the evidence at trial (or during the preliminary investigation) or in the stage of evaluating the evidence (for instance, in judgment reasons).

In the bulk of the literature, this distinction is ignored in favor of a rather superficial distinction between *admissible* and *inadmissible* evidence, determined by the method of the collection of the evidence. Among the older generation of theoreticians, this approach is taken by Bayer, Damaška, Aleksić and Vasiljević, whereas among contemporaries, it is espoused by Grubač, Feješ and Škulić. This is similar to the Anglo-American concept of the exclusion of evidence, though only to

[47] HCS, Kž. I o.k. 6/2005(2)(14 December 2006); HCS, Kž. I 1360/2004 (17 October 2005).

[48] See Gless, Ch. 5, p. 116; Thaman, Ch. 17, p. 141.

[49] Krapac (1990, 13–14).

a certain point, mainly attributable to the fact that the principle of material truth still holds strong sway in Serbia and exclusionary rules are seen as limiting this goal of criminal procedure. A second distinction, is that evidentiary prohibitions in Europe are normally introduced by the legislator, whereas in Anglo-American law exclusionary rules are overwhelmingly a product of the case law.

In Serbia, since the constitution is silent about both exclusionary rules and the search for truth, the interrelation of the two has been left to the legislator. But, until the CCP (2011), the legislator's approach has been inconsistent, largely due to the continued adherence to the principle of material truth, which is unfriendly towards the exclusion of relevant evidence. The development of exclusionary rules has been extensive, but has not proceeded in a straight line. As far as the jurisprudence of the High Court of Serbia is concerned it has often acted to overturn erroneous decisions of the lower courts, though it has, on occasion, been hesitant and contradictory in its rulings and has sometimes returned to outmoded precedent. It must be emphasized, however, that the case law is not as important in Serbia, as it is in a common law country like the United States.

The debate as to the future essence of Serbia's exclusionary rule was stuck at an "intermediate stage" during the time when the CCP (2001) was still in force, and while the highly criticized, and now moribund CCP (2006) was still awaiting to go into force. This quandary is now a thing of the past, now that the amendments of 2009 have taken effect, and the CCP (2011) is on the verge of going into effect on January 15, 2013.

The CCP (2011) introduces two key innovations. First, it abandons the principle of material truth, thus relieving the court from the obligation of itself determining the facts. Evidentiary initiative lies nearly exclusively with the parties, while the burden of proof lies with the prosecutor. This removes a traditional and huge obstacle to a wider promotion of the concept of legally invalid evidence. Secondly, the new code, for the first time, expresses the legislator's commitment to the doctrine of the "fruits of the poisonous tree", which will certainly eliminate the inconsistencies that have plagued the theory and the judicial case law.

Bibliography

Bayer, V. 1978. Pravno nevaljani dokazi i posljedice njihove upotrebe kod donošenja sudskih odluka u krivičnom postupku. *Pravni život* 1978(5): 3–20.

Beljanski, S., G.P. Ilić, and M. Majić. 2011. *Zakonik o krivičnom postupku*. Beograd: Službeni glasnik.

Damaška, M. 1960. Procesne posledice upotrebe dokaza pribavljenih na nezakonit način. *Naša zakonitost* 1960(6): 220–229.

Damaška, M. 1962. *Okrivljenikov iskaz kao dokaz u suvremenom krivičnom postupku*. Zagreb: Narodne novine.

Feješ, I. 1990. *Procesne sankcije,* Pravni fakultet u Beogradu. An unpublished PhD thesis.

Grubač, M. 2006. *Krivično procesno pravo*. Beograd: Službeni glasnik.

Ilić, G. 2006. Žalba protiv prvostepene krivične presude—osvrt na nova zakonska rešenja. *Revija za kriminologiju i krivično pravo* 2006(2): 117–128.

Kobe, P. 1985. Rezultati prisluškivanja kao dokaz u krivičnom postupku. *Naša zakonitost* 1985(12): 1280–1294.

Krapac, D. 1990. Prilog razmatranju pojma dokaznih zabrana u suvremenom krivičnom postupku. *Pravni vjesnik* 1990(6): 11–31.

Munda A. 1956. Dokazne prepovedi v jugoslavanski kazenski zakonodaji. *Zbornik znanstvenih razprav* XXVI letnik 1956, 123–139.

Šimatović, D. 1981. Protuzakonito pribvljanje dokaza. *Odvjetnik* 1981(11–12): 31–32.

Škulić, M. 2007. *Krivično procesno pravo, opšti deo*. Beograd: Službeni glasnik.

Subotić, D. 2007. Nedozvoljeni dokazi u krivičnom postupku. *Sudska praksa* 2007(3–4): 68–70.

Trajković, S. 1978. Posledice upotrebe dokaza dobijenih na zakonom zabranjeni način prema odredbama novog Zakona o krivičnom postupku. *Glasnik Advokatske komore Vojvodine* 1978(11): 1–11.

Vasiljević, T., and M. Grubač. 2003. *Komentar Zakonika o krivičnom postupku*. Beograd: Službeni glasnik.

Part III
The Fair Trial Test for Exclusion

Chapter 14
England and Wales: Fair Trial Analysis and the Presumed Admissibility of Physical Evidence

Andrew L.-T. Choo

14.1 The General Theory of Admissibility of Illegally Gathered Evidence

The law governing the use of illegally gathered evidence in criminal trials in England and Wales[1] is derived from statute law, case law and the European Convention on Human Rights (hereafter ECHR). There are, in essence, three automatic exclusionary rules. First, as we shall see below, any evidence obtained by torture is automatically inadmissible. Secondly, the Regulation of Investigatory Powers Act 2000 has been held to prohibit impliedly the admission in evidence of any intercepted communications to which the Act applies, including communications intercepted illegally. Thirdly, as will be discussed in greater detail below, a confession made by an accused person that was obtained by oppression, or by words or actions conducive to unreliability, is automatically inadmissible in evidence at the behest of the prosecution.

Any illegally gathered evidence not falling in one of the above three categories is presumptively admissible, but may be excluded in the exercise of the judicial discretion to exclude prosecution evidence to ensure a "fair trial". This "fair trial" discretion has long been recognized at common law,[2] and is also encapsulated in § 78(1) of the Police and Criminal Evidence Act 1984 (PACE), which provides:

> In any proceedings the court may refuse to allow evidence on which the prosecution proposes to rely to be given if it appears to the court that, having regard to all the circumstances, including the circumstances in which the evidence was obtained, the admission of the evidence would have such an adverse effect on the fairness of the proceedings that the court ought not to admit it.

---

[1] In this paper, I have drawn on work published elsewhere, particularly in Choo (2012).

[2] R v. Sang, [1980] A.C. 402 (H.L.).

A.L.-T. Choo (✉)
Professor of Law, Law School of the City University of London, Matrix Chambers, Griffin Building, Gray's Inn, London WC1R 5LN, UK
e-mail: andrew.choo.1@city.ac.uk

S.C. Thaman (ed.), *Exclusionary Rules in Comparative Law*, Ius Gentium: Comparative Perspectives on Law and Justice 20, DOI 10.1007/978-94-007-5348-8_14,

The Human Rights Act 1998, which came fully into force on 2 October 2000, has the effect of "incorporating" the ECHR into domestic law by making certain Convention rights "directly enforceable in domestic courts".[3] In very brief terms, the purport of the Human Rights Act is as follows. Despite preserving the principle of Parliamentary sovereignty as far as primary legislation is concerned,[4] the Act provides that, in so far as it is possible to do so, all legislation must be read and given effect in a way that is compatible with the Convention rights.[5] If, however, primary legislation cannot be read in a way that renders it compatible with the Convention rights, the court must still apply it, but will be able, if it is a superior court, to issue a declaration of incompatibility.[6] Furthermore, public authorities, including courts and tribunals,[7] are obliged to act in a way which is compatible with the Convention rights[8] unless provisions in primary legislation require them to act differently.[9] "A court or tribunal determining a question which has arisen in connection with a Convention right must take into account any … judgment [or] decision … of the European Court of Human Rights [hereafter ECtHR]… whenever made or given, so far as, in the opinion of the court or tribunal, it is relevant to the proceedings in which that question has arisen".[10]

Determination of the extent to which criminal evidence doctrine has been reshaped by Art. 6(1) ECHR, which guarantees the right to a fair trial, has proved crucial in recent years, and has particular relevance to the subject matter of this paper.

14.2 Rules of Admissibility/Exclusion in Relation to Violations of the Right to Privacy

Art. 8 ECHR, which essentially guarantees the right to privacy, provides as follows:

1. Everyone has the right to respect for his private and family life, his home and his correspondence.
2. There shall be no interference by a public authority with the exercise of this right except such as is in accordance with the law and is necessary in a democratic society in the interests of national security, public safety or the economic well-being of the country, for the prevention of disorder or crime, for the protection of health or morals, or for the protection of the rights and freedoms of others.

The evidential implications of a violation of Art. 8 ECHR will now be considered.

---

[3] See generally Berger (2007), Choo and Nash (2003), Emmerson et al. (2007), Friedman (2002), Jackson (2005), Mirfield (2003), Ovey (1998), and Sharpe (2007).

[4] Human Rights Act 1998, c. 42, § 3(2)(b) (U.K.).

[5] Ibid, § 3(1).

[6] Ibid, § 4(2). The superior courts include the House of Lords (or, from October 2009, the Supreme Court), the High Court and the Court of Appeal. See § 4(5).

[7] Ibid, § 6(3)(a).

[8] Ibid, § 6(1).

[9] Ibid, § 6(2).

[10] Ibid, § 2(1)(a).

14.2.1 The Jurisprudence of the European Court of Human Rights

A useful starting point is the May 2000 judgment of *Khan v. United Kingdom.*[11] Having failed in both the Court of Appeal[12] and House of Lords,[13] Khan took his case to Strasbourg. The essential facts were that on being interviewed at a police station after his arrival from Pakistan, Khan denied any offense and declined to answer most of the questions put to him. He was released without charge. Some months later he visited the home of a person whom the police suspected of involvement in the supply of heroin on a large scale. As a result of these suspicions they had installed an aural surveillance device on the exterior of the property, without the knowledge or consent of the owner or occupier of the property. An audio recording was obtained of a conversation that took place between Khan and others in which Khan made statements plainly demonstrating his involvement in the importation of heroin. The ECtHR observed: "There was ... no domestic law regulating the use of covert listening devices at the relevant time. ... It follows that the interference in the present case cannot be considered to be 'in accordance with the law', as required by Article 8(2) of the Convention. Accordingly, there has been a violation of Article 8".[14] On the issue of exclusion the Court commented as follows:

> With specific reference to the admission of the contested tape recording, the Court notes that ... the applicant had ample opportunity to challenge both the authenticity and the use of the recording. He did not challenge its authenticity, but challenged its use at the '*voir dire*' and again before the Court of Appeal and the House of Lords. The Court notes that at each level of jurisdiction the domestic courts assessed the effect of admission of the evidence on the fairness of the trial by reference to section 78 of PACE...[15]
>
> The Court would add that it is clear that, had the domestic courts been of the view that the admission of the evidence would have given rise to substantive unfairness, they would have had a discretion to exclude it under section 78 of PACE.[16]
>
> In these circumstances, the Court finds that the use at the applicant's trial of the secretly taped material did not conflict with the requirements of fairness guaranteed by Article 6(1) of the Convention.[17]

The fact that the evidence "was in effect the only evidence against the applicant" was considered irrelevant in the circumstances of the case:

---

[11] Khan v. United Kingdom (2001), 31 E.H.R.R. 45, 1016. See generally Nash (2000), and Tain (2000).

[12] R. v. Khan, [1995] Q.B. 27.

[13] R. v. Khan, [1997] A.C. 558.

[14] Khan, 31 E.H.R.R. 45, 1023, §§ 27–28. See also Elahi v. United Kingdom (2007), 44 E.H.R.R. 645. Note that there is now legal regulation of covert surveillance in the Regulation of Investigatory Powers Act 2000.

[15] Khan, 31 E.H.R.R. 45, 1027, § 38.

[16] Ibid, § 39.

[17] Ibid, § 40.

> The relevance of the existence of evidence other than the contested matter depends on the circumstances of the case. In the present circumstances, where the tape recording was acknowledged to be very strong evidence, and where there was no risk of it being unreliable, the need for supporting evidence is correspondingly weaker.[18]

Two themes emerge clearly from this judgment: first, that the reliability of the evidence is treated as a paramount consideration; and, secondly, that compliance with the right to a fair trial guaranteed by Art. 6 ECHR will be considered to be secured by the appropriate use of § 78(1) of PACE. The later judgment of the ECtHR in *Allan v. United Kingdom*[19] brings into sharp focus the respective approaches of the Court to different types of evidence obtained in violation of Art. 8 ECHR. When Allan was in custody with one Leroy Grant on suspicion of having committed a robbery, the police received information that Allan had been involved in a murder. Authority was accordingly granted by the Chief Constable for the cell and visiting areas used by Allan and Grant to be fitted with audio and video equipment. When Allan was subsequently arrested for the murder he exercised his right to remain silent. However, recordings were made of Allan's conversations (1) with a friend, JNS, in the prison visiting area, (2) with Grant in the cell in which they were held, and (3) with H, a police informant who was placed in Allan's cell for the purpose of eliciting information from him. He argued, *inter alia*, that the use of the evidence of these recordings (which, together with the testimony of H, constituted the principal evidence against him) violated Art. 6(1) ECHR.

The ECtHR Court was "not persuaded that the use of the taped material concerning Leroy Grant and JNS at the applicant's trial conflicted with the requirements of fairness guaranteed by Art 6(1) of the Convention":

> …the applicant's counsel challenged the admissibility of the recordings in a *voir dire*, and was able to put forward arguments to exclude the evidence as unreliable, unfair or obtained in an oppressive manner. The judge in a careful ruling, however, admitted the evidence, finding that it was of probative value and had not been shown to be so unreliable that it could not be left to the jury to decide for themselves. This decision was reviewed on appeal by the Court of Appeal which found that the judge had taken into account all the relevant factors and that his ruling could not be faulted. At each step of the procedure, the applicant had therefore been given an opportunity to challenge the reliability and significance of the recording evidence.[20]

In relation to the conversations with H, however, there had been a violation of Art. 6(1) ECHR:

> In contrast to the position in the *Khan* case, the admissions allegedly made by the applicant to H, and which formed the main or decisive evidence against him at trial, were not spontaneous and unprompted statements volunteered by the applicant, but were induced by the persistent

[18] Ibid, 1026–1027, § 37. See also P.G. v. United Kingdom (2008), 56 E.H.R.R. 51, 1272; see generally Nash (2002); Bykov v. Russia, No. 4378/02, ECHR, 10 March 2009, Lee Davies v. Belgium, No. 18704/05, ECHR, 28 July 2009.

[19] Allan v. United Kingdom (2002), 36 E.H.R.R. 12, 143. See generally Nash (2003).

[20] Allan, 36 E.H.R.R. 12, 143, 157–158, § 48.

> questioning of H, who, at the instance of the police, channelled their conversations into discussions of the murder in circumstances which can be regarded as the functional equivalent of interrogation, without any of the safeguards which would attach to a formal police interview, including the attendance of a solicitor and the issuing of the usual caution. While it is true that there was no special relationship between the applicant and H and that no factors of direct coercion have been identified, the Court considers that the applicant would have been subject to psychological pressures which impinged on the 'voluntariness' of the disclosures allegedly made by the applicant to H: he was a suspect in a murder case, in detention and under direct pressure from the police in interrogations about the murder, and would have been susceptible to persuasion to take H, with whom he shared a cell for some weeks, into his confidence.[21]

It is no surprise, in the light of the stance taken earlier by the ECtHR in *Khan*, that the admission of evidence of undisputed reliability was considered not to violate Art. 6 ECHR, while Art. 6 was held to have been violated by the admission of evidence of questionable reliability.

14.2.2 The Domestic Jurisprudence

A few illustrations from English case law of the courts' approach to the exclusion of illegally gathered evidence in the light of Arts. 8 and 6 ECHR may now be provided. In *R v. Sanghera* the search of the defendant's premises had been conducted in breach of what was then § 1.3 (now 2.3) of Code of Practice B, PACE, in that his consent to the search had not been obtained. The Court of Appeal held that appropriate consideration of § 78(1) was sufficient to ensure compliance with the ECHR. The Court was of the view, however, that the trial judge had exercised his discretion appropriately in not excluding the evidence:

> It is important to note that ... the appellant did not challenge the fact of the discovery of the money. ... There was no issue as to the reliability of the evidence. ... In addition, there is the fact that there is no suggestion that the police were acting other than bona fide. ... The money was in the box above the safe. ... If the judge had acceded to the submissions that were made to him, the result of the failure to obtain formal written consent ... would have had the consequence of interfering with the achievement of justice.[22]

Once again, the commitment to accurate fact-finding is immediately apparent.

In *R v. Loveridge*, the Court of Appeal held the secret filming by police of defendants in the cell area of a magistrates' court to be in contravention of § 41 of the Criminal Justice Act 1925 and a breach of Art. 8 ECHR:

> However, so far as the outcome of this appeal is concerned, the breach of Article 8 is only relevant if it interferes with the right of the applicants to a fair hearing. Giving full weight to the breach of the Convention, we are satisfied that the contravention of Article 8 did not

---

[21] Ibid, 159, § 52.

[22] R. v. Sanghera, [2001] 1 Crim. App. 20, ¶ 299, [15]–[17].

> interfere with the fairness of the hearing. The judge was entitled to rule as he did. The position is the same so far as section 78 of the Police and Criminal Evidence Act 1984 is concerned. We would here refer to the judgment of Swinton Thomas LJ in the case of *Perry* … [23]

The remarks of Swinton Thomas LJ in *R v. Perry*,[24] a decision on video identification evidence obtained in consequence of breaches of Code of Practice D, probably represent the high-water mark of judicial antagonism to the idea that the law on the exclusion of illegally gathered evidence may be altered by the Human Rights Act 1998:

> The purpose underlying the [Human Rights] Act is to protect citizens from a true abuse of human rights. If, as it seems to us has happened in this case, it is utilised by lawyers to jump on a bandwagon and to attempt to suggest that there has been a breach of the Act or of the Convention when either it is quite plain that there has not or alternatively the matter is amply covered by domestic law, then not only will the lawyers, but the Act itself (which is capable of doing a great deal of good to the citizens of this country) will be brought into disrepute. … In our judgment questions of breaches of the European Convention on Human Rights or the Act should not have formed any part of this appeal. All the submissions which have been made can properly and readily be dealt with under the provisions of our national law. It is devoutly to be hoped that the court's time will not be utilised in the future in this way.[25]

In *R v. Button* the Court of Appeal observed: "The intrusion or interference has already occurred, the evidence obtained is admissible under English law and so the court's obligation is confined to deciding whether or not, having regard to the way in which the evidence was obtained, it would be fair to admit it".[26] The idea that a breach of Art. 8 ECHR might be able to result in the automatic inadmissibility of any resulting evidence was greeted with horror: "What [counsel for the appellants] is saying is that the court is bound to exclude any evidence obtained in breach of Article 8 because otherwise it would be acting unlawfully. This is a startling proposition and one which we are pleased and relieved to be able to reject".[27]

In sum, therefore, the approach taken is that a court's "powers to regulate the admission of evidence, pursuant inter alia to s 78 and its inherent jurisdiction, represent means of ensuring that Article 6 is not infringed. … unlawfully obtained evidence may be inadmissible but is not *ipso facto* so. Nor is a trial in which it is relied upon necessarily unfair".[28] It is undeniable that the maintenance of this approach by the domestic courts of England and Wales has been assisted in no small measure by *Khan v. UK* and other jurisprudence from the ECtHR.

---

[23] R. v. Loveridge, [2001] EWCA (Crim) 973 2 Crim. App. 29 ¶ 591, [33] (2001). See also R. v. Lawrence, [2002] Crim. LR 584.

[24] *The Times*, Apr. 28, 2000.

[25] Quotation from transcript from Smith Bernal.

[26] R. v. Button, [2005] EWCA (Crim) 516, ¶ 23.

[27] Ibid, ¶ 24.

[28] R. v. Hardy, [2002] EWCA (Crim) 3012, [2003] 1 Cr. App. R. 30, ¶ 494, [18]–[19] (2003).

14.3 Rules of Admissibility/Exclusion in Relation to Violations of Article 3 of the European Convention on Human Rights

Art. 3 ECHR provides: "No one shall be subjected to torture or to inhuman or degrading treatment or punishment". In *A v. Secretary of State for the Home Department*,[29] the House of Lords considered the issue of evidence obtained by torture. While the case concerned evidence of statements, which carry obvious dangers of unreliability, the Law Lords clearly assumed that their ruling would cover *any* evidence. The House of Lords held that there is a rule of law that evidence obtained by torture is automatically inadmissible in proceedings in the United Kingdom, regardless of where, by whom and against whom the torture was committed. Lord Hoffmann noted that

> the law has moved on. English law has developed a principle ... that the courts will not shut their eyes to the way the accused was brought before the court *or the evidence of his guilt was obtained*. Those methods may be such that it would compromise the integrity of the judicial process, dishonour the administration of justice, if the proceedings were to be entertained *or the evidence admitted*. In such a case the proceedings may be stayed *or the evidence rejected* on the ground that there would otherwise be an abuse of the processes of the court.[30]

In the words of Lord Carswell, "the duty not to countenance the use of torture by admission of evidence so obtained in judicial proceedings must be regarded as paramount and ... to allow its admission would shock the conscience, abuse or degrade the proceedings and involve the state in moral defilement".[31]

The decision in *A* represents an acknowledgement that there may be circumstances in which a court should be prepared, "on moral grounds",[32] to exclude reliable evidence because of the manner in which it was gathered. How far the spirit of *A* will be extended in the coming years remains to be seen.

The House of Lords made it clear in *A* that the exclusionary rule in question covered evidence obtained by torture only, and did not extend to evidence obtained by inhuman or degrading treatment. Such evidence was considered in *Jalloh v. Germany*.[33] As a result of the forced administration of emetics, the defendant regurgitated a bag of cocaine that he had swallowed. The Grand Chamber of the ECtHR held that the evidence had been obtained as a result of "inhuman and degrading

---

[29] A. v. Sec'y of State for the Home Dep't (No. 2), [2005] UKHL 71, [2006] 2 A.C. 221. See generally Choo and Nash (2007), Foster (2006), Grief (2006), Mackie (2006), Rasiah (2006), and Samiloff (2006).

[30] A. v. Sec'y of State for the Home Dep't (No.2), [2005], UKHL 71, 87 (italics added).

[31] Ibid, 150.

[32] Ibid, 148 per Lord Carswell.

[33] Jalloh v. Germany (G.C.) (2007), 44 E.H.R.R. 32, 667.

treatment" and therefore in breach of Art. 3 ECHR.[34] The Court did not consider that the evidence had been obtained by torture under Art. 3 ECHR; if it had been, it would have had to be automatically excluded,[35] an approach consistent with that of English law. The Court considered that the question whether evidence obtained as a result of inhuman and degrading treatment, but not torture, was also subject to an automatic exclusionary rule could be left open.[36] The Court concluded on the facts of the case, however, that the admission of the evidence did violate the defendant's right to a fair trial under Art. 6 ECHR:

> The Court notes that, even if it was not the intention of the authorities to inflict pain and suffering on the applicant, the evidence was obtained by a measure which breached one of the core rights guaranteed by the Convention. Furthermore, it was common ground between the parties that the drugs obtained by the impugned measure were the decisive element in securing the applicant's conviction. It is true that, as was equally uncontested, the applicant was given the opportunity, which he took, of challenging the use of the drugs obtained by the impugned measure. However, any discretion on the part of the national courts to exclude that evidence could not come into play as they considered the administration of emetics to be authorised by the domestic law. Moreover, the public interest in securing the applicant's conviction cannot be considered to have been of such weight as to warrant allowing that evidence to be used at the trial. ... the measure targeted a street dealer selling drugs on a relatively small scale who was finally given a six months' suspended prison sentence and probation.[37]

The judgment in *Jalloh*, like that in *Khan*, suggests therefore that, outside the specific context of torture, what is being advocated is effectively a balancing approach to the question whether evidence obtained in breach of the Convention should be excluded. Factors that will be considered by the ECtHR in determining whether Art. 6 ECHR has been breached by the admission of the evidence include the effect of the misconduct on the ability of the trial to make an accurate determination of guilt, the nature of the right that has been breached, the existence or otherwise of adequate mechanisms in domestic law for the misconduct to be taken into account, and the public interest in bringing to conviction the perpetrator of such an offense. It is interesting to speculate whether the ECtHR would have decided *Jalloh* differently if the relevant German law had permitted the possibility of exclusion to be given due consideration.

---

[34] Ibid, 689, § 82.

[35] Ibid, 693, § 105: "incriminating evidence—whether in the form of a confession or real evidence—obtained as a result of acts of violence or brutality or other forms of treatment which can be characterised as torture—should never be relied on as proof of the victim's guilt, irrespective of its probative value".

[36] Ibid, 694, § 107.

[37] Ibid.

14.4 Rules of Admissibility/Exclusion in Relation to Illegal Interrogations

14.4.1 Confession Evidence

14.4.1.1 Definition of Confession

§ 76(1) PACE provides that "a confession made by an accused person may be given in evidence against him in so far as it is relevant to any matter in issue in the proceedings and is not excluded by the court in pursuance of this section". A confession is defined in § 82(1) PACE as *including* "any statement wholly or partly adverse to the person who made it, whether made to a person in authority or not and whether made in words or otherwise."

14.4.1.2 Mandatory Exclusion

§ 76(2) PACE provides that there are two grounds[38] on which a confession sought to be used at trial by the prosecution must be excluded from evidence:

> If, in any proceedings where the prosecution proposes to give in evidence a confession made by an accused person, it is represented to the court that the confession was or may have been obtained—
>
> (a) by oppression of the person who made it; or
> (b) in consequence of anything said or done which was likely, in the circumstances existing at the time, to render unreliable any confession which might be made by him in consequence thereof,
>
> the court shall not allow the confession to be given in evidence against him except in so far as the prosecution proves to the court beyond reasonable doubt that the confession (notwithstanding that it may be true) was not obtained as aforesaid.

The two grounds for the mandatory exclusion of confession evidence will now be considered in turn.

Oppression

A confession must be excluded from evidence if it was obtained by *oppression* of the person making it. The word "oppression" is defined in § 76(8) PACE as *including* "torture, inhuman or degrading treatment, and the use or threat of violence (whether or not amounting to torture)". This, then, is a wider ground for automatic exclusion than that applicable to *non-confession* evidence. The decisions of the Court of

[38] See generally Biçak (2001).

Appeal on confession evidence in which the meaning of "oppression" has been considered suggest, however, that it connotes fairly harsh treatment of the confessor, and therefore that it is only in rare cases that the prosecution would be unable to prove that a confession was *not* obtained by oppression. In the leading case of *R v. Fulling*, the Court of Appeal held that

> 'oppression' in section 76(2)(*a*) should be given its ordinary dictionary meaning. The *Oxford English Dictionary* as its third definition of the word runs as follows: 'Exercise of authority or power in a burdensome, harsh, or wrongful manner; unjust or cruel treatment of subjects, inferiors, etc.; the imposition of unreasonable or unjust burdens.' One of the quotations given under that paragraph runs as follows: 'There is not a word in our language which expresses more detestable wickedness than oppression.'[39]

Thus the Court of Appeal found no oppression in *R v. Emmerson* where one of the interviewing officers, giving the impression of impatience and irritation, "raised his voice and used some bad language".[40] By contrast, in *R v. Paris*, one of the co-accused, Miller, was

> bullied and hectored. The officers, particularly Detective Constable Greenwood, were not questioning him so much as shouting at him what they wanted him to say. Short of physical violence, it is hard to conceive of a more hostile and intimidating approach by officers to a suspect. It is impossible to convey on the printed page the pace, force and menace of the officer's delivery.[41]

The Court of Appeal held that this conduct clearly amounted to oppression.

Words or Actions Conducive to Unreliability

In essence, § 76(2)(b) PACE is directed at the issue of potentially unreliable confession evidence. It requires the court to determine whether the confession was obtained *in consequence of* something *said or done* which, taking into account *all the circumstances* prevailing at the time, was *likely* to cause *any confession* which might be made to be *unreliable*.

The condition that the confession be one made in consequence of something "said or done" has been interpreted narrowly. In *R v. Goldenberg*, the defendant, a heroin addict, had *himself* requested the interview with the police during which the relevant confessions were made, apparently because he was suffering from withdrawal symptoms and wished to obtain bail in order to feed his addiction. The Court of Appeal held that as there was no suggestion that Goldenberg had confessed in consequence of anything said or done *by the interviewing officers*, §76(2)(b) PACE could not be invoked. The words "anything said or done" "do not extend so as to include anything said or done by the person making the confession", but, rather, are "limited to something external to the person making the confession".[42]

---

[39] R. v. Fulling, [1987] Q.B. 426, 432.

[40] R. v. Emmerson, (1991) 92 Crim. App. 284, 287. See also R. v. Foster [2003] EWCA (Crim) 178.

[41] R. v. Paris, (1993) 97 Crim. App. 99, 103.

[42] R. v. Goldenberg, (1989) 88 Crim. App. 285, 290. *See also* R. v. Wahab, [2002] EWCA (Crim) 1570, [2003] 1 Crim. App. 15, ¶ 232, [41].

The confession must have been obtained *in consequence of* whatever is alleged to have been "said or done". In *R v. Law-Thompson*[43] the Court of Appeal thought that § 76(2)(b) PACE could not have been invoked because there was no suggestion that the confessions had been obtained in consequence of the absence of an appropriate adult during interview.[44]

In determining whether what was said or done was likely to render any resulting confession unreliable, the court must consider the circumstances *actually* existing at the time. It is relevant to have regard, for example, to the suspect's physical condition and emotional state at the time,[45] the suspect's mental condition (including his or her mental age,[46] his or her suggestibility and vulnerability,[47] and the presence of any personality disorder[48]); the suspect's fitness to be interviewed (a suspect under the influence of drugs[49] or suffering from withdrawal symptoms may obviously be unfit, although "the mere fact that someone is withdrawing, and may have a motive for making a confession, does not mean the confession is necessarily unreliable"[50]); and the absence of an appropriate adult.[51]

14.4.1.3 Discretionary Exclusion

Even if a confession cannot be excluded from evidence under § 76 PACE, it may still be possible for it to be excluded in the exercise of the "fair trial" discretion, on the ground that it was improperly obtained. Indeed, "it is evident that many cases which could have fallen to be decided under section 76 are instead being considered by the courts under section 78(1)", and it is for this reason "that the jurisprudence on section 76 remains surprisingly underdeveloped given the difficulties of interpreting it".[52]

The appellate courts have exhibited a marked reluctance to provide guidelines for the assistance of trial judges. The following comment is typical: "It is undesirable to attempt any general guidance as to the way in which a judge's discretion under section 78 ... should be exercised. Circumstances vary infinitely".[53] Furthermore,

---

43 R. v. Law-Thompson, [1997] Crim. LR 674.

44 See also R. v. Samuel, [2005] EWCA (Crim) 704, [45].

45 R. v. McGovern, (1991) 92 Crim. App. 228.

46 Ibid., See also R. v. Sylvester, [2002] EWCA (Crim) 1327.

47 Ibid.

48 R. v. Walker, [1998] Crim. LR 211.

49 Ibid.

50 R. v. Crampton, (1991) 92 Crim. App. 369.

51 Sylvester, [2002], EWCA (Crim) 1327.

52 Grevling (1997, 667–668).

53 R. v. Samuel, [1988] Q.B. 615, 630. See also R. v. Jelen, (1990) 90 Crim. App. 456, 465: "The circumstances of each case are almost always different, and judges may well take different views in the proper exercise of their discretion even where the circumstances are similar. This is not an apt field for hard case law and well-founded distinctions between cases".

"the Court of Appeal does not set aside the exercise of the trial judge's discretion under section 78 unless it concludes that the decision to admit the confession was unreasonable …".[54]

An examination of the cases reveals, however, that a number of general principles have indeed emerged. First, a "significant and substantial" breach of the rules will weigh heavily in favor of exclusion, but will not lead automatically to exclusion. Exclusion is unlikely to be ordered if the defendant is not considered to have been actually disadvantaged by the breach.[55] The court may consider, for example, that the confession is likely to have been made even if the breach had not occurred. Second, a breach may, by its very nature, be significant and substantial; in other words, it will be significant and substantial even if the police acted in good faith. Bad faith can, however, convert a breach which is not otherwise significant and substantial into one which is.[56] Finally, exclusion is not to be used directly to discipline the police.[57]

A simple illustration, in the context of the denial of access to legal advice, may be provided. In *R v. Walsh*, the Court of Appeal held that the confession evidence in question ought to have been excluded under § 78(1) PACE, since, "having considered the matter, we can see nothing in this case which could properly lead the court to the conclusion that the breach of section 58 [of PACE, which provides for access to legal advice for persons arrested and held in custody] made no difference; or in other words that it was likely that the appellant would have made the admissions in any event. The very highest it could be put, to our minds, was that it was perhaps uncertain whether or not the presence of a solicitor would have made any difference".[58]

By contrast, in *R v. Alladice*,

> the appellant himself said in evidence … that he was well able to cope with the interviews; that he had been given the appropriate caution before each of them; that he had understood the caution and was aware of his rights. … His reason for wanting a solicitor was to have some sort of check on the conduct of the police during the interview. … It may seldom happen that a defendant is so forthcoming about his attitude towards the presence of a legal adviser. That candour does however simplify the task of deciding whether the admission of the evidence "would have such an adverse effect on the fairness of the proceedings" that it should not have been admitted. Had the solicitor been present, his advice would have added nothing to the knowledge of his rights which the appellant already had.[59]

---

[54] Thompson v. R., [1998] 2 W.L.R. 927, 949. See also R. v. O'Leary, (1988) 87 Crim. App. 387, 391; R. v. Christou, [1992] Q.B. 979, 989.

[55] R. v. Samuel, [1988] Q.B. 615; R. v. Alladice, (1988) 87 Crim. App. 380; R. v. Parris, (1989) 89 Crim. App. 68; R. v. Keenan, [1990] 2 Q.B. 54; R. v. Walsh, (1990) 91 Crim. App. 161; R. v. Canale, [1990] 2 All E.R. 187; R. v. Dunn, (1990) 91 Crim. App. 237; R. v. Dunford, (1990) 91 Crim. App. 150; R. v. Aspinall, [1999] 2 Crim. App. 115; R. v. Kirk, [2000] 1 W.L.R. 567; Watson v. DPP, [2003] EWHC (Admin) 1466, (2004) 168 J.P. 116; R. v. Gill, [2003] EWCA (Crim) 2256, [2003], 4 All E.R. 681.

[56] R. v. Walsh, (1990) 91 Crim. App. 161.

[57] R. v. Mason, [1988] 1 W.L.R. 139; R. v. Delaney, (1989) 88 Crim. App. 338.

[58] R. v. Walsh, (1990) 91 Crim. App. 161, 163. See also R. v. Parris, (1989) 89 Crim. App. 68.

[59] Alladice, 87 Crim. App. 380, 386–7.

It had not, therefore, been wrong for the confession evidence not to have been excluded under § 78(1) PACE.[60]

The notion that a confession will not be excluded from evidence under §78(1) PACE if it is determined that the presence of a legal adviser would have "made no difference", since the defendant would have made the confession in any event, is a problematic one. It is clear that such a determination can involve courts in a certain amount of post hoc rationalisation of events. The desirability of this may be questioned.

14.4.2 Indirect Evidence/Fruits of the Poisonous Tree

14.4.2.1 Tainting of Subsequent Confessions

There has been judicial consideration of the issue of whether a particular confession may be regarded as "tainted" by an earlier illegality. Thus the fact that something "said or done" has caused a confession to be inadmissible under § 76(2)(b) PACE may mean that a later but properly obtained confession is similarly tainted and thus also automatically inadmissible under § 76(2)(b).[61] Equally, an earlier illegality may render a later but properly obtained confession liable to be excluded from evidence in the exercise of the "fair trial" discretion.

Whether a later but properly obtained confession will be deemed to be "tainted" by an earlier illegality will naturally depend on the circumstances of the particular case. Some illegalities will be of such a nature that they cannot be "cured"[62] by a properly conducted later interview, with the result that there "must inevitably be a continuing blight"[63] on any confessions subsequently made. The question for the court is whether there is any suggestion of oppression, inducement, stress or pressures in the earlier interview which may have continued to exert a "malign influence" during the later interview.[64] A relevant consideration is whether the earlier breach was a flagrant or merely technical one.[65] Ultimately, however,

> where an early interviewing is excluded admission of a later interview must be a matter of fact and degree. It is likely to depend on a consideration of whether the objections leading to the exclusion of the first interview were of a fundamental and continuing nature, and, if so, if the arrangements for the subsequent interview gave the accused a sufficient opportunity to exercise an informed and independent choice as to whether he should repeat or retract what he said in the excluded interview or say nothing.[66]

---

[60] See also R. v. Dunford, (1990) 91 Crim. App. 150.

[61] R. v. McGovern, (1991) 92 Crim. App. 228.

[62] R. v. Ismail, [1990] Crim. LR 109.

[63] R. v. Glaves, [1993] Crim. LR 685.

[64] Y. v. DPP, [1991] Crim. LR 917. See also, R. v. Canale, [1990] 2 All E.R. 187; R. v. Gillard, (1991) 92 Crim. App. 61.

[65] R. v. Wood, [1994] Crim. LR 222.

[66] R. v. Singleton, [2002] EWCA (Crim) 459, [10].

Thus in *R v. Neil*[67] the Court of Appeal held that the judge should have exercised his discretion to exclude the evidence, since Neil would have considered himself bound to the admissions in the first statement, and the circumstances of the second interview were insufficient to provide him with a safe and confident opportunity to withdraw the admissions.[68] In *R v. Singleton*, on the other hand, "the objections leading to the exclusion of the earlier interviews were not continuing and the appellant plainly had ample opportunity to decide whether or not to volunteer a repetition of what he had earlier said".[69]

14.4.2.2 Facts Discovered in Consequence of Confessions Contravening Section 76(2)

There is specific provision in PACE on the admissibility of non-confession evidence that has been discovered by the police in consequence of a confession that is inadmissible in evidence under § 76(2) PACE. The effect of § 76(4)(a) PACE, read in conjunction with § 76(6) PACE, is as follows. The fact that a confession is wholly or partly excluded pursuant to § 76(2) PACE "shall not affect the admissibility in evidence … of any facts discovered" as a result of the wholly excluded confession, or the excluded part of the confession, as the case may be. In other words, derivative evidence is admissible as a matter of law (though subject to the usual "fair trial" exclusionary discretion[70]). The prosecution is, however, forbidden by § 76(5) PACE from introducing evidence that the fact which was discovered was discovered as a result of a statement made by the accused; only the defense may introduce such evidence if it so wishes.

The prohibition of the introduction by the prosecution of evidence that the non-confession evidence was discovered as a result of a confession by the accused can have important practical implications, and prove a substantial impediment for the prosecution. This is because, in cases where the non-confession evidence was discovered in a "neutral" place unconnected with the defendant, such evidence will be of little relevance or value in the absence of evidence of what led the police to its discovery.

---

[67] R. v. Neil, [1994] Crim. LR 441.

[68] See also R. v. Nelson, [1998] 2 Crim. App. 399, in which *Neil* was distinguished.

[69] Singleton, [2002] EWCA (Crim) 459, [11]. See also R. v. Ahmed, [2003] EWCA (Crim) 3627.

[70] See Mirfield (1997, 225).

14.4.3 Erosion of the Right to Silence: § 34 of the Criminal Justice and Public Order Act 1994

"Until the enactment of section 34, judges and juries were severely constrained by a common law rule applicable in England and Wales against drawing an adverse inference against a defendant if he failed to mention during police questioning a matter on which he later relied in his defence".[71] Acknowledged to be "a notorious minefield"[72] and "a very difficult area",[73] § 34 provides in pertinent part:

> (1) Where, in any proceedings against a person for an offence, evidence is given that the accused—
>
> (a) at any time before he was charged with the offence, on being questioned under caution by a constable trying to discover whether or by whom the offence had been committed, failed to mention any fact relied on in his defence in those proceedings; or
> (b) on being charged with the offence or officially informed that he might be prosecuted for it, failed to mention any such fact,
> (c) being a fact which in the circumstances existing at the time the accused could reasonably have been expected to mention when so questioned, charged or informed, as the case may be, subsection (2) below applies.
>
> (2) Where this subsection applies—
>
> (d) the court or jury, in determining whether the accused is guilty of the offence charged, may draw such inferences from the failure as appear proper.
>
> (2A) Where the accused was at an authorised place of detention at the time of the failure, subsections (1) and (2) above do not apply if he had not been allowed an opportunity to consult a solicitor prior to being questioned, charged or informed as mentioned in subsection (1) above.

14.4.3.1 On Being Questioned Under Caution

The terms of the caution are prescribed by §10.5 of Code of Practice C: "You do not have to say anything. But it may harm your defence if you do not mention when questioned something which you later rely on in Court. Anything you do say may be given in evidence".

This is rather more complex than the old caution: "You do not have to say anything unless you wish to do so, but what you say may be given in evidence". In the light of evidence that even the old and simpler caution was misunderstood by many

[71] R. v. Webber, [2004] UKHL 1, [2004] 1 W.L.R. 404, [16].
[72] R. v. B., [2003] EWCA (Crim) 3080, [20].
[73] R. v. Bresa, [2005] EWCA (Crim) 1414, [51].

suspects,[74] the likelihood of the "new" one being properly understood may well be questionable. A research study has found: "Police officers and legal advisers both expressed doubts about the extent to which suspects understand the content and implications of this statement. … even if police officers explained the caution in lay terms, they expressed a degree of scepticism about whether suspects fully comprehended it".[75]

14.4.3.2 Was It "a Fact Which in the Circumstances Existing at the Time the Accused Could Reasonably Have Been Expected to Mention"?[76]

Some general observations have been made by the Court of Appeal on the determination of whether the failure to mention a fact was one

> which in the circumstances existing at the time the accused could reasonably have been expected to mention … The time referred to is the time of questioning, and account must be taken of all the relevant circumstances existing at that time. The courts should not construe the expression 'in the circumstances' restrictively: matters such as time of day, the defendant's age, experience, mental capacity, state of health, sobriety, tiredness, knowledge, personality and legal advice are all part of the relevant circumstances; and those are only examples of things which may be relevant. When reference is made to "the accused" attention is directed not to some hypothetical, reasonable accused of ordinary phlegm and fortitude but to the actual accused with such qualities, apprehensions, knowledge and advice as he is shown to have had at the time. It is for the jury to decide whether the fact (or facts) which the defendant has relied on in his defence in the criminal trial, but which he had not mentioned when questioned under caution before charge by the constable investigating the alleged offence for which the defendant is being tried, is (or are) a fact (or facts) which in the circumstances as they actually existed the actual defendant could reasonably have been expected to mention.
>
> Like so many other questions in criminal trials this is a question to be resolved by the jury in the exercise of their collective common-sense, experience and understanding of human nature. Sometimes they may conclude that it was reasonable for the defendant to have held his peace for a host of reasons, such as that he was tired, ill, frightened, drunk, drugged, unable to understand what was going on, suspicious of the police, afraid that his answer would not be fairly recorded, … acting on legal advice, or some other reason accepted by the jury.
>
> In other cases the jury may conclude, after hearing all that the defendant and his witnesses may have to say about the reasons for failing to mention the fact or facts in issue, that he could reasonably have been expected to do so.[77]

An issue that has proved troubling for the courts is the extent to which adverse inferences may be drawn where the suspect *acted on legal advice* in failing to mention a fact in interview.[78] In *Condron v. UK*, the ECtHR remarked that "the very fact that an accused is advised by his lawyer to maintain his silence must … be

---

[74] Zander (2007, 170).

[75] Bucke et al. (2000, 27); See also Lindsay (2006).

[76] See generally Leng (2001).

[77] R. v. Argent, [1997] 2 Crim. App. 27, 33.

[78] See generally, Cooper (2006) and Wolchover (2005).

given *appropriate weight* by the domestic court".[79] What are the implications of this? Would *genuine* reliance on legal advice to remain silent, regardless of the quality of that advice, be sufficient of itself to prevent the drawing of adverse inferences under § 34? It is arguable that an affirmative answer would be justifiable from the viewpoint of principle: it would undermine the fundamental importance accorded by the law to the right to legal advice[80] if a suspect who was advised to remain silent was required in effect to make his or her own assessment of the quality of that advice. However, after some earlier uncertainty in the case law, the Court of Appeal confirmed in 2004, in *R v. Hoare*[81] and *R v. Beckles*,[82] that *reasonable* reliance on legal advice to remain silent was necessary to prevent adverse inferences from being drawn. The Court stated in *R v. Beckles*:

> ...in a case where a solicitor's advice is relied upon by the defendant, the ultimate question for the jury remains under section 34 whether the facts relied on at the trial were facts which the defendant could reasonably have been expected to mention at interview. If they were not, that is the end of the matter. If the jury consider that the defendant genuinely relied on the advice, that is not necessarily the end of the matter. It may still not have been reasonable for him to rely on the advice, or the advice may not have been the true explanation for his silence. ... If ... it is possible to say that the defendant genuinely acted upon the advice, the fact that he did so because it suited his purpose may mean he was not acting reasonably in not mentioning the facts. His reasonableness in not mentioning the facts remains to be determined by the jury. If they conclude he was acting unreasonably they can draw an adverse inference from the failure to mention the facts.[83]

14.4.3.3 The Contribution of the European Court of Human Rights

In essence, provided that it is interpreted in a manner which ensures that a fair balance is achieved between the exercise of the suspect's right to remain silent and the drawing of adverse inferences by the jury, § 34 will be regarded as compliant with the ECHR. In *Murray v. United Kingdom*[84] the ECtHR addressed the drawing of inferences under the provisions of the Criminal Evidence (Northern Ireland) Order 1988[85] upon which § 34 of the Criminal Justice and Public Order Act 1994 was later modelled. The Court was satisfied that, having regard to the weight of the prosecution evidence, and provided appropriate safeguards are in place, pre-trial silence may be taken into account by the tribunal of fact when assessing the

---

[79] Condron v. United Kingdom (2001), 31 E.H.R.R. 1, 21, §60 (italics added).

[80] In fact, as § 34(2A) makes clear, the drawing of inferences is prohibited unless the accused has been granted access to legal advice.

[81] R. v. Hoare, [2004] EWCA (Crim) 784, [2005] 1 Crim. App. 22, ¶ 355. See generally, Emanuel and Jennings (2004).

[82] R. v. Beckles, [2004] EWCA (Crim) 2766, [2005] 1 All E.R. 705. See generally, Malik (2005).

[83] Beckles, [2004] EWCA (Crim) 2766, [46].

[84] Murray v. United Kingdom (1996), 22 E.H.R.R. 29.

[85] Criminal Evidence (Northern Ireland) Order, 1988, SI 1988/1987 (N. Ir.).

persuasiveness of the prosecution case without compromising Convention rights. It was stressed, however, that domestic law and practice must strike a balance between the exercise of the suspect's right to remain silent and the circumstances in which an adverse inference might be drawn from silence.

In *Murray*, the tribunal of fact was an experienced judge who was obliged to give a judgment setting out the reasons for the decision, to draw inferences and the weight attached to them. Furthermore, this judgment and thus the exercise of the judge's power to draw inferences were subject to review by the appellate courts. In the subsequent case of *Condron v. United Kingdom*[86] the ECtHR acknowledged that these factors provided important procedural safeguards against unfairness. In this case, which concerned the drawing of inferences under § 34, it was noted that this provision specifically entrusted the task of assessing the evidential value of silence to the jury. The ECtHR considered that in the absence of a mechanism to assess the evidential weight attached to silence, it was of paramount importance that the jury be properly directed. The ECtHR was unanimous in finding fault with the trial judge's summing-up, which had left the jury with the option of drawing adverse inferences. It considered that "as a matter of fairness, the jury should have been directed that it could only draw an adverse inference if satisfied that the applicants' silence at the police interview could only sensibly be attributed to their having no answer or none that would stand up to cross-examination".[87] Accordingly, on the basis of the inadequacy of this direction rather than any inherent deficiency in the legislative scheme, the Court concluded that the applicants had been denied the right to a fair trial under Art. 6 ECHR.

Likewise, the ECtHR later found a violation of Art. 6 ECHR in *Beckles v. United Kingdom* on the basis that

> the trial judge failed to give appropriate weight in his direction to the applicant's explanation for his silence at the police interview and left the jury at liberty to draw an adverse inference from the applicant's silence notwithstanding that it may have been satisfied as to the plausibility of the explanation given by him ... Quite apart from the fact that the trial judge had undermined the value of the applicant's explanation by referring to the lack of independent evidence as to what was said by the solicitor and by omitting to mention that the applicant was willing to give his version of the incident to the police before he spoke to his solicitor, it is also to be noted that he invited the jury to reflect on whether the applicant's reason for his silence was 'a good one' without also emphasising that it must be consistent only with guilt.[88]

The contribution of the ECtHR has thus been relatively modest. Rather than to impugn the legislative strategy as a whole, the concern of the Court has been to ensure that the legislative scheme is *administered* properly, notably through strong directions to the jury.[89]

---

[86] Condron v. United Kingdom (2001), 31 E.H.R.R. 1. See generally Jennings and Rees (2000) and Stanley (2000).

[87] This quotation is taken from the website of the ECtHR. The wording of the passage as reported in Condron v. United Kingdom (2001), 31 E.H.R.R. 1, 22, § 61, is slightly different.

[88] Beckles v. United Kingdom (2003), 36 E.H.R.R. 13,162, 179–180, §64.

[89] The Judicial Studies Board specimen direction on § 34 is accessible via http://www.jsboard.co.uk.

14.5 The Privilege Against Self-Incrimination

By permitting adverse inferences to be drawn in certain circumstances, § 34 of the Criminal Justice and Public Order Act 1994 may be regarded as imposing an *indirect* sanction for a defendant's failure to mention a fact in interview. On occasion, however, a statutory provision may prescribe a criminal sanction for refusing to provide information to the authorities. In *Saunders v. United Kingdom* the ECtHR held that the privilege against self-incrimination "presupposes that the prosecution in a criminal case seek to prove their case against the accused without resort to evidence obtained through methods of coercion or oppression in defiance of the will of the accused".[90]

The jurisprudence of the ECtHR on the privilege against self-incrimination[91] is notable for its uncertainty and inconsistency.[92] Two separate questions arise for consideration. First, would a prosecution, under the statutory provision in question for the failure to provide information, breach Art. 6 ECHR? Secondly, if information is in fact provided, would the use in evidence of the "compelled information" constitute a violation of Art. 6 ECHR? Both questions were considered by the Grand Chamber of the ECtHR in *O'Halloran and Francis v. United Kingdom*,[93] in the context of legislation (§172(2) of the Road Traffic Act 1988) requiring the registered keeper of a vehicle (§ 172(2)(a)) or any other person (§ 172(2)(b)) to provide the police with information relating to the identity of the driver of the vehicle on an occasion when the driver allegedly committed an offense. Both O'Halloran's and Francis's vehicles were "caught" on speed cameras, and they were served with requests under § 172(2)(a). O'Halloran responded that he had been driving and was prosecuted for speeding. Francis refused to provide the information requested and was prosecuted under § 172(3), which made it an offense to fail to comply with a request under § 172(2). The Grand Chamber held, in effect, that, in determining in either situation whether Art. 6 ECHR had been violated, a balancing approach should be adopted. A number of factors were regarded as relevant in this case. First, "those who choose to keep and drive motor cars can be taken to have accepted certain responsibilities and obligations as part of the regulatory regime relating to motor vehicles".[94] Secondly, "a further aspect of the compulsion applied in the present cases is the limited nature of the inquiry which the police were authorised to undertake. Section 172(2)(a) applies only where the driver of the vehicle is alleged to have committed a relevant offence, and authorises the police to require information only, 'as to the

---

[90] Saunders v. United Kingdom (1997), 23 E.H.R.R. 313, 337, §68.

[91] On the privilege against self-incrimination, see generally, Berger (2006), Penney (2003), Redmayne (2007), and Sedley (2001).

[92] See generally Butler (2000), Choo and Nash (2003, 37–43), Dennis (1995), Naismith (1997), Sudjic (2002), Ward and Gardner (2003), and Emmerson et al. (2007, 615–25).

[93] O'Halloran and Francis v. United Kingdom (G.C.) (2008), 46 E.H.R.R. 21, 397. See generally Birdling (2008), Burns (2007), and Spencer (2007).

[94] O'Halloran and Francis, 46 E.H.R.R. 21, 397, 414, § 57.

identity of the driver.'" Thirdly, "s. 172 does not sanction prolonged questioning about facts alleged to give rise to criminal offences," with the penalty for declining to answer being moderate and non-custodial.[95] Fourthly, "no offence is committed under s. 172(2)(a) if the keeper of the vehicle shows that he did not know and could not with reasonable diligence have known who the driver of the vehicle was. The offence is, thus, not one of strict liability, and the risk of unreliable admissions is negligible."[96] Fifthly, in the case of O'Halloran, "the identity of the driver is only one element in the offence of speeding, and there is no question of a conviction arising in the underlying proceedings in respect solely of the information obtained as a result of s. 172(2)(a)".[97] The Court concluded, therefore, that Art. 6(1) ECHR had not been violated: "Having regard to all the circumstances of the case, including the special nature of the regulatory regime at issue and the limited nature of the information sought by a notice under s. 172 of the Road Traffic Act 1988, the Court considers that the essence of the applicants' right to remain silent and their privilege against self-incrimination has not been destroyed".[98]

Whatever the merits of the conclusion reached by the Court in relation to both O'Halloran and Francis, its judgment may be criticized for endorsing too heavily a vague approach involving "balancing" competing considerations.[99] One objection to the approach might be a practical one: one might "question whether there is now *any* coherent guidance"[100] to aid the determination of whether Art. 6 ECHR has been violated in a particular case. There may, additionally, be a more principled objection to the approach, which is that the very essence of a right would seem to be devalued if it can simply be "balanced away" on an apparently ad hoc basis.

It is of note that the Court of Appeal held in a recent decision, which concerned information that the defendant had disclosed under compulsion, that the "balance" should come down in favor of upholding the privilege. The Court stated:

> A wilful refusal to comply with an order for disclosure will amount to a contempt of court which may attract the not insignificant sanction of imprisonment. The nature of the compulsion that may be applied to enforce compliance with the obligation to disclose information that is of an incriminating nature is therefore severe. The social purpose for which the Crown seeks to adduce the evidence in criminal proceedings is the suppression of tax evasion. No doubt the protection of the public revenue is an important social objective, but the question is whether the admission of evidence obtained from the accused under threat of imprisonment is a reasonable and proportionate response to that social need. In our view it is not. ...[W]e do not think that the need to punish and deter tax evasion is sufficient to justify such an infringement of the right of the accused not to incriminate himself.[101]
>
> For these reasons, ... the use of the admissions made by K ... would deprive K of the fair trial to which he is entitled under Article 6 of the Convention.[102]

---

[95] Ibid, 415, § 58.

[96] Ibid, § 59.

[97] Ibid, 415–416, § 60.

[98] Ibid, 416, § 62.

[99] Cf., Meyerson (2007).

[100] Birdling (2008, 61) (italics in original).

[101] R. v. K., [2009] EWCA (Crim) 1640, [42].

[102] Ibid, [43].

Some doubt remains about whether the privilege against self-incrimination applies to documentary evidence. In *Funke v. France*[103] the ECtHR was satisfied that this right attached to bank documents and chequebooks in the applicant's possession. However, in *Saunders v. United Kingdom* the Court drew a distinction between compelled statements and real evidence, finding that the right against self-incrimination did not apply to material having "an existence independent of the will of the suspect such as, *inter alia*, documents acquired pursuant to a warrant, breath, blood and urine samples and bodily tissue for the purpose of DNA testing".[104] This is further subject to *Jalloh v. Germany*, in which the Grand Chamber of the Court held that the privilege against self-incrimination was applicable where the defendant regurgitated a bag of cocaine that he had swallowed as a result of the forced administration of emetics. The Court, distinguishing this situation from the obtaining of samples such as breath, blood, urine or DNA samples, held that

> the degree of force used in the present case differs significantly from the degree of compulsion normally required to obtain the types of material referred to in the *Saunders* case. To obtain such material, a defendant is requested to endure passively a minor interference with his physical integrity (for example when blood or hair samples or bodily tissue are taken). Even if the defendant's active participation is required, ... this concerns material produced by the normal functioning of the body (such as, for example, breath, urine or voice samples). In contrast, compelling the applicant in the instant case to regurgitate the evidence sought required the forcible introduction of a tube through his nose and the administration of a substance so as to provoke a pathological reaction in his body. ... this procedure was not without risk to the applicant's health.[105]

In *J.B. v. Switzerland*[106] the ECtHR found that a prosecution for failing to produce possibly incriminatory documents breached Art. 6(1) ECHR, evidently adopting *Funke* in preference to *Saunders* on this point. The quality of the Court's reasoning in this case has been subjected to some criticism.[107] Noting the inconsistencies in the ECtHR jurisprudence, the Court of Appeal in *A-G's Reference (No 7 of 2000)*[108] suggested that where no clear answer could be found there, it would be appropriate to follow domestic authorities.[109] Drawing a distinction between compelled statements on the one hand, and the production of a pre-existing document or real evidence on the other, the Court of Appeal accepted that it would be objectionable to use evidence which the accused was forced to create by the use of compulsory powers. However, using compulsory powers to oblige the defendant

---

[103] Funke v. France (1993), 16 E.H.R.R. 297. See generally Butler (2000).

[104] Saunders v. United Kingdom (1996), 23 E.H.R.R. 313, 337–338, § 69.

[105] Jalloh v. Germany (G.C.) (2007), 44 E.H.R.R. 32, 667, 695, § 114.

[106] J.B. v. Switzerland (2001), 30 E.H.R.R. CD 328.

[107] Ashworth (2001) and Dennis (2010, 169).

[108] A-G's Reference (No. 7 of 2000), [2001] EWCA (Crim) 888, [2001] 2 Crim. App. 19, ¶ 286. See generally, Henderson (2001).

[109] Those particularly identified were the decisions of the House of Lords in R. v. Director of Serious Fraud Office, ex p Smith [1993] A.C. 1, AT&T Istel Ltd v. Tully [1993] A.C. 45, and R. v. Hertfordshire County Council, ex p Green Industries Ltd [2000] 2 W.L.R. 373.

to deliver up evidence which was already in existence and had an existence independent of the will of the accused would not be contrary to the fair trial guarantees provided by Art. 6 ECHR.

In *R v. Allen*[110] the House of Lords held that a prosecution for submitting a tax return containing false information would not be contrary to Art. 6 ECHR. The House observed that citizens had an obligation to pay taxes and a duty not to cheat the Revenue. In order to ensure the payment of taxes, the State had to have the power to require individuals to provide information about their annual income, and to have sanctions available to enforce the provision of this information.[111]

14.6 Conclusion

The law of England and Wales on the use of illegally gathered evidence in a criminal trial may be said to be characterized by the general absence of fixed rules of automatic inadmissibility and other "bright-line" rules. Rather, a case-by-case approach is favored. This appears to be accompanied by a commitment to the idea that the trier of fact should have access to as much prosecution evidence as possible, regardless of its source and regardless of how it was gathered. Thus, § 34 of the Criminal Justice and Public Order Act 1994 has the effect of shoring up the prosecution's armory by permitting adverse inferences to be drawn, in appropriate circumstances, from the accused's failure to mention facts when questioned or charged. Further, the use of specific legislation compelling the provision of potentially incriminating information may be tolerated if it is considered to constitute a "proportionate response" to some social problem. Still further, the prevailing view in England and Wales is that a trial court will generally be justified in admitting an item of illegally gathered evidence so long as it has given due consideration to whether to exclude the evidence in the exercise of discretion, taking into account in particular any danger that it might be unreliable. The introduction of the Human Rights Act 1998, which some may regard as constituting a Bill of Rights, has not brought about radical change to evidence doctrine in England and Wales.

The above review has demonstrated the large extent to which, evidence obtained by torture aside, evidential reliability is at the forefront of the appellate courts' thinking, the primary concern apparently being with the determination of the truth rather than with upholding due process. It now remains to be seen whether the more flexible reasoning in *A v. Secretary of State for the Home Department*, premised on the importance of the need to protect integrity, will be confined in the future to evidence obtained by torture, or whether courts will take the opportunity to extrapolate from it.

---

[110] R. v. Allen, [2001] UKHL 45, [2002] 1 A.C. 509.

[111] Ibid, 29–30. An application to the ECtHR was held to be inadmissible: Allen v. United Kingdom (2002), 35 E.H.R.R. CD289, The Law, § 1. See also King v. United Kingdom (2003), 37 E.H.R.R. CD1.

Bibliography

Ashworth, A. 2001. The self-incrimination saga. *Archbold News* 5: 5–6.

Berger, M. 2006. Compelled self-reporting and the principle against compelled self incrimination: Some comparative perspectives. *European Human Rights Law Review,* 25–38.

Berger, M. 2007. Self-incrimination and the European Court of Human Rights: Procedural issues in the enforcement of the right to silence. *European Human Rights Law Review,* 514–533.

Biçak, A.V. 2001. Police and criminal evidence Act 1984, S 76(2): Re-emergence of the involuntariness test. *Journal of Criminal Law* 65: 85–92.

Birdling, M. 2008. Self-incrimination goes to Strasbourg: O'Halloran and Francis v United Kingdom. *International Journal of Evidence and Proof* 12: 58–63.

Bucke, T., R. Street, and D. Brown. 2000. *The right of silence: The impact of the Criminal Justice and Public Order Act 1994.* Home Office Research Study 199. Available at http://www.homeoffice.gov.uk/rds/pdfs/hors199.pdf.

Burns, S. 2007. Good to talk? *New Law Journal* 157: 1454.

Butler, A.S. 2000. Funke v France and the right against self-incrimination: A critical analysis. *Criminal Law Forum* 11: 461–505.

Choo, A.L.-T. 2012. *Evidence*, 3rd ed. Oxford: Oxford University Press.

Choo, A.L.-T., and S. Nash. 2003. Evidence law in England and Wales: The impact of the Human Rights Act 1998. *International Journal of Evidence and Proof* 7: 31–61.

Choo, A.L.-T., and S. Nash. 2007. Improperly obtained evidence in the Commonwealth: Lessons for England and Wales? *International Journal of Evidence and Proof* 11: 75–105.

Cooper, S. 2006. Legal advice and pre-trial silence—Unreasonable developments. *International Journal of Evidence and Proof* 10: 60–69.

Dennis, I. 1995. Instrumental protection, human right or functional necessity? Reassessing the privilege against self-incrimination. *Cambridge Law Journal* 54: 342–376.

Dennis, I.H. 2010. *The law of evidence*, 4th ed. London: Sweet & Maxwell.

Emanuel, D., and A. Jennings. 2004. Legal advice to remain silent. *Archbold News* 5: 6–9.

Emmerson, B., A. Ashworth, and A. Macdonald. 2007. *Human rights and criminal justice*, 2nd ed. London: Sweet & Maxwell.

Foster, S. 2006. Detention without trial and the admissibility of torture evidence. *Justice of the Peace* 170: 64–67.

Friedman, D. 2002. From due deference to due process: Human rights litigation in the criminal law. *European Human Rights Law Review,* 216–238.

Grevling, K. 1997. Fairness and the exclusion of evidence under section 78(1) of the police and criminal evidence act. *Law Quarterly Review* 113: 667–685.

Grief, N. 2006. The exclusion of foreign torture evidence: A qualified victory for the rule of law. *European Human Rights Law Review,* 201–216.

Henderson, A. 2001. Defining the limits of silence. *Solicitors' Journal* 145: 432–433.

Jackson, J.D. 2005. The effect of human rights on criminal evidentiary processes: Towards convergence, divergence or realignment? *Modern Law Review* 68: 737–764.

Jennings, A.F., and E. Rees. 2000. Is silence still golden? *Archbold News* 5: 5–7.

Leng, R. 2001. Silence pre-trial, reasonable expectations and the normative distortion of fact-finding. *International Journal of Evidence and Proof* 5: 240–256.

Lindsay, J. 2006. We caution you—This is English but you might not understand it. *The Times*, 25 Apr 2006, Law (online version).

Mackie, J. 2006. Life in crime. *Solicitors' Journal* 150: 62.

Malik, B. 2005. Silence on legal advice: Clarity but not justice?:R v Beckles. *International Journal of Evidence and Proof* 9: 211–216.

Meyerson, D. 2007. Why courts should not balance rights against the public interest. *Melbourne University Law Review* 31: 873–902.

Mirfield, P. 1997. *Silence, confessions and improperly obtained evidence.* Oxford: Oxford University Press.

Mirfield, P. 2003. Silence, innocence and human rights. In *Essays for Colin Tapper*, ed. P. Mirfield and R. Smith, 126–146. London: LexisNexis UK.

Naismith, S.H. 1997. Self-incrimination—Fairness or freedom?. *European Human Rights Law Review*, 229–236.

Nash, S. 2000. Secretly recorded conversations and the European convention on human rights: Khan v UK. *International Journal of Evidence and Proof* 4: 268–274.

Nash, S. 2002. Balancing convention rights: PG and JH v United Kingdom. *International Journal of Evidence and Proof* 6: 125–129.

Nash, S. 2003. Surreptitious interrogation and notions of fairness: Allan v United Kingdom. *International Journal of Evidence and Proof* 7: 137–141.

Ovey, C. 1998. The European convention on human rights and the criminal lawyer: An introduction. *Criminal Law Review*, 4–15.

Penney, S. 2003. What's wrong with self-incrimination? The wayward path of self-incrimination law in the post-charter era—Part I: Justifications for rules preventing self-incrimination. *Criminal Law Quarterly* 48: 249–266.

Rasiah, N. 2006. A v Secretary of State for the Home Department (No 2): Occupying the moral high ground? *Modern Law Review* 69: 995–1005.

Redmayne, M. 2007. Rethinking the privilege against self-incrimination. *Oxford Journal of Legal Studies* 27: 209–232.

Samiloff, J. 2006. Interrogating evidence. *New Law Journal* 156: 5.

Sedley, S. 2001. Wringing out the fault: Self-incrimination in the 21st century. *Northern Ireland Legal Quarterly* 52: 107–126.

Sharpe, S. 2007. The European convention: A suspects' charter?. *Criminal Law Review*, 848–860.

Spencer, J.R. 2007. Curbing speed and limiting the right of silence. *Cambridge Law Journal* 66(3): 531–533.

Stanley, P. 2000. European briefing. *Solicitors' Journal* 144: 512.

Sudjic, B. 2002. Self incrimination: Has the fat lady sung yet?. *Scots Law Times*, 328–330.

Tain, P. 2000. Fair trial and the ECHR. *Solicitors' Journal* 144: 590.

Ward, T., and P. Gardner. 2003. The privilege against self incrimination: In search of legal certainty. *European Human Rights Law Review*, 388–399.

Wolchover, D. 2005. Silent triumph of the coach and horses. *Archbold News* 9: 5–6.

Zander, M. 2007. *Cases and materials on the English legal system*, 10th ed. Cambridge: Cambridge University Press.

Chapter 15
Taiwan: The Codification of a Judicially-Made Discretionary Exclusionary Rule

Jaw-Perng Wang

15.1 The General Theory of Admissibility of Illegally Gathered Evidence

15.1.1 The Duty to Ascertain the Truth in Taiwan

The Constitution of Taiwan (hereafter Const.) does not have any provisions or words regarding exclusionary rules or the court's duty to determine the truth. Such rules are normally found in statutes. Specific statutory exclusionary rules dealing with confessions and physical evidence found through violations of the right to privacy will be discussed in the sections below dealing with those narrower areas.

Traditionally, Taiwan's Code of Criminal Procedure (CCP) has recognized the principle of material truth and the Supreme Court of Taiwan considered the duty to ascertain the truth as being binding on the courts and law enforcement officials. Before 2002, § 163(I) CCP provided that: "Due to the necessity to discover the truth, the court *must*, on its own initiative, investigate evidence". Bound by this statutory provision, the trial court bore the primary duty of both discovering evidence and ascertaining the truth. Even if the parties admitted or did not contest the facts, the court still had an independent duty to discover and decide the material facts. The Taiwan Supreme Court also declared: "The evidence that shall be investigated and examined at trial is not limited to that introduced by the parties. The trial court must, on its own initiative, investigate whatever evidence is relevant to the elements of the crimes in order to discover the truth".[1] Failure to adequately investigate the evidence was reversible error (§ 379(10) CCP).

[1] Supreme Court, 61 Tai-Sun 2477 (1972), *overruled* in September 4, 2001.

J.-P. Wang (✉)
College of Law, National Taiwan University,
1 Roosevelt Road Sect. 4, Taipei, 10617, Taiwan
e-mail: jpwang@ntu.edu.tw

S.C. Thaman (ed.), *Exclusionary Rules in Comparative Law*, Ius Gentium: Comparative Perspectives on Law and Justice 20, DOI 10.1007/978-94-007-5348-8_15,

In 2002, the Legislative Yuan amended § 163 CCP so that it now reads: "Due to the necessity to discover the truth, the court *may*, on its own initiative, investigate evidence. However, in the interest of justice or in matters significant to the defendant's interests, the court *must*, on its own initiative, investigate evidence". Pursuant to this new reading, the parties, and no longer the trial court, bear the primary duty of discovery. Following an amendment in 2001, § 161(1) CCP now provides that "The public prosecutor shall bear the burden of proof as to the facts of the crime charged against an accused, and shall indicate the method of proof". The Supreme Court interpreted this new article that "the court shall certainly acquit the defendant if the evidence offered by the prosecutor at trial could not prove the facts of the crime".[2] In other words, the court has no duty, in principle, to ascertain the truth any more.

15.1.2 General Rules of Admissibility/Exclusion of Illegally Gathered Evidence

It is important to note, that the exclusionary rule in Taiwan, like in the United States, was judicially created. Before 1998, evidence which was the fruit of an illegal search or seizure was definitely admissible at trial. Except for the exclusion of confessions obtained through torture or other improper methods, the CCP had no other provisions authorizing the trial court to exclude physical evidence under any circumstances. Whether the evidence was illegally obtained was always an irrelevant issue in which a trial judge had no interest or obligation to investigate as long as he could find out the truth of the case. On the other hand, it could have been reversible error for the trial judge to exclude illegally obtained evidence. However, in a 1998 breakthrough decision, Taiwan's Supreme Court declared that a court may exclude illegally obtained evidence when it believes that the admissibility of the evidence will undermine justice and fairness.[3] The Court based its decision on the constitutional command that liberty cannot be abridged without due process of law, and that the defendant has the right to a fair and public trial.

Following this judicial creation of the exclusionary rule, the Legislative Yuan repeatedly reinforced the rule in the CCP after 2001. In 2001 and 2002, the legislature amended §§ 416 and 131 CCP dealing with exclusion of evidence following unlawful searches (see Sect. 15.2.2 below). In 2003, however, the Legislative Yuan added § 158-4 CCP, a general exclusionary rule which gave the judge discretion to suppress evidence gathered in violation of the law upon a discretionary basis, after "balancing the protection of human rights and the preservation of public interests".

In interpreting § 158-4 CCP, the Supreme Court required that a trial court shall consider the following factors in deciding whether or not to exclude evidence: (1)

[2] Supreme Court, 92 Tai-Sun 128 (2003).

[3] Supreme Court, 87 Tai-Sun 4025 (1998).

the extent of the violation; (2) the good or bad faith of the officer when violating the law; (3) the circumstances of the violation; (4) the nature and seriousness of the rights which were violated; (5) the gravity of the charged offense and the harm it caused; (6) the deterrent effect suppression will have on future violations; (7) the possibility that the evidence would have inevitably been discovered; and (8) the detriment of the violation to the defendant's defense.[4] In practice, courts tend not to exclude evidence in cases involving very serious offenses, such as murder or rape. Guns are also unlikely to be excluded by many courts. As to drugs, suppression often depends on the quantity and type of drug in question.

15.2 Rules of Admissibility/Exclusion in Relation to Violations of the Right to Privacy

15.2.1 General Provisions Protecting the Right to Privacy and to Develop One's Personality

Nowhere in Taiwan's Constitution can one find expressions such as the "the right to privacy" or "the right to develop one's personality". However, these rights are implicitly guaranteed in the Constitution following a decision of the Grand Justices, Taiwan's equivalent of the United States Supreme Court.

In 2004, Grand Justices' Interpretation No. 582 explains that, "although the right of privacy is not among those rights specifically enumerated in the Constitution, it should nonetheless be considered as an indispensable fundamental right and thus protected under Art. 22 Const. for purposes of preserving human dignity, individuality and moral integrity, as well as preventing invasions of personal privacy and maintaining self-control of personal information".[5]

In its Interpretation No. 630 in 2007, the Grand Justices again emphasized that "To preserve human dignity and to respect the free development of personality is the core value of the constitutional structure of free democracy". After repeating the language from the 2004 Interpretation No. 582 relating to the right of privacy, the Grand Justices continued: "As far as the right of informational privacy is concerned, which regards the self-control of personal information, it is intended to guarantee that the people have the right to decide whether or not to disclose their personal information, and, if so, to what extent, at what time, in what manner and to what people such information will be disclosed. It is also designed to guarantee that the people have the right to know and control how their personal information will

[4] Supreme Court, 93 Tai-Sun 664 (2004).

[5] Art. 22 Const. provides "All other freedoms and rights not detrimental to social order or public welfare shall be guaranteed under the Constitution".

be used, as well as the right to correct any inaccurate entries contained in their information".[6]

There are also many statutes in Taiwan aimed at the protection of the right to privacy and to develop one's personality. For example, it constitutes a criminal offense to open a sealed letter without a justified reason.[7] § 24 of the Act of Communication Protection and Surveillance (ACPS) punishes illegal surveillance of another's communication with up to 5 years imprisonment. The CCP also requires the exclusion of evidence gathered pursuant to illegal searches and seizures under some circumstances, as was noted above.

15.2.2 *Protection of Privacy in the Home or Other Private Premises*

Up until 2001, the CCP was silent in relation to the admissibility of illegally gathered physical evidence. In 2001, however, § 416 CCP was amended to allow defendants to move for court review of the legality of searches which turned up evidence used against them in a criminal trial. If the court were to find a search was illegal, it could exclude the evidence obtained. This was the first legislative recognition of the exclusionary rule in Taiwan's legal history. In 2002, § 131 CCP was also amended to strengthen the exclusionary rule. It now requires that after a search is conducted under exigent circumstances, prosecutors or the police shall report to the court within 3 days after the search and seek ratification of its legality. The court may ratify or annul the search if it was conducted in an illegal fashion. If police or prosecutors do not report to the court within 3 days, or the search is revoked by the court after so reporting, the court may exclude the evidence at trial.

The exclusionary rules provided in §§ 131, 416 CCP are limited to the situations therein described. In 2003, however, a much broader exclusionary rule was promulgated. § 158-4 CCP provides that the court may generally exclude evidence obtained in violation of the legally prescribed procedure. It is not limited to illegal searches or violations of the right to privacy. The exclusionary rule of § 158-4 CCP is not

---

[6] The Grand Justices also indicated that the Constitution does not make the right of informational privacy absolute and the State may impose appropriate restrictions on such right by enacting unambiguous laws as far as such laws do not transgress the scope contemplated by Art. 23 Const. Art. 23 Const. provides "All the freedoms and rights enumerated in the preceding Articles shall not be abridged by law except as may be necessary to prevent infringement upon the freedoms of others, to avert an imminent danger, to maintain social order, or to promote public welfare".

[7] § 315 of Taiwan's Criminal Code (hereafter CC): "A person who without reason opens or conceals a sealed letter or other sealed document belonging to another shall be punished with jail or a fine of not more than 300 *yuan*".

mandatory, however, but allows the judge to balance the protection of human rights against the public interest in prosecuting criminals in deciding whether to admit or exclude illegally gathered evidence.

Although the Constitution nowhere includes the words "right to privacy", the home is protected by Art. 10 Const. which states: "The people shall have freedom of residence and movement". In 2004, Grand Justices Interpretation No. 585 held that the constitution protects "a person's private zone of living from invasion by others". Here the phrase of "private zone of living" certainly includes the home. Protection of privacy in one's home is the subject of many different statutes. For example, § 308 CC provides: "A person who without reason breaks and enters a dwelling house or structure of another, the adjacent or surrounding grounds, or a vessel belonging to another shall be punished with imprisonment for not more than one year, detention, or a fine of not more than 300 *yuan*". While the ACPS allows the government to intercept people's communications in some circumstances, § 13 ACPS provides that: "It is not allowed to install in private dwellings any machine or equipment which is capable of recording voice or images or any other methods of surveillance".

§ 146 CCP(I) provides, as well, that: "No occupied or guarded dwelling or other premises may be entered and searched or property seized at night unless the occupant, watchman, or his representative gives permission, or the circumstances are urgent". § 146(II,III) CCP also regulate the conditions under which night searches may be carried out. It is settled that the government's violation of the above provisions might lead to exclusion of evidence upon application of the § 158-4 CCP balancing test.

The CCP, however, does not explicitly provide for the application of the doctrine of "fruits of the poisonous tree". While many Taiwanese scholars advocate its adoption, Taiwan's Supreme Court is vague in its position. On the one hand, it has recognized that the doctrine of "fruits of poisonous tree" is accepted and applied in the United States, but it refused to adopt it in Taiwan, holding that the balancing test of § 158-4 CCP is the sole test regulating exclusion.[8] In a later case, the Supreme Court held that the doctrine of "fruits of the poisonous tree" will only apply if a second legal police act, following closely on the heels of an initial illegal act, directly leads to the discovery of the disputed evidence.[9] Lower courts, however, have explicitly applied the doctrine of "fruits of the poisonous tree" and excluded indirect evidence. For instance, in an appellate court case, the police illegally searched the defendant's house and thereafter illegally took the defendant to the police station for interrogation. After the interrogation, the police took a urine sample from the defendant. The appellate court excluded the urine and its laboratory test simply on the ground of the doctrine of "fruits of the poisonous tree".[10]

[8] Supreme Court, 96 Tai-Sun 4177 (2007).
[9] Supreme Court, 97 Tai-Sun 4797 (2008).
[10] Supreme Court, 93 Sun-Ii 2056 (2004).

15.2.3 Protection of Privacy in One's Communications

Art. 12 Const. provides: "The people shall have freedom and privacy of correspondence". The Grand Justices interpreted this provision as follows:

> Its purpose is to protect the people's right to choose whether or not, with whom, when and how to communicate and the contents of their communication without arbitrary invasion by the State and others. Any measure of restraint adopted by the State shall have a legal basis. In addition, requirements for taking such measures of restraint must be specific and explicit without exceeding what is necessary, and the procedures should be reasonable and legitimate to fulfill the purpose of protecting the freedom of privacy of correspondence guaranteed by the Constitution.[11]

Protection of privacy in one's communications is reflected in many different statutes. For example, § 1ACPS states that one of its purposes is to "protect people's freedom and privacy of correspondence from unlawful invasion, to ensure national security and to maintain social order". Illegal surveillance of another's communication is punishable by up to 5 years imprisonment under § 24 ACPS, and illegal opening of mail is punishable by jail or a fine under § 315 CC.

It is noteworthy that §§ 5,6,7 ACPS include the first and only statutory provisions recognizing the mandatory exclusionary of evidence which carries over to indirect evidence, or "fruits of the poisonous tree". This is clearly distinguishable from the discretionary exclusionary rule of § 158-4 CCP. § 5 ACPS sets out the requirements for acquiring a surveillance warrant, which includes the presence of probable cause and restrictions to a catalogue of listed offenses. § 5(5) ACPS provides that "evidence obtained in *serious* violation of this Article, as well as its derivative evidence, shall not be admissible during the prosecutorial investigation, the trial, or any other proceedings". The legislative intent was the reinforcement of the protection of human rights. The question of whether a violation was "serious" was to be determined by the courts case by case. § 6 ACPS sets out the rules for conducting surveillance in cases of exigent circumstance, and § 6(3) ACPS includes the same language as § 5(5) ACPS related to exclusion and its extension to derivative evidence. §7 ACPS regulates surveillance on the ground of national security, and § 7(3) again includes similar language as to mandatory exclusion and "fruits of the poisonous tree", but without a restriction to "serious violations".[12]

---

[11] Grand Justices Interpretation No. 631 (2007).

[12] Evidence will be mandatorily excluded under § 7 ACPS as long as it is obtained in violation of this Article. Evidence will be mandatorily excluded under §§ 5,6 ACPS only when the violation of the two Articles is *serious*. It is unclear why the legislators draw a line between these two categories.

15.3 Rules of Admissibility/Exclusion in Relation to Illegal Interrogations

15.3.1 The General Right to Remain Silent/Privilege Against Self-Incrimination

The Constitution does not mention the criminal accused's right to silence or privilege against self-incrimination.

Unlike in the United States, a defendant in Taiwan is not sworn to tell the truth if he decides to testify at trial. The defendant testifies without being sworn and his/her testimony is admissible and often very influential in the court's ultimate decision. No statute requires the accused to make a statement, nor punishes him/her upon remaining silent at any stage of criminal proceedings. The defendant is also not subject to perjury charges if he/she lies while testifying at trial.

Although § 156(IV) CCP provides that an accused's "guilt shall not be presumed merely because of his refusing to testify or remaining silent", it was disputed whether this rule was tantamount to the declaration of a right to silence. All agreed, however, that the CCP had no explicit provision laying out the defendant's right to refuse to answer questions when doing so would incriminate him/her. In 1997, the Legislative Yuan (Taiwan's legislative branch) amended § 95 CCP to explicitly provide for a right to silence and also to require that the accused be advised of this right before interrogation at all stages of criminal proceedings.[13]

Besides the accused, a witness also has an explicit privilege against self-incrimination under the terms of § 181 CCP, which provides that: "A witness may refuse to testify if his testimony may subject himself …to criminal prosecution or punishment". In addition, before a witness testifies, § 186(2) CCP requires that a prosecutor or a judge inform him/her of the right to refuse to testify.

15.3.2 The Protection Against Involuntary Self-Incrimination

The Constitution mentions nothing about the protection of an accused from torture, coercion, threats, etc., or other conduct which tends to undermine the free will of a criminal defendant. However, such protection is abundant in the CCP. § 98 CCP provides that "[a]n accused shall be examined in an honest manner; violence, threat, inducement, fraud, exhausting examination or other improper means shall

[13] § 95 CCP provides that "While being interrogated, the defendant shall be told what act he is accused of, which provisions of the criminal law may apply, that he does not have to make statements against his will, and that he may retain his lawyer".

not be used". § 156(1) CCP provides that the "confession of an accused may not be extracted by violence, threat, inducement, fraud, exhausting interrogation, unlawful detention or other improper means". A confession which is not in violation of § 156(1) CCP, and whis is consistent with the facts, imay be admitted into evidence. Statements taken in violation of the statute are inadmissible.

It is undisputed in Taiwan that a confession will be excluded if it is obtained through *physical* torture, threat, or bodily invasion. Taiwan's Supreme Court also excludes confessions if they are obtained though the use of *psychological* pressure or threats. For example, it excluded a confession when a prosecutor told the accused that "if you confess the offense of robbery, I will give you a chance. If not, you will be detained". The Court reasoned that the prosecutor's comments constituted an inducement and threat.[14] For similar reasons, the Court excluded a confession when the police told the accused that "you could go home after you confess", that a "confession can lead to a suspended, reduced, or remitted sentence", and that "you will not be able to cope with the government". [15] The police used "improper means", the Court held, when they told the accused that "other accused was still detained, but others were released without bail because they have confessed". [16]

If a second confession has close ties with a first involuntary confession, the second confession will also be excluded even though the interrogator did not use any illegal measures. In a 2006 case, the Supreme Court held if the conditions of fear or pressure, caused by the first illegal measure, carried over into the second interrogation, the second confession would not be admissible even though the police at the second interrogation did not do anything illegal.[17] In a 2007 case, a defendant was interrogated illegally by the police and transferred to the prosecutor for further interrogation. While the prosecutor did not use any illegal measures, the Supreme Court still cast doubt on the admissibility of the confession made before the prosecutor because it was obtained only 4 h after the police's illegal interrogation. The Court reversed the case and remanded it to the lower court to determine whether the second confession was still influenced by the coerced initial confession.[18]

It is interesting to answer the question, whether evidence gained from torturing one person, may be used against another person who wasn't subject to unlawful coercion. The issue is treated as one of hearsay in Taiwan. In 2003, § 159 CCP was amended to recognize the hearsay rule. It provides that out-of-court statements of any person other than the defendant are inadmissible unless otherwise provided by law. Under the new provision, statements of any person, other than the defendant, given to the police are inadmissible unless they fall within two exceptions.

[14] Supreme Court, 93 Tai-Sun 5189 (2004).
[15] Supreme Court, 94 Tai-Sun 5654 (2005).
[16] Supreme Court, 96 Tai-Sun 3104 (2007).
[17] Supreme Court, 95Tai-Sun 1365 (2006).
[18] Supreme Court, 96 Tai-Sun 829 (2007).

Accordingly, another person's out-of-court statement, whether or not a product of torture, cannot, in principle, be used against the defendant.

The first exception is when the same witness testifies at trial, in which case his prior statement could be admissible as a "prior inconsistent statement" provided that the prior statement is more "reliable".[19] The second exception is when the witness is unavailable to testify at trial and special circumstances surrounding his prior statement at the police station indicate its "reliability".[20] The Supreme Court interpreted the term "reliability" in the above provisions as meaning whether the statement was made voluntarily, as opposed to being obtained by illegal means.[21] Based on the Court's decision, therefore, a person's statement gained from torture cannot be admissible against another person as a hearsay exception.

On the other hand, it is clear that physical evidence discovered as a result of an involuntary confession would have been admissible at trial before 1998, even if obtained through torture. Physical evidence was never excluded for any reason at trial until the Supreme Court created the exclusionary rule in 1998. Since 1998, however, the Supreme Court has not had occasion to decide this particular issue. In theory, physical evidence could be excluded under the balancing test of § 158-4 CCP, the general exclusionary rule, which provides that the court has the discretion to exclude evidence if it is obtained in violation of the law.

While the Supreme Court has no seminal decision interpreting the scope or protected interests covered by the right to remain silent, it has decided a case dealing with the admissibility of a polygraph test. In that case, the Supreme Court implied that the government is required to get free and sincere consent from the accused before conducting any measures which might implicate his right to silence, among them the use of a polygraph. It reasoned that a polygraph test is employed to evaluate the functioning of a suspect's mind and is of a nature as to undermine a person's free will. Such an invasion of personality rights was considered to be more serious than a violation of the defendant's right to silence.[22]

---

[19] § 159-2 CCP provides: "When a statement made, at the investigation stage, by a person other than the accused to the public prosecutor, judicial police officer, or judicial policeman are inconsistent with that made at trial, the prior statement may be admitted as evidence, provided that special circumstances exist indicating that the prior statement is more reliable, and is necessary to prove the facts of the criminal offense".

[20] § 159-3 CCP: "Statements made at the investigation stage by a person other than the accused to the public prosecutor, judicial police officer, or judicial police may be admitted as evidence, if one of the following circumstances exists in trial and after proving the existence of special circumstances indicating its reliability and its necessity in proving the facts of criminal offense: (1) The person died; (2) The person has lost his memory or has been unable to make a statement due to physical or emotional impairment; (3) The person cannot be summoned or has failed to respond to the summons due to the fact that he is staying in a foreign country or his whereabouts are unknown; (4) The person has refused to testify in court without justified reason".

[21] Supreme Court, 94 Tai-Sun 629 (2005).

[22] Supreme Court, 95 Tai-Sun 2254 (2006).

15.3.3 The Protection Against Unknowing Self-Incrimination: The Miranda Paradigm

Taiwan's Constitution, as was mentioned above, does not address any aspects of the privilege against self-incrimination or the right to silence.

Before 1982, the right to counsel only applied once prosecution had commenced in the trial court. For this reason, an accused's lawyer could not be present at the pretrial-investigation stage, nor at police or prosecutorial interrogations. For the same reason, if a defendant was detained at the investigation stage, his lawyer was not allowed to meet or communicate with him. The period of investigative detention could also last up to 4 months.

In 1982, the police victoriously announced they had a suspect's confession in Taiwan's first bank robbery case. However, the suspect jumped off a bridge after confessing, while he was allegedly leading the police on a search for the stolen money, and drowned. The case was simply closed, and the police made no attempt to find the stolen money. Several days later, however, a civilian, unrelated to the previous suspect, found that a bag left in his house by a friend was full of bank notes. This lead to the arrest of the actual perpetrator of the bank robbery who then confessed. As to the original suspect, the investigation found that he was beaten to make a full confession and killed himself because he could not bear the torture anymore.

This case outraged society. The accused's right to a lawyer at the pretrial stage was therefore established. In 1982, § 27 CCP was amended to allow the accused to retain a lawyer *before* trial. Relevant provisions were also amended to allow the attorney to appear during police and prosecutorial interrogations. In addition, during the investigative stage, an attorney may at any time, unless otherwise provided by the law, meet or communicate with the accused while in police custody.

Although the accused has had the right to retain a lawyer at the pre-trial stage since 1982, the police did not have a corresponding duty to advise the accused of this right. Only when the accused was arrested by the police without a warrant under § 88-1(4) did the Code require that the police advise the accused of the right to retain an attorney and to have him be present during the interrogation.[23]

In 1997, however, as was mentioned in Sect. 15.3.2, above, Taiwan's Legislative Yuan finally gave statutory recognition to the right to silence with the enactment of § 95 CCP, which also required police to advise arrestees of the right to silence and the right to counsel, admonitions tantamount to those required by the famous US *Miranda* decision. However, the Code at that time said nothing about the effect of the police's failure to warn the accused of his right to silence or counsel on the admissibility of statements thereafter taken and a violation of the *Miranda*-type

[23] § 88-1 (4) CCP provides: "When arresting an accused under Sect. 15.1 of this Article, the prosecutor, judicial police officer, or judicial policeman shall advise the accused and his family that they may retain an attorney to appear at interrogations".

warnings required by § 95 CCP was unlikely to lead to the exclusion of confessions obtained. Even before the amendment to § 95 CCP in 1997, § 88-1 CCP provided that police advise arrestees of the right to retain an attorney and have them present during interrogations. However, Taiwan's Supreme Court declared in a 1983 decision that police violation of the § 88-1 CCP duty to warn the accused does not bear any effect on the statements subsequently obtained as long as the violation does not affect its voluntariness.[24] This conservative decision of the Supreme Court encouraged police to ignore 188-1 CCP and not to warn the accused of his rights.

In order to change this police practice, § 158-2 CCP was added in 2003. It provides that the police's failure to warn an arrestee of his right to silence and to a lawyer leads to the exclusion of any confession thereafter obtained, unless there is proof that the police's violation of the duty to warn was in good faith and the confession was voluntary. § 158-2 CCP also provides for exclusion of confessions obtained in violation of § 100-3 CCP's prohibition of police interrogation during the nighttime, unless there is a showing of good faith and voluntariness.[25]

§ 158-2 CCP is very similar to the American *Miranda* rule in that it applies only to accuseds who are in custody following arrest. One difference is, however, that the arrestee does not have the right to a public-paid lawyer if he is indigent. Warning the accused of his rights before interrogation has today become a common police practice.

However, the CCP does not require that police cease questioning when the arrestee asserts his right to silence or right to attorney, as is the case in the US.[26] In 2007, however, the Supreme Court implied that the police indeed have such a duty. The defendant in that case was interrogated by the police at 2:13 p.m. He refused to answer questions after telling police that his lawyer would arrive at the police station at 5:00 p.m. At 2:28 p.m., however, the defendant answered police questions for unknown reasons. The Supreme Court criticized the police for starting the interrogation, without waiting for the lawyer's appearance, even after knowing the defendant had a lawyer. The Court reversed the defendant's conviction and remanded the case to the lower court to determine whether the admissibility of the confession was influenced by this factor.[27]

In addition, the Code provides an incentive for the police to cease questioning when an arrestee asserts his right to an attorney. Under the Code, an arrestee must be turned over to a competent court within 24 h for arraignment, unless certain circumstances specified by law exist. In practice, the police bring the arrestee to a

---

[24] Supreme Court, 72 Tai Sun 1332, *overruled* in March 25, 2003.

[25] "The police may interrogate the accused at nighttime only in one of the following conditions: 1. The accused consents to the interrogation. 2. In the case of arresting the accused at nighttime, the police must check whether a wrongful arrest occurs. 3. A prosecutor or a judge permits the interrogation. 4. In exigent circumstances". § 100-3 (1) CCP. The definition of "nighttime" under the Code is the time between sunset and sunrise.

[26] See Cammack, Ch. 1, at *need cite.*

[27] Supreme Court, 96 Tai-Sun 3104 (2007).

prosecutor within 16 h after the arrest. According to § 93-1 CCP, if an interrogation cannot take place because the police have to wait for the lawyer to arrive, up to 4 h of this period of waiting is not counted against the 24-h limitation. In practice, some policemen stop questioning when the arrestee demands that his attorney be present, because in waiting for the lawyer's presence, the police get an additional 4 h to keep the arrestee in custody. For various reasons, the police love to keep the arrestee as long as possible.

To prevent police manipulation of this provision, § 93-1 CCP also mandates that the police shall not interrogate the accused when waiting for the lawyer to arrive. Violation of this provision will lead to the exclusion of confessions thereafter obtained except if there is proof that the police acted in good faith and the confession was voluntary.

However, in some police stations, the accused's right to counsel means nothing more than that his attorney may be present during interrogations.[28] Even if the accused's attorney appears at the police station, some police officers will not allow the attorney to speak with the accused. They sometimes ask the attorney to sit far behind the table at which they conduct interrogations. The major function of an attorney at the police station is not to consult with the accused, but rather to watch for torture or other improper actions by the police. In this regard, Taiwan probably should do more to protect human rights.

Although an accused has the right to retain his attorney during the preliminary investigation, the government did not have a corresponding duty to appoint a lawyer for the accused under any circumstance before 2006. In that year, however, the legislature in dramatic fashion, under protest by the Minister of Justice, amended the Code and required a prosecutor to appoint a lawyer for an accused who, due to unsound mind, is unable to properly exercise his rights. This was the first time in Taiwan's legal history that the government's duty to appoint a lawyer for the accused was extended from the trial stage to the pre-trial stage, even though the scope of the right is, of course, limited to a narrow range of accuseds. It is not impossible, however, that the same right might be extended to the indigent accused in the near future.

The Supreme Court implied that a confession could be excluded if the police attempt to evade the above provisions. In a 2008 case, the police summoned a person to appear at the police station using the rubric of "relevant person", a term which does not appear in the CCP. The Supreme Court stated that this person's confession could not be excluded under § 158-2 CCP because he was not an *arrestee* as required by that section. The Court, however, indicated that the confession was still obtained in violation of the code because of the use of the unofficial rubric of "relevant person" in the summons. It concluded that the admissibility of the confession should be decided under the general exclusionary rule of § 158-4 by balancing human rights and the public interest.[29]

[28] § 245 (II) CCP: "The attorneys for defendants or suspects may be present when prosecutors, judicial police officers, or judicial policemen interrogate defendants or suspects".

[29] Supreme Court, 97 Tai-Sun 225 (2008).

It may be recalled, that the courts never excluded physical evidence before 1998, when the Supreme Court created the exclusionary rule. Since 1998, however, the Supreme Court has not had a chance to decide whether physical evidence which is the fruit of an unlawful confession, whether involuntary or in violation of the *Miranda* rule, would be admissible. In theory, physical evidence could, however, be excluded under § 158-4 CCP, the general exclusionary rule.

15.3.4 Derivative Exclusion of an Otherwise Valid Confession as Fruit of an Unlawful Search or Seizure

§ 156(1) CCP explicitly provides for the exclusion of a confession which comes on the heels of an unlawful detention: "The confession of an accused not extracted by...unlawful detention or other improper means and consistent with the facts may be admitted as evidence". The use of the term "detention" in § 156(1) CCP is the same as used in the code sections dealing with pretrial "detention". It was, therefore, a common understanding that an unlawful "arrest" would not necessarily lead to the exclusion of an otherwise valid confession.

In a recent case, however, the Supreme Court held that an unlawful arrest leads to the exclusion of a confession obtained thereafter. The defendant in that case was arrested unlawfully by the police and turned over to the prosecutor for interrogation. The Court concluded that the confession before the prosecutor was *involuntary* because the physical and psychological coercion caused by the unlawful arrest obviously had extended to the prosecutorial interrogation.[30] The Court did not explain, however, why the coercion caused by the unlawful arrest obviously extended to the prosecutorial interrogation. It is noteworthy, nevertheless, that the Court excluded the confession on the ground that it was involuntary and not on the theory of fruits of the poisonous tree.

15.4 Conclusion

Illegally gathered evidence can be divided into two categories: confessions (or other statements) and physical evidence.

Involuntary confessions are excluded on the ground that they are unreliable and often inconsistent with the truth. It has been the practice of the courts and the consensus in the literature in Taiwan since the enactment of the CCP, that involuntary confessions should be excluded. The CCP even prohibits the government from using fraud, inducement, or any other improper means to obtain confessions.

[30] Supreme Court, 96 Tai-Sun 3102 (2007).

In practice, however, it is sometimes very difficult to distinguish involuntary confessions from voluntary ones. Confessions, may, on their fact, appear to be voluntary, though in reality the opposite may be true. Due to this confusion, involuntary confessions are sometimes admitted at trial. Nonetheless, in Taiwan one could not accept the idea that an otherwise valid and decisive confession should be excluded only because it could have been the product of improper inducements and thus involuntary, if this could not be proved.

It was also firmly rooted in Taiwan that the purpose of criminal prosecution and trial is to discover the truth. Unlike a confession which might be untrue, physical evidence could never contradict the truth. People believed, that to exclude physical evidence would be to exclude justice. As a result, physical evidence was never excluded even it was obtained through illegal means. It was never an issue which a trial court would waste its time to deal with.

Due to the strong dissatisfaction with the judiciary, Taiwan's people demanded the overhaul of the whole judicial system in the last decade. Protection of human rights became one of the top priorities. The right to silence, the right to counsel, and the right to privacy became highly valued principles in criminal procedure. People started to accept the idea that the ends (truth finding) might not always justify the means, even in criminal procedure. It became an acceptable theory that the exclusion of evidence is necessary to deter the government from disregarding the law.

Thus, the Supreme Court created the exclusionary rule in 1998 and Taiwan's legislature reinforced this step of the Supreme Court with repeated legislation after 2001. This included the amendment of § 416 CCP in 2001, and the amendment of § 131 CCP in 2002, both relating to evidence gathered from illegal searches. In 2003, a much broader general exclusionary rule was added in the form of § 158-4 CCP, which allows the judge to balance the protection of human rights against the public's interest in efficient law enforcement, when deciding whether or not to admit evidence gathered in violation of the law and public interest. It has also gradually been accepted that physical evidence could also be excluded under this balancing test.

With respect to the law of confessions, substantial reform began in1997, when the Legislative Yuan amended § 95 CCP to explicitly guarantee the accused's right to silence and to require admonitions as to the right to silence and counsel, similar to those required in the US *Miranda* case, before interrogations at all stages of criminal procedure. In the same year, § 100-3 CCP was enacted to limit nighttime interrogations. In 1998, § 100-1 CCP was amended so as to require taperecording of the entirety of all confessions in order to guarantee their reliability. The section also provides for videotaping when necessary and requires the exclusion of any transcript of an interrogation which is inconsistent with what is in the audio or videotape. Finally, § 158-2 CCP was added in 2003, providing that the police's failure to warn an arrestee of the right to silence and right to a lawyer leads to the exclusion of a confession thereafter obtained, unless the police were acting in good faith and the confession was voluntary.

Before 2003 it was unclear which party bore the burden of proof when it came to showing the voluntariness or involuntariness of a confession. In an early decision, the Supreme Court even held that without sufficient evidence the court could not exclude a confession contained in the file due to involuntariness. Thus, in practice, the defendant seemed to bear the burden of proving the involuntariness of confessions. Without actual injury to his body, a defendant almost always lost his claim that the confession was involuntary in the "swearing contest" with the police at trial. In 2003, §156 (III) CCP was amended and now requires that the prosecutor prove the voluntariness of a confession whenever a defendant asserts that it was obtained through improper methods.

As a result, the courts in Taiwan are now very willing to exclude confessions even if they are voluntary or their involuntariness cannot be proven.

I will not say "due process" trumps "truth finding" in Taiwan's criminal procedure. But, based upon the recent developments as described above, it is obvious that "truth finding" is not the first priority any more in Taiwan, and that "due process" is playing an increasingly important role in criminal procedure.

Chapter 16
The European Court of Human Rights: The Fair Trial Analysis Under Article 6 of the European Convention of Human Rights

F. Pınar Ölçer

16.1 Introduction

Binding on the 47 members states of the Council of Europe – and therewith potentially affecting the lives of some 800 million European citizens – The European Convention on Human Rights (ECHR) is widely recognized as "the most successful human rights treaty in the world".[1] Much of that success has to do with the extensive case law of the supranational court charged with supervision of the ECHR, namely the European Court of Human Rights (ECtHR). Famously, through an active judicial policy, the ECtHR has in a sense "multiplied" the content of the ECHR through its judicial interpretations, providing Europe with an intricate normative framework for human rights protection that interfaces with a wide range of distinct fields of law. One of the fields of law in which the ECtHR has adopted a highly active policy is that of criminal procedure.

Evidently, as criminal procedural law has a strong intrinsic connection with human rights law, the ECHR explicitly addresses criminal procedure itself, particularly in Art. 6 ECHR,[2] provision of which guarantee, the right to a fair trial. Nevertheless, the body of criminal procedural law that the ECtHR has added to the Convention, through sometimes highly extensive interpretations, again, of Art. 6

This chapter is a summary of the ECHR-report presented at The XVIIIth International Congress of the International Academy of Comparative Law (Criminal Procedure Section, "The Exclusionary Rule"), which took place in Washington D.C. from July 25 to August 1, 2010.

[1] Myjer (2002, 5), referring to: Lawson and Myjer (2000, xiii).

[2] Art. 6(1) ECHR provides, in pertinent part: "In the determination…of any criminal charge against him, everyone is entitled to a fair and public hearing…".

F.P. Ölçer (✉)
Leiden Law School,
Steenschuur 25, 2311 ES Leiden, The Netherlands
e-mail: f.p.olcer@law.leidenuniv.nl

S.C. Thaman (ed.), *Exclusionary Rules in Comparative Law*, Ius Gentium: Comparative Perspectives on Law and Justice 20, DOI 10.1007/978-94-007-5348-8_16,

ECHR in particular, is much more vast than could be guessed from the text of the Convention alone. Often making quite fundamental (and detailed) determinations as to how member states should arrange their criminal procedural affairs, the ECtHR has thus become a foremost authority in European criminal procedural human rights law.

One of the areas of criminal procedure in which the ECtHR has become quite active is that of rules regarding the admission and/or exclusion of illegally obtained evidence. While this issue is not explicitly addressed in the Convention at all, the ECtHR has gradually interpreted various provisions of the Convention – and again, mainly Art. 6 ECHR – to develop an important normative protective structure in this regard. On the one hand, this judicially crafted framework is oriented to the pretrial stage itself, and as such describes substantive norms which must be adhered to in pretrial criminal procedural investigations (such as the privilege against self-incrimination, the right to counsel, or the right to privacy in one's home or private communications). On the other, the framework determines rules for the admission and/or exclusion of evidence obtained through violation of such substantive norms in the pretrial phase.

This chapter will concentrate on the ECtHR's case law in relation to both aspects of this normative framework, i.e. the mechanism through which the ECtHR determines if and how illegally obtained evidence may (or may not) be used as evidence, as well as (some of the) substantive pretrial ECHR norms which may be violated in pretrial criminal investigations. The substantive pretrial norms which will be discussed in this chapter are: (1) the privilege against self-incrimination and the right to remain silent, protected under Art. 6 ECHR; (2) Art. 3 ECHR's prohibition on torture or inhuman or degrading treatment in the context of the interrogation of criminal suspects; (3) the right to counsel during the pretrial investigation, guaranteed by Art. 6(3)(c) ECHR and (4) violations of the right to privacy guaranteed by Art. 8 ECHR.

We will see, that in its relatively brief case law history in dealing with these violations, the ECtHR has developed strong case law in the area of Art. 3 ECHR violations, to the extent that the use of evidence gained from such a violation is apt to result in the finding of a violation of the Art. 6 ECHR fair-trial guarantee. The same is true for violations of the right to counsel during the criminal investigation, following the landmark decision of *Salduz v. Turkey* by the Grand Chamber of the ECtHR in November, 2008[3] and the privilege against self-incrimination or the right to remain silent. In relation to violations of other norms however, the Court will engage in balancing, and is not averse to finding that use of evidence obtained through such violations will not necessarily violate the right to a fair trial, if certain conditions are fulfilled.

[3] Salduz v. Turkey (G.C.)(2009), 49 E.H.R.R. 19, 421.

16.2 The General Theory of Admissibility of Illegally Obtained Evidence in the Case Law of the European Court of Human Rights

16.2.1 The Right to the Fair Use of Evidence and the Two-Tiered Analytical Approach

In ECtHR jurisprudence, the admissibility and exclusion of illegally obtained evidence can best be understood in terms of a "right to the fair use of evidence". In its early case law dealing with complaints regarding the use of unlawfully obtained evidence the ECtHR adhered to a cautious approach. This cautious approach is still reflected in the general principles the Court refers to when evaluating such complaints. As the Court stated in *Schenk v. Switzerland*: "(w)hile Article 6 guarantees the right to a fair hearing, it does not lay down any rules on the admissibility of evidence as such, which is primarily a matter for regulation under national law".[4] The Court also typically notes that:

> It is therefore not the role of the Court to determine, as a matter of principle, whether particular types of evidence – for example, evidence obtained unlawfully in terms of domestic law – may be admissible. The question which must be answered is whether the proceedings as a whole, including the way in which the evidence was obtained, were fair. This involves an examination of the 'unlawfulness' in question and, where the violation of another Convention right is concerned, the nature of the violation found (...).[5]

In its early case law, the ECtHR nearly always concluded that Art. 6 ECHR had *not* been violated, therewith fortifying the notion that Art. 6 ECHR does *not* contain rules of admissibility or exclusion with regards to illegally obtained evidence.[6] However, importantly, nearly all the early cases dealt with violations of the right to privacy under Art. 8 ECHR. In later jurisprudence, as cases concerning other types of substantive norm violations were submitted to the ECtHR – and the Court did find violations of Art. 6 ECHR because of the use of evidence so obtained – it became apparent that the Court's early cautiousness had more to do with its (low) appraisal of the effect of Art. 8 ECHR violations on the fairness of the use of evidence, rather than a general reticence in formulating and imposing human rights standards for evidence exclusion and admission.

The right to fair use of evidence can best be depicted as a protective system based on a two-tiered analytical model. In the first tier, the analysis seeks to determine if

---

[4] Schenk v. Switzerland (1991), 13 E.H.R.R. 1342, 265–266, § 46.

[5] Gäfgen v. Germany (2011), 52 E.H.R.R. 1, 41, § 163, citing Khan v United Kingdom (2001) 31 E.H.R.R. 45, 1016, 1025–1026, §34; PG v United Kingdom (2008) 46 E.H.R.R. 51, 1272, 1294–1295, §76; and Allan v United Kingdom (2003) 36 E.H.R.R. 12, 143, 155–156, §42.

[6] In reflecting on this case law, Bradley predicted that it "(...) will likely solidify the resistance of other countries to America's mandatory exclusionary rule" Bradley (2001, 376).

convention rights were violated during the preliminary or pretrial investigation of the case in the form of violations of Art. 3 ECHR (torture or inhuman and degrading treatment); Art. 8 ECHR (right to privacy); Art. 6(3)(c) ECHR (right to counsel) and the privilege against self-incrimination and the right to remain silent, also protected by Art. 6 ECHR.

In the second tier of analysis, the court looks to see if the admission (or use) of evidence obtained through the violation of a first tier norm violated Art. 6 ECHR. One may distinguish three scenarios in the ECtHR case law. The first regards a category of illegally obtained evidence which presents a low risk to trial fairness, to which, in the court's view, violations of the right to privacy belong. The second category regards illegally obtained evidence, the use of which generally presents a high risk to fairness, such as violations of Art. 3 ECHR, not amounting to torture. The third category regards illegally obtained evidence which presents so high a risk to fairness, that it may absolutely not be used, such as evidence obtained through torture. The Court will engage in balancing in all scenarios, except the last. Otherwise, the greater the risk, the more care must be taken in the balancing process, i.e. the more must be done to restore or recuperate the balance of (overall) fairness.

In determining whether balancing was achieved, the ECtHR conducts the following tests. The defense must have been presented with adequate opportunity to invoke defense rights in challenging the manner in which the evidence was obtained, as well as the use thereof. Thus, the defendant must have been able to exercise information rights,[7] have the benefit of legal assistance at trial and be able to present this type of evidentiary challenge in an adversarial setting.[8] Finally, in testing whether balancing was achieved, the ECtHR looks to see whether the trier of fact gave reasons for its decisions on admissibility and checks to make sure that the conviction was not based solely on the illegally obtained evidence.[9]

In determining in first-tier analysis whether a Convention right was violated, the ECtHR, especially when dealing with implied rights, not explicitly articulated in the language of the ECHR (such as the privilege against self-incrimination), will also

[7] Information rights in Art. 6 ECHR can be understood as the aggregate of the right to information as that right follows from the principle of equality of arms (implicitly read in the notion of fairness in Art. 6 (1) ECHR) and the various explicit information rights enumerated in Art. 6 (3) ECHR.

[8] See Bykov v. Russia [GC], no. 4378/02, ECHR, 21 January 2009, § 90 and more recently, Lisica v. Croatia, No. 20100/06, ECHR, 25 Feb. 2010, § 49: "In determining whether the proceedings as a whole were fair, regard must also be had to whether the rights of the defence were respected. It must be examined in particular whether the applicant was given the opportunity of challenging the authenticity of the evidence and of opposing its use".

[9] Ibid., § 95–96, where the Court noted that "the impugned recording, together with the physical evidence obtained through the covert operation, was not the only evidence relied on by the domestic court as the basis for the applicant's conviction" and pointed to what it saw to be the "key evidence" in the form of a "statement by V., who had reported to the FSB that the applicant had ordered him to kill S., and had handed in the gun".

look to broader factors, such as public interest concems, needs brought about by the rise in organized crime, national security interests, the interests of witnesses, etc.

Second-tier analysis is more particular to ECHR law, and not found in many national approaches to evidentiary exclusion. Here, in evaluating whether or not an overall balance of fairness was achieved the court will also weigh: (1) the gravity of the norm violation established during first-tier analysis; (2) the probative value of the evidence obtained through that violation; and at times the seriousness of the crime being investigated, and thus the public interest in solving the crime and punishing the guilty culprit.

16.2.2 Dynamism in Art. 6 ECHR

In understanding the ECtHR's protective model regarding the admission and exclusion of illegally obtained evidence, it is important to keep in mind that because it is of judicial construct, the Court has a good degree of latitude in shaping its composite rules and adapting them as it sees fit. Certainly, the Court's approach to illegally obtained evidence and its use at trial, may be characterized as dynamic, in the sense that the Court quite frequently adds to and adapts its own model. In doing so, the Court may create new areas of protection on its own without necessarily referring to shared European standards, or may refer to developments in the legal systems of member states of the Council of Europe or more generally to international law.

With regard to departing from its own precedent, the ECtHR is straightforward: "(w)hile it is in the interests of legal certainty, foreseeability and equality before the law that the Court should not depart, without good reason, from precedents laid down in previous cases, a failure by the Court to maintain a dynamic and evolutive approach would risk rendering it a bar to reform or improvement. It must be remembered that the Convention is designed to 'guarantee not rights that are theoretical or illusory but rights that are practical and effective'.[10]

Besides the rights explicitly mentioned in the subsections of Art. 6 ECHR, i.e., the presumption of innocence, the right to notice, counsel and confrontation, the ECtHR has explicitly extended the protections of Art. 6 ECHR to include further implicit rights, some of which may already apply pretrial, such as the privilege against self-incrimination and the right to remain silent, the right not be incited or entrapped into committing crimes and the right to legal counsel.[11]

The right to fair use of evidence is itself an implicit addition, and as such constitutes a protective bridge between the pretrial and trial phase, functioning to determine whether or not pretrial unfairness can be resolved at trial. The Court is

[10] Micallef v. Malta (G.C.)(2010), 50 E.H.R.R. 37, 920, 940, § 81.

[11] See for early pretrial application of Art. 6 ECHR, Imbrioscia v. Switzerland (1994), 17 E.H.R.R. 441, § 36.

also aware of other remedies for Convention violations, where it does not find a violation of the right to a fair trial in the second-tier analysis. One is, of course, monetary compensation, which may be accomplished under Art. 41 ECHR.[12] The Court also occasionally refers to other remedies, such as discipline, or criminal prosecution of the officials who violated the petitioner's rights which are used, sometimes in lieu of exclusion, in some European Countries.[13]

16.2.3 *The General Balancing Test*

In its Art. 6 fair trial analysis, the Court engages in a broad and flexible umbrella test of balancing, allowing for restrictions of sub-rights, as long as the proceedings as a whole were fair. Restrictions of some rights may be allowed, if they are grounded in a legitimate necessity, are kept to a minimum, and are adequately compensated for. Whether or not compensation is achieved depends on the manner in which other rights are affected. In any analysis of Art. 6 ECHR, an important point of departure is that "(i)n a democratic society within the meaning of the Convention, the right to a fair administration of justice holds such a prominent place that a restrictive interpretation of Article 6 para. 1 would not correspond to the aim and the purpose of that provision".[14]

High as its status may be however, the intricate structure of Art. 6 ECHR, which consists of a catalogue of different types of rights, creates interpretative difficulties: "(w)hile the right to a fair trial under Article 6 is an unqualified right, what constitutes a fair trial cannot be the subject of a single unvarying rule but must depend on the circumstances of the particular case".[15] In a similar way, the ECtHR's act of "balancing" in the Art. 6 ECHR context defies reduction to precise rules. The ECtHR's decisions have been seen to reflect, first, a "case-by-case approach" and second, a use of "multi-prong tests".[16] Yet, as Gerards has noted in relation to (aspects of) other Convention rights, where the Court has adopted multi-pronged tests, in practical interpretation, it "does not seem to pay equal attention to the various parts" of those tests.[17] "It is clear from many analyses of the Court's case law that there is no logical order between the various elements of (…) [the tests], and that hardly any explanation can be given" for the use of some tests in some cases, and other tests in other instances.[18] Gerards continues:

---

[12] See Allan v. United Kingdom (2003), 36 E.H.R.R. 12, 143, 160, § 60, where the petitioner was awarded € 1642 for non-pecuniary damages for violations of the right to privacy, though no Art. 6 violation was found.

[13] See Gäfgen v. Germany (G.C.)(2011), 52 E.H.R.R. 1, 31–33, §§ 122–125.

[14] Delcourt v. Belgium (1979–1980), 1 E.H.R.R. 355, 366–367, § 25.

[15] O'Halloran and Francis v. United Kingdom (G.C.) (2008), 46 E.H.R.R. 21, 397, 413, § 53.

[16] Gerards (2009, 420).

[17] Ibid, 422.

[18] Ibid.

> In fact, in the largest proportion of cases, the Court just plunges into a general test of balancing. Indeed, the language of balancing would seem to explain its case-law much better than the use of multi-prong tests would seem to do. Indeed, in applying its balancing test, the Court mostly mentions a variety of aspects which would seem to stress the importance and weight of the interests at stake, and then it considers that one or the other tips the scale.[19]

In a similar manner, the Court's Art. 6 ECHR balancing is not always well-structured and is complicated by its at times unclear applications of what appears to be a well-conceived approach. This sometimes makes it difficult to ascertain how and why a particular outcome was reached in a concrete case.

16.2.4 Balancing of the Gravity of the Violation, the Seriousness of the Crime Investigated, and the Probative Value of the Evidence

In making its "second-tier" evaluation as to whether use of the evidence would be "fair" under Art. 6 ECHR, the ECtHR weighs the gravity of the underlying substantive pretrial norm violation against the probative value of the evidence obtained through that violation. When a norm violation is considered to be "grave", such as intentionally threatening a suspect with torture, as in *Gäfgen v. Germany*, then the court leans toward exclusion and considers the necessity of deterring such egregious conduct, much as would an American court when making a finding that an officer in violating the constitution did not act in "good faith". As the ECtHR stated in *Gäfgen*, "the use of evidence absolutely prohibited by Art. 3 might be an incentive for law-enforcement officers to use such methods notwithstanding such absolute prohibition".[20]

The ECtHR has weighed the truth-telling nature of the evidence in many cases dealing with alleged violations of Art. 6(3)(d) ECHR which guarantees criminal defendants the right to confront and examine prosecution witnesses. In this area, a crucial aspect of hearsay testimony is its inherent unreliability, so the ECtHR is quick to find that the use of such evidence as the main evidence of guilt in a criminal case constitutes a violation of Arts. 6(1), and 6(3)(d) ECHR.[21] Once the probative value of evidence becomes a factor in the ECtHR's fair-trial analysis under Art. 6 ECHR, its approach begins to look more like that of a continental European country steeped in the inquisitorial tradition which "admit all evidence that is logically relevant" rather than a common law system, which is "mainly concerned with the

---

[19] Ibid.

[20] Gäfgen v. Germany (G.C.)(2011), 52 E.H.R.R. 1, 45, § 178.

[21] Delta v. France (1993), 16 E.H.R.R. 574 and Kostovski v. Netherlands (1990), 12 E.H.R.R. 434, and discussion in Thaman (2008, 129–130, 137–140).

issue of admissibility".[22] Continental European countries are less likely to exclude evidence for "reasons extraneous to truth-finding considerations", such as reliable evidence obtained in an illegal manner.[23] Especially the US will consciously sacrifice "factfinding accuracy for the sake of other values".[24]

Outside the realm of substantive norm violations the ECtHR has identified as particularly grave, the ECHR "fair-use" model is oriented to remedying unfairness so that illegally obtained evidence can be used, rather than preemptively protecting fairness by keeping evidence out, which more reflects the traditional US approach. It allows unfairness to be processed away through compensation mechanisms (balancing) that are unrelated to the issues that make evidence problematic in the first place (the substantive norm, the violation of which led to its acquisition). The ECtHR appears to "recuperate" fairness while allowing evidence-use much more readily if the evidence is of high probative value, as is physical evidence. This can explain the unwillingness of the court to find a fair trial violation when the evidence was obtained in violation of Art. 8 ECHR's right to privacy, which often leads to discovery of physical evidence or freely spoken words accessed through wire-tapping.

In privacy cases, the ECtHR consistently holds that "(…) regard must be had to the quality of the evidence, including whether the circumstances in which it was obtained cast doubts on its reliability or accuracy *and* that (w)hile no problem of fairness necessarily arises where the evidence obtained was unsupported by other material, it may be noted that where the evidence is very strong and there is no risk of its being unreliable, the need for supporting evidence is correspondingly weaker".[25] Yet, where the violation is of a different nature, such as the use of inhuman and degrading treatment in violation of Art. 3 ECHR, the Court has found the use of highly probative evidence (cocaine extracted through the use of emetics) to be a violation of Art. 6 ECHR.[26] This is even more so the case if the violation amounted to torture. In *Gäfgen v. Germany*, which featured real evidence obtained "indirectly" through ill-treatment consisting in the threat of torture, the ECtHR stated:

> The use of such evidence, secured as a result of a violation of one of the core and absolute rights guaranteed by the Convention, always raises serious issues as to the fairness of the proceedings, even if the admission of such evidence was not decisive in securing a conviction. Accordingly, the Court has found in respect of confessions, as such, that the admission of statements obtained as a result of torture or of other ill-treatment in breach of Article 3 as evidence to establish the relevant facts in criminal proceedings rendered the proceedings as a whole unfair. This finding applied irrespective of the probative value of the statements and irrespective of whether their use was decisive in securing the defendant's conviction.

---

[22] Damaška (1973, 513).

[23] Ibid.

[24] Ibid, 525.

[25] Allan v. United Kingdom (2003), 36 E.H.R.R. 12, 143, 156, § 43.

[26] Jalloh v. Germany(G.C.) (2007), 44 E.H.R.R. 42, 667, 694, § 106.

> As to the use at the trial of real evidence obtained as a direct result of ill-treatment in breach of Article 3, the Court has considered that incriminating real evidence obtained as a result of acts of violence, at least if those acts had to be characterised as torture, should never be relied on as proof of the victim's guilt, irrespective of its probative value (...).[27]

In conclusion, the ECtHR appears to not consider violations of the Art. 8 ECHR right to privacy to be as fundamental as torture or infliction of inhuman or degrading treatment under Art. 3 ECHR, and will exclude probative evidence in the latter cases, but seldom in the former. The ECtHR has also never considered the probative value of evidence obtained in violation of the pretrial right to counsel and seems also not to attach weight to high probative value where the right to remain silent is concerned.

In *Jalloh*, the ECtHR stresses another factor, "the weight of the public interest in the investigation of the particular offence at issue", yet stresses that the "public interest concerns cannot justify measures which extinguish the very essence of an applicant's defence rights".[28] And in cases involving the violation of Art. 3 ECHR, the court indicated that evidence obtained as a result thereof could not be used "irrespective of the seriousness of the offence allegedly committed".[29]

As for violations of the privilege against self-incrimination and right to silence, protected by Art. 6 ECHR, the ECtHR has stated: "the general requirements of fairness contained in Article 6, including the right not to incriminate oneself, apply to criminal proceedings in respect of all types of criminal offences without distinction from the most simple to the most complex. The public interest could not be relied on to justify the use of answers compulsorily obtained in a non-judicial investigation to incriminate the accused during the trial proceedings".[30]

The same is true of violations of the right to counsel during the pretrial stage of criminal proceedings. There, the Court holds that the protective principles expounded in that case "are particularly called for in the case of serious charges, for it is in the face of the heaviest penalties that respect for the right to a fair trial is to be ensured to the highest possible degree by democratic societies".[31] This reversal might appear confusing, unless one is to rank the right to counsel during the preliminary investigation, reinforced by the *Salduz* judgment, along with the protections of Art. 3 ECHR as absolute rights, brooking of no balancing whatsoever in relation to truth-finding or the public interest in solving serious cases.

Thus one can ascertain three discernible categories of violations which bring with them different approaches in relation to exclusion of evidence: (1) privacy violations, which can easily be purged so as to allow evidence admissibility; (2) violations of other Convention rights, which require more exacting balancing, and; (3) violations that ineluctably lead to a violation of the right to a fair trial under Art.

---

[27] Gäfgen v. Germany (G.C.)(2011), 52 E.H.R.R. 1, 42, §§ 165–167.

[28] Jalloh v. Germany (G.C.)(2007), 44 E.H.R.R. 42, 692–693, § 97.

[29] Ibid, 693–694, § 106.

[30] Saunders (1997), 23 E.H.R.R. 313, 340, § 74.

[31] Salduz v. Turkey (GC)(2009), 49 E.H.R.R. 19, 421, 437, § 54.

6 ECHR if the evidence is used at trial. Probative value then will always be a decisive factor in the first category, will go into the balance in the second, yet will have no effect in the third.

But what makes privacy violations, which are serious enough to merit protection in human rights conventions and national constitutions, less serious than other rights violations, such as violations of the privilege against self-incrimination, violations of Art. 3 ECHR, or violations of the right to counsel? The explanation seems to be that the EctHR does not discount privacy violations as serious in an of themselves, but rather finds them to be less offensive to fairness. Thus, even the most serious privacy violation is not considered to be grave from a *criminal procedural perspective* and thus the use of evidence so obtained is seen to be less problematic.

Violations of the various rights included in Art. 6 ECHR which affect suspects during the pretrial stage of criminal proceedings, such as the privilege against self-incrimination, the right to remain silent, the right to pretrial legal assistance and, the "right not to be incited to commit a crime", are part and parcel of the "fairness" protected by the ECHR and have no application outside of realm of criminal procedure.

Privacy violations are different, and, according to the ECtHR, do not necessarily require a remedy *within* criminal procedure. The Court has never found a fair trial violation based on the use of evidence obtained through a violation of Art. 8 ECHR, though it has found many important violations of Art. 8 ECHR itself because of illegal investigative acts. In contrast, the Court has often found violations of Art. 6 ECHR because of the use of evidence where other types of pretrial norm violations were concerned.

16.2.5 *Fruits of the Poisonous Tree, Independent Source, Inevitable Discovery*

In its second-tier decision as to whether use of evidence would result in a violation of the Art. 6 ECHR right to a fair trial, the ECtHR takes into consideration many of the doctrines developed by the United States Supreme Court, such as attenuation of the taint of a violation, or whether the evidence was found through a source independent of the violation, or would have inevitably been discovered despite the violation.

In *Schenk v. Switzerland,*[32] one of the Court's considerations in finding no violation of Art. 6 ECHR was that the same information could have been introduced at trial through other means, thereby applying the hypothetical independent source doctrine. The ECtHR Grand Chamber in *Gäfgen v. Germany* applied the "attenuation doctrine" when it found that the defendant's confession at trial followed

[32] Schenk v. Switzerland (1991), 13 E.H.R.R. 242, 266, § 48.

a "break in the causal chain" in relation to the confession which was obtained in violation of Art. 3 ECHR,[33] and clearly recognized the doctrine of "inevitable discovery", when discussing whether the victim's body would have been found even if the defendant had not shown the police its location as a result of the violation.[34]

16.3 Substantive Norm Violations: First-Tier Analysis in Relation to Violations Involving the Taking of Confessions

16.3.1 The Privilege Against Self-Incrimination and the Right to Silence

In ECtHR case law, the privilege against self-incrimination and the right to remain silent have a high status. The Court describes them as "(...) generally recognised international standards which lie at the heart of the notion of a fair procedure under Article 6".[35] Therefore, "public interest concerns cannot justify measures which extinguish the very essence"[36] of those rights.

The privilege against self-incrimination and the right to remain silent have given rise to a multitude of questions in ECtHR case law. In relation to their pretrial application, several issues are of particular importance. In the first place, the rationale of these norms in ECHR law is not entirely clear. In the second place, the scope of both norms fluctuates in case law.

What is clear, is that the privilege against self-incrimination and the right to remain silent have a broad range and can encompass distinct categories of violations, which may differ in severity or in type. The most severe violations will occur through acts that entail violation of not only the privilege against self-incrimination and/or the right to silence, but also – concurrently – of the prohibition of torture per Art. 3 ECHR. A second category consists of violations of the privilege against self-incrimination and/or the right to silence that concurrently qualify as ill-treatment, again within the terms of Art. 3 ECHR. A third category (which is not necessarily less severe than the second, as that will depend on the gravity of the ill-treatment in question), constitutes acts that do not simultaneously violate Art. 3 ECHR: there is no torture or ill-treatment, but there is direct compulsion. A fourth category is relatively new in ECHR case law and regards violations that do not feature compulsion, but deception.

---

[33] Gäfgen v. Germany (G.C.)(2011), 52 E.H.R.R. 1, 46, § 180.

[34] Ibid, 44, § 174.

[35] Jalloh v. Germany (G.C.) (2007), 44 E.H.R.R. 42, 693, § 100.

[36] Ibid, § 97.

16.3.1.1 The Development of the Privilege Against Self-Incrimination and the Right to Silence in ECtHR Case Law

According to the ECtHR, the rationale of the privilege against self-incrimination consists, "(…) inter alia, in the protection of the accused against improper compulsion by the authorities, thereby contributing to the avoidance of miscarriages of justice and to the fulfillment of the aims of Article 6".[37] Some connection seems to exist between the privilege against self-incrimination and the presumption of innocence, expressly guaranteed by Art. 6(2) ECHR, but what that connection is, is not abundantly clear.[38] While the ECtHR has never directly stated that the protection of human dignity is a basis for the privilege against self-incrimination and the related right to silence, Judge Martens, dissenting in *Saunders v. United Kingdom*, clearly felt the Court was heading in that direction:

> In this context I note that legal writers and courts have frequently accepted a further rationale. Its formulations vary, but they all essentially boil down to the proposition that respect for human dignity and autonomy requires that every suspect should be completely free to decide which attitude he will adopt with respect to the criminal charges against him. On this view it would be improper, because incompatible with such respect, to compel an accused to cooperate in whatever way in bringing about his own conviction. This rationale often seems to be the main justification for the broader privilege against self-incrimination.
>
> This present judgment strongly suggests that the Court now has embraced this view… [T]he Court now underlines that the privilege against self incrimination is primarily concerned 'with respecting the will of an accused person'. That comes very near to the rationale outlined above which allies both immunities to respect due to human dignity and autonomy.[39]

The ECtHr currently defines the privilege against self-incrimination and the right to remain silent as follows:

> The right not to incriminate oneself, in particular, presupposes that the prosecution in a criminal case seek to prove their case against the accused without resort to evidence obtained through methods of coercion or oppression in defiance of the will of the accused. (…) In examining whether a procedure has extinguished the very essence of the privilege against self-incrimination, the Court will have regard, in particular, to the following elements: the nature and degree of the compulsion, the existence of any relevant safeguards in the procedures and the use to which any material so obtained is put. (…) The Court has consistently held, however, that the right not to incriminate oneself is primarily concerned with respecting the will of an accused person to remain silent. As commonly understood in the legal systems of the Contracting Parties to the Convention and elsewhere, it does not extend to the use in criminal proceedings of material which may be obtained from the accused through the use of compulsory powers but which has an existence independent of the will of the

---

[37] Ibid, § 100.

[38] In Murray v. United Kingdom (1996), 22 E.H.R.R. 29, 44, §§ 56, 57, the court eventually held that allowing comment on a suspect's exercise of the right to silence and its use to justify a judgment of guilt did not violate the presumption of innocence. Ibid, 46–47, § 65.

[39] Saunders v. United Kingdom (1997), 23 E.H.R.R. 313, 352-353 (§ 9, Martens, dissent).

suspect such as, inter alia, documents acquired pursuant to a warrant, breath, blood, urine, hair or voice samples and bodily tissue for the purpose of DNA testing.[40]

Although the ECtHR continues to hold that both the privilege against self-incrimination and the right to remain silent are not absolute, an important distinction was made in the *Saunders* case, in which no exceptions were tolerated in relation to the right to remain silent, while the privilege was not deemed to be absolute. That difference hinged on the distinction between real and testimonial evidence, or, in terms of the Court, evidence that does and does not have existence independent of the will of the suspect. Evidence that exists independently of the will of the suspect, such as physical evidence, already exists: the suspect does not have to *willfully* produce it. The right to remain silent on the other hand protects all written and verbal testimony, the production of which is dependent on the will of the suspect. Thus, suspects could never be directly compelled to produce written and verbal evidence that might tend to incriminate (even through impeachment of the suspect's credibility), but could be compelled to provide real evidence, already in existence.[41]

An exception, however, was made in *Jalloh v. Germany*, when the Grand Chamber of the ECtHR held that when Art. 3 ECHR is violated by the use of inhuman or degrading treatment (in that case forced use of an emetic to induce vomiting and make the defendant expel swallowed narcotics from his body), in order to secure physical evidence, then this enhanced compulsion constitutes a violation of the privilege against self-incrimination under Art. 6 ECHR as well, and use of the evidence violates the right to a fair trial.[42]

In *O' Halloran and Francis v. United Kingdom*, the applicants claimed that a statute which compelled them to produce information as to the identity of the driver of an automobile registered to them which was photographed in the context of speeding violations, violated their privilege against self-incrimination. The ECtHR found no violation after engaging in a balancing test, one major component of which was the minor nature of the offense in question and the fact that the regulation of automobiles is necessary as they can cause serious bodily harm and their owners and drivers have accepted certain responsibilities and obligations.[43] The Court also stated that "even if a clear distinction could be made in every case between the use of compulsion to obtain incriminatory statements on the one hand and "real" evidence of an incriminatory nature on the other" it emphasized that *Jalloh* was not decided on the basis of the type of evidence yielded, but on the fact that physical coercion was used to get the suspect to turn it over.[44]

---

[40] Jalloh v. Germany (G.C.)(2007), 44 E.H.R.R. 32, 667, 693, §§ 100–102.

[41] Saunders v. United Kingdom (1997), 23 E.H.R.R. 313, 337–339, §§ 69–71.

[42] Jalloh v. Germany (G.C.)(2007), 44 E.H.R.R. 32, 667, 695, §§ 113–116.

[43] O'Halloran and Francis v. United Kingdom (G.C.)(2008), 46 E.H.R.R. 21, 397, 414–415,§§ 57–58.

[44] Ibid, 413–414, § 54.

16.3.1.2 The Treatment of Involuntary Confessions or Declarations

Violations of Art. 3 ECHR: Torture and Inhuman and Degrading Treatment

In *Gäfgen v. Germany* police threatened a Frankfurt law student with torture and other brutality, if he did not reveal the whereabouts of a child kidnap victim, whom they thought may still be alive. He made incriminating statements and took them to the lake where he had disposed of the child's body. A report of the autopsy conducted on the boy's body, and evidence of the tire tracks of defendant's car near the lake were used at trial, though all his statements were suppressed.[45] The ECtHR Grand Chamber deemed that the threats constituted "inhuman and degrading" treatment and were thus in violation of Art. 3 ECHR, but did not rise to torture. Since the defendant confessed his guilt at trial, the court found that his courtroom testimony was no longer the fruit of the Art. 3 ECHR violation, since he was represented by counsel, and the court based its guilty judgment on the courtroom confession alone, only using the ill-gotten "fruits" to corroborate its truthfulness.[46]

The Grand Chamber of the ECtHR found that the non-derogable Art. 3 ECHR "enshrines one of the most fundamental values of democratic societies" and thus "makes no provision for exceptions" even in "the most difficult circumstances, such as the fight against terrorism and organised crime" or in relation to the "nature of the offence allegedly committed".[47]

Whether the acts of law enforcement officials constitute "torture" or "inhuman and degrading treatment" depends on "all the circumstances of the case, such as the duration of the treatment, its physical or mental effects", the "sex, age and state of health of the victim", the "purpose for which the treatment was inflicted together with the intention or motivation behind it", and the "context, such as an atmosphere of heightened tension and emotions".[48] The ECtHR has found treatment to be "inhuman" when it was "premeditated, was applied for hours at a stretch and caused either actual bodily injury or intense physical and mental suffering", and "degrading" when it arouses in its victims "feelings of fear, anguish and inferiority capable of humiliating and debasing them and possibly breaking their physical or moral resistance, or when it was such as to drive the victim to act against his will or conscience".[49] To be qualified as "torture" there must be "deliberate inhuman treatment causing very serious and cruel suffering" coupled with a "purposive element" such as "obtaining information, inflicting punishment or intimidating".[50] A threat to

[45] Gäfgen v. Germany (G.C.)(2011), 53 E.H.R.R. 1, 6–7, 9–10, §§ 15–18, 29–31.

[46] Ibid, 44–46, §§ 177–183.

[47] Ibid, 23, § 87.

[48] Ibid, 23, § 88.

[49] Ibid, § 89.

[50] Ibid, § 90.

commit any act prohibited by Art. 3 ECHR, such as a treat to torture, "may constitute at least inhuman treatment".[51]

The violation of Art. 3 ECHR must be proved beyond a reasonable doubt, though it may be based on inferences or unrebutted presumptions of fact. For instance, where an individual enters police custody uninjured but is injured at release, "it is incumbent on the State to provide a plausible explanation of how those injuries were caused", which, if not done, will imply a violation of Art. 3 ECHR.[52] When a violation of Art. 3 ECHR is alleged, the court must make a "particularly thorough scrutiny" but may not substitute its own assessment of the facts for that of the domestic courts".[53]

In *Gäfgen*, the Grand Chamber found that the threats had caused the applicant "considerable fear, anguish and mental suffering", but did not find any "long-term adverse psychological consequences". It determined that the threats were premeditated in order to "extract information" in an "atmosphere of heightened tension and emotions" and that the motivation was to save the child's life.[54] Yet the Court emphasized:

> the prohibition on ill-treatment of a person applies irrespective of the conduct of the victim or the motivation of the authorities. Torture, inhuman or degrading treatment cannot be inflicted even in circumstances where the life of an individual is at risk. No derogation is allowed even in the event of a public emergency threatening the life of the nation. Article 3, which has been framed in unambiguous terms, recognises that every human being has an absolute, inalienable right not to be subjected to torture or to inhuman or degrading treatment under any circumstances, even the most difficult. The philosophical basis underpinning the absolute nature of the right under Article 3 does not allow for any exceptions or justifying factors or balancing of interests, irrespective of the conduct of the person concerned and the nature of the offence at issue.[55]

In determining whether a threat of torture itself constitutes torture, or only inhuman or degrading treatment, the Grand Chamber stated: "the classification of whether a given threat of physical torture amounted to psychological torture or to inhuman or degrading treatment depends upon all the circumstances of a given case, including, notably, the severity of the pressure exerted and the intensity of the mental suffering caused". Applying this test, the Grand Chamber found that the threats in the case amounted to inhuman treatment, but not torture.[56]

The Grand Chamber compared Art. 3 ECHR with Art. 8 ECHR violations, which are always subject to a "totality of the circumstances" balancing test in determining whether the violation would trigger in turn a fair-trial violation under Art. 6 ECHR. It noted that "particular considerations apply in respect of the use in criminal

---

[51] Ibid, 24, §91.

[52] Ibid, § 92.

[53] Ibid, § 93.

[54] Ibid, 26–27, §§ 103–107.

[55] Ibid, 27, § 107.

[56] Ibid, § 108.

proceedings of evidence obtained in breach of Article 3" because the "use of such evidence, secured as a result of a violation of one of the core and absolute rights guaranteed by the Convention, always raises serious issues as to the fairness of the proceedings, even if the admission of such evidence was not decisive in securing a conviction".[57]

Because the coerced statements were not used at Gäfgen's trial, the Grand Chamber had to deal with the issue of the physical fruits of the poisonous tree, i.e., the discovery of the victim's body and the tiretracks from Gäfgen's vehicle, which were used at trial. The Grand Chamber established in this regard that "incriminating real evidence obtained as a result of acts of violence, at least if those acts had to be characterised as torture, should never be relied on as proof of the victim's guilt, irrespective of its probative value", as "(a)ny other conclusion would only serve to legitimise, indirectly, the sort of morally reprehensible conduct which the authors of Article 3 of the Convention sought to proscribe or, in other words, to 'afford brutality the cloak of law'".[58]

As for the question "whether the use of real evidence obtained by an act classified as inhuman and degrading treatment, but falling short of torture, always rendered a trial unfair, that is, irrespective of, in particular, the weight attached to the evidence, its probative value and the opportunities of the defendant to challenge its admission and use at trial", the Grand Chamber pointed out that it had left this issue unanswered in the case law.[59] While the Grand Chamber found that the discovery of the victim's body and the tiretracks were definitely caused by the Art. 3 ECHR violation,[60] it pointed to conflicting applications of the doctrine of the "fruits of the poisonous tree" in the law of the member states to the ECHR, including the exception of "inevitable discovery".[61] The Grand Chamber then appeared to engage in some "balancing" of rights and interests, despite the presence of an Art. 3 ECHR violation:

> On the one hand, the exclusion of – often reliable and compelling – real evidence at a criminal trial will hamper the effective prosecution of crime. There is no doubt that the victims of crime and their families as well as the public have an interest in the prosecution and punishment of criminals, and in the present case that interest was of high importance. Moreover, the instant case is particular also in that the impugned real evidence was derived from an illegal method of interrogation which was not in itself aimed at furthering a criminal investigation, but was applied for preventive purposes, namely in order to save a child's life, and thus in order to safeguard another core right guaranteed by the Convention, namely Article 2. On the other hand, a defendant in criminal proceedings has the right to a fair trial, which may be called into question if domestic courts use evidence obtained as a result of a violation of the prohibition of inhuman treatment under Article 3, one of the core and absolute rights guaranteed by the Convention. Indeed, there is also a vital public interest in

[57] Ibid, 41–42, § 165.

[58] Ibid, 42, § 167.

[59] Ibid.

[60] Ibid, 43, § 171.

[61] Ibid, 44, § 174.

> preserving the integrity of the judicial process and thus the values of civilised societies founded upon the rule of law.[62]

Despite the relevance of the physical evidence in the case, the Grand Chamber indicated that its use "raises serious issues as to the fairness of the proceedings" and may serve as an "an incentive for law-enforcement officers to use such methods notwithstanding such absolute prohibition", thus leading it to conclude that:

> (t)he repression of, and the effective protection of individuals from, the use of investigation methods that breach Article 3 may therefore also require, as a rule, the exclusion from use at trial of real evidence which has been obtained as the result of any violation of Article 3, even though that evidence is more remote from the breach of Article 3 than evidence extracted immediately as a consequence of a violation of that Article. Otherwise, the trial as a whole is rendered unfair.[63]

But the Grand Chamber stopped short of finding that use of evidence gained in violation of Art. 3 ECHR will ineluctably lead to a violation of the Art. 6 ECHR guarantee of a fair trial, and articulated a type of "harmless error" doctrine, indicating that "both a criminal trial's fairness and the effective protection of the absolute prohibition under Article 3 in that context are only at stake if it has been shown that the breach of Article 3 had a bearing on the outcome of the proceedings against the defendant, that is, had an impact on his or her conviction or sentence".[64] The Grand Chamber then, following the lead of the German courts, found that Gäfgen's conviction was based on his open-court confession at his trial and that the physical evidence, while having been used to corroborate the in-court confession, was not necessary to the finding of guilt, as other evidence which had been obtained independently of the coerced confession, also corroborated the veracity of the in-court confession.[65] It also found that the in-court confession was no longer a "fruit of the poisonous tree" in relation to the Art. 3 ECHR violation, because Gäfgen was told after the coerced confession, that he had a right to remain silent, and that the coerced statements could not be used against him, and he was represented by counsel at trial and stressed that he was confessing out of remorse.[66]

Involuntary Confessions Neither Obtained in Violation of Art. 3 ECHR nor Compulsion or Coercion

The ECtHR has also dealt with cases involving use of methods, such as deception, or other manipulation, which may also constitute violations of the privilege against self-incrimination or the right to remain silent guaranteed by Art. 6 ECHR. In *Allan v. The United Kingdom*, a police informant was placed in the same cell as the applicant,

---

[62] Ibid, § 175.
[63] Ibid, 45, § 178.
[64] Ibid.
[65] Ibid, 46, §§ 179, 180.
[66] Ibid, §§ 181–183.

in order to induce him to incriminate himself. The Court found that his right to remain silent had been violated. The reasoning of the Court in that regard was as follows:

> (w)hile the right to silence and the privilege against self-incrimination are primarily designed to protect against improper compulsion by the authorities and the obtaining of evidence through methods of coercion or oppression in defiance of the will of the accused, the scope of the right is not confined to cases where duress has been brought to bear on the accused or where the will of the accused has been directly overborne in some way. The right, which the Court has previously observed is at the heart of the notion of a fair procedure, serves in principle to protect the freedom of a suspected person to choose whether to speak or to remain silent when questioned by the police. Such freedom of choice is effectively undermined in a case in which, the suspect having elected to remain silent during questioning, the authorities use subterfuge to elicit, from the suspect, confessions or other statements of an incriminatory nature, which they were unable to obtain during such questioning and where the confessions or statements thereby obtained are adduced in evidence at trial.[67]

In determining whether an informer, who is not expressly a state agent, should be qualified as such in a particular case, the ECtHR referred to Canadian case law in taking into consideration "both the relationship between the informer and the State and the relationship between the informer and the accused" and concluded that "the right to silence would only be infringed where the informer was acting as an agent of the State at the time the accused made the statement and where it was the informer who caused the accused to make the statement", that is, if the "exchange between the accused and the informer would (not) have taken place, and in the form and manner in which it did, but for the intervention of the authorities". Evidence is to be regarded as "having been elicited by the informer" if the conversation between the informer and the accused can be qualified as "the functional equivalent of an interrogation".[68]

The Court attached weight in this case to the fact that the applicant had invoked his right to silence during police interrogation and that the police informer, who had been placed in the same cell for the specific purpose of eliciting self-incriminating evidence, had been "coached" and "instructed" by the police. Furthermore, the Court found that the statements made by the applicant "were not spontaneous and unprompted statements volunteered by the applicant, but were induced by the persistent questioning of H., who, at the instance of the police, channelled their conversations into discussions of the murder in circumstances which can be regarded as the functional equivalent of interrogation, without any of the safeguards which would attach to a formal police interview, including the attendance of a solicitor and the issuing of the usual caution".[69] Although there was no special relationship between the informer and the applicant and there was no indication of direct coercion being applied, the Court nevertheless found a violation of the privilege against self-incrimination under Art. 6(1) ECHR, because "the applicant would have been

---

[67] Allan v. United Kingdom (2003), 36 E.H.R.R. 12, 143, 158, § 50.

[68] Ibid, 158, § 51.

[69] Ibid, 159, § 52.

subjected to psychological pressures which impinged on the 'voluntariness' of the disclosures allegedly made by the applicant to H.: he was a suspect in a murder case, in detention and under direct pressure from the police in interrogations about the murder, and would have been susceptible to persuasion to take H., with whom he shared a cell for some weeks, into his confidence".[70]

The decision in *Allan* can be compared with that in *Bykov v. Russia*,[71] where the surreptitious interrogation by a police informant was not carried out in police custody. In *Bykov*, the police informer was a member of Bykov's entourage who had approached law enforcement authorities, alleging that Bykov had asked him to murder a former business associate. The authorities arranged for false media coverage, indicating that the former business associate had indeed been found dead in his home, together with another victim. Wearing a bug, the police informer then went to Bykov's estate for the purpose of eliciting self-incriminating evidence. He took with him some objects that he claimed to have taken from the victim's house and told Bykov that he had committed the murder. Police officers recorded their conversation from outside the estate.[72]

The Court found no violation of the right to silence in this case, because there had been no psychological pressure on Bykov, due to the fact that the conversation had taken place on his own estate.[73] Judge Spielmann, writing for four other judges, disagreed in his dissenting opinion. Despite the lack of custody, he stressed that the police informer had operated as an agent of the State, was under its control, and that "the applicant's conduct was therefore not solely, or mainly, guided by events which would have taken place under normal circumstances" and because he had been the "victim of a ruse, his statements and reaction cannot reasonably be said to have been voluntary or spontaneous".[74]

In comparing *Allan* with *Bykov* it appears that the ECtHR places great weight on the inherent coerciveness of custody in determining whether police deception sufficed to render a confession involuntary and therefore in violation of the privilege against self-incrimination and the right to silence.

16.3.1.3 Pretrial Right to Counsel as a Protection of the Privilege Against Self-Incrimination and the Right to Silence

In its November 2008 Grand Chamber judgment in *Salduz v. Turkey*,[75] the ECtHR found that Art. 6 ECHR, the right to a fair trial was violated, because the applicant in that case was denied the pretrial right to legal assistance during custodial police

---

[70] Ibid.

[71] Bykov v. Russia (G.C.), No. 4378/02, ECHR, 10 March 2009.

[72] Ibid, §§ 10–14.

[73] Ibid, §§ 101–102.

[74] Ibid, §§ 30–35 (partly dissenting opinion of Judge Spielmann).

[75] Salduz v. Turkey (GC), (2009), 49 E.H.R.R. 19, 421.

interrogation, and because the self-incriminating statement he made to the police (which he later retracted), was used as (the main) evidence of his guilt. The constituted a drastic change vis-à-vis the ECtHR's earlier case law.[76]

Formerly, the ECtHR had recognized a pretrial right to legal assistance, but had allowed for restrictions of what was then considered to be a non-absolute right for "good cause".[77] In each case, the test was "whether the restriction was justified and, if so, whether, in the light of the entirety of the proceedings, it has not deprived the accused of a fair hearing, for even a justified restriction is capable of doing so in certain circumstances".[78] That standard not only generally represented a low enough threshold to allow for broad, if not structural, limitations of the right, its application in the earlier second section chamber judgment in *Salduz* itself resulted in the finding that Art. §6(3)(c) ECHR had not been violated.[79] The Grand Chamber did more than reverse the chamber decision, opting to change the test by which the effective guarantee of the right to pretrial legal assistance must henceforth be judged.

The new test contains three separate rules. In the first place, the standard for restrictions has been raised from "good cause" to "compelling reasons", which may only "exceptionally" justify limitation. In the second place, even if compelling reasons are to be given, that does not mean that the rights of the accused will automatically not have been prejudiced. That leaves open a range of situations in which the right to a fair trial may still be violated due to a restriction, regardless of a justification for it. Those situations are as of yet mainly undefined, except for one: the *use as evidence of self-incriminating statements* made during police interrogation without access to a lawyer will almost certainly always violate Art. 6 ECHR. This has become a nearly absolute rule of exclusion.

The ECtHR obviously means business with regards to early pretrial legal assistance. As of March 2012, the Court has confirmed *Salduz* in some 125 further judgments, though many did not result in a finding of a violation of Art. 6 ECHR. In Europe, this case law has had deep impact. The legal systems of more than a few Council of Europe member states do not (or, at the time of the judgment, did not) provide for legal assistance in (the early phases) of police custody, notably before or during police interrogation.[80] *Salduz*-case law compels member states to alter that situation.

---

[76] Ibid, 436–437, §§ 52–55.

[77] The right to pretrial legal assistance in relation to police interrogation was first recognized in Imbrioscia v. Switzerland (1994), 17 E.H.R.R. 441, 455–456, §§ 36–38. The principles deployed with regards to this right prior to the enunciation of Salduz-rules were formulated in Murray v. United Kingdom (1996), 22 E.H.R.R. 29, 47, § 67.

[78] Salduz (GC)(2009), 49 E.H.R.R., 19, 421, 436, § 52.

[79] Salduz v. Turkey, No. 36391/02, ECHR, 26 April 2007, §§ 22–24. That decision was not unanimous, the Court's Second Section finding by five votes to two that there had been no violation of Article 6 § 3 (c) ECHR.

[80] As of February, 2009, the right to legal assistance during police interrogation was provided for by law in only 17 out of the 27 member states of the European Union. Spronken (2009, 94–95).

As may already be understood from the original *Salduz*-judgment itself, the only way "out" of *Salduz*-rules seems to be a valid waiver, which in the case of waiver of the right to counsel during interrogation, must be "knowing and intelligent" and will not be lightly presumed if the suspect has not had the chance to talk with a lawyer before the waiver.[81] But the impact of *Salduz* will likely extend to contexts other than interrogation, such as line-ups, or, as was the case in *Lisica v. Croatia*, where the ECtHR held that the search of a vehicle conducted in the absence of the suspect, his lawyer or an independent civil witness should have led to exclusion of evidence.[82]

The Grand Chamber in its decision in *Salduz v. Turkey*, emphasized that the right to counsel pretrial "relates in particular to the protection of the accused against abusive coercion on the part of the authorities".[83] It stressed that "an accused often finds himself in a particularly vulnerable position at that stage of the proceedings", and that "this particular vulnerability can only be properly compensated for by the assistance of a lawyer whose task it is, among other things, to help to ensure respect of the right of an accused not to incriminate himself", because "[t]his right indeed presupposes that the prosecution in a criminal case seek to prove their case against the accused without resort to evidence obtained through methods of coercion or oppression in defiance of the will of the accused".[84] Thus, early access to legal assistance "is part of the procedural safeguards to which the Court will have particular regard when examining whether a procedure has extinguished the very essence of the privilege against self-incrimination".[85]

16.4 The Protection of Privacy Rights in Criminal Procedure: The Application of Art. 8 ECHR

16.4.1 Art. 8 ECHR and Restriction Requirements

Art. 8 ECHR provides:

(1) Everyone has the right to respect for his private and family life, his home and his correspondence.
(2) There shall be no interference by a public authority with the exercise of this right except such as is in accordance with the law and is necessary in a democratic society in the interests of national security, public safety or the economic well-being of the country, for

[81] See notably, Pishchalnikov v. Russia, No. 7205/04, ECHR, 24 Sept. 2009, §§ 77–79.
[82] Lisica v. Croatia, No. 20100/06 ECHR, 25 Feb. 2010, §§ 55–61.
[83] Salduz v. Turkey (G.C.) (2009), 49 E.H.R.R. 19, 421, 436, § 53.
[84] Ibid, § 54.
[85] Ibid.

> the prevention of disorder or crime, for the protection of health or morals, or for the protection of the rights and freedoms of others.

The Court has had ample opportunity in its case law to frame rules in relation to Art. 8 ECHR for a wide array of criminal procedural pretrial investigative measures, including searches of residences and businesses, wiretapping, various other forms of surveillance,[86] and the registering and use of data in a criminal procedural context.[87] In all cases, testing follows the same general framework. Firstly, the Court will determine whether or not a particular measure actually interfered with the right (or rights) enumerated in the first subsection of Art. 8 ECHR.[88] If the Court finds that a particular measure did indeed "interfere", that interference will then be tested against the conditions of the limitation clause contained in the second subsection of Art. 8 ECHR, in order to determine whether or the interference was justified. Those conditions may roughly be depicted as follows: there must have been a sufficient basis for an investigative measure in law, the application of the measure must have been necessary in a democratic society (in which regard the Court "(…) relies heavily upon the principle of proportionality",[89] and the application of the measure must have corresponded to one or more of the aims (interests) enumerated in the second subsection of Art. 8 ECHR.

The "in accordance with the law" condition, which may be regarded as the most important requirement for restrictions in the context of criminal procedure (and also represents the basis on which most violations are founded in this regard), may be understood as a test of legality. This test entails evaluation not only of the existence of a (sufficient) legal basis, but also of the quality of that legal basis, given the type and/or degree of interference involved. In *Perry v. The United Kingdom*, the Court described this condition as follows:

> (t)he expression 'in accordance with the law' requires, firstly, that the impugned measure should have some basis in domestic law; secondly, it refers to the quality of the law in question, requiring that it should be accessible to the person concerned, who must moreover be able to foresee its consequences for him, and that it is compatible with the rule of law (…). It also requires that the measure under examination comply with the requirements laid down by the domestic law providing for the interference.[90]

[86] See, amongst others, P.G. v. The United Kingdom (2008), 46 E.H.R.R. 51, 1272 (use of a covert listening device at a residence and at a police station and telephone metering); Perry v. The United Kingdom (2004), 39 E.H.R.R. 3, 76 (covert video-taping at a police station) and Uzun v. Germany (2011), 53 E.H.R.R. 24, 852 (observation via GPS in a vehicle).

[87] See, again, amongst others, P.G. v. The United Kingdom, 46 E.H.R.R. 51, 1272, 1288, § 57, and Perry v. The United Kingdom, 39 E.H.R.R. 3, 19, 85, § 38.

[88] Ibid: "The monitoring of the actions of an individual in a public place by the use of photographic equipment which does not record the visual data does not, as such, give rise to an interference with the individual's private life (…). On the other hand, the recording of the data and the systematic or permanent nature of the record may give rise to such considerations".

[89] Van Dijk et al. (2006, 747).

[90] Perry v. The United Kingdom (2004), 39 E.H.R.R. 3, 76, 87, §45.

It may be generally stated that the graver an interference, the stricter will be the standards in relation to the quality of the law.[91]

As for requirements such as judicial authorization or "probable cause" for interferences in the protected privacy sphere during the criminal investigation, which are required by most democratic constitutions in the absence of exigent circumstances or danger in delay,[92] ECtHR case law has accepted that such requirements may exist, depending on the type of measure and contemplated interference at issue.

The ECtHR had occasion to decide several cases dealing with the powers of French customs officials to order searches of suspect's homes and businesses. In all three cases the searches, which were conducted without judicial authorization, were found to have violated Art. 8 ECHR.[93]

The ECtHR did, however, uphold a search authorized by a non-judicial official in *Camenzind v. Switzerland.*[94] The area director of the Swiss Post and Telecommunications Authority (PTT) in Berne issued a warrant to search the petitioner's home to find and seize an unauthorized cordless telephone. The search was carried out by a single PTT official in the petitioner's presence. The official checked to see whether the petitioner's telephones and television sets were approved under Swiss law.[95] In assessing the law and facts, the ECtHR noted that: "it must be particularly vigilant where, as in the present case, the authorities are empowered under national law to order and effect searches without a judicial warrant. If individuals are to be protected from arbitrary interference by the authorities with the rights guaranteed under Article 8, a legal framework and very strict limits on such powers are called for".[96]

The Court then assessed the statute, which required a warrant and limited the time searches could be carried out, and the facts and held: "Having regard to the safeguards provided by Swiss legislation and especially to the limited scope of the search, the Court accepts that the interference with the applicant's right to respect for his home can be considered to have been proportionate to the aim pursued and thus "necessary in a democratic society" within the meaning of Article 8. Consequently, there has not been a violation of that provision".[97]

---

[91] See P.G. v. The United Kingdom (2008), 46 E.H.R.R. 51, 1272, 1286 § 46: "What is required by way of safeguard will depend, to some extent at least, on the nature and extent of the interference in question. In this case, the information obtained concerned the telephone numbers called from B.'s flat between two specific dates. It did not include any information about the contents of those calls, or who made or received them. The data obtained, and the use that could be made of them, were therefore strictly limited".

[92] Thaman (2008, 56–59).

[93] Funke v. France (1993), 16 E.H.R.R. 297, 329, §§ 53–59; Miailhe v. France (1993), 16 E.H.R.R. 332, 354, §§ 36–40; Cremieux v. France (1993), 16 E.H.R.R. 357, 376, §§ 36–41.

[94] Camenzind v. Switzerland (1999), 28 E.H.R.R. 458.

[95] Ibid, 461, §§ 8–11.

[96] Ibid, 475–476, § 45.

[97] Ibid, 477, § 47.

Although the *Camenzind* decision could be seen as supporting the possibility of non-judicially authorized searches, the careful language in the holding would appear to limit such searches to very narrow circumstances relating to violations of an administrative-criminal regulation scheme. The US Supreme Court has also allowed for the use of "administrative search warrants" issued by administrative officials to search homes and businesses for violations of administrative health and safety regulations when the owner denies consent to enter, as long as the inspection sought is part of a non-discretionary administrative program and is not used explicitly to investigate criminal conduct against identified suspects.[98]

16.4.2 Privacy Violations in the Context of Wiretapping, Bugging, the Interception of Confidential Communications and Other Forms of Surveillance

In the area of wiretapping, the ECtHR in *Klass v. Germany*,[99] dealt with a special system for approving wiretaps used in Germany before enactment of its current statute, which requires judicial authorization. Although the ECtHR accepted parliamentary control of wiretapping in the particular case, it clearly asserted, that the "rule of law implies, inter alia, that an interference by the executive authorities with an individual's rights should be subject to an effective control which should normally be assured by the judiciary, at least in the last resort, judicial control offering the best guarantees of independence, impartiality and a proper procedure". It continued that "in a field where abuse is potentially so easy in individual cases and could have such harmful consequences for democratic society as a whole, it is in principle desirable to entrust supervisory control to a judge.[100] In *Kruslin v. France*[101] the ECtHR found an Art. 8 ECHR violation in a case where an investigating magistrate had authorized a wiretap. The court stated, that "[t]apping and other forms of interception of telephone conversations represent a serious interference with private life and correspondence and must accordingly be based on a 'law' that is particularly precise. It is essential to have clear, detailed rules on the subject, especially as the technology available for use is continually becoming more sophisticated".[102] The Court found that the French legislation was defective on several counts, in that it nowhere defined the crimes for which the measure could be ordered, placed no limits on the length of a wiretap order, nor did it specify any procedure for preparing reports containing the intercepted conversations, nor for allowing judicial or defense

---

[98] Camara v. Municipal Court, 387 US 523 (1967); Marshall v. Barlow's, 436 U.S. 307 (1978).

[99] Klass v. Germany (1978), 2 E.H.R.R. 214 (1978).

[100] Ibid, 234–235, §§ 55, 56.

[101] Kruslin v. France (1990), 12 E.H.R.R.547.

[102] Ibid, 563–564, § 33

inspection of the intercepted conversations.[103] The Spanish wiretap law was also twice declared to be in violation of Art. 8 ECHR due to similar insufficiencies.[104]

In relation to secret surveillance measures, the Court has determined that:

> (a) As to the requirement of legal 'foreseeability' in this field, (...)in the context of covert measures of surveillance, the law must be sufficiently clear in its terms to give citizens an adequate indication of the conditions and circumstances in which the authorities are empowered to resort to any such measures (...). In view of the risk of abuse intrinsic to any system of secret surveillance, such measures must be based on a law that is particularly precise, especially as the technology available for use is continually becoming more sophisticated (...).[105]

However, as is the case in the context of Art. 7 ECHR (the principle of legality in relation to substantive criminal law):

> however clearly drafted a legal provision may be, there is an inevitable element of judicial interpretation. There will always be a need for elucidation of doubtful points and for adaptation to changing circumstances. Indeed, in the Convention States, the progressive development of the criminal law through judicial law-making is a well entrenched and necessary part of legal tradition. The Convention cannot be read as outlawing the gradual clarification of the rules of criminal liability through judicial interpretation from case to case, provided that the resultant development is consistent with the essence of the offence and could reasonably be foreseen.[106]

Nevertheless,

> '(...)in the context of secret measures of surveillance by public authorities, because of the lack of public scrutiny and the risk of misuse of power, compatibility with the rule of law requires that domestic law provides adequate protection against arbitrary interference with Article 8 rights (...)', which means that '(t)he Court must be satisfied that there exist adequate and effective guarantees against abuse. This assessment depends on all the circumstances of the case, such as the nature, scope and duration of the possible measures, the grounds required for ordering them, the authorities competent to permit, carry out and supervise them, and the kind of remedy provided by the national law'.[107]

16.4.3 Rationale for the Failure to Find Fair Trial Violations Based on the Use of Evidence Obtained in Violation of Art. 8 ECHR

Although the ECtHR sets high standards for the protection of privacy in the investigation of criminal cases, and has interpreted Art. 8 ECHR extensively, it does not rigorously enforce its own standards by punishing the use of evidence obtained in violation of privacy rights protected by Art. 8 ECHR.

---

[103] Ibid, 564, § 35.

[104] Valenzuela Contreras v. Spain (1998), 28 E.H.R.R. 43; Prado Bugallo v. Spain, No. 58796/00, ECHR, 18 Feb 2003.

[105] Uzun v. Germany (2011), 53 E.H.R.R. 24, 852, § 61.

[106] Ibid, § 62.

[107] Ibid, § 63.

This was already apparent in one of the first cases dealing with exclusion of evidence, *Schenk v. Switzerland*, but in that case there was also evidence other than that gained by an unlawful interception of conversations upon which to base guilt.[108] In *Khan v. United Kingdom*,[109] however, a "bug" or listening device was placed in a suspect's home by the police without judicial authorization and without there even having been a law regulating such invasions of privacy, thus violating all of the rules laid out for interceptions of conversations in *Klass*, *Kruslin* and later cases.[110] And unlike in *Schenk*, the only evidence used to convict the applicant of narcotics offenses was gained through the illegal bugging. The ECtHR, however, found no violation of the Art. 6 ECHR fair trial right, because the applicant had been able to challenge the admissibility of the evidence in the English courts which use a test, similar to the Court's own fair-trial test, and had admitted the evidence.[111]

One explanation for the Court's ambivalent approach may lie in the broadness of the Art. 8 ECHR right to privacy, which extends far beyond the realm of criminal investigation.[112] The ECtHR has also expanded the reach of Art. 8 ECHR protection in areas not directly related to criminal procedure, such as in the area of personal data protection. Perhaps the Court compensates for the breadth of its interpretation of Art. 8 ECHR by coupling it with an extraordinarily reluctant exclusionary rule.

In *Bykov*, the Grand Chamber, for instance, found that the applicant's right to privacy had been violated by surreptitious recording made by Bykov's associate at the behest of the police. But the applicant did not even challenge the use of the recordings based on the Art. 8 ECHR violation, relying solely on the violation of the privilege against self-incrimination protected by Art. 6(1) ECHR. The Grand Chamber also never discussed the possibility of an Art. 6(1) ECHR fair trial violation based on the Art. 8 ECHR violation.

The sheer number of the dissenting or concurring judges in *Bykov*, who question the insignificance of Art. 8 ECHR privacy violations in the fair trial analysis of Art. 6(1) ECHR (seven judges), perhaps portends a change in the court's approach in the future. Judge Cabral Barreto, for instance, argues that the Court should focus more on the type of privacy violation at issue, namely if it is one that is procedural or substantive: "we must distinguish between what strikes at the heart of a fair trial, what shocks the sensibilities of a democratic society, what runs counter to the fundamental values embodied in a State based on the rule of law, and a breach of procedural rules in the gathering of evidence".[113]

---

[108] Schenk v. Switzerland (1991), 13 E.H.R.R. 242, 266, § 48.

[109] Khan v. United Kingdom (2001), 31 E.H.R.R. 45, 1016.

[110] Ibid, 1023, §§ 27–28.

[111] Indeed, the applicant alleged that the House of Lords had ruled that evidence obtained in violation of the right to privacy is not excludable under the applicable rule in England and Wales. Ibid, 1028, §§ 38–40.

[112] Van Dijk et al. (2006, 664–744).

[113] Bykov v. Russia [G.C.], No. 4378/02, ECHR, 10 March 2009, § 3.3 (concurring opinion of Judge Cabral Barreto).

16.5 Conclusion

Art. 6 ECHR provides no more than the most summary description of what constitutes due process, or a fair trial. The ECtHR, in interpreting Art. 6 ECHR, thus is not bound by any specific systemic approach as might exist in the countries which make up the Council of Europe, yet its case law must be understandable and applicable in the member countries, despite their different legal traditions. It thus has (relatively) free range to develop an eclectic model. Yet some aspects are pre-determined by the language of the ECHR. Art. 6 ECHR, for instance, clearly has an adversarial signature, which is reflected in the Court's case law. Yet, at the same time, the Court's case law is famously "hybrid", for the jurisprudence must be applicable in non-adversarial systems as well.

The ECtHR's approach to pretrial convention violations and how they affect the fairness of the use of illegally obtained evidence at trial, through what I have called the "fair-use-of-evidence" model, is perhaps a "hybrid" solution, which may go down well in some member countries, who already use similar balancing tests, but might be more difficult in others, which might use exclusionary rules of a more absolute character. However, we have shown, that the Court moves from absolute exclusionary rules (for violations of Art. 3 ECHR and violations of fundamental pretrial norms contained in Art. 6 ECHR itself) to open balancing tests for Art. 8 ECHR violations.

Keeping in mind that the ECtHR's protective model regarding pre-trial norm violations and the admission and exclusion of evidence so obtained is relatively young, it is important to take note of its dynamism, and understand that it continues to develop. Certainly there are areas which may be considered to be weaker aspects of the model, such as the Court's approach to privacy violations, which it seems to disregard entirely from the perspective of the fairness of use of evidence so obtained, unless the evidence in question is of questionable probative value. Although there is a chance, due to the substantial divergent opinions of the judges in *Bykov*, that the ECtHR will change course and attach more evidentiary importance to Art. 8 ECHR violations. But the court could also move in the other direction. Thus, in *Al-Khawaja and Tabery v. United Kingdom*, the Grand Chamber in 2011 backed off of its case-law, in which the Court had repeatedly held that no criminal judgment could be based "solely or to a decisive extent" on hearsay witness testimony, when courts in the United Kingdom refused to apply the rule following the decision of the chamber in 2009.[114] It rationalized as follows, in holding that use of such hearsay will "not automatically" lead to a violation of the right to a fair trial per Art. 6(1) ECHR:

> It would not be correct, when reviewing questions of fairness, to apply this rule in an inflexible manner. Nor would it be correct for the Court to ignore entirely the specificities of the particular legal system concerned and, in particular its rules of evidence, notwithstanding judicial dicta that may have suggested otherwise (…). To do so would transform the rule into a blunt and indiscriminate instrument that runs counter to the traditional way in which

[114] For the chamber judgment, see Al-Khawaja and Tabery v. United Kingdom (2009), 49 E.H.R.R. 1, 16–18, §§ 39–48.

> the Court approaches the issue of the overall fairness of the proceedings, namely to weigh in the balance the competing interests of the defence, the victim, and witnesses, and the public interest in the effective administration of justice.[115]

In their joint partly dissenting and partly concurring opinion, the Judges Sajó and Karakaş noted that: "(t)o our knowledge this is the first time ever that this Court, in the absence of a specific new and compelling reason, has diminished the level of protection. This is a matter of gravest concern for the future of the judicial protection of human rights in Europe".[116]

It would be undesirable if the weight the Court attaches to probative value in the context of privacy violations and the testimony of absent witnesses were also to be extended to other types of substantive norm violations. In this regards, but also more generally, it is crucial that the ECtHR enhances the clarity of its balancing tests, and creates "bright lines" where they should exist, i.e. in relation to particularly grave norm violations.

Even if there are weak spots in the case law, however, the fact that the ECtHR has introduced a protective framework in relation to pretrial norm violations and the use of evidence so obtained into the Convention and often applies it in a strict manner, is vital. The Court's reasons for its turnabout in *Salduz* are telling in this regard: "legislation on criminal procedure tends to become increasingly complex, notably with respect to the rules governing the gathering and use of evidence".[117] While the ECtHR itself has contributed to that complexity continuing to formulate new standards in this regard, its case law with regards to pre-trial substantive norms and evidentiary remedies for violations responds to a true need.

Pre-trial criminal procedural norms have indeed become more diffuse and Europe needs guidelines in this respect, especially in view of the steadily developing legal co-operation in criminal law enforcement, which requires proper definition of (old and new) communal boundaries. Constructing a model regulating the admission and exclusion of evidence obtained in breach of pretrial norms that may be workable in all the legal systems of the 47 member states of the Council of Europe is, however, no easy task. The ECtHR's contribution to criminal procedure in this respect is in any event, highly valuable.

Bibliography

Bradley, C.M. 2001. Mapp goes abroad. *52 Case Western Law Review* 52: 375–400.

Damaška, M. 1973. Evidentiary barriers to conviction and two models of criminal procedure: A comparative study. *University of Pennsylvania Law Review* 121: 506–589.

---

[115] Al-Khawaja and Tabery v. United Kingdom [G.C.], Nos. 26766/05, 22228/06, ECHR, 15 Dec. 2011, § 146.

[116] *Joint partly dissenting and partly concurring opinion* Judges Sajó and Karakaş attached to *Al-Khawaja en Tahery*.

[117] *Salduz*, § 54.

Gerards, J.H. 2009. Judicial deliberations in the European Court of Human Rights. In *The legitimacy of highest courts' rulings. Judicial deliberations and beyond*, ed. N. Huls, M. Adams, and J. Bomhoff, 407–436. The Hague: T.M.C Asser Press.

Lawson, R.A., and E. Myjer. 2000. Ten geleide. In: R.A. Lawson, E. Myjer (ed.), "50 jaar Europees Verdrag voor de Rechten van de Mens 1950-2000, Bijzondere aflevering NJCM-Bulletin", *Nederlands Tijdschrift voor de Mensenrechten*, 25, 1, XIII–XIV.

Myjer, B.E.P. 2002. *De vijftig voorbij. Aantekeningen over het 'Europees Verdrag tot bescherming van de rechten van de mens en de fundamentele vrijheden' en de Nederlandse strafrechtspleging*. Nijmegen: Wolf Legal Publishers.

Spronken, T. 2009. Ja, de zon komt op voor de raadsman bij het politieverhoor! *Nederlands Juristenblad* 2: 94–100.

Thaman, S.C. 2008. *Comparative criminal procedure: A casebook approach*, 2nd ed. Durham: Carolina Academic Press.

Van Dijk, P., F. Van Hoof, A. Van Rijn, and L. Zwaak (eds.). 2006. *Theory and practice of the European Convention on Human Rights*, 4th ed. Antwerp/London: Intersentia.

Part IV
A Comparison of Exclusionary Jurisprudence

Chapter 17
Balancing Truth Against Human Rights: A Theory of Modern Exclusionary Rules

Stephen C. Thaman

17.1 Introduction

The notions of "truth" and "evidence" have been inextricably intertwined in the history of Western criminal procedure since the advent of inquisitorial criminal procedure on the European Continent in the late Middle Ages. The justice achieved by early customary and lay courts in pre-inquisitorial times often had little to do with either truth or evidence. The only criminal evidence that was accepted as being "true", was the hard facts produced by the flagrant crime, when "hand-having" thieves or "redhanded" assailants were caught in the act and either summarily killed,[1] or hurriedly sentenced to death by *ad hoc* courts.[2] Mediation conducted by respected community figures or elders, and restoring the peace between victim (or victim's family or clan) and culprit enjoyed priority over the meticulous determination of "what happened" [3] in the era of duels,[4] swearing contests among

---

This chapter was originally published, except for some minor changes to bring it up to date, as "Constitutional Rights in the Balance: Modern Exclusionary Rules and the Toleration of Police Lawlessness in the Search for Truth" in *University of Toronto Law Journal*, Vol. 61, 692–735 (2011).

[1] Weigend (1989, 36). This rule applied to murderers, adulterers, and thieves Diamond (1971, 295). In Mesopotamia, adulteresses caught in the act were thrown bound into the river VerSteeg (2002, 70).

[2] For such procedures in medieval Germany, see Esmein (1913, 302) and Weigend (1989, 36–37).

[3] Glenn (2007, 68–69). Use of punishment or death penalties always risked stoking a feud (Diamond 1971, 293).

[4] Also called "trial by battle" Bartlett (1986, 103).

S.C. Thaman (✉)
School of Law, Saint Louis University,
3700 Lindell Blvd., St. Louis, MO 63108, USA
e-mail: thamansc@slu.edu

S.C. Thaman (ed.), *Exclusionary Rules in Comparative Law*, Ius Gentium: Comparative Perspectives on Law and Justice 20, DOI 10.1007/978-94-007-5348-8_17,

compurgators[5] and divine ordeals.[6] There was little truth in these procedures, but also little punishment, because punishment triggered anger, feud and blood revenge. Compensation to the victim was the rule, if the suspect was not finished off *in flagrante*.[7] Even when juries or *Schöffengerichte* replaced these primitive procedures, their roles had more to do with appraising whether the accused should be accepted back into the community and on what terms, than evidence analysis and truth determination.[8]

It was with the "scientization" of criminal procedure[9] and the displacement of lay judges and irrational procedures by professional judges with their "truth-seeking" inquisitorial powers of evidence gathering and preservation, that the link between "evidence" and "truth" was soldered and took priority over more humane concerns of smoothing over the conflict the wrongful act caused in the community. The growing ascension of inquisitorial procedure was dictated by the needs of the central powers of church and state, which sought to subjugate local governments and their systems of dispute-resolution. The "truths" the governments sought to prove through their courts were often self-perpetuating myths or fictions upon which the central powers' domination rested: the crimes which arguably gave rise to this system were crimes against the state or religion, which could not be proved adequately by mere witnesses or victims (there were none): they had to be proved by judges learned in the science of the law secretly, without being nettled by victims, accuseds, lawyers or the public.[10]

But the dominance of inquisitorial procedure on the European continent did not, despite the advances in evidence-taking and the greater predictability of professional decision making, bring with it a humanization of the resolution of criminal

---

[5] According to one Tibetan proverb: "[If the case is] clear, [decide it] by law; [if the case is] unclear, [decide it] by oath" French (1995, 132). Cf. Diamond (1971, 270). According to § 131 of the Code of Hammurabi, if a man accuses his wife of adultery, and she is not caught *in flagrante*, she can cleanse herself by oath VerSteeg (2002, 66).

[6] Ordeals were usually used in the absence of proof, but among some European tribes the ordeal was used to deter lying under oath Diamond (1971, 228, 296).

[7] Paid in livestock, trinkets or money Diamond (1971, 228). On the usefulness of compensation in terms of livestock, because, quoting Tacitus, "enmities are very dangerous for a free people" Montesequieu (1749–1979, Vol. II, 152).

[8] Customary law courts were often presided by a tribal chief, a king or heads of local communities, but leading members of local families had a right and duty to serve as members of the court, and anyone present could participate. These courts then gave way to trials by sworn neighbors in places as diverse as England and Ethiopia Diamond (1971, 273, 391).

[9] The "right solution" was based on "textual analysis and logical penetration of its meaning". Law "came increasingly to be regarded as a self-contained, or closed system—a 'science'" Damaska (1986, 31). This science "needed no illumination" because it was a science of text Luhmann (1995, 48).

[10] On how the secret victimless crime of heresy required a new procedure Vogler (2005, 25). The procedure in ecclesiastical courts for heresy and magic was the most "ferocious" and required the forced cooperation of the accused Ferrajoli (1998, 577).

disputes. Enlightenment thinkers complained that more terror and inhumanity were perpetrated by the administration of the law in these times than was committed by common criminals.[11] More innocent persons were convicted and sentenced to death in this era than in any other era of European history, often based on confessions extorted through legalized torture or the threat thereof.[12]

Although torture was officially abolished in Europe by the end of the eighteenth and beginning of the nineteenth centuries,[13] continental Europe experienced political convulsions throwing most countries back and forth between the extremes of absolute monarchist police state and liberalism during the nineteenth and early twentieth centuries. All pretenses of a state under the rule of law, of course, were erased with the rise of Bolshevism in Russia, Nazism in Germany, Fascism in Italy and Francoism in Spain.

It was in reaction to the horrors of the holocaust and Soviet totalitarianism that the human rights movement was launched after 1945, resulting in the promulgation of the Universal Declaration of Human Rights (UDHR),[14] the European Convention on Human Rights (ECHR)[15] and the International Covenant on Civil and Political Rights (ICCPR).[16] The American Convention on Human Rights (ACHR) followed in 1969.[17] After emerging from Fascist domination after World War II, Germany and Italy, enacted new constitutions which reflected the priority given to the protection of citizens against the threat of violence and arbitrariness by the state. Spain followed in 1978. A similar explosion of new constitutions and criminal procedure reforms occurred in the 1990s as Latin America emerged from decades of authoritarian military regimes and the collapse of the Soviet Union and Yugoslavia gave rise to a host of new aspiring democracies in Eastern and South Eastern Europe and Central Asia. It is still too early to predict whether the domino-effect of the so-called "Arab Spring" which has resulted in the toppling of repressive dictatorships in Tunisia, Egypt, and Libya will extend further and actually lead to a similar democratization and respect for the rule of law.

The experience in Common Law countries has been a bit different. England had no experience of Fascism and, due to its unique tradition, no written constitution or

---

[11] Ibid, 339,382. On criminal procedure of this epoch as a "science of horrors", ibid, 578.

[12] On the conviction of the innocent, Beccaria (1764–1995, 62). *La Bruyere* once said: "Torture is a wonderful invention and may be counted upon to ruin an innocent person with a weak constitution and exonerate a guilty person born robust". And further: "I might almost say in regard to myself, 'I will not be a thief or a murderer'; but to say, 'I shall not some day be punished as such', would be to speak very boldly" Esmein (1913, 352, 380).

[13] Langbein (1977, 10).

[14] Universal Declaration of Human Rights, G.A. Res. 217A (III), U.N. Doc. A/810 at 71 (1948).

[15] Convention for the Protection of Human Rights and Fundamental Freedoms, Nov. 4, 1950, Europ.T.S. No. 5; 213 U.N.T.S. 221.

[16] International Convenant on Civil and Political Rights, Dec. 16, 1966, 999 U.N.T.S. 171; S. Exec. Doc. E, 95–2 (1978); S. Treaty Doc. 95–20, 6 I.L.M. 368 (1967).

[17] American Convention on Human Rights, Nov. 21, 1969, O.A.S. T.S. No. 36; 1144 U.N.T.S. 143; S. Treaty Doc. No. 95–21, 9 I.L.M. 99(1969).

Bill of Rights listing specific protections for its citizens. Lawlessness of state officials, where it existed, did not, generally, affect the admission of evidence in the common-law tradition. In Britain, the courts did not worry about the methods used to acquire evidence if it was otherwise relevant and material.[18]

The United States (US), on the other hand, had its Bill of Rights of 1791, the purpose of which was to restrict the new federal government against passing any laws which would impact on the freedoms of the citizens of the 13 states which made up the new Union at that time. In the early days, however, nearly all criminal cases in the US were handled in the state courts, governed by state laws and constitutions. Until the end of the Civil War in 1865, African-American slaves had few rights under the laws of the states or the federal government. The enactment of the Fourteenth Amendment to the US Constitution in 1865 granted the freed slaves "due process of law" in relation to the States, yet it was only in the 1930s that the US Supreme Court (USSC) began overturning state criminal convictions based on torture, and the use of other coercive tactics which undermine the freedom of will of the accused as "violations of due process".[19]

Already in 1914 the USSC adopted an exclusionary rule which prevented the use of evidence seized by Federal officials in violation of the Fourth Amendment.[20] The problems this rule addressed were made abundantly clear:

> The tendency of those who execute the criminal laws of the country to obtain conviction by means of unlawful seizures and enforced confessions, the latter often obtained after subjecting accused persons to unwarranted practices destructive of rights secured by the Federal Constitution, should find no sanction in the judgments of the courts which are charged at all times with the support of the Constitution and to which people of all conditions have a right to appeal for the maintenance of such fundamental rights.[21]

The USSC only became a true constitutional court for the entire country, however, when, influenced by the civil rights movement in the 1950s and 1960s, it decided that the Fourth, Fifth[22] and Sixth Amendments[23] to the US Constitution, were binding on the states, thus enabling it to affect racist practices in many, mainly Southern, states which deprived African-American citizens of the protection of the law in criminal cases.

---

[18] Blackstone's Criminal Practice (2003, 1974).

[19] The most notorious of the dozens of cases decided in this area was Brown v. Mississippi, 297 U.S. 278 (1936), which involved the torture of Black suspects in a murder case and their hurried sentence to death 3 days later in a kangaroo jury court.

[20] The Fourth Amendment of the US Constitution reads: "The right of the people to be secure in their persons, houses, papers and effects against unreasonable searches and seizures shall not be violated, and no Warrants shall issue but upon probable cause, supported by Oath or affirmation, and particularly describing the place to be searched and the persons or things to be seized."

[21] Weeks v. United States, 232 US 383, 392 (1914). See also Cammack, Chap. 1, pp. 8–9.

[22] The Fifth Amendment of the US Constitution provides, *inter alia*, that: "No person…shall be compelled in any criminal case to be a witness against himself"(…).

[23] The Sixth Amendment, provides, *inter alia*, "In all criminal prosecutions, the accused shall have the Assistance of Counsel for his defense".

The notion that evidence obtained as a result of police violation of the constitution could not be used in a criminal trial was finally established nationwide and made applicable to the states during the years that Earl Warren was Chief Justice of the USSC.[24] The landmark decisions in this respect were: (1) *Mapp v. Ohio*,[25] which made the Fourth Amendment exclusionary rule of *Weeks*, binding on the States; (2) *Wong Sun v. United States*,[26] which re-articulated the exclusionary rule in relation to derivative evidence causally linked to preceding constitutional violations[27]; (3) *Massiah v. United States*,[28] which provided for exclusion of statements made to government agents by charged defendants, in violation of the Sixth Amendment right to counsel; and, of course (4) *Miranda v. Arizona*,[29] which provided for exclusion of confessions and admissions made during custodial interrogation, where the suspect was not advised of the right to silence and the right to counsel or did not effectively waive those rights, in violation of the Fifth Amendment privilege against self-incrimination.[30]

These landmark decisions, especially *Mapp* and *Miranda*, have been very influential overseas, but so have some of the limitations placed on the exclusionary rule by the USSC under Chief Justice Warren Burger,[31]foremost of these being the exceptions to the doctrine of the "fruits of the poisonous tree" known as "inevitable discovery"[32] and "independent source",[33] and the "good faith" exception to violations of the Fourth Amendment.[34]

Long before the innovations of the Warren Court, inquisitorial systems on the European continent had developed rules to address violations of the law by organs of law enforcement at a time when Common Law courts never questioned the provenance of the evidence before them. Continental European codes of criminal procedure prescribed rather strict rules for the gathering of evidence and the performance of other acts during the preliminary criminal investigation and provided

---

[24] From 1953 to 1969.

[25] 367 U.S. 643 (1961).

[26] 371 U.S. 471 (1963).

[27] The term "fruit of the poisonous tree" was originally coined by Justice Frankfurter in Nardone v. United States, 308 U.S. 338 (1939), but the idea that the government could not use derivative evidence was articulated 19 years earlier by Justice Holmes in Silverthorne Lumber Co. v. United States, 251 U.S. 385 (1920).

[28] 377 U.S. 201 (1964).

[29] 384 U.S. 436 (1966).

[30] For more detail on the importance of these decisions, Cammack, Chap. 1, p. 1.

[31] Warren Burger was Chief Justice of the USSC from 1969 to 1986.

[32] First articulated in Nix v. Williams, 467 U.S. 431, 444–50 (1984).

[33] First articulated in Silverthorne Lumber Co. 251 U.S. 385, 392, but then reaffirmed in Murray v. United States, 487 U.S. 533, 537–39 (1988).

[34] United States v. Leon, 468 U.S. 897, 918–25 (1984). For more on these exceptions, Cammack, Chap. 1, pp. 19–20.

for the nullification of the efficacy of these acts if they were performed in violation of the statutory rules. So-called "nullities" could and did lead to exclusion of evidence.[35] In fact, one of the most influential treatises on exclusionary rules was written in Germany before the USSC's decision in *Weeks*, and is one of the first scholarly attempts to create a balancing test for the introduction of illegally gathered evidence.[36]

The thesis of this attempt to synthesize the varying approach to exclusionary rules is that while all lawmakers and courts "balance", i.e., make value judgments, when navigating between the Scylla of fundamental or constitutional rights and the Charybdis of truth and accuracy in criminal trials, some kinds of official law violations are so serious that they should trigger a very strong presumption of non-use of the evidence resulting therefrom. True "balancing" of various considerations should occur only where the violation is not properly characterized as fundamental.

The value judgment that a violation is fundamental is sometimes made at the level of international law, such as with the prohibition of torture, sometimes in constitutions and codes, and sometimes by the courts. The prevailing view is that the violations must be "serious", i.e., must be of fundamental or constitutional rights. Even if a constitutional violation has been identified, which could trigger exclusion or "non-use" of evidence, judges must again decide whether the evidence the prosecution seeks to use is actually the "fruit of the poisonous tree", i.e., does it derive inexorably from the constitutional violation? And finally, even if it is agreed that a constitutional right has been violated and the evidence sought to be admitted is the fruit thereof, some jurisdictions still require the judge to engage in a balancing of other important interests before deciding on admissibility, for instance: (1) the seriousness of the constitutional violation (was it intentional, reckless, negligent, etc.); (2) the gravity of the crime which is before the court; (3) the character of the evidence subject to exclusion (its credibility, importance for proving guilt, whether it constitutes the *corpus delicti* of the crime or is "mere evidence", etc.); (4) whether use of the evidence would violate the defendant's right to a fair trial, and other factors.

While courts will inevitably engage in balancing, I do not think that determining the material truth in a criminal proceeding should be considered to be a higher goal than the respect for the international and constitutional protection of the right to human dignity and related guarantees respecting the right to silence and privacy. But the principle of material truth, which I believe nowhere has explicit constitutional status, still holds sway in the criminal courts. Yet, a legal system, which employs explicit loopholes or vague balancing principles in order to use evidence

---

[35] on how inquisitorial Europe developed "extrinsic" exclusionary rules relating to "values unrelated to the pursuit of truth" at a time when the Common law only knew "intrinsic" rules relating to the probative value of evidence Damaska (1997, 12–17).

[36] Beling (1903). For more detailed discussion of Beling's contribution to the German doctrine. Gless, Chap. 5, p. 116.

gathered directly or indirectly by means of unconstitutional acts of its investigative organs, only with difficulty incorporates the spirit of a state under the rule of law. As long as such loopholes exist, constitutional rights will be routinely violated by state officials.

A dismissal or acquittal in a criminal proceeding, even when the evidence seems to point to the guilt of the accused, violates no fundamental human rights. The victim of an act of violence or theft remains a victim, whether or not the defendant is convicted. In the case of victim-less drug crimes, which constitute the overwhelming majority of cases involving illegal searches and a large number of those with illegal wiretaps, a dismissal does not prevent future surveillance and legal apprehension of what are usually repeat offenders involved in illegal enterprise.

In the US, the power in the hands of law enforcement is awesome. Life imprisonment is possible for first-time drug dealers[37] and recidivist thieves.[38] Around 731 of every 100,000 residents of the U.S. are behind bars.[39] The coercive nature of the plea bargaining system means that no more than 5 % of those convicted actually have a trial which results in an ascertainment of "the truth" based on the full panoply of due process rights.[40] A healthy skepticism, if not mistrust, of the powers of the state, even in a modern democracy, may still be warranted and the warnings of the authors of *Weeks* and subsequent decisions, should not be dismissed as being antiquated.[41]

In order to provide an effective remedy for violations of rights during criminal investigations, evidence obtained in violation of fundamental constitutional rights should presumptively be excluded, subject only to narrowly-drawn exceptions for good-faith errors and emergencies. Exclusion of such evidence should not depend on the balancing of interests; otherwise, fundamental human rights will be lost in the balance. But evidence obtained through unlawful state conduct that does not rise to the level of violating a fundamental constitutional right may properly be considered for admission on the basis of a balancing test. As in the other chapters of this book, I will concentrate my analysis on (1) police commission of constitutional violations in acquiring confessions; and (2) violations of constitutional rights in the invasion of the privacy

---

[37] Harmelin v. Michigan, 501 U.S. 957 (1991).

[38] Ewing v. California, 538 U.S. 11 (2003); Lockyer v. Andrade, 538 U.S. 63 (2003).

[39] Gopnik (2012, 73).

[40] Thaman (2010, 327–328).

[41] I disagree with the majority of the USSC when they intimate that improved police training, disciplinary regimes, and the possibility of civil suits, which were not available when *Mapp v. Ohio* was decided, might make the exclusionary rule no longer valid. Hudson v. Michigan, 547 U.S. 586, 597–599 (2006). The economic crisis has caused drastic cuts in the budgets of police departments (as well as public defender offices) which could lead to an actual decline in the quality of justice delivered both on the investigative and adjudicative end of criminal proceedings in the US. And violations of constitutional rights, such as failure to get a search warrant, are often just cost-cutting, and time-saving measures not linked to any true exigent circumstance.

of the home or private conversations.[42] I will analyze the constitutional, statutory, and court-made doctrine dealing with seemingly absolute exclusionary rules in comparative and international law, which brook of no balancing (or are "pre-balanced" by the law-giver), relative exclusionary rules, which encourage balancing of various interests, and how these absolute and relative exclusionary rules deal with the use of derivative evidence, or "fruits of the poisonous tree". Before beginning my analysis of the various approaches, however, I will briefly discuss the concept of "nullities" as it developed in civil law jurisdictions and try to flush out how "nullities", in the abstract, differ from modern exclusionary rules. The workings of concrete "nullities" and exclusionary rules will then be addressed in the succeeding parts of the article.

17.2 "Nullities" in Modern Criminal Procedure Codes

Many countries in Europe and Latin America still provide for "nullities" when there is a violation of procedural norms. In some countries, such as France, procedural "nullities" are still the only statutory grounds for excluding evidence. In others, such as Italy, Spain, Brazil or Colombia, codes have maintained the doctrine of "nullities" and yet added modern statutory or even constitutional prohibitions on the use of illegally gathered evidence.

The relationship between modern rules of exclusion or "non-usability" (*inutilizzabilità*, to use the Italian term), which were often inspired by the American case law of the last 50 years, and the more venerable "nullities", which originally related to procedural acts and not necessarily to the evidence these acts might have produced, is often difficult (at least for a lawyer schooled in the common law!) to understand. For instance, one category of nullities, called "nullities of general order" relates to defects in the procedure which do not necessarily touch on the collection of evidence, yet are treated as grave violations which can even lead to dismissal of the prosecution.[43]

§ 171 CCP-France provides: "There is a nullity when a failure to recognize a substantial formality contained in a provision of the present Code or any other provision of criminal procedure has infringed on the interests of the party to which it applies".[44] This formulation appears close to limiting France's nullity-based

---

[42] I will be largely ignoring another substantial area of exclusionary doctrine in the US relating to statements and physical evidence gathered as fruits of unlawful detentions or arrests.

[43] See § 178 CCP-Italy. See References at end of chapter for cites to all Codes of Criminal Procedure, Judicial Codes and Constitutions. See Illuminati, Chap 10, p. 252. On "general order" nullities in France, Frase (2007, 213).

[44] Brazil also limits nullities to violations which infringe on the interests of the prosecution or the defense (§ 563 CCP-Brazil) or which impact on the ascertainment of the truth or the outcome of the trial (§ 566 CCP-Brazil). § 238 Ley del Poder Judicial (hereafter LOPJ-Spain), provides for a "nullity" when: "the essential rules of procedure are not respected and this may have caused an actual restriction of defense rights". See Bachmaier, Chap. 9, p. 224.

exclusionary rule to constitutional violations, at least when the "party to which it applies" is the defendant. § 174(3) CCP-France further provides that the annulled act will be removed from the case dossier. In civil law systems the withdrawal of the document memorializing an investigative measure from the dossier traditionally meant that no use could be made of it or its contents at the trial.[45] Since the document is excluded before the case reaches the trial court, the trial judge will be as insulated from the tainted evidence as would be a jury following a successful pre-trial motion to exclude evidence in the US.[46]

The CCP-Italy distinguishes between "relative nullities", which must be raised by the parties and, if recognized, may be "sanitized" or purged by waiver by the affected party or by the official who violated the law,[47] and "absolute nullities," which are usually of constitutional importance, may be raised at any stage of the proceedings, may not be sanitized or purged and may lead to exclusion of evidence.[48]

Some nullity provisions also explicitly refer to derivative evidence. Thus, according to § 174(para.3) CCP-France: "the annulled acts or documents are withdrawn from the investigative dossier" and it is "prohibited to derive any information against the parties from the annulled acts or documents".[49] §185(1) CCP-Italy also provides that: "The nullity of an act renders the subsequent acts invalid which depend on that declared to be annulled".[50]

In Italy, the term "nullity" usually refers to acts, whereas the term "non-usability" (§ 191 CCP-Italy) refers to evidence.[51] "Non-usability" has been limited in the literature to cases where there is a statutory prohibition on the gathering of the evidence, whereas "nullities" arise when legal formalities are violated in the gathering of what would otherwise be admissible evidence. The courts, however have used the term "non-usability" to apply to both types of illegalities, creating doctrinal murkiness. In 2001 the Italian Constitutional Court made it clear that the "fruits of the poisonous tree" apply only to "nullities" when expressly provided by statute,

---

[45] In systems where the written trial still dominates, such as in the Netherlands or the French trial in the correctional courts, the documents in the dossier could historically be read at the trial. This is now changing because the European Court of Human Rights (hereafter ECtHR), has held that the use of written statements may violate Art. 6(3)(d) ECHR, which guarantees the right to confrontation. See, *inter alia*, Delta v. France, 16 E.H.R.R. 574 (1993) and discussion in Thaman (2008, 125–135).

[46] For more on the French treatment of nullities, Pradel, Chap. 6, pp. 151–152.

[47] §§ 183, 184 CCP-Italy. For similar provisions, *see* § 171 CCP-Argentina-Federal; §§ 191, 195 CPP-Venezuela.

[48] § 179 CCP-Italy. Cf. Illuminati, Chap. 10, p. 251.

[49] French courts have based exclusion of "fruits" on these sections. Pradel, Chap. 6. See also Pradel (1997, 604–605).

[50] For similar language, see § 573(1) CCP-Brazil; § 172 CCP-Argentina-Federal, and § 196(para.1) CCP-Venezuela.

[51] Tonini (2005, 175); cf. Illuminati, Chap. 10, p. 243.

whereas § 191 CCP-Italy, providing for "non-usability", has no language referring to derivative evidence.[52]

§ 359a CCP-Netherlands, which appears to be an adaptation of traditional nullity rules, and applies to any "procedural rule", gives the court discretion to exclude evidence or impose other sanctions, such as barring prosecution or mitigating sentence, and obligates it to "take account of the interest that the breached rule serves, the gravity of the breach and the harm it causes".[53]

17.3 Categorical "Pre-balanced" Exclusionary Rules

17.3.1 A Categorical Exclusionary Rule in International Law: The Case of Torture and Cruel, Inhuman and Degrading Treatment

Although international and regional human rights conventions firmly protect the privilege against self-incrimination,[54] and the right to privacy,[55] they do not categorically prescribe exclusion of evidence gathered as a direct or indirect result of the violations of these provisions. Indeed, the treaty language itself indicates that the right to privacy is not absolute. It may be violated, according to Art. 8 (2) ECHR: "in accordance with the law" and when "necessary in a democratic society in the interests of national security, public safety or the economic well-being of the country, for the prevention of disorder or crime, for the protection of health or morals, or for the protection of the rights or freedoms of others".[56]

The prohibition against torture or other cruel, inhuman and degrading treatment, however, is treated as absolute. There is no qualifying language in the treaty texts,[57] and states may not derogate from this protection, even in times of war or public emergency.[58] Although the human rights treaties do not have built-in exclusionary rules, § 15 of the Convention Against Torture and Other Cruel, Inhuman or Degrading

[52] Italian Constitutional Court, Decision No. 332/2001. For discussion, Illuminati, Chap. 10, p. 253, and Conso, Grevi (2002, 339).

[53] For a discussion, see Borgers and Stevens, Chap. 8, pp. 188–194.

[54] Art. 14(3)(g) ICCP; Art. 8(2)(g) ACHR. The ECHR recognized the right to silence as being part of the right to a fair trial guaranteed under Art. 6(1) ECHR. Murray v. United Kingdom (1996), 22 E.H.R.R. 29, 60.

[55] Art. 12 UDHR; Art. 17(1) ICCPR; Art. 8(1) ECHR; Art. 11(2) ACHR.

[56] Art. 12 UDHR prohibits "arbitrary" interference, Art. 17(1) ICCPR "arbitrary and unlawful" interference and Art. 11(2) ACHR, "arbitrary and abusive" interference.

[57] Art. 5 UDHR; Art. 7 ICCPR; Art. 3 ECHR; Art. 5(2) ACHR.

[58] Art. 4(2) ICCPR; Art. 15(3) ECHR.

Treatment (CAT) to which 146 nations are a party,[59] clearly prohibits the use of statements gathered through torture. But, oddly enough, the CAT does not provide an explicit exclusionary rule for statements gathered through use of "cruel, inhuman or degrading treatment".[60] § 16 of the U.N.'s "Body of Principles for the Protection of All Persons Under Any Form of Detention or Imprisonment", however, requires prosecutors to refuse to use as evidence statements obtained by torture "or other ill treatment except in proceedings against those who are accused of using such means".[61] The Grand Chamber of the ECt.HR also has clearly held in the case of *Gäfgen v. Germany*, that the use of any statements gathered through use of torture *or* inhuman or degrading treatment would result in an unfair trial in violation of Art. 6 ECHR.[62]

Although the CAT does not mention exclusion of the "fruits of the poisonous tree" derived from tortured confessions, it is presumed that the use of physical or other evidence derived from torture would also violate the treaty and international law. The ECtHR held in *Gäfgen* that use of fruits of a tortured confession would automatically result in the violation of the right to a fair trial, though it admitted that its case law was not as categorical when it came to the fruits of "inhuman or degrading" treatment, also prohibited categorically by Art. 3 ECHR.[63]

In *Gäfgen*, police threatened a Frankfurt law student with torture and brutality, if he did not reveal the whereabouts of a child kidnap victim, whom they thought was still alive. He made incriminating statements and took them to the lake where he had disposed of the child's body. A report of the autopsy conducted on the boy's body, and evidence of the tire tracks of defendant's car near the lake were used at trial, though all his statements were suppressed.[64] The ECtHR Grand Chamber deemed that the threats constituted "inhuman and degrading" treatment and were thus in violation of Art. 3 ECHR, but did not rise to torture. It also found that in such a case, the use of the fruits would not violate the Art. 6 ECHR right to a fair trial, using a kind of harmless error analysis. Since the defendant confessed his guilt at trial, the court found that his courtroom testimony was no longer the fruit of the Art. 3 ECHR violation, since he was represented by counsel, and the court based its guilty

[59] G.A. Resolution 39/46, Dec. 10, 1984, 39 U.N. GAOR, Supp. No. 51, at 197,U.N. Doc A/39/51. 146. http://treaties.un.org/Pages/ViewDetails.aspx?src=UNTSONLINE&tabid=2&mtdsg_no=IV-9&chapter=4&lang=en#Participants.

[60] Scharf (2008, 140).

[61] Ibid, 145.

[62] Gäfgen v. Germany (2011), 52 E.H.R.R. 1, 42 (§ 166). It appears here, that the ECtHR is treating the use of statements at trial, which were obtained as a result of the violation of Art. 3 ECHR as absolute reversible error, not subject to any "harmless error" analysis. US Courts would likely apply the doctrine of "harmless constitutional error" to such a situation, for so-called "structural errors", which will constitute automatic reversible error, are usually not related to the erroneous admission of evidence, and thus are much like "nullities of general order" in civil law systems. On structural, and harmless constitutional error in the US, see LaFave et al. (2009, 1323–1331).

[63] Gäfgen, 52 E.H.R.R. 1, 42 (§§ 166–167).

[64] Ibid, 6–7, 9–10 (§§ 15–18, 29–21).

judgment on the courtroom confession alone, only using the ill-gotten "fruits" to corroborate its truthfulness.[65]

Despite the fact that the ECtHR in *Gäfgen* recognizes certain exceptions to an absolute exclusionary rule for fruits of inhuman and degrading interrogation practices not amounting to torture, such as harmless error, "inevitable discovery",[66] and attenuation of the taint of the illegality, it also expressly disallows any "balancing" of this "absolute" violation against other interests, such as the "the seriousness of the offence under investigation or the public interest in effective criminal prosecution",[67] which are at the core of Germany's balancing test, which will be discussed below.

Long before the adoption of the CAT, national legal systems provided for categorical exclusion of statements obtained by threats, force, deception, promises or other means, such as to render them "involuntary", which might fall short of cruel, inhuman and degrading treatment or torture. Thus, § 136a CCP-Germany prohibits the use of "maltreatment, fatigue, physical intervention, the administration of substances, torture, deception, hypnosis, threats to apply measures not applicable according to the rules, or promises of a benefit not provided by law" during questioning and provides for a mandatory exclusionary rule if the prohibitions are violated.[68]

In 1897, the USSC held that, for statements taken in police custodial interrogation to be admissible under the Fifth Amendment privilege against self-incrimination, they must "not be extracted by any sort of threats or violence, nor obtained by any direct or implied promises, however slight, nor by the exertion of any improper influence".[69] Between 1936 and 1966 the USSC also condemned interrogation practices ranging from clear torture, to lesser modes of coercion, threats, promises, deception, etc., which might or might not today rise to the level of cruel, inhuman or degrading treatment, as violations of "due process" and required reversals of 35 convictions based thereon.[70] I will discuss exclusionary rules dealing with "involuntary" confessions which were induced by practices which do not rise to the level of torture or cruel, inhuman and degrading treatment, below.

17.3.2 Categorical General Exclusionary Rules Applying to Violations of Constitutional and Sub-Constitutional Statutory Law

A number of constitutions adopted by democratizing countries emerging from the clutches of totalitarian, authoritarian or dictatorial regimes specifically require the exclusion of illegally gathered evidence. This is an important step, because,

[65] Ibid, 44–46 (§§ 177–183).

[66] Ibid, 44 (§ 174).

[67] Ibid, § 175–176. For more on the *Gäfgen* case, Ölçer, Chap. 16, pp. 388–393.

[68] Similar rules are common in other modern CCP's as well. Cf. § 64(3) CPP-Italy and § 9 CCP-Russia.

[69] Bram v. United States, 168 U.S. 532, 542 (1897). See Cammack, Chap. 1, p. 22.

[70] For a summary of these "voluntariness" cases, see LaFave et al. (2009, 343–349).

some courts which require suppression of evidence following a constitutional violation, do not acknowledge that the exclusionary rule, itself is of constitutional stature.[71]

Some of these exclusionary provisions apply to evidence gathered in violation of statutory provisions which do not rise to violations of fundamental or constitutional rights. For instance, Art. 50(2) Const.-Russia (1993)[72] provides: "In the administration of justice the use of evidence gathered in violation of federal law is not permitted".[73] Similarly, Art. 5(LVI) Const.-Brazil provides for inadmissibility of evidence obtained by "illegal means".[74] Here, the constitutional legislator has already balanced, or to put it another way, has pre-empted all balancing by law-givers or lower-court judges. In Russia, the extension of the provisions to errors of non-constitutional gravity has been criticized.[75]

There are equally broad-sounding exclusionary rules in some new codes of criminal procedure. § 191 CCP-Italy (1988), provides for a sanction of "non-usability" in relation to "evidence acquired in violation of prohibitions established by the law". § 16 CCP-Serbia (2011) goes even further: "Court decisions may not be based on evidence which is, directly or indirectly, in itself, or by the manner in which it was obtained, in contravention of the Constitution, this Code, other statute, or universally accepted rules of international law and ratified international treaties".[76]

These broad rules seem to hearken back to equally broad "nullity" provisions which are rooted in a strict legality principle, according to which any law violation nullifies the validity of the acts which are the results thereof. We will see, however, that, that the blind eye exercised by courts in relation to the admissibility of otherwise relevant evidence seized in violation of statutory "nullities" in traditional civil law regimes, also lacks acuity when it comes to interpreting modern exclusionary rules.

---

[71] I am, of course, referring to the convoluted attempts by the USSC to characterize *Mapp*'s Fourth Amendment exclusionary rule and *Miranda*'s Fifth Amendment exclusionary rule as "prophylactic" rules not required by the constitutional amendments they were originally designed to safeguard. *See* United States v. Leon, 468 U.S. 897 (1984), in relation to the Fourth Amendment exclusionary rule, and most recently United States v. Patane, 542 U.S. 630, 631 (2004), in relation to the *Miranda* rule.

[72] English translations of all world constitutions are available at CONSTITUTIONS OF THE COUNTRIES OF THE WORLD, http://www.oup.com/online/us/law/oceanalaw/?view=usa#ccwo (all constitutions will be referred to as Const.-).

[73] For similar language, *see* Art. 42(7) Const.-Georgia; Art. 71(3) Const.-Azerbaijan; Art. 27(2) Const.-Belarus; Art. 77(3)(9) Const.-Kazakhstan. § 75(1) CCP-Russia (2001), includes the same, broad, exclusionary mandate, as does § 105(4–5) CCP-Belarus; § 116(4) CCP-Kazakhstan; § 6(3) CCP-Kyrgyzstan; and § 125(4) CCP-Turkmenistan.

[74] Cf. § 38(para.8) Const.-Turkey and § 206(a)(2) CCP-Turkey, which use similar language.

[75] See Thaman (1995, 90–94), discussing exclusionary practices and criticism of the broad rule in jury trials in 1993–1994.

[76] For a US statutory exclusionary rule extending to non-constitutional statutory violations, *see* Vernon's Ann. Texas C.C.P. § 38.23.

17.3.3 Categorical General Exclusionary Rules Restricted to Violations of Fundamental or Constitutional Rights

I believe the better approach is to limit categorical exclusionary rules to situations where fundamental or constitutional rights are violated.[77] A statute which I believe could be a model for other jurisdictions, and which expressly extends to the "fruits of the poisonous tree" is § 11.1 LOPJ-Spain which provides: "Evidence obtained, directly or indirectly in violation of fundamental rights and liberties is without effect". In a similar manner, § 23 CCP-Colombia, which provides for exclusion of "[a]ll evidence obtained in violation of fundamental guarantees" extends the prohibition to "[e]vidence which is the consequence of the excluded evidence, or can only be explained by reason of its existence".

Derivative evidence, however, is only a "fruit" of the violation, if there is a close causal connection between the violation and its discovery, and the evidence would not have been discovered, but for the violation. Some recent statutes explicitly provide for exceptions to exclusion developed in US jurisprudence. For instance, § 157 CCP-Brazil (2008), provides: "Illicit evidence, understood to be that obtained in violation of constitutional and legal norms, is inadmissible and should be removed from the trial: (1) the evidence derived from the illicit evidence is also inadmissible except where there is no obvious or causal nexus between the one and the other or where the derived evidence could be obtained from a source independent of the former; (2) An independent source is considered to be such, that when, following the normal procedures used in practice which are proper in criminal investigation, it would be capable of leading to the facts which are the objects to be proved". In a similar vein, §455 CCP-Colombia explicitly makes exceptions for "attenuated connection, independent source, inevitable discovery, and others provided by law".

17.4 What Is a Constitutional or Fundamental Right?

17.4.1 Introduction

Assuming that most jurisdictions will only exclude probative evidence if the police violate a fundamental or constitutional right, it is still not always easy for courts or law-givers to determine which violations fall into this category. Courts thus make value judgments, which could be considered to be a balancing of the seriousness of the violation in relation to the legal interest protected by a constitutional provision. Art. 29 Const.-Colombia states that "evidence obtained in violation of due process

[77] Cf. § 136.4320 Or.Rev.Stats. which limits exclusion of evidence to situations when required by the constitutions of Oregon or the US.

is null in the full sense of the law" (*in pleno derecho*). We know from USSC case law that determining what is a violation of due process in the taking of a confession, or "probable cause" in the issuance of a warrant to search or wiretap can imply a complicated weighing of the "totality of the circumstances".[78] Art. 32(6) Const.-Portugal lists specific constitutional violations which will trigger exclusion: "Any evidence obtained by torture, force, violation of the physical or moral integrity of the individual, wrongful interference in private life, the home, correspondence, or telecommunications is of no effect".

We have already seen that the nullities approach adopted in many civil law criminal procedure codes differentiates between nullities which affect constitutional rights or substantial interests of the defendant, called "absolute" nullities, or nullities of "general order", and those which are only relative, and may be purged, etc. The German Supreme Court, in a similar way, has found that: "[i]f the procedural provision which has been violated, does not, or not primarily, serve to protect the defendant, then a prohibition on use will be unlikely; on the other hand, a prohibition on use is appropriate, when the violated procedural provision is designed to secure the foundations of the procedural position of the accused or defendant in a criminal prosecution".[79]

The right to privacy in one's home and one's communications, and the right to remain silent are core constitutional rights in all democracies, but it is also legal for police to search homes, intercept private communications and interrogate criminal suspects, if they follow the correct procedures. Some of the procedures are directly required by constitutions, or constitutional decisions of high courts because they impact upon the core interests protected by the constitutional rights if violated. Other rules dictated by statute are often considered to be of lesser importance. I will assess what I believe to be the core rules in these two areas which should usually trigger exclusion of evidence if violated.

§ 177(2) CCP-Greece provides for mandatory exclusion, including "fruits of the poisonous tree" if the police evidence-gathering violation constitutes a crime and in Greece, this would of course apply to coerced confessions, illegal wiretaps and some other violations, but not to what we in the US call *Miranda* violations.[80] This appears to be a straight-forward approach with which criminal law scholars could not in all honesty fail to agree, as *ignorantia legis neminem excusat* (ignorance of the law is no excuse). Indeed, 18 U.S.C. § 242 punishes violations of constitutional rights as a misdemeanor and 18 U.S.C. § 2236 makes it a misdemeanor to participate in illegal searches. No federal officer, however, has apparently ever been prosecuted under the latter section.[81]

---

[78] On the "totality of the circumstances" approach related to the admissibility of arguably "involuntary confessions", LaFave et al. (2009, 343–349). In relation to determining "probable cause", see Illinois v. Gates, 462 U.S. 213, 267–274 (1983).

[79] BGHSt 38, 214, 218–222 (1992). English translation in Thaman (2008, 111).

[80] Triantafyllou, Chap. 11, pp. 288–290.

[81] Saltzburg and Capra (2010, 509).

17.4.2 The Constitutionality of Limitations on Governmental Invasions of Privacy

17.4.2.1 The Requirement of Probable Cause and Judicial Authorization

If a dwelling search or wiretap is based on probable cause and is judicially authorized, its constitutional underpinnings are normally guaranteed. I believe that these are the two core factors which, to use the language of Art. 8 ECHR, are "necessary in a democratic society" before invading protected areas of privacy for the purposes of criminal investigation. If the investigative measure violates statutory rules which are unrelated to the amount of suspicion necessary to search or wiretap, or the fact of judicial authorization, then the Spanish courts, for instance, consider the violation to be an "irregularity", rather than an "illegality", and treat it like a "relative nullity" which would not lead to exclusion of evidence.[82] For example, in one Spanish case, the police conducted a search which was authorized by the investigating magistrate and based on sufficient suspicion, but neither the investigating magistrate nor his secretary were present during the search, violating a statutory norm regulating the execution of searches. The Spanish Supreme Court held that this error did not impact upon a fundamental right, and therefore the sanction was merely the annulment of the act documenting the search, making it inadmissible at trial. This, however, did not prevent the police who conducted the search from testifying in court to prove the seizure of the drugs and the *corpus delicti* of the crime.[83]

In principle, the USSC has also categorized certain violations of the laws regulating wiretaps and search warrants as being of sub-constitutional status, the violation of which does not require suppression. Thus, mistakes in the execution of an otherwise valid search warrant,[84] or wiretap,[85] will not lead to exclusion. By refusing to suppress the fruits of an otherwise constitutionally valid, judicially authorized search in *Hudson v. Michigan*,[86] despite a violation of the "knock and announce" requirement, the USSC has come to a result similar to that of the Spanish Supreme Court,

---

[82] On the notion that "illicit evidence" is suppressible under § 11.1 LOPJ-Spain and that "irregular" evidence falls under § 238 LOPJ-Spain, the nullity provision, and does not lead to suppression of fruits of the violation, Aguilera Morales (2008, 93); Bachmaier, Ch. 9, p. 219.

[83] Supreme Court of Spain, Decision of July 9, 1993, English translation in Thaman (2008, 106–108).

[84] See the following two cases in which aspects of Fed. R. Crim. P. 41, regulating serving of search warrants, were violated: United States v. Schoenheit, 856 F.2d 74 (8th Cir. 1988) (violation of prohibition of night service); United States v. Charles, 883 F.2d 355 (5th Cir. 1989) (serving officer did not have warrant in hand).

[85] In relation to the wiretap statute, the provision must "directly and substantially implement" the congressional intention to restrict the use of electronic surveillance or be "intended to play a central role in the statutory scheme". United States v. Giordano, 4 16 U.S. 505, 527 (1974); United States v. Chavez, 4 16 U.S. 562, 574 (1974).

[86] 547 U.S. 586, 594 (2006).

but had to resort to contorted reasoning because of a previous decision in which the "knock and announce" rule was declared to be constitutionally required.[87]

There will, of course, be differences in the interpretation of what is an unconstitutional search, because, while the US requires "probable cause" for the issuance of a search warrant or wiretap,[88] some other countries, such as Germany, Spain or France, appear to require a lesser degree of suspicion.[89]

17.4.2.2 The Constitutional Exception for Exigent Circumstances

Both the German and Italian Constitutions provide for an exception to the warrant requirement in cases of exigent circumstances, or what the Germans call "danger in delay". [90]

This exception is universally recognized, but can easily be abused so it is important that it be narrowly construed to prevent large-scale evasion of the requirement of pre-search, or pre-wiretap judicial authorization.

Although it was well-known that German law enforcement officials seldom if ever acquired search warrants,[91] and always (successfully) defended their warrantless searches retrospectively[92] with a perfunctory incantation of the words "danger in delay", often attributed to the fact that there were no evening duty judges to issue warrants, the appellate courts winked at this sleight of hand, claiming the trial judge's discretion could not be reviewed on appeal.[93] The German Constitutional Court finally took note of this scandalous situation in 2001 and attempted to rectify the situation by limiting the exception for "danger in delay" to cases that are clearly documented, and by requiring judges to be on duty 24 h for the purposes of issuing warrants.[94]

---

[87] See Wilson v. Arkansas, 514 U.S. 927 (1995). The court had to base its decision on the fact that the seizure of the evidence was not a "fruit" of the unlawful entry. Hudson, 547 U.S. at 586–587.

[88] Described as a "fair probability" that the thing searched for will be present in the indicated location. Illinois v. Gates, 462 U.S. 213, 238.

[89] On the near complete discretion of French judges to search any place and seize any thing that the judge deems "useful to the manifestation of the truth" Frase (2007, 210–211). On the low substantive barriers to searches in Germany, where mere "suspicion" is sufficient Weigend (2007, 249–250). For a Spanish investigating magistrate to order a search there need only be "indications" that the person or objects sought are located therein. § 546 CCP-Spain.

[90] Art. 13(2) Const.-Germany; Art. 14 Const.-Italy.

[91] Weigend (2007, 250), estimated that only 10 % of searches were conducted with warrants.

[92] In Germany and many other countries, police must acquire judicial validation of exigent searches within 2 or 3 days after the search. See § 98(2) CCP-Germany.

[93] In effect, only the most arbitrary searches ever led to exclusion of evidence Ransiek (2002, 566).

[94] BVerfGE 103, 142 (2001).

To prevent such manipulation, the exception for "exigent circumstances" should be limited to two fact situations, the "flagrant crime"[95] and real emergency situations involving threat to human life, health or property. An example of a statute which puts clear restrictions on the invocation of "exigent circumstances" is the US-federal wiretap statute, which allows warrantless wiretaps only in emergency situations that involve "immediate danger of death or serious physical injury to any person", or conspiratorial activities which threaten "the national security interest" or are "characteristic of organized crime".[96] The USSC has also created an exception to the warrant requirement which allow police to enter a house with less than probable cause to save live, prevent injuries, or protect property.[97]

The "flagrant crime" exception would apply to "hot pursuit" cases,[98] where probable cause develops suddenly upon commission of a crime, and escape of the culprit or destruction of evidence is likely. If the suspicion of the presence of drugs in a dwelling, for instance, comes, however, as a result of an investigation, then in principle a warrant should be obtained. The police should not be able to create the need for exigent circumstances by, for instance, walking up to the target house and announcing they are present so as to create a pretext for entering to prevent the destruction of evidence.[99]

17.4.2.3 Instances Where a Constitutional Violation Permits of No Further Balancing

Thus, when a home has been searched without a search warrant based on probable cause or without exigent circumstances, this should be considered to be a clear constitutional violation and exclusion should be the presumptive remedy. This was traditionally the approach of the USSC following *Mapp*, until the "good faith" test and "cost-benefit" balancing was introduced in 1984,[100] as it was for the Spanish courts in interpreting § 11.1 LOPJ-Spain, until balancing was introduced in 1998. The Irish Supreme Court, which initially employed a simple balancing test to determine admissibility of evidence,[101] changed course in 1990 and recognized a categorical exclusionary rule in cases where police clearly violate the constitutional rights of citizens,

---

[95] An exception specifically included in Art. 18(2) Const.-Spain.

[96] 18 U.S.C. § 2518(7)(a). The federal prosecutor must then request *post factum* approval of a judge within 48 h. Such immediate review after an emergency invasion of privacy is otherwise not required for emergency searches in the US.

[97] Brigham City, Utah v. Stuart, 547 U.S. 398, 403 (2006). I disagree with the USSC majority, however, and believe that such searches should not be used solely as pretexts for searches for evidence of crime.

[98] See Warden v. Hayden, 387 U.S. 294, 310 (1967).

[99] I thus disagree with the recent decision of the USSC in Kentucky v. King, 131 S.Ct. 1849, 1857–1862 (2011), which allows such creation of exigent circumstances.

[100] United States v. Leon, 468 U.S. 897, 918–925 (1984). See Cammack, Chap. 1, pp. 19–20.

[101] See People (A.G.) v. O'Brien [1965] I.R. 142, 160–161.

rejecting even the "good faith" exception recognized by the USSC. According to Judge Finlay: "[t]he detection of crime and the conviction of guilty persons, no matter how important they may be in relation to the ordering of society, cannot, however, in my view, outweigh the unambiguously expressed constitutional obligation as far as practicable to defend and vindicate the personal rights of the citizen".[102]

Categorical statutory exclusionary rules are otherwise clearly less common in relation to violations of the right to privacy, than they are for violations of the right to counsel or silence in the context of interrogations. The great exception, however, is with violations of the wiretap statutes. Thus, when core provisions of the US. wiretap statute have been violated, 18 U.S.C. § 2515 provides: "no part of the contents of such communication and no evidence derived therefrom may be received in evidence in any trial, hearing, or other proceeding in or before any court, grand jury, department, officer, agency, regulatory body, legislative committee, or other authority of the United States, a State, or a political subdivision thereof". This is likely the broadest explicit statutory exclusionary rule in US law and clearly extends to "fruits of the poisonous tree". It also brooks of no exceptions based in "standing" or good faith mistakes.[103] § 271 CCP-Italy also expressly prohibits use of the "results of interceptions" made in violation of the wiretap statute.

A key reason for court reluctance to exclude evidence gained from violations of the right to privacy, has been that such violations usually occur unrelated to the violation of any trial right, such as the privilege against self-incrimination, and thus, in the words of the German Supreme Court, will not affect the "procedural position" of the defendant, or in the approach of the ECtHR, will not affect the right to a fair trial protected by Art. 6 ECHR.[104]

17.4.3 Constitutional Limitations on Interrogation Practices

17.4.3.1 Admonitions as to the Right to Silence and to Counsel

While the use of means such as torture, cruel, inhuman and degrading treatment, and lesser tactics which render a confession "involuntary" clearly constitute a fundamental rights violation which leads to suppression of an ensuing statement,

---

[102] People (D.P.P.) v. Kenny, [1990] 2 I.R. 110, 134; [1990] I.L.R.M. 569, 579. For a comprehensive discussion of the Irish cases and approach, Cras and Daley, Chap. 2, pp. 38–40.

[103] See United States v. Rice, 478 F.3d 704, 711–712 (6th Cir. 2007) which accepts no "good faith" exception to the wiretap exclusionary rule.

[104] In *Leon*, the USSC stated that the wrong perpetrated by the Fourth Amendment violation is "fully accomplished" at the time of the illegal search and no "new Fourth Amendment wrong" is perpetrated by admitting illegally seized evidence into the trial. United States v. Leon, 468 U.S. at 906. The "fair trial" test of the ECtHR will be discussed, *infra.*, and in detail in Ölčer, Chap. 16, p. 402.

another very important procedural rule, is the requirement that a suspect or defendant be aware of the right to silence and the right to counsel before being questioned.[105] Whereas the former, more egregious violation constitutes an attack on human dignity and sometimes bodily integrity, the latter is more of a procedural error, which undermines the defendant's defense capabilities during the criminal trial.

The warnings made famous in the USSC's landmark decision of *Miranda v. Arizona*,[106] were deemed by the majority in that case to be firmly rooted in the Fifth Amendment, and therefore constitutionally required to dissipate the inherent coerciveness of custodial interrogation. The consequence of a violation of the rules the court laid down was exclusion of the statements gathered following the violation. The USSC also claimed that it is with custodial interrogation that "our adversary system of criminal proceedings commences".[107] In a similar vein, the German Supreme Court has proclaimed, that the German variant of *Miranda* warnings are "designed to secure the foundations of the procedural position of the accused". Exclusion of a statement taken in violation of the German *Miranda*-warnings is mandated even if the suspect interrogated was out of custody, as long as probable cause existed to arrest him for the crime which was the subject of the interrogation.[108]

Although most democratic countries have adopted the teachings of *Miranda*, the constitutional underpinnings of the rule have been called into question in the country of their origin. The USSC in 1971 began permitting the use of statements taken in violation of the *Miranda* rules in order to impeach a defendant whose courtroom testimony contradicted it.[109] By 1974, the violation of the *Miranda* rules was no longer characterized as a violation of the Fifth Amendment privilege against self-incriminationor or the Sixth Amendment right to counsel, but as a "prophylactic rule" the violation of which would not affect the use of the "fruits of the poisonous tree".[110] Although the USSC reversed course in 2000 and declared that the *Miranda* warnings were of constitutional stature,[111] it refused to reverse the exceptions to the exclusionary rule previously based in its purportedly sub-constitutional status, and a plurality of the court has recently returned to calling *Miranda* warnings mere "prophylactic" safeguards not themselves required by the Fifth Amendment, in holding that physical evidence found as a result of a *Miranda*-defective confession, is admissible.[112]

---

[105] Most European and Latin American jurisdictions now require that persons subject to police interrogation be admonished of their right to confer with counsel and their right to remain silent before being interrogated Thaman (2008, 85–96). In general, see Thaman (2001, 591–624).

[106] Miranda v. Arizona, 384 U.S. 436 (1966).

[107] 384 U.S. at 477.

[108] BGHSt 38, 214, 218–222, 224–225 (1992). For an English translation of this case, Thaman (2008, 91–92, 110–112). See also Gless, Chap. 5, p. 137.

[109] Harris v. New York, 401 U.S. 222, 225–226 (1971).

[110] Michigan v. Tucker, 417 U.S. 433, 438–439, 450 (1974).

[111] Dickerson v. United States, 530 U.S. 428, 437–438 (2000).

[112] United States v. Patane, 542 U.S. 630, 632 (2004).

17.4.3.2 The Actual Right to Counsel Before and During Interrogations

Although the *Miranda* decision clearly intimated that an uncharged suspect in custody must be advised of the right to have counsel present during the entire interrogation,[113] the Court never required that police assure that those facing interrogation will actually be able to speak to lawyers before deciding whether they will waive their rights.[114] Police can even tell suspects that no lawyer will be provided until they are charged and go to court,[115] or refuse to tell a suspect that a lawyer has been actually retained.[116] An invocation of the right to counsel will certainly prevent any further legal interrogation of a jailed uncharged suspect, even as to different charges, unless the defendant reinitiates contact with the interrogators,[117] but the dissent of Justice White in *Miranda* already expressed doubt, as to whether a waiver of the right to counsel, allowed by the majority, could ever truly considered to be voluntary, if custody was *per se* coercive in the first place.[118]

As a result, the overwhelming majority of suspects in the US waive their *Miranda* rights and speak to police without ever having talked to a lawyer.[119] Although the USSC originally held that once a person is charged and is represented by counsel or has requested or been assigned counsel, no interrogation may take place in the absence of counsel nor without counsel's consent. But that rule was recently overruled by the USSC, and the *Miranda* rules now apply whether or not the suspect is represented by counsel.[120]

Unlike in the US, however, in Europe the right to actually consult with counsel before and during interrogation is obtaining indubitable constitutional status as a fundamental right. According to § 75(2)(1) CCP-Russia, for example, no pretrial statement made by a defendant to law enforcement officials which was given in the absence of counsel, even if the suspect waived the right to counsel, may be used at

---

[113] Miranda v. Arizona, 384 U.S. 436, 492 (1964) This was also clearly reaffirmed in Florida v. Powell, 130 S.Ct. 1195, 1211 (2010).

[114] The *Miranda* court said it was not necessary to have a system of "station house lawyers" ready to advise incarcerated suspects, 384 U.S. at 474, as is required in England and Wales under the system of "duty solicitors". Code of Practice (C) § 6.6 (a–c) Police and Criminal Evidence Act 1984 (hereafter PACE-England and Wales).

[115] California v. Prysock, 453 U.S. 355, 361 (1981); Duckworth v. Eagan, 492 U.S. 195, 203–204 (1989).

[116] Moran v. Burbine, 475 U.S. 412, 422 (1986). The Court stated: "No doubt the additional information would have been useful to respondent; perhaps it even might have affected his decision to confess".

[117] Edwards v. Arizona, 451 U.S. 477 (1981); Arizona v. Roberson, 486 U.S. 675 (1988).

[118] Miranda v. Arizona, 384 U.S. at 536–537 (White, dissenting).

[119] According to one study, only around one quarter of suspects elected to remain silent Leo (1996, 657–659).

[120] Montejo v. Louisiana, 556 U.S. 778, 129 S.Ct. 2079, 2085, 2089–2091 (2009).

trial if the defendant retracts the statement at or before trial.[121] A similar rule has been recognized in Spain.[122] In Italy, the denial of the assistance of counsel constitutes a nullity of general order, and, in the context of police interrogation, an "absolute nullity" which cannot be purged and must be raised *ex oficio* by the judge.[123] Exclusion follows even if the suspect offers a statement voluntarily in the absence of counsel.[124]

Traditionally, some European regimes gave the police a determinate period of time to interrogate suspects (called *garde à vue* in France and Belgium), and the right to counsel was only recognized during subsequent interrogation by an investigating magistrate.[125] In 2008, however, the Grand Chamber of the ECtHR in *Salduz v. Turkey* held that the right to counsel, guaranteed by Art. 6(3)(c) ECHR, applies not only at trial, but also during the investigative stage, and most assuredly during the first police interrogation. Any conviction based on an admission or statement taken in violation of this right constitutes a violation of the general right to a fair trial guaranteed under Art. 6(1) ECHR. The Court said: "The rights of the defense will in principle be irretrievably prejudiced when incriminating statements made during police interrogation without access to a lawyer are used for a conviction".[126] The Grand Chamber did, however, allow for waivers of fair trial rights,[127] and this could be interpreted as allowing waiver of the right to counsel during the first interrogation.[128]

The decisions subsequent to *Salduz*, however, indicate that the ECtHR has in mind a right to counsel during pretrial interrogation that is significantly stronger than that articulated in *Miranda*, or its diluted post-Warren-Court progeny.[129] First of all, the Court makes it clear that a waiver of the right to counsel must be

---

[121] This provision was introduced due to the prevalent use of coercion by Russian criminal investigators, not only in inducing confessions, but also in inducing waivers of counsel prior to interrogation Thaman (2007, 375–378).

[122] See § 520(2)(a–c) CCP-Spain. See also De Urbano Castrillo, Torres Morato (2003, 78) and Bachmaier, ch. 9, p. 237.

[123] §§ 178(1)(c), 179 (1), 350(3) CCP-Italy, and discussion in Colamussi (1996, 37).

[124] § 350(6,7) CCP-Italy.

[125] On how much easier it was for police to get confessions in the absence of counsel than it was during questioning by the *juge d'instruction* Pradel (1997, 397). In Belgium, there was no right to counsel even during interrogation before the investigating magistrate Van Puyenbroeck (2010, 78).

[126] Salduz v. Turkey (G.C.)(2009), 49 E.H.R.R. 19, 421, 435–439.

[127] Ibid, 438,§ 59.

[128] However, in a later case, the ECtHR held that Art. 6 ECHR had been violated in a case where the defendant signed a waiver of the right to counsel and confessed, because he credibly alleged that police had coerced him to waive the right. Oleg Kolesnik v. Ukraine, no. 17551/02, § 37, ECHR 2009.

[129] For more detail on the post-*Salduz* cases, Ölçer, Chap. 16, pp. 396–397. See for instance the USSC's trivialization of the right to counsel during post-charge interrogations in Kansas v. Ventris, 556 U.S. 586, 129 S.Ct. 1841 (2009), discussed in Cammack, Chap. 1, pp. 29–30.

unequivocal and cannot be presumed from the fact that the suspect answers questions after having acknowledged understanding of his rights. A valid waiver must be knowing and intelligent, which means that "he could reasonably have foreseen what the consequences would be."[130] The ECtHR further held, that it violates the right to counsel to continue questioning a suspect who has asked for counsel, unless the suspect has spoken to counsel or reinitiates the contact with police.[131] It also found that subsequent confessions, where defendant did arguably waive his *Miranda* rights, did not attenuate the taint of the previous confessions given without counsel.[132] Finally, the ECtHR clearly links the right to remain silent with the presumption of innocence, and the notion that the prosecution must prove its case "without resort to evidence obtained through coercion or oppression in defiance of the will of the accused".[133]

The decisions in *Salduz* and its progeny have led to substantial changes in the *garde à vue* procedures in France and Belgium,[134] and are quickly leading to changes in other parts of Europe.

17.4.3.3 Exigent Circumstances in Relation to Interrogations?

The *Salduz* court admitted that there are possible restrictions on the right to counsel at the first interrogation: "The question, in each case, has therefore been whether the restriction was justified and, if so, whether, in the light of the entirety of the proceedings, it has not deprived the accused of a fair hearing, for even a justified

---

[130] Pishchalnikov v. Russia, no. 7025/04, §§ 76, 77, ECHR 2009. The ECtHR emphasized that defendant was questioned about grave crimes, such as murder, after having been arrested for another crime and that only with counsel could he have assessed the consequences of agreeing to the interrogation. ibid, § 80. On the contrary, the USSC recently ruled that an unequivocal waiver of *Miranda* rights, including the right to counsel, is no longer necessary, and may be inferred from the fact that the defendant eventually answers questions. Berghuis v. Thompkins, 130 S.Ct. 2250, 2260–2262 (2010).

[131] Pishchalnikov v. Russia, no. 7025/04, § 79. The language seems plucked from Edwards v. Arizona, 451 U.S. 477, 484 (1981).

[132] Pishchalnikov v. Russia, no. 7025/04, §§ 81–82. Here the ECtHR makes a finding similar to that in Missouri v. Seibert, 542 U.S. 600, 601 (2004), which held that a *Miranda* waiver after a preceding statement taken in willful violation of the *Miranda* rules could not be deemed to be knowing.

[133] Zaichenko v. Russia, no. 39660/02, § 38, ECHR 2010.

[134] In early March, 2011, the Belgian Senate approved a law providing for counsel before the first interrogation. *Le Sénat adopte la loi Salduz: les droits des justiciables renforcés*, RTBF.BE.INFO, March 3, 2011, http://www.rtbf.be/info/belgique/detail_le-senat-adopte-la-loi-salduz-les-droits-du-justiciable-renforces?id=5714303; in France, the *Conseil constitutionnel* ordered in April 2011 that *Salduz* be implemented in France and lawyers stormed the jails demanding to represent their clients. Marion Isobel, *Salduz fever sweeps Europe*, BLOG OPEN SOCIETY, April 26, 2011, http://blog.soros.org/2011/04/case-watch-salduz-fever-sweeps-europe/. For the new sections implementing the right to counsel in France, see §§ 63-3-1, 63-4, 63-4-1, 63-4-2, added by Law 2011–392 of 14 April 2011.

restriction is capable of doing so in certain circumstances".[135] A typical example would be the restriction allowed in § 6.6(b)(i) Code of Practice C, of PACE-England and Wales, which allows for the postponement of the right to speak to a duty solicitor if "delay will involve an immediate risk of harm to persons or serious loss of, or damage to, property". The USSC has also recognized an exception to the need to give a suspect the *Miranda* warnings when "prompted by a concern for the public safety".[136]

On the other hand, the ECtHR has made it clear that there are no exceptions to the prohibition against torture or inhuman and degrading treatment provided by Art. 3 ECHR even in the "fight against terrorism and organised crime" or to save human life.[137]

17.5 Balancing by the Courts

17.5.1 Introduction

I have tried to articulate what violations would constitute fundamental or constitutional violations in a democratic country which respects human rights. This is clearly the case when interrogation methods are used that violate CAT or render a statement involuntary and the consensus is growing for imposing a bright-line rule for interrogations in violation of the right to counsel. I would also make this claim in relation to violations of the right to privacy in one's domicile and private communications, when law enforcement authorities proceed without judicial authorization and probable cause in the absence of exigent circumstances. In some jurisdictions, the primary evidence, and sometimes the actual "fruits of the poisonous tree" are suppressed upon such a finding.

But this is not the case in the majority of jurisdictions where courts tend to balance even clear constitutional violations against other important interests, and often will suppress neither the direct, nor the derivative evidence resulting from them. The use of any balancing test where fundamental rights have been violated therefore threatens to subordinate the right to other interests that have less (if any) constitutional significance; on the other hand, unlawfully obtained evidence that does not involve violations of fundamental rights may be admitted or excluded, depending on the balance of interests. In the rest of this section, I review the main tests and factors that courts have used in balancing interests. I will first examine three general tests, which I call the "fair trial" test, the "judicial integrity" test, and the "public

[135] Salduz v. Turkey(G.C.)(2009), 49 E.H.R.R. 421, 436, § 52.

[136] New York v. Quarles, 467 U.S. 649, 656 (1984).

[137] Gäfgen v. Germany (G.C.) (2011), 52 E.H.R.R. 1, 23, 27, §§ 87, 107.

interest" test. I will then examine separate factors used in these tests such as the "good faith" of the violating officer, the seriousness of the violation, whether the evidence was actually the "fruit" of the violation, the importance of the evidence to determine the truth, and the seriousness of the offense, for the proof of which the illegally gathered evidence has been proffered.

17.5.2 The "Fair Trial" Assessment

§ 78(1) PACE-England and Wales, provides: "(1) In any proceedings the court may refuse to allow evidence on which the prosecution proposes to rely to be given if it appears to the court that, having regard to all the circumstances, including the circumstances in which the evidence was obtained, the admission of the evidence would have such an adverse effect on the fairness of the proceedings that the court ought not to admit it".

In employing its "fair trial" test, the ECtHR traditionally defers to domestic exclusionary practices. Thus, although the court has found violations of the right to privacy under Art. 8 ECHR in many cases involving illegal wiretapping or interception of private conversations, it has consistently held, that: "It is not the role of the Court to determine, as a matter of principle, whether particular types of evidence – for example, unlawfully obtained evidence – may be admissible or, indeed, whether the applicant was guilty or not. The question which must be answered is whether the proceedings as a whole, including the way in which the evidence was obtained, were fair. This involves an examination of the 'unlawfulness' in question and, where violation of another Convention right is concerned, the nature of the violation found".[138]

When the Spanish Constitutional Court held in 1984 that evidence seized in violation of the constitution had to be suppressed, it grounded the prohibition of use on: (1) the violation of a fair trial with all the guarantees established by law (Art. 24 Const.-Spain); (2) a denial of equality of arms, in the sense that the defense is *not* allowed to violate the law in order to produce evidence; and (3) a violation of the presumption of innocence, which in Spanish law restricts the prosecutor to the use of legally gathered evidence to rebut the presumption.[139]

Thus, whereas Spain finds a categorical violation of the right to a fair trial if the fruits of a violation of constitutional magnitude are used at trial, § 78(1) PACE-England and Wales, gives the court, what has been described in the literature as

---

[138] Allan v. United Kingdom (2003), 36 E.H.R.R. 12, 143, 155–156, § 42. The first important case taking this approach was Schenck v. Switzerland (1988), 13 E.H.R.R. 242, 264, § 46. To my knowledge, the ECtHR has never found a violation of the Art. 6 ECHR right to a fair trial based solely on the use of evidence seized in violation of the right to privacy under Art. 8 ECHR.

[139] STC 114/1984 (Nov. 29, 1984), discussed in De Urbano Castrillo, Torres Morato (2003, 41–42) and Aguilera Morales (2008, 84–88). See also Bachmaier, Chap. 9, p. 218.

"broad and unstructured" discretion to balance a plethora of factors against the illegality of police actions, such as: the seriousness of the offense, good faith of the officers, the type of evidence and its reliability, the existence of corroborative evidence, the type of illegality and the type of right infringed.[140] We can see here, that the "fair trial" criterion is flexible enough, that each judge can give his or her own stamp on what is a "fair trial" when so many factors are in the balance.[141]

17.5.3 *Preserving the Integrity of the Courts*

Duff correctly notes that, if exclusionary rules are to have any meaning they must be "extrinsic", and not anchored in the "intrinsic" emphasis on probative value and credibility. The notion of "judicial integrity" is such an "extrinsic" justification for exclusion, yet scholars differ as to its theoretical underpinnings, differentiating between: (1) the "disciplinary" model adopted by the US which focuses on deterrence of unconstitutional police conduct; (2) the "vindicatory" model, which focuses on protecting citizens' constitutional rights and would tend to automatic exclusion once a significant violation has been ascertained[142]; and (3) the "moral legitimacy" approach, which balances the seriousness of the constitutional violation and the harm to the public if a dangerous criminal were to go free.[143]

For the *Mapp* court, of course, the "imperative of judicial integrity" was vindicatory, and meant, that "the criminal goes free, if he must, but it is the law that sets him free. Nothing can destroy a government more quickly than its failure to observe its own laws, or worse, its disregard of the charter of its own existence".[144] The USSC in *Leon* abandoned this high ground by equating judicial integrity with the exclusively disciplinary rationale, aimed at deterring only police, and not judicial errors.[145]

Art. 24(2) of the Canadian Charter clearly proclaims judicial integrity as the basis for exclusion: "where…a court finds that evidence was obtained in a manner that infringed or denied any of the rights or freedoms guaranteed by this Charter, the evidence shall be excluded if it is established that, having regard to all the

---

[140] Ormerod (2003, 64).

[141] According to Andrew Ashworth, "if courts are allowed simply to pick and choose the guiding principle(s) in the circumstances of any individual case, there is unlikely to be a consistent approach and a danger of the question of admissibility being left to the 'whim of the particular court'". Cited in Duff (2004, 159).

[142] The New Zealand courts have rejected the deterrent rationale and focus exclusively on "vindication of the right" that has been breached, though they still engage in balancing Mahoney (2003, 610).

[143] Duff (2004, 160–174).

[144] Mapp v. Ohio, 367 U.S. 643, 659 (1961).

[145] United States v. Leon, 468 U.S. 897, 916 (1984).

circumstances, the admission of it in the proceedings would bring the administration of justice into disrepute".[146] In interpreting this provision, Canadian courts originally developed two separate tests to determine whether exclusion was appropriate. Under the first test, exclusion would result, regardless of the seriousness of the violation, if it had as a consequence that a suspect-defendant was "conscripted" to produce evidence against himself. The second test focused exclusively on the seriousness of the violation such that a failure to exclude would bring the administration of justice into disrepute. Important factors here were the intentionality of the violation and whether police acted in "good faith", but not whether there might have been a hypothetical clean path to the evidence (i.e. inevitable discovery).[147] Recently the Canadian courts have moved to a simpler balancing test, which now includes the "moral legitimacy" criterion. The test involves the weighing of three factors: (1) the severity of the violation; (2) whether the admission of the evidence would bring the administration of justice into disrepute from the perspective of society's interest in respect for Charter rights; and (3) the effect of admitting the evidence on the public interest in having the case adjudicated on its merits.[148]

17.5.4 The Public Impact of the Admissibility Decision

§ 158-4 CCP-Taiwan (as amended in 2003), requires the court to balance "the protection of human rights and the preservation of public interests" in deciding whether or not to exclude illegally gathered evidence.[149] In 1950, the Scottish High Court developed a test which balanced: "(a) the interest of the citizen to be protected from illegal or irregular invasions of his liberties by the authorities, and (b) the interest of the State to secure that evidence bearing upon the commission of crime and necessary to enable justice to be done shall not be withheld from Courts of law on any merely formal or technical ground".[150]

But what is the "public interest"? This could mean that the public would be appalled if evidence resulting from torture or pervasive warrantless wiretapping were used in the courts.[151] It could also refer to "the public's interest in maintaining the integrity of the courts and in ensuring the observance of the law and minimum

---

[146] Canadian Charter of Rights and Freedoms, Enacted by the Canada Act 1982 [U.K.] c.11; proclaimed in force April 17, 1982. Art. 35(5) Const.-South Africa, contains similar language, mandating exclusion if "the admission of that evidence would render the trial unfair or otherwise be detrimental to the administration of justice" (Schwikkard, van der Merwe 2007, 487–488).

[147] Roach (2007, 71–72).

[148] See R. v. Grant, 2009 S.C. 32 §§ 95–97; R. v. Harrison, 2009 SC 34, § 2. For a positive assessment of this change, Stuart (2010, 316–319).

[149] See discussion in Wang, ch. 15, pp. 362–365.

[150] Lawrie v. Muir, 1950 JC 19, 26. See Stark and Leverick, Chap. 3, pp. 70–71.

[151] Duff (2004, 155), providing examples of this sort.

standards of propriety by those entrusted with powers of law enforcement", as stated by the Australian High Court, which returns us to the interests of judicial integrity.[152]

In *Leon*, the USSC proclaimed: "The substantial social costs exacted by the exclusionary rule for the vindication of Fourth Amendment rights have long been a source of concern. Our cases have consistently recognized that unbending application of the exclusionary sanction to enforce ideals of governmental rectitude would impede unacceptably the truth-finding functions of judge and jury". The court continued: "particularly when law enforcement officers have acted in objective good faith or their transgressions have been minor, the magnitude of the benefit conferred on such guilty defendants offends basic concepts of the criminal justice system".[153]

Thus, the USSC posits a "public interest" in "having juries receive all probative evidence of a crime".[154] More recently, the court bemoaned the exclusionary rule's "costly toll upon truth-seeking", which consists in "letting guilty and possibly dangerous defendants go free".[155] Exclusion, for the USSC, is now a "last resort"[156] subject to a balancing test which pits the exclusionary rule's "deterrence benefits" against its "substantial social costs".[157]

With the USSC's disciplinary, cost-benefit approach, the "intrinsic" emphasis on not losing probative evidence is pushing back the vindicatory interest in protecting constitutional rights, paving the way for a possible return to the old Common Law presumption of admissibility of relevant evidence, or its inquisitorial counterpart which prioritized truth over rights.

17.5.5 Application of the Balancing Tests Once a Constitutional Violation Has Been Determined

17.5.5.1 Was the Constitutional Violation Excusable? Questions of "Good Faith" and Lack of Intentionality

Once the German courts determine that the interest violated is of constitutional magnitude, they next examine the gravity of the violation, that is, whether it was in conscious disregard of the law, or only inadvertent or negligent.[158] A similar test has

---

[152] Ridgeway v. the Queen, (1995) 184 C.L.R. 19, 38, cited in Bradley (2001, 380).

[153] United States v. Leon, 468 U.S. 897, 907–908 (1984).

[154] Murray v. United States, 487 U.S. 533, 537 (1988).

[155] Herring v. United States. 555 U.S. 135, 141 (2009).

[156] Ibid, 140.

[157] Hudson v. Michigan, 547 U.S. 586, 591 (2006).

[158] Weigend (2007, 251).

been adopted by the Australian High Court, whereby the court should taken into consideration whether there was bad faith on the part of the police and the ease with which the law might have been complied with.[159] The Scottish courts also occasionally refer to whether there was bad faith on the part of the police in deciding whether to exclude.[160] § 359a(1) CCP-Netherlands gives the court discretion to exclude evidence and obligates it to "take account of the interest that the breached rule serves, the gravity of the breach and the harm it causes".

In 1998 the Spanish Constitutional Court allowed for a "good faith" exception to the otherwise categorical exclusionary rule codified in § 11.1 LOPJ-Spain. It made the nice distinction between "natural" and "juridical" causation. The court analyzed the extent to which an illegal wiretap tainted the other evidence in terms of the right to a "fair trial", referring directly to the approach taken by the ECtHR in this respect. It analyzed whether the violation was of a required "intensity" and then used a balancing test to determine whether there was an "anti-juridical" nexus between illegality and the derivative evidence. It determined, that the violation was not so "intense" due to the fact that the police did get a wiretap order, and the violation was based on a lack of probable cause. The court also noted that such an "error" was not intentional and not grossly negligent, and that under the totality of the circumstances, the derivative evidence could be used.[161] Here we see an incorporation of the "good faith" rule articulated in *Leon* in relation to wiretaps, a step even the USSC has not yet taken.

In *Leon*, the USSC introduced the "good faith" exception to the Fourth Amendment exclusionary rule in a case in which a magistrate erroneously issued a search warrant based on what a police officer believed in "good faith" constituted probable cause. The USSC held that, though the Fourth Amendment was violated, excluding the illegally obtained evidence would only be appropriate to deter unlawful police conduct if the officer intentionally or recklessly submitted a clearly inadequate or "bare bones" affidavit of probable cause or false evidence to the magistrate.[162]

The USSC has also extended the "good faith" exception to other areas where the magistrate erred, such as where the search warrant itself contained an erroneous or inadequate descriptions of the things to be seized or the places to be searched,[163] or where an unlawful detention was based on erroneous court records.[164] Finally, however, the court has lowered the bar recently to allow admission of evidence which was gathered when the police were guilty of "isolated negligence" in believing there was probable cause.[165]

---

[159] Bunning v. Cross, (1978) 141 C.L.R. 54, cited in Bradley (2001, 380).

[160] See Edgley v. Barbour, 1994 SCCR 789, 792, cited in Duff (2004, 165). See also Stark and Leverick, Chap. 3, pp. 72–73.

[161] STC 81/Feb. 4, 1998. Discussion in Bachmaier, Chap. 9, pp. 222–223.

[162] United States v. Leon, 468 U.S. 897, at 915–923.

[163] Massachusetts v. Shepard, 468 U.S. 981, 988–990 (1984), decided on the same day as *Leon*.

[164] Arizona v. Evans, 514 U.S. 1, 14–15 (1995).

[165] United States v. Herring, 555 U.S. 135, 137 (2009). For more on the "good faith" exception. Cammack, Chap. 1, pp. 19–20.

Since the assessment of probable cause, i.e. a "fair probability" that a crime has been committed or that evidence of that crime is to be found in a particular place, is a value judgment based on the "totality of the circumstances", I believe that a narrow exception can be allowed in borderline cases where "reasonable minds may differ on the question whether a particular affidavit establishes probable cause",[166] when the officer has followed the search warrant procedure and submitted the case to an impartial magistrate. I also believe that "good faith" could save evidence derived from police procedures which were allowed by law or high court jurisprudence when they were performed, but where the standards became stricter after the measure was undertaken.[167] I believe, however, that the exception for police negligence goes too far. I agree with Justice Ginsburg's dissent in *Herring*, that tort liability for negligence is considered to deter careless conduct in citizens, and if the Fourth Amendment exclusionary is meant to deter, it should encompass negligent conduct as well.[168]

17.5.5.2 Was the Evidence the "Fruit" of the Constitutional Violation?

Introduction

Even if a system recognizes the extension of the exclusionary rule to derivative evidence, the question still remains, as to whether the evidence sought to be used in the criminal trial really owes its existence to the constitutional violation, i.e., is actually its "fruit". And it is here that the famous exception of "attenuated taint", and its closely related subcategories "inevitable discovery" or "independent source", are invoked to admit arguably derivative evidence.

Each of these exceptions has been recognized and applied by the Spanish courts despite Spain's categorical exclusionary rule in relation to derivative evidence.[169] Since the aforementioned Constitutional Court decision in 1998, Spain's courts now engage in a balancing test to determine whether to exclude the fruits of a constitutional violation and the test is framed in terms of a limitation on the doctrine of the "fruits of the poisonous tree". An exception to the otherwise categorical rule can exist, "even when there is a factual causal nexus between the illegality and the evidence, if the causal link is not based in the illegality" (is not "anti-juridical"). In assessing the existence of a legally relevant connection, the following elements should be taken into account: (a) The significance of the constitutional infringement; (b) The importance of the evidence for proving guilt; (c) whether there was a

---

166 United States v. Leon, 468 U.S. 897, at 914.

167 The USSC recently recognized this exception in Davis v. United States, 131 S.Ct. 2419, 2428–2429 (2011).

168 United States v. Herring, 555 U.S. at 153–154 (Ginsburg, dissenting).

169 See Decision of June 5, 1995 (Spanish Supreme Court), RJ 1995. No. 4538, 6058, at 6060, English translation in Thaman (2008, 118–119). See also Bachmaier, Chap. 9, p. 222.

hypothetical clean path to discover the evidence (i.e. inevitable discovery); (d) whether the right violated requires special protection; and (e) whether the violating officers acted intentionally, or erred in good faith, and thus whether exclusion is necessary for deterrent purposes.[170]

We will now discuss how courts approach the issue of "fruits" in deciding whether to suppress fruits of both privacy violations and unconstitutional confessions.

Fruits of Illegal Dwelling Searches

Independent Source and Inevitable Discovery

The courts will generally admit evidence that has been discovered through an illegal "search" if it is actually "seized" by independent legal means.[171] The courts will also admit evidence which is seized illegally, if it would have inevitably been discovered through legal means.[172] The doctrine of "inevitable discovery", however, can serve as a gaping loophole in constitutional protections if interpreted in too broad a manner. Some American courts have recognized this exception if the police, who had probable cause, were already in the process of getting a search warrant, when they erroneously but in good faith felt that exigent circumstances existed which allowed them to make a warrantless entry.[173] However the most dangerous extension of this notion of a "hypothetical independent source" is when the court allows the introduction of evidence because probable cause existed and a judge would have approved a warrant application had it been submitted.[174] The German Courts, however, have routinely used this latter rationale, and almost never exclude the direct fruits of warrantless searches.[175]

---

[170] STS 127/2004 of January 19, cited in Bachmaier, Chap. 9, pp. 222–223.

[171] The doctrine of "independent source" is applied in cases where there have been two searches, an illegal one and a legal one, independent of the illegality. It is applied, for instance, when police discover the presence of evidence illegally, but actually seize it pursuant to a search warrant based on information they possessed before the illegal search. Segura v. United States, 468 U.S. 796, 805 (1984); Murray v. United States, 487 U.S. 533, 537 (1988).

[172] This doctrine of "inevitable discovery" is applied where there is only one search and seizure, but other investigative procedures independent of the illegality *would have* discovered the evidence legally. Nix v. Williams, 467 U.S. 431, 444 (1984). The Germans call this the "hypothetical independent source" or "hypothetical clean path" Weigend (2007, 253).

[173] United States v. Cabassa, 62 F.3d 470, 473 (2d Cir. 1995); United States v. Whitehorn, 829 F.2d 1225, 1232–1233 (2d Cir. 1987) (search warrant signed after the search); United States v. Curtis, 931 F.2d 1011, 1013 (4th Cir. 1991).

[174] The overwhelming majority of US courts have rejected this argument, for it would make the warrant requirement meaningless. See e.g., United States v. Johnson, 22 F.3d 674, 680 (6th Cir. 1994); United States v. Echegoyen, 799 F.2d 1271, 1279 (9th Cir. 1986); State v. Handtmann, 437 N.W.2d 830, 838 (N.D. 1989); United States v. Brown, 64 F.3d 1083, 1085 (7th Cir. 1995).

[175] Ransiek (2002, 566). In 1989, the German Supreme Court held that the evidence found in an unconstitutional search will be admissible as long as it is otherwise legally seizable (i.e., is contraband, fruits, or instrumentalities of crime—and not a protected diary) and a judge would have issued a search warrant had the police sought one Weigend (2007, 252).

The Seizure Is Not a Fruit of the Unlawful Search

In overseas jurisprudence one finds doctrines which sever the causal connection between a constitutional illegality and its "fruits" in ways unknown in the US. One of these is the notion that seizures are conceptually independent of searches, and that if the seizure is "legal" then the nexus of illegality has been attenuated. Another, is that a seizure which is a causal result of an illegal search, can nevertheless be attenuated by judicial balancing of other factors.

It is a doctrine firmly entrenched in Italy and accepted by courts in Germany, that the seizure of drugs, for instance, is not the fruit of a clearly unconstitutional search, even where the express object of the search was to find those selfsame drugs. The Italian courts reason, that since § 253(1) CPP-Italy requires the police to seize the *corpus delicti* of a crime, that is, fruits, instrumentalities and contraband, then this *legal* seizure cannot be vitiated by an antecedent unconstitutional search, be it without probable cause or judicial authorization.[176] The courts have held that searches and seizures have different juridical presuppositions and functions and cannot be viewed as linked due to their convergence in reality.[177] As was noted in Sect. 17.2, *supra*, the doctrine of "fruits of the poisonous tree" applies only to "nullities" when expressly provided by statute, and not to the general exclusionary rule in § 191 —CCP-Italy.[178] This doctrine is baffling, because the Italian literature, like the Spanish, asserts that "nullities" relate only to non-constitutional violations in the gathering of evidence, whereas "non-usability" applies only to violations of fundamental rights.[179]

By separating an unlawful search, which is a tool to find evidence to use in a criminal case, from its object, the evidence sought, the Italian and German courts ignore the plain meaning of their constitutional prohibitions on unwarranted searches in order to achieve a goal, the conviction of a guilty person at any cost, which is no longer the purported goal of criminal procedure. It is clear that the prohibition of the violation of privacy of the dwelling is not only rooted in the protection of privacy, but also constitutes a limitation on the ability of the state to gather information or seize evidence in those spaces. Search and seizure cannot be logically separated into different actions with different motivations.[180]

[176] Decision of Italian Supreme Court of March 27, 1996, English translation in Thaman (2008, 122–124). See also Illuminati, ch. 10, p. 254.

[177] Decision of Italian Supreme Court of April 24, 1991, cited in Conso and Grevi (2002, 550).

[178] Decision No. 332/2001, Italian Constitutional Court, *Gazzetta Ufficiale*, n. 38 (Oct. 3, 2001). See Illuminati, ch.10, pp. 253–254 and Conso and Grevi (2002, 339).

[179] Fanuli (2004, 5–6).

[180] Ransiek (2002, 568). At least one section of the Italian Supreme Court has rejected the prevailing doctrine and recognizes a strict functional relationship between the act of searching and the seizure. Decision of March 13, 1992, cited in Conso, Grevi (2002, 550). See also Illuminati, Chap. 10, pp. 253–254.

Fruits of Unconstitutional Interceptions of Confidential Conversations

Unlike in America, where the fruits of a violation of the wiretap statute are explicitly inadmissible, the approach in Europe is less rigorous. In Germany, for instance, the testimony of witnesses who were discovered through an illegal interception has been admitted at trial.[181] Although § 271(1) CCP-Italy mandates "non-usability" of illegally intercepted conversations, § 271(3) CCP-Italy makes an exception for physical fruits which can prove *corpus delicti*. There is also no restriction on using the contents of the "non-usable" conversations to further the investigation, discover new crimes, etc.[182] New wiretaps may also be based on the information gained from antecedent illegal ones.[183]

Up until the new approach of the Spanish Constitutional Court in 1998, physical evidence found as a result of an unconstitutional wiretap or bugging was routinely suppressed per § 11.1 LOPJ-Spain and could not be used at trial.[184] For example, in one case police used a scanner to intercept cellphone conversations without having obtained judicial authorization. The information gathered led to an arrest and the search incident thereto uncovered drugs. The Supreme Court held that the drugs were fruit of the poisonous tree and could not be used.[185] Since the new case law, however, the decision depends on the new balancing test mentioned *supra*. In the seminal 1998 case, the Spanish Constitutional Court used the doctrine of inevitable discovery to dissociate the arrest of the defendant in possession of drugs from an unconstitutional wiretap, by arguing that the defendant had already been under heavy police surveillance and the arrest was therefore not sufficiently tainted by the antecedent illegality.[186]

"Fruits" of "Involuntary" Confessions Which May or May Not Be the Product of Cruel, Inhuman, or Degrading Treatment

I submit, based on the analysis *supra* in Sect. 17.3.1, that any fruits, even physical evidence, of confessions induced by torture or cruel, inhuman or degrading treatment, must be suppressed, provided that the taint has not been attenuated. The USSC has also indicated that the "fruits of the poisonous tree" of "involuntary" confessions, which were not induced by cruel, inhuman or degrading treatment, would also not be usable in a criminal trial. Thus, in *Oregon v. Elstad*, the Court held

---

[181] Weigend (2007, 253).

[182] Cordero (2000, 804).

[183] Conso, Grevi (2002, 399).

[184] See Gómez Colomer (1998, 162–163).

[185] STS 137/1999 of 8 Feburary, available at http://sentencias.juridicas.com/index.php.

[186] STC 81/1998, discussed in Bachmaier, Chap. 9, pp. 222–223.

that a voluntary confession following proper *Miranda* warnings would be subject to exclusion if it followed on the heels of a confession deemed to be involuntary under the due process analysis.[187] In *Patane*, a plurality of the court also said that physical evidence would be subject to exclusion if found as a result of a "coerced" confession.[188] Because the USSC based its reluctance to apply the fruits-of-the-poisonous-tree doctrine to *Miranda* violations on their supposed sub-constitutional "prophylactic" character, it would follow, therefore, that a clear constitutional violation of due process resulting in an involuntary confession would necessarily require exclusion of the "fruits", whether they be in the form of subsequent confessions or physical evidence.[189] In addition, no evidence derived in any way from a statement compelled through a grant of immunity may be admissible in a trial of the person who was granted immunity.[190]

In some jurisdictions, however, the fruits of involuntary statements may be used. Although § 76(2)(a) PACE-England and Wales provides that a confession "may" be rendered inadmissible "where it is the product of "oppression", § 76(4–6) of the same statute provides that this "shall not have any influence on the admissibility in evidence of "any facts" discovered by utilizing the suppressed confession".[191] Argentine courts have also allowed use of information from involuntary confessions to further the investigation.[192]

Fruits of "Unknowing" Confessions Taken in Violation of the Right to Counsel or Without Admonitions as to the Right to Silence

Following the *Patane* decision, there is no bar in the US federal courts to using physical evidence gathered as a result of a violation of the *Miranda* rule. Many European countries take a similar approach. For instance, the Italian courts do not recognize the doctrine of fruits of the poisonous tree for physical evidence or witnesses discovered through otherwise unlawful confessions.[193] In Germany, which has given *Miranda* warnings constitutional status, the courts do not extend the evidentiary prohibition to the "fruits" of a confession taken without the proper warnings, whether in the form of physical evidence or subsequent confessions.[194]

---

187 470 U.S. 298, 340 (1985).

188 United States v. Patane, 542 U.S. 630, 632 (2004).

189 Supporting this interpretation, LaFave et al. (2009, 543).

190 18 U.S.C. § 6002. "The prosecution has a burden to prove the evidence it uses is derived from a legitimate source wholly independent of the compelled testimony". Kastigar v. United States, 406 U.S. 441,460 (1972).

191 § 76(5) PACE-England and Wales provides, albeit, that the jury shall not be told that the "facts" were derived from the statements of the defendant. Duff (2004, 152), alleges that there are no English cases upholding the suppression of physical evidence.

192 Carrió, Garro (2007, 32–33).

193 Di Palma (1996, 115).

194 Weigend (2007, 261).

Some U.S. state courts, however, have suppressed physical evidence resulting from a *Miranda* violation, whether or not the violation was intentional or inadvertent.[195]

In Canada police are not constitutionally required to advise detained suspects of the right to silence before questioning them, but § 10(b) of the Charter does accord arrested persons the right to attempt to contact counsel before being interrogated.[196] If the right to counsel has been violated, however, and derivative evidence is found that could not have been found but for the violation, the Canadian courts considered this to be "conscripted" evidence and traditionally suppressed it. Thus, if a suspect pointed out incriminating evidence in his own house, which would have been searched anyway, this would be admissible, but if the accused, while being denied the right to counsel, informed police that the murder weapon is at the bottom of a frozen river, this would have been suppressed.[197] Whether the "conscription" doctrine is still viable is questionable, since the Canadian Supreme Court has recently adopted a new approach to exclusion in two 2009 cases.[198]

17.5.5.3 Balancing the Quality or Importance of the Evidence

Introduction: Distinguishing Among Different Kinds of Evidence

Prior to 2002 in New Zealand, there was a rebuttable presumption that illegally gathered evidence was inadmissible. The New Zealand Court of Appeal, however, adopted a new multi-factor "fairness" test in 2002 which gives the trial judge broad discretion in deciding whether to exclude illegally gathered evidence, and provides a list of criteria to be weighed, including the "seriousness of the offense" and the "importance of the evidence".[199] A similar test was adopted by the Australian High Court, which required trial courts to consider whether there was bad faith on the part of the police, the importance of the evidence, the seriousness of the offense, and the ease with which the law might have been complied with.[200]

The right to privacy in Germany and some other countries is grounded in the right to human dignity and most importantly the "right to develop one's personality".[201] This approach has led to declaring certain items non-seizable, even where

---

[195] Commonwealth v. Martin, 827 N.E.2d 198, 215 (Mass. 2005); State v. Knapp, 700 N.W.2d 899, 905–906 (Wis. 2005); State v. Peterson, 923 A.2d 585, 588–591 (Vt. 2007); State v. Vondehn, 236 P.3d 691, 695 (Or. 2010).

[196] Roach (2007, 75–77).

[197] Ibid, 71.

[198] See R v. Grant [2009] SCC 32, § 16, where the court balanced a non-egregious unlawful detention and questioning, by virtue of which the defendant was "conscripted" to admit possession of a gun, against the importance of the rights impinged on thereby, and the importance of the physical evidence to determine the truth of the charges, and admitted the gun.

[199] Shaheed [2002] 2 N.Z.L.R. 377, CA , cited in Mahoney (2003, 607).

[200] Bunning v. Cross, [1978] 141 C.L.R. 54, cited in Bradley (2001, 380).

[201] Art. 2(1) Const-Germany

the government has probable cause that they would be material to prove guilt in a criminal case. In Germany, for instance, this protection extends to personal diaries[202] and to a person's spoken words when surreptitiously recorded by another, whether the recorder is, or is not a state official.[203]

This doctrine is reminiscent of the old "mere evidence" doctrine of the USSC which was overruled in 1967.[204] According to that doctrine, the government only had a right to seize the *corpus delicti* of crime, that is, objects to which it had a superior title: such as fruits and instruments of crime, and contraband. Personal papers were protected, unless they were instruments of crime.[205] In fact, to search for and seize a person's words, even where put to paper or uttered under no compulsion, was considered to be tantamount to compelling self-incrimination. As the *Boyd* court noted: "...we have been unable to perceive that the seizure of a man's private books and papers to be used in evidence against him is substantially different from compelling him to be a witness against himself".[206]

The now overruled "mere evidence" rule and the current German limitations on using highly personal evidence to prove guilt, are examples of *prima facie* intrinsic prohibitions on the seizure of what may be highly probative evidence, not merely prohibitions on "use" due to the irregular or illegal methods of seizure.[207]

Evidence of Questionable Reliability

Coerced or otherwise involuntary confessions were traditionally excluded in the US due to their lack of credibility, rather than on constitutional grounds.[208] Today, even potentially probative evidence may be excluded if the judge decides that its prejudicial nature outweighs its probative value.[209]

A number of post-Soviet codes have exclusionary rules which limit exclusion to situations where the violation "influenced or could have influenced the credibility of

---

[202] See Decision of German Supreme Court of Feb. 21, 1964, BGHSt 19, 325, 326–328 (1964), English translation in Thaman (2008, 82).

[203] See Decision of German Supreme Court of June 14, 1960, BGHSt 14, 358, 359–360, 364–365 (1960), English translation in Thaman (2008, 72–73).

[204] Warden v. Hayden, 387 U.S. 294, 309–310 (1967).

[205] Boyd v. United States, 116 U.S. 616, 628 (1886); Weeks v. United States, 232 U.S. 383, 391–392 (1914).

[206] 116 U.S. at 633. Note the similarity with the now outdated Canadian exclusionary rule based on constitutional violations which "conscript" the defendant to give evidence against himself. For a similar comparison of a subpoena *duces tecum* with an involuntary confession, see Beling (1903, 14).

[207] On the distinction between *Beweiserhebungsverbot* (evidentiary gathering prohibition) and *Beweisverwertungsverbot* (evidentiary use-prohibition), Roxin (1995, 164).

[208] Hopt v. Territory of Utah, 110 U.S. 574, 585 (1884).

[209] Fed. Rule of Evidence 403, § 352 Cal. Evidence Code.

the evidence".[210] Such emphasis on the credibility of the evidence also constitutes one prong of the tests which have been adopted by the International Criminal Tribunals for the Former Yugoslavia (ICTY) and Rwanda (ICTR) and for the International Criminal Court (ICC). Rule 95 of the ICTY Rules of Procedure and Evidence provides: "No evidence shall be admissible if obtained by methods which cast substantial doubt on its reliability or if its admission is antithetical to, and would seriously damage, the integrity of the proceedings".[211] Identical language was incorporated into § 69(7) of the Rome Statute for the International Criminal Court.[212]

Exclusionary rules based on the questionable reliability of evidence are unremarkable, for courts should generally only admit reliable and relevant evidence, or, at the least, should prevent judges from relying on questionable evidence when formulating the reasons for their decisions.

Physical Evidence That Proves Corpus Delicti

We have discussed in Sect. 17.5.5.2, above, how in Italy the police duty to seize contraband, fruits and instrumentalities of crime, i.e., the *corpus delicti*, breaks the nexus between a patently unconstitutional search and its intended fruits, and allows the use of the evidence collected. The other side of this equation, is that "mere evidence" discovered in a patently illegal search would be "non-usable", much as it was under *Boyd* even following a warranted search based on probable cause.

The unwillingness of most courts to suppress physical evidence which is a fruit of a violation of the right to privacy, or the *Miranda* rules, and of some to do so when the evidence is the fruit of an unconstitutional wiretap or an involuntary confession speaks to the preponderance of truth-finding over constitutional rights, at least when dealing with the most reliable of evidence. This balancing is justified by some courts with the assertion that the admission of physical evidence can never violate the right to a fair trial because it is not really the "fruit" of the violation, nor dependent thereon, having pre-existed the violation.[213]

17.5.5.4 The Gravity of the Crime Which Is Being Prosecuted

Beling's treatise on evidentiary prohibitions clearly provided for more liberal admissability of illegally seized evidence in capital cases, than in less serious ones: "the interest in solving high treason or a murder, is infinitely greater than the interest

[210] § 105 CCP-Armenia. Similar language is used in § 125(2)(1) CCP-Azerbaijan; § 94(2) CCP-Moldova; and § 125 CCP-Turkmenistan.

[211] United Nations, IT/32/Rev.40, July 12, 2007.

[212] The Rome Statute of the International Criminal Court. July 17, 1998. U.N. GAOR, 53d Sess, U.N. Doc.A/CONF. 183/9 (1998).

[213] This rationalization is employed in South Africa, Schwikkard, van der Merwe (2007, 488).

in investigating and punishing a cyclist who drives on the wrong side of the road, or a sassy young man who gives his desire for singing too long a rein during nighttime hours".[214] Beling's approach has now been squarely adopted by the German courts. Thus, even if a court is dealing with a grave violation of the right to develop one's personality which would normally lead to exclusion of a diary, for instance, the court must still weigh the seriousness of the crime charged before deciding whether to exclude.[215]

Andrew Ashworth has, in my view correctly, asserted that the seriousness of the charges facing the defendant should never go into the balancing process, because the more serious the charge, the more detrimental will be the introduction of the evidence to the defendant due to the more severe punishment awaiting him.[216] A compromise position here, would be to mandate a reduction of punishment if the state violated the constitution in order to bring someone to justice.[217]

In another context I have suggested that all interrogations should take place only after counsel has been provided, and that confessions should be negotiated, much like plea-bargains, thus allowing the defendant to negotiate a discounted punishment before agreeing to help the state in proving his own guilt. The truth might better be ascertained through a grant of leniency than through the typical psychological coercion of custodial interrogation.[218] Criminal codes could also provide statutory mitigation whenever the use of unconstitutionally acquired evidence is required to prove guilt. In other words, the maximum punishment should only be allowable if the state can prove guilt without any help from the defendant, whether obtained voluntarily or involuntarily.

17.5.6 Appropriate Balancing

The balancing doctrines discussed in this part of the paper are applied to illegal evidence gathering of all kinds. As argued above, they should not be applied where the illegality in question involves a violation of fundamental constitutional rights. Nonetheless, these doctrines should be available where I believe balancing is appropriate, that is, when the illegality does not rise to the level of a violation of the constitution or human rights guarantees. In such cases, factors relevant to the seriousness

---

[214] Beling (1903, 35).

[215] Thus, the German Supreme Court allowed use of a diary in a brutal rape-murder case, but not in a perjury case. Thaman (2008, 113).

[216] Ashworth (1977, 732), discussed in Duff (2004, 169–171).

[217] This is allowed under § 359a CCP-Netherlands, and suggested by some U.S. commentators. See Calabresi (2003, 116).

[218] Thaman (2003, 314).

of the violation (e.g., good or bad faith) can be balanced against factors relevant to the effect of the evidence on the trial (e.g., trial fairness; reliability). However, for the reasons given by Ashworth, the seriousness of the offense should not be a factor.

17.6 Conclusion

Only a few jurisdictions, notably those which have recently emerged from totalitarian or authoritarian regimes (former Soviet and Yugoslav republics, Turkey, Latin American countries) have foreclosed all balancing in relation to the use of any evidence which was gathered illegally, whether or not the illegality was of constitutional proportions. Otherwise, the international community has clearly prohibited any balancing in relation to statements obtained through torture or cruel, inhuman and degrading treatment and appears to be moving in that direction in relation to statements given either involuntarily, or in the absence of counsel. Although most countries will suppress confidential communications that were obtained in violation of wiretap legislation, a blanket exclusionary rule which includes fruits, as exists in US legislation, is not yet a commonplace either in relation to illegal wiretaps or involuntary or counsel-less statements.

Once a country advances from a police state to an entrenched democratic society, should we allow more balancing (i.e. tolerate more police lawlessness) or less? Should we extend categorical exclusion, including that of "fruits", to privacy and *Miranda* violations, got the other way and even admit of balancing in relation to what are considered to be more serious violations? The categorical exclusionary rule of § 11.1 LOPJ-Spain, was arguably still a reaction to the abuses of the Francoist police, but has now given way to a moderate balancing test. In the US the harsh language of *Weeks* condemning widespread police violation of rights led to seemingly categorical exclusionary rules in *Mapp* and *Miranda*, but the recent cases, which propose doing more balancing, seem to intimate that our police have now developed to such an extent that the old toughness is no longer required.[219] But if police have become more professional, shouldn't they be aware of constitutional rules and follow them? Or do our modern constitutional rules prevent police from solving crimes, or make it too time-consuming?

Once such a violation of constitutional importance has been ascertained, there should be a presumption that any evidence directly or indirectly gathered as a result of the violation should be excluded. Valid exceptions, such as for good faith mistakes, or emergency situations should be narrowly construed in the way I have argued above. "Fruits of the poisonous tree", even physical evidence, should be excluded, when the taint of the violation has not been attenuated, there is no true

[219] See Hudson v. Michigan, 547 U.S. 586, 598–599 (2006).

independent source, and the evidence would not inevitably have been discovered. The seriousness of the crime under investigation should play a role in the assessment of whether emergency or exigent circumstances will obviate the necessity to secure a warrant, or administer *Miranda* warnings, but should not be an omnibus reason to admit evidence where there has been a clear and unforgivable constitutional violation. The area of "good faith" of the violating official should be limited to cases where the officer was using what were formerly accepted practices at the time of the investigative measure, which were subsequently deemed to violate constitutional principles, or where a search warrant was obtained, based on evidence which was close to being "probable cause". A police officer who acts negligently is not acting in "good faith", especially in a case like *Herring*, where police were negligent in looking for a pretext to arrest someone as to whom they had no reasonable suspicion.[220]

Finally, the importance of the evidence to convict the defendant should never be a factor. The ECtHR has ruled that evidence gathered in violation of Art. 3 ECHR, following use of torture or cruel and inhuman treatment, can never be justified due to the seriousness of the charges, especially if it is the main evidence of guilt. The same now applies to violations of the right to counsel in *Salduz* and I believe they should extend it to violations of the right to privacy as well.

The area where true judicial balancing should have free rein, is where the violation is truly not of constitutional significance, such as errors in the execution of a search or wiretap warrant otherwise based on probable cause. Here the seriousness of the violation can be weighed against the seriousness of the offense, the intentionality of the violations, etc.

When balancing is allowed, it should also not be undertaken by the trial judge, especially in those systems based in the civil law, where the trial judge is simultaneously a trier of the facts and is considered to be an investigator of the material truth of the charges. A judge with such inquisitorial duties will intentionally or instinctively give priority to the principle of material truth in exercising the Herculean evidentiary balancing act and neglect the equally important role as constitutional guarantor. Therefore, if judicial balancing is to persist, it should be carried out by a neutral judge of the investigation, or liberty judge, and not the trial judge or investigating magistrate, who is also duty-bound to seek truth.

Bibliography

Aguilera Morales, M. 2008. Regla de exclusión y acusatorio. In *Proceso penal y sistemas acusatorios*, ed. L. Bachmaier Winter, 73–108. Madrid: Marcial Pons.

Ashworth, A. 1977. Excluding evidence as protecting rights. *Criminal Law Review* 723–735.

---

[220] United States v. Herring, 555 U.S. 135, 137–138 (2009), noting that the reason for stopping the defendant was that he was "no stranger to law enforcement".

Bartlett, R. 1986. *Trial by fire and water*. Oxford: Clarendon.

Beccaria, C. 1764, 1995. *Dei delitti e delle pene*, 4th ed. Feltrinelli: Milan.

Beling, E. 1903. *Die Beweisverbote als Grenzen der Wahrheitserforschung im Strafprozess*. Breslau: Schletter'sche Buchhandlung.

Bradley, C.M. 2001. Mapp goes abroad. *Case Western Reserve Law Review* 52: 375–400.

Calabresi, G. 2003. The exclusionary rule. *Harvard Journal of Law and Public Policy* 26: 111–118.

Carrió, Alejandro D., and A.M. Garro. 2007. Argentina. In *Criminal procedure: A worldwide study*, 2nd ed, ed. C. Bradley, 3–55. Durham: Carolina Academic Press.

Colamussi, M. 1996. In tema di deducibilitá della nullitá derivante dalla violazione del diritto dell'imputato in stato di custodia cautelare di conferire con il proprio difensore. In *Percorsi di Procedura Penale. Dal garantismo inquisitorio a un accusatorio non garantito*, ed. Vincenzo Perchinunno, 37–39. Milan: Giuffrè.

Conso, G., and V. Grevi. 2002. *Commentario Breve al Nuovo Codice di Procedura Penale*, 4th ed. Padua: CEDAM.

Cordero, F. 2000. *Procedura penale*, 5th ed. Milan: Giuffrè.

Damaska, M.R. 1986. *The faces of justice and state authority*. New Haven: Yale University Press.

Damaska, M.R. 1997. *Evidence law adrift*. New Haven: Yale University Press.

De Urbano Castrillo, E., and M.A. Torres Morato. 2003. *La Prueba Illícita Penal: Estudio jurisprudencial*, 3dth ed. Navarra: Thomson, Aranzadi.

Diamond, A.S. 1971. *Primitive law: Past and present*. London: Methuen & Co.

Di Palma, E.M.T. 1996. Riflessioni sulla sfera di operativitá della sanzione di cui all'art. 191 c.p.p. In *Percorsi di Procedura Penale. Dal garantismo inquisitorio a un accusatorio non garantito*, ed. Vincenzo Perchinunno, 113–121. Milan: Giuffrè.

Duff, P. 2004. Admissibility of improperly obtained physical evidence in the Scottish criminal trial: The search for principle. *Edinburgh Law Review* 8: 152–176.

Esmein, A. 1913. *History of continental criminal procedure with special reference to France*. Boston: Little, Brown, & Co.

Fanuli, G.L. 2004. *Inutilizzabilità e nullitá della prova nel giudizio abbreviato, nel "patteggiamento" e nell'istituto della acquisizione degli atti su accordo delle parti*. Milan: Giuffrè.

Ferrajoli, L. 1998. *Diritto e ragione: teoria del garantismo penale*, 5th ed. Rome: Laterza.

Frase, R. 2007. France. In *Criminal procedure: A worldwide study*, 2dth ed, ed. C. Bradley, 201–242. Durham: Carolina Academic Press.

French, R.R. 1995. *The golden yoke: The legal cosmology of Buddhist Tibet*. Ithaca/London: Cornell University Press.

Glenn, H.P. 2007. *Legal traditions of the world*, 3rd ed. New York: Oxford.

Gómez Colomer, J.-L. 1998. La intervención judicial de las comunicaciones telefónicas a la luz de la jurisprudencia. *Revista Jurídica de Catalunya* 1: 145–167.

Gopnik, A. 2012. The caging of America. *The New Yorker*, Jan 30, 2012, 72–77.

LaFave, W.R., J.H. Israel, and N.J. King. 2009. *Criminal procedure*, 5th ed. St. Paul: West.

Langbein, J.H. 1977. *Torture and the law of proof: Europe and England in the Ancien Régime*. Chicago: University of Chicago Press.

Leo, R. 1996. The impact of Miranda revisited. *Journal of Criminal Law and Criminology* 86: 621–692.

Luhmann, N. 1995. *Das Recht der Gesellschaft*. Frankfurt am Main: Suhrkamp.

Mahoney, R. 2003. Abolition of New Zealand's prima facie exclusionary rule. *Criminal Law Review* 607–617.

Montesequieu, C. 1748, 1979. *De L'Esprit des Lois*. Paris: Garnier Flammarion.

Murphy, P., and E. Stockdale (eds.). 2003. *Blackstone's criminal practice*, 13th ed. London: Oxford Press.

Ormerod, D. 2003. ECHR and the exclusion of evidence: Trial remedies for Article 8 breaches?. *Criminal Law Review* 61–80.

Pradel, J. 1997. *Procédure pénale*, 6th ed. Paris: Cujas.
Ransiek, A. 2002. Durchsuchung, Beschlagnahme und Verwertungsverbot. *Der Strafverteidiger* 10: 565–571.
Roach, K. 2007. Canada. In *Criminal procedure: A worldwide study*, 2dth ed, ed. C. Bradley, 57–90. Durham: Carolina Academic Press.
Roxin, C. 1995. *Strafverfahrensrecht: ein Studienbuch*, 24th ed. Munich: Beck.
Saltzburg, S.A., and D.J. Capra. 2010. *American criminal procedure: Cases and commentary*, 9th ed. St. Paul: West.
Scharf, M.P. 2008. Tainted provenance: When, if ever, should torture evidence be admissible? *Washington and Lee Law Review* 65: 129–172.
Schwikkard, P.J., and S.E. van der Merwe. 2007. South Africa. In *Criminal procedure: A worldwide study*, 2dth ed, ed. C. Bradley, 471–518. Durham: Carolina Academic Press.
Stuart, D. 2010. Welcome flexibility and better criteria from the supreme court of Canada for exclusion of evidence obtained in violation of the Canadian Charter of Rights and Freedoms. *Southwestern Journal of International Law* 16: 313–332.
Thaman, S.C. 1995. The resurrection of trial by jury in Russia. *Stanford Journal of International Law* 31: 61–274.
Thaman, S.C. 2001. Miranda in comparative law. *Saint Louis University Law Journal* 45: 581–624.
Thaman, S.C. 2003. Gerechtigkeit und Verfahrensvielfalt: Logik der beschleunigten, konsuellen und vereinfachten Strafprozessmodelle. In *Recht-Gesellschaft-Kommunikation. Festschrift für Klaus F. Röhl*, ed. S. Machura and S. Ulbrich, 306–320. Nomos: Baden-Baden.
Thaman, S.C. 2007. The nullification of the Russian jury: Lessons for jury-inspired reform in Eurasia and beyond. *Cornell International Law Journal* 40: 355–428.
Thaman, S.C. 2008. *Comparative criminal procedure: A casebook approach*, 2dth ed. Durham: Carolina Academic Press.
Thaman, S.C. 2010. A typology of consensual criminal procedures: An historical and comparative perspective on the theory and practice of avoiding the full criminal trial. In *World plea bargaining*, ed. S.C. Thaman, 297–396. Durham: Carolina Academic Press.
Tonini, P. 2005. *Manuale di Procedura Penale*, 6th ed. Milan: Giuffrè Editore.
van Puyenbroeck, L. 2010. Belgium. In *Effective criminal defence in Europe*, ed. E. Cape, Z. Namoradze, R. Smith, and T. Spronken, 78–123. Oxford: Intersentia.
VerSteeg, Russ. 2002. *Law in the ancient world*. Durham: Carolina Academic Press.
Vogler, R. 2005. *A world view of criminal justice*. Burlington: Ashgate.
Weigend, T. 1989. *Deliktsopfer und Strafverfahren*. Berlin: Duncker & Humblot.
Weigend, T. 2007. Germany. In *Criminal procedure: A worldwide study*, 2nd ed, ed. C. Bradley, 243–272. Durham: Carolina Academic Press.

Codes of Criminal Procedure (CCP) and Judicial Codes

ARGENTINA (FEDERAL): Código Procesal Penal Argentino, Ley No. 23,984, Sept. 4, 1991, available at http://www.robertexto.com/archivo4/cod_proc_penal.htm
ARMENIA: Ugolovno-protsessual'nyy kodeks Respubliki Armenii, available at http://www.base.spinform.ru/show.fwx?Regnom=7460
AZERBAIJAN: Ugolovno-protsessual'nyy kodeks Azerbajdzhanskoy Respubliki, confirmed by Law of the Azerbaijan Republic No. 907-IG, July 14, 2000, available at *km.undp.sk/.../Azerbaijan_Criminal_Procedre_Code_Russian.doc*

BELARUS: *Ugolovno-protsessual'nyy Kodeks Respubliki Belarus'*. Priniat Palatoy predstaviteley 24 June 1999. Odobren Sovetom Respubliki 30 June 1999. St. Petersburg: Yuridicheskiy tsentr Press (2001). Augmented by web version with changes of to July 22, 2003.

BRAZIL: Codige de processo penal , Decreto-Ley 3,689 of Oct. 3, 1941, as amended by Law No. 11,690 of June 9, 2008, http://www.scribd.com/doc/6284936/Codigo-de-Processo-Penal-Atualizado-2008

COLOMBIA: Law 906 of Aug. 31, 2004, Diario Oficial No. 45,658 of Sept. 1, 2004, available at http://domiarmo.iespana.es/index-52.htm, also at *Código Penal, Ley 599 de 2000, Códigos de Procedimiento Penal, Ley 906 de 2004-Ley 600 de 2000 177*, Bogotá: Códigos Básicos (2009).

ENGLAND AND WALES: Police and Criminal Evidence Act 1984, all cites from M. Zander, *The Police and Criminal Evidence Act* 1984 (5th ed.)(2005)

FRANCE: Code de procédure pénale, Version of Jan. 16, 2010, available at http://www.legifrance.gouv.fr/affichCode.do;jsessionid=3B9DC1BE6591A6616746EF79D132D061.tpdjo10v_3?cidTexte=LEGITEXT000006071154&dateTexte=20100117

GERMANY-Strafprozessordnung. 1. Februray1887 (RGBl 253), in Meyer-Goßner, L., *Strafprozessordnung, Gerichtsverfassungsgesetz, Nebengesetze und ergänzende Bestimmungen* (50th ed.)(2007).

ITALY. Codice di procedura penale. Entered into force Oct. 24, 1989. Published in *Gazzetta ufficiale* on Sept. 22, 1988, no. 447. Available at http://studiocelentano.it/codici/cpp/03/disp_gen.htm

KAZAKHSTAN: *Ugolovno-protsessual'nyy Zakon Respublika kazakhstan*. Almaty: Yurist (2003). Changes up to Sept. 25, 2003. Originally passed Dec. 13, 1997. No. 206-I.

KYRGYZSTAN: Ugolovno-protsessual'nyy Kodeks Kyrgyzskoy Respubliki, Zakonov KR, No. 55, June 22, 2001, Changes up to Oct. 26, 2009, available at http://www.medialawca.org/document/-4460

MOLDOVA (MO): *Ugolovno-protsessual'nyy kodeks Respubliki Moldova*, Kishinev: S.A. Cartea (2003). No. 122-XY. March 14, 2003. Went into force June 12, 2003.

NETHERLANDS: Wetboek van Strafvordering, available at http://wetten.overheid.nl/BWBR0001903/TweedeBoek/TitelVI/Vierdeafdeeling/Artikel359a/geldigheidsdatum_17-01-2010, translation by M.J. Borgers, L. Stevens.

RUSSIA: *Ugolovno-protsessual'nyy kodeks Rossiyskoy Federatsii* (contents up to October 1, 2010), Moscow: Prospekt (2010).

SERBIA: The Criminal Procedure Code, PR No. 89, Promulgated Sept. 26, 2011. Signed by President Boris Tadic, Sept. 28, 2011, available at www.legislationonline.org/documents/id/8918/

SLOVENIA: Criminal Procedure Act (2007), http://www2.policija.si/portal_en/zakonodaja/pdf/CriminalProcedureAct2007.pdf

SPAIN: Ley de Enjuiciamiento Criminal, Promulgated by Royal Decree on Sept. 14, 1882, available at http://noticias.juridicas.com/base_datos/Penal/lecr.html

Ley Orgánica del Poder Judicial (Organic Law on the Judicial Power), Ley Orgánica 6 (July 1, 1985), available at http://noticias.juridicas.com/base_datos/Admin/lo6-1985.html (LOPJ-Spain)

TAIWAN: Code of Criminal Procedure of Taiwan (as amended on Feb. 6, 2003), English translation available at http://db.lawbank.com.tw/Eng/FLAW/FLAWDAT0201.asp

TURKEY. *Turkish Criminal Procedure Code*. 4.12.2004-5271, RG. 17.12.2004, Nr. 25673. Beta-Istanbul. 2009.

TURKMENISTAN, Ugolovno-protsessual'nyy kodeks Turkmenistana http://www.turkmenistan.gov.tm/_ru/laws/?laws=01fe

VENEZUELA: Código Orgánico Procesal Penal, G.O. 38,536, Oct. 4, 2006, available at http://www.mipunto.com/venezuelavirtual/leyesdevenezuela/codigos/codigo_organico_procesal_penal.html

Constitutions (Const.)

AZERBAIJAN: Constitution of the Republic of Azerbaijan (1995), Russian version in Y.O. Buluktaev (ed.), *Konstitutsii stran SNG*, Almaty: Zheti Zharghy (1999).

BELARUS: Constitution of the Republic of Belarus, Russian version in Y.O. Buluktaev (ed.) *Konstitutsii stran SNG*, Almaty: Zheti Zharghy (1999).

BRAZIL: Constitution of Brazil (1988), http://www.v-brazil.com/government/laws/constitution.html

CANADA: Canadian Charter of Rights and Freedoms, Enacted by the Canada Act 1982 [U.K.] c.11; proclaimed in force April 17, 1982. http://www.efc.ca/pages/law/charter/charter.text.html.

GEORGIA: Constitution of the Republic of Georgia (1995), Russian version in Y. O. Buluktaev (ed.), *Konstitutsii stran SNG*, Almaty: Zheti Zharghy (1999).

GERMANY: Basic Law for the Federal Republic of Germany (Grundgesetz) published in First Issue of the *Federal Law Gazette*, May 23, 1949. http://www.iuscomp.org/gla/statutes/GG.htm

KAZAKHSTAN: Constitution of the Republic of Kazakhstan (1995), Russian version in Y.O. Buluktaev (ed.), *Konstitutsii stran SNG*, Almaty: Zheti Zharghy (1999).

KYRGYZSTAN: Constitution of the Republic of Kyrgyzstan (1996), Russian version in Y.O. Buluktaev (ed.) *Konstitutsii stran SNG*, Almaty: Zheti Zharghy (1999).

RUSSIA: Konstitutsiia Rossiyskoy Federatsii, adopted by popular referendum, 12 Dec 1993, http://www.consultant.ru/popular/cons/

SPAIN: Constitución Española de (Dec. 27, 1978), http://noticias.juridicas.com/base_datos/Admin/constitucion.html#

TURKEY: Constitution of the Republic of Turkey (1982), http://www.anayasa.gov.tr/images/loaded/pdf_dosyalari/THE_CONSTITUTION_OF_THE_REPUBLIC_OF_TURKEY.pdf

TURKMENISTAN: Constitution of the Republic of Turkmenistan (1992), Russian version in Y.O. Buluktaev (ed.), *Konstitutsii stran SNG*, Almaty: Zheti Zharghy (1999).

Contributing Authors

Lorena Bachmaier Winter is Professor of Law at Complutense University, Madrid. She is the author of various books and more than 90 academic articles. She is Alexander von Humboldt fellow and international expert for the Council of Europe. She also holds a degree in Political Science. Her fields of specialization are criminal, civil and constitutional procedure from a comparative point of view, as well as European judicial cooperation.

Marie-Aude Beernaert is Professor of Law at the University of Louvain, where she completed a Ph.D. in 2002 on repentant collaborators with justice (*pentiti*). She currently teaches criminal procedure, European Union criminal law and the law on the execution of criminal sanctions, and has published widely on all these matters.

Matthias Borgers is Professor of Criminal Law and Criminal Procedure at the VU University Amsterdam and honorary judge in the Amsterdam Court of Appeal. In 2001 he obtained his Ph.D. *cum laude* at Tilburg University. The subject of his Ph.D. thesis was the confiscation of criminal assets in the Netherlands and in Germany. His current research focuses on criminal procedure, European criminal law and money laundering.

Snežana Brkić has a Ph. D. in law and is Professor of Law at the Novi Sad Faculty of Law in Serbia. She has published four books and more than 100 academic articles. She was a member of the working group which drafted the Codes of Criminal Procedure of Yugoslavia (2001) and Serbia (2004).

Mark Cammack is Professor of Law at Southwestern Law School in Los Angeles, California. He got his J.D. from the University of Wisconsin and writes extensively in the areas of criminal procedure and Indonesian law. He writes extensively on criminal procedure and Indonesian law and is co-author of "Islamic Law in Contemporary Indonesia" (Harvard University Press, 2007), and "Advanced Criminal Procedure in a Nutshell" (West, 2nd ed. 2006).

S.C. Thaman (ed.), *Exclusionary Rules in Comparative Law*, Ius Gentium: Comparative Perspectives on Law and Justice 20, DOI 10.1007/978-94-007-5348-8,

Andrew L.-T. Choo is Professor of Law at the Law School of City University, London. He has his B.Com. and LL.B. from the University of New South Wales, and his D.Phil. from Oxford. He is also a barrister with Matrix Chambers in London. He writes widely on criminal procedure and evidence, including "Evidence" (2012) and "Abuse of Process and Judicial Stays of Criminal Proceedings in Criminal Proceedings" (2008) both published by Oxford University Press.

Arnaud Cras graduated from the University of Paris (Licence: 1970), (DES: 1971), (IHEI: 1970) specializing in comparative law and international law. He lectured at Warwick University, Trent Polytechnic and University College Dublin in Public International Law, Comparative Law, and French Law. His fields of specialization are state sovereignty and armed conflicts and comparative criminal procedure. He has published in international and European law.

Yvonne Marie Daly lectures in Criminal Law and Law of Evidence at the School of Law and Government, Dublin City University where she is a member of the Socio-Legal Research Centre. She has degrees from University College Cork (BCL: 2003) and Trinity College Dublin (Ph.D.: 2008). She is co-author of "Irish Criminal Justice: Theory, Process and Procedure" (Clarus Press, 2010), contributes to the blog www.humanrighs.ie and writes primarily on pretrial process.

Sabine Gless teaches at the University of Basel (Chair for Criminal Law and Criminal Proceedings). Her research and writing encompasses several studies on the Law of Evidence in national criminal justice systems as well as in transnational and international legal frameworks, including matters of judicial assistance and European criminal law. Her key interests therein especially lie with evidence transfer across borders.

Giulio Illuminati is Professor of Criminal Procedure at the University of Bologna, and Head of its Juridical Sciences Department. He also lectures in Criminal Procedure at L.U.I.S.S. "Guido Carli" in Rome. In 1987–1989 he was a member of the Committee for the Reform of the Italian Criminal Process, drafted the Italian Code of Criminal Procedure. He is on the Editorial Board of *Cassazione Penale* and vice-president of the *Associazione fra gli Studiosi del Processo Penale.*

Rinat Kitai Sangero is a Senior Lecturer at the Academic Center of Law & Business in Israel.

Fiona Leverick is a Senior Lecturer (Professor) in law at the University of Glasgow. She has written two books on criminal law and is in the process of writing a third. She has published extensively on issues of criminal law, justice and procedure and has undertaken research for various government organisations on criminal justice issues.

Yuval Merin is a Senior Lecturer at the Striks School of Law, College of Management Academic Studies, Israel. He received his LL.B. from the Hebrew University of Jerusalem and his LL.M and J.S.D. from New York University School of Law. His main research and teaching fields are Evidence Law, Civil Procedures, and Law and Gender.

F. Pınar Ölçer is Assistant Professor of Criminal and Criminal Procedural Law at the Leiden Law School, Leiden University and in is Visiting Professor at the Faculty of Law of Istanbul University.

Jean Pradel is Emeritus Professor of Criminal Law at the Faculty of Law of the University of Poitiers in France. From 1960 through 1969 he was a *juge d'instruction*. For 12 years he was President of the French Association of Penal Law. He is the author of authoritative books such as *Procédure pénale* (Cujas) and *Droit pénale comparé* (Dalloz), and collaborated with G. Corstens and G. Vermeulen in the book *Droit pénale européen* (Dalloz).

Öznur Sevdiren teaches criminal law and procedure and international criminal law at Uludağ University Law Faculty in Bursa and Boğaziçi University in Istanbul. She received her law degree from the University of Istanbul, and a masters degree from the University of Sheffield. She worked as a research assistant at the University of Cologne and served as a member of the Curriculum Commission of the Law Faculty of Turkish-German University.

Adem Sözüer is Dean of the Law Faculty of Istanbul University and is Professor of Criminal Law. He graduated from Istanbul University Faculty of Law in 1983, and received his Ph.D in law in 1993 with a dissertation on the law of attempt. He is a member of the Justice Committee in the *Grand National Assembly* of *Turkey* he played a key role in drafting Turkish Criminal Code, Criminal Procedure Code, and the Law on Execution of Sentences and Security Measures.

Findlay Stark is a College Lecturer and Fellow in Law at Jesus College, University of Cambridge. He is a graduate of the Universities of Aberdeen (LL.B. (Hons.), LL.M. (Res.)) and Edinburgh (Ph.D.).

Lonneke Stevens is Associate Professor of Criminal Law and Criminal Procedure at the VU University Amsterdam and honorary judge in the Court of Alkmaar. She graduated in law from Maastricht University in 2001, finished her Ph.D. on the privilege against self-incrimination at Tilburg University in 2005 and worked as a criminal defense lawyer. Her research focuses on procedural topics such as the right to counsel during police interrogation and pre-trial detention.

Stephen C. Thaman, is Professor of Law at Saint Louis University, in the U.S. He has a J.D. from the University of California, Berkeley, and a Dr. iur. from the University of Freiburg. He is a member of the Scientific Advisory Board of the Max-Planck-Institute for Foreign and Comparative Criminal Law. He has published widely in the area of comparative criminal law and procedure, including a casebook on comparative criminal procedure.

Philip Traest is professor in criminal law and criminal procedure at the Department of Penal Law and Criminology at Ghent University, Belgium. He studied law and criminology at the same university and obtained in 1992 a Ph.D. degree with a thesis on Criminal Evidence. He is the author of many publications in the field of criminal law, criminal procedure and criminal evidence. He is also lawyer at the Brussels Bar.

Georgios Triantafyllou is Assistant Professor of Criminal Law and Criminal Procedure at the School of Law, University of Athens. He is a member of the Athens Bar Association, and practices as defense counsel in all fields of criminal litigation.

Jaw-Perng Wang is the Vice Dean of National Taiwan University College of Law. He has his Bachelor of Law from NTU College of Law, LL.M. from Columbia University, a second LL.M. and an S.J.D. from the University of Chicago. He has been a member of the Judicial Yuan's Committee on Research and Revision of the Code of Criminal Procedure and the Minister of Interior's Committee on Human Rights. He has widely published in the area of criminal justice.

Index

S.C. Thaman (ed.), *Exclusionary Rules in Comparative Law*, Ius Gentium: Comparative Perspectives on Law and Justice 20, DOI 10.1007/978-94-007-5348-8,

MIX
Papier aus verantwortungsvollen Quellen
Paper from responsible sources
FSC® C105338
www.fsc.org

If you have any concerns about our products,
you can contact us on
ProductSafety@springernature.com

In case Publisher is established outside the EU,
the EU authorized representative is:
Springer Nature Customer Service Center GmbH
Europaplatz 3, 69115 Heidelberg, Germany

Printed by Libri Plureos GmbH
in Hamburg, Germany